Course   HIST 151 World History II
           NICHOLLS STATE UNIVERSITY

http://create.mheducation.com

ISBN-10: 1308164904   ISBN-13: 9781308164908

Contents

Online Supplements

Credits

Online Supplements

Instructor Resources for Panorama: A World History

More Primary Sources in Create

The World History Document Collection in McGraw-Hill's Create (www.mcgrawhillcreate.com) allows you to choose from over 100 primary and secondary sourcesÐ each with a headnote and questionsÐ that can be added to your print text. Create also allows you to rearrange or omit chapters, combine material from other sources, and/or upload your syllabus or any other content you have written to make the perfect resources for your students. You can search thousands of leading McGraw-Hill textbooks to find the best content for your students, then arrange it to fit your teaching style. When you order a Create book, you receive a complimentary review copy in three to five business days or an electronic copy (eComp) via e-mail in about an hour. Register today at www.mcgrawhillcreate.com and craft your course resources to match the way you teach.

Instructor Resources on the Online Learning Center

The Online Learning Center for *Panorama* at www.mhhe.com/panorama1e contains a wealth of instructor resources, including an Instructor's Manual, Test Bank, and PowerPoint presentations for each chapter. All maps and most images from the print text are included. A computerized test bank powered by McGraw-Hill's EZ Test allows you to quickly create a customized exam using the publisher's supplied test questions or add your own. You decide on the number, type, and order of test questions with a few simple clicks. EZ Test runs on your computer without a connection to the Internet.

CourseSmart e-books

CourseSmart offers thousands of the most commonly adopted textbooks across hundreds of courses from a variety of higher education publishers. It is the only place for faculty to review and compare the full text of a textbook online, providing immediate access without the environmental impact of requesting a printed exam copy. At CourseSmart, students can save up to 50 percent off the cost of a printed book, and gain access to powerful web tools for learning, including full text search, notes and highlighting, and e-mail tools for sharing notes among classmates. Learn more at www.coursesmart.com.

McGraw-Hill Campus

McGraw-Hill Campus is the first-of-its-kind institutional service providing faculty with true single sign-on access to all of McGraw-Hill's course content, digital ·tools, and other high-quality learning resources from any learning management system (LMS). This innovative offering allows for secure and deep integration and seamless access to any of our course solutions such as McGraw-Hill Connect, McGraw-Hill Create, McGraw-Hill LearnSmart, or Tegrity. McGraw-Hill Campus includes access to our entire content library, including e-books, assessment tools, presentation slides, and multimedia content, among other resources, providing faculty open and unlimited access to prepare for class, create tests and quizzes, develop lecture material, integrate interactive content, and much more.

List of Maps

An Interview with the Authors of *Panorama: A World History*

Ross Dunn and Laura Mitchell discuss how they came to write *Panorama* and how they believe it contributes to the study of the human past.

Q: Tell us about the unique approach you have taken in *Panorama*.

A: In *Panorama*, we have created a unified narrative of world history, assuming that the primary subject we are investigating is humankind as a whole, and the primary setting of the narrative is the globe. We have organized the chapters chronologically, by consecutive historical periodsÐ never repeating a period from different regional or thematic angles. Our aim is to advance the mission of conceptualizing the human experience in ways that are more holistic and integrated. To do this, we have had to select the very broad developments that define particular historical periods and that we think readers ought to understand.

Q: Why did you choose this approach?

A: We wanted to contribute to the important work of making the history of humankind intelligible, to write a unified narrative that is clear and coherent and that gives readers a sturdy framework for thinking about the global past. We believe we can begin to understand big and rapid changes in the world today only if we have a mental scaffolding of ideas and words for thinking, talking, and writing about the world as a whole. Similarly, we can begin to grasp how the world got to be the way it is only if we have world-scale narratives that help us connect the histories of particular groupsÐ nations, civilizations, religions, corporationsÐ to patterns of change in human society writ large.

Q: How do you balance large historical generalizations with knowledge about particular peoples, places, and events?

A: We know from experience that if the presentation is too broad, abstract, or theoretical, students may have a hard time grasping the generalizations. But if the writing is too loaded with historical details (all of which may be significant at some level), then the big pictures of change tend to get lost in thickets of information about particular societies, individuals, conquests, wars, philosophies, artistic movements, and so on.

Like all writers of world history, we have made choices to leave out a great deal of perfectly useful and interesting knowledge. Only by doing this are we able to keep our sights on the panoramic view and on the unified narrative. We have also, however, aimed to write in concrete, descriptive language, recognizing that history is fundamentally about human beings, individually or in groups, thinking, working, fighting, and creating.

Q: How are you able to combine the telling of "large-scale" history with in-depth, "small-scale" knowledge of people and events?

A: In every chapter, we shift between larger- and smaller-scale narratives, but we aim consistently to relate developments at relatively small scales to those at much larger scales. We cannot understand the Industrial Revolution as the world event it was by studying just one English factory town, but historians might write about such a town as an example of how large-scale changes played out on a local level and affected people's lives.

Q: Does *Panorama* have a central theme?

A: Yes, it does. This theme is the growing complexity of human society from the early era of stone toolmaking to today. Looking over the very long term of history, we see a nearly continuous though by no means inevitable trend toward greater complexity in the relations of human groups with one another and with the earthly environment. This movement from lesser to greater complexity has been manifested across the ages in several nearly continuous trends of growth, even though the rates and dimensions of change in these areas have been uneven:

- Global population (more people and more groups interacting with one another)
- Human use of the planet's energy supply to produce food and other goods
- Human intervention to alter the natural and physical environment
- The intricacy and sophistication of technology and science
- The density and speed of systems of communication and transport

- The density of human networks of interchange, including movement of people, goods, and ideas
- The size of governments and their capacity to manage and control people
- The technical capabilities of weaponry to kill people and destroy property
- The size and elaborateness of systems of belief, including religions, ethical structures, and philosophies

Throughout the book, we pose the same question in different ways: How and why did the world move relentlessly toward greater cultural complexity, despite breaks and unevenness in that trend, for example, short-term drops in global population, periods of economic contraction, or the disappearance of particular languages and local religions?

Q: How did you decide on the topics for each chapter?

A: In aiming to write a unified narrative of history, we followed the basic principle of bringing to the fore historical developments that had (and may still have) an impact on relatively large numbers of people, that is, developments of large scale. We let these big developments generally determine the chronological frame of each chapter, and we investigate them in whatever geographical context seems appropriate for clear discussion of their importance. If most chapters focus in part on developments in a region, it is because a development of large-scale significance happened or started there in that particular period. For example, we devote a primary chapter section to developments in China under the Song dynasties of the eleventh and twelfth centuries because China in those centuries generated exuberant economic innovation and growth, a phenomenon that had effects all across the Eastern Hemisphere.

Q: What is distinctive about *Panorama*'s periodization of the past?

A: As a unified narrative, *Panorama* proposes a plan for dividing the past into specific chunks of time, with the beginnings and endings of those chunks determined by the important historical developments that occurred within them. Our periodization plan is a single chronology, or timeline moving from the remote to the recent past. One way that *Panorama*'s periodization differs from the majority of world history books is its greater attention to very early human history, that is, to the long paleolithic era that preceded the coming of agriculture. The whole paleolithic era (old stone age), which started perhaps 2.5 million years ago, constitutes about 99.6 percent of the history of humankind and its near biological ancestors. Attention to early history encourages readers to think about how and why humans made radical changes in the way they livedÐ taking up farming, building cities, creating mechanized industries, populating the world

with billionsÐ when they got along without doing these things for hundreds of thousands of years.

Q: You refer to your narrative as "unified"; can you elaborate?

A: One element of our approach to a unified narrative is to conceive of Africa, Asia, and Europe together as a single land mass, a sort of ªsupercontinentº within which humans interacted, or at least had the physical possibility of interacting, since paleolithic times. As discussed in our Introduction, we refer to this supercontinent as Afroeurasia. For periods of world history up to 1500 C.E., we conceive of the world as divided into four primary geographical regions: Afroeurasia (where the great majority of human beings have always livedÐ about 86 percent today), the Americas (North and South together), Australia, and Oceania (the Island Pacific). Within these regions, human groups interacted with one another, though with greater or lesser intensity and from different chronological starting points. On the other hand, people did not interact, at least not in any sustained way, between one of these regions and another because wide expanses of ocean and to some extent contrasting climatic conditions prevented or discouraged it. For periods up to 1500 C.E., therefore, we explore developments in these regions in different chapters or sections of chapters, even though we also introduce points of historical comparison between one region and another. Starting in the late fifteenth century, the four regions began to throw out lines of communication to one another, though not all at once. The Great World Convergence, as we call it, began when sea captains established regular transport routes between Afroeurasia and the Americas. For periods after 1500, we treat the entire world as a single zone within which human interrelations became increasingly complex and large-scale developments occurred. From that chronological point to the present, all the chapters are global in scope.

Q: How does *Panorama* cover the significance of individuals—both men and women—in the course of human history?

A: *Panorama* endeavors to take full account of the historical fact that men and women share the planet. Even though much of the narrative is not explicitly gender specific, it aims to be ªgender sensitive.º This has meant repeatedly asking ourselves as we move from topic to topic how both men and women, whether aristocrats, city workers, peasants, or forager-hunters, acted as agents of change.

In every chapter of this book, the cast of characters is necessarily very large. We aim, however, to remind readers of the importance of individuals as agents of change by introducing a chapter feature titled ªIndividuals Matter.º It presents a biographical sketch of an individual whose life in some way illuminates the period the chapter addresses. In most cases, this individual is a person of public importance, for example, Empress Wu of the Chinese Tang dynasty, or Diego Rivera, the twentieth-century Mexican artist. In a few chapters, however, the individual is an ªordinary° woman or man whose life or deeds illustrate some aspect of the periodÐ for example, Ötzi, the ascribed name of a neolithic traveler in the Alps, or Olga Lisikova, a Russian combat pilot in World War II.

Q: Does *Panorama* incorporate primary sources?

A: Yes. A feature titled ªWeighing the Evidence° appears in every chapterÐ and in the accompanying Connect History programÐ offering students an opportunity to critically examine a piece of historical evidence relating to the chapter content. The selection is usually a written document (for example, a nineteenth-century Moroccan diplomat's description of France), though in a few chapters a visual artifact (for example, an image of a giant stone head from ancient Mexico) is included. In some chapters, we present two pieces of evidence to compare with each other. ªWeighing the Evidence° includes questions that prompt readers to analyze, interpret, and discuss the selection. This feature reminds readers that the *Panorama* narrative rests on the work of thousands of professional historians and other scholars who have examined, authenticated, and interpreted written documents, works of art, fossilized bones, and numerous other kinds of primary evidence.

Q: Is there a theme to your chapter-opening vignettes?

A: Yes. A key element of the trend toward greater complexity in world history has been the development of systems of communication that have allowed humans to move from one place to another and to create networks for exchanging ideas and things in increasingly complicated ways and at faster and faster speeds. To highlight this aspect of human complexity, we open each chapter with a brief story or vignette that has to do with some kind of communication, transport, or movement pertinent to the historical period under study. The subjects of these stories range widely from camel caravans to the profession of telephone operator.

Q: Is *Panorama* available as an e-book?

A: Even betterÐ it is available as a SmartBook, which means not only that students can read it online, but they can quiz themselves after every section. The SmartBook then adapts to their response, highlighting areas in the narrative that they need to study more.

Q: Are any other digital resources available?

A: Absolutely. The Connect History program offers activities with *Panorama*'s maps, primary sources, key concepts and terms, as well as auto-gradable test items and essay questions.

Interconnections and Their Consequences 900–1500

part 4

Interconnections and Their Consequences

900–1500

A blue-green porcelain vase from China's Song Dynasty.

L ooking at the human past through a very wide-angle lens, we might say that the world did not change much between the era we explored in Part 3 and the six centuries we now investigate in Part 4. Between 900 and 1500, the agrarian age continued as before. In other words, agriculture, including both crop and domestic animal raising, remained the economic foundation of both rural villagers and the builders of complex societies with their cities, centralized governments, and grand buildings. The ability of humans to produce food, fiber, and fuel remained as strictly dependent on the soil as it had throughout the agrarian age. Even though people continued to invent practical new tools—better plows, horse harnesses, sails, water-lifting machines—the number of daily calories of useful energy an individual could control barely doubled from the dawn of agriculture to 1000.[1] And that number did not begin to accelerate at a much faster rate until the nineteenth century, when our species devised ways to exploit immense underground stores of energy from coal, oil, and gas.

If we view history through a somewhat narrower lens, we see that several large-scale patterns of change under way in the first millennium C.E. continued into the second. World population, economic output, and interregional trade all continued to increase, while societies fashioned more complex social and economic institutions and accumulated more scientific and technical knowledge. We saw in Part 3 that these trends, all generally characteristic of the agrarian age, could be interrupted by unforeseen slumps in population and economy accompanied by more intense social and political turmoil. This happened between the third and sixth centuries. As we shall see in Part 4, it happened again in the 1300s, a depressive period marked by the great

Afroeurasian disease pandemic we call the Black Death. But as in the first millennium, the downturn was temporary. Recovery took hold in the fifteenth century, and between 900 and 1500, the population of Afroeurasia managed to double.

If we focus even more closely on hemispheric and regional landscapes, we see that the 900–1500 period looks very different from the previous millennium. In Part 4 we explore changes that had broad regional or hemispheric effects in those six hundred years:

■ In China under the Song (960–1276) and Jin (1115–1234) dynasties, manufacturing, commerce, urbanization, and technical innovation all surged forward. China's economic growth outpaced that of all other regions. And because China both exported and imported larger quantities of goods, its prosperity affected the livelihoods and business activities of peoples as far distant as East Africa and western Europe.

■ Pastoral nomads of Inner Eurasia had a greater impact on Afroeurasia's history between 900 and 1500 than in any period before or after. Beginning in the late tenth century, Turkic-speaking nomads migrated in large numbers into densely settled lands of Southwest Asia, and they raided and conquered along an even wider arc of territory. By the twelfth century, Turkic populations, or at least military elites, dominated societies from Egypt to South Asia's Ganges valley. These movements caused social and political upheavals, but the great cities of Southwest Asia and Egypt continued to prosper as centers of manufacturing and commerce.

■ Among Afroeurasia's major belief systems, Islam spread more widely than any other during these centuries. Because Turkic migrants and conquerors were Muslims, they introduced their faith to new regions. Merchants, scholars, and wandering preachers also founded new Muslim communities from West Africa to China.

■ In Europe, improving political stability and new agricultural inventions fueled more towns and trade, a development that paralleled events in Song China on a smaller scale. By the eleventh century, a new center of urban civilization under the moral and cultural guidance of the Catholic Christian church was taking shape. Europeans linked themselves more firmly to the web of hemispheric exchange, a process interrupted but not halted by climatic change and the Black Death.

■ In Africa south of the Sahara Desert, population levels remained lower than in the agrarian lands of Eurasia and northern Africa. Nevertheless, farming and cattle-herding societies continued to grow and with them more interregional trade, cities, and large states. In the thirteenth and fourteenth centuries, for example, the West African empire of Mali stimulated Afroeurasian trade by exporting large quantities of gold.

■ Pastoral nomadic conquests resumed on a spectacular scale in the early thirteenth century, when Mongol and Turkic horse cavalry stormed across Eurasia, forging the largest land empire the world had ever seen. The Mongol conquests from China to Hungary were terrifying, but once the victors founded new governments, they rebuilt cities and patronized art and learning. For more than a century, Mongol rulers encouraged the flow of goods, technologies, and religious ideas across Afroeurasia.

■ In the Americas, total population may have been only a fifth of China's as of 1200, but numbers grew as farmers experimented with irrigation and land-reclaiming techniques and as maize cultivation spread more widely. Several new monument-building states appeared, culminating in the fifteenth century with the rise of the Aztec and Inca empires. Those two states demonstrated that human labor and creativity could be mobilized on an enormous scale despite the absence of iron technology or wheeled transport.

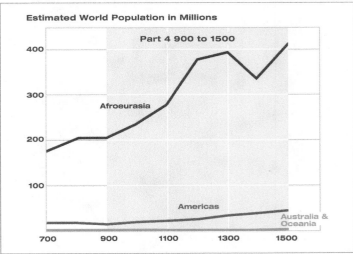

15 Calamities and Recoveries across Afroeurasia

1300–1500

In *The Holy Trinity,* the Florentine painter Masaccio applied new principles of linear perspective to achieve an illusion of three-dimensional space.

If you drive a car along a straight, flat stretch of country highway, your eyes will tell you that the road ahead narrows. The two edges gradually converge to a point, and the road disappears altogether. If you should see a line of ten school buses coming toward you, you will perceive that the closest bus is bigger than the most distant one. You will *see* these things, but at the same time your brain, reasoning logically and drawing on stored knowledge, will tell you that neither perception is accurate. The road will almost certainly not vanish, and the buses will turn out to be all the same size.

No doubt, humans figured out tens of thousands of years ago that the way objects look to us depends on where we position ourselves in relation to those objects. Throughout most of our history, artists who tried to make pictures that represent objects and spaces just as they appear to the eye relied mostly on trial and error, using their powers of imagination. Early in the fifteenth century, however, architects and painters working in the Italian city of Florence formulated rules of linear perspective. These were a set of optical and mathematical principles for depicting how the eye views a particular scene from a given stationary position. In achieving this breakthrough, these artists drew on knowledge about optics found in translations of Greek and Arabic texts.

Masaccio (MUH-sah-chee-oo), a young Florentine artist (1401–1428), created one of the earliest known works that clearly shows the principles of linear perspective in action. Titled *The Holy Trinity* (1425), this fresco, a picture made by applying paint to a moist plaster surface, occupies a wall in the church of Santa Maria Novella in Florence. It depicts the crucified Jesus Christ and three other figures as though they were inside a room with an arched ceiling. The illusion of spatial depth is convincing because, in accord with the rules of perspective, all the diagonal lines in the pattern of the ceiling converge at a single point in the picture. Other artists in Florence adopted the new technique, and it subsequently spread throughout Europe. For the next few centuries, the idea that painters should apply rules of perspective so that their canvases appear as "windows" on the natural world became fundamental to European art.

Linear perspective was one of the remarkable innovations in art and architecture that Florentines achieved in the period of European history conventionally called the late Middle Ages. Ironically, the city's cultural flowering, the period that later became known as the Italian Renaissance, took place, not in a time of political and social calm, but when Europe was just beginning to recover from several decades of severe social and economic upheaval. The young Masaccio and numerous other talented Florentines went about their creative labor in a city troubled by disease, war, and poverty.

In fact, Florence was representative of several Afroeurasian cities that sparkled as points of artistic and scholarly light despite repeated episodes of epidemic, violence, and economic disruption. Beginning early in the fourteenth century, the expansionary trend of population, economic output, and long-distance trade that had characterized much of Afroeurasia for about seven hundred years went into reverse. This general downturn, recalling the prolonged economic contraction of the fourth to sixth centuries C.E., involved several crises. One was a serious decline in food production and consequent famine in the Northern Hemisphere linked to climatic change. A second was the outbreak of infectious disease in several parts of Afroeurasia, a pestilence whose initial assault became known in history as the Black Death. A third was a swell of regional wars that reconfigured Afroeurasia's political map. Finally, commercial and cultural exchange along the trans-Eurasian silk roads declined following a century of unprecedented activity. The first part of this chapter explores the environmental catastrophes of the fourteenth century. The second part investigates the economic, political, and social consequences that attended those calamities, focusing here on China, the central Muslim lands, and Europe.

In the third section, we explore how and why demographic and economic motors began to rev up again in the 1400s

• • •

in much of Afroeurasia. Several vigorous new monarchies appeared, some of them eventually to become imperial giants. Silk road traffic picked up again, the shipping lanes along Afroeurasia's chain of seas flourished as never before. The technology of mechanical printing spread along the exchange routes from East Asia to Europe, allowing knowledge to be produced and circulated on a vastly larger scale. The secrets of gunpowder weaponry also spread across the hemisphere, amplifying human capacity to kill and destroy but also enhancing the power of centralized states.

The multiple troubles of the 1300–1500 period, like earlier cycles of retrenchment, revealed humankind's extraordinary talent for adapting to jarring change. Moreover, in the very long term of history, the era represented a short and only partial interruption of the human tendency to devise ever more complex systems of economy, social organization, and cultural exchange.

A Panoramic View

MAP 15.1 Spread of the plague pandemic (Black Death), 1330–1355.
The Black Death was one of several human catastrophes to strike Afroeurasian lands during the fourteenth century. What geographical factors might help explain why the plague pandemic spread in the general directions it did?

Environmental Crises of the Fourteenth Century

FOCUS What historical developments may account for significant population decline in parts of Afroeurasia in the fourteenth century?

After about seven hundred years of steady growth, the population of Afroeurasia as a whole plunged suddenly in the mid-fourteenth century, dropping about 16 percent between 1300 and 1400. This demographic slump did not take place everywhere, nor did it occur all at once. It did not, as far as we know, happen in Subsaharan Africa. In China, Inner Eurasia, and parts of Southwest Asia, on the other hand, numbers started sinking in the 1200s in connection with Mongol destruction, then kept on sinking straight through the 1300s. After three centuries of vigorous growth, Europe's numbers leveled off in about 1300 and then nose-dived between 1340 and 1400. Afroeurasia's overall demographic recovery did not get under way until the second half of the fifteenth century.

The economies of China, Inner Eurasia, the central Muslim lands, and Europe all appear to have slowed significantly in the fourteenth century, especially set against the dramatic growth that had occurred between 1000 and 1200. Subsaharan Africa was almost certainly an exception to this trend. There, towns and trade routes multiplied throughout the crisis decades, though from a lower starting base compared, say, to China.

Monumental changes also took place in the political sphere. Two of the great Mongol statesÐ the Yuan dynasty in China and the khanate of Iran-Iraq (Ilkhanate)Ð disintegrated before 1370. The other two major Mongol empiresÐ the khanate of Chagatai in the eastern steppes and Central Asia and the Golden Horde in the western steppes and RussiaÐ started imploding before the end of the century as a result of dynastic wars and rebellions. In the Mediterranean basin, the Turkic Mamluk empire of Egypt and Syria had increasing trouble maintaining its economic and financial health, and the three Muslim sultanates that shared North Africa all experienced serious internal troubles after 1350. In West Africa, the Mali empire, the world's most important gold-supplying state as of 1300, also shrank in the later decades of the fourteenth century amid royal succession disputes and provincial revolts.

These economic and political traumas had no single cause, and explanations for stagnancy or upheaval in one region do not necessarily apply in others. We have no index of wars and revolts to prove that the fourteenth century was more violent than any of several previous ages in world history. Russia, for example, certainly suffered more material destruction from the Mongol invasion of 1237±1240 than from any stresses that occurred in the following two hundred years. Nevertheless, we can identify, at least in northerly parts of Afroeurasia, environmental crises that profoundly disrupted the lives and livelihoods of tens of millions of people in the fourteenth century.

Downpour and Drought

As we saw in earlier chapters, the Northern Hemisphere experienced a small but ecologically significant warming trend, known as the North Atlantic Warm Period, between the ninth and thirteenth centuries. This trend ended sometime after 1200. Temperatures in Arctic and northern temperate latitudes dropped, and this cooling cycle continued erratically to the mid-1800s. Climatologists have labeled this temperature decline the **Little Ice Age** because of the advance of polar and alpine glaciers that accompanied it. Drawing on evidence from Europe and the North Atlantic, researchers have also suggested three general types of environmental change and accompanying social upheavals centered on the fourteenth century. First, in the Baltic Sea and the North Atlantic, sea ice and colder water temperatures extended farther south, reducing fish stocks and making voyages between Europe and the Norse communities of Iceland and Greenland more dangerous. Second, annual weather patterns became more erratic. Beginning in the 1200s, brutal wind storms and sea floods periodically smashed into the North Atlantic, North Sea, and Baltic Sea coasts, inundating low-lying farmland and in some years killing tens of thousands of people. Third,

> **Little Ice Age** A trend of climatic cooling that affected weather conditions chiefly in the Northern Hemisphere approximately from the late thirteenth to the mid-nineteenth century.

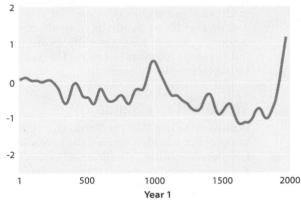

Temperature deviation (°C)

Global temperature changes, 1–2000 c.e. In what one-hundred-year period did the temperature peak of the North Atlantic Warm Period occur? In what one-hundred-year period did the lowest temperature point of the Little Ice Age occur?

summers became generally cooler and wetter all across northern Europe. In northern Britain and Scandinavia, grain farmers had to retreat south, leaving behind hundreds of deserted villages. English vintners found they could no longer produce decent wine.

Between 1315 and 1322 a succession of cool, rainy summers in northern Europe shortened the growing season, hampered crop harvesting, and made sheep and cattle more susceptible to epidemic diseases. Massive famine ensued, disrupting all economic life, expanding the ranks of the destitute, and killing perhaps 5±10 percent of the population. A modern historian, drawing on fourteenth-century chronicles, describes the sufferings of people in the region that is today Belgium during rains that started in May 1315 and continued nearly uninterrupted for a year: ªThe local harvest was wholly insufficient and the customary imports ceased almost entirely. In Antwerp the moans of the famishing could almost move a stone to pity. . . . They died in large numbers and great pits were dug outside the town into which were cast as many as sixty bodies.º¹ Better weather returned after 1322, but climatic conditions remained highly volatile. Regional famines continued to occur throughout the century in both northern and Mediterranean Europe.

The Little Ice Age hit western Europe just when economic growth was leveling off following several centuries of robust expansion. By the later 1200s, farm production could no longer keep pace with population growth. Good cropland in the more densely populated regions of western and central Europe filled up, and the migration of German and other western European farmers to conquered frontier territories in eastern Europe and Spain slowed down (see Chapter 12). Consequently, food prices increased, living standards shrank for all but the very rich, and at the low end of the social scale many serfs and tenant farmers descended into extreme poverty. The famines of 1315 to 1322 made all these problems worse. But even though hunger and disease killed hundreds of thousands, Europe's population appears to have generally recovered in the second quarter of the fourteenth century. The real demographic catastrophe struck in midcentury.

The Great Pestilence

Writing in the late 1370s the North African historian and philosopher Ibn Khaldun recalled the horror he had witnessed two decades earlier: ªCivilization both in the East and the West was visited by a destructive plague which devastated nations and caused populations to vanish. It swallowed up many of the good things of civilization and wiped them out. . . . Cities and building were laid waste, roads and way signs were obliterated, settlements and mansions became empty, dynasties and tribes grew weak. The entire inhabited world changed.º² The infectious disease that Ibn Khaldun described did not in fact affect ªthe entire inhabited world.º But it no doubt seemed that way to him, because

it killed a substantial percentage of North Africa's population and triggered years of economic and political disorder. Next to the massive die-off that American Indians endured when they first came in contact with Afroeurasian pathogens in the sixteenth century, the **Black Death** of 1346 to 1352 stands as the most deadly known disease crisis up to modern times. It broke upon populations from Inner Eurasia, and perhaps China, to as far west as Greenland (see Map 15.1). Everywhere that it struck, immune systems failed to defend human bodies against the invading microorganism. Millions died after days, or even just hours, of acute suffering from raging fevers, vomiting, and dark painful swellings called buboes. Though as many as 40 percent of infected victims recovered, depending on the locality, people who contracted pneumonic plague, that is, infection of the lungs, almost always died. And before they expired, they often transmitted the pathogen to others by coughing, sneezing, or just breathing. In Afroeurasia the Black Death reached the proportions of a pandemic, a contagion that spread from one region to another, in this case nearly across the hemisphere.

> **Black Death** An infectious disease, probably plague, that caused significant population decline in parts of Afroeurasia in the mid-fourteenth century.

Origins of the Black Death. Since the late nineteenth century, epidemiologists and historians have argued that plague was the infection associated with the Black Death. We sometimes use the word *plague* to characterize any serious epidemic or, metaphorically, any sudden calamity, such as a ªplague of locusts.º By a stricter definition, however, plague refers to a particular disease having a range of symptoms and biological strains associated with the disease-producing bacterium, or bacillus, called *Yersinia pestis* (*Y. pestis*). For longer than anyone knows, plague has thrived among ground-burrowing rodents that live in certain parts of the world, notably in Inner Eurasia, the Himalayan Mountain foothills, East Africa, and the American Southwest. The principal vector, or carrier, of *Y. pestis* is a type of flea that inhabits the fur of living animals and feeds on their blood. In certain environmental conditions, the bacillus may spread through a large rodent population. Animals infected with *Y. pestis* soon die, forcing equally infected fleas to jump to a living animal to feed, thereby spreading the disease further. If infected animals come into sustained contact with humans, fleas that can find no other hosts may look for blood meals on human bodies, thereby passing *Y. pestis* to them. According to recent research, *Y. pestis* infections caused the first plague pandemic, the Plague of Justinian, which occurred in the mid-sixth century (see Chapter 9).³

Some researchers have argued recently that the Black Death had nothing to do with *Y. pestis*, pointing to differences in symptoms and other factors between the fourteenth-century pandemic and modern plague. Nevertheless, current genetic studies, including analysis of DNA from the bones of plague victims buried between 1348 and

1350 in a cemetery in London, have confirmed the presence of *Y. pestis*.[4] This research contends that the Black Death was more virulent than modern plague because infected people were already suffering from malnutrition associated with food shortages linked to the Little Ice Age.

The precise region where the Black Death originated is also debated, but the dominant theory contends that humans mingled with infected rodent communities somewhere in Inner Eurasia in the late thirteenth or early fourteenth century (see Map 15.1). Turkic and Mongol horse soldiers may have been the first to spread the disease widely. Infected rodents and fleas could have infiltrated grain stores in saddlebags and wagons, thus traveling far and wide to contaminate both humans and more rodents. Some scholars have also hypothesized that Little Ice Age conditions helped propel the disease because drier weather on the Inner Eurasian steppes forced rodents to migrate in search of water. As infected creatures moved east or west from areas of sparse to denser human habitation, they set off epidemics.

According to contemporary Chinese reports, a terrible pestilence struck the Hebei region of northern China in 1331, killing nine-tenths of the population. Though we lack a description of symptoms, it is possible that the Black Death enacted its first scene in East Asia. To the west, epidemics occurred in Inner Eurasia in the late 1330s and in the Golden Horde territories north of the Black Sea in the following decade. About 1345, disease erupted in Kaffa (Theodosia) on the Black Sea coast, infecting the resident community of Genoese Italian merchants. Ships leaving the port carried sailors, merchants, and black rats, all infected or soon to be, to other ports around the Black Sea rim. From there the pathogen spread on the sailing ships that linked the Black Sea to the Mediterranean. A ghastly epidemic hit Constantinople in 1347. That same year the contagion spread to Sicily and Egypt, almost certainly carried by Italian seafarers. The Muslim historian al-Maqrizi tells of a ship limping into the port of Alexandria. Out of a company of 332 souls, all had perished of disease at sea except for forty sailors, four merchants, and one slave, and all of those unfortunates died a short time later.[5]

In the grim year of 1348, ships coursing through the Mediterranean deposited their lethal cargo in one port after another. From those towns, caravans and wagon trains distributed the ailment to inland regions of Europe, North Africa, and Southwest Asia. In the spring and summer, epidemics hit dozens of citiesÐ Genoa and Venice, Barcelona and Paris, Damascus and Tunis. An epidemic struck the holy city of Mecca in Arabia in 1348±1349, no doubt carried there by Muslim pilgrims. Florence, already weakened by a succession of famines, may have lost as much as 75 percent of its population of about eighty thousand. Cairo, capital of the Mamluk empire and probably the largest Afroeurasian city west of China, may have lost 300,000 of its estimated 500,000 residents. In his famous collection of stories titled *The Decameron*, the fourteenth-century Florentine writer Boccaccio describes the terrors of the pestilence in both city and countryside:

Fleas in search of blood meals bite rodents infected with plague bacillus.

Bacilli multiply in fleas' gut, causing starvation.

Starving fleas jump from rodent to rodent to try to feed.

Fleas infect healthy rodents with plague bacillus and disease spreads.

When sick rodents die, fleas look for new living hosts.

If infected rats and fleas live near humans, hungry fleas may infect them.

Infected humans become sick; 50 percent or more may die.

If lungs are infected, sick people may transmit bacillus to others through respiration; pneumonic plague is almost always fatal.

How plague spread in the fourteenth century. What are some ways in which humans may have unintentionally transported plague-infected fleas or rats from one village or city to another?

The condition of the common people (and also, in great part, of the middle class) was yet more pitiable to behold, because these . . . fell sick by the thousand daily and being altogether untended and unsuccored, died well-nigh all without recourse. Many breathed their last in the open street, by day and by night, while many others, though they died in their homes, made it known to the neighbors that they were dead rather by the stench of their rotting bodies than otherwise. . . . Throughout the scattered villages and in the fields, the poor miserable peasants and their families without succor of physician or aid of servant, died not like men, but well-nigh like beasts.[6]

In 1349 the pandemic spread like wildfire, advancing simultaneously up the Nile River valley, along the North African coast, and across the English Channel to Britain. It advanced northwestward to Ireland, Iceland, and even Greenland, where it appears to have obliterated one of the

Perspectives on the Black Death

The Black Death spawned innumerable treatises on causes and treatments. Although writers proposed theories and made recommendations that today seem illogical, and perhaps dangerous, these texts help us understand the medical and religious debates that circulated as the epidemic raged. The two selections below discuss the issue of contagion. Document 1 is from a plague tract that a French court physician wrote around 1364. A Swedish bishop republished the text in the mid-fifteenth century under the name Bengt Knutsson. Document 2 is from a work by Lisan al-Din Ibn al-Khatib, a celebrated poet, philosopher, and physician who lived in Granada, Spain, when it was a Muslim-ruled city. Ibn al-Khatib wrote "A Very Useful Inquiry into the Horrible Sickness" about 1349–1352, just when the Black Death was spreading around the Mediterranean rim.

DOCUMENT 1 Bengt Knutsson

I say that pestilence sores are contagious because of infectious humors, and the reek or smoke of such sores is venomous and corrupts the air. And therefore one should flee such persons as are infected. In pestilence time nobody should stand in a great press of people because some man among them may be infected. Therefore wise physicians visiting sick folk stand far from the patient, holding their face towards the door or window, and so should the servants of sick folk stand. . . .

Now it is to be known by what remedies a man may preserve himself from the pestilence. First see the writings of Jeremiah the prophet that a man ought to forsake evil things and do good deeds and meekly confess his sins, for it is the highest remedy in time of pestilence: penance and confession to be preferred to all other medicines. Nevertheless I promise you verily it is a good remedy to void and change the infected place. But some may not profitably change their places. Therefore as much as

they can they should eschew every cause of putrefaction and stinking, and namely every fleshly lust with women is to be eschewed. Also the southern wind, which is naturally infective. Therefore spar the windows against the south . . . until the first hour after the middle of the day then open the windows against the north. Of the same cause every foul stench is to be eschewed, of stable, stinking fields, ways or streets, and namely of stinking dead carrion and most of stinking waters where in many places water is kept two days or two nights. . . .

Also let your house be sprinkled especially in summer with vinegar and roses and with the leaves of the vine. Also it is good to wash your hands oft times in the day with water and vinegar and wipe your face with your hands.

Source: Rosemary Horrox, ed. and trans., *The Black Death* (Manchester: Manchester University Press, 1994), 175±177.

DOCUMENT 2 Ibn al-Khatib

If it were asked, how do we submit to the theory of contagion, when already the divine law has refuted the notion of contagion, we will answer: The existence of contagion has been proved by experience, deduction, the senses, observation, and by unanimous reports, and these aforementioned categories are the demonstrations of proof. And it is not a secret to whoever has looked into this matter or has come to be aware of it that those who come into contact with [plague] patients mostly die, while those who do not come into contact survive. Moreover, disease occurs in a household or neighborhood because of the mere presence of a contagious dress or utensil; even a [contaminated] earring has been known to kill whoever wears it and his whole household. And when it happens in a city, it starts in one house and then affects the visitors of the house, then the neighbors, the relatives, and other visitors until it spreads throughout the city. And coastal cities are free of the disease until it comes from the sea through a visitor from another city that has the disease, and thus the appearance of the disease in the safe city coincides with the arrival of this

man from the contagious city. And the safety of those who have gone into isolation is demonstrated by the example of the ascetic, Ibn Abu Madyan, who lived in the city of Salé [on the coast of Morocco]. He believed in the contagion, and so he hoarded food and bricked up the door on his family (and his family was large!), and the city was obliterated by the plague and not one soul [except Ibn Abu Madyan] was left in that whole town. And reports were unanimous that isolated places that have no roads to them and are not frequented by people have escaped unscathed from the plague. . . . And it has been confirmed that nomads and tent dwellers in Africa and other nomadic places have escaped unscathed because their air is not enclosed and it is improbable that it can be corrupted.

Source: M. J. Müller, "Ibnulkhatib's Bericht über die Pest," Sitzungsberichte der Königl. Bayerischen Akademie der Wissenschaften, 2 (1863): 2±12. Translated from the Arabic with assistance from Dr. Walid Saleh. In John Aberth, *The First Horseman: Disease in Human History*, 1st Edition, 44±46, © 2007. Reprinted by permission of Pearson Education, Inc., Upper Saddle River, New Jersey.

Thinking Critically

What did Knutsson think caused the deadly disease to spread? How could people avoid contracting it? How does religion figure in Knutsson's list of treatments for the disease? How is Ibn al-Khatib's understanding of contagion similar to or different from Knutsson's? How do the two authors compare in their discussion of "corrupt air" as a cause of epidemic? If fourteenth-century city officials were to consult these two texts, what public health measures might they have taken to combat the spread of the malady?Perspectives on the Black Death

A dying plague victim. In this illustration from a Czech codex (1376), Death, depicted here as a ghoulish demon, strangles a plague sufferer. Why might strangulation be an appropriate image if the victim were suffering from pneumonic plague?

two remaining Viking settlements there. To the east, it assaulted Germany, Scandinavia, and the eastern Baltic lands, reaching Moscow, though with declining virulence, in 1352.

Coping with the calamity. Fourteenth-century societies had no effective remedy for either the Black Death or the terrible epidemics that recurred every several years in different localities for another century or more. People suffered not only physical pain but also terror, helplessness, and despair. In both Europe and the Muslim Mediterranean lands, groups who lived in tight communities or administered to the sick endured particularly high mortality rates. Priests, nuns, religious scholars, university faculties, urban artisans, and soldiers living in barracks all proved highly vulnerable. Epidemics swept through armies in Germany and Italy. In southern Spain in 1349±1350, both Muslim and Christian troops battling for control of the city of Gibraltar lost large numbers to the contagion, the Black Death favoring neither side. The pestilence devastated not only crowded cities but also rural hamlets. Peasants who fled their homes to escape the scourge unwittingly passed it on to neighboring villages. A Muslim chronicler who witnessed scenes of flight in Egypt wrote of ªthose dead who are laid out on the highway like an ambush for others.º[7]

No one understood the biology of contagion, nor was there much agreement about treatment. In both Europe and the Muslim world, learned observers blamed the high mortality on a polluted wind coming from the east, a foul corruption of the air, or a bad alignment of stars. Preventive and curative advice abounded: flee your home, do not flee your home, burn clothes, get fresh air, eat pickled onions, pray, and gather in houses of worship. Christians, Jews, and Muslims all struggled to give the catastrophe divine meaning. Christian doctrine invited the conclusion that the sins of humankind obliged God to teach his creation a lesson it would never forget. In Germany and other European countries, penance-doers, called **flagellants,** tried to expiate the sins of the world by parading through towns while beating themselves savagely with iron-studded leather thongs. Other terrified believers blamed the pandemic on Jews rumored to have ªpoisoned the wells.º In Switzerland and Germany, **pogroms** wiped out Jewish communities in many towns. Thousands of Jews consequently fled eastward to Poland and Russia, where they established new communities that thrived in the following centuries. Despite great social trauma, Muslims interpreted the disaster mostly as a manifestation of the Creator's unknowable plan for his creation. Terror and despair abounded, but this particular catastrophe did not incite significant Muslim maltreatment of Christian or Jewish minorities.

> **flagellants** In Christian Europe in the thirteenth and fourteenth centuries, individuals who whipped, or flagellated, themselves as an act of public penance for sin.

> **pogrom** A violent attack on a minority community characterized by massacre and destruction of property; most commonly refers to assaults on Jews.

Wherever the pandemic hit hard, economic disruption immediately followed. In western Europe, Egypt, and Syria, peasant farmers died or fled their homes in such large numbers that crops rotted in the fields. In hundreds of cities, manufacturing industries temporarily ground to a halt as entire neighborhoods of skilled artisans perished. People who performed vital servicesÐ priests, doctors, teachers, lawyers, mule drivers, riverboat crews, even gravediggersÐ became scarce and expensive. On the brighter side, the plague completely skipped some parts of Europe and Southwest Asia altogether, though the reasons are not clear. We have no sound evidence that the pandemic spread to West Africa, South Asia, or Southeast Asia. We know that severe epidemics occurred in China in 1331, 1333, and 1353±1354, though they could have been outbreaks of diseases other than plague.

Crises in the Political and Social Realms

FOCUS What evidence indicates that the fourteenth century was a period of unusual crises and instability in several parts of Afroeurasia?

A surge of political and social instability rocked large parts of Afroeurasia in the later fourteenth century. By comparison with the previous hundred years, when the great Mongol empires kept order over much of Eurasia, the century after 1350 looks troubled indeed. Several large states either shrank or collapsed, and in some regions warfare took a particularly vicious turn. We cannot conclude that famine or infectious disease were the primary causes of those upheavals because other known historical factors came into play. Nevertheless, the occurrence of a number of wars, rebellions, and regime changes corresponded with times of food shortage and pestilence, which disrupted the social order.

China: The Collapse of Mongol Rule

The Mongols first invaded China under the great conqueror Chingis Khan in 1211. By 1276 they dominated all of it (see Chapter 13). Kubilai Khan, the grandson of Chingis, founded the Yuan dynasty and ruled China to 1294. Under him and his first few successors, the empire remained unified and generally stable. By the 1320s, however, political factions within the imperial palace at Beijing (known then as Khanbaliq) descended into chronic factional infighting. The Mongol court paid less and less attention to firm administration of the provinces, and emperors lacking Kubilai's backbone became pawns of one power group or another. Togon Temur, the last Mongol emperor, reigned as little more than a figurehead for thirty-six years (1333±1368).

Below the turbulent surface of palace politics, deeper structural shifts helped undermine the Mongol state. The government had allowed military and administrative costs to swell, so that taxes ate up a burdensome portion of people's income. Worse than that, revenues dropped in the fourteenth century, partly because the population kept declining amid successive regional famines and epidemics. An extended cold snap in the second quarter of the century, almost certainly linked to the general global cooling trend, cut both food supplies and tax receipts in the northern provinces. Struggling to finance the regime, Mongol officials churned out more paper money, which accelerated price inflation and pushed down standards of living.

As chains of command broke down, discontented peasants, soldiers, and local warlords felt emboldened to protest poverty and government neglect. In 1351 an uprising flared among tens of thousands of abused and underpaid peasants whom the Mongol regime had drafted to rechannel a section of the Yellow River. Several more insurgencies broke out in the following years, especially in the south. Bandits, smugglers, peasant marauders, and fervent new religious sects all contributed to spreading turmoil. By the 1360s the beleaguered central government had to compete for authority with a dozen or so local rebel groups. Zhu Yuanzhang (JOO yuwen-JAHNG), the leader of one of these insurgent bands, built up a power base in the Yangzi River valley and then sent his army against Beijing. In 1368 he forced the emperor and his entourage to flee to Mongolia. Once in control of the capital, Zhu Yuanzhang moved vigorously to restore China's unity, this time under Chinese, not foreign, leadership. Suppressing all competing rebel movements, he proclaimed the new Ming dynasty. We return to it later in this chapter.

Political and Economic Troubles in the Central Muslim Lands

The Mongol khanate of Iran-Iraq crumbled in 1335, twelve years before the Black Death even appeared in Southwest Asia. This realm was not economically healthy. Farming in the Tigris-Euphrates valley had been shrinking gradually for several centuries. The Mongol conquest in the previous century did more damage to the economic infrastructure there, as well

Harvest of Victory. Timur, seated on a throne, receives soldiers carrying severed heads. Decapitated enemies lie sprawling in the foreground. The painting comes from a fifteenth century Persian history of the Timurid dynasty. What do you think the structure in the upper center of the picture represents?

as to Iran's irrigated agricultural lands. A few of the khanate's rulers experimented with reforms to improve farm production but made only modest headway. The regime fell, not amid popular revolt as in China, but as a consequence of internal feuding among Mongol and Turkic princes for supreme command. The regime's collapse left the region splintered into several, relatively weak military states.

The Mamluk sultanate of Egypt and Syria, a Turkic state that had defended itself successfully against Mongol assaults, remained intact. But the population plunged in the aftermath of the Black Death and recurring epidemics. As the skilled workforce dwindled, manufacturing became depressed. To take the example of Egypt's once-thriving textile industry, the city of Alexandria had 12,000±14,000 skilled cotton and linen weavers in 1394, but only 800 by 1434.[8] The rural peasant economy suffered as well. Reduced urban populations cut demand for grain; therefore, prices fell. To compensate for their income losses, Turkic and Arab estate lords tightened the screws on peasants, demanding higher rents and taxes. Thus, millions of men and women who farmed the Nile valley and the Syrian plains fell into deeper poverty in the later fourteenth century. On the other hand, the scarcity of labor in the aftermath of the pandemic meant that urban workers who managed to survive, especially those with skills, could command higher wages, at least for a time.

As if the peoples of Southwest Asia did not suffer enough from disease and economic troubles, they also had to endure another episode of massacres and city burnings, a dismal sequel to the Mongol invasions of the previous century.

This time the perpetrator was Timur, also known later in European history as Timur the Lame, or Tamerlane. Born in Central Asia, the young Timur began his career as a local Turkic war captain. Like his role model, Chingis Khan, he bested opposing tribal lords and amassed a large following of mounted archers. He began his ascent to power in Central Asia in the 1360s. His core state embraced vast grazing lands and the fertile valley of the Amu Darya (Amu River), plus Samarkand, Bukhara, and several other silk roads cities. Taxation of these resources paid for his expanding army, and, like Chingis, he ensured the allegiance of fractious warrior clans by continually leading them on huge plundering expeditions. From 1370 to 1405 he kept on the move, incorporating fighters of many origins into his forces as they advanced. Sacking one city after another, he outdid the Mongols in cruelty, raping and enslaving women by the tens of thousands and burying prisoners alive or starving them to death.

Timur led his forces north, east, and west (see Map 15.2). In the early 1390s he advanced north of the Caspian Sea to assault the Mongol khanate of the Golden Horde, destroying several cities in the Volga River valley and seriously weakening Mongol domination of Russia. In 1399 his cavalry rode from Afghanistan to the Indus River valley, where the invaders wrecked the great city of Delhi and permanently crippled the Delhi sultanate, which had once ruled all of northern India. In 1400±1401 he took Damascus, the Mamluk capital in Syria, but then withdrew. Apparently convinced that all great steppe lords should conquer China, he set off in that direction in 1405. But he died just when the expedition was getting under way.

MAP 15.2 The empire of Timur in 1404.
When Timur died in 1405, he was planning to lead an army against China. From a geographical and political perspective, how difficult a task might that have been?

Timur had a genealogy worked up to show, without compelling evidence, that he descended from Chingis Khan and was therefore the right man to fulfill the Mongol ambition to rule the whole world. Though we know little of his thoughts on religion, he professed Islam and appears to have regarded himself as a special agent of God destined to punish both unbelievers and apathetic Muslims. He twice laid waste to the Christian kingdom of Georgia in the Caucasus Mountains and nearly extinguished the Nestorian Christian communities of Inner Eurasia. Muslims who displeased him for one reason or another got no better treatment.

Timur did not, however, match Chingis in the art of empire building. He did little to set up a firm chain of command or administration in conquered cities. He sent thousands of captured artisans and engineers to Samarkand to create a magnificent capital, but he rarely went there himself. He encouraged caravan traffic and thereby won the support of merchants, but his devastating campaigns hampered agriculture and trade. When he died suddenly, power struggles immediately erupted among his four sons and various tribal warlords. The empire soon fell apart, though the most vigorous of his descendants held Central Asia and part of Afghanistan together as a regional state. Timur deserves recognition as the last of the great Inner Eurasian steppe conquerors, but his predations only aggravated Southwest Asia's long-term economic problems.

Europe in the Aftermath of the Black Death

Like the Muslim Mediterranean, western Europe continued to lose population for about a century after 1350. In turn, labor shortages in nearly every occupation slowed economic recovery. As in Egypt and Syria, the demographic plunge reduced the market for grain and simultaneously raised the cost of labor. Land became cheap as people abandoned farms and villages or fell to the pestilence. Like the Mamluk military elite, European aristocrats who owned great manors had a harder time keeping up farm production and generating new wealth.

Population decline and the end of serfdom in western Europe. Peasants lucky enough to escape lethal contagion found that the population fall-off increased the value of their labor, giving them a measure of leverage over their landlords. Especially in northwestern Europe, farmers had some success negotiating with estate owners to lower rents, eliminate customary payments, and ease restrictions on their mobility. In other words, men and women whose labor enjoyed strong demand might bargain their way out of serfdom, the condition of legal bondage that forced them to live and work on a particular estate. Many thousands of serfs simply abandoned their lords and fled to towns, which needed their labor as well. Aristocrats desperate to preserve

their agricultural incomes retaliated by joining with royal governments, notably in France and England, to fight the rising cost of labor and the deterioration of serfdom. These regimes legislated ceilings on wages, imposed new rural taxes, and insisted that peasants meet their manorial obligations, though to little long-term avail.

In some places farmers and landless workers who thought the increased value of their labor deserved more just compensation took up knives and pitchforks in revolt. Rural rebellions flared from England to Hungary in the later fourteenth century. Indeed, these movements paralleled the uprisings that broke out in China in the 1350s and 1360s in similarly unsettled economic conditions. The Jacquerie rebellion in northern France in 1358 and the Peasants' Revolt in England in 1381 were among the most violent insurgencies. Describing the Jacquerie, a disapproving chronicler lamented that "these mischievous people thus assembled without captain or armor, robbed, burnt, and slew all gentlemen that they could lay hands on, and forced and ravished ladies and damosels, and did such shameful deeds that no human creature ought to think on any such."[9] Commanding far better fighters and weapons than the rebels did, landowning elites soon snuffed out these insurgencies. In contrast to what happened in China, none of the rebel groups came close to removing a dynasty.

Nevertheless, serfdom virtually disappeared in western Europe in the fifteenth century. Landowners discovered economic sense in paying wages to workers, collecting money rents from them, or selling them land outright, rather than trying to force labor from aggrieved serfs. Peasants became "free" in the sense that they could legally move from one place to another and to sell their labor for cash. In some Mediterranean cities, however, slaves imported from eastern Europe or Africa continued to perform domestic labor.

Long wars. Warfare among Europe's several competing states may have been no more ferocious in the fourteenth century than in earlier times. But the leveling off of economic growth, followed by famine, disease, and mass die-off, intensified political stresses and raised the stakes for control of resources. The prolonged conflict between England and France known as the Hundred Years' War (1337±1453) merely extended three centuries of hostility between the two monarchies over territories that are today part of France but were then under English rule. At first, English cavalry, as well as infantry troops armed with longbows, won most of the battles, but in the end England had to cede nearly all its continental territory to France, which emerged in the later fifteenth century as western Europe's most powerful state.

The war was marked by episodes of terrible violence alternating with extended lulls, sometimes made necessary by wet summers or epidemics. Fought mostly in France, the conflict involved long urban sieges, scorched earth tactics that destroyed cropland, and deployment on both sides of great bands of hired mercenaries, who sometimes

Ibn Khaldun: A Thinker for Troubled Times

Many scholars from China to Europe wrote narrative descriptions of the tumultuous events of the later fourteenth century. Abd al-Rahman ibn Khaldun (1332–1404) went much further, creating an elegant political theory to explain those wrenching changes. Born of a long line of Muslim scholars who made their mark in both Spain and Tunisia, Ibn Khaldun wrote on subjects as diverse as philosophy, theology, history, law, ethnology, and mathematics.

In his most celebrated work, titled *The Muqaddima* (Introduction to History), Ibn Khaldun theorized that change in human political affairs is not haphazard but follows a pattern of cycles. New dynasties arise when an energetic leader organizes a band of warriors into a sturdy, cohesive military force, which then seizes power. This conquering elite founds a state, but it soon starts to deteriorate because its members become caught up in urban luxury, political squabbling, and selfish oppression of their subject population. Eventually, the dynasty collapses under pressure from a new band of hardy warriors, and a fresh cycle begins. In formulating this theory of change, Ibn Khaldun contended that history has an identifiable shape to it and that finding the underlying pattern depends on close scrutiny of human events. Because he built his theory on concrete observation and research, not simply philosophical conjecture, he foreshadowed the methods of the modern social sciences.

Ibn Khaldun saw enough political and economic instability in the later fourteenth century to hypothesize that Muslim civilization was in jeopardy. In his view the Black Death, which struck his native city of Tunis in 1348, hastened the process of decay, overtaking "the dynasties at the time of their senility." Only a teenager at the time, he lost both of his parents to the pestilence. This personal tragedy, however, drove him to try to explain rationally why social calamities recur.

His learned family provided him with a strong education, and after his parents died he entered a career of public service. Ambitious, a bit snobbish, and sometimes politically meddlesome, he moved in and out of princely favor, holding government posts under several rulers in Tunisia, Morocco, Algeria, and Granada and even going to jail in Morocco for two years for taking part in a court conspiracy. In 1382 he traveled to Egypt, where he accepted posts as judge and law professor in the Mamluk sultanate. His wife and daughters sailed from Tunis to join him in Cairo, but they all died in a shipwreck. He gave brilliant lectures in Cairo's colleges, but he also made enemies. He got fired from every prestigious position he held.

In 1400, after making a pilgrimage to Mecca, Ibn Khaldun traveled to Damascus in Syria in the entourage of the Mamluk sultan. Later, he helped negotiate the city's surrender to Timur. He even got an interview with the conqueror and seems to have regarded Timur as the leader who might restore political unity to the Muslim world. Ibn Khaldun later returned to Cairo, where he continued his academic and legal career until his death in 1406.

Ibn Khaldun is represented as a member of the scholarly class in this modern statue on display in his native city of Tunis.

Ibn Khaldun typified the cosmopolitan spirit among educated Muslims, traveling widely to seek knowledge, serving numerous rulers without giving any of them permanent allegiance, and finding time to observe and write about the human condition. Modern scholars stand in wonder at his immense project to synthesize human history and to discover meaning in the directions it takes.

Thinking Critically

How would you argue that Ibn Khaldun's life and thought might help us better understand the era in which he lived?

---

abandoned the fighting to terrorize country peasants. In short, the brutality of the struggle only aggravated the economic problems that came in the wake of the Black Death.

The Church divided. In the fourteenth century the political authority and moral prestige of the Catholic Church plummeted along with Europe's population. The church had developed into a highly centralized and wealthy organization with its own law courts, diplomatic service, businesses, and vast properties. However, the people who managed these enterprises were generally more interested in worldly affairs than in spiritual ministry. In the political sphere, the pope directly ruled a large part of central Italy from his seat in Rome. But he also continued to press his claim, as divinely appointed shepherd of western Christendom, to supreme authority over all monarchs and princes. In fact, as powerful centralized states arose in western Europe, this assertion no longer had much force. The kings of France and England had particularly strong convictions about their independent authority to tax members of the Christian clergy, require their political allegiance, and prosecute them in royal courts of law, all practices that the pope tried to oppose.

In the fourteenth century the old ideal of Europe as a moral empire under the guiding hand of a benevolent pope perished once and for all. In 1309 the French king Philip IV pressured a newly chosen pope to move his throne from Rome, where it had always been, to Avignon in southern France. There, Philip's officials could make sure that the Holy Father led the church in ways favorable to the French crown. Palace extravagance and financial corruption thrived in Avignon, a state of affairs that appalled ordinary Christians. Moreover, thousands of nuns, monks, and priests died in the Black Death, including many of the best-educated clerics. This led to a chronic shortage of spiritual caregivers, local church leaders, and teachers. In 1378 the church hierarchy fell into near chaos when two popes, one in Avignon and one in Rome, competed for legitimacy. At one point, three men claimed the papal throne. The schism ended finally in 1417 with some church theologians and legal experts leading a reform effort, known as the Conciliar Movement, to transfer supreme church authority from the person of the pope to councils of high clergy. Since the majority of Catholics preferred a strong and morally righteous pope to fractious gatherings of clerics, the movement faded. Nevertheless, the church's prestige continued to suffer, encouraging a new generation of moral critics and reformers to come forward.

Fifteenth-Century Recuperation

FOCUS What factors may account for a trend of demographic and economic recovery in several parts of Afroeurasia in the fifteenth century?

The population crisis that affected so much of Afroeurasia in the fourteenth century proved to be a short-lived cyclical phenomenon, just as the downturn of the fourth to sixth centuries C.E. had been. By 1500 the supercontinent's overall population reached about 416 millionD about 8 million more than the 1340 level. Long-distance trade almost certainly slowed on both land and sea routes in the immediate

Peasants killing nobles. This miniature illustration from the *Chronicles of France* depicts the outbreak of the Jacquerie uprising in France in 1358. Peasants with daggers and swords are making short work of four unarmed aristocrats. Do you think the artist reveals a particular political bias? In favor of which side?

aftermath of the Black Death. But demand for luxury goods and exotic imports swelled among city dwellers who survived the pandemic and therefore commanded higher incomes. Ironically, cities made smaller by epidemic, famine, and war frequently entered the fifteenth century more important than ever as storehouses of wealth, knowledge, and skill. Several cities emerged as vibrant capitals of new states and dynasties, and in some regions those centers blazed with artistic and literary light.

Technologies for the Future

Both the sources of useful energyD human muscle, animal traction, wind, and waterD and the technologies for moving people and goods from place to place remained largely unchanged in most of Afroeurasia between 1300 and 1500. To be sure, entrepreneurs and technicians across Afroeurasia continued to refine mechanical devices and undertake great building projects. In China, for example, engineers expanded the already immense inland waterway system, and shipwrights built ever-larger oceangoing vessels. In Europe, labor shortages and declining land values prompted estate lords and urban manufacturers to improve the technologies of textile production, mining, and wind and water mills. Medical scholars did not learn much about infectious diseases from the Black Death, but European and Muslim physicians gained a little more understanding of the mechanisms of contagion. Two technical advances that spread widely in the fifteenth century were gunpowder weaponry and printing.

Guns. Back in the thirteenth century, Mongol conquerors adopted Chinese techniques for making bombs, rockets, and incendiary weapons by mixing salt peter (potassium nitrate), sulfur, and charcoal to make gunpowder. Mongol and Mamluk armies used explosive devices in the late thirteenth century. About the same time, the gun made its world debut. In elemental form a gun is simply a tube of durable material. A charge of gunpowder is inserted into the tube's base and then ignited to propel a missile out the front end, presumably with destructive, or at least loud, effect. The earliest physical evidence of gun making is a bronze tube that archeologists found in Manchuria (northeastern China) at

the site of a 1288 battle. No doubt, military commanders regarded the earliest firearms merely as new-fangled devices to supplement other types of machines for hurling objects against enemy soldiers or fortifications.

Gunpowder and recipes for making it almost certainly became known in Europe as a result of diffusion westward across Inner Eurasia during the Mongol era. By the 1320s, European soldiers were using gunpowder to propel arrows or stones from pot-shaped metal tubes, though with little force or accuracy. In the following decades, artisans in the employ of princes or towns experimented widely with barrel castings, firing mechanisms, and gunpowder blends. By the end of the century, rulers began using firearms on the battlefield. Some European monarchs had sufficient wealth to cast and deploy rudimentary cannons, which launched stone or iron balls against castle or city walls. In the late phase of the Hundred Years' War, French kings organized Europe's first artillery corps to transport and maintain guns. They used these weapons to help blow the English out of

Early artillery. Near the end of the Hundred Years' War, a French army dislodged the English from the fortress of Cherbourg on the northern coast of France. This fifteenth-century illustration documents French deployment of cannons that fired stone balls. The horse in the foreground is wearing a caparison, or fabric covering, decorated with fleurs-de-lis (lily flowers), a symbol of the French monarchy. How effective do you think artillery of this type might have been in siege warfare compared to the longbows that both sides used?

their remaining continental strongholds. In the same period, rulers in China, India, Southwest Asia, and North Africa all fielded increasing numbers of cannons and handguns. Until the sixteenth century, these weapons had limited military value. Mounted archers with composite bows, as well as infantry carrying crossbows or longbows, could load and fire their weapons much faster than could either hand gunners or artillery crews. Nevertheless, world history's age of gunpowder was well under way by 1450.

Printing. Books printed on paper circulated widely in China during the Song and Yuan (Mongol) dynasties (eleventh to fourteenth centuries) and contributed much to the spread of knowledge across East Asia. The idea of printing words or pictures by pressing sheets of paper onto carved wooden blocks brushed with ink reached Southwest Asia in the later thirteenth century. There, the government of the Mongol khanate of Iran-Iraq tried, and failed, to introduce the Chinese idea of printed paper money. Local merchants wanted no part of it. Neither in India nor in the central Muslim lands did printing for any purpose take hold in the fourteenth or fifteenth century. We should be careful, however, not to equate printing with the hand production of books on paper. In the Muslim world, for example, rulers, religious institutions, colleges, and wealthy families possessed libraries that might contain thousands of hand-copied books, mainly in Arabic or Persian.

Libraries in fifteenth-century Europe were far smaller than in the Muslim lands or China, but Europeans warmed quickly to the idea of printing. By the 1200s, western Europe had a thriving papermaking industry, another technology that originated in China and spread to Europe by way of the Muslim Mediterranean. Italian artisans knew something about block printing images, such as stamping illustrations on playing cards. But the idea of mechanically reproducing books probably reached Europe directly from China, perhaps when Christian travelers returned from Mongol lands carrying Chinese volumes in their packs.

> **movable type printing** A technology in which characters, especially alphabetic letters and punctuation, are individually carved or cast on pieces of wood, ceramic, or metal and then assembled into a text, inked, and printed on paper or other material.

European artisans used block printing for many purposes, but in the fifteenth century they also adopted the technology of **movable type.** Metalsmiths fashioned individual characters; printers arranged them as needed in a frame, inked the frame, and printed a sheet on a press. These individual pieces of type could be used over and over. Chinese printers had invented movable type made of wood or ceramic in the eleventh century, and as early as the thirteenth century Korean artisans discovered the superior durability of metal type produced in molds. In East Asia, however, this technology proved less efficient than block printing because the particular Chinese writing system, which is logographic, not alphabetic, required production of thousands of distinct characters rather than multiple copies of the thirty or fewer signs that make up an alphabet. Nevertheless, East Asia's book industry using block technology continued to expand.

In Europe in the 1440s a team of German craftsmen led by the goldsmith Johannes Gutenberg invented movable metal type for the Latin alphabet, almost certainly independently of the Korean invention a century or more earlier. Gutenberg printed a Latin Bible in 1455 and from that date printing presses multiplied across Europe. Scribes who hunched over desks to copy books could not come close to matching the speed with which a movable type press could produce multiple copies of an absolutely uniform text. In the 1460s, printing presses opened in several cities in Italy, which already led Europe in papermaking technology. In the following decade, printers began to ply their trade in France, the Netherlands, Hungary, Poland, England, and Spain.

A screw press in Hungary. This press, shown here in a woodcut, operated for a short time in the city of Buda (modern Budapest). The man in front on the left is turning the screw to lower the flat surface of the metal platen to press a sheet of paper firmly against a set of inked type. The man in back on the left is holding inking pads. What do you think the worker on the right might be doing?

Ming China: New Prosperity and a Maritime Thrust

After the rebel leader Zhu Yuanzhang expelled the Mongols in 1368, he founded the Ming dynasty (Dynasty of Light), a thoroughly Chinese regime. Ruling for thirty-one years (1368±1398) under the imperial name Taizu, he ordered a torrent of reforms to transform China into a more centralized and efficient monarchy than the Mongols had ever imagined. Under Taizu and his early successors, China's huge economy maintained steady growth. After nearly two centuries of decline, the population recovered as well, rising from about 85 million in 1393 to about 155 million by 1500. By the mid-seventeenth century, when the Ming era ended, about one-third of the world's people lived in China.[10]

The style of early Ming government. As the son of a poor farmer, in fact the first Chinese ruler to come from such humble origins, the emperor Taizu extolled the toiling peasant as the pillar of China's agricultural economy. He aimed to model his imperial government not on the Song dynasties (960±1276), which had given loose rein to business enterprise and technical innovation, but on the more agrarian-oriented Tang empire of the seventh and eighth centuries. He even discouraged the use of paper money, which went largely out of circulation by the mid-fifteenth century. In contrast to what some European kings did in the aftermath of the Black Death, Taizu lowered taxes on ordinary farmers and raised them on the rich. Early in his reign he decreed a comprehensive census of people, occupations, and landholdings to systematize revenue collection. To encourage social stability he prescribed laws that impeded rural people from changing occupations or migrating from village to cityÐ again, contrary to the trend in western Europe. He also encouraged conformity to standards of Neo-Confucian morality, including restrictions on women's social and legal liberties.

Because he improved the state bureaucracy's efficiency and raised living conditions for millions of peasants, Taizu enjoyed broad popular support. Distrusting the landed aristocratic families that had traditionally dominated government offices, he reformed the Neo-Confucian school and examination system to allow talented young men from a wider range of social backgrounds to take up government careers. Also a master of political fear tactics, he created an elaborate apparatus of spies and secret police, and he periodically purged officials who he thought had failed him in one way or another.

The Ming government's policies, which favored a state-regulated, stable agrarian society, ran counter to the interests of private entrepreneurs and merchants, who yearned to pick up where the Song dynasty had left off. Yet despite the state's close supervision of commerce, China became more economically and geographically integrated than ever before. It already had the world's most complex canal and road system, but the Ming extended the Grand Canal so that it ran about a thousand miles from the Yangzi River to Beijing, which after Taizu's death became the imperial capital. The waterway had forty-seven locks, fifteen of them to move barges through hill country. Because Beijing could receive 400 million pounds of grain a year by canal, its population soared in the fifteenth century to over two million.

The Ming and its neighbors. Like the Mongols before them, Taizu and his fifteenth-century successors insisted on government supervision of external trade. Commercial exchange with foreign states had to conform to a protocol that imagined neighboring rulers not as trading partners but as payers of tribute in the form of material goods. In turn, the sublime emperor offered these presumably dependent princes comparable ªgifts.º China's neighbors often played this ritual game on Ming terms in the interests of profitable commerce. And although the Ming outlawed private overseas trade, Chinese merchants routinely defied this prohibition.

The Ming never tried to conquer deep into Inner Eurasia, as the Tang dynasty had done seven centuries earlier. Even so, early emperors pursued a forceful foreign policy. In Korea the monarchs of the Choson dynasty (1392±1910) accepted a formal tributary relationship with China, while in fact governing independently. They also energetically advanced Chinese Neo-Confucian teachings. Sejong (SAY-johng, reigned 1418±1450), the strongest Korean king of the fifteenth century, patronized Neo-Confucian culture and also inspired the invention of Hangul. This remarkable Korean alphabet used a system of phonetic signs that complemented Chinese logographic writing. In relations with Japan, which was then politically fragmented, the early Ming emperors encouraged diplomatic and cultural exchanges. These initiatives did not last, but private sea trade between the islands and the mainland continued to flourish.

In the subtropical hill country of the far southwest, today Guizhou and Yunnan provinces, landless peasants and discharged soldiers opened a new frontier of Chinese settlement. These lands were by no means empty, however, and non-Chinese ethnic peoples put up stiff though finally unsuccessful resistance. In the longer term, Chinese immigrants and local peoples interacted in complex ways, including marriage. This gave the region a distinct cultural flavor. Further south, a Chinese army invaded the Vietnamese kingdom of Annam in 1407 and occupied it for two decades. Annam's ruling class had already embraced Chinese Confucianism, but it tenaciously fought the intruders. Finally deciding to cut its losses, the Chinese force withdrew in 1427, leaving little to show for the adventure. Similarly to Korea, however, Annam pragmatically accepted the formal role of Chinese tributary by sending annual ªgiftsº to Beijing.

The Ming government kept a close eye on the northwestern frontiers facing Inner Eurasia, putting three million soldiers under arms to defend the imperial borders. Though the Mongols had retreated to their homeland, they could still command tens of thousands of mounted archers. At

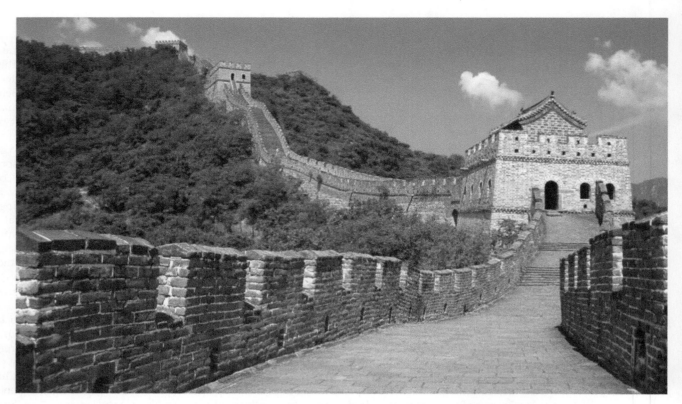

The Great Wall of China. This section of the restored wall near Beijing crosses extremely rugged country. Why do you think historians have characterized the wall as a physical barrier rather than as a series of frontier fortifications?

first, the Ming combined diplomacy and gift giving with military thrusts into pastoral nomad territory. This forward strategy, however, did not go well, and in 1449 Mongol cavalry defeated a huge Chinese army and even captured the reigning emperor. After that humiliation, the state pulled the military frontier further back. It also spent huge sums to extend and connect frontier defensive fortifications, creating most of the 1,500-mile-long Great Wall. Masons reinforced long sections of the barrier to an average height and width of twenty-five feet, and they built guard towers at close intervals to permit soldiers to send signals along the wall at great speed. The project was a stupendous engineering feat, though the northwestern frontier remained turbulent into the next century, causing Ming bureaucrats no end of worry and debate.

The Ming maritime voyages. The Yongle (YAWNG-leh) emperor (r. 1403±1424), Taizu's son and successor, shared his father's grand vision of China as the world's Middle Kingdom surrounded by satellite states. Not only did Yongle attack Mongolia and Vietnam, but he also sought to gather rulers far west of China into the tributary net. In 1405 he placed Zheng He (JUNG-huh), a talented naval officer, in charge of a new seaborne mission to make a show of Ming imperial power and glory in the Indian Ocean (see Map 15.3).

Zheng He was an interesting choice for this project. His life reflected a creative, yet sometimes violent mix of cultural influences. He came from a Muslim family, and his

father had made the four-thousand-mile holy pilgrimage to Mecca. Given the name Ma He at birth, he grew up in Yunnan in the southwest, where Ming forces expelled the Mongols when he was about ten years old. Chinese soldiers seized him and other local boys and made him a eunuch to serve in the army as an orderly. The lad, however, distinguished himself as a warrior. He made influential friends in the imperial court and became a trusted member of the corps of eunuchs, which did duty in the palace as bodyguards and administrators, as they had for many centuries. Yongle gave him the new name of Zheng, the name of a battlefield where the young eunuch distinguished himself.

At the emperor's request, Zheng He assembled a massive fleet of 287 junksÐ 62 enormous ᵃtreasure shipsº and 225 smaller ones. They carried a total crew of about 27,000. The largest vessel may have been more than twice the length of the Santa Maria, the little flagship that Christopher Columbus sailed to America almost a century later.[11] Between 1405 and 1433, Admiral Zheng He commanded seven major expeditions westward, leading his ships into the Indian Ocean and ultimately to the Persian Gulf, the Red Sea, and the East African coast. Many of the common sailors on these ships were recruited from the criminal classes, but the fleets also carried soldiers, doctors, herbalists, astrologers, diplomatic protocol experts, and Arabic and Persian translators.

Zheng He and the ship captains serving under him navigated with compasses, star charts, and coastline maps, as well as ready advice from local Muslim mariners who knew

MAP 15.3 The Zheng He expeditions, 1405–1433.
In the fifteenth century, sailors of many Asian and African lands sailed the routes that Zheng He navigated. How would Zheng He and his crews have taken advantage of their knowledge of seasonal monsoon winds in making these long-distance voyages?

the Indian Ocean intimately. He would also have been able to draw on a store of Chinese knowledge. Since the eleventh century or earlier, private traders had been sailing junks from Chinese ports to the coasts of India and possibly farther, accumulating from these journeys a rich fund of navigational and geographic information. About sixty-five years before Zheng He's first expedition, Ibn Battuta, the Moroccan traveler, saw thirteen large Chinese vessels in the port of Calicut on the southwestern Indian coast, ships of four decks, he reports, outfitted with ªcabins, suites, and salons for merchants,º a s well as in-room latrines.[12]

Zheng He's fleet did a good deal of ordinary trading during the expeditions, but their larger mission was to magnify the influence and splendor of the Yongle emperor. The admiral returned from his second voyage with envoys from thirty South and Southeast Asian kingdoms to pay homage to the emperor. On several occasions, violent encounters took place between Chinese visitors and local populations. But Zheng He seized no ports nor founded any imperial colonies.

Not all factions in the royal court supported Yongle's initiative, and when he died in 1424, the chorus of opposition grew louder. Many of the government's scholar-bureaucrats despised palace eunuchs like Zheng He as political opportunists

Zheng He's treasure fleet sets sail. This modern bronze relief depicts the size of the admiral's ships relative to other vessels and to buildings on land. Why might Ming emperors have funded the construction of such enormous vessels? What does their size suggest about the state of Chinese shipbuilding technology in the fifteenth century?

with too much power. These officials reasoned that they might undermine eunuch influence by scuttling any more voyages. Imperial accountants fretted that the expeditions cost far too much and that public money would be better spent on northwestern frontier defenses and internal economic projects. Another factor may have been long-term deforestation in southern China, which made the cost of building more oceangoing ships prohibitive. Yongle's successor permitted a final expedition in 1433, but Zheng He died that same year, perhaps on shipboard. Thereafter, the government dismantled the yards that built the big ships, which eventually rotted away in dry dock. Ming officialdom took no further interest in long sea voyages. As East Asia's population and economy grew, however, Chinese merchants continued to traffic in the China seas at least as far west as the Strait of Malacca.

South Asia: A Steadier Course of Change

Though the international ports of South Asia remained busy throughout the fourteenth and fifteenth centuries, the region appears to have experienced a significant population decline. Evidence is lacking for a massive pandemic in India in the years of the Black Death. It is more likely that people died in larger numbers as a consequence of regional famines or epidemics having no connection to the disease that ravaged Southwest Asia or Europe.

Like Europe, India was a region of many states of varying sizes that competed for territory and resources. In the fourteenth century the Muslim Turkic military lords who ruled the North Indian sultanate of Delhi made a bid to unify the entire subcontinent. Expansion sputtered, however, and after Timur's army pillaged Delhi in 1399, the sultanate carried on as merely one of several monarchies sharing northern and central India. Islam, however, became the dominant faith in both the upper Indus valley and the Ganges watershed, as the sultans encouraged Muslim farmers to move in to clear land and build towns. The Muslim population of Bengal, the region of the Ganges delta, grew steadily, laying the religious foundation of the modern state of Bangladesh. Sufi Muslim clerics and preachers fanned out across central India, converting Hindu villagers in some places.

By contrast, the southern part of the subcontinent became more politically consolidated and remained largely Hindu. In the 1340s a victorious warrior band founded the Vijayanagar (vizh-ah-na-ya-GAR-ah) monarchy in semiarid south central India. In the ensuing decades, this upstart Hindu kingdom conquered or put under tribute several other southern states, recruiting Muslim mercenaries from the north and deploying gunpowder artillery against enemy strongholds. Revenues subsequently poured into Vijayanagar city from both the lush rice-growing valleys of the southeast and the great trade entrepôts along the southern coasts. Gold and silver coins circulated widely, market

Royal elephant stables. Fifteenth-century monarchs of Vijayanagar housed war elephants in the large arched rooms in this grand structure. The open space in front of the stables probably served as a parade ground. Why do you think a ruler would construct such an elaborate and expensive building to keep his elephants?

towns multiplied, and the farming population appears to have enjoyed prosperity.

The Hindu elite also spent great sums building magnificent temples in the capital and other cities. These buildings ingeniously combined southern Indian techniques and styles with architectural elements, including domes and arches, imported from northern India and, more broadly, from Iran. The empire remained quite loosely organized, however, held together on the strength of alliances with local potentates and frequent campaigns against rebels. Nevertheless, Vijayanagar continued to dominate southern India until the mid-1500s.

Astronomy and Empire Building in the Central Muslim Lands

Shortly after his death in 1405, the conqueror Timur's huge but fragile empire broke apart, leaving Central and Southwest Asia in the hands of several competing princes and military lords, as it had been before his rise. Political divisions and economic doldrums persisted across Southwest Asia. Against this background, however, two dynamic developments stand out, one of them artistic and intellectual, the other political.

The Timurids. In the core region of Timur's empire, his offspring managed to preserve a much smaller but nevertheless prosperous state for about a century after 1405. The main urban poles of the Timurid sultanate, as this dynasty was called, were Samarkand in what is now Uzbekistan and Herat in western Afghanistan. Through much of the fifteenth century, these two cities functioned as capitals of largely self-governing northern and southern sections of the kingdom. In both places Timurid princes erected splendid palaces using tax revenues from irrigated farming and trade. In contrast to Timur, most of these rulers cared more about knowledge and literature than military glory, and their capitals attracted scholars from throughout the Muslim world.

In the first half of the fifteenth century, Ulugh Beg (r. 1447±1449) oversaw the transformation of Samarkand into a center of art and intellect. Timur had started to beautify Samarkand with mosques and palaces, and Ulugh Beg added a grand college of advanced learning (madrasa), whose walls inside and out sparkled with the reflected light of millions of multicolored tiles. This institution expanded the traditional Muslim college curriculum from law and the religious sciences to mathematics, astronomy, history, and several other subjects. Ulugh Beg sponsored scientific research and built an imposing observatory. Indeed, Timurid scholars made important advances in algebra, trigonometry, and astronomy. Most notably, they produced a comprehensive star catalog in the form of astronomical tables, the most advanced gazetteer of the heavens produced anywhere in the world to that point. In the following centuries, scientists in Europe used the catalog as a key research tool.

In the second half of the fifteenth century, Herat took over as the leading cosmopolitan center. Combining Persian with Chinese elements of art and design, Herat's intellectual elite excelled in painting and calligraphy, especially the art of the illustrated book. In both Herat and Samarkand, poets and prose writers composed in Persian and Arabic, as well as Chagatai, a Turkic language. The reputations of Jami and Navai, fifteenth-century Herat's most famous poets, remain very much alive today. Early in the sixteenth century, political troubles and a shift of wealth and power to other capitals sent Samarkand and Herat into cultural eclipse, though they remained important emporia on the trade routes between Southwest Asia and India.

The Ottoman Turkish state. In 1300, Anatolia (modern Turkey) was among the most politically fragmented regions of Southwest Asia. The Mongols based in Iran and Iraq ruled the eastern half of Anatolia with declining competence. Several Turkic principalities shared western Anatolia, and the Christian Byzantine monarchy clung to a chip of territory across the Bosporus from Constantinople, the Greek capital. During the fourteenth century, however, this landscape changed radically. The House of Osman, a line of Muslim warrior sultans later known as the Ottoman dynasty, rose to dominate not only much of Anatolia but also Europe's Balkan Peninsula. The transformation of Anatolia from a Greek-speaking Christian land to a Turkish-speaking

The Observatory in Samarkand. Like many of the other buildings constructed during the rule of Ulugh Beg, the observatory was beautiful as well as functional. The building is now in ruins, but this nineteenth-century watercolor offers a representation of how it might have looked to the leading astronomers of the fifteenth century. Why might this building have been important in the eyes of a European artist four centuries later?

Muslim land, a process that had started with Turkic migrations in the eleventh century (see Chapter 12), accelerated along with the Ottoman expansion.

The Turkish warlord Osman (r. 1281±1324) founded the new state, but his successors Orkhan (r. 1324±1360) and Murad I (r. 1360±1389) made it a regional power by defeating rival sultanates in Anatolia and sending cavalry across the Dardanelles, first to raid, then to occupy Christian territory deep in the Balkans. As Ottoman forces amassed booty and slaves, more warriors joined in, including many from conquered states. As in the case of the early Mongol empire, every military success bred more of the same. By the end of the century, the empire had absorbed Christian Bulgaria and reduced the kingdom of Serbia to dependency. Writing in the later fifteenth century, the Greek chronicler Kritovoulos described the Ottoman advance in Europe: ªThus they came down into the plain, and there nothing was any obstacle to them any more. They occupied the level country, sacked the villages, and captured the cities, overthrew castles, defeated armies, and subdued many peoples.º[13]

Boisterous and loosely organized, the young empire kept growing, though more as a result of the sultans' skills negotiating with local chiefs than owing to any well-organized central administration. The Turkic warrior tradition of *ghaza*, a code of military honor having to do with the accumulation and division of plunder, imposed some order on the wars of conquest. Moreover, Greek Christian aristocrats and their mounted knights joined the Ottoman offensive in significant numbers. Turkic warriors, or *ghazis*, coalesced around personal loyalty to the ruler, who promised land and loot. However, *ghazi* frontier fighters tended also to be unruly and opportunistic, too undisciplined for single-minded empire building.

In the late fourteenth century, Murad I addressed this problem by creating a professional standing army. To do this, he adopted a system of drafting healthy boys from Christian families in the Balkans every three to seven years as the need arose. These recruits, called **janissaries,** had the legal status of slaves of the sultan. As sons of Christian peasants, conscripts had, in contrast to members of Turkic warrior families, no stake in Ottoman politics or factional feuding and could be expected to give absolute personal allegiance to the ruler. Moreover, Christian families did not necessarily lament the loss of these children, since at least some lads rose to positions of responsibility and influence within the Ottoman

> **janissaries** An elite infantry corps in the Ottoman Turkish state whose members were conscripted as boys from Christian families in southeastern Europe.

The Ottoman capture of Constantinople. This illustration from a fifteenth-century French chronicle conveys the intensity of the battle to control the city. We see evidence of Ottoman naval power and the infantry using ladders to scale the city walls built by Emperor Theodosius ten centuries earlier. What features communicate the artist's impressions of this battle? Does the painting convey sympathy for the conquering Ottomans or the besieged Byzantines?

state. Young janissaries had to convert to Islam and undergo rigorous training before taking military or administrative posts. About the same time, the Ottoman state began to build powerful cavalry regiments (*sipahis*). These units ensured order in rural provinces, and their commanders received in return rights to collect taxes on their own account from an assigned number of villages.

The capture of Constantinople. For more than a century after crossing the Bosporus and Dardanelles straits to penetrate the Balkans, Ottoman forces either bypassed or failed to penetrate the great Byzantine bastion of Constantinople. They absorbed nearly all other Greek-ruled territories, and by the early fifteenth century, the Byzantine emperor found himself effectively surrounded. Finally, in 1453, Sultan Mehmed II, known as the Conqueror (r. 1451±1481), breached the city's triple walls, deploying gunpowder artillery and handguns. The Greek historian Kritovoulos described the hours preceding the victory:

> The day was declining and near evening, and the sun was at the Ottomans' back but shining in the faces of their enemies. . . . First they exchanged fire with the heavier weapons, with arrows from the archers, stones from the slingers, and iron and leaden balls from the cannon and muskets. Then, as they closed with battleaxes and javelins,

and spears, hurling them at each other and being hurled at pitilessly in rage and fierce anger. . . . Many on each side were wounded, and not a few died.[14]

Mehmed gave his troops free rein to plunder the city for three days, and they murdered or enslaved much of the Christian population. In imitation of Mongol conquerors before him, however, Mehmed called a halt to the carnage and immediately set to work to restore and repopulate the city as the Ottoman capital. For example, the sultan recruited a diverse team of architects, including Italians, to build his magnificent palace of Topkapi Saray, an architectural complex that blended Muslim, Greek, Roman, and Italian elements. Western European rulers reacted to the fall of the greatest of Christian cities with shock and dismay, but they soon established diplomatic contacts with the new regime. The Ottoman empire would play a key part in the politics of Europe, the Mediterranean basin, and Southwest Asia for the next 450 years.

The Meaning of Recovery in Europe

Although Europe's population began to climb again after about 1450, many of its cities showed new vigor well before that date. Urban dwellers who survived epidemics found they could command higher prices for their labor, products, and professional services. They had more money to spend on food, luxuries, and capital investment in business and property. Consumers demanded a wide range of high-quality goods, stimulating both European industry and import trade. Europe's banking industry, which nearly collapsed during the Black Death, thrived once again. Florence emerged as the leading financial hub. From there, the Medici family and other rich firms built up pan-European commercial and banking empires. In Florence, Venice, Cologne, Paris, Bruges, London, and other cities, socially well-placed families piled up great wealth.

The bourgeoisie, that is, the nonaristocratic propertied class, took advantage of business success to build bigger houses, purchase better educations for their children, and carve out solid social positions between the privileged nobility above and the working masses below. Urban women also gained a measure of social and cultural status following the plague era. Scarce labor meant that male heads of households felt obliged, if grudgingly, to concede more value to women's homemaking and artisanry. In the fifteenth century, both urban and rural women enjoyed somewhat greater freedom to earn money as spinners, weavers, teachers, and business owners. Literary works of the fifteenth century showed a new regard for the cultural worth of motherhood and wifery. As the all-male priesthood lost prestige (especially after the pope decamped to Avignon) and as the psychological gloom of the Black Death persisted, more women emerged as spiritual guides and reformers. Christian practice in the fifteenth century paralleled in some ways Sufi tendencies in Islam, as men and women turned to personal, inward worship centered on adoration of God, Jesus, and the Virgin Mary and on acts of communal service and humble living. Among female mystics, Catherine of Siena (1347±1380) achieved renown across Europe, urging both spiritual renewal and church reform in her writings. A radical ascetic, she practiced self-denial to the point of sleeping and eating as little as possible, a habit that may have cost Catherine her life at the age of thirty-three.

Catherine of Siena. A lay member of a society associated with the Dominican monastic order, Catherine reported numerous mystical experiences, including a spiritual marriage to Christ. She also had political influence, working to end war between Florence and Rome and successfully urging Pope Gregory XI to move the papal court from Avignon, where it had been under French domination for sixty-eight years, back to the Vatican in Rome. How would you describe the way the Italian artist represents Catherine in this painting made around 1462?

Royal power. Several of Europe's numerous states achieved new strength between 1350 and 1500 (see Map 15.4). The troubles of the church, the declining incomes of local aristocrats, and the renewed economic growth of the fifteenth century offered able and ambitious rulers opportunities to assert their authority in creative ways. Out of Italy's crazy-quilt of princedoms and city-states, five polities emerged in the 1300s to tower over the peninsula: the kingdom of Naples in the south, the papal states centered on Rome, and the northern

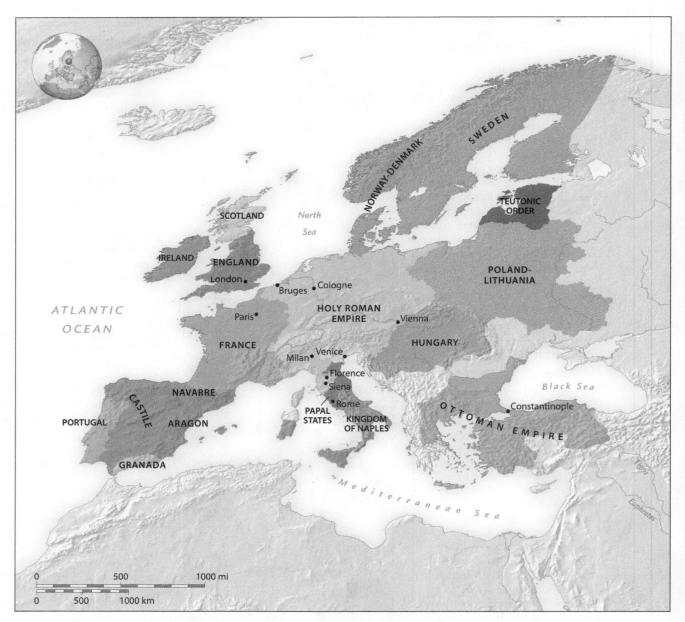

MAP 15.4 Europe in 1455.

The mid-fifteenth century was a time of prosperity in many European states. What geographical factors might help account for lavish financial patronage of the visual arts in cities of the Italian Peninsula in the fifteenth century?

city-states of Milan, Florence, and Venice. Together, these five dominated or absorbed weaker cities and small states.

The kingdoms of France, England, Spain, and Portugal all consolidated royal power. The French and English monarchs invented new taxes to impose on their subjects to pay for larger armies and more officials. Sometimes using cannons to smash castle walls, they subdued local estate lords and put royal bureaucrats directly in charge. France devoted large sums to a standing professional army, equipping it with artillery units that no unruly duke or rebel leader could hope to afford. England endured a bitter civil war near the end of the fifteenth century (the Wars of the Roses), but Henry VII (r. 1485±1509), the first king of the Tudor dynasty, took the state to new levels of bureaucratic efficiency. In Iberia, Queen Isabella of Castile (r. 1474±1504) and King Ferdinand of Aragon (r. 1479±1516) formed a powerful alliance in 1469, unifying their two kingdoms at the dynastic level through marriage. Along the Atlantic, the kingdom of Portugal also built a sturdy central administration. In all of these states, rulers claimed supreme authority but nonetheless governed in consultation with various advisory bodies made up of aristocrats and bishops, and sometimes town leaders and rich commoners. Only in England, however, did the head of state formally share power with a representative body. In the fourteenth century, Parliament's House of Commons (see Chapter 12) evolved into a genuine legislative body, making many laws and obliging the monarch to get its approval before imposing new taxes.

Poland-Lithuania emerged as Europe's territorially largest monarchy, when in 1385 Queen Jadwiga of Poland married the Grand Duke of Lithuania to merge the two kingdoms. This state claimed sovereignty over a huge area stretching from the Baltic to the grassland frontier of the Mongol Golden Horde. Formerly pagan, Lithuanians moved steadily into the Catholic Christian fold. Especially in Poland, urbanization, commercialization, and higher education developed rapidly, bolstered by a continuing inflow of German migrants, as well as thousands of Jewish families who fled persecution in western Europe during the Black Death. In contrast to the trend in western Europe, however, local Polish, Lithuanian, and German aristocrats retained much power within the empire. Royal governance in rural areas remained relatively weak, despite the empire's impressive size. Similarly in central Europe, the Holy Roman Empire continued to exist under the sovereignty of the Habsburg dynasty, but the emperor had limited power and functioned mainly to legitimize the regional authority of several German dukes.

The Italian Renaissance. At particular historical moments starting in ancient times, certain cities have shone more brightly than any others. Athens in the fifth century B.C.E., Baghdad in the ninth century C.E., and Hangzhou in the twelfth century produced innovations in art, literature, and science that have endured in the world's imagination. In the fourteenth and fifteenth centuries, Beijing, Vijayanagar, Delhi, Samarkand, and Cairo numbered among Afroeurasia's most creative centers of intellect and skill. In the decades following the Black Death, Florence in north central Italy emerged as Europe's liveliest hub of cultural genius. The movement that began there in the 1300s and that historians later labeled the Renaissance, or ªrebirth,º spread rapidly to other Italian cities and, in a variety of expressions, to the rest of Europe.

Florence in the late fifteenth century. The Arno River divides the walled city. Locate the Duomo, the cathedral that Filippo Brunelleschi completed.

Located in the Arno River valley amid the rolling hills of Tuscany, Florence had, despite its severe population loss in the later fourteenth century, the right mix of ingredients to achieve cultural distinction. It possessed sufficient wealth from manufacturing, trade, and banking to support ambitious artistic and literary projects. In that era, no city could excel in the arts or sciences without the backing of elite men and women who possessed both surplus wealth and urban cultural refinement. Often, the ruler of a city or state stepped forward as the most generous cultural patron, as in the case of Ulugh Beg in Samarkand. In Florence the eight hundred or so wealthiest families, including the Medici banking family, patronized the arts by offering stipends, commissioning projects, and purchasing sculptures, paintings, and numerous other art objects.

In Florence rich aristocrats and merchants competed with one another to spend money on art and buildings, confident that some of the glory would reflect back on them. As the city's reputation grew, artists and writers flocked there from around Europe. Other important Italian towns, some of them political enemies of Florence, vied for attention. Poets, painters, and fine metalsmiths traveled from one city to anotherÐ Milan, Siena, Rome, VeniceÐ to look for books, find patrons, and exchange ideas with like-minded individuals. By the later fifteenth century a network of cultural exchange inspired by Italian ideas spread across Europe to embrace educated men and women from Portugal to Poland.

humanism European movement of the fourteenth to sixteenth centuries dedicated to rediscovering, investigating, and reinterpreting ancient Greek and Roman civilization.

The cultural movement centered on Florence took shape around the multifaceted philosophy called **humanism.** Today, that word is commonly associated with secularism, a human-oriented, nonreligious attitude or way of life. Six hundred years ago, however, humanism was fundamentally a project to search out and retrieve the surviving literary and aesthetic achievements of ancient Rome and, by extension, Greece. Inquisitive Italians could see Rome's physical ruins everywhere, and they knew that more of the record of classical civilization lay moldering in churches, monasteries, and palace cellars. Humanists argued that anyone wishing to restore, analyze, or interpret ancient knowledge should master the *studia humanitatis,* that is, the study of the ª humanisticº disciplines of grammar, rhetoric, poetry, moral philosophy, and history. These disciplines, they said, must form the core of young people's education and should be dedicated to recovering ancient wisdom, which humanists regarded as intellectually and morally superior to anything Europe had produced in the intervening centuries. Three of the most important pioneers of this rebirth of classical culture came from Tuscany. The epic poet Dante Alighieri (1265±1321), the lyric poet Petrarch (1304±1374), and the classical scholar and storyteller Boccaccio (1313±1375) all devoted their careers to finding and elucidating ancient literary and philosophical texts and to reviving classical arts.

Humanists put forth numerous ideas. They considered Greek and Roman achievements to be the proper point of reference for moral thought and behavior. Human beings, they argued, had responsibilities not only to perform religious duties but to better themselves as individuals through education and constructive thought. Taking the early Roman republic as their model, humanists also encouraged public service as a moral obligation, though no genuinely democratic republic existed anywhere in Europe. Indeed, the classicist and diplomat Niccolò Machiavelli (1469±1527) argued in his book *The Prince* that rulers who wished to strengthen Italy against foreign invaders should be guided by ruthless pragmatism, not Christian morality. Machiavelli's humanism emphasized political activism, even violent or deceitful measures, to defend the freedom and integrity of the republican city-state.

Renaissance men and women found much to criticize about the dogmatism and corruption they witnessed in the Roman church. Somewhat like Muslim scientists and philosophers in the same era, humanist scholars gravitated mainly to princely courts and aristocratic households for support, not to established centers of learning. They tended to consider Europe's universities as preserves of narrow-minded theologians and lawyers. Eventually though, humanist ideas penetrated the universities.

The Italian Renaissance embraced all expressions of art and craft. Gifted sculptors of the era, such as Donatello (1386±1466) and the relentlessly creative and long-lived Michelangelo (1475±1564), studied classical models to create sublime naturalist images in marble and bronze. As we saw at the beginning of the chapter, early Renaissance painters, such as Masaccio, strove to recreate the ª real,º three-dimensional world using new techniques of perspective. Artists also depicted not only Christian subjects but also historical, mythological, and everyday secular themes. Architects such as Filippo Brunelleschi (1377±1446) built churches and other monumental structures that combined Roman engineering with clever new techniques. For example, in building a great dome for Florence's cathedral (known as the Duomo), he constructed in effect two domes, one inside the other and connected together, in order to reduce the weight of the structure on the supporting walls.

Brilliant achievements like these gave rise to the modern phrase ª Renaissance manº to describe someone of wide-ranging interests and skills. It was indeed a man's world. Humanist ideology made little room for urban women to express themselves except in perfecting the arts of household management and social adornment. However, a few women achieved fame in the arts, several applying their aesthetic talents as painters, calligraphers, and book illuminators. Other upper-class women patronized male artists and scholars from behind the scenes. Among the early humanists, Christine de Pizan (1364±1431) stands out.

Daughter of an Italian astrologer who lived at the court of King Charles V of France, she made a living after the death of her husband writing poetry, biography, and political treatises under the patronage of various aristocrats. Modern historians have paid special attention to her because of her spirited writings challenging medieval male stereotypes of women as slow witted and wanton.

The Renaissance beyond Italy. The movement of Renaissance art and ideas from Italy to the rest of Europe in the later fifteenth century occurred in tandem with the spread of printing technology. The early presses of the fifteenth century put out Bibles, catechisms, and sermons, but literate Europeans soon demanded poetry, stories, histories, classical texts, scientific works, and advertising broadsheets. By 1500, just a half-century after the invention of metal movable type, presses had already turned out somewhere between six and fifteen million books. Many of these volumes appeared in regional vernacular languages, not Latin. By the sixteenth century, therefore, mechanically produced books added a revolutionary new dimension to the collective sharing of wisdom and information.

The early Renaissance evolved from an Italian into a European phenomenon, but we should also think of it as taking place within the larger Mediterranean world. Although the humanists tapped much ancient knowledge that Europeans had forgotten, they also used numerous philosophical and scientific texts that reached Europe owing to contacts with Muslim and Byzantine cities. The works of Plato, Aristotle, the Jewish philosopher Maimonides, and numerous Muslim savants were already part of Europe's intellectual library when humanism appeared. Books in ArabicÐ as well as Muslim textiles, art objects, and numerous ideas about design, architecture, and fine cuisineÐ continued to stream into Italy. When Byzantine travelers and Greek Orthodox Church envoys visited Rome, they often brought copies of ancient texts. It is no surprise that images of Muslim philosophers, Egyptian landscapes, decorative Arabic inscriptions, and Syrian textile designs turned up in early Renaissance paintings.

Although Latin Christians bemoaned the fall of Constantinople to the Turks in 1453, the new Ottoman capital quickly became a participant in Renaissance exchange. Sultan Mehmed II collected printed books from Europe to add to existing stores of Arabic and Persian literature, and

An Italian portrait of Sultan Mehmed II. The Venetian painter Gentile Bellini spent a year in Constantinople, where he painted the Ottoman ruler in royal robe and voluminous turban. Can you identify elements of Muslim art in the painting?

he took keen interest in Greek and Roman philosophy. In 1479 the Italian artist Gentile Bellini (1429±1507) painted a Renaissance-style portrait of Mehmed. Sultan Bayezid II (r. 1481±1512) invited both Michelangelo and Leonardo da Vinci (1452±1519) to Istanbul (Constantinople) to undertake commissions, though neither went. The early designs for St. Peter's Basilica in Rome, begun in 1506, emulated Constantinople's Hagia Sophia, even though Mehmed II had turned this great Byzantine church into a mosque. Lively cultural exchange between the Ottoman empire and Renaissance Europe continued into the sixteenth century, even as Turkish and Christian armies fought fiercely for control of southeastern Europe.

• • •

Conclusion

If we take a very long historical perspective, Afroeurasia's fourteenth-century population crisis and all the suffering that attended bad weather, epidemics, and war looks slightly less gloomy. In the past 200,000 years, the world's population increased fairly steadily until about three centuries ago, when it began to grow at a much faster rate. Thus, the demographic and economic decline that started around 1330 fits into the longer trend as just one of many recurring but short-lived downturns.

The fourteenth-century plunge *looks* calamitous partly because we have a richer documentation of it than of any earlier slump. It *was* calamitous because by that century human society in Afroeurasia had become so intermeshed that a demographic shift of that scope inevitably caused great upheaval. In fact, the trans-hemispheric pandemic likely occurred only because the dense exchange network strengthened by Mongol rulers was still in place to transmit infectious microbes from one person to another across steppe, mountain, and sea.

In the fifteenth century, economic growth began to accelerate again in many parts of Afroeurasia. The Zheng He voyages demonstrated spectacularly the prosperity of commerce in the southern seas. The larger classes of Chinese junks were probably seaworthy enough to brave any of the world's oceans, but Chinese officialdom decided after 1433 that it could no longer spend great sums on overseas power displays. Meanwhile, economic conditions in western Europe were improving, and shipbuilders were making incremental changes to small but buoyant sailing craft in order to explore Atlantic fishing grounds, look for new islands, and probe commercial possibilities along the North African and Saharan coast. These Italian, Portuguese, and Spanish mariners, like the crowd of Asian and African merchants who crisscrossed the Indian Ocean, no doubt anticipated that seaborne trade would continue to grow, though within networks already known. Well-traveled, cosmopolitan Afroeurasians thought the world was theirs. They had no inkling of America.

• • •

Key Terms

Black Death 428
Choson dynasty 439
flagellants 431
Great Wall 440
Gutenberg Bible 438
humanism 448
Hundred Years' War 434

janissaries 444
Little Ice Age 427
Ming dynasty 432
movable type printing 438
Ottoman Turks 443
papal schism 436
pogrom 431

Renaissance 447
Timur (Tamerlane) 433
Timurid sultanate 443
Vijayanagar kingdom 442
Zheng He expeditions 440

Change over Time

Late 13th–mid-19th century	Temperatures in the Arctic and northern latitudes drop (Little Ice Age), contributing to environmental changes and social upheavals of the 14th century.
1280–1324	Osman rules over the newly created Ottoman Turkish state.
1315–1322	Massive famines hit northern Europe.
1340s–early 17th century	The Vijayanagar state in southern India prospers from agriculture and trade links.
1337–1453	France and England wage the Hundred Years' War over territorial dispute.
1346–1352	The Black Death pandemic hits Inner Eurasia, Southwest Asia, North Africa, and Europe.
1350s and 1360s	Rural rebellions erupt in China and western Europe.
1368–1644	Mongols are expelled from China, ushering in several centuries of rule under the Ming dynasty.
1370–1405	From a Central Asian base, Timur leads conquests to the north, east, and west.
1378–1417	Papal schism disrupts the Catholic Church.
1392–1910	The Choson dynasty rules in Korea; Hangul, a Korean alphabet, is invented under Sejong.
1394–1449	Ulugh Beg rules the Timurid state in Central Asia and Afghanistan.
1405–1433	Zheng He leads Chinese maritime expeditions.
1453	Ottomans capture Constantinople.
1455	Johannes Gutenberg produces a printed Bible.
1474–1516	Queen Isabella of Castile) and King Ferdinand of Aragon create a powerful Christian state in the Iberian Peninsula.

Please see end of book reference section for additional reading suggestions related to this chapter.

The Great World
Convergence 1450–1750

part 5
The Great World Convergence
1450–1750

F rom about 1450 C.E. the pace of change in human society quickened markedly. Regional economies and populations grew again across much of Afro-eurasia, after a century of economic and political troubles associated most conspicuously with recurring epidemics. In the Americas, farming based on maize continued to spread to new areas, encouraging population growth, social innovation, and larger state-building projects. On the whole, humankind was moving toward greater social complexity at a moderately accelerating speed.

We can only wonder how this trend might have played out if not for the spectacular "accident" that occurred near the end of the fifteenth century. In 1492 the Genoese sea captain Christopher Columbus, sailing into the Atlantic in search of Japan or China, stumbled onto an island off the coast of North America. Other mariners followed, and in the next few decades, trans-Atlantic voyages became commonplace. After about 12,000 years of no significant human migration between them and 250 million years of limited biological exchange of any kind, this sudden convergence of Afroeurasia and the Americas had enormous consequences for our species. The opening of Atlantic passages, as well as Pacific crossings soon thereafter, added multiple complexities to relations among human groups and between all peoples and their natural environments.

In Part 5 we investigate global and regional developments in the period just before and for about two and a half centuries after this great world convergence began. Historians conventionally call this period the early modern era. We use this term to signal the magnitude of changes taking place between 1450 and 1750 and to distinguish that period from the modern age, which emerged fully in the mid-eighteenth century.

Among world-scale developments of the early modern period, we highlight these eight:

Brass figure of a Portuguese soldier holding a musket, from Benin, Nigeria, seventeenth century.

■ The entire era lay within the cycle of slight global temperature decline that climatologists call the Little Ice Age (thirteenth to nineteenth century). Within this cyclical downturn, temperatures oscillated from one year and decade to the next. This produced erratic and unpredictable weather changes in the Northern Hemisphere, including shorter growing seasons in some regions and torrential rains, floods, or extended droughts in others. Historians associate famines, population displacements, and political upheavals with the unstable conditions this cycle generated.

■ Infectious diseases that were common in human populations in Afroeurasia but not in the Americas took a catastrophic toll among Native American societies when people carried microbes westward across the Atlantic. Horrendous epidemics extending into the seventeenth century threw Indian societies into disarray, rapidly depleted their numbers, and hobbled their capacity to control the terms of their encounters with intrusive Europeans interested in conquest, economic exploitation, and settlement.

■ The opening of transoceanic passages also permitted the transfer of a multitude of plants and animals to regions where no one had ever seen them before. This Columbian exchange profoundly affected ecological and economic conditions in most of the world. It allowed Europeans to grow Afroeurasian commercial crops on vast acreages of American land. It also introduced a variety of nutritious American plants to Afroeurasia, contributing to faster population growth in both Eurasia and Africa.

■ The great world convergence involved the interlinking of nearly all regions of the world, including Australia and Oceania, by the late eighteenth century. Consequently, mariners and merchants carried material goods over long distances in all directions. A mesh of trade routes soon encircled the globe, and economic life changed in some measure in every locality connected to this expanding network.

■ The densely populated regions of Asia remained the world's richest centers of production and commerce. Western Europe, which until the sixteenth century was perched on the edge of the Afroeurasian exchange system, suddenly became a crossroads of seaborne trade. New wealth stimulated more investment in agriculture, manufacturing, and intercity trade.

■ Firearms came into worldwide use in this era. Artillery and handguns not only transformed warfare—making it much deadlier—but also permitted rulers who could finance expensive gunpowder armies to tighten their authority, seize more territory, and coerce their subjects to pay the taxes that permitted even greater military buildup. A relatively small number of states consolidated power on an unprecedented scale. Some of them founded transoceanic empires.

■ Empire building and the emerging world economy animated migration on a growing scale—from countryside to town and from one region to another. The largest seaborne movement between 1500 and 1750 was the forced migration of more than 3.6 million enslaved Africans to the Americas to perform hard labor, mainly on commercial plantations.

■ Maritime communication, empire building, and migration contributed to the spread of major religious traditions, especially Islam and Christianity, into regions where they had previously been unknown. At the same time, educated thinkers in Europe began working out a new way of making sense of nature and the universe. It was founded, not primarily on ancient philosophical and religious writings, but on systematic observation and analysis of phenomena to arrive at general principles—in other words, the modern scientific method.

Though no one could have guessed it at the time, these three hundred years represent the last phase of the agrarian age, the 10,000 years or so when humans met their energy needs mainly by growing crops, raising animals, and burning biomass. An assortment of technical advances—more powerful ships, new farming methods, the invention of firearms—permitted our species to harness larger amounts of energy, but still at the incremental rates of increase that had characterized the whole agrarian era. The revolutionary breakthroughs in humankind's ability to exploit energy were yet to come.

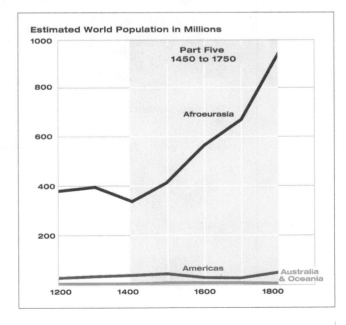

Estimated World Population in Millions

453

16 Oceans Crossed, Worlds Connected

1450-1550

This 1532 map by German cartographer Sebastian Münster demonstrates a new but still incomplete knowledge of world geography.

According to al-Umari, a renowned Muslim geographer of the fourteenth century, a fleet of ships set forth from the West African empire of Mali early in that century to explore the Atlantic Ocean. As al-Umari tells the story, Mansa Muhammad, the king of Mali, believed the ocean could be crossed. "He wished to reach the other side and was passionately interested in doing so. He fitted out 200 vessels and filled them with men and as many again with gold, water, and food supplies for several years." These watercraft would almost certainly have been canoes carved from single logs, though big enough to carry several dozen paddlers. According to al-Umari, the king told the officers in charge of the embarkation, "Do not return until you have reached the other side of the ocean or if you have exhausted your food or water." The ships set sail, and after a long time just one vessel returned, reporting that a mighty current had gripped the rest of the fleet and carried it away. Mansa Muhammad then organized a much bigger expedition, leading it himself. This second flotilla ventured into the deep but was never heard from again.[1]

West Africans, North Africans, and Europeans—inhabitants of the eastern rim of the Atlantic—had all learned well before the fourteenth century how to build boats that could negotiate ocean waters, at least close to shore. No doubt, mariners in all three regions wondered what rich lands they might find if they dared to push west. From as early as the sixth century, Europeans told stories of Irish monks or other adventurers sailing into the setting North Atlantic sun. Vikings, we know, occupied a trading base on the coast of Newfoundland in Canada for a decade or two in the eleventh century. But medieval sailors had little knowledge of how the Atlantic's winds and currents worked, limiting their ability and inclination to venture far out to sea.

During the fifteenth century, however, mariners gained knowledge essential for attempting a roundtrip trans-Atlantic voyage. They began to understand that the North Atlantic's wind system forms a gigantic clockwise wheel. Once they realized that this pattern was relatively dependable, they became more confident about sailing out of sight of land for long stretches of time, as Christopher Columbus did in 1492. About that time, other European skippers discovered that a twin, though counterclockwise wind wheel ruled the South Atlantic.

The permanent opening of passages across the Atlantic, and shortly thereafter the Pacific, produced the "great global convergence." By this we mean not only that Europe and the Americas became permanently conjoined, but also that nearly all regions of the world became connected to one another. The convergence had revolutionary consequences because it involved a sudden, vast, and unprecedented exchange of living organisms—people, animals, plants, and microbes. To one extent or another, this exchange disturbed existing ecological and economic systems, especially because Afroeurasia and the Americas had been virtually sealed off from each other for at least 12,000 years. It enabled some people to exploit new resources in land, minerals, and human labor, whereas others became victims of that exploitation. Also for the first time, maritime routes spanned and connected all the world's big oceans. By the mid-sixteenth century, a genuinely globe-girdling economy was taking shape.

The first part of this chapter surveys the global scene in the mid-fifteenth century, just before the great world convergence got under way (see Map 16.1). This was a time of demographic, economic, and commercial recovery in Afroeurasia. It was in this context that western European sailors stepped up the tentative probes they had been making

Chapter Outline

• • •

into the Atlantic to try to tap the trade of uncharted islands, tropical Africa, or even Asia. On the other side of the globe, the Americas had only 10 to 15 percent of the world's population before Columbus, but it displayed a somewhat similar pattern of population and economic growth, as maize farming continued to spread and as empires of unprecedented size arose in Mexico and the Andes Mountains.

In the second part of the chapter, we consider the conditions in which the opening of new oceanic passages took place. First we investigate Portugal and Spain, exploring the geographical knowledge and technical innovations that made back-and-forth ocean crossings possible, as well as the motives and aims of the Europeans who took part in seaborne adventures. The section describes early encounters between Portuguese newcomers and peoples on the Atlantic side of tropical Africa. We also trace Columbus's transatlantic voyages and describe the early impact of the sudden arrival of Europeans on Caribbean societies.

A Panoramic View

MAP 16.1 Major states in the mid-fifteenth century.
On the eve of the great global convergence, several large territorial states shared Afroeurasia with small monarchies, city-states, and nomadic societies. Two large empires and many smaller polities occupied the Americas. What basic technologies did most Afroeurasian states have in the mid-fifteenth century that American states lacked?

In the third section, we describe developments in the Americas from 1492 to about 1550. This period was catastrophic for Native Americans, especially in the Caribbean and densely populated regions of Mesoamerica and the Andes. American Indians died off in massive numbers, chiefly because they lacked immunities to infectious microorganisms introduced from Afroeurasia. At the same time, Spanish and Portuguese soldiers and colonists undertook to subjugate American societies and to exploit land and labor for commercial profit. Disease, warfare, and rampant social dislocation led in short order to the collapse of the Aztec and Inca empires. In the sixteenth century, Spain and

Portugal expanded their conquests beyond those states to found territorial empires of their own.

Beginning in 1498–1499, Portuguese captains started sailing around Africa to the Indian Ocean. In stark contrast to the empty Atlantic, the chain of waterways extending from the Arabian Sea to the East China Sea teemed with maritime activity. The final part of the chapter addresses patterns of change that occurred in the southern seas in the half-century after Portuguese ships arrived there. We describe early encounters between Indian Ocean peoples and the Portuguese, and the initial effects of the European armed incursions on prevailing patterns of power and trade.

On the Eve of the Great World Convergence

> **FOCUS** What important changes were taking place in economic and political life in both Afroeurasia and the Americas as of about 1450?

The European mariners who crossed the Atlantic, Pacific, and Indian Oceans in the late fifteenth and early sixteenth centuries had primarily, though not exclusively, economic aimsÐ the desire to trade, raid, and find treasure. An understanding of when and how those sailors set forth, unwittingly starting the great world convergence, requires a global context, particularly regarding political and commercial aspects of change. Here, we look at developments in two geographical arenas. The first is Afroeurasia and its long-distance exchange system as it existed about 1450. The second is the Atlantic rim. As of 1450, the European, tropical African, and American societies that faced the Atlantic knew absolutely nothing or, in the case of Europeans and Africans, very little about one another. Those societies were playing out their own histories with no expectation of the transformations that encounters among them would set in motion.

Changes in the Afroeurasian Trade Network

After a century and a half of contraction associated with the Black Death and recurring infectious plague epidemics in Eurasia and northern Africa, Afroeurasia's population swung upward again from about 1450. Regional plague outbreaks diminished, and Eurasia's northerly latitudes experienced a moderate (and temporary) warming trend that brought longer growing seasons. These improving environmental conditions encouraged greater food production and accelerating population growth, notably in China, South Asia, and Europe. Although about 90 percent of Afroeurasia's population lived rural lives, cities grew and multiplied. The center of gravity for economic production, trade, population, and urbanization was in Asia. By one estimate, Asia had seventeen of Afroeurasia's twenty-five largest cities in 1450. Four were in northern Africa or Muslim-ruled parts of Europe. Christian Europe claimed the remaining four.[2]

Caravan traffic on the overland silk routes of Inner Eurasia prospered in the later fifteenth century, but maritime shipping routes carried goods in much greater volume. The busiest trade circuits connected the South China Sea, the Bay of Bengal, and the Arabian Sea. In addition to luxury wares, including silks, spices, drugs, aromatic woods, gemstones, and fine ceramic ware, ships carried everyday commodities such as lumber, rice, salt, and cheap textiles. Men dominated trading operations in the southern seas, but in many regions, production of food, fiber, and cloth depended heavily on the labor of women and girls, who planted and harvested rice and other foods, spun and wove silk and cotton, and traded goods in local markets.

Antonio Galvão, a Portuguese official who lived in the spice-producing Molucca Islands of Indonesia in the early sixteenth century, observed that ᵃthe more daughters a man has, the richer he is.º[3]

The Chinese trade pump. In the fifteenth century, significant changes took place in the ports, routes, and people involved in the southern seas trade. In 1433 China's imperial Ming government stopped sponsoring large naval expeditions, which in the previous three decades had sailed as far west as the Red Sea and the East African coast (see Chapter 15). Nevertheless, the Chinese economy, the largest regional one in the world, continued throughout the century to power maritime commerce. China's internal network of roads, rivers, and canals was highly developed; urban incomes were rising; and production of silk, porcelain, and numerous other wares flourished. Some of these goods were mass produced for export. At the same time, rich elites and prosperous city-dwellers craved luxury imports. This meant that economic activity in China reverberated across the hemisphere. Chinese merchants and artisans continued to visit or migrate to foreign cities, mainly in Southeast Asia, and to ship goods at least as far west as the Strait of Melaka, which connects the South China Sea with the Bay of Bengal. Conversely, traders from many lands called at southern Chinese ports.

Southern seas entrepôts: Melaka. Numerous cosmopolitan seaports faced the southern seas, though the fortunes of particular entrepôts (OH-truh-poh) rose and fell with changes in political conditions or factors of supply and demand. Early in the fifteenth century, for example, the city of Melaka (also, Malacca) emerged as a magnet of seaborne commerce. In 1403 the ruler of Singapore founded this port after being expelled from his home city by a rival prince. Melaka enjoyed a protected harbor along the narrowest stretch of the Strait of Melaka. The streets of the port soon thronged with traders of different ethnic groups, languages, religions, customs, and cuisines. According to Tomé Pires, a Portuguese druggist who lived there between 1512 and 1515, this was ᵃa city that was made for merchandise, fitter than any other in the world; . . . the trade and commerce between different nations for a thousand leagues on every hand must come to Melaka.º[4]

Merchants of Gujarat. Another fifteenth-century development was the commercial expansion of Gujarat, a Muslim state on the northwestern coast of India. In 1401 Gujarat's rulers successfully broke away from the sultanate of Delhi, South Asia's largest land empire. On its own, the region prospered by exporting cotton, as well as goods that arrived overland from greater South and Central Asia. From Cambay and other ports, Gujarati merchants fanned out across the Arabian Sea and eastward to Melaka. When Tomé Pires visited Gujarat early in the sixteenth century, he observed: ᵃThey are men who understand merchandise. . . . They are diligent, quick men in trade. . . . Those of our people who want to be clerks or factors ought to go there and learn, because the business of trade is a science in itself which does not hinder any other noble exercise, but helps a great deal.°5

Gujarati merchants helped animate the trade of the Arabian Sea, which connected South Asia to East Africa, the Persian Gulf, and the Red Sea. Duarte Barbosa, a Portuguese official who sailed to the Indian Ocean early in the sixteenth century, wrote about Muslim merchants who shipped goods westward from India. In the southern Indian port of Calicut, he observed, the traders ª took on board goods for every place, and every monsoon [the seasonal wind shifts] ten or fifteen of these ships sailed for the Red Sea, Aden, and Meca [Mecca], where they sold their goods at a profit. . . . These goods were pepper (great store), ginger, cinnamon, cardamoms, . . . precious stones of every kind, seed pearls, musk, ambergris, rhubarb, aloes-wood, great store of cotton cloths, porcelains.°6 This immensely valuable merchandise, he reported, went ª to Cairo, and from Cairo to Alexandria, and thence to Venice whence they came to our regions.°

Europeans looking east. In the early fifteenth century, the western European and North African societies located at the far western end of the trans-hemispheric trade system had generally smaller populations, fewer cities, and more modest manufacturing economies than did India, China, or the central Muslim lands. A much greater volume of goods flowed into the far west than out of it. Wealthy Europeans had access to gold from West Africa, silks from East Asia, and spices, drugs, and dyes from Indonesia. But the merchants who relayed these items along the exchange network practiced the usual profit-seeking rule: buy cheap and sell dear. Consequently, people in the west usually paid prices marked up many times over the cost of production. In the 1400s, for example, Indian pepper sold in England for about £200 per ton, whereas construction of a seagoing ship there cost only £2 or £3 per ton. Europe's workshops turned out a variety of products, for example, fine woolens, ironware, and weaponry, which commanded respectable markets in Mediterranean ports. But the balance of trade remained heavily tipped toward Asia, requiring European importers to buy Asian products with gold or silver coins. That exchange worked quite well because neither South Asia nor China had large endowments of those metals. Europeans mined silver in Germany, Bohemia, and other regions, though gold reached Europe principally by camel caravan trade from Sudanic West Africa.

Indians harvesting pepper. This illustration comes from a fifteenth-century edition of Marco Polo's travels, *Book of Wonders of the World*. Look for the artist's depiction of three phases of the global pepper trade: harvesting, transporting to market, and commercial exchange. Why might the artist have shown these three phases happening simultaneously?

For about a century and a half before 1350, bands of Italian and other European merchants traveled overland in small numbers to Iraq, Iran, India, and even China. Marco Polo (1254±1324) was among the Venetians who journeyed to East Asia and back. These traders found opportunities to the east because the rulers of the Mongol states that existed at the time, as well as some Muslim and Hindu princes who controlled Indian Ocean ports, allowed foreigners of just about any origin to pass through to conduct business. Western Europeans therefore acquired greater knowledge of the trans-hemispheric web as well as keen aspirations to penetrate it on a larger scale.

Unfortunately for them, the political situation changed. The Mongol state that ruled Persia collapsed in 1335, and the rulers that succeeded it regarded the presence of Franks, as Muslims called western Europeans, as a potential threat to local mercantile groups. In Egypt the Muslim military state known as the Mamluk sultanate allowed Venetian ships to enter the port of Alexandria but not to sail on the Nile or the Red Sea. Then, in 1453, Ottoman Turkish armies captured Constantinople, eradicated the Christian Byzantine empire, and took control of the sea passage between the Black Sea and the Mediterranean (see Chapter 15). The Ottoman emperor Mehmed II (reigned 1451±1481) at first encouraged European merchants to visit Aegean ports. But as the sixteenth century approached, commercial relations soured. Ottoman forces warred intermittently with Venice for control of eastern Mediterranean islands, and the merchants of Genoa lost access to ports they had frequented in the Black Sea. Thereafter, Italian traffic in the eastern Mediterranean ports fell off. In addition to that, Turkish armies seized both southern Iraq and Egypt early in the sixteenth century, positioning themselves to send naval vessels into the Indian Ocean.

The Eastern Atlantic Rim

In the fifteenth century, three major clusters of relatively dense agrarian population faced the Atlantic Ocean. Along the eastern rim of the Atlantic (see Map 16.2), one cluster extended from the British Isles southward to the northern edge of the Sahara Desert. The second cluster, also along the eastern Atlantic rim, was tropical West and Central Africa. The third was the American lands rimming the western Atlantic, around the Caribbean Sea and the Gulf of Mexico. In the late century, these three regions quite suddenly found their previously separate histories coming together.

MAP 16.2 The eastern Atlantic rim, 1470.
The Sahara Desert separated the relatively densely populated regions of western Europe and North Africa from the agrarian lands of West Africa. What factors help explain increased maritime activity in the eastern Atlantic in the late fifteenth century?

Focus on the Strait of Gibraltar. In the fourteenth and fifteenth centuries, the Atlantic presented an alluring challenge to the monarchs, merchants, and navigators inhabiting the European and African lands on either side of the Strait of Gibraltar. Since ancient times, the Iberian Peninsula (modern Spain and Portugal) and western North Africa (modern Morocco and Algeria) had constituted a single zone of human interaction, especially from the eighth century, when Arab Muslim forces crossed the strait to unite the two regions in a single religious, cultural, and political sphere. By the mid-thirteenth century, three Christian monarchiesÐ Castile, Aragon, and PortugalÐ wrested most of Iberia from Muslim control. Nevertheless, merchants, pilgrims, and diplomats continued to move back and forth across the strait. In the fourteenth century, the Christian states, the Muslim kingdom of Granada, and three Muslim monarchies in North Africa competed in peace and war, forming and breaking alliances and exchanging one another's goods without much regard to religious differences.

By the late thirteenth century, the Strait of Gibraltar was becoming a ªriver° of commerce connecting the Mediterranean world with the eastern Atlantic. Italian and other European vessels frequented the strait and the ports along its shores. Some of those ships probed Morocco's Atlantic coast to buy grain, horses, and gold. In 1291 the Genoese Vivaldi brothers conceived a much more ambitious plan to lead a small fleet of galleys southward until they found a passage around Africa to the Indian Ocean. The hulls of Italian galleys, however, were too shallow to withstand high Atlantic seas. The Vivaldis disappeared without a trace, and another 197 years passed before a Portuguese captain reached Africa's southern extremity.

Other Italian sea merchants who passed through the strait turned north, sailing around Iberia to the ports of the English Channel, North Sea, and Baltic Sea. That route could be highly profitable, since the costs of direct water transport from southern to northern Europe were much lower than hauling goods overland. From the fourteenth century, in effect, the Strait of Gibraltar fused the Mediterranean and the whole northeastern Atlantic into one network.

In those conditions, ports in southwestern Spain and Portugal attracted sailors, shipbuilders, and cartographers, who talked together about routes, hull designs, and navigation techniques. Portuguese shippers and fishermen began to grope their way farther into the Atlantic to see what landfalls they might discover. Iberians, Italians, and French-speaking Normans visited the Madeira and Canary Island groups in the first half of the fourteenth century and began to plant trading stations and small settlements.

The Madeira Islands had no native inhabitants, but sometime early in the Common Era people who spoke a Berber language voyaged across open water from Morocco to the Canaries. These small bands of migrants survived as farmers, stock breeders, or foragers on the archipelago of seven mountainous islands, though they apparently lost all contact

A Guanche man. This sixteenth-century Spanish engraving, originally published in a book about styles of dress around the world, shows a muscular, well-armed man representing the hunting and herding inhabitants of the Canary Islands. Why might the artist have portrayed the figure in this particular way?

with North Africa. When the islanders, known collectively as Guanches (HWAN-chehs), began to encounter Europeans, the consequences ranged from wars and enslavement to alliances, intermarriage, and conversion to Christianity. The long-isolated population lacked immunities to infectious diseases that Europeans introduced and therefore died in large numbers in the fifteenth century as epidemics, perhaps of typhus or pneumonia, swept across the islands. As more Europeans arrived to trade, farm, and set up sugar plantations, the Guanches gradually lost all distinctive physical or cultural identity.

The Canaries became a base for deeper Atlantic probes. Portuguese seafarers found the uninhabited Azores by 1331, an archipelago located nearly a third of the way to America. Advancing southward along the Atlantic coast, European sailors reached the Senegal River south of the Sahara Desert in 1444 and the uninhabited Cape Verde Islands twelve years later. By the mid-fifteenth century, in short, the communication network that spanned Afroeurasia east to west extended a significant distance into the eastern Atlantic and to the northern edge of tropical West Africa (see Map 16.2). But what, experienced sea dogs asked, might lie even farther south and west?

Meanwhile, the political climate around the Strait of Gibraltar became increasingly hostile. Portugal, a small, mostly rural kingdom that nonetheless became an effectively centralized monarchy, launched seaborne assaults on Morocco, a land of around seven million Arabic- and Berber-speaking Muslims. In 1415 Portugal took advantage of instability within Morocco's ruling Marinid dynasty to seize the port of Ceuta (SYOO-tah) on the African side of the strait. Throughout the following century, Portuguese marauders continued to raid Moroccan coastlands for loot and slaves and, despite local resistance, captured several more ports. Both Portugal and the other Iberian kingdoms coveted Morocco's grain and cane sugar, as well as the gold that camel trains brought from West Africa. In 1469 Ferdinand II of Aragon married Isabella of Castile, laying the political foundations of the Spanish monarchy. Shortly thereafter, the king and queen turned their combined forces against mountain-bound Granada. Victory and annexation of Granada in 1492 allowed Spain to commit more resources to two other military projects. One was war against the Ottoman Turkish navy, which presented a growing threat in the western Mediterranean. The other was further expansion into Atlantic waters in search of new territories to seize and exploit.

Tropical Africa facing the Atlantic. In the fifteenth century, most populations on the Atlantic side of tropical Africa formed either stateless societies or small monarchies supported by agriculture or cattle herding. Nevertheless, growing wealth from agriculture, mining, and trade supported a number of large state-building projects in both savanna lands and tropical forests. Moreover, the savanna region just south of the Sahara known historically as the Western Sudan had a long tradition of monarchy, including the empires of Ghana and Mali.

Along the rainforested coasts of West and Central Africa, farming societies grew rice, yams, bananas, oil palms, and other tropical crops. Forest populations rose steadily in the first millennium c.e., and state building got under way around 700 c.e. In fifteenth-century West Africa, several kingdoms occupied the lands facing the Gulf of Guinea. Those states founded their economies on forest agriculture and on tradeÐ in palm oil, kola nuts, salt, and goldÐ with savanna societies to the north.

Among forest kingdoms of the region bordering the lower Niger River (modern Nigeria), Benin had probably the largest population. We know that this monarchy had sufficient resources to support state-sponsored building and creative arts. Ewuare, one of Benin's fifteenth-century *obas*, or kings, built massive walls and a moat to protect his palace, a project that testifies to skilled workmanship and the state's ability to mobilize labor. Archaeologists have recovered some of Benin's intricate, naturalistic ivory and brass sculptures depicting humans and animals.

Southeast of the Gulf of Guinea, the Kongo kingdom emerged in the late fourteenth century along the lower reaches of the Congo River. Within another hundred years, the kings of Kongo ruled a 250-mile stretch of coastline and territory stretching deep into the forested interior just south of the equator. Agriculture and mining of both copper and iron sustained the state's economy, along with trade on long stretches of the Congo and several of its tributaries. This commerce included ivory, copperware, iron goods, and pottery. Kongolese weavers produced large

Ivory hip mask from Benin. The kings of Benin wore masks like this seventeenth-century example tied to their left hip during ceremonial occasions. The figures across the top of the head represent Portuguese traders. Why do you think the kings incorporated Portuguese figures into their regalia?

quantities of textiles for regional markets. These cloths were made from fibers extracted from tree bark and the fronds (leaves) of certain palm species. According to the Portuguese captain Pacheco Pereira, writing in the early sixteenth century, ª In this Kingdom of Conguo [Kongo] they make cloths of palm-leaf as soft as velvet, some of them embroidered with velvet satin, as beautiful as any made in Italy.º⁷ At its fifteenth-century peak, Kongo may have had a population of about 500,000. From his capital on an inland plateau, the Mwene Kongo, or king, commanded an army and a growing urban population.

States in the Americas

Even though peoples of Afroeurasia and the Americas developed entirely separately from each other for thousands of years, fundamental interactions with local environments were not so different. In some parts of the Americas, mobile bands of foragers and hunters discovered efficient ways to share land, extract wild resources, and govern small communities, as they did in Afroeurasia. In others, farming peoples created complex societies, built cities, and formed states of varying organization and size. Maize farming spread steadily across the Americas in the first millennium C.E., and by the fifteenth century, maize was the basic staple that sustained growing populations and complex settlements from Canada to the southern Andes.

The Aztec empire. Especially large agrarian populations arose in Mesoamerica, where state and city building started in the second millennium B.C.E. In the fifteenth century, the Aztec empire, centered in the Valley of Mexico (where Mexico City is today), expanded territorially and enclosed a growing circle of subject peoples (see Chapter 14). The Nahuatl-speaking Mexica, the core imperial population, incorporated numerous neighboring groups into the empire by armed conquest or the mere threat of it. Like some premodern empire builders in Afroeurasia, the Aztecs ruled their subjects largely indirectly, allowing conquered groups to retain their own leaders, as long as they pledged loyalty and sent regular tribute in food and cotton to Tenochtitlan, the capital city located on an island in Lake Texcoco.

In the early sixteenth century, the Aztec state, whose core was a ªtriple allianceº of Tenochtitlan and two other city-states, commanded tens of thousands of warriors and a population of about twenty-five million. Trade in gold, silver, jade, feathers, fine textiles, and an array of foodstuffs circulated throughout the empire and far beyond it. Under the emperor Motecuzoma II (also, Moctezuma or Montezuma), who reigned from 1502 to 1520, stability and prosperity generally prevailed. On the other hand, the social distance between the noble class and commoners was widening, growing numbers of ordinary men and women occupied low rungs of society as landless laborers or tenants of rich estate lords, and slaves abounded. This was cause for chronic social tension. The Aztecs' dependent allies and tributaries also resented their subordination, and the Tenochtitlan elite imposed order by taking violent reprisals at any sign of rebellion.

The Inca empire. Along South America's Andean Mountain spine and the coastal deserts running parallel to it, a history of urbanization and state formation extends back even earlier than in Mesoamerica. The Inca state, founded in the Valley of Cuzco in what is now southern Peru, emerged as an expansive empire about 1438. Its power was based on the irrigated agriculture of highland valleys. A century later it constituted the largest territorial state the Americas had ever seen, embracing fewer people than the Aztec empire but extending along the Andean chain about 2,400 miles. In contrast to the Aztecs, Inca armies broke up the smaller Andean states they conquered and integrated local chiefs into a large centralized bureaucracy. Inca rulers also ordered involuntary population exchanges. They brought recently

Aztec tribute list. This sixteenth-century document records the tribute that Aztec rulers collected from a single city. Why would both Aztec rulers and Spanish conquerors have kept these tribute lists?

Machu Picchu. The Inca built this citadel, perched at 7,900 feet in the Andes, in the mid-fifteenth century. It was apparently abandoned after the Spanish conquest of Peru. Probably constructed as a retreat for Inca rulers, the site has distinct residential, agricultural, and religious sectors. Why might the Inca ruler have wished to build a residence on a mountainside fifty miles from Cuzco, his capital city?

conquered peopleÐ especially rebellious groupsÐ to live close to the capital and moved loyal peasants to the frontiers. Only at the village level did local kinship groups manage daily affairs with little government interference.

Like all other American societies, the Inca lacked wheeled vehicles or iron tools. But they drew on a long Andean state tradition of mobilizing labor on a large scale to build mountain roads and bridges, erect grain storehouses, field a large army, and meticulously collect information about social and economic conditions using a system of knotted and variously colored strings, or *quipus.* An early Spanish observer wrote that at the start of a new year village chiefs brought *quipus* to the capital city of Cuzco to report births, deaths, and other social facts. [a] In this way the Inca and the governors knew which of the Indians were poor, the women who had been widowed, whether they were able to pay their taxes, and how many men they could count on in the event of war, and many other things they considered highly important.[8] Just as in the Aztec and several Afroeurasian empires of the same era, the government gathered this information to support its own interests rather than that of the people, counting on tax revenues to maintain the army,

feed peasant workers drafted for public works, and support the lavish lifestyle of the royal court, noble families, and high religious and political officials.

Under a succession of three capable rulers, Inca armies incorporated more than 772,000 square miles of Andean and Pacific coastal territory into the empire between the 1430s and about 1520. By that date, the state was nearly three and a half times the size of Spain and Portugal together. Emperor Huayna Capac died about 1527, and that event set off an internal power struggle between two of his sons. This civil war was just coming to an end in 1532, when a band of pale, long-haired strangers in metal armor appeared suddenly on the Peruvian coast.

The Birth of the Atlantic World

FOCUS What factors contributed to the establishment of regular seaborne communication across the Atlantic Ocean in the late fifteenth century?

When European sailors explored the eastern Atlantic in the fourteenth and fifteenth centuries, they had limited, profit-seeking objectives, not grand plans to find direct sea routes to Asia. These mariners looked for islands or African coastal points where they might trade, raid, fish, or even settle. They also reasoned that they might not have to sail too many hundreds of miles to reach the sources of West African gold, a commodity they had always had to buy from North African merchants at elevated prices. But they had no firm knowledge that they could ever reach the Indian Ocean by going south, and America was still *terra incognita*Ð unknown territory.

Even so, scholars and merchants of Mediterranean Europe had for centuries theorized about a southern sea passage to Asia. The Vivaldi brothers, as we have seen, tried to test that theory in 1291, but they never came back to report. The rise of Ottoman power in the eastern Mediterranean, which dashed European hopes of traveling freely across Southwest Asia to Indian Ocean ports, ignited new interest in a South Atlantic route. Some EuropeansÐ gallant nobles and pious churchmen more than hard-headed merchantsÐ dreamed of carrying the successful Christian crusade for control of Iberia southward into tropical Africa. There, they imagined, monarchs might be found willing to accept the Christian gospel. Better yet, contact might be made with Prester John, a mythical ruler almost certainly associated with the very real Christian kingdom of Ethiopia. Once formed, this Christian alliance would move to encircle the Ottomans and other Muslim states and eventually squeeze them into oblivion.

European rulers who dreamed of such a crusade, however, had little urge to pay for it. For example, Prince Henry of Portugal (1394±1460), later known as Henry the Navigator, saw himself as a chivalrous warrior for Christ, and he enthusiastically supported maritime expeditions, technical improvements, and cartography. But he had little money. He dedicated much of his career to the strategically short-range goals of conquering the Canary Islands for Portugal, which he failed to do, and encouraging expeditions that might divert West African gold to Portuguese ships. The kings of Portugal awarded charters to private groups to explore southward but did not directly finance such expeditions until the 1480s.

Changing Maritime Technology

The shipwrights, pilots, cartographers, and astronomers who frequented Iberian ports in the fifteenth century made up a diverse crowd. They came not only from various parts of Portugal and Spain but also from Italy, North Africa, France, England, Germany, and Poland. The Iberian region of Catalonia and the Mediterranean island of Mallorca (Majorca), both part of the kingdom of Aragon after 1344, emerged as creative centers for making maps, navigational charts, and nautical instruments. Jewish scholars and artisans specialized in this profession. They collected information from sailors who braved gale-prone Atlantic waters. They also drew on a large fund of technical and maritime knowledge that filtered to them from northern Europe, the Muslim lands, and the Indian Ocean rim.

Shipbuilding. European traditions of shipbuilding definitely needed improvement if captains were going to venture far into the Atlantic. As of the early fifteenth century, Chinese seagoing junks, with their massive hulls, multiple masts, and watertight compartments, were probably technically capable of braving Atlantic or Pacific waters. Chinese captains, however, never tested these craft, so far as we know, beyond the China seas or the Indian Ocean. The ships that plied the Baltic and North Seas in the medieval centuries were not strong enough to carry large loads of cargo long distances. High-sided, broad-beamed vessels called round ships used in northern waters usually had only one mast. It supported a square sail that worked most efficiently when the wind blew generally from behind the vessel to push it forward. In the Mediterranean Sea, galley ships that supplemented sail power with dozens of rowers were more common. Human muscle allowed galleys to make progress in any wind condition, but they had to carry food and water for the rowers. That increased costs and restricted space for paying cargo.

Starting in the fourteenth century, western European shipwrights gradually revolutionized ship design. In earlier times, carpenters built hulls by attaching wooden planks to each other, then constructing a frame around them. In the fifteenth century they reversed this process, assembling the hard ªskeletonº of the hull first, then attaching the planks to this frame. This method reduced construction time and labor; it also yielded sturdier hulls that withstood Atlantic seas and could bear heavier cargos. This innovation coincided with the introduction of gunpowder artillery in warfare. Stronger hulls made it possible to mount heavy cannons on the decks of oceangoing vessels without destabilizing them.

Stronger ships could also support multiple masts and a combination of types of sails, which provided more propulsion power and greater maneuverability. If a vessel had three masts, the two farthest forward typically carried square sails for moving downwind. The mast at the stern (the back end) held a lateen, or triangular sail. This type had been in use in the Mediterranean for many centuries and perhaps in the Indian Ocean before that. Its particular shape and construction allowed a vessel to make progress even when it was heading nearly straight into the wind. This power and flexibility gave sailors more confidence to buck contrary winds and helped reduce travel times between ports.

In the later fifteenth century, two generic models of sailing ships were in use in the Atlantic. The Portuguese-designed **caravel** was a stout fireplug of a ship equipped with two or three lateen sails. It measured only sixty-five to eighty feet long but had

> **caravel** A type of light, highly maneuverable sailing vessel used by Iberian sailors in the Atlantic in the fifteenth and sixteenth centuries.

room for crew supplies, small cannons, and cargo. It became the preferred vehicle of early exploration, well suited to sail along coasts and up rivers and estuaries. Near the end of the century, builders modified caravels to combine square and lateen sails. The **carrack,** the second general vessel type, evolved into a much larger craft designed to make long sea voyages and mount heavier cannons for defense against pirates and rival naval powers. Carracks had multiple decks for storing different types of cargo and for crew quarters. High ᵃcastles,° or platforms were constructed at each end of the ship. These gave cannoniers and soldiers armed with handguns or crossbows commanding positions from which to repel seaborne attacks. In the sixteenth century, carracks became the workhorses of transoceanic trade.

carrack An oceangoing ship, larger than a caravel, used extensively by Iberian mariners in the Atlantic and Indian Oceans in the fifteenth and sixteenth centuries.

Navigation.
Open-ocean sailing required not only better ships, but also new navigation techniques to plot location on a map, plan routes, calculate a ship's speed, follow a course, and avoid hazards. Before the fifteenth century, navigation depended on landmarks. Pilots determined their ship's position at sea by estimating its distance from known coastal points. This required them to sail within sight of land as much as possible. A captain could maintain a constant heading by looking at the Pole Star (North Star) or other heavenly bodies. From the thirteenth century, he could also use a compass, a device that Chinese mariners invented and that Indian Ocean mariners passed to the Mediterranean.

Deep sea navigators could not rely on landmarks, but they knew how to estimate their latitude, that is, their location between the earth's poles and the equator. They did this by sighting the distance from the Pole Star to the horizon to reveal their approximate distance south of the North Pole. Abraham Zacuto, a Portuguese Jew, drew on the earlier work of Muslim scholars to come up with another way to measure latitude. He compiled tables indicating the sun's declination, that is, its distance north or south of the equator at noon on any given day of the year. Captains could observe the sun to verify when it was at its highest point in the sky, then use the tables to determine the ship's latitude. European sailors also used astrolabes and quadrants, devices perfected in earlier centuries by Muslim artisans, to calculate the height of heavenly bodies. Determining longitude, a vessel's position east or west of a particular point, was a much greater challenge. It required knowing the difference between the time on shipboard at a given moment and the time at a place from which the

ship had embarked. That calculation could not be made precisely until the late eighteenth century, when clocks were invented that could keep accurate time on a rolling vessel.

Charting Atlantic winds and currents.
Ship captains who ventured into the Atlantic recorded latitudes, compass directions, and landforms from day to day, thereby building up a body of geographical knowledge for sailors who wished to follow the same routes later and perhaps push deeper into unknown waters. The most useful maps displayed the swirling patterns of wind and current. Sailors embarking from Iberian ports learned in the fourteenth century that they could easily sail southwestward along the African coast or to the Canary Islands because the strong Canary Current and associated trade winds sucked them in that direction. On the return voyage, however, they usually faced contrary winds. Crews discovered, however, that they could make headway slowly by sailing diagonally across a head wind, then turning sharply to sail on the opposite diagonal, in other words, tacking (zigzagging) across the wind and current. Caravel pilots took advantage of their lateen sails to perform these maneuvers. Even more important for venturing far into the Atlantic, Portuguese mariners who frequented the Azores after 1431 discovered that those northerly islands, located eight hundred miles due west of Portugal, lay in the path of winds that blew from the west and toward Europe. If ships returning from the African coast sailed northwestward and farther out to sea, they

A Portuguese caravel. This mosaic adorns a fountain at the home of Vasco da Gama's brother, Paulo, a noted ship builder. Two of the masts carry square sails for running before the wind. The third carries a lateen sail for sailing close to the wind—close to the direction from which the wind is blowing. Sturdy decks could support artillery. What do you think the two symbols on the sails represent?

could catch the westerlies in the vicinity of the Azores and return at good speed to the Iberian coast. Soon thereafter, navigators began to understand that the trade and westerly winds formed a single clockwise wind wheel that circulated above the entire North Atlantic.

How big is the world? Fifteen-century scholars generally agreed on the roundness of the world but not on its circumference. The Italian Renaissance, the fifteenth-century intellectual and artistic movement that sought to rediscover and emulate the cultural achievements of ancient Rome and Greece (see Chapter 15), involved study of Latin and Greek geographical texts. One key document was the *Geography* (*Geographia*) of Ptolemy, a scholar who lived in Roman Egypt in the second century C.E. In 1406 Renaissance sages translated the *Geography* from Greek into Latin, triggering debate about the size of the earth. Ptolemy conceived of a round globe about 18,000 miles in circumference. In 1410 Pierre d'Ailly, a Catholic cardinal, published *Imago Mundi,* a treatise that drew on both ancient and Muslim writings to argue that European sailors could reach Asia by heading west. In 1474 Paolo Toscanelli, a Florentine businessman and geographer, wrote to the king of Portugal, arguing that Europe and China lay on opposite sides of the Atlantic a mere five thousand miles apart. Those fifteenth-century hypotheses were wrong, but they nevertheless motivated adventurous sailors, including Christopher Columbus, to test them.

Europeans and West Africans: Early Encounters

Portuguese mariners began to explore the African coast south of the Senegal River in the second half of the fifteenth century. There, they came into contact with much denser populations than they had seen in the arid Saharan latitudes. Interaction between agrarian West Africa and the rest of Afroeurasia had until then depended entirely on overland communication either across the desert or, much more irregularly, eastward across equatorial Africa to the Indian Ocean. Now, however, European sailors pioneered a new sea route that connected West Africans to the Mediterranean world. This route had much greater commercial potential than the trans-Saharan camel trails because it could carry goods and people faster, cheaper, and at much greater capacity.

Portuguese sea venturers aimed to profit from gold and other products that African agrarian societies had to sell. They also believed they could combine peaceful exchange with violent raiding and seizure of territory, just as Europeans were doing in the Canary Islands. They soon discovered, however, that such tactics would not work well in the long term. Africans were eager for trade, but they had the means to resist landward assaults, just as Moroccans had in North Africa. West Africans could usually mobilize much larger military forces than the Portuguese could, including fighters who put to sea in giant canoes to shower arrows on hostile ships and landing parties. In contrast to Canary Islanders, mainland Africans and Europeans had not been

biologically isolated from one another during the preceding millennia and therefore shared partial immunities to the same infectious diseases. Consequently, Portuguese visitors to West Africa did not often leave socially disruptive epidemics in their wake. On the contrary, Europeans who resided in tropical West Africa for even a short period frequently contracted tropical diseases, especially malaria or yellow fever. Somewhere between 25 and 50 percent of Europeans who went to tropical Africa in the fifteenth century died within a year. Thus, Africans had effective biological allies against seaborne invaders.

Portuguese expeditions continued to sail to Africa year after year, first advancing eastward along the Gulf of Guinea, then turning south toward the Cape of Good Hope. These visitors realized that they could profit handsomely from trade as long as they understood that African rulers and merchants largely controlled its terms. In 1471, for example, the Portuguese merchant Fernão Gomes reached the area known later as the Gold Coast. The local Fante-speaking rulers offered gold and other commodities and permitted Gomes to establish a trading station and later to build a coastal fort named Elmina. The Fante collected duties on cargo moving in and out, and they required European captains to seek royal permission to dock. Ships from Europe brought iron bars and tools, woolen cloth, copper, brass, alcohol, Moroccan horses, and various other products to trade for gold, pepper, ivory, African textiles, and slaves. The Portuguese shipped some of those items to Europe, but they found they could also make money by purchasing slaves or goods at one port on the African coast and selling them at another. In effect, Europeans engaged in this ªcarrying tradeº became participants in African exchange networks.

Benin and Kongo meet the Portuguese. Before the end of the century, the Portuguese entered into relations with both Benin and Kongo, two of the most populous Atlantic-facing states. These relations, however, moved in two very different directions. Portuguese merchants obtained authorization from the king of Benin to buy pepper for export to Europe and cloth for shipment to other parts of the coast. They also bought slaves. In that period, Benin was engaged in wars to conquer and colonize neighbors and therefore generated numerous war prisoners. The king agreed to send a diplomatic mission to Lisbon and to accept Christian missionaries, but these initiatives went nowhere. In the 1550s, with the wars of expansion at an end, the king decided to stop selling slaves, a policy that continued to the late seventeenth century. Benin continued to trade with Europeans, but it strictly controlled foreign activities.

In the Kongo kingdom, by contrast, the arrival of Europeans led to severe political and social disruption. Relations between the Portuguese and the Kongolese monarchy started out as they had in BeninÐ amicable diplomatic formalities and plans for commercial and cultural exchanges. Portuguese priests evangelized some members of the royal family, and in 1506 a young prince who had already converted

Pompe & magnificence du Roi de Congo en donnant audience aux Etrangers.

King Afonso I of Kongo receives a Portuguese delegation. Ceremonial meetings like this ratified the formal diplomatic relations that Kongo had with Portugal. Notice the Catholic priests standing by Afonso's right hand, the weapons carried by both Portuguese and Kongolese soldiers, and captive slaves in the background. This European engraving was made a century after the occasion, probably by an artist who never visited Kongo. Which elements in this image are likely realistic, and which are a product of the artist's imagination?

to Christianity mounted the throne under the name Afonso I (r. 1506±1543). In the following years, the Portuguese sent him technicians, mercenary soldiers with guns, more missionaries, and a printing press. In turn, the king dispatched young Kongolese to Lisbon for education, and he opened correspondence with both the Portuguese crown and the Vatican in Rome. He also used Portuguese support to expand his territories and gain more central control over provincial noble families.

Even before Afonso came to power, however, Portuguese entrepreneurs began to set up sugar plantations on the uninhabited island of São Tomé in the Gulf of Guinea. Even though it was far south of the Madeira and Canary Islands, São Tomé was in a sense the last of the eastern Atlantic islands that Europeans colonized before 1500. Plantation owners on Madeira and the Canaries enslaved Guanches, Moroccans, and West Africans to work in fields and mills. Similarly, European planters who arrived on São Tomé in the 1490s (and who had no interest in cultural exchanges with Kongo) met their labor needs by purchasing slaves from anyone on the neighboring mainland willing to supply them in exchange for European goods. Afonso had great difficulty throughout his reign controlling the disruptive effects of slave trading. In 1526 he wrote to the Portuguese king João III:

Sir, in our Kingdoms there is another great inconvenience which is of little service to God, and this is that many of our people, keenly desirous as they are of the wares and things of your Kingdoms, which are brought here by your people, and in order to satisfy their voracious appetite, seize many of our people, freed and exempt men, and very often it happens that they kidnap even noblemen and the sons of noblemen, and our relatives, and take them to be sold to the white men who are in our Kingdoms.[9]

Nevertheless, the slave trade continued to grow, especially after 1530 when São Tomé became an important assembly point for captives destined to be shipped to new sugar plantations in Brazil. Afonso grew increasingly dependent on Portuguese advisors and mercenaries to keep the kingdom stable. A quarter-century after he died, his kingdom nearly collapsed. Meanwhile, Portuguese slavers expanded their regional operations. In 1576 they carved out a permanent if initially small territorial base at Luanda, the future colony of Angola. Afonso's hopes of his kingdom's technical development, Christianization, and diplomatic standing in the world came to almost nothing.

Rounding the Cape. In 1479, after five years of maritime war, Portugal and Spain resolved festering territorial and trade disputes by signing the Treaty of Alcáçovas. By

Martin Behaim's Fifteenth-Century Globe

In 1492, merchant and mariner Martin Behaim presented a globe to the city of Nuremberg, Germany. He called his gift "der Erdapfel," or "the Earth apple." Such a plain name, however, hardly does justice to the ornately decorated globe, its map sprinkled with miniature paintings of animals, saints, kings, and ships. Today, the globe's vibrant colors are faded, but the map still commands great interest. It is one of the oldest terrestrial globes in existence and presents a window on western European geographical knowledge on the eve of Columbus's first trans-Atlantic voyage.

Though we associate the globe with Behaim, many other people contributed to its construction. Craftsmen built the papier-mâché-like form at the center, then strengthened it with wooden hoops. A blacksmith crafted two iron rings to stabilize the sphere. In drawing the globe's map, Behaim gleaned knowledge from the ancient Greek geographer Ptolemy, the Venetian traveler Marco Polo, and Sir John Mandeville, the pseudonym of a fourteenth-century French author. After Behaim compiled the map, artist Georg Glockendon spent fifteen weeks painting it on the sphere and adding decorative elements.

The globe stood in the Nuremberg town hall for over a century. In the early 1700s, Behaim's descendants asked to have it back, and the city complied. It remained in a Behaim family home until 1907, when its owners transferred it to Nuremberg's Germanic Museum. Der Erdapfel has remained in remarkably good shape, permitting modern scholars to have some idea of how fifteenth-century sailors envisioned the world they set out to explore.

Thinking Critically

How is the relationship between western Europe and East Asia depicted on the globe? What landforms are missing from the map? How accurate do you think the map's land and sea features are? Why do you think Behaim put in the Atlantic so many islands that had never been identified? If a sailor were working from this map, why would a western route from Europe to Asia seem preferable to an eastern one?

its terms, Spain acquired sovereignty over the Canary Islands and Portugal over the Azores and Madeira. Portugal also secured rights to African trade south of the Canaries. This provision deflected Spanish interest from seeking an African route to the Indian Ocean, leaving that field to its smaller neighbor. Portuguese captains who explored the Central African coast south of Kongo gradually accumulated knowledge of South Atlantic winds and currents. Bartholomew Dias was investigating what is today the coast of Namibia in 1488 when his two small caravels were blown far southwest in a storm. When he tried to return to shore, he found himself sailing past the Cape of Good Hope and into the Indian Ocean. Deferring to his crew, who threatened mutiny if he tried to push farther, he made for Lisbon. Drawing on Dias's experience ten years later, however, Vasco da Gama led five ships into the South Atlantic, sailing southwest until he caught westerly winds that brought him back to the coast just north of the Cape. By accomplishing that maneuver, he demonstrated the existence of a South Atlantic wind wheel that revolved counterclockwiseÐ the opposite direction of the North Atlantic one. Continuing around the Cape of Good Hope, he continued up the East African shore and on to South Asia. The Atlantic and the Indian Oceans were now connected directly by sea.

Columbus's Atlantic Crossing

While Dias confirmed an eastward sea passage to Asia in 1488, the possibility of a westward route remained a matter of debate among Iberian sailors and cartographers. Christopher Columbus (1451±1506) was consumed by the question. Born in Genoa, he sailed extensively in the Mediterranean and along the Atlantic coast during his adolescence. When he was not at sea, he pursued occupations as a weaver, bookseller, and mapmaker. Sometime in his early twenties, he settled in Portugal, where he married the daughter of a nobleman who had served Prince Henry in the Madeira Islands. As a wedding present, Columbus's father-in-law gave him his maps and navigational papersÐ a rare treasure in that era. In 1482 Columbus made a voyage to the Gulf of Guinea.

Though he had a flawed conception of the size of the world, he became convinced that an ocean voyage between Iberia and East Asia was possible. An enthusiastic risk-taker, he spent more than seven years trying to persuade first the Portuguese king and then Ferdinand and Isabella of Spain to finance a westward voyage. The possibility of finding a lucrative trade route to Asia not blocked by Muslim navies finally persuaded the Spanish monarchs. At the least, Columbus might discover new Atlantic islands before the Portuguese did.

Ferdinand and Isabella elevated Columbus to the rank of admiral and gave him funds to acquire ships and engage a crew. He chose two caravels, the *Niña* and the *Pinta,* and a flagship carrack, the *Santa Maria.* He and his little fleet first sailed south to the Canaries, then continued into the deep, sighting land thirty-six days later. We know that he reached the Bahamas or Turks and Caicos archipelago on the western edge of the Caribbean, but the location of his initial landfall has never been confirmed. Taino (TEYE-noh) Indians, who would have spoken an Arawakan language, greeted the strangers on the beach and graciously offered parrots and cotton thread for red Spanish caps and glass beads. Columbus had read Marco Polo's description of China, but nothing he discovered looked like thatÐ no gold-roofed temples, no cities, no bustling wharfs. In his own account of the voyage, Columbus emphasized the nakedness of the locals he encountered, but he also declared them fully rational and human, thus disposed to Christian conversion. The islanders were no doubt equally amazed by the hairy-faced visitor.

For two months Columbus continued to search the eastern Caribbean, including the coast of Cuba. He encountered numerous settlements but not much in the way of commercial opportunity. In December 1492 the fleet began the homeward voyage, minus the *Santa Maria,* which ran aground. The returning company, which reached Portugal in March 1493, included ten Tainos, the first American Indians, as far as we know, to cross the Atlantic west to east. Columbus made three more trips to the Caribbean, many other Europeans followed, and within barely three decades round trips were becoming nearly routine.

In time Europeans came to understand that they had found, not some islands close to China, but two enormous land masses, a New World, as they came to call the Western Hemisphere, teeming with exotic people and other life forms. At the start of the sixteenth century, however, neither Tainos nor Iberians had any idea of the historic significance of Columbus's voyages. Spain and Portugal, still in competition with each other for overseas possessions, scrambled to make geographical sense of his discoveries. In 1494 Pope Alexander VI mediated the Treaty of Tordesillas, an agreement between the two monarchies that imagined a longitudinal line in the Atlantic approximately midway between the Cape Verde Islands, a Portuguese possession, and the islands that Columbus claimed for Spain. By the terms of the treaty, a breathtaking exercise in royal self-importance, the Portuguese crown could lay claim to any territory east of the line, which included the Indian Ocean basin. Spain could claim land to the west. Neither power intended to ask the inhabitants of newly discovered territories whether they *wished* to be claimed by a European monarch. The treaty did, however, give the two states assurance of continuing their maritime adventures without immediate risk of war.

American Catastrophes

FOCUS In what circumstances did large states in North and South America fall to European invaders between 1492 and 1550?

Early encounters between Europeans and American Indians took a very different course than between Europeans and Subsaharan Africans. Europeans developed increasingly complex relations with African societies in the fifteenth and sixteenth centuries. With just a few exceptions those relations involved no significant colonial subjugation of one group by another. African political leaders and merchants often squabbled and sometimes skirmished with Europeans along the coasts, but interactions involved mainly trade, including slave trade, and in some places intermarriage and cultural interchange. In startling contrast, Europeans who ventured to America took just a few decades to overrun the Caribbean, bring down the mighty Aztec empire, seize large areas of Mesoamerica, and destroy the highly centralized Inca state in the central Andes (see Map 16.3). Spain went on to lay the foundations of a mammoth American empire, and Portugal took control of coasts and hinterlands of Brazil. The Netherlands, Britain, and France arrived early in the following century to carve out territories of their own.

Why such contrasting histories in Africa and the Americas? At least in general terms, the explanation is uncomplicated. Both Europeans and Africans had iron weaponry; Americans did not. Tropical African states started acquiring firearms soon after their first commercial contacts with the Portuguese. Both Europeans and some African kingdoms deployed horse cavalry in their wars; Americans had no horses. Europeans who went to Africa died at alarming rates because they lacked immunities to malaria, yellow fever, and other tropical diseases; in America, it was the indigenous people who fell in great numbers when exposed to the pathogens introduced from Afroeurasia.

American Death and the Columbian Exchange

Europeans moved as quickly to colonize Caribbean islands as they had the Canaries and Azores. On his second voyage, Columbus founded a settlement on Hispaniola (today Haiti and the Dominican Republic). Ferdinand and Isabella

Explorer	Sponsoring Country
António de Abreu	Portugal
Afonso de Albuquerque	Portugal
John Cabot	England
Pedro Álvares Cabral	Portugal
Juan Sabastián del Cano	Spain
Jacques Cartier	France
Christopher Columbus	Spain
Hernán Cortés	Spain
Vasco da Gama	Portugal
Bartolomeu Dias	Portugal
Francis Drake	England
Ferdinand Magellan	Spain
Rafael Perestrello	Portugal
Francisco Pizarro	Spain

MAP 16.3 Major European maritime voyages, fifteenth and sixteenth centuries.
Within just a few decades, European mariners transformed the Atlantic, the Pacific, and the southern Indian Ocean into channels of intercontinental communication. How did the Treaty of Tordesillas influence Spanish and Portuguese maritime voyages after 1494?

American Catastrophes **471**

granted him the title ª Viceroy of the Indies,° sharing his anticipation that ª India° lay nearby. Columbus led a fleet of seventeen ships and 1,500 settlers, all of them men. These colonists, however, quickly bonded with local Taino women, and the resulting *mestizo,* or mixed-race children, contributed to the colony's growth. The Spanish crown awarded land grants to loyal subjects, including minor nobles with limited prospects in Spain, as well as farmers and artisans who hoped to strike it rich across the sea. As more Europeans arrived, they looked for additional places to colonize. In 1508 Juan Ponce de León founded a colony on Puerto Rico, where he became governor. Two years later, Vasco Núñez de Balboa started the first permanent mainland colony on the coast of present-day Colombia. Both men continued to explore: Ponce de León reached Florida, and Balboa discovered a route across the Isthmus of Panama to the Pacific.

European accounts of early colonization report that islanders identified as Taino or Caribe sometimes resisted the newcomers and, once conquered, repeatedly rose in revolt. Nevertheless, Europeans found progress easier than they might have expected from earlier African experience. Cavalry mounts, vicious attack dogs, guns, and steel swords gave them military advantages. Brutal tactics, including massacres and creative forms of torture, terrified some populations into flight or submission. The colonizers also noticed that islanders seemed to die of their own accord in large numbers from disease. Europeans died, too, both from shipboard infectious and tropical American illnesses such as dysentery or intestinal worms. Indians, however, suffered and died in raging epidemics.

A biological revolution gets under way. An Italian gentleman who accompanied Columbus on his second voyage recorded that ª we brought pigs, chickens, dogs, and cats, they reproduce there in a superlative manner, especially the pigs.°¹⁰ He could not have known that these animals, along with various plants that Columbus introduced, were about to initiate what historians call the **Columbian Exchange**Ð a monumental transfer of foods, fibers, weeds, animals, microorganisms, and people across the Atlantic in both directions. These were living organisms that had not spanned either the Atlantic or the Pacific for, in many cases, 180 million years or more. Consequently, on each side of the oceans, biological evolution followed different paths. Humans migrated in recent geological time from Eurasia to North America by way of the northern Pacific coast or a land bridge linking Siberia with Alaska. That migration stopped, however, about 12,000 years ago. Columbus and the mariners who followed him made the trans-Atlantic linkup permanent, and as traffic grew, numerous life-forms, indeed thousands of them, moved back and forth between Afroeurasia and the Western Hemisphere for the first time.

> **Columbian Exchange** The transfer of living organisms, including plants, animals, microorganisms, and humans, between Afroeurasia and the Americas starting in 1492.

These transfers had growing social, economic, and cultural consequences, not only for Native Americans and Europeans, but also for peoples around the world.

In its effects on human societies and their environments, the Columbian Exchange played itself out over several centuries. As of 1550, human societies were in many respects just beginning to experience ecological and social consequences of the great biological swap. We return to the long-term, global consequences of the Columbian Exchange in Chapter 18.

In one respect, however, the Atlantic linkup had immediate, shocking, and socially transforming effects. In addition to pigs, cows, and food plants, Columbus and his companions introduced a zoological garden of living pathogens resident in human and animal bodies. Sailors who reached America infected with a communicable disease could quickly pass on their malady to biologically vulnerable Caribbean islanders. Smallpox appears to have first arrived on Hispaniola in 1518. According to two Spanish Catholic friars, a smallpox epidemic among the islanders ª does not cease. From it have died and continue to die to the present almost a third of the said Indians.°¹¹ The same two friars reported that the epidemic apparently spread to nearby Puerto Rico. Additional illnesses arrived from either Europe or Africa (carried by African slaves) as the sixteenth century proceeded. And as foreign sailors, soldiers, and traders penetrated the North and South American mainlands, they introduced new ailments to Indians in ever-widening arcs.

In that era no one understood why Native Americans suffered and died in such great numbers. From modern science, however, we know that Indians lacked immunities to many diseases that were endemic, or permanently present, in much of Afroeurasia but previously unknown in the Western Hemisphere. For example, in Europe, small children often died after exposure to infectious maladies such as smallpox or measles, but if they survived they carried lifelong immunities. When the pathogens that caused these diseases, as well as tuberculosis, typhus, chickenpox, dengue fever, and other pestilences, infected Indians, neither children nor adults could biologically cope with these invaders, and mortality soared.

Afroeurasian illnesses could be transmitted through many kinds of contact. Outbreaks of disease could be set off by something as innocent as a sneeze, cough, or touch. The smallpox virus, for example, could move from one human host to another through the air or by a contaminated object. Once a pathogen became established in an Indian community, it spread easily to neighboring ones as people traveled to trade or visit relatives. Epidemics could reach areas hundreds of miles beyond the frontiers of any European settlement.

A few disease organisms endemic in America traveled eastward across the Atlantic to afflict unsuspecting Afroeurasians. Members of the crew that returned to Spain with Columbus after his first voyage introduced the bacteria that causes syphilis. Scholars think this sexually transmitted

The Seminole Indians of Florida treat the effects of Afroeurasian diseases. French artist Jacques le Moyne de Morgues accompanied an early expedition to North America. His images are an important source of information about the period. This engraving made in 1565 was widely reproduced in the sixteenth century. One man lies on his back while a woman sucks blood from a slit made in his forehead. Another lies on his stomach and inhales smoke from burning seeds. The man in the background smokes a tobacco pipe, believing the leaves have medicinal properties.

pathogen (*Treponema pallidum*) mutated quickly after the first encounter between Native Americans and Europeans and adapted readily to Afroeurasian environmental conditions. It appeared in different forms and produced a variety of symptoms. Syphilis began to spread across Europe in 1495, moving along roads and rivers in the company of soldiers, merchants, and pilgrims. It arrived in the Low Countries and England as early as 1496. It also accompanied Portuguese sailors to Africa and the Indian Ocean, reaching the port of Canton in China by 1505. Syphilis caused much suffering in Afroeurasian societies but nowhere near the mortality and upheaval that Old World diseases triggered among Americans after 1492.

The European ᵃlabor problem.° The two Spanish friars who bemoaned the terrible smallpox epidemic on Hispaniola in 1518 also worried that too many Taino deaths would cause a labor shortage and hold up gold-seeking operations.[12] Wherever Europeans founded settlements in the Caribbean and mainland coasts, they aimed to exploit any economic opportunity that promised quick wealth,

whether trade, farming, or mining. To set up any commercial operation, they needed workers. Local labor supplies, however, declined as Indians died not only from disease and Spanish violence but also from starvation as fields were abandoned and trade networks were disrupted. European conquistadors (conquerors) and hopeful entrepreneurs knew well that slave labor on eastern Atlantic island plantations cut production costs and raised profits. As a result, colonizers began to enslave Caribbean Indians shortly after Columbus's first voyage. They could never get as many as they wanted, however, and local people could also flee to islands or hinterlands beyond European reach.

Another approach to the labor problem was the **encomienda** (ehn-koh-mee-EHN-dah). This was a Spanish system of labor regulation that rewarded conquerors by giving them control of groups of people and their labor. In principle, an encomendero, or holder of an

> **encomienda** A grant from the Spanish crown to its conquistadors or other Spanish settlers in the Americas, giving them the rights to the labor services and tribute payments of the indigenous people in a particular area.

encomienda, was entrusted to protect his people and give them Christian instruction in exchange for work and taxes. During the first half of the sixteenth century, the Spanish government and church debated the biological and moral nature of American Indians. Should they be regarded as human savages or even as less-than-human brutes naturally suited for lifelong slavery? Or were they fully human ᵃbrothersº capable of assimilation into civilized Christian society? The Spanish state ultimately pronounced that Indians were indeed ᵃbrothers.º They were to be ranked below Europeans in the colonial social hierarchy but nonetheless were entitled to legal freedom, property ownership, and wages for labor. In America, however, encomenderos seeking profits and sumptuous lifestyles often treated their Indian workers harshly and ignored their rights under Spanish law.

As more Europeans crossed the ocean to invest in mines, lumbering, and plantations, the greater the labor demand became, especially in regions where the Native American population declined sharply. Few Spanish or Portuguese peasants felt motivated to migrate to tropical America to take jobs as field hands or mine diggers, and Europeans had no legal or moral basis to enslave other Europeans. Shackling Africans, however, was another matter. Europeans had already started putting bonded Africans to work on the Atlantic islands. There were no serious legal or logistical obstacles to bringing Africans to America to help make up for shortages of Indian labor. For European agricultural entrepreneurs in tropical America, African slave labor was the answer to their prayers (see Chapter 18).

The End of the Aztec Empire

In 1502, the year Columbus made his fourth and last voyage to the Caribbean, Motecuzoma II became monarch of the Aztec empire, or Triple Alliance. This sprawling state loomed over central Mesoamerica, but ill will festered between the elite class and the mass of the population, as well as between the dominant Mexica rulers and other Mesoamericans who had been subjugated to them. Some groups, notably Tarascans in the northwest and Tlaxcalans in the east, continued to resist Aztec conquest.

In 1517, as Spanish colonizers completed the occupation of Cuba, European explorers crossed the Gulf of Mexico to the Yucatán Peninsula, site of the once-flourishing Maya civilization. There, they discovered gold objects and impressive stone buildings, finds that encouraged the search for more riches. Hernán Cortés was the son of a minor Castilian noble who, like other Spanish aristocrats lacking strong political connections at home, regarded the Caribbean as a frontier of opportunity. The king granted him an encomienda in Cuba, and he subsequently achieved wealth, respectability, and an administrative office there. In 1519, however, he sailed for the Mesoamerican mainland with a force of eleven ships, sixteen war horses, about six hundred men, many of whom were former artisans or farmers also seeking their fortunes.

He reached the western gulf shore near the modern city of Veracruz, then marched inland.

Motecuzoma had already received reports of large, fantastically shaped boats and strange bands of pale and bearded men. Aztec envoys visited Cortés and his motley army shortly after they landed. The Spaniards had cannons and handguns, though, given the state of firearms technology in the early sixteenth century, they were likely to cause more fright than casualties. According to Aztec traditions later recorded, the emissaries described the artillery they saw: ᵃA thing like a ball of stone comes out of its entrails; it comes out shooting sparks and raining fire. . . . If the cannon is aimed against a mountain, the mountain splits and cracks open. If it is aimed against a tree, it shatters the tree into splinters.º¹³

It was not an Aztec army but Tlaxcalan warriors who first clashed with the strangers, trying to push them back to the coast. Failing that, the Tlaxcalans decided the outlanders might be militarily useful and negotiated an alliance with Cortés against the dominant Mexica. The Spaniards and as many as three thousand Indian fighters then marched on Tenochtitlan, the great Aztec capital. Other groups, weary of Aztec oppression, joined them. In effect, Cortés rode the crest of an explosive local rebellion against Mexica oppression. The attackers quickly captured Motecuzoma in his own palace, much to his surprise. But Cuitláhuac, the emperor's younger brother, soon drove the assailants out of the city. Motecuzoma was killed in the melée. Cuitláhuac reigned for three months, then contracted smallpox, which raged along

Aztecs acknowledge defeat. Ritual weeping was part of Aztec political culture, a public sign of deference or humility. This drawing comes from the Florentine Codex, a sixteenth-century study of Mesoamericans compiled by the Spanish friar Bernardino de Sahagún with the collaboration of many indigenous artists and informants. Both men (on the left) and women lament defeat at the hands of Cortés. How might people in Europe who read the codex have explained or interpreted this image?

Malinche: Translator, Diplomat, and Slave

In modern times, Mexican nationalists have twisted her name into an insult, calling those suspected of betraying their heritage "malinchistas," meaning traitors. At birth, around 1505, she was named Malinal and later known as Malinche or Doña Marina. She was the daughter of a wealthy *cacique*, or chief, on the Yucatán Peninsula, but when her father died, her mother remarried and bore a son. To erase any claim to property that the girl might make, Malinche's mother and stepfather sold her to Maya merchants.

Since slavery was practiced in Maya society, Malinche's fate was not uncommon. She lived in the region of Tabasco when Cortés arrived there in the months before his march into the Aztec empire. As tribute payment from local rulers, Cortés claimed her and nineteen other young women to serve the conquistadors. Bernal Diaz del Castillo's firsthand account of the Spanish invasion describes Malinche as a pretty woman with a "warm-hearted manner" and quick wit. He reports that she rapidly became "a person of great importance." Because enslavement had taken her to several different regions, she could communicate in both Mayan and Tabascan, as well as in Nahuatl, the principal language of the Aztec empire. She learned Spanish quickly, and as a talented translator, she helped the strangers understand how local people might interpret their gestures and behavior, how best to impress important *caciques,* and how to avoid hostile ambushes.

Cortés promised Malinche her liberty if she served the Spanish cause. He consulted her about strategy as his small army made its way toward Tenochtitlan. She mingled with local villagers, made friends, gained confidences, and collected intelligence. She persuasively conveyed Cortés's declaration that if subjugated peoples united they could throw off Aztec rule. She also assisted him in alliance negotiations with the Tlaxcalans.

Foot soldiers like Bernal Diaz developed affection for Malinche, whose forewarnings of ambush saved them more than once. He reported that she went on every expedition and "although she heard every day how the Indians were going to kill us and eat our flesh with chili, . . . [she] never allowed us to see

any sign of fear in her, only a courage exceeding that of woman."[15] When the expedition finally reached Tenochtitlan, it was Malinche who explained to Motecuzoma that he would have to submit to capture or be killed.

She bore Cortés his first son, and later she married another Spaniard with whom she had a daughter. The conquistador awarded her two estates, including land at Chapultepec that previously belonged to the Aztec emperor.

Judging her according to what historians call a "presentist" perspective—analyzing the past by the standards of the present—she betrayed the Mexican people by joining with the invaders. But in fact thousands of other Mesoamericans collaborated with the Spanish to end Aztec domination. Malinche was not Mexica, nor even a free woman. She was given as a slave to the Spanish and served them competently, managing in the process to secure her own survival.

This drawing from the Florentine Codex depicts Malinche as a translator during a meeting between Hernán Cortés and Motecuzoma II.

Thinking Critically

How do you think Malinche's status as a woman and a slave might have contributed to her success serving as an intermediary between Spanish conquistadors and Native Americans?

---

the capital's densely inhabited streets and canals. Within another few months, perhaps a third of the population of central Mexico succumbed to this and perhaps other imported diseases. Meanwhile, Cortés regrouped, raised reinforcements, and laid siege to Tenochtitlan, where according to one Spaniard's report, ª the streets were so filled with dead and sick people that our men walked over nothing but bodies.º[14]

Cortés took the city and made the Tlaxcalans privileged allies of Spain. More armed Europeans arrived to extend Spanish control across Mexico and Central America in the

following decades. As this conquest proceeded, Mesoamericans continued to die. The population of the Aztec realm alone may have dropped from 25.2 million on the eve of European contact to 0.7 million by 1623. As for the Caribbean, its native population had nearly gone extinct by 1550.

Assault on the Inca Empire

The conquest scenario that Cortés enacted in central Mexico was repeated elsewhere in the Americas, with local variations: Small numbers of Europeans with horses, steel weapons, metal armor, and earsplitting cannons suddenly appeared, sowing confusion among local leaders. Deadly diseases accompanied the trespassers or even preceded them, quickly producing economic and social disorder. Certain groups joined the invaders, believing they could use them to advance their own interests against political rivals or oppressors. This alliance, in which local warriors far outnumbered the Europeans, then attacked and defeated the common enemy. But initial victory produced more political disarray, and amid epidemics and much violence, the Europeans, through some combination of military skill, doggedness, and dumb luck, seized control of the strategic centers of power. Subjugation of large regions, however, typically required more years of fighting owing to tenacious local resistance.

This was certainly the general pattern of events in the central Andes, where the Spanish conquistador Francisco Pizarro, an illiterate adventurer of petty noble origin and a veteran of campaigns in Mexico and coastal South America, displaced the ruler of the Inca empire with amazing speed. About 1527, five years before Pizarro arrived on the coast of Peru with fewer than two hundred men, the emperor Huayna Capac died suddenly of smallpox, along with the son he had designated as his successor. The king appears to have caught the disease during a campaign to extend the empire further north. By this time, smallpox had already infected Indian populations on the Isthmus of Panama, and it subsequently spread southward along the Pacific coast. The death of Huayna Capac and his son left two other offspring competing for the throne. Atahualpa, a son who controlled the northern provinces, captured and killed his rival in 1532 and was on the verge of ending the war when Pizarro suddenly arrived at the town of Cajamarca. Like Motecuzoma in Mexico, Atahualpa unwisely agreed to meet the stranger and got himself taken prisoner in a Spanish ambush. The invaders fired cannons and charged on horseback, throwing Atahualpa's escort of three thousand

The Battle of Cajamarca. This engraving depicts Pizarro's capture of Atahualpa in 1532. It was made by Theodore de Bry, a Belgian artist known for his images of the Americas, though he never crossed the Atlantic. It was published over a half-century after the event. How does de Bry portray Spanish military power? Does his image seem realistic to you?

soldiers into panic. According to Francisco de Xeres, Pizarro's secretary, ªIt was a very wonderful thing to see so great a lord taken prisoner in so short a time, who came in such power.º[16]

To try to save himself, Atahualpa ordered his loyalists to present Pizarro with numerous llama loads of gold and silver objects, which the Spaniards melted into ingots. Despite the ransom, Pizarro had his captive executed. Then, with the help of some of Atahualpa's former enemies, he marched on the capital city of Cuzco, where he placed himself and his lieutenants at the top of the Inca political hierarchy and administrative system. European soldiers, officials, priests, and merchants began arriving in force, and the empire was transformed into a dependency of Spain. In remote Andean valleys, however, popular resistance continued for another forty years or more.

Spanish Empire-Building

The quick destruction of both the Aztec and Inca empires launched the Spanish domination of the Americas from California to the tip of South America (see Map 16.4). This process demanded different strategies from settlement in the Caribbean, where mortality among Taino and Caribe Indians virtually wiped out indigenous communities. Colonization on the mainland required effective control over huge territories and large numbers of people of diverse languages and life waysÐ the same challenges Aztec and Inca state builders had faced earlier. Dense agrarian societies in Mesoamerica and the Andes, though reduced and weakened by Afroeurasian diseases, fighting, and labor exploitation, nonetheless survived initial contact. The Native American population continued to drop for about a century and a half, but the rate of decline slowed and recovery set in about 1650.

In zones of conquest, the Spanish crown moved early in the sixteenth century to impose its authority over both Native American political leaders and freebooting conquistadors, who operated largely as they pleased in the early decades. Like the rulers of Portugal, France, and England, the Spanish monarchy aimed to strengthen and centralize state power at home. Its high officials also intended to impose that model on the American colonies, which meant reining in the likes of Cortés and Pizarro. The crown instituted the Council of the Indies to serve as the supreme legislative, financial, judicial, and executive authority for the new colonies. It authorized creation of a complex set of civic, legal, and religious institutions to run local colonial affairs. The monarchy also founded the House of Trade (*Casa de Contratación*) to closely regulate and tax the flow of commerce in and out of American ports. During most of the colonial

MAP 16.4 Iberian colonization in the Americas to 1550
The territory of the two Spanish viceroyalties incorporated the lands of the former Aztec and Inca empires. Might the argument be made that the Spanish did not destroy these empires but rather replaced the former imperial governments with their own?

era, Spanish territory was organized into two huge jurisdictions, each headed by a crown-appointed **viceroy.** One viceroyalty was New Spain, governed from the former Aztec capital

viceroy An official appointed by a monarch to govern a colonial dependency as the sovereign's representative. *Vice* is a Latin prefix meaning "in place of" and *roy* means king. The territory administered by a viceroy is called a viceroyalty.

of Tenochtitlan, renamed Mexico City. The other was Peru, with its capital at the new colonial town of Lima. Both cities became thriving administrative and commercial centers by the middle of the sixteenth century. Royal judicial courts, called *audiencias,* had jurisdictions within each of the viceroyalties. They heard civil and criminal cases involving colonists, Native Americans, and slaves. Local chiefs retained authority over Indian settlements, whereas councils, usually comprised of wealthy European landowners, governed colonial towns.

The Catholic Church, including religious orders such as Franciscans, Dominicans, and later Jesuits, set about converting Indians. By 1560 there were over eight hundred priests, monks, and nuns in New Spain serving in more than 160 churches, missions, or monasteries. Many Catholic clerics had amicable relations with Indians. Their documented observations tell us much about the devastating changes the conquest imposed on Native Americans. Bartolomé de las Casas (1484±1566), a Dominican friar and bishop of Chiapas in southern Mexico, served as the first Protector of the Indians, a royal post created to speak for indigenous interests. His book, *A Short Account of the Destruction of the Indies,* documented atrocities that colonizers committed against native peoples. He influenced the enactment of the ªNew Lawsº of 1542, which provided greater protection for Indians, including a ban on enslavement. He also spoke out against the encomienda system, arguing that holders of rights to Indian labor had too much latitude to abuse their workers. Under his influence, Spain gradually phased out the encomiendas, replacing them with direct bureaucratic rule from Mexico City or Lima.

Portuguese Stakes in Brazil

In 1500, after Vasco da Gama returned to Portugal from the Indian Ocean, Pedro Álvares Cabral set out for the same destination. After crossing the equator, however, he sailed so far on the southeast trade winds that he bumped into the coast of Brazil. This unexpected landfall opened another theater of encounter between Europeans and Native Americans. Like Columbus, Cabral was not sure where he had landed. He found no large agrarian states comparable to Benin or Kongo, and he reported that the ªislandº he thought he had found offered little wealth compared to the silks and spices of India. Nevertheless, more expeditions headed for the Brazilian coast, and forest-dwelling Tupi people offered trade in timber, which they floated down rivers to coastal points, in exchange for steel axes and other useful items. Europeans also initiated a profitable trade in tropical woods from which textile dyes could be extracted.

European activity on the Brazilian coast remained limited until the 1530s, when the Portuguese monarchy, fearing French explorations in the region, encouraged crown subjects to claim land in northeastern Brazil. Indian populations there may have been quite dense when the Portuguese first arrived. But as in the Caribbean, large numbers succumbed

to new diseases. Europeans found cane sugar cultivation profitable, and planters quickly adopted the economic model that had worked well on the Atlantic islands: labor-intensive harvesting, milling, and shipping of sugar on plantations using gangs of laborers. It became apparent by the later sixteenth century that Indians could not supply the demand and that economic success required large importations of African slaves (see Chapter 18). Meanwhile, Portuguese pathfinders continued to lead expeditions to Brazil's southern coasts and up river valleys to the deep interior.

New Power Relations in the Southern Seas

FOCUS In what ways did political and commercial systems change in the Indian Ocean region in the first half of the sixteenth century?

In the last quarter of the fifteenth century, merchants of the Indian Ocean and the China seas carried on flourishing trade from one busy port to another with no idea that their entire commercial network was about to be shaken. No single maritime power dominated or monopolized the southern seas trade or, as far as we know, had ever tried to do so. In the early part of the century, Ming Chinese emperors had dispatched seven mammoth expeditions to the Indian Ocean under the command of Admiral Zheng He (see Chapter 15). But their purpose, so far as we understand it, was primarily to expand the number of states that paid formal tribute to the Ming ruler, not to seize territory or drive local merchants out of business. In any case the Ming government terminated those voyages in 1433 owing to other political priorities, and Indian Ocean trade continued much as before. Merchants of diverse origin sailed lightly armed vessels, selling and buying in accord with local customs, prevailing political conditions, and fluctuating prices. The greatest dangers they faced were pirates and storms at sea.

This system came under threat in the new century when armed Portuguese carracks entered the region. The captains of these vessels attempted from the outset to control as much as they could of the trade in spices and other commodities, an aggressive strategy not previously witnessed in those waters. A Portuguese nobleman captured the spirit of this grand mission when he remarked that immensely valuable South Asian black pepper was no mere commodity. Rather, ªpepper should be a sacred thing.º[17] The level of seaborne violence rose markedly in the Indian Ocean between 1500 and 1550. Portuguese intruders attacked both ports and the ships of competing traders, and those traders fought back. The Ottoman imperial navy also joined the fray.

To Capture the Spice Trade

Vasco da Gama rounded Africa's Cape of Good Hope in 1498 on ships armed with artillery, and he used it in the Indian

Ocean to display his military clout and to force favorable terms of trade. He returned to Lisbon with a cargo of Indian pepper and other goods that paid huge profits. Dom Manuel, the king of Portugal, was delighted: "With the help of God, that the great trade which now enriches the Moors [Muslims] of those parts, through whose hands it passes.° might now be diverted to the natives and ships of our own kingdom.°[18] New expeditions were soon on their way around the Cape. The fleet sent in 1505 returned with 1,100 tons of pepper.

Afonso de Albuquerque, who first sailed to South Asia in 1503 and subsequently commanded Portugal's coastal territories there, well understood that Asians had little demand for European goods other than gold and silver. If, therefore, the Portuguese were to acquire all the products they wished either to carry back to Europe or to sell in various Asian ports, they would have to force their way into the commercial system. Albuquerque's fleet seized several key ports in quick succession: Mombasa in East Africa (1505), Hormuz in the Persian Gulf (1507), Goa in South Asia (1510), and Melaka on the strait of the same name (1511). The threat of this new and heavily armed trading power was not lost on local rulers. According to one chronicle, Portuguese invaders sacked the port of Mombasa in what is today Kenya. Afterward the local Swahili-speaking ruler wrote a warning letter to his fellow sultan in a neighboring port: "May God's blessing be upon you, Sayyid Ali! This is to inform you that a great lord has passed through the town, burning it and laying it waste. . . . He not only killed and burnt men but even the birds of the heavens were shot down. . . . I give you these sad news for your own safety.°[19]

Trading post empire. By the 1530s Portugal had several fortified enclaves facing the Indian Ocean, as well as one on Macau, an island off southern China (see Map 16.5). They

MAP 16.5 The southern seas in 1550.
The Portuguese concentrated their seaborne conquests on ports of South Asia, the pivot points of the southern seas trade. How would you compare the territorial claims of the Portuguese in Asia with those of the Ottoman or Ming empires?

bought spices for gold and silver but also began quickly to buy and sell numerous Asian commodities. They threatened naval action when necessary to require local shippers to buy trade permits and put in at Portuguese-controlled harbors to pay taxes on cargo. Similarly to their policy in Atlantic Africa, Portugal did not try to control more than coastal enclaves around the Indian Ocean rim. The one notable exception was the Zambezi River valley in southeastern Africa, where Portuguese traders pushed into the interior to found a number of small settlements. Portugal could not hope to command enough soldiers or weapons to seize densely populated interior regions or confront strong Asian or African states on land. Instead, it created a **trading post empire** aimed at controlling key ports, strategic points, and sea lanes. "I would like . . . to affirm," observed one Portuguese official in Goa, "that in no circumstances should the Portuguese enter as much as a hand-span into the interior . . . of India, because nothing keeps the peace and conserves our friendship with the kings and lords of India except that they believe and consider it most certain that we are content with the sea."[20]

In 1505 King Manuel I formalized Portugal's claims in the Indian Ocean and China seas by establishing the Estado da India (State of India), a governing body paralleling Spain's Council of the Indies. The Estado had charge of colonial administration, finance, and military operations over Portuguese coastal colonies from southeastern Africa to China. Though Lisbon was the imperial capital, Goa became the Estado's actual headquarters under the authority of a crown-appointed viceroy. Asian rulers did not necessarily respond to this development with hostility. Some of them either tolerated the Europeans or actively partnered with them to advance their own commercial interests. Ming imperial officials, for example, strictly limited foreign merchant activity in China's ports, but they allowed Portuguese venturers to establish a trading post on Macau as long as they paid tribute.

Challenges to Portuguese monopoly. Asian rulers and merchants also realized by the mid-sixteenth century that Portugal's monopolistic ambitions were fading. Voyages around southern Africa remained expensive and dangerous. No more than seven ships a year went out from Lisbon, and in the sixteenth century nearly a third of them foundered in rough seas or were lost in Indian Ocean naval battles. The Portuguese hoped to monopolize India's pepper trade, but they could buy and transport only 10 percent of production. Many Asian sea merchantsÐ Arabs, Chinese, Gujaratis, MalaysÐ eluded Portuguese patrols, and they far outnumbered Europeans. As the century progressed, the Portuguese looked less like a maritime superpower and more like one more Asian commercial firm competing for business. Nevertheless, Portugal's spice trade profits were more than enough to entice the Netherlands, England, and France to send their own naval vessels around the Cape to plant their own trading posts. As the global economy emerged, so too did a new age of armed commerce.

Ottoman naval expansion. Part of Portugal's early Indian Ocean strategy was to intercept the flow of trade from the Arabian Sea to both the Red Sea and the Persian Gulf by seizing ports at the southern approaches to those waterways. Initially, this strategy worked well enough to hurt

Fort Jesus commands the port of Mombasa, Kenya. Built on the orders of King Philip I of Portugal in 1591, this bastion was the first one the Portuguese designed in the Indian Ocean region to withstand artillery attacks from non-European powers. How might the construction of this type of fort reflect changes in the nature of warfare in the Indian Ocean during the previous century?

the commercial economies of Muslim Egypt and Southwest Asia as well as the Italian merchants who had for centuries visited Alexandria and other eastern Mediterranean ports. The Mamluk sultanate of Egypt, which had a small naval force in the Red Sea, allied with Gujarat in South Asia to expel the European interlopers from the region. This Muslim alliance defeated a small Portuguese fleet off the coast of India in 1507 but two years later lost a battle in which shipboard artillery proved decisive. Portuguese victory gave them freer run of the Arabian Sea for several years.

In 1517, however, the Ottoman Turkish army occupied Egypt and thereafter sent its own fleet down the Red Sea to confront the Portuguese and restore lost Asian trade. From then until the 1550s, Ottoman envoys and merchants cultivated relations with Muslim Asian powers, and Turkish squadrons periodically clashed with Portuguese carracks. Ottoman captains also mounted artillery on board in imitation of their adversary. Turkish expeditions sailed as far east as Aceh in Indonesia to provide its sultan with cannons. Ottoman forces expelled the Portuguese from Aden at the entrance to the Red Sea, but warfare between the two powers remained indecisive. As the ships

A Portuguese ship in a Japanese port. A sixteenth-century Japanese depiction of "Southern Barbarians" repairing their ship and offloading luxury goods conveys the curiosity and wonder that early maritime encounters with Europeans elicited. This is a detail from a large screen that served as a room divider in an elite household. What might the picture tells us about Japanese perspectives on trade with foreigners?

of other European powers began to enter the Indian Ocean, however, the Ottomans abandoned their aggressive but expensive southern seas strategy.

The Trans-Pacific Link

While Portugal exploited the Cape route to Asia, mariners in the service of Spain continued to search for a way to get there by going west, despite the troublesome geographical complications that the discovery of America presented. Balboa's crossing of the Isthmus of Panama in 1513 raised new hope of a sea passage to Asia. A Spanish-funded expedition headed by Ferdinand Magellan, a Portuguese subject, finally found the westward route and demonstrated just how large the spherical earth really was. Magellan had already visited Southeast Asia as part of a Portuguese expedition, and he persuaded the Spanish crown in 1519 to sponsor

a westward voyage. Commanding a fleet of five caravels, he sailed across the Atlantic and down the eastern coast of South America, then made his way through the strait that now bears his name and into the Pacific. Continuing northwestward on an interminable voyage that reduced the crew to eating leather and rats, he got as far as the Philippines. There he died in a fight with local warriors, though not before claiming the islands for Spain. It was Sebastián del Cano, Magellan's navigator, who actually circumnavigated the globe by piloting a single vessel westward across the Indian Ocean and back to Spain. Despite the expedition's success, few Europeans showed interest in the long and arduous voyage around the tip of South America as an oceanic trade route. Forty years after Magellan's journey, rather, Spain initiated colonization of the Philippines, a strategic pivot point, as we shall see, for immensely valuable trade across the northern Pacific between Mexico and China.

• • •

Conclusion

Magellan's crossing of the Pacific in 1520 filled the last gap in transoceanic communication and made genuinely globe-encircling interchange among human communities a reality. Afroeurasia and the Americas became connected from both east and west. Only Australia, as well as numerous islands here and there, remained for the time being in worlds of their own.

In the fifteenth century the world's densest and economically richest systems of production, trade, and finance were in Asia. Because Europeans understood this and because their own economies were expanding in that period, they searched for strategies to reach Asian markets without having to undertake long, immensely expensive, and probably futile wars against Muslim states to gain full access to the most direct routes to the Indian Ocean through Egypt or Southwest Asia. European mariners were well aware of educated speculation about the possibility of reaching Asia by sailing either around Africa or by heading west to the other side of the spherical earth. The Iberian countries, however, pursued exploration, trade, war, and settlement in the eastern Atlantic and along the African coast for more than a century and a quarter before they confirmed both theories and began to act on them.

Within a half-century of Columbus's voyages, the Atlantic Ocean became known territory—a "basin" of intercommunication like the Mediterranean or Arabian Sea, only much bigger. But as the sixteenth century progressed, the Atlantic also became smaller in the sense that marine technologists continually invented new ways to make ocean crossings faster, safer, and more cost-efficient. The regions of Europe and Africa that bordered the Atlantic no longer lay at the western edge of the intercommunicating world but suddenly became hubs for the movement of goods, people, and ideas in every direction. An Atlantic-centered economy began to take shape, though only very gradually did it compete with the Indian Ocean system in size, complexity, and wealth.

The way the Atlantic economy emerged is inseparable from the cataclysmic loss of Native American life. The population of the Americas in 1492 dropped by as much as 90 percent in the ensuing 150 years, a disaster that allowed Europeans to take control of the Western Hemisphere with a speed and depth that would otherwise have been impossible. Ironically, the population of Afroeurasia grew at an accelerating rate during the same time period. In Chapter 17 we return to Afroeurasia, to survey developments there in the sixteenth century, when societies were just beginning to experience the effects of the great world convergence.

• • •

Key Terms

Aztec empire 462
caravel 464
carrack 465
Columbian Exchange 472
conquistadors 473

encomienda 473
Guanches 460
Kongo kingdom 461
Melaka 457
New World 469

Portuguese trading post empire 479
sultanate 457
Treaty of Tordesillas 469
viceroy 477

Please see end of book reference section for additional reading suggestions related to this chapter.

Change over Time

1290s–early 14th century	European sailors begin sailing deeper into the Atlantic, encountering the Guanches of the Canary Islands.
1394–1460	Henry the Navigator, a prince of Portugal, supports maritime technical improvements and expeditions along the Atlantic coast of Africa.
1403	Singapore's ruler founds the port of Melaka in Southeast Asia, which becomes a magnet for southern sea merchants.
1415	Portugal seizes the port of Ceuta on the coast of Morocco.
1433	China's imperial Ming government ceases its large naval expeditions ("Ming voyages") in the Indian Ocean.
1444	Portuguese mariners reach the Senegal River in West Africa.
1453	Ottoman Turks capture Constantinople, terminating the Byzantine state and taking control of sea trade between the Black Sea and the Mediterranean.
1469	The crowns of Castile and Aragon unite, laying the political foundation of the Spanish monarchy.
1492	Christopher Columbus sails from Spain across the Atlantic to the Caribbean Sea.
1494	Spain and Portugal settle claims to overseas possessions with the Treaty of Tordesillas, drawing an imaginary dividing line in the Atlantic.
1498	Vasco da Gama rounds the Cape of Good Hope to the Indian Ocean.
1502–1520	Motecuzoma II begins his reign over the Aztec empire, or Triple Alliance, in Mesoamerica.
1506–1543	Afonso I reigns in the Kongo kingdom and promotes political and cultural relations with Portugal.
1510	Afonso de Albuquerque's fleet captures Goa, which becomes the capital of Portugal's Asian trading post empire.
1517	The Ottoman empire's naval reach into the Indian Ocean expands following the conquest of Egypt.
1518	The first smallpox epidemic to result from the Columbian Exchange strikes Hispaniola in the Caribbean Sea.
1520	A Spanish expedition initially led by Ferdinand Magellan circumnavigates the globe.
1521	Spanish conquistadors led by Hernán Cortés defeat the Aztec Triple Alliance.
1527	The death of Inca emperor Huayna Capac and his son from smallpox leads to a battle for succession.
1532	Francisco Pizarro initiates the Spanish conquest of the Inca empire and Andean Peru.

17 Afroeurasia and Its Powerful States

1500–1600

The Ottoman army, like Al-Mansur's Moroccan forces, used artillery to capture new territory in the sixteenth century.

amel caravan merchants who crossed the western Sahara Desert in the sixteenth century may have thought that Ahmad al-Mansur, the sultan of Morocco, had taken leave of his senses. He proclaimed that he planned to send a large military expedition equipped with muskets, mortars, and cannons across a thousand miles of arid waste to launch a surprise attack on the West African empire of Songhay. A monarch of the Sa'adian dynasty, al-Mansur (reigned 1578–1603) commanded the northern terminals of the trans-Saharan camel routes, but the southern entrepôts were under the authority of Songhay. The sultan calculated that if he invaded Songhay and seized its desert ports, especially Timbuktu, he would control the entire western Saharan network and its immensely valuable trade in gold, salt, and slaves. Intelligence reports had informed him that factional struggles had weakened the Songhay state and that, despite its large cavalry, it had no guns. He scolded his advisors who opposed his scheme as too risky: "Our predecessors would have found great difficulty if they had tried to do what I now propose; . . . gunpowder was unknown to them, and so were firearms and their terrifying effect. Today, the Sudanese [people of Songhay] have only spears and swords, weapons which will be useless against modern arms."[1]

Al-Mansur won over his counselors, and in October 1590 a force of about five thousand infantry, horse cavalry, and support personnel departed from Marrakech, crossed the High Atlas Mountains, and advanced into the wilderness. The commanding officer was Judar Pasha, a Christian convert to Islam who had made a name for himself in the Moroccan army. He had never led such an ambitious expedition, however, and about half of his soldiers died along the route from exhaustion, sunstroke, or illness. In February 1591 the column reached the banks of the Niger River, where it skirts the southern edge of the desert.

Askiya Ishaq II, the emperor of Songhay, either did not know or failed to believe that a hostile army was about to materialize from the desert. Nevertheless, he managed to assemble a large force of cavalry and foot soldiers. Somewhere near the Niger the adversaries met. Though the emperor's army was by far the larger, Judar Pasha's disciplined gunners killed many defending troops and probably terrified many more. The emperor left the field of battle, and his remaining troops fled. Disorder and rebellion then spread through the Songhay realm, and within a few years it collapsed. Al-Mansur, however, did not get the trans-Saharan empire he wanted. The distances were simply too great. Rather, his officers settled in as lords of a small West African state and within a few decades lost political contact with Morocco.

Al-Mansur's desert adventure, as anticlimactic as it turned out to be, illustrates a major world-scale development in the sixteenth century. Morocco was just one of several Afroeurasian states that amassed formidable political power based on firearms technology. The rulers of these states created large, disciplined armies, which they deployed to conquer weaker neighbors and to tighten their authority within their own domain. On the whole, sixteenth-century rulers, in contrast to their predecessors, relied less on the cooperation of local chiefs and estate-owning aristocrats to maintain their power and more on loyal, centrally appointed civil and military bureaucrats. The first section of this chapter surveys the changing political map of Afroeurasia, focusing on regions where rulers consolidated authority over their subjects and pushed their borders outward.

The second section examines the significance of firearms technology and its spread across Afroeurasia. As this happened, armies became more lethal than they had ever been. Rulers, however, had to finance expensive armies and administrations, and this raised the stakes for control of agrarian resources, commercial routes, and subject populations that could be made to pay taxes. The immense cost of equipping land and naval forces with the new weaponry produced a revolution in political organization and finance, and it strictly limited the number of states that could compete for power on a large scale.

Chapter Outline

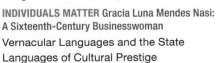

• • •

The third section investigates some of Afroeurasia's key sixteenth-century cultural developments, changes closely related to the rise of more powerful states and the expanding global economy. In the sphere of religious and moral systems, intense controversies took place over matters of belief and practice, notably in neo-Confucian China, the central Muslim states, and Christian Europe. A second important development was the ascendancy of particular regional languages and the distinctive cultural styles associated with them. In the sixteenth century, more local tongues gave way to languages associated with expanding states, universalist religions, and international merchant groups.

A Panoramic View

MAP 17.1 Major states of Afroeurasia, late sixteenth century.

The sixteenth century is notable for the growing number of relatively large, politically centralized states. What factors might help explain why most of these states were located in Afroeurasia's north temperate latitudes?

Afroeurasia's Political Panorama

FOCUS What developments in Afroeurasia in the sixteenth century account for the rise of more powerful centralized states?

In the sixteenth century, almost all major states in Afroeurasia had access to roughly equivalent technologies for farming, mining, communications, and war making. And most of those states shared in the population surge and accompanying economic expansion that generally characterized the period. With a few exceptions, states were organized as monarchies. Their kings, queens, emperors, sultans, or shahs occupied the apex of a hierarchy of officials, and they claimed to rule as agents of divine power. Beyond those common features, states varied widely in population, political institutions, and cultural diversity, and in the strategies they adopted to assert power and accumulate wealth (see Map 17.1).

By capitalizing on some combination of firearms technology and more efficient political organization, several states achieved remarkable success in the sixteenth century in at least one of two respects. First, those states became more efficient at controlling, regulating, keeping track of, and taxing their own populations; that is, they achieved greater political and economic centralization. Second, a number of them also used a large part of their financial resources to undertake campaigns of imperial expansion. Conquered states, which had previously been sovereign and perhaps powerful in their own right, either became tribute-paying dependents of bigger states or disappeared altogether. The number of political units in the world dropped steadily in the sixteenth century as powerful, expansionary states absorbed relatively weaker kingdoms, city-states, and self-governing clans and tribes.

The parallel trends toward greater state centralization and territorial expansion, the themes we highlight in this part of the chapter, were, however, not conspicuous in China, at least not in the sixteenth century. The Ming dynasty (1368±1644) reigned over the most populous and in many respects the most economically developed society in the world, and the state had achieved more effective central bureaucratic organization in the previous 130 years. The imperial palace generated laws and policies in consultation with commissions of administrative officials ideally guided by Confucian moral and political values. The dynasty's line of sixteen potentates ranged in leadership ability from brilliant to inept, but the bureaucrats that formed a chain of authority reaching from the capital to the most distant provinces continued for the most part to do their jobs whether the emperor was effective or not.

Nevertheless, China experienced growing political troubles after 1500. Both Confucian officials and imperial eunuchs (who served the emperor as bodyguards and palace administrators) became increasingly factionalized and hostile to one another. Local estate lords found new ways to avoid taxes and make the rural peasantry pay more. In the later century an influx of silver from American mines caused serious economic and financial turbulence. (We return to that issue in Chapter 18.) The later emperors largely rejected imperial expansion and adopted defensive strategies to protect their Inner Eurasian borderlands from Mongol or other nomad assaults. The government extended the Great Wall across western China. As Chinese emperors had long done, the Ming represented the empire as the world's ªmiddle kingdom,º deserving of the formal allegiance of all neighbors. Missions from Korea, Vietnam, and various Inner Eurasian power groups traveled periodically to Beijing to offer tribute. But these relationships served more to stimulate trade between China and societies that in fact ran their own political affairs.

The Ottoman Empire's Dramatic Expansion

The Ottoman Turkish sultanate, founded in Anatolia (modern Turkey) in the late 1200s, achieved the most spectacular territorial and seaborne expansion of any sixteenth-century state, with the exception of Spain and its American conquests. The Ottoman sultanate emerged as a major Afroeurasian empire after 1453, when its army seized Constantinople (modern Istanbul) and eradicated the Greek Byzantine empire (see Chapter 15). From that city, which overlooked the Bosporus Strait, the sultans commanded the immensely valuable shipping that passed between the Mediterranean and the Black Seas. By the start of the sixteenth century, the empire embraced the agrarian lands of Anatolia and a large part of the Balkan Peninsula in southeastern Europe. The central government evolved as a system in which the sultan reigned over a hierarchy of advisors and administrators, all of whom had the formal status of imperial slaves. This meant that the sultan commanded the absolute personal loyalty of this ruling elite and could appoint, dismiss, or execute any of its members at will. Starting with the reign of Selim I (1512±1520), the government marshaled its rich farm and commercial resources to undertake a new round of territorial conquests in almost every direction.

Ottoman army and state. All departments of the Ottoman government, except for the system of judicial courts run by Sunni Muslim legal scholars, had a strong military character. In one way or another, those ministries devoted themselves to imperial defense and relentless frontier expansion. In the sixteenth century, Ottoman forces consisted of three major elements. First were cavalry regiments, either Turkish frontier fighters (*ghazis*) or mounted units whose officers (*sipahis*) raised imperial troops in return for the right to tax peasants. The second element were the janissaries, the corps of slave infantry that in the sixteenth century numbered up to about thirty-seven thousand combatants and

Topkapi Palace. The center of Ottoman imperial administration for over 400 years, the palace buildings overlook the Bosporus —then as now a vital commercial waterway. Note the palace's location within a dense urban landscape.

that could match any land force in the world in martial skill and discipline (see Chapter 15). The third arm of Ottoman might was the navy, which in the early century supplanted Venice and Genoa as the preeminent maritime power in the eastern Mediterranean and Black Seas and which advanced into the Arabian Sea nearly simultaneously with the arrival there of Portuguese warships.

Like all early modern monarchs, the Ottoman sultans claimed to rule with divine consent. Their authority was limited only by the requirements of the *shari'a,* or Muslim law. The political nucleus of the empire from the later fifteenth century was the Topkapi Palace, resplendently situated on a site in Istanbul above the Bosporus. A continually growing complex of elaborate pavilions, chambers, and courtyards, Topkapi eventually had room for some five thousand residents, including members of the imperial family, state officials, soldiers, concubines, and a host of servants. From within the palace, the sultan's high council (*divan*) and a sort of prime minister holding the title of *vizir* gave advice and directed the various offices. Government in the provinces was less centralized than, for example, in Ming China. Cavalry officers, not civil bureaucrats, administered local affairs, and they forwarded to the capital fixed proportions of the revenue they collected from peasants.

Sixteenth-century conquests. The most aggressive Ottoman expansion took place in the reigns of Selim and his successor Suleyman I, called ªthe Magnificentº (r. 1520±1566). Selim extended Ottoman power to the south by conquering the populous Arabic-speaking lands of Syria and Egypt. To the east, he warred repeatedly with the Safavid (SAH-fah-vihd) empire of Persia, mainly for control of the cities and agricultural resources of Iraq. Ottoman forces invaded Egypt

in 1517, overthrowing the Sunni Muslim Mamluk dynasty that had ruled there for two and a half centuries. Shortly after that, Turkish privateers sailing under the Ottoman flag seized Tunis, Algiers, and other Mediterranean ports, thereby controlling North Africa's coastline as far west as the frontier of Morocco. Ottoman successes in the Mediterranean, plus persistent threats to invade Italy, set off several decades of warfare with Habsburg Spain and Venice on both land and sea. The tide of battle shifted repeatedly during Suleyman's reign, though in 1580 the adversaries agreed to an extended maritime peace, recognizing that neither of them was going to achieve complete dominance in the Mediterranean.

On the European front, Ottoman land armies invaded Romania in 1504 and subjugated the kingdom of Hungary in 1526. Three years later Suleyman's forces advanced up the Danube River valley and surrounded Vienna, the capital of Habsburg Austria. Though this siege alarmed western Europe, an early winter forced the attackers to retreat. Some historians have referred to the prolonged conflict between the Ottomans and several European powers as the ªsixteenth-century world warº because the contending forces fought battles from the western Mediterranean to the coasts of India. The struggle was not, however, a straightforward clash between Muslims and Christians. Both France and several independent German princes allied with the Turks out of shared hostility to the Habsburgs.

The sprawling Ottoman state embraced many ethnolinguistic groups and a total population of about twenty-two million by the later seventeenth century. The ruling class proudly identified with the Turkic-speaking people that in earlier centuries had migrated from the Inner Eurasian steppes and after 1000 C.E. achieved dominance over Anatolia. As the empire grew, however, the Turkic population

A European Ambassador Compares Armies

In 1554 Ogier Ghiselin de Busbecq (1522–1592) traveled to Constantinople as the Habsburg or Holy Roman empire's ambassador to the Ottoman court. Raised in Flanders and educated in western European universities, Busbecq entered diplomatic service only months before receiving this important mission. During his eight years in Constantinople, he wrote numerous letters to his friend and fellow diplomat Nicholas Michault. In this correspondence he recounted travel stories and his observations of Ottoman life. Busbecq was especially interested in comparing the Holy Roman and Turkish empires. He was worried that Ottoman forces might defeat western European states because they seemed to him much hardier and better disciplined. Busbecq compiled his Turkish Letters *for publication in 1589, long after he left Constantinople. They remain a precious source of knowledge of the Ottoman state.*

The Turkish monarch going to war takes with him over 40,000 camels and nearly as many baggage mules, of which a great part, when he is invading Persia, are loaded with rice and other kinds of grain. These mules and camels also serve to carry tents and armor, and likewise tools and munitions for the campaign. . . . The invading army carefully abstains from encroaching on its magazines [stored supplies] at the outset; as they are well aware that when the season for campaigning draws to a close, they will have to retreat over districts wasted by the enemy, or scraped bare by countless hordes of men and droves of baggage animals. . . . Then the Sultan's magazines are opened, and a ration just sufficient to sustain life is daily weighed out to the Janissaries [imperial slave soldiers] and other troops of the royal household. The rest of the army is badly off, unless they have provided some supplies at their own expense. And this is generally the case, for the greater number, and especially the cavalry, having from their long experience in war already felt such inconveniences, lead with them a sumpter horse [packhorse] by a halter, on which they carry many of the necessities of life; namely, a small piece of canvas which they use as a tent, for protection against sun and rain, with the addition of some clothes and bedding; and as provisions for their private use, a leathern bag or two of the finest flour, with a small pot of butter, and some spices and salt, on which they sustain life when they are hard pressed. . . .

From this you will see that it is the patience, self-denial and thrift of the Turkish soldier that enable him to face the most trying circumstances and come safely out of the dangers that surround him. What a contrast to our men! Christian soldiers on a campaign refuse to put up with their ordinary food, and call for thrushes, beccaficos [a small bird], and suchlike dainty dishes! If these are not supplied, they grow mutinous and work their own ruin; and, if they are supplied, they are ruined all the same. For each man is his own worst enemy, and has no foe more deadly than his own intemperance. . . . It makes me shudder to think of what the result of a struggle between such different systems must be; one of us must prevail and the other be destroyed, at any rate we cannot both exist in safety. On their side is the vast wealth of their empire, unimpaired resources, experience and practice in arms, a veteran soldiery, an uninterrupted series of victories, readiness to endure hardships, union, order, discipline, thrift, and watchfulness. On ours are found an empty exchequer, luxurious habits, exhausted resources, broken spirits, a raw and insubordinate soldiery, and greedy quarrels; there is no regard for discipline, license runs riot, the men indulge in drunkenness and debauchery, and worst of all, the enemy are accustomed to victory, we, to defeat. Can we doubt what the result must be?

Source: Charles Thornton Forster and F. H. Blackburne Daniell, *The Life and Letters of Ogier Ghiselin de Busbecq,* vol. 1 (London: Kegan Paul, 1881), 219±222.

Thinking Critically

What particular traits does Busbecq believe that Ottoman soldiers possess, compared to European Christian troops? Why does he consider Turks a threat to the Holy Roman empire? How do you think a European reading this letter might react to Busbecq's characterization of the Ottoman army? Do you think that Busbecq might be exaggerating differences between Ottoman and Christian European armies? If so, what attitude or feelings might lead him to exaggerate?

came to be outnumbered by conquered peoples speaking Arabic, Persian (Farsi), Greek, Armenian, several Slavic languages, and a variety of other tongues. In its religious complexion, Muslims accounted for only a slight majority of the empire's total population. Christians in eastern Anatolia, Syria, Egypt, and especially southeastern Europe comprised more than 30 percent of the sultan's subjects. Jews accounted for another 10 percent in the sixteenth century. Indeed, the sultans welcomed thousands of Jews following their expulsion from Christian Spain in 1492. The state organized Greek and Armenian Christian groups, plus Jews, into *millets*, or legally constituted religious communities that were permitted to run their own internal affairs, including courts, schools, and tax collection. But Christians and Jews did not enjoy legal and social equality with Muslims. Members of these communities could not serve in the government or army, and they paid a tax (the *jizya*) that did not apply to Muslims.

An empire of trade. As it expanded, the Ottoman state spilled across the east±west trade arteries running between the Mediterranean and both Inner Eurasia and the Indian Ocean. In the later sixteenth century, after Portuguese commercial aggression in the Arabian Sea quieted down, Muslim sea traders returned in large numbers, enjoying Ottoman naval protection on the routes through the Red Sea and Persian Gulf. Muslim, Jewish, and Armenian merchants moved goods from one part of the empire to another. Egypt exported rice and sugar, Syria supplied dates and pistachios, Anatolia shipped dried fruit and silk, and the Balkans traded wheat, timber, and wine. To encourage Italian and other European shippers to visit Ottoman ports to buy textiles, carpets, and other products, the government offered them special commercial privileges, beginning with a treaty with France in 1536. Under these **capitulations,** European merchants enjoyed reduced tariffs, freedom from Ottoman taxes, and if they became involved in civil or criminal cases the right to try them in their own consular courts rather than before Muslim judges.

capitulations International agreements in which one state awarded special privileges within its borders to subjects or citizens of another state.

The Safavid Empire of Persia

After more than a century and a half of political division, a new political force arose in the early sixteenth century to unify Persia, the region centered on the Iranian plateau. Like the Ottoman governing elite, the new Safavid dynasty traced its ancestry to Turkic horse archers who had entered Southwest Asia in the tenth and eleventh centuries. Isma'il, the first Safavid king, began his political career in the late fifteenth century and at the tender age of seven as chief of a Turkic military state located in the hill country that is today Azerbaijan and northwestern Iran. He also headed a Muslim Sufi association, which gave its name to the Safavid political movement. This mystical brotherhood, dedicated to individual spiritual enlightenment, attracted Turkic pastoral groups that inhabited the grassy valleys south of the Caucasus Mountains.

The Safavid state and the ascendance of Shi'a Islam. Beginning in 1501, Isma'il's cavalry vanquished one after another of the several small Turkic states that dominated Iran and Iraq. Isma'il's fighters were known as the Qizilbash, or Red Heads, because of the red Sufi headgear they wore. Advancing down the Tigris-Euphrates River in 1508, warrior bands seized Baghdad in 1508 and in a short time most of the commercial and manufacturing cities of Persia.

Isma'il also declared his devotion to Shi'ism, the wing of Islamic belief and practice that was taking militant forms

Shah Isma'il and the Red Heads. This miniature painting depicts the Safavid ruler and his elite warriors, identified by their red hats. Compare this picture to the chapter's opening image. What differences do you notice between Safavid and Ottoman visual representations of military action?

in Southwest Asia in the fifteenth century. Sunni Islam, the faith of the great majority of Muslims, affirmed that supreme spiritual authority belonged with the Muslim community as a whole. The caliphs, or ªdeputies,º who had succeeded the Prophet Muhammad since the seventh century, were obligated to implement and defend the community's will. Shi'ism proclaimed to the contrary that authority rested with the blood descendants of Ali, who was the fourth caliph and a kinsman of the Prophet. Ali's successors, called imams, were, according to Shi'a teaching, the rightful leaders of all Muslims. Isma'il came to profess the particular variant of Shi'ism that venerates the twelfth imam in the line of succession after Ali. According to Shi'a belief, this imam had gone into an occult, or hidden, state

Imam Mosque in Isfahan, Iran. Shah Abbas commissioned this mosque as part of the reconstruction of Isfahan as his new capital city in the early seventeenth century. The walls and domes are covered with inscriptions from the Quran and floral patterns formed from hundreds of thousands of glistening tiles. This type of ornamentation is a distinctive feature of Persian architecture. What architectural elements let you know this building was intended to communicate the power and splendor of a Muslim ruler?

but would one day return to reign over the world with divine authority. Claiming leadership as earthly representative of the Hidden Imam, Isma'il and his warriors strove to impose Shi'a doctrines on subjugated Sunni populations. Shi'a scholars and theologians, many from Iraq and Syria, formed a new religious elite. Gradually, Shi'ism became, by armed pressure or willing conversion, Iran's majority religion, though in many respects Sunni and Shi'a teachings and devotions are identical. In southern Iraq, a province of the Safavid state, Arabic-speaking populations converted to Shi'ism in large numbers. In this period, therefore, Iran and Iraq took on the religious profiles they largely have today.

The reign of Shah Abbas. After Isma'il's death in 1524, his early successors, who claimed the ancient Persian royal title of ªshah,º had a hard time holding the state together. It survived, however, by balancing the power of Red Head cavalry officers, who had rights to extract taxes from the mass of population, against the influence of urban, educated Iranian and Iraqi families, who ran the central government and enforced Shi'ism as the state religion.

The Safavid empire came to full flower under Shah Abbas, a ruler of unusual talents. Ascending the throne in 1587, he reigned for forty-three years (r. 1587±1629). To check the power of rural tribal commanders, he created a standing professional army. This force of as many as thirty-seven thousand troops included artillery and musket units advised by a group of English mercenaries. Healthy male prisoners seized in wars against the Christian kingdoms of Georgia and Armenia in the Caucasus Mountains were trained to serve in elite military units. These soldiers had the legal status of slaves of the shah, as the janissaries did in the Ottoman state. The shah's gunpowder army showed its mettle in victories over Ottoman forces in Iraq and over the Mughal

(MOO-guhl) empire of India in Afghanistan. The Safavids had no navy, but in 1622 Abbas evicted the Portuguese from their fortress at Hormuz on the Persian Gulf with the aid of gunships supplied by friendly English trading partners.

The Persian empire had more limited resources than the Ottomans did. About 70 percent of Iran is extremely arid, and most farming required intensive irrigation. Shah Abbas, however, strengthened the economy by investing in water management, improving the trans-Iranian road and trail system, encouraging silk textile and carpet exports, and striking trade deals with European merchant firms. To boost overland traffic, he appointed Armenian Christian merchants as his special agents. They operated a commercial network linking the Volga River valley in Russia with both Europe and Southwest Asia. The shah's capital at Isfahan, a city built around an expansive central square flanked by spectacular domed mosques and an enormous covered bazaar, attracted a population of about 400,000. The government invited both Armenian and Roman Catholic clerics to build churches in Isfahan, no doubt finding friendly contacts with Christian powers a useful counterweight to the Ottoman empire, its enduring enemy.

Mughal Power in South Asia

Like Persia, South Asia experienced a long period of political fragmentation before achieving unification in the sixteenth century under a new and militarily aggressive dynasty. From the thirteenth to the early sixteenth centuries, several Muslim dynasties in succession dominated the river plains of northern India and the majority population of Hindu farmers and town dwellers. These regimes also fought, and sometimes allied with, local Hindu kingdoms. In 1526, however, Babur, ruler of a minor state in Afghanistan, led an assault on northern India, seizing most of it by fielding an army that included both traditional horse archers and gunpowder cannons. A descendant of the thirteenth-century Mongol conqueror Chingis Khan and a lover of Persian art and poetry, Babur (r. 1526±1530) founded a dynasty that became known as Mughal, a corruption of the word *Mongol*. As in both the Ottoman and Safavid empires, the ruling military elite boasted descent from Inner Eurasian warriors.

The reign of Akbar the Great.

Babur governed for only four years, and his son Humayun failed to gain firm control of northern India until just before his death in 1556. It was Babur's grandson Akbar (r. 1556±1605) who put the Mughal state on a firm footing and transformed it into a powerful regional empire. He organized an elaborate system of administration and taxation and during his half-century rule sent armies in all directionsÐ south into the subcontinent's central plateau (the Deccan), north into Himalayan Kashmir, southwest into the cloth-producing region of Gujarat, and east into Bengal, the rice-rich lower Ganges River valley. He made no investment in a navy but relied on Indian Ocean merchants, including Portuguese and other Europeans, to export South Asian cotton textiles and other goods to the wider world.

Akbar had the same ambitions as many other monarchs of that era: to make war on neighboring states, confiscate their treasuries, tax his subjects, ensure public order, and display imperial power on a magnificent scale. To pursue these aims, he organized the upper level of officialdom into thirty-three ranks of imperial commanders, or *amirs*. These officers, including both Muslims and Hindus, raised cavalry troopsÐ the higher the rank, the greater the number of horsemen requiredÐ to defend or extend imperial territory. The state paid them salaries or gave them rights to income from farm land. In this way Akbar created a **service nobility.** This was a governing class that enjoyed imperial income and privilege but did not constitute a land-owning aristocracy. It could not pass on property to heirs or build a power base independent of the state. Akbar also bolstered central authority by appointing agents to conduct surveys to determine the value of agricultural land. He then named local princes, landlords, or simply profit-minded entrepreneurs, who used survey information to collect taxes from Hindu and Muslim peasants. These intermediaries transferred a predetermined portion of revenue to the state but kept the balance for themselves to help maintain local order and pay for their own luxurious households.

Akbar founded the Mughal dynasty's authority on absolute loyalty and service to the monarchÐ the Royal Person. In this spirit, he and his successors demanded continuous, breathtaking displays of power, including intricate court rituals and lavish consumption of goods. Akbar proclaimed himself *padshah,* or king of kings, a title that recalled ancient

> **service nobility** A privileged governing class whose members depended entirely on the state rather than on inherited property and titles for their status and income.

Gathering the almond crop. This painting from the *Baburnama*, the memoir of the Mughal conqueror Babur, is included in an illustrated edition published after the ruler's death. Peasants gather the nuts and load bags onto pack animals while more elaborately dressed men weigh the harvest. Why would a ruler's memoirs include a depiction of agricultural activity?

Persian and Hindu ideas of the ruler as a semidivine personality. Antonio Monserrate, a Catholic missionary who resided at the imperial palace in the 1580s, described the subservience of Akbar's courtiers:

> His court is always thronged with multitudes of men of every type, though especially with the nobles, whom he commands to come from their provinces and reside at court for a certain period each year. When he goes outside the palace, he is surrounded and followed by these nobles and a strong body-guard. They have to go on foot until he gives them a nod to indicate that they may mount. All this adds greatly to the wonderful majesty and greatness of the royal court.[2]

Among early modern rulers, Akbar championed peculiarly liberal views on religion. He came to the throne as a Muslim, but much to the dismay of orthodox clerics, he proclaimed a divine religion centered on a Sufi, or mystical, fraternity that taught that all faiths have spiritual insights to offer. He invited Muslim theologians, Sufis, Hindu sages, and even visiting Roman Catholic priests to debate questions of morality and doctrine. He also took a benevolent view of Sikhism, a new Indian religion whose founder Nanak (1469±1539) taught reconciliation of Hinduism and Islam through simple love of God, pacifism, and strict moral conduct. He gave the Sikhs land in the city of Amritsar to build their Golden Temple, which remains today the world headquarters of the Sikh faith. He also abolished a number of taxes that Hindus had to pay, and he allowed them to build new temples. Akbar's religious movement died with him, but his creative mix of political might and cultural tolerance almost certainly contributed to the social stability that characterized India for nearly a century after his reign.

Akbar had the fortune to come to power at a time of accelerating demographic and economic growth in South Asia. Its population approached 100 million, and the cities of Agra, Bijapur, and Ahmedabad were among the largest in the world. The subcontinent had immense resources in grain, cotton, silk, pepper, sugar, indigo, gems, and timber. Indian spinners and weavers had for centuries led the world in cotton textile production, and once European mariners opened the oceanic routes, global demand for Indian cottons swelled. Akbar obliged his subjects to pay taxes in copper, silver, or gold coins, a policy that pushed more rural farmers into the commercial market to earn money. The economy of Bengal, the rainforested region of the lower Ganges River, was particularly dynamic. Mughal armies conquered Bengal, then encouraged peasants from other parts of India, predominantly Muslims, to migrate there to clear forests, drain swamps, and transform the Ganges delta into endless tracts of rice paddy.

Akbar's successors. Akbar had three intelligent, strong-willed successors: Jahangir (r. 1605±1627), Shah Jahan (r. 1628±1658), and Aurangzeb (r. 1658±1707). These kings maintained Akbar's administrative system for the most part, and they continued to add territories to the empire. Jahangir, one of Akbar's sons, consolidated his father's achievements, though in fact his Iranian wife Nur Jahan had a huge influence on state affairs, promoting Persian styles in imperial art and craft, and for a time acting as the de facto ruler. Jahangir's son Shah Jahan also looked toward Muslim Persia for models of civilized art and letters, launching a splendid building program that included the glorious Taj Mahal.

Aurangzeb, the last of the great Mughals, waged wars of conquest throughout the central plateau and sent armies into India's far south. His campaigns, however, consumed twenty-six years of bloody, immensely expensive fighting. To keep revenue flowing in, he taxed rural populations more harshly, which in the later years of his reign provoked rural uprisings and banditry. In stark contrast to Akbar, he also rigorously enforced Muslim orthodoxy, forcing Hindus out of government service, pulling down Hindu temples, and making war on the pacifist Sikhs, who had to take up arms to survive. His narrow view of religion clearly weakened social and cultural bonds within the empire. After he died, the empire deteriorated rapidly, making way for new power groups to carve out local bases of their own. As we will see in Chapter 18, these groups included armed merchants of the English East India Company.

Russia: From Principality to Empire

Russia joined the club of multiethnic empires near the end of the sixteenth century. This state encompassed a much smaller population than the Mughal or Ming Chinese states, but it expanded so rapidly over such great distances that by 1800 it was the world's largest monarchy, in square miles.

St. Basil's Cathedral, Moscow. Ivan the Terrible commissioned this Russian Orthodox cathedral following military victories along the Volga. The building, located on Moscow's Red Square, blends Byzantine arches, towers that resemble northern Russian churches, and features of Asian minarets. Why might the tsar build a monumental church in the center of Moscow after conquering territory in Inner Eurasia?

This was a striking phenomenon considering that Russia originated in the mid-fifteenth century as Moscovy, a small state centered on the city of Moscow.

The rise of Moscovy. Mongol conquerors had subjugated the Russian-speaking lands in the 1240s, but when their power waned two centuries later, the Moscovite princes Ivan III (r. 1462±1505) and his son Vasily III (r. 1505±1533) progressively eliminated rival regional rulers. Their conquests yielded extensive wheat and timber lands, plus key commercial towns, notably the northern fur trade emporium of Novgorod. The early Russian monarchs, or tsars (ZAHRS, from the word ᵃcaesar°), allied closely with the Russian Orthodox Church and represented themselves as agents of God and guardians of Christian truth. They also imposed their authority over the land-owning Russian aristocracy, known collectively as the boyars. They did this partly by creating a new governing class drawn largely from a pool of talented military and civil officers who received revenues from farm estates in return for unconditional loyalty. Like the Mughals in India, the tsars aimed to create a service nobility that had no large properties or aristocratic family attachments and could counterbalance the influence of the traditional boyar families.

Ivan IV, who ruled for fifty-two years (1533±1584), pursued the centralizing policies of his predecessors so pitilessly that his subjects came to know him as ᵃIvan the Terrible.° He founded new ministries of state, as well as a special group of imperial enforcers that dressed in menacing black uniforms and carried brooms as emblems of their mission to cleanse the land of treason. In 1550 he founded the *streltsy*, a professional force of musketeers. These soldiers resembled the janissaries in the Ottoman empire, though they were freemen rather than military slaves. Deeply suspicious of the Russian aristocracy, Ivan periodically terrorized nobles families and seized their lands.

Russia's Eurasian empire. Between 1552 and 1556 Ivan IV's armies seized the middle and lower Volga River valley from regional Muslim rulers. These victories had great significance. First, they gave Russia control of the strategic north-south trade route linking the Baltic Sea with Southwest Asia and India. Second, they pushed Russian power closer to the Black Sea and the political orbit of the Ottoman empire. In the later 1500s, the two empires entered into diplomatic and commercial exchanges, but relations also became increasingly tense, leading to wars in later centuries. To the east, cavalry in service to the tsar crossed over the Ural Mountains in the 1580s to penetrate western Siberia. These gun-toting horse soldiers, known as Cossacks, had diverse origins. Many were former Muslim herders, others landless Slavic peasants. They made their living by trading furs and plundering Siberian villages, but they also spearheaded the conquests that gave the tsars access to boundless resources in furs, timber, and potential wheat land.

To the west, the early tsars sought stronger political and cultural contacts with Europe's Catholic states. In the fifteenth century, Russian merchants, envoys, and scholars began traveling regularly to Germany, Italy, France, and England. Relations with western neighbors, however, were not all happy. Starting in 1558, Ivan IV engaged in a prolonged war with the kingdoms of Sweden and Poland-Lithuania over control of Baltic coastlands. He coveted a warm-water port on the west, but he failed to get it after a quarter-century of fighting.

The high cost of Ivan's wars put heavy pressure on Russian and other Slavic peasants to pay taxes and generate income for aristocratic estate lords. To escape their lot, many peasants fled to sparsely populated lands in the Ukraine or western Siberia. To prevent such flight and to meet rising demand in Europe for Russian wheat, the imperial government placed new

Yermak Timofeyevich, conqueror of Siberia. This lithograph depicts a Cossack leader responsible for key military victories that enabled Russian expansion into Siberia in the late sixteenth century. This picture, made 300 years later, combines military symbols and images from several regions and time periods. Why might a nineteenth-century artist depict a sixteenth-century soldier in Roman battle dress? What other elements in the lithograph suggest warriors from different places and eras?

restrictions on farm tenants, gradually reducing them from legally free rent-paying peasants to serfs. This status bound them to live on a particular estate and pay dues to its master. Ironically, serfdom spread widely in Russia at the same time it was disappearing in western Europe.

Ivan's political repression and exhausting wars contributed after his death to a severe ªtime of troubles.º Between 1598 and 1613, central authority nearly collapsed amid civil war, famine, peasant rebellion, and Polish and Swedish border invasions. The state returned to stability, however, after Russian nobles elected Mikhail Romanov tsar (r. 1613±1645). The new Romanov dynasty initiated more conquests in Inner Eurasia and reigned over the empire for more than three hundred years.

Japan and the Tokugawa

Among relatively smaller Afroeurasian states, Japan advanced toward political unity and strong central government in the late 1500s. In the previous two and a half centuries, the Japanese island chain had been politically divided into territories of numerous self-governing estate lords, known as daimyo. Supported by paid knights, or samurai, the daimyo constituted Japan's aristocratic ruling class. The emperor, who resided in the city of Kyoto, had only ritual functions. He appointed a shogun, or ªgreat general,º who ideally ruled Japan as his agent. But under the Ashikaga shoguns (1336±1573), named for the noble family that controlled that office, local daimyo did largely as they pleased. After Portuguese merchants introduced firearms to Japan in 1543 and local gunsmiths learned how to make them, warfare among the most powerful daimyo grew in intensity.

Starting in the 1550s, however, Oda Nobunaga (1534±1582), a local warlord from the big island of Honshu, made effective use of both long pikes and muskets to defeat several rival lords. At his death by assassination, his forces controlled a large part of Honshu. Toyotomi Hideyoshi (1536±1598), a general who built his career in service to Nobunaga, assembled an army of 300,000 soldiers and within a few years emerged as military lord of three of the archipelago's four major islands. Flush with victories at home, he also launched an amphibious invasion of Korea in 1592, even boasting, ªI shall take even China in hand, and have control of it during my lifetime.º[3] By assaulting Korea, however, he overreached badly. The Korean navy, which included heavily timbered ships equipped with artillery, harassed Japanese military supply lines in the Korea Strait. After six years of intermittent fighting, the Chinese government, which had close ties with Korea's Choson dynasty, sent an army that helped expel the intruders.

Hideyoshi died a much weakened ruler. Nevertheless, Tokugawa Ieyasu (r. 1603±1616), a Hideyoshi ally, held the state together. He took the title of shogun (made legitimate by the endorsement of the ceremonial emperor) and inaugurated the long era of the Tokugawa (TOH-koo-GAH-wah) shogunate (1603±1867). Similarly to other centralizing

powers in Afroeurasia, this new regime required a strong army and a steady revenue flow to reduce the power of local magnates and provincial town leaders. Ieyasu and his successors accumulated immense tracts of taxable farm land, forbade ordinary people to own weapons, tore down many castles held by samurai knights, and obliged the 250 or so regional daimyo to contribute to the central treasury. To keep these aristocrats on a short political leash, the shoguns made them live in the capital city of Edo (modern Tokyo) every other year. The Tokugawa did not, however, try to govern the countryside in the direct way that imperial bureaucrats did in Ming China. Rather, they worked out a pragmatic

Tokugawa Ieyasu. The first Tokugawa shogun is depicted here as a ruler rather than a warrior. He is seated formally and framed by drapery displaying the Tokugawa family crest—three hollyhock leaves in a circle. In what ways does this silk hanging scroll symbolically legitimize the shogun's centralization of political power in Japan?

bargain with the daimyo that allowed these lords to run local administration and maintain small armies. This division between central and provincial power permitted the shogunate and the daimyo to work together to keep the peace and extract wealth from millions of farmers. From the perspective of ordinary men and women, all levels of government were authoritarian and demanding. On the other hand, Japan achieved greater political stability in the seventeenth century than it had enjoyed for several hundred years.

Strong Monarchies in Southeast Asia

In Indochina (mainland Southeast Asia), the tropical rice-growing lands south of China, trends toward political consolidation got seriously under way in the late fifteenth century. Three kingdomsÐ Burma (Myanmar), Thailand, and VietnamÐ gained control of most of Indochina, which had a population in 1600 of perhaps ten million (see Map 17.2). These three Buddhist monarchies conquered and assimilated numerous smaller states and mountain chiefdoms, using some of the same state-strengthening techniques as other Afroeurasian monarchies. They acquired firearms, organized conscript armies, and adopted new governing strategies for wringing revenue from their subjects. In the sixteenth century they hired foreign advisors and mercenaries, mainly Europeans but also Japanese. All three kingdoms financed centralization with wealth from flourishing rice economies centered on the region's great river valleys.

The Burmese state launched a centralizing project shortly after 1500, conquering neighbors up and down the Irrawaddy

MAP 17.2 Major Southeast Asian states, sixteenth century.

In the premodern centuries, China and its Confucian values wielded great cultural influence in Vietnam. South Asia's Hindu and Buddhist traditions had comparable impact on Burma, Thailand, and Cambodia. What geographical factors might help account for this difference?

River valley. Similarly, Vietnam expanded from the state's core region in the Red River valley southward along the coast of the South China Sea. Near the end of the sixteenth century, two aristocratic families, one in the north and the other in the south, divided Vietnam into two autonomous power centers, though these leaders kept up a fiction of unity by paying allegiance to the same, politically feeble emperor. Thailand also had great military success. In the later fifteenth century the energetic King Trailok (r. 1448±1488) colonized Cambodia and the Mekong River valley, codified royal laws, and reduced independent noble strongholds to the status of tax-paying provinces. After several fierce wars with Burma in the later sixteenth century, Thailand emerged as the stronger power.

The European States

In the fifteenth century, Europe west of Russia was a jumble of sovereign kingdoms, principalities, city-states, and mountain chieftaincies. By the end of the sixteenth century, however, a small number of regional powers extended their authority at the expense of weaker monarchs and princes. This centralization process took place in the larger context of Europe's expanding population, production, and trade. Agricultural and commercial wealth gave the strongest states the means to build armies and administrative bureaucracies.

Large states and small. In rough terms, the most successful experiments in state consolidation took place at the western and eastern extremes of Europe (see Map 17.3). In the west, France, England, Portugal, Spain, and, after 1600, the Netherlands emerged as larger and more tightly centralized states, though in all of them rulers had regularly to negotiate and compromise with rich noble families and other local power groups. If we recognize that the Strait of Gibraltar was a negligible barrier to communication between the Iberian Peninsula and North Africa, we may add Morocco to this list. That Muslim sultanate was involved deeply with both Spain and Portugal in trade, diplomacy,

MAP 17.3 Major European states, 1600.

Consolidation of royal power over larger territories characterized some parts of Europe in the sixteenth century. How would you account for differences in the size and number of states in Europe compared to South Asia, Southeast Asia, or East Asia in the sixteenth century?

St. Bartholomew's Night, August 24, 1572. Huguenot artist François Dubois painted this image after fleeing to Switzerland. It is not known whether Dubois witnessed this event in Paris, but the painting depicts two incidents described or illustrated in other sources. The French queen Catherine de Medici, dressed in black, stands outside the palace to inspect a pile of dead bodies. The slain Huguenot leader Gaspard de Coligny hangs out a window. Does the artist reveal a pro-Protestant bias in this painting? If so, in what ways?

and war. It lost coastal enclaves to Portugal, but from the 1570s the Saadian dynasty (1554±1659) emerged as a strong and economically prosperous monarchy. Moroccan forces repelled a Portuguese invasion in 1578, and under Sultan Ahmad al-Mansur undertook, as we saw in the chapter introduction, a bold campaign to control trade across the Sahara Desert.

In eastern Europe, Poland-Lithuania, a state created in 1569 by the merger of two dynasties, encompassed more territory than any other European polity west of Russia. But its rulers continued to share power with the leading noble families, which collectively dominated financial and military affairs. In Scandinavia, Sweden emerged as a strong monarchy and, for a time, a leading player in European diplomacy and war. Most of southeastern Europe, by contrast, was incorporated into the Ottoman empire.

Europe's middle zone remained politically splintered. The Italian peninsula was divided into the city-states of Genoa, Florence, Milan, Venice, and a few others, together with the papal states (lands ruled directly by the Catholic pope) and territorial dependencies of Spain. In Germany, as well as in the Netherlands before 1600, a conglomeration of

more than 150 dukedoms and free cities blanketed the land. Most of these small states paid formal allegiance to the Holy Roman emperors of the Habsburg dynasty, whose core territory was Austria. But on the local level, German princes and city councils remained largely free of royal interference.

Wars of religion. Between 1500 and 1650 the states of Europe fought multiple wars with one another over territory, resources, and the future of the Christian church. In 1517 Martin Luther (1483±1546), a German monk and a native of the Duchy of Saxony in central Germany, touched off the movement later labeled the Protestant Reformation when he publicly accused the Catholic hierarchy of rampant corruption and false doctrines. Initially Luther wanted to spark Christian reform, not rebellion, but events escalated quickly. Within barely two decades of his first public statements, new Protestant churches, which renounced the pope's authority, began to spring up across Europe. Moreover, religious quarrels broke out not only between loyal Catholics and Protestants in general but also between one Protestant community and another. All of Europe's rulers chose sides in these clashes, at the cost of much bitterness and bloodshed.

In that era, Europeans, like societies in most of the world, took it for granted that rulers had the right to specify the religious allegiance of their subjects. When a ruler opted for one or another Protestant church, the entire population was expected to conform. Protestant princes typically persecuted or expelled men and women who remained loyal to the Catholic Church. Catholic rulers did the same to Protestants. (We return to doctrinal and organizational changes in sixteenth-century Europe later in the chapter.)

Even before the religious wars broke out, two alliances of states, one headed by the Habsburg empire and the other by France, fought to shape Europe's political future. In 1519 Charles V (r. 1519±1556) succeeded to the Habsburg throne, inheriting sovereignty over a large part of central Europe (German- and Slavic-speaking regions), most of the Netherlands, parts of Italy, Spain, and the young Spanish empire in America and the Philippines. A pious and resolute Catholic, he envisioned himself transforming Europe from a conglomeration of squabbling kingdoms into a unitary Christian empire under Habsburg family leadership. Once Europe's states were united, Charles predicted, they would drive the Ottoman Turks from southeastern Europe and the Mediterranean. In fact, Charles spent more time warring with other Christian states than with the Ottomans. The French kings Francis I (r. 1515±1547) and Henry II (r. 1547±1559) had no intention of being absorbed into Charles's Christian empire and violently resisted the idea. France even allied with the Turks against him. After fighting France, Ottomans, and several German Protestant princes for three decades, Charles finally exhausted himself and his treasury. When he abdicated his throne in 1555, his brother Ferdinand (r. 1558±1564) inherited the German lands and the office of emperor; his son Philip II (r. 1556±1598) took Spain and the Spanish empire. Thereafter, European rulers accepted the reality that multiple centers of power would have to coexist, at least for the time being.

France, the Netherlands, and England.
In the later sixteenth century the titanic struggle between the Habsburgs and French alliances yielded to a series of smaller conflicts, civil wars, and popular rebellions, many of them colored by religious hostility. In France, battles between Catholic and Protestant factions continued on and off from 1562 to 1598, punctuated by urban massacres and assassinations. In 1572, for example, Catholic officials and soldiers marked St. Bartholomew's Day on August 24 by conspiring with Parisian mobs to murder thousands of Protestants. The slaughter then spread to other cities. France's civil war finally ended in compromise. The monarchy remained Catholic, but French Protestants

(Huguenots) received limited religious rights. Under King Henry IV (r. 1589±1610), France returned to political stability, and the monarchy amassed more power.

Traditionally the French king took advice on taxation and other matters from the Estates-General. This was a council of delegates from the country's social hierarchy of three ªestates°: the high Catholic clergy, the nobility, and the common population. The third estate was represented by merchants, lawyers, and other members of the bourgeoisie, or urban middle class. Louis XIII (r. 1610±1643), however, never called the Estates-General in to session after 1614, putting forward the doctrine that the ruler had responsibilities to his subjects for law, order, and territorial defense but that he answered directly to God, not to the three estates. In fact, no French king called the Estates-General for another 175 years. Meanwhile, the monarchs continued to consolidate power as salaried officials whittled away at the customary rights and powers of provincial aristocrats and notables, much as rulers were striving to do in other parts of Afroeurasia.

In the Netherlands, which belonged to the Habsburgs, several commercially prosperous cities revolted against Philip II, who followed Charles V on the Habsburg throne. In 1579 the rebels proclaimed independence as the United Provinces of the Netherlands, or simply the United Netherlands. (This new state was also known as the Dutch Republic and the United Provinces.) Fighting with Habsburg armies, however, dragged on intermittently for eighty years.

The *Armada Portrait* of Queen Elizabeth I. This late sixteenth-century portrait of the English queen exists in at least three different versions, attesting to the monarch's popularity and the powerful symbolism of the image. The windows behind Elizabeth offer two views on the English victory over the Spanish invasion fleet. Note that she has her back to the nighttime storm and turns toward the calmer scene on the left. What other symbols of the monarch's power can you identify in this picture?

Though Catholics and Protestants fought on both sides, the United Netherlands emerged eventually as a thoroughly Protestant country, whereas the Spanish Netherlands, the region that gained independence centuries later as Belgium, remained predominantly Catholic.

England entered the sixteenth century a much smaller, militarily weaker monarchy than either France or the Habsburg empire. King Henry VIII (r. 1509±1547) tried to reconquer territory that the English crown had once held in France but with no success. Henry also provoked a major religious crisis when in the 1530s he repudiated papal authority, made himself head of what became the Church of England, and seized the extensive lands held by Catholic monasteries. He did this, not because of any heartfelt conversion to Protestantism, but because of a dispute with the pope over his marital affairs and a larger ambition to gain religious as well as political supremacy in his realm. Under Elizabeth I (r. 1558±1603), Henry's daughter and successor, England enjoyed political stability and stayed out of foreign wars until the 1580s when it supported the Dutch fight for freedom from Spain. Elizabeth invested energetically in naval ship building, and in 1588 the English fleet defeated the Spanish Armada, a force Philip II launched in a failed attempt to invade Britain.

Like France, England traditionally had a royal advisory council, but this parliament, as it was called, gained rather than lost power in the early modern era. Parliament's members were landed aristocrats, high churchmen, lesser nobles, and, on occasion, town leaders. Henry VIII and Elizabeth pressured Parliament to bend to their will, but they also depended on it for taxes and loans, especially if they wished to fund wars. Gradually, Parliament won the authority to approve new taxes before the ruler had the legal right to collect them. This assembly of notables thus emerged as a more effective counterweight to kingly power than such advisory groups managed to do in other centralizing monarchies of the era.

The Songhay Empire

Population growth, agricultural expansion, and the development of trade networks all encouraged the formation of more and larger centralized states in Africa south of the Sahara in the fifteenth and sixteenth centuries (see Chapter 16). Trans-Saharan caravan trade, which linked the Mediterranean world with tropical Africa, spurred the development of monarchies in the Sudan, that is, the agrarian and partially urbanized region of open or wooded savannas just south of the desert.

Named for the ethnolinguistic population that inhabited a region along the Niger River where it passes close to the Sahara, Songhay was the largest African empire in the sixteenth century. It began as a modest chieftaincy paying tribute to Mali, the giant Sudanic state that had flourished in the thirteenth and fourteenth centuries. Mali's gradual deterioration left a regional power vacuum that Sunni Ali

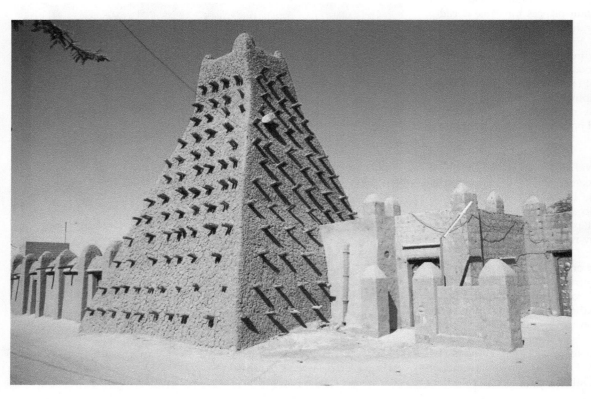

Sankore Mosque, Timbuktu. Like the structure in the city of Jenne (see Chapter 13, p. 382), this building combines the shape of a mosque—minaret and an interior courtyard—with Sudanic mud-brick architecture. The Sankore mosque was the focal point of Timbuktu's leading madrasa, or college of religion and law. It emerged as an important site of Muslim scholarship in the sixteenth century. What geographic and economic factors do you think contributed to Timbuktu's growth as a center of learning?

(r. 1464±1492) and Askiya Muhammad (r. 1493±1528), the two most energetic Songhay monarchs, rose to fill. Centered on Gao, a key commercial center on the Niger, Songhay at its height extended for more than seven hundred miles along the Niger and incorporated farming and herding peoples speaking numerous languages. The governing and commercial classes were largely Muslim, though the majority of the population adhered to traditional polytheistic beliefs and rituals.

Songhay exported gold, ivory, and slaves across the Sahara, but its economic foundation was farming and cattle herding. In Askiya Muhammad's time, Niger valley farmers constructed canals, dykes, and reservoirs, expanding irrigation to produce rice on a large scale. Around 1500 the region experienced the start of a climatic wet cycle. Over the ensuing decades, average annual rainfall increased, and summer rains extended farther into the fringes of the desert, opening up new areas for grain growing and cattle.

Askiya Muhammad undertook a pilgrimage to Mecca in 1495, and he funded mosques and patronized numerous Muslim scholars, both local intellectuals and visitors from North Africa. In the sixteenth century, Timbuktu gained a wide reputation as a center of Arabic learning. The Muslim scholar Leo Africanus, who crossed the Sahara from Morocco about 1510, described Timbuktu in his *History and Description of Africa:* [a] Here are many shops of artificers and merchants, and especially of such as weave linen and cotton cloth. And hither do the Barbarie [North African] merchants bring cloth of Europe. . . . Here are great store of doctors, judges, priests [Muslim clerics], and other learned men, that are bountifully maintained at the king's cost and charges. And hither are brought diverse manuscripts or written books out of Barbarie.[o] [4]

Songhay had no firearms that we know of, but like the Ottomans and Safavids it recruited a standing army of military slaves to fight alongside local militias called up when needed. It fielded a massive cavalry force, its bowmen and lancers clothed in armor of thick cloth quilting. The king appointed royal kinsmen to provincial governorships, and scholars literate in Arabic constituted a central administration of secretaries and scribes organized in ministries.

As we described in the chapter introduction, Songhay's imperial history ended abruptly. The Moroccan musket and artillery troops that appeared suddenly from out of the desert in 1591 dispersed the Songhay cavalry in a single battle. In short order, chiefs and nobles who had paid tribute to the king rose in rebellion, and the central regime disintegrated. No monarchy of the scale of Mali or Songhay appeared again in the western Sudan until the nineteenth century.

The New Era of Guns

FOCUS In what ways did the wide adoption of gunpowder technology affect political, economic, and social patterns in Afroeurasia in the sixteenth century?

Among the instruments of centralizing power that Afroeurasian states deployed in the early modern era, none was more important than firearms. At the start of the thirteenth century, the world had no guns. In the sixteenth century it bristled with them, and they were beginning to transform the way humans waged war, organized governments, and kept public order.

In the two centuries from 1300 to 1500, artisans working in several lands progressively transformed primitive metal tubes that fired stone balls in wildly unpredictable directions into lethal artillery that could demolish castles, gouge gaping holes in the sides of ships, and kill many soldiers all at once. As technological and tactical innovations enhanced the power and accuracy of guns, wars became progressively more deadly. One scholar has estimated that in the first 1,500 years of the Common Era about 3.7 million men and women died from war-related causes, including famine and disease. But in the sixteenth century alone, about 1.6 million people died in wars. In the seventeenth century, the number jumped to 6.1 million.[5]

The Citadel of Turin, Italy, in 1644. Star forts, or *traces italienne*, replaced circular defensive walls in parts of Europe where rulers could afford these expensive strongholds. The triangular bastions, or projections, allowed soldiers on facing ramparts to give each other defensive cover. A deep moat or ditch and an outer defensive wall of loosely packed earth kept enemy artillery at a distance and forced advancing infantry into vulnerable positions before they could reach the inner stone walls. What other changes in military organization and tactics do you think the development of gunpowder weapons brought about?

New and Deadly Armies

By the later 1400s, rulers learned that gunpowder weapons worked best when manufactured in large numbers and issued to ranks of troops who fired volleys of shot at defensive fortifications or charging cavalry. Small states and stateless societies invariably lacked the material wealth to deploy such massed firepower. Even those states that could afford large arsenals had to solve numerous logistical and tactical problems that armies had never previously faced.

One key advance was recruitment of much larger infantry forces to fight alongside cavalry, which had traditionally enjoyed higher social status than foot soldiers. An infantry unit armed with muskets and marching in close order could devastate an advancing enemy with a wall of fire. Muskets, however, took longer to load than crossbows or longbows because the infantryman had to swab out the barrel and insert a powder charge and ball. Officers could speed up the firing rate, however, by organizing troops in ranks, or rows. In a battle, the front rank would fire, then move back to reload as the second row stepped forward. The earliest use of this tactic may have been in sixteenth-century Japan, where Oda Nobunaga taught soldiers to fire in multiple ranks. A short time later, Dutch officers refined this tactic by exhaustively drilling infantry to maneuver, load, and shoot in synchronized harmony. In the seventeenth century, massed infantry tactics spread to all armies in Europe, as well as to the Ottoman empire. Mounted warriors also got better at controlling handguns. Cavalry in sixteenth-century Morocco may have been the first in the world to master the art of firing guns from horseback.[6]

Rulers also had to recruit bigger armies to accommodate the complex technology of both artillery and the defenses against it. Bronze, brass, and cast iron artillery required large teams to transport and repair them. Sixteenth-century cannons did their most damage smashing holes in defensive walls. In response, Italian engineers made cities and castles less vulnerable by constructing earthen ramparts and ditches that kept enemy artillery from approaching too close and by placing defensive guns on high bastions. Consequently, rulers had to recruit even more soldiers to build and garrison massive fortifications.

After 1500 the size of armies catapulted upward. By 1595 France had 80,000 fighters on duty, and by 1710, around 360,000. Ming China maintained the largest military in the world, posting several hundred thousand soldiers along its frontier with Inner Eurasia. These figures would be even larger if they included the great numbers of noncombatants that almost always accompanied early modern armies on the march. Support personnel included supply contractors, mechanics, horse grooms, merchants, servants, and construction laborers. They also included many women, who went along as traders, cooks, laundresses, prostitutes, and caregivers to the sick and wounded. Wives and children frequently accompanied soldiers on the march, foraging for food not provided by the army. A Dutch document of 1622 describes

MAP 17.4 Spread of firearms, fourteenth through sixteenth centuries.
In the sixteenth century gunpowder weaponry reached every continent except Australia. What differences do you notice in the direction of the spread of firearms in the fourteenth century compared to the sixteenth? What might explain these differences?

The Invention of Gunpowder and the First Casting of Bronze Cannon. This engraving by Dutch artist Philip Galle appeared in 1600 in a collection called *New Discoveries*. The image depicts many facets of arms production. Skilled craftsmen are at work while assistants stoke the fires and provide mechanical power—look carefully at the wheel on the left. Describe the action portrayed outside the foundry in the background on the right. Why might the engraver have included that detail?

ᵃa small army of carts, baggage horses, nags, sutlers [traders], lackeys, women, children, and a rabble which numbered far more than the army itself.º [7]

The Military Revolution

In the fourteenth and fifteenth centuries, gunpowder technology spread westward from China across Afroeurasia. After 1450, however, the patterns of innovation and diffusion became more complicated. The Ottoman Turks, for example, pioneered muskets with strong steel barrels. Indian metalsmiths excelled at making brass cannons, and French technicians led the way in designing light, mobile field artillery. Rulers aspiring to compete for wealth and territory had little choice but to join the stampede for guns.

The spread of firearms. States that lacked gunpowder weapons might face disaster, as the Songhay empire discovered in 1591 when Moroccan musketeers turned up. Firearms contributed, if much less decisively than disease epidemics, to Spain's rapid defeat of the Aztec and Inca empires. Ottoman forces seized Egypt and Syria in 1517 because musket and cannon units were not well integrated into the Mamluk army. Its aristocratic cavalry preferred to fight with bows, lances, and swords. The Ottoman army entered Egypt with guns booming and quickly overran the Mamluk horse regiments. Japan was something of an exception to the dominant pattern. The founders of the Tokugawa shogunate triumphed with the aid of cannons and musketry. In 1637, however, the shoguns had to put down a serious revolt led by musket-wielding Japanese

Christian converts. In the aftermath of that disturbance, the state gradually abolished the manufacture and sale of firearms and let its arsenal rust away. Since the shogunate enjoyed political stability and faced no imminent external threat, radical gun control worked well. Tokugawa Japan remained practically war free for more than 250 years.

After European sailors opened new transoceanic passages, knowledge of firearms spread faster, and heavy guns could be transported from one part of the world to another in a matter of months (see Map 17.4). Private gun merchants, mercenaries, and freelance technical advisors offered their services far and wide. German and Hungarian gunners advised the Ottoman army. Japanese musketeers fought for the king of Thailand. In China, the Ming government enlisted foreign advisors to strengthen firepower along its Inner Eurasian frontier. Ming commanders studied Turkish, Portuguese, and Dutch artillery designs and ordered Chinese metal founders to copy them. One observer described how Ming artillerymen in 1626 saved a northern city from an assault of Manchurian horse archers: ᵃAs the cannon went off, one could see in the light of the fires the barbarians and their horses being thrown up in the air; those who fell in the confusion were countless, and the villains, being badly defeated, ran away.º [8] States also sent guns and military missions to allies. The Ottoman sultans shipped artillery to Southeast Asia to help Aceh, a Muslim kingdom on the island of Sumatra, fight off Portuguese assailants. In northeastern Africa, the Christian monarchy of Ethiopia bolstered its army with four hundred Portuguese musketeers, while neighboring Muslim states accepted help from Ottoman gunners.

Many Afroeurasian states with access to the sea supported navies of one size or another, and from the midsixteenth century, several rulers adopted the Iberian tactic of mounting cannons on ships (see Chapter 16). China, Korea, Japan, Vietnam, and Thailand, as well as Southeast Asian maritime kingdoms, built vessels to accommodate mortars or artillery, if only to defend ports and protect local sea trade. The Ottoman Turks built hundreds of armed galleys, which operated on all the seas from the Mediterranean to the Indian Ocean. Near the end of the sixteenth century, England, the United Netherlands, and France, the three richest states of northwestern Europe, began to deploy shipboard artillery to challenge Spanish and Portuguese dominance of the oceanic routes. These powers interloped on Portugal's lucrative spice trade in the Indian Ocean and negotiated their own deals with Asian sellers.

Paying for gunpowder armies. Historians have called the worldwide transition to gunpowder-based armies and navies a ᵃmilitary revolution° because of its far-reaching impact on economy and society. States aiming to make war on neighbors, subdue local aristocrats, and turn defiant peasants into submissive taxpayers had to recruit and pay fighters, expand chains of command, and procure guns, uniforms, horses, ships, and countless supplies. They had to ensure production of iron, copper, and other metals and build roads, bridges, and harbors to move troops and materiel. They had to employ metalsmiths, engineers, accountants, doctors, and commercial agents. In other words, no state could accumulate power without investing great sums of public money. Therefore, the military revolution also involved, as some historians have called it, a ᵃfiscal revolution.° That is, rulers

| **fisc** The treasury of a sovereign state; a state department concerned with financial matters. | had to put heavy demands on the **fisc** if they hoped to achieve armed advantage over their rivals. The most |

powerful states sometimes dedicated 70 to 90 percent of their total annual budgets to military expenses, a much larger proportion of expenditure than any country allocates today.

European monarchs invented an array of new taxes to harvest revenue. In the seventeenth century, the tsars of Russia collected at least 280 different taxes, including levies on honey, salt, bathhouses, and the contracting of third marriages.[9] Some states strengthened direct rule in the provinces, sending officials from the capital to collect taxes, set up legal courts, and keep the peace in collaboration with local nobles, town magistrates, and religious leaders. Where they had the military backing to do it, royal agents bypassed these local authorities altogether. Many governments also borrowed from rich private families to get infusions of cash for wars. In Europe, bankers, such as the Fugger family of southern Germany, became immensely rich advancing funds to rulers. Big loans, however, pushed states deeper into debt, periodically destabilizing financial markets. The Spanish Habsburg emperor Philip II spent so much on his wars that, despite his access to American silver, he had to declare bankruptcy four different times.

The Limits of Central Power

We should not overemphasize the power of early modern regimes to monitor and regulate their subject populations. States learned how to do it on a much larger scale in later centuries. In the 1500s, communication technology, dependent as it was on animals, wagons, and boot leather, prevented micromanagement of far-flung provinces. Midsized states, such as France or Thailand, tended to have more success at direct rule than did giant ones like the Ottoman or Mughal empires. Central regimes also left economic improvements and education mostly to local communities and religious institutions. Some rulers undertook censuses and land surveys to maximize revenue collection, but early modern states had limited knowledge of the numbers, incomes, and whereabouts of the people they ruled, certainly compared to the databases that government agencies work with today.

Some monarchs strengthened their authority over local aristocrats and town authorities, though at the price of incessant negotiations over long-established rights, privileges, and legal jurisdictions. After dispatching soldiers to reduce a rural area to submission, rulers often found it less expensive and bothersome to let local leaders continue to run affairs and perhaps grant rights of **tax farming** to landed nobles or private contractors.

| | **tax farming** A system in which a government awards the right of tax collection to a private individual or group in return for a fee or a percentage of the taxes gathered. |

State intrusions in local affairs rarely went uncontested. Revenue-hungry monarchs had to confront aristocratic resistance movements, urban uprisings, peasant rebellions, and banditry. Between 1514 and 1551, for example, the kings of France, fixated on raising money for wars, had to suppress tax revolts in ten different cities and six different regions.[10] The long Dutch revolt against the Spanish Habsburgs began as a violent tax protest in 1571. Rural men and women also slipped from the grasp of centralizing rulers simply by fleeing. In Mughal India, farmers frequently avoided burdensome taxes by running away to forests or sparsely populated frontiers where state agents would not venture. In Russia, tax-loathing peasants ran off to the Ukraine or Siberia to get beyond the tsar's reach.

Trends in Religion, Language, and Culture

FOCUS In what ways did political and economic changes in the sixteenth century affect patterns of cultural life in different parts of Afroeurasia?

The number of sovereign states in the world shrank in the sixteenth century because rulers with guns absorbed weaker states and societies into their own expanding territories. Similarly, and partly as a consequence of political centralization, consolidation also took place in religion, language, and styles of culture. By 1500, all of the major belief systems that exist today had already appeared in Afroeurasia. Three of themÐ Buddhism, Christianity, and IslamÐ reached out to millions of potential converts as missionaries, as well as merchants, soldiers, and scholars with religious messages to share, moved out along the global communication networks. These three universalist faiths progressively assimilated, modified, or displaced many purely local religious beliefs and practices, a phenomenon that had been occurring in earlier centuries. Global communication and interchange also sped up what linguists have labeled **language death.** Scholars have estimated that in the past one thousand years, the number of languages spoken in the world has fallen

language death A process in which the number of native or fluent speakers of a particular language declines over time until no community of speakers remains.

from between 10,000 and 15,000 to fewer than 7,000, and the process continues to accelerate. By one current estimate, one language goes extinct every two weeks.[11] In the early modern era, local tongues and the cultural ideas and practices that those tongues expressed lost ground to ascendant languages associated with expanding states, universalist religions, or merchant networks.

Afroeurasia's religious landscape changed significantly in early modern times, not only because ªbig religionsº spread more widely, but also because accelerating global change raised numerous new questions about humankind, nature, and the cosmos. Transoceanic communication confronted societies in both Afroeurasia and the Americas with ideas and things that seemed strange, unexplainable, and perhaps dangerous. Christians, for example, debated whether American Indians descended from Adam and Eve or, because the Bible does not account for them, represented an entirely separate divine creation. Chinese Confucian scholars who hosted European missionaries tried to wrap their minds around such novel ideas as the supreme being's taking a three-part formÐ Father, Son, and Holy Ghost. Practitioners of local polytheistic religions in Indonesia or West Africa met Muslims who urged them to renounce their nature spirits and household deities and submit to the One God.

The major universalist faiths had for many centuries experienced internal divisions or disagreements about belief and practice. The very fact that Buddhism, Christianity, and Islam spread so widely and crossed so many linguistic and ethnic frontiers made it inevitable that doctrinal differences and organizational splits would occur. The early modern era witnessed intense religious debates and ruptures, especially when popular movements to improve society or recharge moral energies gathered support.

Intellectual and Moral Ferment in China

In the last century and a half of the Ming dynasty, people in Beijing and several coastal cities began to debate the nature and proper direction of Chinese society. Rapid economic change, the growth of city populations, and new contacts with people and products from abroad stimulated

their thinking. Roman Catholic missionaries were among the new influences, bringing Christian teachings, as well as astronomy, geometry, and clock making. These newcomers generated lively debate with Chinese intellectuals, though they had little impact on popular beliefs.

Millions of Chinese performed Buddhist and Daoist devotions, and the educated classes, especially the huge Ming bureaucracy, looked to the moral and ethical precepts of neo-Confucianism for guidance in social and public life. An amplification of the teachings of Confucius (551±479 B.C.E.) and other ancient sages, neo-Confucianism emphasized righteous moral behavior, daily ritual, respect for hierarchy, and dedication to family and local community. To encourage social harmony throughout the land, the Ming state made neo-Confucianism the imperial orthodoxy and closely regulated the activities of religious groups, including Muslims and Christians.

Chinese intellectuals nonetheless argued over neo-Confucian ideas during this period. Corruption and cronyism plagued the imperial government in the sixteenth century, and to some educated people, neo-Confucian doctrines appeared sterile and elitist. One response was a lively reform movement initiated by Wang Yangming (1472±1529), a Chinese military officer, public official, and philosopher. He argued that, contrary to neo-Confucian orthodoxy, all human beings possess innate moral knowledge and can therefore discern good from evil. Ordinary men and women may discover intuitively how to lead an honest life without mastering Confucian texts or performing complex rituals. Wang's proposition that neo-Confucian scholars had no corner on truth or virtue won him a large following among young literate people, including Buddhists and Daoists already inclined to personal introspection. After Wang died, some of his disciples expanded on his ideas to preach individual creativity, education for the poor, and respect for women's inherent intellectual abilities. Neo-Confucian officials who championed strict hierarchy and male authority struck back, and some of Wang's disciples ended up in prison or dead. Nevertheless, Wang's movement freed up and broadened the scope of Chinese intellectual life.

Tension between Sunni and Shi'a Muslims

Although Islam spread to more people than any other major faith in the early modern era, quarrels between Sunni Muslims and adherents of Shi'ism caused serious political and social distress. Sunni and Shi'a communities had shown for centuries that they could live near one another in mutual toleration. But when Shi'a doctrine became the ªofficialº religion of the Safavid state, which occupied the geographical heart of the Muslim world, ill feelings were aggravated. The neighboring Ottomans, whose Sunni sultans claimed the title of caliph, doubted the loyalty of Shi'a communities within their empire. For their part, Shi'a clerical leaders rejected the legitimacy of the Ottoman caliph. Safavid and Ottoman armies fought each other mainly over territory, not doctrine, but mutually hostile religious rhetoric fueled this chronic conflict. Indeed, in the sixteenth and seventeenth centuries, the idea hardened that Sunni and Shi'a Islam constituted two distinct and mutually exclusive forms of the faith.

Religious Crisis in Europe

Religious organization in both Islam and Buddhism tended to be fluid, informal, and no more than loosely centralized. In Christianity, by contrast, churches formally supervised doctrine and practice. The Roman Catholic Church, the exclusive Christian organization in western and central Europe up to the sixteenth century, was a huge administrative, financial, and educational institution. When church leaders clashed over belief and worship, the crisis affected nearly everyone (see Map 17.5).

The Roman church had presided over western Europe's medieval cultural flowering. By 1400, however, the church's moral light was dimming. Its integrity depended on principled men and women occupying the highest officesÐ pope, cardinals, bishops, and the heads of monasteries and nunneries. In the 1300s the clergy's reputation plummeted. Many Christians faulted the church for failing to prevent or relieve the horrors of the Black Death, and they watched in bewilderment as two, and at one point three, rival popes struggled for supremacy for forty years (the Western Schism, 1378±1417). Across Europe, dismayed Christians told stories of corrupt and greedy bishops, priests with bastard children, and materialistic popes dedicated mainly to their family's fortunes. Higher-minded clerics bewailed this state of affairs but achieved little change.

The Protestant Reformation. Martin Luther reiterated the protests of earlier critics when in 1517 he published a scholarly disputation in the form of Ninety-Five Theses, directed mainly against the sale of indulgences. This was a church practice in which clerics took donations from people on the promise of offering special prayers to help deceased friends and relatives move up to heaven from purgatory (the place of temporary punishment for earthly sin). Luther denounced this ªindulgences market,º and he deplored priestly immorality and church wealth. He damned the pope as the antichrist and proposed bold new interpretations of biblical scripture. In 1520, to no one's surprise, the church excommunicated him. Resolute and brave, but also bad tempered and tactless, Luther might have died a martyr at the stake had not the Elector of Saxony and other German princes protected him from arrest. Those rulers had complex motives for supporting a religious rebel. In varying degrees they sympathized with Luther's religious ideas. But they also resented the flow of German wealth to the Vatican treasury, and they saw an opportunity to assert their rights of self-government against Charles V, the Holy Roman emperor and a staunch Catholic. Because mechanical printing presses were just then appearing across Europe, Luther's books, pamphlets, and hymns spread faster than they would have in any earlier age. He became something of a religious sensation, and within two decades, supportive Christians were organizing independent worship communities in Germany, Switzerland, and other countries.

All these protesters, or Protestants, rejected the pope's authority, but not all of them became ªLutherans.º Other emerging leaders disagreed with Luther on various points of theology and church organization. For example, disputes arose among Protestants over the display of images of Jesus in church buildings, how churches should be governed, and what exactly Jesus meant at the Last Supper when he took a piece of bread and said, ªThis is my body.º The most prominent early Protestant scholars and preachers included Ulrich Zwingli (1484±1531), who pioneered reform in Switzerland, and the French lawyer John Calvin (1509±1564), who set up a church in Geneva that became a model for Protestant organization across Europe. More radical groups, such as Anabaptists, Quakers, and Unitarians, variously advocated baptism for adults rather than infants, political pacifism, vows of poverty, and the principle that God's nature is singular rather than a separate but united trinity. In short, Protestant sects multiplied, and the Roman church permanently lost its monopoly over Christian doctrine and worship.

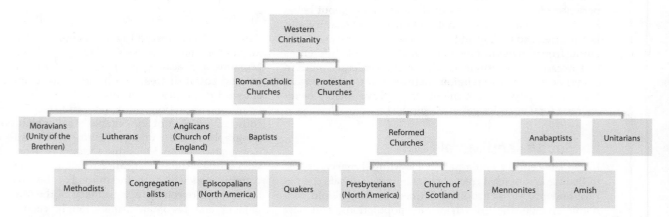

Principal divisions of western Christianity, sixteenth through eighteenth centuries.

MAP 17.5 Religions of Europe, 1560.

Where do religious boundaries match political borders on this map? Can you account for the places where religion and political rule coincide, and where they are different?

Legend:
- Anglican
- Calvinist
- Calvinist-influenced
- Roman Catholic
- Lutheran
- Lutheran-influenced
- Boundary of the Holy Roman Empire

Protestant teachings. Despite their differences, Protestants shared certain precepts that generally distinguished them from Roman Catholics, and still do. One was the doctrine that the Holy Bible is the only valid Christian authority. Believers must seek divine truth through scripture alone. No bishop, priest, or saint has divine authority to intercede between an individual and God. This doctrine did much to encourage people to read their Bibles and stimulate literacy, but it also meant that Protestantism was sure to branch out in several directions.

Protestants also professed that human beings are justified, that is, redeemed or saved, exclusively by faith in God's love, not by anything they may do to overcome sin or to gain divine favor. The Catholic Church encouraged Christians to perform ªgood worksº in expectation of realizing God's forgiveness and entry to heaven. These works included acts of kindness and charity but also obedience to church doctrines, laws, and sacraments. Protestant reformers countered that if people have heartfelt faith in God's grace, good works will follow naturally. In Luther's view, unconditional surrender to the divine willÐ without expectation that this devotion will guarantee any particular resultsÐ liberates Christians from the fear that they can never do enough good deeds or conquer enough of their sins to receive God's grace. Somewhat differently, John Calvin asserted that God predestined some to salvation and others to hell regardless of how many good works they might do. To Catholics, such a teaching suggested that God could be fickle and punitive.

Protestant churches also allowed members of the clergy to marry. The Catholic Church taught that priests and nuns must remain celibate, devoting themselves totally to God's service and remaining free of family cares and obligations. Protestant leaders argued to the contrary that wholesome family life would educate children in Christian virtue, help ministers avoid sexual sin, and provide pastors with female companions and helpmeets. In the early Protestant churches, women sometimes took on leadership roles as writers and organizers. Catholic and Protestant clerics mostly agreed, however, that although males and females are spiritually equal, women should keep silent in churches, submit themselves to the will of male relatives, and accept intellectual inferiority as part of the divine order of things. A few brave women retorted that Christians should challenge traditional gender roles inherited from the medieval

Religious differences in Germany, 1529. This woodcut depicting rival Christian services circulated in Europe in the new and inexpensive print medium aimed at popular audiences. On the right, a Catholic priest in elaborate robes preaches to a somewhat distracted congregation. On the left, a Protestant minister uses a Bible to preach to congregants, who are also reading Bibles. What other differences do you notice in the two scenes? What message do you think the creator of this woodcut aimed to convey?

church. As a German woman wrote in 1524, ªAlthough St. Paul [in the New Testament] forbade women to preach in churches and instructed them to obey their husbands, what if the churches were full of liars?º[12] For the most part, however, these women's voices went unheard.

Europe became religiously plural after 1550, but no Protestant denomination advocated religious freedom. Rather, they all insisted on the correctness of their own particular version of Christian truth. Consequently, Lutherans, Calvinists, and members of other sects frequently persecuted (and sometimes murdered) one another. Catholic Spain convened special courts known as the Holy Inquisition to rid the country of all religious deviantsÐ Muslims, Jews, and Protestants alike. Intolerance took a particularly abhorrent turn in the later sixteenth century, when trying, torturing, and executing people accused of witchcraft became a popular civic pastime in both Protestant and Catholic countries. The great majority of victims were women, often poor, elderly, socially isolated individuals who had few defenses against richer and more powerful people who accused them of conspiring with Satan.

The Catholic Reformation.

Once a significant number of European rulers aligned themselves with Protestantism, the Roman church could not simply go on as before. Many Catholic clerics wanted reform as badly as Luther did but from within the existing church. Internal reform initiatives got under way in the 1540s, and they had two major aims: to frustrate Protestant success and to reinvigorate the church's

moral authority, tacitly recognizing that critics had made some legitimate points.

A Catholic reform council, which met intermittently between 1545 and 1563 in the Italian city of Trent, reaffirmed most of the church's fundamental doctrines but also took numerous actions to strengthen the clergy's moral and spiritual fiber. Church leaders insisted, for example, that priests and monks become literate. A series of devout church fathers, beginning with Pope Paul III (1534±1549), also worked for change. The Catholic Reformation, sometimes called the Counter Reformation, approved the creation of several new religious orders committed to restoring the church's integrity and energy. The Society of Jesus, or the Jesuits, founded in 1540 by the Spanish nobleman Ignatius Loyola (1491±1556), became most active on a world scale. Loyola argued that the spiritual weapons against Protestantism must include advanced education and missionary zeal. He established schools to train young priests, and he dispatched Jesuit missionaries to America, Africa, and Asia, where they often learned local languages and offered non-Christian rulers technical and scientific advice. In 1535 Angela Merici (1474±1540), an Italian aristocrat, founded the Company of St. Ursula. Members of this order, called Ursulines, took vows as nuns. But they resided with their families rather than in cloisters, and they dedicated themselves to Christian education of girls in both Europe and overseas colonies.

After 1650, following a century and a half of debilitating warfare among European states, the region's religious map generally stabilized. Most rulers agreed to accept one

A Mennonite minister and his wife. This oil painting by the celebrated Dutch artist Rembrandt van Rijn expresses the values of well-to-do Protestant elites in the Netherlands. Conelis Claesz Anslo, the clergyman, was the son of a successful merchant and leader of Amsterdam's Mennonite community. His wife Aeltje Gerritsdr Schoueten listens attentively to him. Although their dress is somber, the fur trim of his coat and the fine lace of Aeltje's cap display their wealth. The Asian tapestry used as a table covering and large books on the left signal Anslo's connections to the global market and his status as a man of learning. What do you think the image communicates about the status of women in Protestant households?

another's spiritual preferences. States sometimes persecuted minority sects, and Jewish or Muslim residents might be tolerated only as long as they accepted their legal and social inferiority. Northern Europe became predominantly Protestant, whereas the southern and eastern countries remained Catholic. Protestant movements budded early in Bohemia, Hungary, and Poland but then faltered owing to the energy of Catholic reform and the loyalty of rulers to Rome.

Vernacular Languages and the State

The centralization and expansion of states in the sixteenth century had important consequences for language and literate culture. When rulers deployed gunpowder armies to seize new territories or impose direct government on previously autonomous regions, they also often introduced the language and cultural preferences of the state's core area as the medium of administration and law. Moreover, local aristocrats and business leaders usually saw the political and social advantages of learning the language and imitating the fashions and public rituals of the central regime. Consequently, local languages and customs might gradually lose prestige and even disappear.

Across Afroeurasia, language consolidation accompanied nearly every state-centralizing project. In Europe, people babbled in many tongues, but in the early modern centuries a relatively small number of languages, all of them written, spread more widely. The most important of these **vernacular languages** were Italian, French, German, English,

vernacular language The native language commonly spoken by ordinary people in a region.

Gracia Luna Mendes Nasi: A Sixteenth-Century Businesswoman

A bronze medal of Gracia Luna Mendes Nasi.

The Protestant and Catholic Reformations had grim consequences for European Jews. Rivaling one another to display their Christian piety, many clerical leaders fanned the always-smoldering fires of anti-Semitism, urging rulers to more ruthlessly restrict, segregate, or even expel their Jewish minorities. In response to intensifying legal discrimination and social pressures, tens of thousands of Jews left western Europe to resettle in Poland, North Africa, or the Ottoman empire. In those lands they found, not full social equality, but greater odds of living in peace and economic security.

The family of Gracia Luna Mendes Nasi (1510–1569) originated in Spain but moved to Portugal sometime after 1492, when King Ferdinand and Queen Isabella decreed that Jews must either become Catholics or leave the country. A few years later, the Portuguese crown made a similar decree. Not wanting to emigrate again, Gracia Nasi's parents accepted, or were forced to accept, conversion. Nasi therefore grew up a *converso,* or "New Christian," and when she was eighteen she married Francisco Mendes, also a *converso* and an immensely wealthy merchant banker.

Following her husband's untimely death in 1536, Nasi and her young daughter sailed to Antwerp, Europe's most thriving seaport. The Mendes family already had large mercantile interests there, and Gracia soon immersed herself in the business, which included the profitable Indian pepper trade between Lisbon and northern Europe. Plainly a woman of commercial talent, she took full charge of the Mendes fortune after her husband's brother died in 1542.

In the heat of the early Protestant movement, however, *conversos* were vulnerable to charges of being secret Jews bent on persuading other New Christians to renounce their faith. In this threatening climate, Nasi slipped out of Antwerp and made for Venice, where she arrived about 1546. The Mendes firm had commercial agents in several Italian cities, but Nasi found no permanent haven there. She even spent a short time in a Venetian prison and had to deposit part of the family fortune with the public treasury.

Consequently, in 1549, she moved again, this time to the Italian city of Ferrara. She and her fortune received a warmer welcome there, and she openly returned to her Jewish roots. The Roman church, however, demanded that the city enact stronger anti-Jewish legislation. Fortunately for Nasi, she had an invitation from the Ottoman emperor Suleyman to settle in Istanbul, much as a modern government might entice a major corporation to move in. In 1552 she left Christian Europe for good. Once established in the empire, where Jews enjoyed formal legal status, Nasi shed her *converso* identity and moved socially in the Jewish community. She lavishly patronized Jewish scholarship, synagogues, schools, and, some evidence suggests, new Jewish and *converso* immigrants arriving from western Europe.

Nasi never married again and died in 1569 at the age of fifty-nine. Running an international business empire of mammoth proportions, she was hardly typical of a sixteenth-century women, whatever her religion. But she does exemplify the remarkable migratory shift of western European Jews toward eastern Europe and the southern and eastern shores of the Mediterranean.

Thinking Critically

What political, social, cultural, or personal factors do you think were most important in explaining Gracia Mendes Nasi's success as a businesswoman?

Polish, Spanish, Portuguese, and Dutch. In France before the fourteenth century, for example, people spoke the language ancestral to modern French only in the Paris region. Elsewhere, twenty-two or so other tongues could be heard. French, however, was the language of the rising monarchy. Parisian French accompanied royal armies, administrators, and judges into the provinces, where local nobles and town merchants quickly concluded that they should learn it. In

1539 King Francis I decreed that all state documents must be produced ᵃin the maternal French language,° by which he meant Parisian French.[13] Today, only a few of the other old languages, notably Provençal, Breton, and Basque, are still spoken at all. In the British Isles, Henry VIII and other monarchs stipulated English as the state language and tried by various means to stifle use of Celtic tongues like Irish, Welsh, or Cornish in the royal domain. In 1536, for example,

Henry urged inhabitants of Galway, a part of Ireland under English rule, to endeavor [a]to speak English, and to use themselves after the English fashion; and specially that you, and every one of you, do put forth your child to school, to learn to speak English.[o][14]

In Asia, China had long had a standardized written language, but it also accommodated numerous Chinese dialects, as well as tongues of other linguistic families, notably Turkic. Confucian officials favored Mandarin Chinese, the dialect associated with the capital city of Beijing. Consequently, Mandarin evolved into the most prestigious medium of verbal communication throughout the empire. Urban presses generated thousands of books on innumerable subjects, and literacy expanded among both men and women. The Jesuit priest Matteo Ricci, who lived in Beijing from 1601 to 1611, remarked on [a]the exceedingly large number of books in circulation here and the ridiculously low prices at which they are sold.[o][15] In Southeast Asia, the rise of Burma, Thailand, and Vietnam as strong monarchies propelled the Burmese, Thai, and Vietnamese languages to regional primacy, thereby displacing in some measure local tongues that peoples of mountain and forest had traditionally spoken. Tokugawa Japan, by contrast, already had a single dominant vernacular. This circumstance, along with widespread literacy and a flourishing woodblock printing industry, promoted the archipelago's cultural unity.

Languages of Cultural Prestige

Whenever a language spread from one region to another, a full package of ideas and cultural behavior usually went with it because the elements of culture expressed through language, gesture, art, and ritual cannot be disentangled.

Arabic, Persian, and Turkish. Arabic and Persian shared high status as the principal carriers of Muslim theology, philosophy, literature, and science in the early modern centuries. Persian served as a medium of diplomacy and intellectual exchange from Bengal to the Mediterranean. Peoples of South Asia spoke many tongues, but Persian was the chief Mughal administrative language. Urdu, which is a Hindi language infused with Persian loan words, became an important literary medium in northern India. Muslims everywhere esteemed Arabic as the language of the Prophet Muhammad and the Holy Quran. It was the dominant language of all the western Muslim lands from Iraq to the Atlantic in early modern times, and it still is today. Arabic also served as the language of intellectual culture and political administration in Sudanic Africa.

In the Ottoman domains, Oghuz, the Turkic language that evolved into modern Turkish, competed successfully with Persian among government officials and the learned class. From the Topkapi Palace in Istanbul, the sultan dispensed patronage to poets, astronomers, geographers, and historians, who wrote in Arabic, as well as in Persian and Turkish, both of which used a modified Arabic script. By contrast, Greek, the language of the deceased Byzantine empire, went into permanent eclipse as a major carrier of new knowledge, though remaining the language of modern Greece and the Greek Orthodox Church.

Print languages of Europe. In Europe, mechanical printing presses began in the sixteenth century to pour out thousands of books and pamphlets in the leading vernacular languages. These [a]print languages[o] gradually standardized vocabularies and grammars. Partly because inexpensive books became available, more people learned to read vernaculars, especially in northern Europe. Literate women who had little access to classical Greek or Latin found at least narrow avenues for publishing essays, poetry, and religious pamphlets in the regional vernaculars. Novelists, playwrights, poets, and religious writers broadcast their works in vernaculars. Martin Luther produced floods of religious pamphlets in German. Miguel Cervantes's monumental novel titled *Don Quixote* was published in Spanish (in two parts in 1605 and 1615) and quickly translated into several other languages. The poet Anna Bijns (1494±1575) wrote satirical verse in Dutch. And the English writer William Shakespeare (1564±1616) produced much poetry and, we should note, thirty-two plays.

Languages of humanism. The European print languages carried the humanist movement from its base in northern Italy to all parts of the subcontinent. Humanism flowered in the later fourteenth century as an intellectual mission to recover the lost knowledge of the ancient Romans and Greeks (see Chapter 15). Its advocates prized education in grammar, rhetoric, history, and moral philosophy, which they believed gave students the disciplinary tools needed to understand classical texts. Humanist scholars also contended that the Bible should be as open to critical analysis as any other ancient document. In 1516 the Dutch intellectual Desiderius Erasmus (1469±1536), a loyal Roman Catholic but scathing critic of church vice and bigotry, published the first printed edition of the New Testament in Greek. The Oxford University cleric William Tyndale (1490±1536) later translated it from Greek into EnglishÐ before being burned at the stake as a Protestant heretic. Educated men and women in Moscow read Latin scientific works and translated them into Russian. Tsar Ivan III married Sofia Palaiologina (1455±1503), a noblewoman raised in Italy who made a lifelong project of strengthening language and cultural ties between the Russian Orthodox and Roman Catholic worlds.

• • •

Conclusion

The start of the seventeenth century marked a significant transition in world history. By then, most states in Afroeurasia had access to firearms. The most successful ones acquired gunpowder armies, central bureaucracies, and law courts with increased powers to keep the peace, amass revenue, and safeguard commerce. Those states also exerted cultural influence on wider circles of population, persuading their subjects, especially the wealthy and educated classes, to accept greater homogeneity in religion, language, legal custom, and public taste. States had never wielded such power in any earlier era. Nevertheless, limitations on early modern systems of overland communication left plenty of room for subjects of centralizing rulers to protest, rebel, hide, run away, or keep local languages and cultural traditions alive.

As of the early seventeenth century, no single Afroeurasian state, no matter the size of its army, held a decided advantage over the others in commanding resources and labor or marshaling firepower. Because of the great global convergence of the same century, configurations of both regional and global power remained extremely fluid. The circulation of American silver, the spread of food crops to new places, rising population and productivity in many lands, and maritime innovations that made transoceanic travel routine all worked together to produce a genuinely global and increasingly complex system of commercial, cultural, and demographic exchange.

As a result, all but the most remote societies were forced to confront new ideas, products, and cultural challenges. Moreover, some states, social groups, and economic interests benefited from accelerating global change more than others did. Thus the largest centers of population, farm production, and manufacturing remained in Asia, and these resources supported a few mammoth and powerful states, plus numerous smaller ones. Even so, circumstances led western Europeans—not Poles, Russians, Ottoman Turks, or Ming Chinese—to take charge of maritime trade across the Atlantic and to exploit immense mineral and agricultural wealth in the Americas. We explore this emerging Atlantic system and other global developments of the later sixteenth and seventeenth centuries in Chapter 18.

• • •

Key Terms

capitulations 490	Jesuits 508	service nobility 492
Catholic Reformation (also, Counter Reformation) 508	language death 505	Sikhism 492
	Moscovy 494	tax farming 504
fisc 504	Mughal empire 491	Tokugawa shogunate 495
gunpowder armies 491	Protestant Reformation 498	vernacular language 509
Habsburg dynasty 498	Romanov dynasty 495	

Change over Time

1448–1488	King Trailok reigns in Thailand (Siam), creating a strong central state in Southeast Asia.
1453	Ottoman Turks capture Constantinople, strengthening the Ottoman sultanate's position as a major Afroeurasian power.
1469–1539	The sage Nanak lives in India and founds the Sikh religion.
1472–1529	The philosopher Wang Yangming lives in China and challenges the elitist principles of neo-Confucianism.
1493–1528	The Songhay empire in the Sudan region of Africa expands during the reign of Askiya Muhammad.
1516	The Dutch humanist Desiderius Erasmus publishes the first printed edition of the New Testament in Greek.
1517	Martin Luther publishes his Ninety-Five Theses critical of the Catholic Church, launching the movement that would become the Protestant Reformation.
1517	Ottoman forces armed with gunpowder weapons overthrow the Mamluks in Egypt and Syria.
1519–1556	Charles V reigns as Holy Roman emperor and head of the Habsburg dynasty, leading an unsuccessful attempt to unify Europe and drive out the Ottoman Turks.
1520–1566	Suleyman I "the Magnificent" rules the Ottoman empire during a period of expansion in southeastern Europe.
1533–1584	Central government is strengthened in Russia during the reign of Ivan IV ("Ivan the Terrible").
1540	Spanish nobleman Ignatius Loyola founds the Jesuits, a leading religious order of the Catholic Reformation.
1556–1605	Akbar the Great rules in South Asia, transforming the Mughal state into a powerful empire.
1564–1616	William Shakespeare lives in England as a playwright and poet.
1587–1629	The Safavid empire of Persia comes to full flower under the reign of Shah Abbas.
1600–1616	Tokugawa Ieyasu, founder of the Tokugawa shogunate, rules in Japan.

Please see end of book reference section for additional reading suggestions related to this chapter.

18 The Expanding Global Economy: Expectations and Inequalities

1550-1700

This map of the thriving port of Manila circa 1650, painted on the lid of a wooden chest, is centered on the fortified area reserved for Spaniards. Other foreigners and Filipinos lived outside the city walls.

Every day, oil tankers and freighters pass through the channel that connects Manila Bay in the Philippines to the South China Sea. With thousands of stacked shipping containers sprawling over the waterfront, the city of Manila at the eastern end of the bay is one of the busiest ports in the world. It is also a culturally diverse city of more than twenty million people of Filipino, Chinese, Spanish, American, South Asian, and variously mixed ancestry. Four centuries ago, Manila was not so different, though much smaller. Founded by the Spanish explorer Miguel López de Legazpi in 1571, the town blossomed quickly into a major emporium. According to a seventeenth-century Italian traveler, it was "so equally situated between the wealthy kingdoms of the east and west, that it may be accounted one of the greatest places of trade in the world."[1]

Manila attracted merchants from many lands for one reason. Every year, a large vessel arrived from Acapulco, Mexico, loaded with silver from American mines. According to the official register, the cargo for 1602, 316,250 pounds of silver bars and coins. was valued at five million pesos.[2] Spanish merchants traded this specie for the silk garments, cotton cloths, gold, jewelry, porcelain, perfumes, and fine spices that both Asian and European sea traders brought to the port. Dockworkers packed the Acapulco ship with these wares, and it sailed back across the Pacific to Mexico. There, merchants came from New Spain (Mesoamerica), the Caribbean islands, and the Viceroyalty of Peru to buy the Asian cargo at a giant fair. Some of the goods were consumed in the Americas and some transshipped across the Atlantic to Europe. Meanwhile, other merchants carried silver from Manila to China and the lands around the Indian Ocean rim.

With the inauguration of the Manila galleons, which directly linked the Americas with Asia, the last big connection in the global chain of commerce was put in place. After 1572, shipping lanes joined all of the inhabited continents (except Australia) and all the major oceans to one another. By the end of the seventeenth century, it was no surprise to see French aristocrats donning beaver hats from Canada, West African farm women wearing Indian cottons, and Egyptian merchants dining on Chinese porcelain. Silver coins and ingots from American mines streamed across every sea, passed through every port, and lubricated the entire network of exchange. In the later sixteenth and the seventeenth centuries, as one historian has written, "Money went around the world and made the world go round."[3]

The first part of this chapter describes advances in shipping technology and mercantile organization that made possible the emergence of a globe-encircling network of exchange. It also investigates major economic and demographic consequences of the linkup between Afroeurasia and the Americas. In Chapter 16, we described the early and cataclysmic effects of that linkage on Native Americans, who perished by the millions from exposure to previously unknown Afroeurasian diseases. Here, we explore the continuing transoceanic exchange of plants and animals, a phenomenon whose biological and social effects worldwide dawned only gradually on human consciousness in the sixteenth and seventeenth centuries. Finally, we survey the early global exchange of American silver and its part in shaping a world economy.

The second section examines events in Afroeurasia in the later sixteenth and the seventeenth centuries in relation to the developing global exchange system. We first focus on Europe, a region that had occupied the far western edge of the Afroeurasian network but after 1492 was transformed into a hub of world trade. American silver poured into Europe, with

• • •

both beneficial and negative effects on the region's economy. We then move across the hemisphere to East Asia, looking at economic developments in both China and Japan, the first an importer and the second an exporter of tons of silver. Finally, we focus on Afroeurasia's long-distance trade, both the maritime routes of the Indian Ocean and China seas and the ancient silk roads. The advent of trade between Afroeurasia and the Americas strengthened rather than diminished Asia's already mature commercial economy.

In the third section we return to the Atlantic basin, where European entrepreneurs and trading companies acquired rights to land or commerce from their governments and then proceeded to exploit lucrative trade in furs and hides in North America and to set up commercial plantations in northeastern Brazil, the Caribbean, and other warm lowland areas. Plantations required great concentrations of labor, which depleted American Indian societies could not supply. We explore also in this section why New World capitalists turned to African slaves rather than Europeans to solve their labor problems. Finally, we investigate the circumstances under which Africans came to participate in the global economy in a way that enriched rulers and merchants but that inflicted misery on millions more.

A Panoramic View

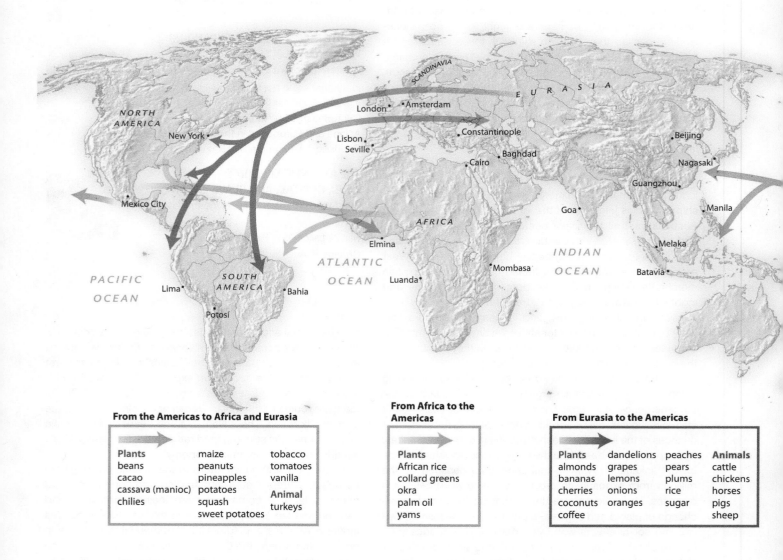

From the Americas to Africa and Eurasia

Plants
beans
cacao
cassava (manioc)
chilies
maize
peanuts
pineapples
potatoes
squash
sweet potatoes
tobacco
tomatoes
vanilla

Animal
turkeys

From Africa to the Americas

Plants
African rice
collard greens
okra
palm oil
yams

From Eurasia to the Americas

Plants
almonds
bananas
cherries
coconuts
coffee
dandelions
grapes
lemons
onions
oranges
peaches
pears
plums
rice
sugar
Animals
cattle
chickens
horses
pigs
sheep

MAP 18.1 The global diffusion of plants and animals, sixteenth to eighteenth centuries.
The Columbian Exchange had a profound effect on human diets. Can you locate the origins of the ingredients of one of your favorite meals?

The Global Network Takes Shape

FOCUS What historical evidence shows that a globe-encircling economy was emerging in the sixteenth and seventeenth centuries?

The great global convergence that started near the end of the fifteenth century proceeded gradually. Within a few decades of Columbus's voyages, sea captains discovered how to sail regularly back and forth between western Europe and both the Caribbean Sea and the Indian Ocean. But as of 1550, only two explorers, Giovanni Verrazano sailing for France and Esteban Gómez for Spain, had explored the length of North America's Atlantic seaboard. Spain and Portugal had barely started to organize their American empires or even to ªdiscover° much of the land that they claimed for themselves. Only four Spanish expeditions had crossed the Pacific.

The era of blind probing from one island or stretch of sea to another, however, ended shortly. Shipwrights steadily improved vessel technology. Governments and merchants set up exploration and trading organizations. Infectious pathogens continued to kill American Indians, but by the early seventeenth century the transoceanic exchange of plants and animals began to have the opposite effect on Afroeurasia. There, new food crops increased supplies and improved nutrition, contributing to accelerating population growth. Shortly after 1550, Spanish entrepreneurs also began to extract silver from stupendously rich mines in Mexico and South America. This development, more than any other, jumpstarted the worldwide economy.

Technology and Organization for Global Exchange

In Chapter 16 we described the advances in ship design and navigation that allowed European sea captains to penetrate the Indian Ocean and cross the Atlantic. But before oceanic trade could become routinely profitable, shipwrights had to build vessels that efficiently combined size and strength with speed and maneuverability, while at the same time reducing production costs. Regular global commerce also required continuous advances in naval armament, navigational skills, geographical knowledge, provisioning methods for long voyages, and reliable sources of money to finance and insure complex and risky operations. In Europe, governments took the lead in organizing sea trade, but large international companies came to dominate exchange in the seventeenth century.

Ships. The type of ship known as the caravel, which carried the first generations of Atlantic explorers, was not adequate for repeated transoceanic voyages. But naval architects rose to the challenge, first in Spain and Portugal, then in northwestern Europe and along the coasts of Asia. Sharing design knowledge from port to port, shipwrights built vessels that were not only stronger but also more cost-efficient because they required smaller crews and therefore fewer provisions, which left more room for paying cargo. The multidecked carrack served as the workhorse of bulk transport between Europe and distant shores from about 1500 to 1630. Those vessels, however, were slow and difficult to maneuver in bad weather. The **galleon**, developed in the later sixteenth century, represented a key advance. It combined the long, narrow hull of the medieval galley and the sails of the caravel with the imposing mass of the carrack. A strong frame allowed galleons to support both bulky cargos and heavy artillery mounted to fire from gun ports on each side of the hull.

> **galleon** A large, multidecked sailing vessel used for both war and commerce from the sixteenth to the eighteenth century.

Toward the end of the sixteenth century, shipbuilders in the Netherlands introduced the *fluyt*, or fly boat. Constructed of cheaper wood than galleons required, this vessel had a flat bottom, shorter masts, smaller sails, and fewer guns. It required half the crew of a galleon and half the money to build and operate. Though *fluyts* were slow, merchants used them profitably to haul high-volume commodities like timber, grain, fish, and salt. In the seventeenth century, they dominated the shipping lanes of northern Europe and, owing to their cargo capacity, typically returned large profits to their owners.

Trading companies. European governments and private capitalists collaborated in a variety of ways to expand seaborne commercial operations. Early in the sixteenth century, the Portuguese crown founded the House of India (*Casa da India*) to assert control over transoceanic trade. The Spanish government created the House of Trade (*Casa de Contratación*). These institutions compiled nautical information, trained pilots, registered cargo, inspected ships, collected duties, and enforced maritime laws. Through the House of India, Portugal exercised a monopoly on many spices and precious metals imported from Africa and Asia, selling these goods at a fixed price in Lisbon and reaping most of the profits. The Spanish House of Trade functioned more like a regulatory agency than a state-owned business, issuing licenses to private traders. A separate merchant guild settled disputes among traders and controlled access to commerce by restricting membership.

In the later sixteenth century, England experimented with a different form of commercial organization. The crown granted charters to companies that awarded them monopoly rights to trade or plant settlers in specific regions. Though having many of the same functions as the two Iberian institutions, the English entities were private firms that hired captains and crews. A strict division was maintained between managers, who ran the company, and investors,

A *fluyt* and other vessels in stormy seas. This seventeenth-century painting of Dutch coastal shipping shows the stern of a three-masted *fluyt*. The lateen-rigged third mast is not flying a sail. Other large ships are indistinctly visible in the distance, suggesting a busy shipping lane, where oceangoing vessels were provisioned and serviced by smaller craft, including the rowboat in the foreground. Why do you think so many different kinds of boats were used in seventeenth-century shipping?

chartered company A type of corporation in which the state granted specific rights and obligations to private investors to engage in exploration, commerce, or colonization.

who supplied capital and received dividends (shares of profit).

The English **chartered company** model soon spread to the Netherlands, France, Sweden, Denmark, Italy, and, eventually, even to Spain and Portugal. Stock markets that traded shares in chartered companies emerged in Amsterdam and London. In fact, a financial transformation began to take place in Europe as aristocrats and other affluent individuals redirected some of their capital from land, traditionally the principal source of wealth, to stocks, commodities, slaves, and other forms of investment associated with international trade.

The Continuing Columbian Exchange

When human beings began to cross the Atlantic to the Americas in the later fifteenth century, they brought all sorts of living organisms with them, from wheat and dandelions to horses, honeybees, brown rats, and, as we have seen, measles and smallpox. When people made the return trip, they introduced American organisms to Afroeurasia, including maize, potatoes, tomatoes, turkeys, rattlesnakes, and the bacterium that causes syphilis. In time the Columbian Exchange produced a worldwide biological revolution, though some organisms found niches in new environments much later than others. For example, European weeds began to crowd out native plants on Caribbean islands shortly after Columbus arrived. By contrast, the climbing vine called kudzu, native to Japan, did not begin to overrun the southeastern United States until the 1870s. North American raccoons made homes for themselves in Europe only in the mid-twentieth century.

Afroeurasian biota in the Americas. Columbus and the voyagers who followed him introduced many new plant and animal species to the Caribbean and Mesoamerica without thinking they were abetting a biological revolution (see Map 18.1). Ships had to carry enough food to sustain crews for months, so sailors kept live chickens, pigs, and cattle in their cargo holds, slaughtering them for meals as needed. Some of these animals survived the voyage and began immediately to multiply on land, frequently escaping their human owners, running into forests and swamps, and reverting to a feral, or wild, state. Within eight years of Columbus's first voyage, European pigs, which in that era looked more like wild boars than today's farm hogs, infested the island of Hispaniola and competed with indigenous animals for food.

Early colonizers also brought food plants on their ships in order to grow familiar homeland crops, wherever natural conditions permitted, rather than experiment with strange American ones. They understood how to cook Old World foods, preferred their taste, and knew they would not be poisoned by them. On his second voyage, Columbus introduced seeds or cuttings of chickpeas, melons, onions, radishes, lettuce, cabbage, and cauliflower, all of which eventually spread across the Western Hemisphere. Subsequent travelers imported bananas and rice, both of which became staples in tropical America. Grapevines and olive trees flourished in the coastal valleys of Peru and Chile. By the middle of the sixteenth century, Mexico grew so much wheat that it began exporting it to other regions. Old World cultural obligations might dictate the introduction of particular foods. For example, Europeans in America grew grapes and wheat partly because they needed wine and unleavened bread to celebrate the Catholic mass. Wherever Europeans established their dominance over Native Americans, they put them to work raising Afroeurasian crops and herds compatible with local climates. But Indians rarely added wheat or other foreign grains to their own diets, any more than early European colonizers wished to eat maize unless they had no alternative.

Livestock came to America with Europeans but then swarmed out ahead of them. Feral pigs made their homes on every island and coastal lowland they could reach. By the end of the sixteenth century, hundreds of thousands of cattle and sheep grazed in northern Mexico, and cattle herds doubled in size every year and a half. Cattle also accompanied Spanish conquistadors to Peru, then made their way through Andean mountain passes to the grasslands of Argentina. When Spanish settlers founded Buenos Aires in 1580, they found the surrounding area already teeming with cattle, perhaps forty-eight million of them by 1700. Horses followed a similar trajectory. Observing the herds near Tucumán in Argentina, one chronicler wrote, ª They cover the face of the earth, and, when they cross the road, it is necessary for travelers to wait and let them pass, for a whole day or more.º 4

Europeans also brought species to America that neither they nor Native Americans wanted. These included various weedsÐ ferns, thistles, nettles, clover, and bluegrassÐ which invaded open spaces and stifled native vegetation. A most unwelcome import was various species of rats. These rodents multiplied faster than cattle and hogs and easily threatened village food supplies. By devouring grain, rats

Embarcadero de los Cavallos.

Loading horses for the voyage to the Americas. This engraving from about 1550 shows the precision required and risks involved in shipping livestock across the Atlantic. Given the difficulties, why would Spaniards have taken the trouble to transport large animals such as horses and cattle?

nearly forced early colonizers at both Buenos Aires and Jamestown, Virginia, to abandon their settlements. The chronicler Garcilaso de la Vega reported from Peru that they ª bred in infinite numbers, overran the land, and destroyed the crops.º 5

American foods in Afroeurasia. Though initially reluctant to try American foods, Europeans brought many back to their homelands. These included plants that added variety, color, and spice to humdrum diets, including tomatoes, chilies, avocadoes, pineapples, and cacao beans. They also introduced plants that in time became nutritious and calorie-rich staples, notably maize, potatoes, sweet potatoes, and manioc (cassava). By the seventeenth century, these foods and others began to have profound effects on Afroeurasia's demography and dietary culture.

Columbus carried maize to Spain in 1493, and within another century, it became a major food crop for both humans and domestic animals throughout Iberia and in parts of France and Italy. Poor families in those regions gradually incorporated maize into their traditional porridge. Venetian merchants introduced maize to the Ottoman empire. It thrived in several parts of Southwest Asia, in Egypt, and in the Balkan Peninsula, where in the eighteenth century it became a staple crop.

European peasants resisted potatoes for more than a century, not knowing that these tubers produced more calories and a greater variety of nutrients per acre of land than the grains to which they were accustomed. By the 1600s, however, impoverished Irish farmers discovered that they could increase their health and extend their life on a daily diet of hardly anything other than potatoes and milk. In that century and the next, potato cultivation spread across the northern half of Europe, where climate and soils favored it. Even aristocrats served potatoes boiled, baked, or mashed at their lordly tables.

Iberian sailors introduced American food plants to parts of Afroeurasia besides Europe. Manioc, a root crop native to tropical America, has nutritional value mainly in vitamins, and the variety known as bitter manioc had to be specially processed to leech out poisons. But the plant is hardy and productive. From Brazil it encircled the globe, becoming an important food in tropical Africa, Southeast Asia, and southern China. Chinese farmers also began growing American maize, sweet potatoes, and peanuts early in the sixteenth century. Peasants planted sweet potatoes in northern and central highland regions of China where rice did not flourish, thereby enriching Chinese diets and sometimes cheating famine. Cultivators also learned how to rotate rice crops with peanuts, a nourishing legume, to improve soil fertility.

American staple crops added nutritional variety to Afroeurasian diets and bolstered immune systems. For example, in Ireland, where the mostly rural population began eating potatoes, the population rose by more than 450 percent, from about 1.5 to 8.5 million between 1600 and 1800. If a society could grow more than one staple, both potatoes and wheat for example, they might in years of bad weather lose one harvest but not the other, thereby averting hunger. Historians do not doubt that American foods contributed mightily to Afroeurasia's accelerating population growth after 1500.

Showers of silver. Ships returning from America to Europe also carried shiny metal. Europeans who went to the Americas found gold in several regions, but they discovered whole mountains of silver. This metal was a material commodity like any other, but rulers turned much of it into coins, which animated commercial transactions around the world. Between 1550 and 1800, Mexico and Peru produced 150,000 tons of the metal, more than 80 percent of the world's supply.[6]

Three factors were instrumental in launching the sixteenth-century silver boom. First, in 1545 prospectors uncovered an enormous deposit near Potosí, a site located in the highlands of Bolivia at an altitude of more than 13,000 feet. The following year, they found another lode near Zacatecas in north central Mexico. Second, miners initially used a German smelting process that worked well only for high-grade ore. In the 1560s, however, Spanish technicians invented a new method that involved spreading crushed silver ore on flat areas, or ªpatiosº and laboriously mixing it with mercury, water, salt, and copper sulfate. The silver metal and the mercury eventually formed an amalgam, which was then heated to drive off the mercury. Just as this process was being developed, prospectors discovered a large mercury source at Huancavelica in Peru. Transporting mercury to Potosí, mine owners sharply reduced costs and accelerated production. The third factor is that Francisco de Toledo, the Spanish viceroy of Peru, introduced a conscription labor system called the *mita* in order to exploit the mines to their full potential. Andean Indian villages had to supply a certain number of people each year to work at Huancavelica or Potosí. These people trekked long distances to the mines, where they worked in rotating shifts as excavators, carriers, millers, and refiners. Though legally free, they received little compensation and worked in harsh, life-threatening conditions. After visiting Huancavelica in 1616, the Catholic friar and missionary Antonio Vazquez de Espinosa reported:

> The [mercury] ore was very rich black flint, and the excavation so extensive that it held more than 3,000 Indians working away hard with picks and hammers, breaking up that flint ore; and when they have filled their little sacks, the poor fellows, loaded down with ore, climb up those ladders or rigging. . . . Those who carry out the reduction of this ore have to be very careful and test cautiously; . . . otherwise they may easily get mercury poisoning and if they do, they are of no further use; their teeth fall out, and some die.º[7]

Silver production involved a division of labor between government and private interests. Most silver mines and smelters were privately owned, but the Spanish crown controlled the mercury supply and impounded one-fifth of the processed silver in addition to taxes and duties. The imperial authorities also required all silver to pass through the official mints in Potosí or Mexico City to be cast into ingots or coins and stamped with the royal seal. This allowed officials to certify purity and collect the king's share. Not surprisingly, miners and merchants circumvented these regulations whenever possible. Illegal shipments may have surpassed the registered exports.

Silver flowed out of the mining regions by different routes (see Map 18.2). Pack animals hauled loads from Potosí to the coast of Peru, ships carried the cargo to Panama, and more animals lugged it across the isthmus to the Caribbean. From there, armed galleons transported it to Spain. Silver from the Zacatecas mines went overland to Mexico

Harsh labor in a Potosí silver mine. Potosí became one of the largest cities in the world in the seventeenth century. This 1602 image by Theodore de Bry, however, shows us not crowds in a booming city but Native American peasants working deep underground to extract silver for capitalist entrepreneurs. A prolific illustrator, de Bry's engravings provided many Europeans with their only glimpse of the Americas. How would you characterize his depiction of work in the mines?

City, and then from the port of Veracruz to Europe. The Manila galleon runs started in 1572. Meanwhile, smuggled silver poured out of both Mexico and South America. An estimated 15 to 30 percent of Potosí's metal left by an illegal °back door° that ran from Bolivia southeastward along the Rio de la Plata (River of Silver) to the Atlantic and the holds of waiting ships of various European origins.[8]

Afroeurasia and the Expanding World Economy

FOCUS What effects did global communication and exchange have on societies of Afroeurasia in the sixteenth and seventeenth centuries?

Many Afroeurasian societies experienced remarkable economic and demographic growth between 1500 and 1650. A factor in northern Eurasia may have been modest climatic warming. The northern hemispheric cooling cycle called the Little Ice Age (see Chapter 15) lasted from the thirteenth to the nineteenth century, but within that phase weather patterns fluctuated from one decade to another. Northern temperatures rose two or three degrees Celsius in the later fifteenth and the sixteenth centuries. That trend brought more frequent years of warm, dry weather and improved farming conditions in northern latitudes, including China and Europe. Following the serious demographic decline of the fourteenth century, the populations of both regions surged in the sixteenth, China by around twenty-five million, Europe by five million. In all of Afroeurasia, numbers rose from around 418 to 545 million. Since the population of the Americas plunged in the same period, something close to 98 percent of all human beings lived in Afroeurasia as of 1600.[9]

In some regions, rising population meant potentially larger work forces and armies. In turn, generous state spending to build military assets and strategic industries

MAP 18.2 Global flows of silver in the seventeenth century.
Silver flowed both east and west from American mines. Can you think of finished goods or other commodities that circled the globe in both directions in the seventeenth century?

reinforced the upward economic trend. Indicators of this prosperity in densely populated regions included proliferation of rural market towns, increasing job specialization in manufacturing, more widespread use of money, and more sophisticated commercial institutions such as banks. The flow of silver from American mines also greatly stimulated money-based market exchanges.

Western Europe's Economic Surge

The first Portuguese ship laden with Indian pepper docked at Antwerp on the North Sea in 1501, and American silver began flowing into the Spanish port of Seville in the 1530s. But in fact Europe's remarkable economic expansion after 1450 had more to do with regional developments than with overseas trade. Population growth was a fundamental factor. Similarly to China, Europe began to recover from the huge epidemic-related mortality of the previous hundred years. The population plunge had made more farm land available, and that in turn allowed food production to grow faster than population, raising living standards again. Longer growing seasons associated with the temporary easing of the Little Ice Age also contributed to higher farm yields. In the sixteenth century, the population from the Atlantic to Russia surged from about 80 to 100 million. As in China, the growth rate slowed in the late 1500s, accelerating again after 1700.

In 1500, 90 to 95 percent of Europe's people lived in country villages and hamlets, but cities of twenty thousand or more began to multiply. By the end of the century, about 2.5 million people lived in the region's thirty-one largest cities, most of them located either in northwestern Europe or northern Italy. Antwerp, the most important northern center of commerce and banking until about 1570, reached a population of 100,000. Paris, the capital of the expanding French monarchy, grew from about 100,000 to 510,000 between 1500 and 1700, London from 40,000 to 575,000 in the same period.[10] The Netherlands, where Amsterdam replaced Antwerp as the chief financial center in the late 1500s, became the most densely urbanized part of Europe. Hundreds of miles of canals linked the region's towns with one another. Elegant homes and public buildings lined urban canals, and in the 1660s, street lights began to flicker on in the major centers.

Europe's growing markets. The sixteenth-century population surge magnified demand for food, fuel, clothing, and an array of manufactures. In response, entrepreneurs and commercial farmers put disposable wealth into many new capitalist ventures. Merchants moved goods from one part of Europe to another, taking advantage of the region's many navigable rivers for cheap inland transport. English and Spanish landlords raised sheep and exported wool. Scandinavian enterprisers mined copper and iron and

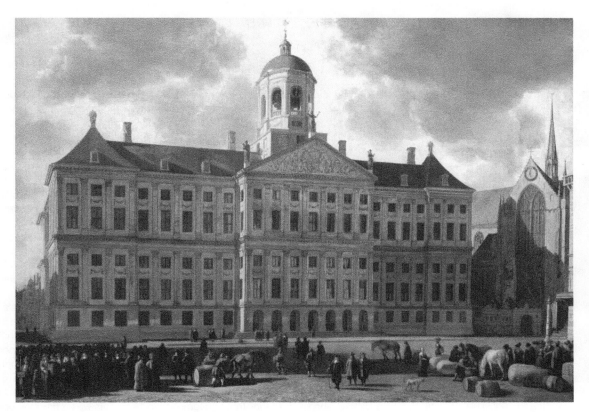

Urban revival in Europe. Gerrit Berckheyde's oil painting *The Town Hall in Amsterdam* (1673) reveals aspects of urban growth and concentrated wealth during the Dutch golden age. The size of the building, its imposing location on the city's main square, and the great cost of imported sandstone for the exterior walls and marble for the interior express the wealth and political clout of the merchant elite. The Town Hall casts a shadow on the Nieuwe Kerk (New Church), while market activity takes place in the square. What do you think the painting reveals about relationships among political, economic, and religious power in Dutch urban life?

felled trees for lumber and charcoal. Knitting, a technology developed centuries earlier in Muslim lands, became an important European industry, especially production of vividly colored stockings. Genoa and other northern Italian cities made fine silk fabrics. Dutch workshops turned out woolen and linen textiles, glassware, printed books, seagoing ships, and beer. Dutch *fluyts* moved bulk cargos of grain, timber, sugar, fish, and wine around the Baltic and the North Seas and into the Atlantic.

Europe needed to grow more grain, but in the western regions small farmers found it harder to acquire land, partly because of increasing population density and partly because many estate lords wanted to turn arable land into pasture to make money raising cattle and sheep for the market. One solution was to transform swamps and marshes into cropland. Ambitious drainage projects got under way, for example, in the Netherlands and in the low-lying area of southeastern England called the Fens. Farmers in northwestern Europe also had great success intensifying production, that is, coaxing greater yields out of a given acreage. One key innovation was the four-field rotation system. One field was devoted to turnips or other crops to feed animals; a second one to alfalfa, clover, or other nitrogen-fixing plants to reinvigorate the soil; and the third and fourth to different grain crops. This strategy also involved more efficient ways of collecting domestic animal manure to fertilize crops. Raising productivity required hard work of all family members. Men and boys did most of the heavy labor, while women and girls gathered grain, looked after animals, and processed food. Waterwheels and windmills supplemented human or animal energy in much of Europe, though agricultural technology did not change radically in the early modern centuries. Meanwhile, in eastern Europe and Russia, aristocratic land-owners found new opportunity to grow grain specifically for export to western Europe, where new city dwellers and wage workers had to buy all their food.

The inflationary spiral. Despite Europe's remarkable economic growth, the gap between affluent minorities

Louis De Geer: A Capitalist Success Story

David Beck's 1649 portrait of Louis De Geer.

The career of Louis De Geer (1587–1652) nicely illustrates European economic dynamism in the early seventeenth century. Born in the Habsburg-ruled city of Liège in what is today Belgium, De Geer moved with his family to the young United Netherlands in 1595. Learning both business and copper making, he established himself as a merchant and financier before he was thirty. In 1615 he settled in Amsterdam, the energetic center of the Dutch economy. He also forged strong business ties with Elias Trip, his brother-in-law, and several other Trip relatives.

In 1618 the conflict known later as the Thirty Years' War broke out. This brutal struggle, which initially pitted Habsburg Catholics against Protestant princes, spread across central Europe, pulling in economically poor Sweden. The war generated huge demand for firearms. Sweden's king Gustavus Adolphus (reigned 1611–1632) needed badly to find ways to finance land and naval forces. Seizing an attractive opportunity, De Geer and Trip extended the king a series of loans, made payments on behalf of the Swedish government, and armed and equipped the royal army. Other private Dutch investors and manufacturers also fueled Sweden's economic expansion, as well as its emergence as an important European military power.

Gustavus Adolphus repaid loans from De Geer and Trip in a variety of ways but rarely directly. Rather, he awarded De Geer monopolies on the copper and iron trades and allowed him to lease agricultural lands and set up a foundry in eastern Sweden. De Geer's complex business interests came to include gun sales, armament works, textile and paper mills, shipping wharves, a brewery, and metal foundries. In fact, De Geer and his Trip associates emerged as arguably the largest weapons traders in Europe, supplying Sweden, Venice, France, England, German states, and the United Netherlands with ships, artillery, muskets, bullets, grenades, and gunpowder.

Although De Geer kept a home in Amsterdam where his wife and children lived, he acquired Swedish citizenship in 1627. Thereafter, he continued moving between Amsterdam and Sweden, attending to his businesses in both locations and caring for his family after his wife died giving birth to their sixteenth child.

In 1640 he applied for recognition as a Swedish nobleman, another good strategic move. Only as a titled aristocrat could he legally own land and pass it to his children. Otherwise, his holdings would revert to the crown upon his death. His request was granted, and he soon became one of Sweden's biggest landholders. In addition to his many other business ventures, he organized and financed the Swedish African Company in 1647. This was a firm that operated under a royal charter. One of De Geer's last projects was sponsorship of a plan to found a joint Dutch-Swedish colony on the West African coast, though the scheme had little success.

De Geer died in 1652, a stupendously rich nobleman. He sired two aristocratic families, one in Sweden, the other in the Netherlands, and both lineages maintained their lucrative relations with the Swedish and Dutch governments for centuries. Political merchants like Louis de Geer personify an age in which power and profit, war and trade, government projects and private initiatives were intricately linked together.

Thinking Critically

In what ways do you think Louis De Geer's career illustrates the partnership between government and private capitalist interests in seventeenth-century Europe?

and the rest of the population yawned wider. Production of basic commodities like bread and firewood failed to keep pace with demand as the population rose. This drove prices relentlessly upward, a phenomenon of monetary **inflation** that historians call the **price revolution.** The continuing influx of silver into Europe also gradually reduced its value, along with that of gold and copper coins. From month to month, therefore, consumers had to spend more coins for a single loaf of bread. Some governments tried to cut military and administrative spending by debasing

inflation A rise in the general level of prices of goods and services in a society over time. Rising inflation means that the purchasing power of a given unit of currency declines.

price revolution A period of sustained inflation in Europe in the sixteenth and seventeenth centuries.

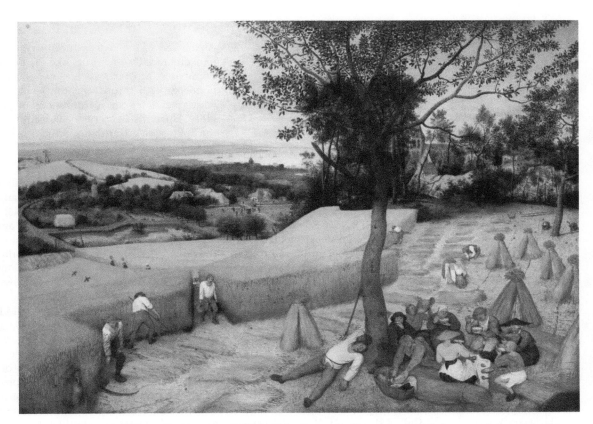

Agricultural life in rural Europe. *The Harvesters* (1565) by Pieter Bruegel the Elder was one of six large panels the celebrated artist painted to depict the seasons. The series originally hung in the home of a wealthy Antwerp merchant. The impression of abundance in this image comes not only from the lush wheat harvest but also from the scene of peasants resting for a meal, the agricultural activity in the background, and the view of commercial ships anchored in the distant bay. How would you compare the portrayal of people engaging in labor in this painting with the depiction on page 521?

coins, that is, by diluting their precious metal content without changing their value. This tactic worked only in the short term because devalued coins bought fewer loaves of bread than fully valued ones, pushing up prices even more.

Except in unusually prosperous regions around big cities, population growth coupled with rising prices made ordinary men and women poorer (see Figure 18.7). Since more people competed to sell their labor, estate lords and urban employers could keep down wages and also raise rents and fees on tenants. The ranks of day laborers and jobless folk consequently swelled. On family farms women often did almost all the work because husbands and sons went off to find wage jobs to bring in food. Although the practice of legally binding men and women to work on a particular estate (serfdom) nearly disappeared from western Europe by the sixteenth century, it actually grew in eastern Europe and Russia. There, the aristocratic class, which dominated government, got expanded legal rights to force peasants to stay put rather than freely sell their labor for wages or resettle on open land. That way, landlords retained the workers

Consumer prices in grams of silver

The "price revolution" in Europe. Why do you think inflation was higher in Antwerp than in London or Valencia?

that brought them fortunes exporting grain. Throughout Europe, governments also raised taxes on ordinary people to finance increasingly expensive armies and bureaucracies. The masses, however, did not necessarily accept their growing impoverishment. Urban bread riots, peasant uprisings, and soldier rampages repeatedly jolted the ruling and moneymaking classes.

Shifting wealth and conflicts across Europe. During the sixteenth century, the geographical center of concentrated wealth in Europe moved gradually northward from Iberia to the Netherlands, France, and England. Spain became immensely rich early in the century, but its silver bonanza turned to stone. The Spanish Habsburg kings Charles V (r. 1519±1556) and Philip II (r. 1556±1598) disposed of huge amounts of silver to pay down debts incurred in European wars and to buy textiles, wine, guns, and other wares to ship to the American empire. ª[Silver] falls on Spain as does rain on a roof,° wrote a Venetian diplomat. ª It pours on her and then flows away.° [11] The Habsburg drive to dominate both Europe and America, including the ill-fated naval armada launched in 1588 to invade England, led the state into bottomless debt. Silver migrated steadily to England, the Netherlands, and northern Italy where entrepreneurs invested it in manufacturing, European trade, and commercial ventures abroad.

The Habsburg dynasty also became immersed in a particularly brutal struggle that engulfed much of Europe between 1618 and 1648. Called the Thirty Years' War, the conflict devastated large areas of Habsburg-ruled Germany. The conflict began as a Habsburg campaign to suppress German princes who had become Protestants. It ballooned, however, into a pan-European war that drew in France, Spain, the Netherlands, Poland, Sweden, and the Ottoman empire. The fighting degenerated into a vicious central European free-for-all as famines, epidemics, and roving mercenary bands stalked the region.

The war nearly wrecked Germany's agricultural and urban economy, and it so exhausted Europe's rulers that they finally agreed to a general settlement. In the Peace of Westphalia, a series of treaties signed in 1648, the Habsburgs gave up their ambition to dominate the German princes. More broadly, rulers agreed to stabilize their mutual frontiers, and they accepted the idea that sovereign states should determine the religion of their own realms. This accord reinforced the principle of territorial sovereignty that has guided international relations ever since: States should regard one another as equals in diplomatic dealings and should not interfere in one another's internal affairs. Following the war, religious passions also subsided, and Europeans generally accepted the reality of multiple Christian denominations rather than a single all-embracing church. Regional wars continued after 1648 but usually on a smaller scale. Only near the end of the century, however, did a new cycle of population and economic growth set in.

Centuries of Silver in East Asia

At the end of the sixteenth century, China, Korea, and Japan embraced something like 30 percent of the world's population. Most of East Asia experienced remarkable economic growth throughout that century. China expanded its market economy in conditions of general political stability. Japan also experienced steady growth, even though the Tokugawa government, which took power shortly after 1600, adopted policies that strictly limited the country's participation in world trade.

China the ªsilver sink.° Like Europe, China moved into a new expansionary cycle in the later fifteenth century. In 1600 the Ming dynasty (1368±1644) ruled somewhere between 125 and 150 million people, and its demographic center continued to shift from the semiarid north toward the rainier rice-growing south. If an orbiting satellite could have produced a map of nighttime city lights in East Asia in the sixteenth century, it would have revealed a belt of illumination extending from Beijing in the north all the way to the southeastern coast. The light would have shone brightest in the densely urbanized lower Yangzi River valley. In the vast and dimly lit rural regions, industrious peasants, like their counterparts in northeastern Europe, coaxed high yields of grain from small plots of land using intensive labor methods. Silk and cotton production expanded in the Yangzi valley. Near the southern coast, sugar cane (an Afroeurasian crop) and tobacco (a new American one) boomed as commercial commodities.

The limited economic information we have suggests that China's population enjoyed life expectancies and living standards as high as people anywhere in the world. Most rural villagers and town dwellers wore warm clothing, consumed nutritious foods, and drank tea. Farm families routinely sold surplus crops in local markets. Nevertheless, even though Ming emperors abolished slave labor and made it harder for estate owners to evict tenants, the elite class lived far better than the masses. As in Europe, Chinese cities harbored large fluctuating populations of criminals, beggars, and underemployed refugees from rural famines or epidemics. Women toiled alongside men to grow and market crops, but few entered the urban labor force except in traditional roles as servants, entertainers, or prostitutes. Women of all classes remained firmly under male supervision.

In the first half of the sixteenth century, the Ming government enforced policies aimed at restricting Chinese participation in international trade. The regime was reluctant to divert public resources from defense of land frontiers. East Asian waters swarmed with Japanese, Malay, and private Chinese ships, plus European carracks, all of them seeking ways, legal or not, to trade for China's silk, tea, porcelain, and dozens of other products in demand across Afroeurasia. Starting in the 1520s, pirates and smugglers, many of them Japanese, repeatedly sacked Chinese ports

Rural life in Ming China. This detail from a Ming-era porcelain vase shows workers watering tea plants. Why might an affluent consumer of a decorative object have valued an image of agricultural work?

In 1551 one of them denounced ᵃunscrupulous merchants who carry away to foreign lands precious commodities of the Middle Kingdom like silk yarn, brocades, damask, cotton, porcelain, and iron, which they exchange not for goods but only for gold and silver.º¹³

Unable to find a workable alternative, the government finally adopted its own silver standard. Beginning in the 1570s it decreed laws, known collectively as the Single Whip Reforms, that converted all tax payments to fixed amounts of silver. In consequence, demand rose even faster. The timing was opportune for the Spanish, whose Pacific galleons were just starting to haul silver between Acapulco on the coast of Mexico and Manila in the Philippines. Some historians have argued that China's unquenchable silver demand allowed Spain to keep its huge American empire intact. If silver were not so cheap at the Potosí and Zacatecas mines and so expensive in China, the Spanish crown would not have reaped enough wealth to fight long wars in Europe and simultaneously pay for its New World colonies.

The silver influx profoundly affected the Chinese economy. The Ming reforms compelled people to pay taxes in silver, but its price kept rising. Consequently, millions of peasant families were hard put to meet their obligations. Many sold more crops and homespun silk or cotton in local markets to acquire coins, and this further stimulated the commercial economy. While the economy continued to expand, living standards for the great majority began to slip. Worse yet, so much metal streamed from American and Japanese mines that the world price began to fall. This meant that the Chinese government got less and less buying power from fixed tax revenues. Then in 1639±1640, silver imports nearly halted owing to political troubles in both Japan and the Philippines. This event sent China's commercial economy into a tailspin, shortly leading to the fall of the Ming and the rise of a new dynasty (see Chapter 19).

Japan and its silver boom. After the founding of the centralized Tokugawa shogunate in 1603 (see Chapter 17), Japan's economy accelerated briskly. Rural men and women converted woodland and dry plains into irrigated rice fields. Market towns multiplied, connected to one another by well-maintained gravel roads. Cargo ships tramped the islands' coasts, carrying rice, metals, and finished goods from one part of the archipelago to another. The Tokugawa encouraged market activity by issuing gold, silver, and copper coins. Japan's population more than doubled in the seventeenth century, from about twelve million to as many as thirty million. Cities also grew in number and size. The greatest were Osaka, a manufacturing and commercial center; Kyoto, the seat of the emperor's court; and Edo (Tokyo), the capital of the shogunate. By the early eighteenth century, Edo was one of the largest cities in the world, with a population of more than one million.

The Ming imperial government formally treated Japan as a subordinate, tributary kingdom like Korea or Vietnam.

and interior towns, exploiting weak coastal security. Manufacturers and merchants who profited from China's robust commercialization appealed to the government to liberalize overseas mercantile policies. Ming forces finally counterattacked the coastal intruders, and in the 1560s agreed to relax trade restrictions on Chinese subjects. It continued, however, to limit the number of ports where foreigners, including Europeans, had permission to enter.

Japanese mines helped ease China's great demand for silver, and in the 1570s American coins and ingots began to flood in. Gomes Solis, a Portuguese merchant, wrote in 1621, ᵃSilver wanders throughout the entire world in its peregrinations before flocking to China, where it remains, as if at its natural center.º¹² Some observers referred to China as a ᵃsinkº into which the world's silver disappeared as into a black hole. But why did Chinese demand for silver soar? The simple answer is that the Ming regime needed a more reliable currency to oil its economy, the world's largest. The government tried to limit money use to paper bills and copper coins, but those currencies easily lost value, causing inflation. Merchants involved in foreign trade much preferred silver. Ming authorities at first bemoaned this metal hunger.

Urban life in Kyoto. This early seventeenth-century decorative screen shows members of the Tokugawa family leaving the Nijo Castle. Tokugawa Ieyasu undertook construction of the castle as a residence for his family in the imperial capital. The fortified compound was situated in the center of the city.

In fact, the relationship between the two states turned mainly on mutually beneficial trade. When the Tokugawa came to power, that trade was doing well. Japanese prospectors discovered major new silver deposits in the early sixteenth century, and the shoguns consolidated their power partly by gaining control of the mines. Technicians began to produce large quantities of high-grade bullion, exporting between 165 and 206 tons of it in the early 1600s. Most of this silver went to China and in larger quantities than the American metal passing through Manila. In return, Japan's affluent classes acquired prestigious Chinese manufactures. Because of difficult political relations, the Ming emperor formally banned direct trade with Japan, but Chinese merchants frequently ignored him.

Early in the sixteenth century, Portuguese and Spanish mariners also turned up in the China seas. They carried silk, sugar, deerskins, and medicines to Japan, exchanging those goods for silver, gold, and copper, which they sold in China or other Asian lands. Iberian Catholic missionaries also reached Japan, and they converted enough souls to establish a strong Christian minority on the southern island of Kyushu. The Tokugawa shoguns wanted to encourage foreign trade. But Catholic clerics, whose followers had plenty of imported guns, began to assert more political influence than the rulers were willing to. In 1613 the government clamped new regulations on foreign residents, prohibited Japanese from traveling abroad, tore down churches, and executed Christians. In 1637 a rural rebellion on Kyushu that displayed Christian symbols to protest famine and government mistreatment prompted closure of all remaining missions and most European trading posts. Legal overseas commerce continued only through a small number of carefully supervised ports. Dutch merchants retained permission to occupy just one entrepôt on a little island in Nagasaki Bay.

The Tokugawa had no desire to cut Japan off from the world economy but rather to ensure that Japanese merchants controlled external trade and that the government harvest its proper share of customs revenue. By the later seventeenth century, however, the silver mines began to give out, leading the shoguns to ban its export. That action reduced foreign trade in general, though the domestic economy continued to grow.

Asians and Europeans in the Southern Seas

European participation in global trade grew slowly for two centuries. Up to 1700 or later, the value of interregional exchange within Afroeurasia far exceeded the value of trans-Atlantic or trans-Pacific trade. Moreover, European captains carried costly spice cargos from Asia to Europe by way of the Cape of Good Hope. This trade, however, had much less value than the exchanges between one big Asian population center and another. In the southern seas, Asian and African sailorsÐ Chinese, Malays, Indians, Persians, Arabs, Ethiopians, and Swahili East AfricansÐ continued to move merchandise, both luxury wares and bulk commodities like rice, timber, and fish, from port to port.

American and Japanese silver pumped energy into the whole southern seas network. The increasing availability of silver stimulated commercial demand. Consequently, producers of agricultural commodities (rice, pepper, and cinnamon) and manufactures (cottons, silks, ceramics) ratcheted up their supply, employing larger numbers of men and women for wages as farm laborers, spinners, weavers, and potters. Silver, gold, and copper money fabricated in the mints of several states circulated as coins. Cowry shells, which came mainly from the Maldive Islands in the Indian Ocean, were also used as money

in certain regions. Silver set the standard of value for other currencies, including Spanish coins such as ᵃpieces of eightº and gold doubloons. Money coursed through the trade network like blood through veins, though clotting up in regions that ran large trade surpluses, including South Asia. In fact, South Asia, which had little silver, became a ᵃsilver sinkº second only to China.

The Dutch move in. The Portuguese venturers who penetrated the Indian Ocean on carracks bristling with artillery gave Asian and African merchants an economic jolt (see Chapter 16). But the government in Lisbon never had nearly enough vessels or firepower to dominate Asian sea trade. The old circuits were not seriously interrupted, and Portuguese shippers eventually joined the ᵃcountry trade,º transporting goods from port to port in the southern seas without going back to Europe. They employed crews mainly of Asian, African, or mixed origin. Portuguese men who resided in coastal ports also became Asianized, marrying Asian women and producing male children who did the same. Portuguese became a *lingua franca,* or medium of trade and interethnic communication, all around the Indian Ocean rim.

In 1602, merchants in the Netherlands organized the Dutch East India Company, or VOC (Vereenigde Oost-Indische Compagnie), to trade in Asian waters. This joint-stock company operated under the authority of the States General, the governing assembly of the United Netherlands. The States General kept basic control but gave the company a monopoly on Dutch commerce in Asia, as well as the right to use force and negotiate treaties. The Netherlands had a population of less than two million, but, as we have seen, its merchants and manufacturers acquired great wealth and therefore capital for overseas investment.

In the first decade of the seventeenth century, VOC vessels sailed into the Indian Ocean with cannons blazing, as the Portuguese had done a century earlier. The United Netherlands was chronically at war with Spain, and in 1580 a royal succession crisis led to the unification of Spain and Portugal under the Spanish crown, a situation that lasted for sixty years. Consequently, the VOC aimed to destroy the bases of both those states and to seize control of the spice trade. In 1614 the company's governor-general told his board of directors: ᵃYou gentlemen ought to know from experience that trade in Asia should be conducted and

A Spanish doubloon. Gold coins such as this one were among the many currencies that facilitated seventeenth-century trade. The coin is inscribed with the name Philippus V (Philip V) and the date 1714. Philip was king of Spain when the coin was stamped.

maintained under the protection and with the aid of your own weapons, and that those weapons must be wielded with the profits gained by the trade. So trade cannot be maintained without war, nor war without trade.[o 14] In 1619 VOC troops invaded the port of Jakarta on the densely populated Indonesian island of Java. After killing or enslaving most of the population, the Dutch renamed the city Batavia (the Latin name for Holland) and from that base campaigned to monopolize the trade in nutmeg, mace, and cloves from the Moluccas Islands. In 1623 Dutch forces invaded the island of Taiwan, and in 1641 they evicted the Portuguese from the strategic port of Malacca. Eleven years later, the VOC established a way station on the South African coast. That settlement became Cape Town.

The English in South Asia. Founded in 1600, the English East India Company (EIC) was a joint-stock enterprise like the VOC. It spent its early decades in a power struggle with the Dutch over the Indonesian spice trade, and it seized some VOC bases. But soon it turned its attention to South Asia, most of which was part of the powerful Mughal empire (see Chapter 17). The Mughals permitted the EIC to set up a few trading posts on the South Asian coasts.

In 1639 the EIC founded a commercial station, or factory (supervised by an agent called the [a]factor[o]), at Madras (Chennai) on the Bay of Bengal to export Indian cotton textiles. Initially, European merchants acquired finished cloth in exchange for silver and other goods purchased elsewhere in Asia. Gradually, however, they became involved in production, depositing raw cotton and dyes with Indian spinners and weavers, then returning a few months later to collect the cloth. Thousands of rural households joined this production system, transforming the economy around Madras from agriculture to export-driven manufacturing. In the later seventeenth century, the EIC also carved out an enclave at Calcutta in Bengal west of the fertile Ganges River delta. Company officers encouraged local artisans to produce cotton and silk fabrics for export. In the same period, the Mughal state experienced growing political problems, prompting the EIC to fortify and extend its enclaves deeper inland.

A multicentered trading world. Neither the VOC nor the EIC had sufficient military power to dominate the southern seas from end to end or to keep out multiple competitors. The Portuguese held on to most of their Asian ports and kept on trafficking much as before. And several other European states—France, Denmark, Prussia, and Russia among them—formed companies that traded in the Indian Ocean with varying success. Muslim merchants from Gujarat in northwestern India maintained a far-flung trade network. The ports of Manila and Batavia attracted tens of thousands of Chinese merchants and craftworkers. As we have seen, the Tokugawa shogunate severely restricted the Dutch presence in Japan after 1637, and in 1662 the VOC abandoned its colony on Taiwan in the teeth of a Chinese invasion. Only in the Indonesian islands did the Dutch

entrench themselves solidly enough to lay the foundation of a territorial colony. Using brutal tactics such as blocking rice supplies from reaching island populations, the VOC tried to control spice production and trade. Even then, conflict with Indonesia maritime states continued on into the next century. For example, the sultanate of Aceh on the northwestern tip of Sumatra deployed a strong navy armed with cannon supplied by the Ottoman Turkish empire. Aceh repeatedly threatened both Portuguese and Dutch rule at Malacca. The Ming, Mughal, and Safavid empires, the giant Asian territorial monarchies, allowed Europeans to trade, not because they were too weak to prevent it, but because foreign commerce benefited their economies.

Overland Trade on the Silk Roads

Commerce along Inner Eurasia's silk roads continued to flourish in the early modern centuries, though on a much smaller scale than the sea trade. The routes and participants, however, changed significantly. First, long-distance movement of goods from China to the Mediterranean or Europe declined in importance relative to exchanges between neighboring regions. Ming China shipped silks, porcelain, paper, tea, and drugs overland to Central Asia in exchange for horses, sheep, and gems. Important routes also connected Central Asia to Mughal India, carrying foodstuffs like melons, apples, grapes, and almonds that did not grow well in South Asia. Central Asians also sent around 100,000 horses a year to the Mughal cavalry.

Second, trade swelled on Inner Eurasian north±south routes that linked the expanding Russian empire to China, India, Persia, and the Ottoman lands. Bukhara, Samarkand, and other Central Asian cities, loosely associated under the Turkic Uzbek dynasty, operated as key entrepôts. Sable and otter fur, which wealthy urban elites wanted nearly everywhere, led export trade from Russia and Siberia. As the Russian empire grew in population and territory, its rich estate lords and merchants desired more Indian textiles, pepper, and other warm-climate wares. Indian traders founded mercantile communities as far north as Astrakhan at the mouth of the Volga River to mediate this traffic.

The Atlantic Economy: Land, Capital, and Slave Labor

FOCUS What effects did the extensive use of African slave labor in the Americas have on economic and political developments in the lands rimming the Atlantic in the sixteenth and seventeenth centuries?

Before 1492 the Atlantic Ocean was a forbidding frontier. By the end of the seventeenth century, port towns lined its rim, nautical maps described its coastlines in detail, and people and goods moved routinely across it. In those two centuries, the demographic picture on the American side of the rim also changed dramatically. As American Indian populations plunged, Europeans crossed the ocean in growing numbersÐ soldiers, royal officials, missionaries, miners, trappers, artisans, plantation entrepreneurs, and workers. European fortune-seekers did not take long to realize the economic potential of not only silver mountains like Potosí, but also tropical lands where climate and soil offered great potential for commercial agriculture. The pace of European immigration, however, did not come close to meeting the demand for labor, and Native American populations could not fill it. Few Europeans without wealth, useful skills, or specific purpose were eager to migrate to America's tropical latitudes, where hard labor and several tropical diseases likely awaited them. Those who did migrate were mostly men, so in the early centuries the birthrate of Europeans in America remained low. Capitalist planters, however, found the solution to their worker problem by bringing in people from tropical Africa, the only dense pool of labor available on the Atlantic rim other than Europe.

In fact, more Africans than Europeans went to America on a yearly basis from the mid-1500s to the 1830s.[15] Tropical Africans did not wish to volunteer for grueling plantation labor in distant America any more than most European peasants did. European governments or private businesses had no moral or legal authority to enslave fellow Europeans in large numbers and ship them to America. But they could do this to Africans, as long as African elites with power or wealth agreed to cooperate in this enterprise. The Atlantic slave trade thus got under way.

The Atlantic Economy and African Slavery

Portuguese and other Europeans who sailed to Subsaharan Africa in the fifteenth and early sixteenth centuries soon discovered that if they wanted to acquire slaves they would not be able to do it by raiding or invading inland territory. African societies, some with armies, successfully fought back and soon acquired guns to help them do it. Also, tropical diseases, notably malaria and yellow fever, took a horrendous toll on Europeans who visited tropical African coasts. For example, British records show that among employees of the Royal African Company who arrived at West African trading ports between 1695 and 1722, six out of every ten died in the first year and only one ever returned home.[16] Until key medical breakthroughs in the later nineteenth century, Europeans died of diseases in Africa at almost the same rate that Native Americans died of Afroeurasian afflictions in the sixteenth century.

Nevertheless, European merchants ambitious or foolhardy enough to go to West or Central African coasts discovered that they could purchase slaves, along with gold, pepper, and other products, from local sellers in return for textiles and other manufactured goods. In the late fifteenth and early sixteenth centuries, Portuguese vessels carried

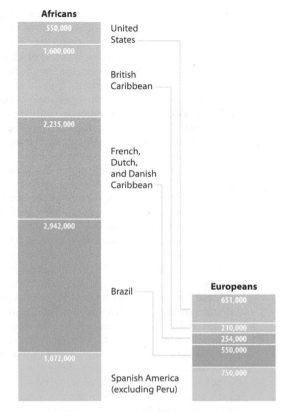

African and European immigration to the Americas, 1500–1820. Which region had the biggest difference between numbers of European and African migrants? Which regions had the greatest parity? What factors explain differences in the numbers of Africans and Europeans migrating to the Americas?

African slaves to the eastern Atlantic islands to perform plantation labor. They also took significant numbers to Europe. In 1550, for example, Lisbon had a population of about 10,000 captive Africans, most of them working as domestic servants, farm laborers, or artisan assistants. After 1520, when European economic exploitation of American territories got seriously under way and demand for labor there grew steadily, slave shippers found no serious technological obstacles to setting sail for Brazil or the Caribbean rather than for the Canary Islands or Portugal.

Why did Africans sell people? In premodern centuries, most agrarian societies in both Afroeurasia and the Americas practiced various forms of **social bondage,** meaning that certain individuals or groups held legal or customary rights to the labor of other people. Many

> **social bondage** A condition in which an individual or a group holds rights to a person's labor or services, whether for a limited period or for a lifetime. Social bondage may take a variety of forms, including slavery, serfdom, or indentured servitude.

societies practiced slavery, defined as the condition of individuals whose lives and labor were at the disposal of others without restriction. Serfdom, common in western Europe down to the fifteenth century, was a type of social bondage, but it had constraints. Masters could not, for example, legally sell serfs as movable property, as they could do with slaves. Also, tens of thousands of Europeans went to the Americas in the sixteenth and seventeenth centuries as bonded, or indentured, servants. Those men and women, typically impoverished or otherwise in desperate straits, agreed to contracts that obligated them to a period of service, often seven years. Their patron paid their passage and agreed to provide food and shelter. Because servants often worked in harsh and unhealthy conditions, many died before their term was up. Indentured servitude was one way for European entrepreneurs or rich families in America to acquire labor, but the numbers never met demand, especially on commercial plantations.

Historians have long debated the history and character of social bondage in Subsaharan Africa. Some scholars contend that slavery was widespread nearly everywhere. Individuals, families, or ruling groups having sufficient wealth accumulated slaves because of the absence of traditions of landed property. Powerful or rich individuals measured their status by how many men and women they controlled rather than by how much land they owned. Land was more abundant in tropical Africa than were potential laborers. Masters made slaves work in a variety of ways, sometimes doing hard farm labor, often serving as domestic servants, artisans, soldiers, or, in the case of women, concubines or wives. Masters also had the right to dispose of their slaves in trade. Because of this practice, Europeans who came to the African coast found they could tap an existing market in ªdisposable persons,º acquiring them in return for manufactured goods.

Critics of this explanation argue that historical evidence for the existence of large numbers of slaves in West and Central Africa in, say, 1450, is limited and questionable. They contend that institutions of social bondage took several different forms and that not all people held in some type of ªunfreeº status should be categorized as slaves. These scholars also claim that if slavery was already extensive in tropical Africa when Europeans first appeared, how could it have expanded so much between the sixteenth and eighteenth centuries, which it clearly did? These historians, rather, see a process in which European merchants began to put great pressure on Africans to sell slaves by offering to buy them at prices that enterprising rulers, well-to-do merchants, and armed kidnappers could not refuse. In other words, if Africans having power and wealth wished to take part in the expanding Atlantic economy, they were going to have to do it partly by selling slaves.

The reign of sugar. From the early sixteenth century, Portuguese merchants contracted with the Spanish crown to supply slaves to its American colonies. By midcentury,

there were about 3,000 Africans in the Viceroyalty of Peru, and within another hundred years, at least 100,000. Another 35,000 lived in New Spain, that is, Spanish North America. In the early empire, African slaves and their descendants lived predominately in towns, working at a variety of jobs, including service in colonial militias. Others toiled in mercury and silver mines.

By the mid-1500s, Europeans also began to open plantations to grow agricultural commodities for the global market, eventually to include sugar, tobacco, indigo, rice, wheat, cotton, cacao, and coffee. In the following two centuries, cane sugar became America's most valuable exportable crop (see Map 18.3). Sugar's journey to the Western Hemisphere was a long one. Farmers probably first domesticated cane in Southeast Asia as many as nine thousand years ago. From there it spread over the millennia to South Asia, where artisans invented processes for making crystalline sugar. From there, it progressed westward to Southwest Asia and from about 1000 C.E. to several Mediterranean islands. The rulers of Aragon in Iberia encouraged cultivation along the western Mediterranean coast, and Muslim land-owners founded a thriving industry in Morocco. By the fifteenth century, cane sugar rivaled honey as a popular sweetener and preservative throughout the Mediterranean basin.

Portuguese, Spanish, and Italian entrepreneurs also planted sugar in the rich volcanic soils of the eastern Atlantic islands. Those growers adopted a set of production methods that combined large capital investment, technically sophisticated mill machinery, tight management, and intensive labor performed increasingly by slaves working in closely supervised gangs. On the island of Madeira, technicians improved the process of extracting sugar juice by crushing cane between horizontal rollers. Workers transferred the sap to copper cauldrons and boiled it down to thick, dark syrup, or molasses. To refine the product further, they poured this liquid into clay vessels, where it dried out gradually, leaving behind solid ªloavesº of tightly packed crystals, ready to be shipped.

In 1485, Portuguese capitalists started planting cane on São Tomé off the Central African coast (see Chapter 16). This successful experiment showed two things. First, planters could harvest and process sugar 1,300 miles from Europe and ship it there for sale at large profit. Second, they could do it entirely with African slave labor, which they obtained from the Kongo kingdom on the nearby mainland. A few decades later, other Portuguese entrepreneurs found that sugar also thrived in northeastern Brazil in conditions of high rainfall and dark rich soil. In a sense, the growing and processing of sugar as an integrated mode of production, including use of African slave labor, was extended from islands on the eastern side of the Atlantic to South America.

When American plantations proved successful, Portuguese shippers began to sail the Atlantic in a triangular pattern. Vessels debarked from Lisbon laden with textiles, metal ware, and other goods. They sailed to one or more African ports, exchanging their cargos for slaves and other

MAP 18.3 The global spread of sugar production.
The world's population developed a taste for this tropical crop. Why do you think it took so much longer for sugar growing to spread across Afroeurasia to the eastern Mediterranean than it took to spread from there to the Americas?

African products. Crossing the Atlantic, they sold their slaves in return for silver, gold, sugar, tobacco, indigo, hides, pearls, and other American merchandise, and then returned to Europe. Brazil seemed to offer endless square miles of fertile land, as well as abundant wood to feed the sugar boilers. As entrepreneurs increased production and improved mill technology, costs declined and profits rose. Trans-Atlantic transport costs also sank as ships came on line that went faster, required smaller crews, and had more cargo space. In 1571 Portugal founded a colony at Luanda on the coast of modern Angola, allying with local Africans to round up captives and bring them to port. From there, captains sailed on trade winds due west to Brazil. Angola soon became the principal source of labor for Portuguese plantations. By 1620, Brazilian mills produced an annual average of 15,000 to 22,000 tons of sugar. Simultaneously, European appetites for sugar began to grow. It provided quick energy to working men and women, and like tea and coffee it was a ᵃdrug food° with mildly addictive properties.

Dutch merchants witnessed the Brazilian bonanza and determined to cut themselves in. In 1621, investors founded the West Indies Company (WIC), a joint-stock firm paralleling the VOC. At first the WIC attacked Portuguese and Spanish ships, ports, and American territories, but this expensive strategy brought diminishing returns. The company therefore made a specialty of carrying the trade of others. Dutch technicians who learned about sugar mills in Brazil helped introduce them to developing English and French colonies in the Caribbean, where cane also flourished. The industry took off initially on the small English island of Barbados. By the 1670s this dot in the sea produced around 65 percent of the sugar England consumed. In the seventeenth and eighteenth centuries, plantation economies came to dominate several French and British islands, including Martinique, Haiti (the western half of Hispaniola), and Jamaica.

As the economic potential of sugar islands and other overseas colonial territories became apparent to western European states, each one formulated policies to try to ensure that it, rather than any rival country, would benefit, exclusively if possible, from the commerce that its dependencies generated. These policies and the ideas that inspired them became known as **mercantilism.**

> **mercantilism** An economic doctrine based on the idea that the world's exploitable wealth could not expand and that a state should therefore erect barriers to keep rival states out of its circuits of trade with its colonies.

Sugar production in the Caribbean. This seventeenth-century engraving shows African slaves driving oxen to power a crushing mill, which extracted juice from fresh sugar cane. The juice was boiled in vats like the two in the foreground to evaporate the water and reduce the juice to crystals. Sugar mill labor was intensive and dangerous. Why would European planters have preferred African slaves as laborers in this industry?

This economic doctrine was founded on the premise that the world's exploitable wealth was finite and on the whole not expandable. Rulers should therefore strive to accumulate more global riches than their rivals did, partly by acquiring productive colonies abroad and binding them to the home country in a closed system that walled off from competitors. A state's wealth was to be measured in reserves of gold and silver, accumulated by selling home manufactures abroad, by strictly regulating colonial imports, and by buying as little as possible from other countries. Central governments should take action to expand domestic manufacturing, encourage population growth, keep import tariffs high, cooperate with national trading firms, and spend generously on military forces to defend colonies and trade lines. As the Atlantic economy grew, mercantilist attitudes contributed to rising political tensions and outbreaks of war among the major European maritime powers. Britain, France, and the Netherlands generally implemented mercantilist strategies more successfully than did Spain or Portugal, which by the seventeenth century had weaker manufacturing economies and naval clout.

Commercial agriculture and slavery.

Forced shipment of African slaves to America became a key element of mercantilist profit-seeking. In Portuguese Brazil, the African slave population rose from about three thousand in 1570 to fifteen thousand by the end of the century. Slave imports also accelerated in the Caribbean after 1640. There, Native American peoples had been all but wiped out. Both the British and the French tried to attract free immigrants from the homelands. That effort failed, largely because the islands gained a reputation in Europe as deadly hellholes. The only feasible alternative was African slave immigration, and by 1680 little Barbados had fifty thousand slaves. Within another twenty years, Africans and their offspring represented a demographic majority in northeastern Brazil and on several Caribbean islands.

Demand for slave labor in America continued to grow for two reasons. One was that the American plantation economy kept expanding, not only to grow sugar but also tobacco, indigo, cotton, and other exportable commodities. The other was that African slave populations in America did not on the whole reproduce themselves by natural increase. Planters

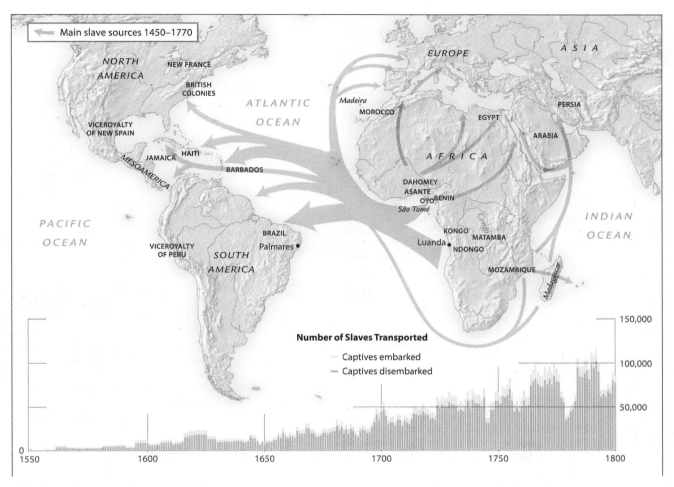

Number of Slaves Transported
— Captives embarked
— Captives disembarked

MAP 18.4 Trade of enslaved Africans, 1500–1800.

High mortality rates on the middle passage across the Atlantic meant that more slaves embarked from African ports than arrived on American shores. Why were the majority of African captives sold into Atlantic markets, despite the demand for slaves in several parts of Afroeurasia? Why were slaves taken in large numbers to some regions but not to others?

wanted to import mainly male slaves for hard field labor. Since enslaved men far outnumbered women, slave deaths consistently exceeded births. (Though women represented a small percentage of imports relative to males, they were not spared the ordeal of slavery. In fact, of all females who crossed the Atlantic to America before 1820, four out of every five were Africans.) Moreover, slaves on tropical plantations were unlikely to live more than about seven years. Consequently, planters made continuous demands on Atlantic merchants to bring more workers, even though slave prices climbed persistently over the long run.

The workings of the slave trade. African rulers and merchants began exporting enslaved men and women long before Europeans appeared on their coasts. Between the years 800 and 1600, for example, something like five thousand slaves, both men and women, crossed the Sahara Desert each year, along with gold and other goods, to serve

in wealthy households, workshops, or army units in Muslim lands. Indian Ocean traders also bought slaves in East Africa for shipment to Arabia, Egypt, Persia, or India. The Atlantic trade, therefore, represented not the advent of African forced migration but rather a major shift in its direction from Afroeurasian to American destinations (see Map 18.4). In the seventeenth century the trans-Saharan trade diminished, whereas more than 2.25 million Africans were taken to America. The Atlantic trade reached its zenith in the 1780s, a decade when about 866,000 Africans endured the ocean crossing, or ªmiddle passage.º[17]

These numbers do not account for the hundreds of thousands, if not millions, of slaves who died in transit. Historians have estimated that in the late seventeenth century as many as 10 percent of captive people perished on their way to the African coast or while waiting to be put on ships. Estimates from Angola suggest 40 percent.[18] Another 10 to 14 percent died at sea and countless more in wars, raids,

Cruelties of the middle passage. The death rate for captives crossing the Atlantic was as high as 15 percent. Slaves who caused trouble faced violent discipline, as we see in the background of this image. Dead and near-dead slaves were thrown to the sharks, but here sailors are casting apparently healthy and valuable slaves overboard. Why might that have happened? Can you speculate about the intended purpose of this mid-eighteenth century engraving?

and kidnappings that fueled the slave trade. Venture Smith, a West African child who was taken to New England in the 1730s but later bought his freedom, composed a narrative of his enslavement and trek to the West African coast, including his father's death at the hands of their captors: ª The women and myself being pretty submissive, had tolerable treatment from the enemy, while my father was closely interrogated respecting his money which they knew he must have. But as he gave them no account of it, he was instantly cut and pounded on his body with great inhumanity. . . . I saw him while he was thus tortured to death. The shocking scene is to this day fresh in my mind, and I have often been overcome while thinking on it.º [19]

From the point of debarkation, the misery of enslavement became progressively worse. The average trans-Atlantic voyage lasted between one and three months. On many ships, slaves spent most of the voyage shackled and confined to dark, stifling holds, where seasickness and other ills produced vomiting, diarrhea, severe dehydration, and sometimes death. In his eighteenth-century narrative, the former slave Olaudah Equiano wrote: ª The stench of the hold . . . was so intolerably loathsome, that it was dangerous to remain there for any time. . . . The closeness of the place and the heat of the climate, added to the number in the ship, which was so crowded that each had scarcely room to turn himself, almost suffocated us.º [20] Slaves who survived the middle passage went on to more trouble and usually an early grave, especially if they were consigned to sugar plantations. At harvest time, field slaves had to meet rigid daily quotas of cut cane. Workers who fed the cane into the mill's crushing

rollers performed repetitive, mind-numbing tasks that invited accidents, notably mangled hands or arms. Boiler tenders worked inside the equivalent of an oven, inhaling smoke and suffering burns.

Slave resistance. Africans frequently resisted their dismal fate. Portuguese sugar planters largely abandoned the island of São Tomé in the seventeenth century partly because escaped slaves waged guerrilla warfare from the interior mountains. In the Americas, men and women found numerous ways to rebel against their condition, ranging from subtle forms of sabotage, attacks on overseers and formation of secret religious or ethnic societies, to outright rebellion. Slaves also resisted by running away. South America and the Caribbean were dotted with remote, hidden communities of escaped slaves, called *macombos* in Portuguese and ªmaroon societies º in English. Some of these communities had no more than a dozen inhabitants; others had populations that rivaled European colonies. The most famous *macombo* was Palmares, a cluster of towns in northeastern Brazil's backcountry. This settlement may have had tens of thousands of residents in the second half of the seventeenth century. Palmares was effectively an African-style state, with a king, a council of nobles, an army equipped with guns, and defensive fortifications. Villagers grew a variety of crops, including sugar cane. Some of them owned their own slaves and occasionally raided European plantations to acquire more. In the 1670s, Portuguese militias launched a series of offensives, finally overrunning Palmares in 1694.

Change in Atlantic Africa

The expansion of the global economy after 1500 had transforming effects on Atlantic-facing tropical Africa. First, population generally declined between the sixteenth and the eighteenth centuries, a period when numbers elsewhere in Afroeurasia were trending rapidly upward. This happened partly because of violence and upheaval in particular regions associated with enslavement, partly because of slave exports, and partly because women of childbearing age who were put on slave ships, even though fewer in number than males, could no longer produce children in their homelands. Population loss might have been even worse, except that when slaving activity and associated warfare devastated a particular area, both African and European traders were obliged to move their operations elsewhere. This allowed the depopulated region time to recover at least some of its numbers.

African economic life also changed. Owing to their participation in international trade, both with slaves and other products, some regions experience significant economic growth. This prosperity, however, tended to benefit mainly small elitesÐ rulers, warlords, merchants, and people who already used slaves for commercial farming or mining. These elites allied themselves, if only indirectly, with their European or American counterpartsÐ company investors, bankers, shippers, planters, and political officialsÐ in order to accumulate wealth. Also, African merchants had for centuries operated

Servants and Slaves on a Barbados Sugar Plantation

In 1647 Richard Ligon (ca. 1585–1662), an Englishman out of money and career options, saw a chance to make a fresh start somewhere in Britain's growing empire. He booked passage on a ship bound for Barbados, where English settlers had first arrived twenty years earlier. During three years in the Caribbean, however, Ligon's fortunes did not improve much. By 1652 he returned to England but then got himself locked up in a London debtors' prison. While behind bars, he wrote The True and Exact History of the Island of Barbadoes, *an account of his Caribbean adventure.*

The early English settlers on Barbados intended to found a predominantly white European society, but African slaves were also brought in from the start. When Ligon arrived there, sugar planters were using both white indentured servant and African slave labor. In this selection from his book, Ligon first describes the troubled lives of white workers and their reasons for plotting an uprising. He portrays African slaves as more contented with their situation than white servants. But he then contradicts this view by giving an account of slaves planning an act of sabotage. In the Caribbean, where potentially great sugar profits depended on relentless labor, such rebellion was far from uncommon.

The Island is divided into three sorts of men, viz. Masters, [white] Servants and [African] Slaves. The slaves and their posterity, being subject to their Masters for ever, are kept and preserv'd with greater care than the servants, who are theirs for but five years, according to the law of the Island. So that for the time, the servants have the worser lives, for they are put to very hard labor, ill lodging, and their diet very sleight. . . .

[S]ome cruel Masters will provoke their Servants so, by extreme ill usage, and often and cruel beating them, as they grow desperate, and so join together to revenge themselves upon them. . . .

A little before I came from thence, there was such a combination [plot] amongst them, as the like was never seen there before. Their sufferings being grown to a great height, and their daily complainings to one another (of the intolerable burdens they labour'd under) being spread throughout the Island; at the last, some amongst them, whose spirits were not able to endure such slavery, resolved to break through it, or die in the act; and so conspired with some others of their acquaintance; So that a day was appointed to fall upon their Masters, and cut all their throats, and by that means, to make themselves [not] only freemen, but Masters of the Island. And so closely [secretly] was this plot carried, as no discovery was made, till the day before they were to put it in act: And then one of them, either by the failing of his courage, or some new obligation from the love of his Master, revealed this long plotted conspiracy; and so by this timely advertisement [alert], the Masters were saved. . . . [W]hereof eighteen of the principal men in the conspiracy, and they the first leaders and contrivers of the plot, were put to death, for example to the rest. . . .

It has been accounted a strange thing, that the Negroes, being more than double the numbers of the Christians that are there, . . . that these should not commit some horrid massacre upon the Christians. . . . But there are three reasons that take away this wonder; the one is, They are not suffered to touch or handle any weapons: The other, That they are held in such awe [dread] and slavery, as they are fearful to appear in any daring act; and seeing the mustering of our men, and hearing their Gun-shot, (than which nothing is more terrible to them) their spirits are subjugated to so low a condition, as they dare not look up to any bold attempt. Besides these, there is a third reason, which stops all designs of that kind, and that is, They are fetch'd from several parts of Africa, who speak several languages, and by that means, one of them understands not another. . . .

I believe . . . that there are honest, faithful, and conscionable people amongst [the African slaves], as amongst those of Europe, or any other part of the world. . . .

A hint of this, I will give you in a lively example; and it was in a time when Victuals were scarce, and Plantins [plantains, which slaves consumed] were not then so frequently planted, as to afford them enough. So that some of the high spirited and turbulent amongst them, began to mutiny, and had a plot, secretly to be reveng'd on their Master. . . . These villains were resolved to make fire to such part of the boiling-house as they were sure would fire the rest, and so burn all, and yet seem ignorant of the fact, as a thing done by accident. But this plot was discovered, by some of the others who hated mischief; . . . and so traduc'd [accused] them to their Master, and brought in so many witnesses against them, as they were forc'd to confess, what they meant should have been put in act the next night.

Source: Richard Ligon, *The True and Exact History of the Island of Barbadoes*, 1657, ed. J. Edward Hutson (St. Michael, Barbados: Barbados National Trust, 2000), 64, 66±67, 75, 76.

Thinking Critically

Why, according to Ligon, did white indentured servants receive worse treatment than African slaves? Why were the indentured servants unable to go through with the plan to kill their masters? What three reasons does Ligon give for the lack of slave resistance on Barbados? According to him, when a group of slaves plotted sabotage, what motivated them and why did they fail?

Queen Nzinga negotiating with the Portuguese governor in Luanda, Angola, about 1620. Legend has it that when the governor refused to offer the queen a chair, a courtesy due to a political leader of equal rank, she refused to be slighted. Instead, she demonstrated both her power over her subjects and her keen negotiating tactics. Why do you think a seventeenth-century European engraving would commemorate this event?

financially sophisticated inland trade networks. Commercial routes, business customs, and credit systems simply became more elaborate in the centuries of the Atlantic trade. African rulers and merchants made rational business decisions to determine how many enslaved men and women should be put to work locally and how many might be sold to Europeans. Rulers hardly ever allowed peaceable and productive members of *their own societies* to be sold into the trade. But individuals having no place or standing in the community might be regarded as disposable, especially prisoners of war (often from wars having nothing directly to do with the slave trade), but also foreign refugees, criminals, outcasts, and kidnap victims.

A third sphere of change was political. The slave trade destabilized some African states but strengthened or helped give birth to others. International commerce offered rulers new economic opportunities, and this encouraged them to centralize political administration more tightly, extract revenue from their subjects more efficiently, and strengthen their control over production and commerce.

Central African states and Portuguese intruders. The Kongo kingdom (see Chapter 16) centered south of the lower Congo River grew powerful in the later fifteenth century but fared poorly after Europeans arrived. Slave trading by both Portuguese and local Africans brought instability that the monarch was unable to prevent, and in the seventeenth century, the kingdom became enmeshed in a series of ruinous wars with the Portuguese in Angola. Internal political struggles followed those wars, generating large numbers of captives, which benefited no one except African and European slave merchants. The kingdom nearly disintegrated, though it managed to reconstitute itself in the next century.

Kingdoms lying south of Kongo connected themselves to the Atlantic economy as suppliers of slaves, ivory, and copper after 1575, when the Portuguese established a fortified post at Luanda, the core of a colony they named Angola. The neighboring Ndongo and Matamba states had to contend with growing Portuguese political and military influence aimed at expanding the supply of slaves for shipment to Brazil. When the king of Ndongo died in 1618, Nzinga (r. 1618±1663), a royal princess, seized power. A remarkable political strategist, she maneuvered among both the Portuguese and various Ndongo factions. But in the 1620s, Portuguese pressures grew too heavy to bear. Nzinga distanced herself from them by leading an army further inland to conquer the Matamba kingdom. She had little trouble establishing her authority because, whereas Ndongo had no tradition of rule by queens, Matamba did. For nearly four decades, Nzinga successfully defended Matamba against both the Portuguese and its African allies. At the same time, she made her own profitable arrangements with rulers and merchants of the Central African interior to direct caravans of slaves, ivory, and copper through Matamba to the Atlantic coast. For many Angolans today, Nzinga remains a mythic national heroine.

West African states.

In the forest and savanna regions of West Africa, several states rose to regional power after 1600. One of these was the kingdom of Oyo, centered in wooded grasslands west of the Niger River. Oyo's rulers took part in slave trading, acquiring European textiles and other goods primarily to purchase horses brought south from the Sahara. Oyo fielded a formidable cavalry army, which pushed out the kingdom's frontiers and, in the process, acquired slaves for home labor or export. Southwest of Oyo, along the fringe between savanna and tropical rainforest, the kingdom of

Dahomey accumulated power in the seventeenth century by trading slaves for guns and building a large professional military. This force expanded to the coast in the early 1700s so that no competing power stood between it and European slave buyers. In the same period, Dahomey and Oyo battled each other, generating more slaves.

Farther west, the gold-producing region that is part of modern Ghana gave rise to a number of small states before 1500. In the late seventeenth century, one of these, the kingdom of Asante (Ashanti), rose under the leadership of Osei Tutu to dominate its neighbors. The common symbol of political authority in the region was a type of stool. According to Asante political legend, Anokye, the principal adviser to Osei Tutu, used magical power to conjure a stool of pure gold from out of the sky. Osei Tutu thereafter inspired intense political loyalty in the region, and several of his successors went on to conquer and incorporate much more territory. War and trade swept growing numbers of slaves into the kingdom. The rulers exported a calculated number of them every year but retained many more to work in fields, gold mines, and households. Slaves not sold off, or at least their children, might gain full integration into Asante society.

Asante royal stool. The golden stool of the Asantehene (king) is a sacred object that only the king himself may touch and few may see. Similarly shaped stools, however, serve ordinary people and are said to be the seat of the owner's soul. Each one is carved from a single block of wood, individually designed and symbolically decorated for the intended owner.

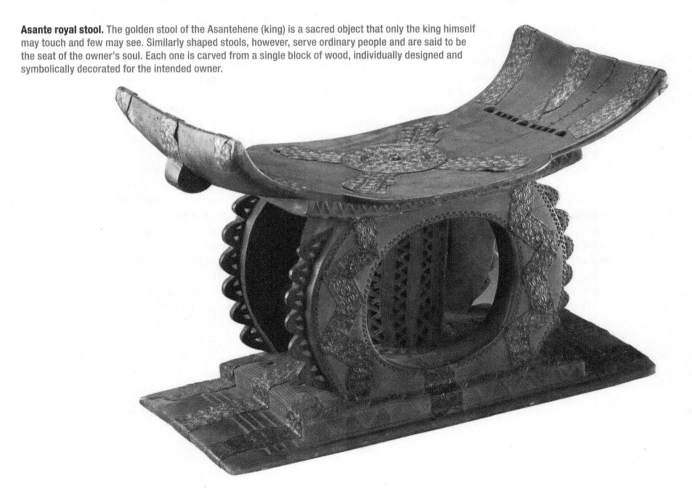

Conclusion

In Afroeurasia the middle decades of the seventeenth century marked a pause between a long period of remarkable demographic and economic growth, which started about 1400, and another, which got under way by 1700. The economic downturn that historians have described in the early and mid-1600s affected many societies, though not all. In both China and Europe, economic output faltered, income declined for many, and population growth slowed. Both the Ottoman and Safavid Persian empires also suffered rising inflation, a serious flight of silver and gold to pay for imports, and worsening poverty. The Atlantic slave trade began to take a significant toll in population and political stability in parts of West and Central Africa. On the other hand, economic growth appears to have characterized South Asia nearly throughout the century. In the West African savanna lands, a climatic wet phase set in around 1500, boosting population and farm production for two or three hundred years. In Europe the United Netherlands had its economic golden age in the mid-seventeenth century, whereas Germany, Spain, and several other states fared badly.

Scholars have linked seventeenth-century recession to a number of possible factors. Some point to declining production of American silver, which caused prices to drop and commerce to languish, notably in China and Europe. Others stress the economic effects of population growth rates leveling off or declining in some regions, a phenomenon that reduced demand for food and other commodities and therefore depressed both production and trade. More recently, historians and climatologists have investigated fluctuations in global temperatures attending the Little Ice Age, which extended altogether from the thirteenth to the nineteenth century (see Chapter 15). Temperatures in the Northern Hemisphere dropped significantly between the 1630s and 1650s. The cold snap was associated with severe winters, cold and rainy summers, floods, or droughts, depending on the region. Scholars have correlated these extreme conditions, including food shortages, with an upsurge of insurrections, revolutions, and wars from western Europe to Japan.[21]

The widespread economic slowdown, which appears to have lasted only a few decades, was a cyclical phenomenon and in the longer term had little effect on the world economy's continuing growth and commercialization. Between 1500 and 1700 the ships and overland transport that linked every part of Afroeurasia and the Americas with every other part spun a web of exchange far bigger and busier than in any previous era. The long-distance movement of commodities, manufactures, food crops, workers, and technical ideas produced new accumulations of wealth, especially in regions that already had large populations and complex agrarian economies. American silver mines, which European entrepreneurs seized from Native Americans, gave the global commercial system a huge dose of adrenaline, though ups and downs in silver supplies could also contribute to periodic or regional slumps.

The new global exchange net affected societies in different ways. As we have seen, it had disastrous consequences for indigenous Americans. In Africa, societies that faced the Atlantic eagerly joined the emerging global trade net but discovered that commerce in people benefited relatively few. Global trade poured great wealth into the agrarian societies of Asia because they had more commodities and manufactured goods to pump into world markets than other regions did. Western European states acquired possession of potentially monumental economic resources in the Americas, and they quickly fell to battling one another for those riches. They did not, however, have to fight Ottoman, Mughal, or Ming armies, which in the circumstances of the early modern era accumulated wealth in other ways than sending navies across the Atlantic or Pacific.

European economic exploitation of the Americas was, with the exception of silver and gold mining, getting under way in the second half of the seventeenth century. Commercial agriculture began to reach bonanza proportions, but only because Europeans found a way to bring in an unwilling African workforce. In Afroeurasia, on the other hand, Europeans were yet to exert much economic power relative to the big Asian states. And, in contrast to their American conquests, they controlled little African or Asian territory other than trading posts and coastal enclaves, almost always under agreements with local rulers. Europeans were to be seen just about everywhere in the world in the seventeenth century, but the circumstances that permitted their global domination two centuries later did not yet exist.

• • •

Key Terms

Asante state 539
chartered company 518
Dutch East India Company (VOC) 529

galleon 517
inflation 524
Manila galleon voyages 521
mercantilism 533

middle passage 535
price revolution 524
social bondage 531
Thirty Years' War 526

Change over Time

1545	Spanish prospectors discover enormous silver deposits near Potosí, Bolivia.
1570s	The Ming government in China requires tax payments in silver.
1572	Manila galleon voyages between America and the Philippines begin, creating the last major connection in the global chain of commerce.
1580s	The African slave population in Brazil starts to grow.
1600	The English East India Company is founded.
1602	The Dutch East India Company (VOC) is founded.
1607	The English found a settlement at Jamestown in North America.
1608	The French found a settlement at Quebec on the St. Lawrence River.
1618–1648	Much of central Europe is embroiled in the Thirty Years' War.
1619	Dutch forces seize the port of Jakarta (Batavia) on Java.
1630s–1650s	The Northern Hemisphere's temperature drops.
1637	The Tokugawa shogunate expels Europeans from Japan.
1650s	A sugar industry is established on the English island of Barbados.
1662	Chinese forces expel the Dutch from the island of Taiwan.
ca. 1680	The Asante state is founded in West Africa.

Please see end of book reference section for additional reading suggestions related to this chapter.

19 The Changing Balance of Wealth and Power
1650–1750

A storm in the Pacific shipwrecked Vitus Bering and his crew in 1741. Bering died on the Aleutian island that was later named in his honor.

T welve thousand years ago, when the last Ice Age was just ending, a land bridge connected the eastern tip of Russia with Alaska. In 1728–1729, Vitus Bering, a Danish sea captain serving in the Russian navy, demonstrated to the world that this isthmus was long gone. Leading an expedition commissioned by Emperor Peter the Great, Bering sailed around the northeastern coastline of Eurasia and through the strait that now bears his name. Before entering the passage, he recorded in his ship's log an encounter with local Siberians. They told him what to expect: "August 8th, having arrived in north latitude 64°30′, eight men rowed to us from the shore in a skin boat, enquiring from whence we came and what was our business there. They said they were Chuikchi . . . and they told us that on the coast lived many of their nation; that the land not far from there takes a decided turn to the westward."[1] In other words, the land did not converge with the North American shore but veered away from it.

Bering did not find Alaska on that first trip, but in 1732 he set sail again, heading a much larger Russian mission. Lasting nearly a decade, the Great Northern Expedition, as it became known, involved more than three thousand people who charted northern Pacific waters and coastlines, collected scientific data, and looked for commercial opportunities. This time Bering reached the coast of North America, but he did not live to return home. His ship broke up on an island (later named Bering Island), and he died there of scurvy in 1741. Surviving crew members managed to build a small craft from the wreckage of their ship and sailed back to Siberia. They carried with them a load of valuable sea otter pelts, which helped inspire Russian trade settlement in Alaska a half-century later. A thread in the web of global connections now traversed the far North Pacific, and by the early 1800s the Russian empire extended from the northern coast of California to eastern Europe, a straight-line distance of more than 5,800 miles.

The integration of northern Pacific lands into global exchange networks is one aspect of the great world convergence that continued to intensify in the later seventeenth and the eighteenth centuries. This chapter focuses on three large-scale manifestations of that convergence: land-based empire building on a spectacular scale; encounters between indigenous peoples and new European settlers in lands distant from Europe; and a new intellectual movement centered in European cities to rethink long accepted explanations of the workings of nature as new knowledge of the world's geography, biology, and diverse human culture flowed in from all directions.

In the first part of the chapter we explore developments in politics and power relations in the century after 1650. The Qing (chihng) dynasty in China, the Romanov rulers in Russia, and the Spanish in America, using gunpowder technology and centralized systems of command, consolidated their power over immense territories. In 1750 these three states together sprawled across about 14,282,000 square miles of land, about 4.5 times more than the continental United States today.[2] By contrast, Europe remained an assemblage of competing states, some of them tiny, others large territorial monarchies that aimed to further centralize royal power. And as we described in Chapter 18, the Netherlands, Britain, France, and Portugal also projected naval and commercial power into Africa, Asia, and the Americas.

In the sixteenth century, Europeans went abroad as explorers, soldiers, merchants, missionaries, business entrepreneurs, and imperial officials. In the second part of the chapter we describe a new type of colonial activity that got under way in the seventeenth century. Increasing numbers of Europeans migrated across the seas or into the forests of Siberia as settlers intending to build farm communities

Chapter Outline

EMPIRES AND BIG STATES
Chinese Prosperity and Imperialism
Russia from the Pacific to Poland
The Spanish Empire in America
Europe: Successes and Failures
of Absolutism

EUROPEAN SETTLEMENT AND THE FATE OF INDIGENOUS PEOPLES
Early European Settlers in North America
Russian Settlement of Siberia
Europeans and Khoisan in South Africa

WEIGHING THE EVIDENCE The Journal
of a Dutch Commander at the Cape of Good Hope

ALTERNATIVE VISIONS OF GOD, NATURE, AND THE UNIVERSE
The Scientific Revolution
The Enlightenment:
Rethinking Human Nature and Society
The Continuing Growth of Islam
and Christianity

INDIVIDUALS MATTER Dona Beatriz Kimpa Vita:
Visionary Christian of the Kongo

• • •

and to reshape land and society, to the extent they could, in the image of Europe. Indigenous peoples, who did not want their land and societies reshaped, naturally opposed these colonizing projects, though to no avail in the long run. By 1750, European settler colonies were well established in North America, Siberia, and South Africa.

Because western Europe began in the sixteenth century to play a new role as a hub of global maritime activity, new information about the world and its peoples poured in. This knowledge circulated widely among literate Europeans just at the time when the Renaissance study of human nature and behavior was reaching into every part of the subcontinent and when various Christian sects and denominations were proclaiming different, often conflicting versions of divine truth. In the final part of the chapter, we look at how these strands of thought converged in an intellectual movement that challenged the ancient wisdom handed down from Greek philosophers and church fathers and that presented radical new ways of describing reality. Yet even as European intellectuals questioned traditional certainties such as divine revelation and God's intervention in human affairs, the world's major belief systems continued to thrive and grow, notably Christianity and Islam.

A Panoramic View

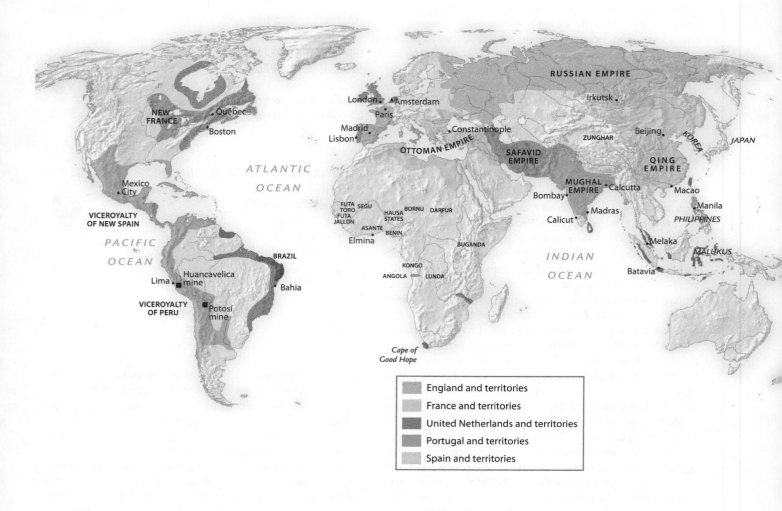

MAP 19.1 Major states and colonial territories, 1700.

By 1700 five European powers had established significant overseas empires. How did these compare in territorial size to the large land empires in Afroeurasia?

Empires and Big States

FOCUS In what ways may the aims and successes of Chinese, Russian, and Spanish land-based empire building in the seventeenth and eighteenth centuries be compared?

The period of world history from 1500 to 1650 saw the growth of two types of states (see Map 19.1). One type comprised the territorial monarchies that marshaled armies of both gun-carrying soldiers and tax-gathering bureaucrats to expand royal power (see Chapter 17). Several of these states, notably Ming China, Mughal India, Safavid Persia, the Ottoman Turkish sultanate, and the Habsburgs of central Europe, may be classed as empires because they incorporated extensive territories and culturally diverse populations. The other type included the European countries that acquired overseas territories in addition to building stronger central governments. Portugal and Spain did this first; Netherlands, England, and France then followed suit (see Chapter 18).

In the century after 1650, important shifts occurred in state power. Both China under the Qing dynasty (1644±1911) and Russia under the Romanov tsars (1613±1917) dispatched armies to conquer immense new areas of Inner Eurasia to exploit its resources and to tax its populations of farmers, herders, and hunters. Spain also emerged in that period as a super-sized imperial power as its soldiers, missionaries, and merchants intruded into new regions of both North and South America. The Ottoman, Habsburg, and French monarchies had all aspired in the sixteenth century to large-scale conquests within Europe. Amid the brutality and confusion of religious wars between Catholics and Protestants, however, none of these states achieved their ambitions. Rather, Europe remained divided among numerous states large and small, simultaneously trading, sharing ideas, making treaties, and fighting one another.

Chinese Prosperity and Imperialism

As we saw in Chapter 18, states in several parts of Afroeurasia experienced economic and political instability in the mid-seventeenth century. China was one of them. The Ming dynasty (1368±1644) became progressively destabilized after 1600. Courtiers, Confucian officials, and relatives of the emperor feuded continually for imperial favor and public influence. The court eunuchs, whose original job had been to guard the emperor, seized direct control of many government functions. Climatic conditions associated with the continuing Little Ice Age worsened across northern China in the 1620s, producing famines. Persistent decline in the price of silver reduced the value of tax receipts, and a sudden stoppage of silver imports in 1639±1640 precipitated an economic crisis. In those tumultuous conditions, peasant uprisings swept the northern and western provinces.

At the same time, the Manchus (also known as Jurchens), a people of the forests, mountains, and plains of Manchuria, or Northeast China, pressed against the Ming imperial borders. Hung Taiji, the Manchu ruler in the mid-seventeenth century, created a strong central government modeled on the Chinese system. He named his dynasty the Qing, meaning ªpure,º and he pushed out the frontiers of his state to incorporate Mongols and Koreans. Ming frontier forces faced Manchu raids while simultaneously battling rural insurgents within China. In 1644 Chinese rebels captured Beijing, the imperial capital, and then Manchu cavalry seized the city from them. Manchu leaders claimed the Mandate of Heaven, or divine authority, to rule in the name of the five-year-old son of the deceased Hung Taiji. This boy reigned under the guidance of a **regent**. Meanwhile, the last Ming emperor committed suicide.

> **regent** An individual who administers the affairs of a state when the ruler is absent, disabled, or has not reached adulthood.

The Qing in power. Though Ming resistance held out in some regions for several years, the new regime made a fairly rapid transition from violent conquest to consolidation of power in both city and countryside. As foreign conquerors, the Qing endeavored to preserve their Manchu ethnic identity separate from the majority Han, or Chinese-speaking population they ruled. The Qing elite prohibited Manchu women from marrying Chinese men, though Manchu men could choose Chinese women as second wives or concubines. A system of parallel ranks characterized the high levels of Qing bureaucracy. That is, a Manchu and a Han Chinese official shared the same position. Each reported to the emperor, who encouraged them to spy on one another to ensure their loyalty to him alone.

Many Manchu-speaking officials learned to communicate in Mandarin Chinese, and government documents were issued in both languages. The Manchus adopted Confucian doctrines of good government, a strategy that achieved important political goals. The Qing emperor represented himself as the symbolic patriarch of a family constituted of all his subjects, and he proclaimed Confucian ideals of fair and just administration. The Ming imperial examination system, designed to train literate, competent, and dedicated public officials, was also retained. Confucianism provided a unifying framework for society but made room for religious toleration. In this respect the Qing carried on the Ming tradition of permitting Buddhists, Daoists, Muslims, and Christians to build places of worship and observe their rituals as long as they did not interfere in state business. The third Manchu emperor explained Qing ideas of religious diversity: ªWe Manchus have our own particular rites for honoring heaven; the Mongols, Chinese, Russians, and Europeans also have their own particular rites for honoring Heaven. . . . Everyone has his way of doing it.º[3]

Qing expansion. Within a few decades of the Manchu victory, China's population and economy resumed the upward trend they had enjoyed in the sixteenth century. The

A display of imperial power. Qianlong, the sixth Qing emperor, used the Grand Canal to tour China's southern provinces in 1751. Such tours were a longstanding practice of Chinese rulers. This painting on silk by an imperial court artist is titled *The Qianlong Emperor's Southern Inspection Tour, Scroll Six: Entering Suzhou and the Grand Canal* (1770). What elements in this image suggest that the emperor's visit was an important event in Suzhou?

ruler named the Kangxi (kang-shee) emperor spent most of his sixty-one-year reign (1661±1722) enlarging the frontiers of China north, west, and east. To the north the Qing intended early on to bring the Amur River valley, a region of fertile land, timber, and fur-bearing animals, into the Chinese political orbit. Shortly before the Manchu victory, however, the Amur region began attracting some of the Russian trappers, traders, and army contingents that spearheaded imperial Russia's eastward advance into Siberia. Inevitably, Russian and Chinese troops came to blows. Fortunately, the two governments decided shortly that the valley might better serve as a middle ground for commerce rather than as a terrain of mutually debilitating war. In 1689 they agreed to the Treaty of Nerchinsk (a town near the Amur). By its terms, Russia relinquished claims to the valley, and the two powers marked out a border. They even erected markers written in Chinese, Russian, Manchu, Mongol, and Latin.

Settling this conflict with Russia freed Qing forces to move westward to deal with Zunghar, a Mongol state in the Inner Eurasian steppe that menaced China's western borders. A Qing army with gunpowder artillery defeated the Buddhist ruler Galdan Khan in 1696, and sixty-four years later Chinese forces fully annexed Zunghar territory. This

victory signaled that China no longer needed to make deals with Mongols or other steppe cavalry armies to secure the empire's western frontiers. Qing troops continued pushing west, subduing other Mongol and Turkic peoples, occupying oasis towns, bringing in Han Chinese immigrant settlers, and absorbing the huge region that is modern China's Xinjiang province. In 1720 a Qing army captured Lhasa, the principal city of Tibet and seat of the Buddhist Dalai Lama. Thereafter, Tibet became a Chinese dependency. These western conquests made the empire much more linguistically and culturally diverse, including absorption of millions more Muslims. In long-term perspective, the Qing and Russian advances together terminated a nearly four-thousand-year history of pastoral nomads forming powerful states in Inner Eurasia.

To the east, Qing seaborne forces captured the island of Taiwan from a Chinese merchant prince whose family ruled there after evicting the Dutch East India Company thirty-eight years earlier. After that victory in 1683, China adopted an ªopen seasº policy, encouraging active collaboration between government officials and Pacific merchants and opening six seaports in the south to shipping. Foreign commercial vessels were permitted to enter the port of

The Kangxi emperor in court dress. This silk scroll by an anonymous court painter depicts Kangxi, the longest-reigning Qing ruler. He was in power for sixty-one years.

Russia from the Pacific to Poland

The reorganized and centralized Russian state that emerged in the fifteenth century suffered both fierce internal struggles and border invasions from Poland and Sweden in the early seventeenth century (see Chapter 17). After claiming the Russian throne, the teenaged tsar Mikhail Romanov (r. 1613±1645) managed to solidify his authority to the advantage of his successors. The early Romanov tsars made land grants to *boyars,* or members of the titled aristocracy, who supported the dynasty. Laws imposed in 1649 reduced free peasants to the status of serfs obligated to work on large estates, making these grants even more valuable. Political stability at the top also permitted Russian rulers to increase spending on territorial expansion, which brought the state more tax wealth, natural resources, and trade.

The ambitions of Peter the Great. Nearly paralleling the reign of the Kangxi emperor in Qing China, Peter I, known as Peter the Great (r. 1682±1725), transformed Russia, first into a regional power, then into both a trans-hemispheric empire and an important member of the European state system. Peter insisted on unlimited authority, an ideal of **absolutism** that Ottoman, Persian, and Mughal monarchs had refined in the previous century and that several European rulers also adopted. Like them, Peter claimed that God granted the monarch a ªdivine rightº to govern and that opposition to the monarch constituted opposition to God. All subjects from noble lords on down therefore owed allegiance to the monarch above all other loyalties. For several millennia kings and queens around the world had associated themselves with godly power. But European rulers, including Peter, tried more forcefully than in the past to nullify the independent authority of aristocratic assemblies, town councils, religious authorities, and other groups that had traditionally claimed social or political privileges and responsibilities. Royal claims of absolutism implied that monarchs had the exclusive right to make decisions for the well-being of their subjects and to impose on them whatever religious practice they thought best.

> **absolutism** A political doctrine asserting that in a monarchy the ruler holds sole and unquestionable power by divine authority.

Peter much admired the technology and administrative techniques that enabled western European states to amass power and establish overseas empires. In 1697±1698, he and an entourage made two trips west to study shipbuilding, sailing, military strategy, administration, and scientific ideas. He consulted with master naval architects in Dutch shipyards, even dressing himself in workers' clothes to labor alongside shipbuilders. He visited textile workshops and museums, conversed with Dutch and English scholars, and corresponded with French intellectuals.

Returning to Moscow, Peter introduced numerous changes, including a stronger central bureaucracy accountable to him and up-to-date armaments to strengthen the army, which by 1715 numbered about 215,000 conscripted soldiers. He

Guangzhou. Qing officials enforced collection of port duties from visiting British, French, Danish, and (after 1789) American merchants. But when British traders asked to build a permanent station, the Qianlong emperor refused. As he wrote to Britain's King George III,

> ªYour request for a small island near Chusan [Zhoushan], where your merchants may reside and goods be warehoused, arises from your desire to develop trade. . . . Consider, moreover, that England is not the only barbarian land which wishes to establish relations with our civilization and trade with our Empire: supposing that other nations were all to imitate your evil example and beseech me to present them each and all with a site for trading purposes, how could I possibly comply? This also is a flagrant infringement of the usage of my empire and cannot possibly be entertained.º4

The ruler was not averse to commerce but insisted on the strict subordination of foreign visitors to imperial authority.

further reduced the local power of the land-owning *boyars* by creating the Table of Ranks, which gave nobles precedence at court based on their meritorious service to the state rather than on their aristocratic family tree. He bolstered royal control of the Russian Orthodox Church, even replacing its patriarch with a council of priests that operated according to the tsar's rules. He initiated westward-looking cultural and education reforms, including a decree that all children of nobles and officials must learn mathematics. He founded a medical school, supported Russia's first newspaper, and set up a scientific academy. To make visible the drastic cultural reorientation he desired, he ordered men to cut off their traditional beards and forced his courtiers to wear western European±style hats, coats, and underwear. To the horror of Orthodox churchmen, he held salons in which men and women socialized together in one room. Not surprisingly, Peter's reforms encountered resistance from conservative leaders, but under his relentless pressure, coupled with Russian military successes, they gained elite support.

Tsar Peter I, imperial modernizer. Peter the Great stands in front of newly constructed St. Petersburg. What symbols of imperial power and of Peter's modernization efforts did artist Grigory Semyonovich Musikiysky incorporate into this miniature enamel portrait?

Empire building west, south, and east. Peter and his successors, especially the empress Catherine II (Catherine the Great, r. 1762±1796), pursued campaigns of overland expansion that tsars had initiated in the fifteenth century. The pace and scope of this expansion was staggering. Imperial territory tripled in the 1700s. Similarly to China in the same period, conquests transformed Russia into a complex multicultural state. The tsars generally tolerated ethnic and religious diversity but insisted on the primacy of Russian cultural and political leadership. They strengthened their historic alliance with the Cossacks, a polyglot collection of mounted fighters and merchants that originated mainly in the Ukraine. Armed Cossack bands, which included both Christians and Muslims and speakers of several different languages, spearheaded many of the emperor's expansionary campaigns.

Looking west, the tsars had long coveted warm water ports on the Baltic Sea, the passage to the wider maritime world. Peter realized this goal after defeating Sweden in the Great Northern War, a struggle that endured from 1700 to 1721. Deploying his newly modernized forces, he obliterated the Swedish army, effectively ending that country's role as a Baltic power and obliging all the major European states to recognize that Russia was going to join their club. In 1703 he set thousands of engineers, artisans, and peasants to work building St. Petersburg, an entirely new city and imperial capital on marshland where the Neva River empties into the Baltic.

To the south and southeast, Peter's forces seized territory in the Ukraine from the kingdom of Poland-Lithuania, and they continued to fight Ottoman Turkish forces for access to the Black Sea. Catherine the Great made huge gains in those directions late in the century. She seized the eastern third of Poland in a coldblooded deal with the Austrian and Prussian monarchies to divide up and eradicate that country as a sovereign state. The army also expelled the Ottomans from the Black Sea's northern shores. To the east, Peter intensified Russian military advances into Siberia, seeking new agricultural lands and commerce. Cossacks subjugated local peoples in the name of the tsar and traded for furs and other forest products. By 1639 Russians reached the Pacific Ocean, then penetrated the Amur River valley. As we have seen, these forays led to the Treaty of Nerchinsk (1689), which calmed border conflict between Russia and China.

After Vitus Bering explored the sea passage between Siberia and North America, Russian trappers and traders began inching their way through the Aleutian Islands and along the Alaskan coast. In 1804 the Russian American Company occupied the little port of Sitka in southern Alaska. Eight years later, the company set up a trading and farming station at Fort Ross in northern California, building a stockade and an Orthodox chapel and making occasional contact with Spanish and later Mexican officers and missionaries advancing from the south. The company occupied this distant post until 1841. Russians interacted with native Siberians and Alaskans in a variety of ways. The newcomers, almost all of them males, frequently married or cohabited with local women, producing children that adapted themselves to two different cultural worlds. Russian merchants and trappers sought mutually beneficial trade with Siberians, offering rewards for collecting furs. But Russians also intimidated and attacked native communities that put up resistance, a portent of the ªRussianizing° of Siberia that was to come.

The Spanish Empire in America

As of 1650, Spain and its colonial possessions constituted an empire second only to Russia in territorial extent. The Spanish monarchy's American lands far exceeded the size of Spain itself. In the mid-seventeenth century, the American empire already had several large Spanish-governed cities, busy trade networks, and control over extensive rural areas, all held together by shared laws, an evolving central governing structure, and the Roman Catholic Church.

Governing Spanish America.

Despite persistent Native American resistance in remote areas and wars with rival European states for trade and land, the empire continued to grow as imperial forces conquered deep interior lands. At its territorial peak in the early 1800s, it stretched from northern California to the tip of South America, including several Caribbean islands. This realm was initially divided into two huge viceroyalties governed by appointees of the Spanish crown. Mexico City became the capital of New Spain, Lima the center of the Viceroyalty of Peru.

In contrast to Beijing and Moscow, Madrid, the imperial capital, was separated from its giant land empire by an ocean. Consequently, viceroys and other colonial officials tended to exercise more autonomous power than the crown would have preferred. The viceroys sometimes disagreed with royal proclamations and dragged their feet in implementing them. Since it could take up to two years to send a message to Spain and receive a reply, officials had plenty of time to do things their own way. The relationship between the crown and colonial elites evolved into a system in which Madrid secured the loyalty of colonial officials, landlords, and mine ownersÐ a tiny percentage of the American populationÐ by allowing them to buy and sell lucrative administrative offices, appropriate Indian land, and evade numerous laws intended to protect ordinary people from labor or tax abuse.

The daily lives of all Spanish American subjects centered on the pueblos (towns), haciendas (large landed estates), Catholic missions, and presidios (garrisons). Provincial governors and judges had legal oversight of Spanish town councils made up entirely of local white men of wealth. In towns distant from the viceroyal capitals, these councils usually had a good deal of freedom to make policies that served their interests. In the countryside, individual estate owners had wide latitude to discipline their families, black slaves, and Indian laborers as they saw fit, echoing the power of feudal lords in medieval Spain. In the huge rural expanses of both Mesoamerica and Peru, the Spanish authorities could only keep order, collect taxes, and recruit workers with the collaboration of local indigenous nobles and chiefs. These heads of villages and kinship groups walked a fine line between Spanish demands for revenue and labor and the pleas of commoners for protection against imperial exactions. As Spanish government and law became entrenched, however, many local leaders transformed themselves into oppressive and wealth-seeking agents of the colonial regime.

Paralleling the viceroy's bureaucracy, imperial judicial courts called *audiencias* judged civil and criminal cases. These tribunals were obligated to recognize the legal standing of people of all social statuses and ethnic backgrounds. The courts typically favored the interests of Europeans, though commoners occasionally won disputes over property ownership or labor abuse. Both the *audiencias* and the viceroys ideally took direction from the Council of the Indies, a body of nobles and court favorites that met in Madrid to advise the king on imperial policies.

The Spanish monarch had the authority to nominate all of the empire's church officials, collect tithes, and found new churches, missions, and monasteries. This tight meshing of church and state meant that Catholic institutions played a particularly prominent role in the Spanish colonies. Several religious orders, including Dominicans, Franciscans, and Jesuits, founded both urban churches, which people of European descent attended, and missions, which primarily served Indians. Missionaries converted Indians, ideally attended to their moral and material needs, and encouraged them to become ªcivilizedº by learning Spanish and adopting European dress and diet. Mission friars also typically made heavy demands on Indians to grow food and pay a variety of fees.

The empire's social profile.

Many Spaniards and other Europeans traveled to the American empire to serve as soldiers, missionaries, or government officials, but others migrated in search of trade, urban business, or plantation ownership. In 1650 the European population living in Spanish America numbered about 600,000, rising to 3.8 million by 1825. This group consisted of both *peninsulares* (pehn-INH-soo-LAH-rayz), the elite class of men and women born

Hacienda Xcanchakan. Many of the haciendas that colonists established in the seventeenth century gave their owners great wealth and endured as large agricultural enterprises for two centuries or more. This estate on Mexico's Yucatan Peninsula caught the eye of the nineteenth-century English artist Frederick Catherwood. How did a small Mexican elite succeed in controlling huge tracts of land and the large Indian and *mestizo* labor forces needed to make estates productive for so long?

creole A person of African or European descent born in the Americas.

in Europe, and **creoles,** that is, people of European descent born in America. Before the nineteenth century, these groups together remained a small minority of the total population. Despite the sixteenth century's catastrophic mortality, Indians continued to far outnumber Europeans throughout most of South America and Mesoamerica. After about 1620, the Indian population began gradually to recover. In some lowland regions and on Caribbean islands, African slaves outnumbered both European and Indian inhabitants. As in Russian Siberia, though with a much larger base population, unions between men and women of different ethnoracial identities became common throughout the Spanish empire. Some of these unions were formalized in marriage; often they were not. Either way, they produced children of mixed ancestry. Social conventions emerged to categorize these *castas*, or mixed ªraces,º according to their various permutations: Spanish father±Indian mother, Spanish mother±African father, Indian father±African mother, and so on. Generally, people of mixed race occupied higher steps in the empire's rigid social hierarchy than Indians or African slaves. In Mexico the *mestizo* population, the group descended predominantly from unions between Indians and Europeans, came to constitute nearly 25 percent of the population by 1650 and about 40 percent by 1810.[5]

Imperial reforms. Changes in the Spanish monarchy had direct consequences for the American empire. Because

of special dynastic circumstances, Philip V, a grandson of the French Bourbon ruler Louis (LOO-ee) XIV, mounted the Spanish throne. Philip and his two Bourbon successors implemented a series of reforms both at home and in the colonies to centralize and modernize economic and political structures. In Spain the king had limited success challenging the long-held power of nobles, town elites, and high church clergy. But across the Atlantic, political reforms to improve government efficiency met with less resistance. To strengthen regional administration, the crown created two new viceroyalties: New Granada (1739), with its capital at Bogotá in modern Colombia; and Rio de la Plata (1776), centered on Buenos Aires in the far south. The reforms also aimed to check the growing power of affluent creoles, who dominated the colonial economy. The crown tended to distrust American-born elites and moved to bar them from high-ranking offices. The main effect, however, was to alienate this economically vital class from the imperial government.

As demand in Europe for sugar, tobacco, hides, and other products continued to climb, the Bourbon government initiated other reforms to increase customs revenues on American exports. After 1770, coffee and cacao joined sugar on the roster of crops exported from the Spanish Caribbean colonies. Cattle ranching in the Rio de la Plata region and a revival of silver mining in Mexico and Peru also signaled higher economic growth. All of these operations depended on intensive use of low-paid manual labor. Even small colonial manufacturing relied on coercion. A German visitor to a Mexican textile factory in 1803 noted troubling conditions ªnot only with the great imperfection of the technical process . . . but . . . also with the unhealthiness of the situation, and the bad treatment to which the workers are exposed. Free men, Indians, and people of color are confounded with the criminals distributed . . . among the manufactories, in order to be compelled to work. All appear half naked, covered with rags, meager, and deformed.º[6] Owing to conditions like these, miners and others who worked for low wages increasingly expressed their grievances in strikes and spontaneous uprisings.

Colonial family life, ca. 1715. This representation of a mixed-race family is typical of a genre known as casta paintings. These works aimed to specify racial identities and depict social hierarchies based on birth, skin color, ethnicity, and place of origin. The painter, Juan Rodriguez Juarez, was a Spaniard who lived and worked in New Spain. What attitude toward interracial families does the painting seem to communicate?

Europe: Successes and Failures of Absolutism

In the first half of the sixteenth century, the Habsburg emperor Charles V imagined himself transforming Europe into a unitary empire under the moral leadership of the Roman Catholic Church. France, the Ottoman empire, and German princes who had converted to ProtestantismÐ all Habsburg enemiesÐ sabotaged this dream, and Europe remained a collection of diverse and competing states (see Map 19.2).

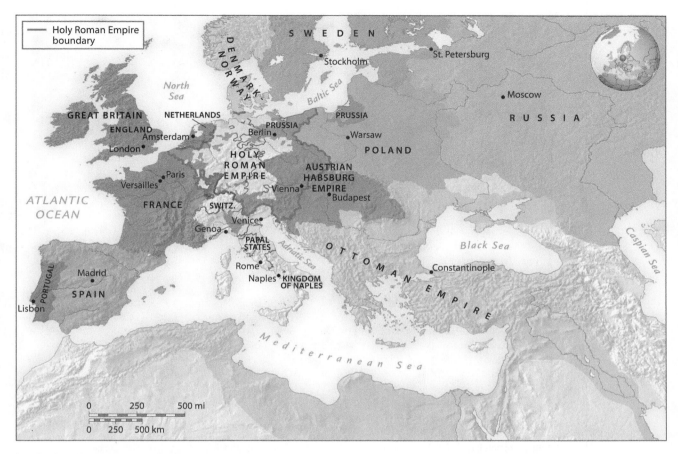

MAP 19.2 European states in 1750.
Many competing states shared the European landscape. What geographical and political challenges were European rulers who sought to expand their territories in this period likely to face?

The religious passions that the Protestant Reformation triggered eventually played themselves out, and by the complex terms of the Peace of Westphalia of 1648, Europe's monarchs and princes resolved a number of troublesome territorial issues and stabilized religious divisions in central Europe between Catholic and Protestant areas. Subsequently, rulers generally resigned themselves, at least for the time being, to a politically segmented Europe, even though they continued as before to try to seize one another's territories and resources. In the century after 1648, wars continued in one part or another of Europe almost without interruption. Generally though, limited strategic objectives rather than religious hatred motivated fighting. European states also fielded more rigorously disciplined armiesÐ professional forces that fought set battles, rather than running riot in the countryside or murdering large numbers of civilians.

In a sense, Europe's monarchs returned after 1648 to the business of strengthening and consolidating state power, a trend that had started back in the fifteenth century before religious and civil strife interrupted it. Not only in Europe but across Afroeurasia, states had undertaken centralizing projects using firearms technology and new approaches to top-down bureaucratic government to expand their borders and to rule their own populations more efficiently. These projects continued in the seventeenth and eighteenth centuries, in some places successfully, as in Qing China and Romanov Russia, and in other places unsuccessfully, as in South Asia, where the Mughal empire began to fragment not long after 1700.

Most Europeans no doubt yearned for social order after decades of violent religious discord and an economic depression in the mid-seventeenth century. Responding to this mood, rulers of several states reactivated projects to reduce the independent power of aristocratic landlords and strengthen the authority of royal officials. Like Peter and Catherine in Russia, western European rulers claimed absolute authority. Jean Domat (1625±1696), a French legal expert and eloquent proponent of absolutism, wrote: ªSince government is necessary for the public good, and God Himself has established it, it is consequently also necessary for

Political resolution. As part of the general Peace of Westphalia in 1648, Dutch and Spanish officials concluded the Treaty of Münster, ending the long war between them and granting independence to the Dutch Republic. Gerard Ter Borch, a noted Dutch portrait painter, rendered both Dutch and Spanish delegates in detail in this work titled *The Swearing of the Oath of Ratification of the Treaty of Münster* (1648). Do you think a Spanish painter might have represented this event differently? Why or why not?

those who are subject to government, to be submissive and obedient. For otherwise they would resist God Himself.[07] Subjects must obey those who head the state, but rulers also have a duty to govern justly, in accordance with God's will. This doctrine contradicted the earlier European tradition of shared governance between the monarch and other influential groups within society. Nevertheless, if rulers improved law, order, and the economy, while winning battles abroad, their subjects tended to go along with absolutist pretensions.

Even the most successful divine right monarchs ruled less absolutely than they might have liked. Communication and transport remained dependent on animal muscle, sail, or oar, and it took about as much time to send troops or government instructions from one province to another in 1750 as it had three hundred years earlier. This meant that village peasants, town elders, and local nobles could often ignore, delay, or resist orders sent out from the capital. Furthermore, all absolutist rulers had greater success negotiating and making deals with local power groups than in violently repressing them. Still, in every European country, provincial groups that did not want the central state nosing deeper into their lives periodically rioted, murdered state officials, or even tried to start civil wars.

French absolutism. Some European monarchs put absolutist ideals into practice more effectively than others. Reigning together for a total of 165 years (1610±1774), the French Bourbon monarchs Louis XIII, XIV, and XV had remarkable success shifting power from provincial aristocrats to themselves and their appointed ministers of state. Like sixteenth-century Russian tsars and Mughal emperors in South Asia, Louis XIII (r. 1610±1643) and his chief minister Cardinal Richelieu introduced a service nobility: an elite class of political administrators who owed their status and livelihoods entirely to the monarchy. These individuals, called ªnobles of the robe,º came largely from the rising urban bourgeois class of merchants and professionals.

Diplomatic splendor of Louis XIV's court. This painting, credited to the studio of the artist Antoine Coypel, depicts the French king receiving an ambassador from the Safavid empire of Persia. What symbolic role might art forms like this have played in legitimizing absolute monarchy?

Louis XIII also transferred provincial administration from local noble families to *intendants*. These were royal officers who held their positions temporarily and had no family or financial interests in the provinces where they served.

Louis XIV (r. 1643±1715) expended much creative energy transforming proud aristocrats into royal subordinates. He showered them with honors, gifts, and other symbols of status while simultaneously undermining their independent action. Jean Domat wrote that sovereigns should have the right ªto make manifest the authority and dignity of such wide-ranging and lofty power.º In line with that doctrine, Louis made himself an object of awe and reverence, building the extravagant palace of Versailles (vehr-SEYE) outside Paris, associating himself with the Greek sun god Apollo, and creating intricate court rituals to celebrate his grandeur. He enticed France's nobles to Versailles, offering them nonstop partying, sexual adventure, and chances to compete with one another, not for land and power, but for the king's personal notice. And he kept a close eye on them for any sign of defiance.

The Bourbon monarchs also wanted religious conformity. On one hand, they tolerated no interference from the pope in the administration of the French church; on the other hand, they had no interest in religious freedom. In 1598 King Henry IV (r. 1589±1610) had signed the Edict of Nantes, which award Huguenots, or French Protestants, limited rights to worship. Louis XIII, however, terminated Protestant control of certain towns. Louis XIV revoked the edict altogether in 1685, ordering churches to close and Huguenot clergy to leave the realm. Indeed, thousands of Protestants fled France, taking their literacy, skills, and successful businesses to places like the Netherlands, Germany, and England, where rulers welcomed them.

Absolutist monarchs across Afroeurasia discovered that political centralization, war making, and magnificent displays of power were hugely expensive; thus they were incessantly thinking up new ways to raise money. The French kings had rich resources to work withÐ a realm of twenty million people (twice the population of Russia), abundant and productive land, burgeoning commercial cities, and a growing overseas empire. They did not try to force the nobility and the clergy to pay direct taxes, but they chose competent financial advisers to help them impose levies on ordinary people more rationally and systematically. They also built canals and roads, subsidized textile and other industries, and promoted shipbuilding and overseas trade. Economic growth, they understood, generated imports, exports, and private money-making, all of which could be taxed.

Like so many other monarchies of the era, however, France continued to let spending far outrun revenue, especially outlays for wars in both Europe and abroad. Louis XIV, believing that absolutist success required military glory, attacked both the Dutch Republic and Habsburg territories and spent the last years of his reign fighting the debilitating War of the Spanish Succession (1701±1714). When he died, France was financially exhausted. Louis XV (r. 1715±1774) returned the country to relative peace, but only until 1740, when new fighting broke out among the European powers. This put even greater strains on the French economy and Bourbon absolutist hopes.

Prussian militarism. In the aftermath of the Thirty Years' War, Germany was divided into about three hundred princedoms, bishoprics, and free cities, most of which paid no more than ceremonial allegiance to the Habsburg emperor in Vienna. Nevertheless, in northern Germany a succession of three rulers of the Hohenzollern family built a formidable professional army and progressively gathered together several discontinuous territories that by the end of the eighteenth century emerged as an important European power. These territories included Brandenburg, location of the modest capital city of Berlin, and Prussia, which had earlier been a dependency of Poland. The Hohenzollern kings, whose state church was Lutheran, financed army and administration by collecting a variety of direct and indirect taxes, promoting industries, and squeezing revenue out of serfs who toiled on dynastic lands. Traditionally, diets, or assemblies of aristocrats and other notables, had local governing powers in Hohenzollern territories. But Frederick William, known as the Great Elector (r. 1640±1688), advanced an absolutist plan to centralize taxation, gutting the diets' taxing authority and making them irrelevant.

Frederick William I (r. 1713±1740), who made clear he answered only to God, organized the state mainly around the needs of the army, increasing its personnel to eighty thousand, including large numbers of draftees. Like the French, he moved to drain the noble class (*junkers*) of local autonomy. But instead of drawing them to a pleasure palace like Versailles, he assimilated them into the army officer corps, where the emphasis was on duty, honor, and loyalty to the crown. He also made the nobility pay direct taxes, which the Bourbons had not dared to do, and he replaced elected city councils with his own officials. Frederick II (Frederick the Great, r. 1740±1786) continued the absolutist policies of his predecessor but also deployed the army more aggressively, seizing important territories from both Austria and Poland. This enlarged state became the core of modern Germany.

Austrian multiculturalism. Although the rise of Prussia much weakened the Austrian Habsburg's already-

Frederick the Great inspects his troops. All of Europe's absolutist monarchs fielded strong armies. This painting portrays Frederick reviewing a regiment from Hesse, one of the component states in the centralized Prussian kingdom. Why did artists frequently depict Frederick as a military commander?

declining authority in Germany, the empire under Leopold I (r. 1657±1705) made dramatic territorial gains to the east. In 1683 Ottoman Turkish forces assaulted the walls of Vienna, the Habsburg capital, as they had done in 1529. The offensive fell short, however, and Austria counterattacked in the 1690s, driving the Ottoman government out of Hungary. This victory transformed the Habsburg state into a more culturally diverse collection of ethnic and religious groups than it had ever been. Leopold claimed absolute authority, but he did not succeed in imposing full centralization and certainly not cultural uniformity. German and Hungarian land magnates retained substantial power. Moreover, German, Hungarian, Serb, Romanian, and several other ethnolinguistic communities held more closely to their separate regional cultural identities than to any concept of a unitary society under the Habsburg crown.

British power sharing. In the Netherlands, Poland for a time, and Britain, political assemblies representing the elite classes of society successfully rejected divine-right absolutism and established governments of collective leadership. When Queen Elizabeth I died in 1603, England's Parliament had already firmly established its authority to debate and approve new taxes. James VI of Scotland, who succeeded Elizabeth as James I of England (r. 1603±1625), had eager hopes of absolutist rule and let his subjects know it: ªIt is atheism and blasphemy to dispute what God can do: . . . so it is presumptuous and high contempt in a subject to dispute what a king can do, or say that a king cannot do this or that.º8 James, who inaugurated the Stuart dynasty, thus put himself at loggerheads with Parliament as soon as he grasped the crown. His son and successor Charles I

King Charles I's last walk. This nineteenth-century painting by Ernest Crofts portrays Puritan soldiers marching Charles I, convicted of treason, to his beheading in January 1649. With this act, Parliament abolished the British monarchy, though its restoration came just eleven years later. Does the artist express sympathy for the king or for the soldiers, or neither?

(r. 1625±1649) took the same view of royal supremacy; consequently, a tug-of-war between king and Parliament continued for nearly four decades.

The Lords and the Commons constituted the two Houses of Parliament, and members of the Commons zealously guarded their right to approve taxes. The merchants, professionals, and members of the gentry (lower nobility) who dominated the Commons also turned England's wheels of industry and commerce. They wanted to expand their participation in government, especially to influence foreign policy. Parliament won some concessions from James because he needed money. The religious strife that engulfed the European continent in the early 1600s also roiled England. The Church of England, or Anglican church, had severed ties with Rome in the previous century. Nevertheless, strict Protestants in the tradition of the Reformation leader John Calvin believed the Anglican faith should replace excessive ceremony and the hierarchy of bishops with simple services, more preaching, lay (nonclerical) church governance, and stern policing of the public's moral behavior. Some of the righteous Puritans who wished to cleanse Christian practice of any vestiges of Catholicism went off to America to found the Massachusetts Bay Colony. Others, however, broadcast their grievances through Parliament.

Charles I tried for a decade to govern without convening Parliament and to force religious uniformity on both English and Scottish Christians. But facing both rebellion in Ireland (whose common people remained Catholic) and an invasion from Scotland, he was obliged to call Parliament into session in 1640 to raise money to deal with these crises. Consequently, the Commons acquired new leverage to make more demands. Charles responded by forming his own army without Parliament's funding. Members of the Commons did the same, and the country descended into civil war. Most European countries faced aristocratic or peasant uprisings in this period, but England had a revolution on its hands.

The British Isles experienced a whirlwind of changes between 1642, when the civil conflict started, and 1660, when Charles II took the throne. In 1645 the Puritan commander Oliver Cromwell assumed charge of the parliamentary army and within four years captured and executed Charles I, an event that stunned the crowned heads of Europe. Parliament declared its supremacy, abolished the monarchy, and wrote a constitution. In effect England became a republic, called the Commonwealth. Cromwell led an army into Ireland and suppressed the rebellion there, killing tens of thousands of Irish Catholics and transferring much land to rich English families. Historians have made the point that English overseas empire building really began in Ireland. Cromwell's forces also invaded and secured Commonwealth rule over Scotland. Despite Parliament, he awarded himself dictatorial powers, ran the country as a military state, and enforced a Calvinist moral code that, among other things, forbade dancing and theaters. He did, however, allow limited freedom of worship.

Cromwell died in 1658 and, amid popular weariness over two decades of turmoil, Parliament moved in 1660 to invite Charles II, son of the executed king, to restore the monarchy. Even so, king and Parliament continued to jockey for political dominance for another three decades. During the Restoration, as the period became known, religious antagonisms also continued between Anglicans, who once again dominated Parliament, and Calvinists and other dissenters who demanded religious toleration for themselves. Both groups feared that Charles II had Catholic sympathies, and his brother James II, who took the throne in 1685, was indeed a Catholic. Both Anglicans and other Protestants turned against him. In 1688 Parliament invited William of OrangeÐ the Protestant *stadholder,* or chief administrator, of the United NetherlandsÐ to take the English throne as coruler with his wife Mary, James II's Protestant daughter.

This sudden change, called afterward the Glorious Revolution, saw Parliament enact a Bill of Rights that established its full lawmaking authority and the principle that legislature and monarch must share sovereignty. Kings and queens would no longer rule by divine or even hereditary right but on the foundation of an unwritten contract with their subjects. Religious toleration was also extended, though restrictions remained on non-Anglicans, especially Catholics. We should not conclude, however, that the Glorious Revolution put Britain on the road to popular democracy. Voting was sharply restricted to property-owning adult males, and for another two centuries the House of Commons remained under the domination of the land-owning gentry together with professionals and wealthy businesspeople whose families frequently intermarried. Nevertheless, the absolutism that continued to loom over the European continent was gone for good in Britain.

European Settlement and the Fate of Indigenous Peoples

FOCUS In what ways may the political, social, and cultural characteristics of early European settler colonies in North America, Siberia, and South Africa be compared, including relations between settlers and indigenous populations?

As political and religious troubles gripped England, men and women began migrating in modest numbers to North America. This small trans-Atlantic stream represented the start of a globe-encircling movement of Europeans to regions thousands of miles from their homelands. This movement continued throughout the eighteenth century and surged mightily in the nineteenth and early twentieth centuries. Europeans migrated as permanent settlers mainly to the world's temperate latitudes both north and south of the equator, where they aimed to create societies founded on the languages, institutions, and cultural practices that they brought with them. Their success at planting settlements resulted in formation of a particular type of society, one in which Europeans living far from Europe came in time to constitute the great majority of the population. Historians have named this type of society a **neo-Europe.** Before 1800, neo-European societies emerged principally in eastern North America,

> **neo-Europe** A region outside of Europe, predominantly in temperate latitudes, where people of European descent came to make up a large majority of the population.

Siberia, and the Cape region of South Africa. (Later they would form in Australia and the southern third of South America.) In terms of both demography and culture, this type of society differed from others where Europeans *ruled* but nonetheless remained a small fraction of the population relative either to indigenous people, as in Mexico or Peru, or African slaves, as in the Caribbean and northeastern Brazil. In Mexico the population of exclusively European ancestry remained small. The *mestizo* population of mixed European and Indian descent evolved into a large minority by the early nineteenth century, but in the neo-Europes mixed populations remained small as percentages of the totalÐ and they became smaller as European settlers continued to arrive.

Most Europeans left home as settlers because of land shortage, poverty, religious persecution, or trouble with the law. Most of these emigrants did not intend to serve an imperial government, convert souls, or make a quick fortune and depart. Free settlers, rather, hoped to work the land, take up craft and commerce, and raise families. Settlers were drawn mainly to temperate zones because those regions were climatically and ecologically similar to western Europe. These destinations promised somewhat healthier disease environments than tropical latitudes did. And newcomers could grow crops (wheat, barley) and herd domestic animals (cattle, sheep) that they already knew about (see Table 19.1).

European settlers also enjoyed an advantage they did not fully understand. In most temperate lands where immigrants appeared, indigenous populations were already seriously declining or soon would be. This happened primarily because infectious diseases of Afroeurasian origin devastated native societies before significant numbers of Europeans even arrived, or else settlers introduced unknown pathogens that set in motion terrible epidemics. New diseases killed millions in Mesoamerica and Andean South America, but the native agrarian populations in those places were so large and dense that they continued to constitute large majorities relative to Europeans. This was not the case in eastern North

TABLE 19.1 Types of Colonial Societies in the Seventeenth and Eighteenth Centuries

Type	Political Organization	Population Profile	Examples
Imperial society	A small minority population of European officials and soldiers administers the imperial territory and rules a large majority of indigenous people.	Over time, a population of mixed European and indigenous descent becomes a significant minority.	Spanish Viceroyalty of Peru British India Russia (excluding Siberia)
Settler society	European officials, soldiers, and settlers administer the colony.	European settlers, most of them farmers and artisans, rise in numbers to constitute a large majority population. The indigenous population declines to a small minority.	British North America St. Lawrence River valley (Canada) Cape of Good Hope (South Africa) Siberia
Plantation society	A small minority of European officials and soldiers rules a large majority population of slaves imported from Africa.	A population of mixed European and African descent rises in numbers to constitute a significant minority. The indigenous population declines to a small minority or disappears.	Northeastern Brazil Caribbean islands Mauritius (Indian Ocean)

America, Siberia, or the South African Cape. In those places, local populations were relatively smaller, and, despite their determination to resist, their numbers dwindled rapidly under the persistent assault of lethal maladies and European settlers with guns.

Early European Settlers in North America

North America's temperate latitudes began to attract European migrants early in the seventeenth century (see Map 19.3). The first settlements were founded in the St. Lawrence River valley and along the Atlantic seaboard, though they remained small and scattered for several decades. Many Europeans crossed the ocean as free settlers, though others left home as indentured servants contracted to work for a master for a specified number of years. Still others traveled as exiled criminals or rebels. Migrants also brought in African slaves, though in far smaller numbers than were transported to the plantations of the Caribbean or Brazil.

Europeans, Indians, and beaver pelts. Attracted by the beavers, black foxes, and other furry creatures whose pelts commanded a market among affluent Europeans, French traders sailed up the St. Lawrence River to found settlements at Quebec (1608) and Montreal (1611). Indians who spoke Algonquian languages bartered with those strangers, offering furs and hides for textiles, liquor, metal ware, and sometimes guns. As the fur trade grew, both Europeans and Indians became locked into the world economy. The merchants, few in number relative to Indian populations, had no choice except to ally with local leaders, accept their trade customs, and employ them as hunters and guides. Conversely, Native Americans warmed quickly to European manufactured goods. As a Montagnais Indian remarked, ªThe beaver does everything perfectly well, it makes kettles, hatchets, swords, knives, bread; in short, it makes everything.º[9]

Native American societies of upper North America had long fought one another for resources, but those conflicts tended to be short. The fur trade changed that, especially when some warrior groups acquired firearms, using them to prey more violently on gunless neighbors to seize their hunting lands. Algonquian groups who allied with French traders also battled Iroquois peoples who lived in what later became New York State. Iroquoians made their own alliances with the Dutch, who built forts along the Hudson River, founding New Amsterdam on Manhattan Island in 1625. Meanwhile, Europeans penetrated Indian lands farther west. French explorers, fur traders, and Jesuit missionaries advanced into the Great Lakes region after 1635, and English sea merchants began building posts on Hudson's Bay in the 1670s.

France's royal government encouraged French peasants to emigrate to the St. Lawrence valley, called New France, to open farms and keep out potential English aggressors. These communities grew slowly. Most settlers had no agricultural knowledge, and the sex ratio remained heavily weighted toward young men. To adjust this imbalance, the crown enlisted Parisian orphan girls to go to the colony. These ªdaughters of the kingº were expected to marry a settler. Nevertheless, New France had only about three thousand European residents in 1663, and immigration all but dried up a decade later. Even so, the few that did come reproduced at a remarkable rate in the long term. Numbers reached about fifteen thousand by 1700 and continued to rise thereafter. Simultaneously, the Indian population of New France, pushed off their lands and suffering from repeated barrages of smallpox and other infections, shrank steadily. Today the French-speaking population of Canada numbers nearly 7.5 million.

English settler colonies. English men and women migrated to North America in the later seventeenth century in much larger numbers than French people did. They landed mainly on the coastlands extending from Massachusetts to Chesapeake Bay. Settler families and indentured servants began to arrive in New England in 1620, hoping to make livings from the land. They left home amid chronic

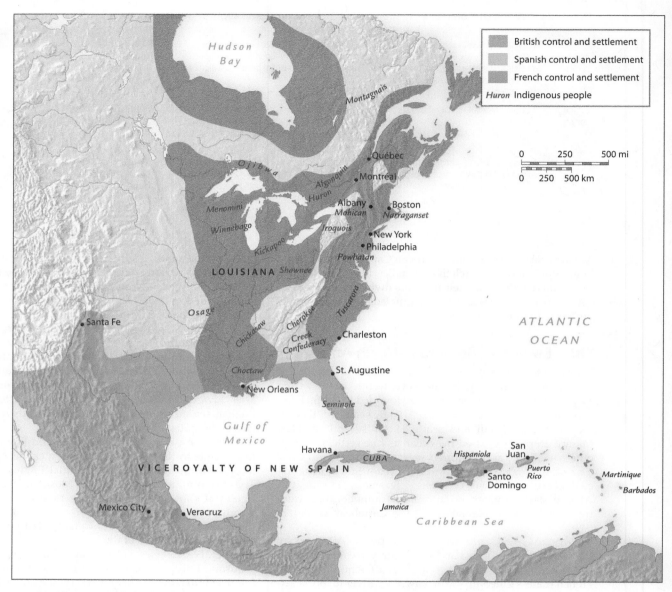

MAP 19.3 North America, 1750.

France claimed all the territory shaded in green. To what extent were its territorial claims supported by colonial occupation and settlement? How would you compare the extent of French and British claims with the reality of political occupation in each case?

political troubles, high population growth, and rising poverty. Large-scale commercial farming in England also pushed growing numbers of peasants off the land and into low-paying jobs or vagrancy. In those circumstances settlement in North America could look appealing.

A large portion of early migrants to New England and the mid-Atlantic region represented religious groupsĐ Pilgrims, Puritans, CatholicsĐ dissatisfied with prevailing trends at home. Puritans, who founded the Massachusetts Bay Colony,

intended to build a ªNew Jerusalem,º a Christian utopia to serve as a beacon of Protestant virtue. Persecuted Catholics later settled in Maryland. Quakers, another dissenting Protestant group, founded Pennsylvania.

From an economic standpoint, Virginia was the most successful early English venture. The Virginia Company of London financed a settlement on the James River in 1607. After a rocky start, villages multiplied and population grew. Small land-owners produced food, while private entrepreneurs opened agricultural estates. Sugarcane did not grow well, but local tobacco did. In 1638, Virginia produced more than three million pounds of leaves. Before long, American tobacco became a popular European addiction.

Entrepreneurs also began to carve out tobacco, indigo, cotton, and rice plantations in the Carolinas and Georgia, at first employing indentured labor. By the late seventeenth century, however, planters realized what sugar growers in the Caribbean already understood. European immigrant labor was not going to meet the needs of expanding plantation economies. Consequently, land-owners adopted the Caribbean system of putting captured Africans to work in closely watched gangs. By 1750 African slaves accounted for about 40 percent of the population in Virginia and Maryland.

Native American resistance and retreat. Early cooperation and neighborly coexistence between Indians and Europeans gave way to increasing hostility. Small numbers of Indian converts to Protestantism learned to read and write. But prospects of social harmony based on shared education and religion faded quickly as Europeans pushed for more land and total social domination. In Massachusetts much of the Native American population had already succumbed to smallpox epidemics in 1617±1619 and 1633. Surviving Indian communities, colonial leaders argued, had no right to the land because they failed to cultivate it properly, or in any case they were guilty of ªgodless ignorance and blasphemous idolatry.º [10] In 1675±1676, Wampanoag, Narragansett, and other New England Indians rose in rebellion against the spreading Massachusetts Bay Colony, briefly threatening its survival. The rising ultimately collapsed, however, and thereafter New England's Indian population steadily withered. In Virginia a violent three-way struggle broke out in 1675 between Powhatan Indians, rebellious land-hungry settlers, and the British governor. This disturbance cost many Powhatan lives. In the face of long-term settler plans ªfor extirpating all Indians without distinction of friends or enemies,º [11] Powhatan groups either retreated westward or resigned themselves to farming or servile jobs in the colonial economy.

In the eighteenth century the English colonies remained overwhelmingly rural. Nevertheless, the settler population swelled, rising between 1680 and 1750 from 150,000 to more than one million. Both agriculture and trade flourished. Boston, New York, Philadelphia, and Charleston grew into respectable cities. As this emerging neo-Europe became more important to the English economy, the imperial government sought to exercise more control. King James II (r. 1685±1688) tried to centralize royal authority in North America. But after the Glorious Revolution of 1688, all twelve of the colonies (Georgia, the thirteenth, was founded in 1732) reclaimed their separate political identities, including both royal governors and representative assemblies of land-owning European males.

Russian Settlement of Siberia

The Russians, Ukrainians, and other eastern Europeans who migrated to Siberia in the seventeenth and eighteenth centuries did not have to cross an ocean to begin building a neo-European society there. But similarly to French and English settlers in North America, they moved into temperate latitudes where wheat, cattle, and hogs could be raised. They had political and military support from the Russian state. They encountered relatively small populations of farmers, herders, and hunters. And they brought with them guns, plows, timber saws, and infectious diseases that would help clear these ªsmall people,º as Russians liked

Resistance to colonial settlement. Although Indians burned Brookfield, Massachusetts, and other villages during the 1675–1676 Narraganset War, they could not sustain their challenge to the expanding Massachusetts Bay Colony. How would you account for the deterioration of relations between Native Americans and settlers in New England?

to call them, out of the way. European settlement of Siberia, however, took a long time, and, like North America, the region did not achieve its full neo-European demographic character until well into the nineteenth century.

The territory that Russian settlers entered beginning in the seventeenth century had fundamental climatic and ecological similarities to northern Canada. In the far north, tundra supported low plant cover and reindeer herds. Farther south were boundless forests of fir, spruce, and pine. In both zones winter temperatures were extreme and rainfall unreliable. Consequently, the indigenous peoples who spoke Tangut, Samoyed, Yakut, and several other languages made their livings hunting, foraging, farming, fishing, and herding, depending generally on the ecological region they occupied. They lived in small, usually mobile groups, and coastal communities hunted seal, whale, and walrus.

Trade and tribute. The fur trade motivated early European colonization in Siberia as it did in upper North America. Russian trappers shipped sable, ermine, and sea otter pelts westward to be sold to affluent folk at huge price markups. As in North America, however, fur-bearing animals were a finite resource. Once traders depleted a region, they had to move on. The relentless search for fur brought Russians to the Pacific by the 1630s.

Encounters between Siberians and Russian settlers had mixed consequences. Compared to upper North American Indians, Siberians had modest defensive power and therefore less leverage to form trading partnerships with Europeans than Iroquois or Hurons did. Russian traders supplied Siberians with axes, cloth, tea, tobacco, and alcohol in return for pelts. But as representatives of the imperial state, Russians also demanded fur as formal tribute. Orders from Moscow declared: ªThe [Russian] serving and trading men should be ordered to bring under the sovereign's exalted hand the . . . diverse foreigners of various tongues who live . . . in new and hostile lands.º[12] Though the government appealed for ªkindnessº in collecting tribute, officials and merchants often held women and children hostage until they received deliveries and conscripted local people to serve as porters, guides, interpreters, and laborers. Furthermore, Siberia was far enough away from the densely populated lands of Eurasia that infections like measles, smallpox, and various venereal diseases were unknown until Russians introduced them. The first smallpox epidemic raged through Siberian communities as early as 1630, and these scourges tended to recur every ten or twenty years.

Advancing farmers. Despite the harsh climate and vast distances, Russian and Ukrainian farmers followed the trappers and merchants into Siberia, especially to its southern, warmer zone. These migrants, who had started moving into western Siberia as early as the fifteenth century, included peasants looking for land, serfs escaping their lords, fugitive criminals, and religious dissenters. Indigenous people were

A sustained demand for furs. Siberian sable and other fur remained an important commodity in Russia's trade with western Europe for centuries after trappers first began to exploit this resource. The affluent woman in this late eighteenth-century drawing from a series on Paris fashions is bedecked in expensive fur. What other products illustrate connections between expanding empires and growing global commerce in the seventeenth and eighteenth centuries?

welcome to live in European settlements as long as they adopted Russian language and dress as well as Christianity.

Peter the Great regarded the ªcivilizingº of Siberians as an important modernizing project. Small cities like Irkutsk began to rise up. By 1760 Irkutsk was connected to Moscow by a muddy trail called the Siberian Road. New towns supported civic life, including local governing councils, churches, libraries, and theaters. Imperial officials, however, had a hard time persuading even the most adventurous Russians to migrate to Alaska or down the North American coast. Those ªoverseasº settlements depended for their survival mainly on residents of mixed European and Indian parentage.

Symbols of colonial power. This well-known painting, *The Landing of Jan van Riebeeck, 6 April 1652*, presents an idealized view of early contact between Dutch settlers and indigenous Khoisan peoples in South Africa. The artist, Charles Davidson Bell, was a British civil servant who worked in South Africa in the mid-nineteenth century. What features of clothing and posture did Bell choose to emphasize in portraying the two groups? How would you account for those choices?

Europeans and Khoisan in South Africa

In the temperate latitudes of the Southern Hemisphere, the first place where Europeans founded a society of farming settlers was in the Cape region at the southern tip of Africa. Like both upper North America and Siberia, this was a region of relatively small-scale human habitation, not dense, city-building populations. Local people spoke languages in the very ancient Khoisan (KOI-sahn) family. Twenty-nine of these languages, characterized by their distinctive clicking sounds, are spoken today, though by relatively few people. In the seventeenth century, Khoisan speakers lived in seasonally mobile foraging and hunting groups. Some Khoisan also herded cattle and sheep. These pastoralists placed great social value on their livestock. Large herds signaled both economic wealth and respectable community status.

The early Dutch outpost. In 1652 the directors of the Dutch East India Company (VOC) issued instructions to land a crew at the Cape of Good Hope to set up a refreshment station for ships making the arduous but profitable six-month passage between Amsterdam and Batavia (modern Jakarta), the principal Dutch enclave in Indonesia. The VOC planned to limit investment at the Cape to a small defensive fort, access to timber for ship repairs, and some farms to supply vessels with grain, vegetables, and meat. The little outpost succeeded, partly because the moderate climate supported food crops familiar to European farmers. VOC officials thought the Khoisan had plenty of surplus cattle to trade, but they did not understand the social significance of herd possession and got limited cooperation. Relations remained tense, and the two groups began rustling each other's cattle.

From outpost to colony. Within five years of its founding, the Cape settlement began to expand. Initially, a few soldiers received grants of land to raise crops and animals. The Dutch lacked sufficient military power to coerce local

The Journal of a Dutch Commander at the Cape of Good Hope

When Dutch East India Company (VOC) officials under Jan van Riebeeck decided to establish a refreshment station on the South African coast, they did not have to negotiate for space with well-armed kingdoms, as they did in Southeast Asia. But they did have to deal with multiple Khoisan groups that hunted, fished, and herded cattle. The early colonists gradually recognized the complexity of Khoisan alliances, animosities, and interests. They also realized that superior weapons did not translate smoothly into immediate political domination. A few Khoisan individuals worked with the colonists, though collaboration put them in the awkward position of not having the full trust of either Europeans or their own communities. After the company began importing slaves in 1658, relationships became even more complicated as runaway captives joined Khoisan groups, strengthening their ability to challenge VOC control.

Van Riebeeck brought his family from the Netherlands to the Cape, and Krotoa, the daughter of a Khoisan chief, joined the household as a servant. She learned Dutch, converted to Christianity, and served as a VOC interpreter. She eventually married a VOC official and had children. But when her husband died, both the Dutch and the Khoisan societies rejected her. She ended her life in prison, a pariah without social identity.

The following excerpts from the VOC journal reveal the company's attempts to understand and manage local conditions. Note the range of dates in these three entries.

February 25, 1652. Aboard the Diamant, *anchored in Table Bay.*

This evening we went ashore . . . to consider where the fort should be built. Also had 2 savages on board this evening, one of whom could speak a little English. We generously filled their bellies with food and drink. As far as we could gather cattle could not be obtained from them for—as they gave us to understand by means of broken English and signs—they were only fishermen and the cattle were always supplied by those from Saldania [farther up the coast].

April 10, 1652. At the site of the fort construction.

About noon a small band of 9 or 10 savages from Saldania arrived, against whom the [fishermen], who sit outside our tents with their wives and children every day, arranged themselves in battle order and advanced toward them with assegais [spears], bows and arrows with such courage and fury that we had sufficient to do to check them. . . . [We] succeeded in arranging a truce between them, so that for the rest of the day they remained at peace with one another in the vicinity of our tents. Those from Saldania, by means of signs and the use of broken English, as well as some Dutch words . . . gave us to understand that for copper and tobacco they would bring cattle and sheep within a few days. By good and liberal treatment we urged them to do so.

July 1, 1658. At the fort.

Today almost all the Hottentots . . . who had been searching for . . . fugitive slaves returned without any and reported that they could find none. Thereupon all the [Khoisan] prisoners and their wives [detained by the Company] began to weep and wail lustily, as they had been told that they would not be released until all the slaves had been brought back to us. They evidently saw little chance of that happening just yet. . . . The interpreter Doman maintains that they had never seen the fugitives, who had run away of their own accord. This we showed him that we did not believe. On the contrary, we feel that we are correct in presuming [the Khoisan are helping the fugitive slaves], for the Hottentot women were too familiar with the slaves in the beginning and gave them many things. The result is that they have to be satisfied to remain in captivity until we recover the slaves or know what has really become of them. This made the interpreter Doman hang his head and seem much depressed, as also Eva [as Krotoa was called by the Dutch], who said that the Hottentots would kill her if we did not release [high ranking Khoisan hostages]. She was told to keep within the fort, and that if anyone harmed her, the Commander would have him captured as well.

To set the minds of the hostages at rest, the Commander in person told them to have no fear for no harm would come to them, and said that everything was being done to recover the runaway slaves. They were given some tobacco, bread, and brandy, which seemed to cheer them up somewhat.

Source: Journal of Jan van Riebeeck, ed. H. B. Thom (Amsterdam and Cape Town: A. A. Balkema, 1952), 1:25, 30; 2:294±295.

Thinking Critically

What do you think may have constituted the colonists' hospitality, generosity, and "liberal treatment" of Khoisan in these passages? What evidence do you find of hostile attitudes? Why would the interpreters Doman and Krotoa feel threatened by the VOC's seizure of Khoisan hostages? What hints, if any, do you think this document offers regarding Khoisan attitudes toward the settlers?

Khoisan into servile labor, so they began bringing in slaves from the VOC's ports on the Indian Ocean. By 1658 the basic demographic profile of the colony was emerging. A minority of European settlers, overwhelmingly men, depended mainly on Asian slave labor to do farm work. In the following decades, the Dutch authorities issued land grants farther away from the Cape fort, and the population of both Europeans and Asians rose gradually, from about four hundred in 1662 to twenty thousand by 1780.[13]

The early Cape colony was culturally diverse. Sexual and marital unions crossed ethnic, linguistic, and religious lines. This happened chiefly because European men continued throughout the eighteenth century to outnumber settler women by three to two.[14] The top level of the VOC governing elite was Dutch and Calvinist Protestant. But new settlers came from across northwestern Europe, including Dutch, German, and Scandinavian farmers, as well as Huguenots escaping religious repression in France. The Afrikaans language, for example, is based on sixteenth-century spoken Dutch but also incorporates words and grammatical influences from French and Portuguese, as well as Southeast Asian languages introduced by slaves. The Cape diet was equally varied, combining European bread, meat, wine, and brandy with African game and Indian Ocean rice, coffee, tea and spices. By the end of the eighteenth century, the population also practiced Protestant Christianity in several forms.

The growth of the colony cost Khoisan hunters and herders dearly. Colonial records point to communities being pushed to the margins of their former hunting and grazing lands. And as Europeans and their slaves advanced along the coast and into the interior to plow land and graze their own herds, Khoisan men and women lost their options for independent life. Consequently, more of them resigned themselves to servile employment on settler farms. Like native Siberians, Cape Khoisan occupied a territorial extremity of Afroeurasia. They therefore lacked effective immunities to a number of infectious diseases. Smallpox, introduced at the Cape by either Europeans or Asians, took an appalling toll. An epidemic in 1713 hit Khoisan communities particularly hard, sparing scarcely one in ten individuals.

In the early eighteenth century, Khoisan society in the Cape region effectively collapsed. As this happened, the Southern Hemisphere's first Neo-Europe began to take shape. In contrast to Siberia, however, greater South Africa was not simply a land of mobile hunters and herders. Not far north and east of the Cape lived much larger, denser farming and cattle-keeping populations of Africans speaking Bantu languages, peoples more resistant to infectious Afroeurasian diseases than were the Khoisan. By the later eighteenth century, these populations met the moving frontier of European settlement with much stiffer economic competition and military resistance than the Khoisan had been able to mount. The South African neo-Europe remained territorially small and, in contrast to North America and Siberia, did not last long.

Alternative Visions of God, Nature, and the Universe

FOCUS How did the scientific revolution and the Enlightenment represent a new system of knowledge, and what factors help explain the continuing growth of Islam and Christianity in the seventeenth and eighteenth centuries?

In the hubs of European overseas empires, especially London, Amsterdam, and Paris, scientists, philosophers, and practical technicians sorted through cascades of new information from across the seas. Africans, Asians, and Native Americans offered much of this knowledgeÐ from Iroquoian kinship relations to West African plant species to Confucian imperial court ceremoniesÐ to European visitors, who returned home with it for study and interpretation. Moreover, the work of making sense of new knowledge took place in a post-Protestant Reformation religious environment in which novel ideas about the natural world no longer had to conform exclusively to the doctrines of the Catholic Church. Growing numbers of intellectuals felt free to challenge truths received from the Bible, the ancient Greeks, and church theologians. An intensive project to reexamine long-accepted explanations of the workings of nature, the cosmos, and human society, an endeavor whose two fundamental elements were the scientific revolution and the Enlightenment, got under way. Also, because peoples around the world participated in interpreting and transmitting this knowledge and because it circulated continuously from one region of the world to another, the project was a global one from the start.

As this rethinking of the nature of things proceeded, people in both Europe and other societies continued their religious quests to understand the operation of the divine in human affairs and come to grips with moral questions, the prospects of salvation, and responsibilities to family and community in a rapidly changing world The world's major religions of salvation and missionary outreachÐ Islam, Christianity, and BuddhismÐ all continued to grow, a phenomenon aided greatly by the new world-girdling routes of transport and travel.

The Scientific Revolution

Since the emergence of *Homo sapiens* more than 200,000 years ago, bright flashes of scientific and technical innovation have occurred periodically in one society or another. One of those moments of illumination took place in the seventeenth and eighteenth centuries, and it was centered in western Europe. This burst of scientific inquiry and invention was not inevitable. Rather, political, economic, and cultural circumstances of the time came together to set it in motion.

After the opening of the oceanic passages in the fifteenth and sixteenth centuries, Europeans had continuous and startling encounters with peoples, plants, animals, landscapes, and climates that they previously knew little or nothing about. This roused great curiosity and a yearning for fresh explanations of natural phenomena and of how the world got to be the way it is. As thinkers sought to make sense of the flood of new knowledge, they brought together three existing intellectual strands: ancient Greek philosophy, especially logic; the medieval European synthesis of this thought; and scientific and mathematical writings of South Asian, Greek, and Muslim thinkers. They also began to work out new methods to verify information to ensure that what people thought they knew about the world was true.

ᵃ Scientific revolution° may be too strong a term to describe these first steps toward a systematic rethinking of what philosophers then called the ᵃ laws of nature.° But over the course of two centuries, this work produced a dramatic shift toward explanations of the world founded on empirical observation, controlled experimentation, careful recording, analytical reasoning, and sharing of knowledge among scholarly communities. By the 1700s European governments and church authorities, whether Catholic or Protestant, interfered less in the publication and circulation of new ideas than they had just a century earlier. New technical instruments such as telescopes and microscopes greatly magnified human powers to observe. Mathematics emerged as the fundamental language for describing phenomena and for communicating and testing scientific hypotheses among educated scholars. European universities, founded in earlier centuries as self-governing corporations, served well as incubators of new theories and speculations. As novel explanations of reality circulated widely, those founded on religious teachings, ancient philosophies, folklore, or other forms of wisdom handed down from earlier generations lost some, though not nearly all, of their power to guide human behavior.

Sun and earth. An early battle between empirical observation and traditional wisdom took place over the celestial relationship between the sun and our planet. Until the sixteenth century, astronomers in both Europe and the major Muslim centers of learning agreed that the earth occupied the center of the universe. This understanding was based on the work of Claudius Ptolemy, the second-century Greek-speaking scholar who lived in Alexandria in Egypt. In his book titled the *Almagest,* he proposed a geocentric, or earth-centered model of the universe in which all other heavenly bodies revolved around our world in nested spheres. Ptolemy remained the accepted authority on astronomy during the next 1,300 years.

Nicolaus Copernicus (1473±1543), a Polish scholar and Catholic cleric, put forth the first serious challenge to the Ptolemaic system in 1543 when he published *On the Revolutions of the Celestial Spheres.* The book tackled problems in Ptolemy's model by proposing that the earth orbited around the sun, along with other planets and stars. Copernicus founded his challenge to Ptolemaic astronomy on his own reading of ancient Greek texts but also on two

mathematical theorems formulated by Muslim scholars during the previous two centuries. Copernicus's heliocentric, or sun-centered theory had significant flaws and failed to attract widespread support. But in the following century, other scholars revised and refined the Copernican model, while theologians grappled with the implications of moving God's earthly creation out of the center of the cosmos. Johannes Kepler built on the work of the Danish astronomer Tycho Brahe to postulate that planetary orbits are elliptical, rather than round. The Catholic Church enlisted its own scholars to refute heliocentric claims as contrary to received truth. In 1633 the church's inquisition pronounced Galileo Galilei a heretic, sentencing him to house arrest for the rest of his life for publicly advocating a heliocentric universe. His *Dialogue Concerning the Two Chief World Systems* (1632) combined logical reasoning with evidence of telescopic observations to argue that the corrected Copernican system had greater explanatory power than the Ptolemaic model.

Sir Isaac Newton (1642–1727) analyzes light. An English physicist, mathematician, astronomer, natural philosopher, alchemist, and theologian, Newton carefully recorded his observations of the natural world, laying foundations for modern scientific knowledge. Here he uses a prism to investigate the constituent colors in a ray of light. What does this nineteenth-century engraving reveal about the tools and methods used in early scientific experiments?

A generation later the English scientist Isaac Newton published *Philosophiae Naturalis Principia Mathematica* (1687), which describes universal gravitation and the laws of motion, demonstrating a connection between gravity and Kepler's laws of planetary motion, thereby confirming the heliocentric theory. Newton's work defined specific laws of physics and set a standard for the next three centuries of scientific writing, combining accessible prose with detailed mathematical explanations of physical motion. Newton's work also had global scope.

Observation and experimentation in many fields.

Remarkable advances took place in a number of fields besides astronomy and physics. Experiments in biology, chemistry, optics, and medicine changed not just what people knew about the world, but how they knew it. The English

Observing and recording the natural world. The German artist Maria Sibylla Merian worked for a time in the Dutch colony of Surinam in South America. Like many of her drawings, this illustration of a pair of common morpho butterflies (ca. 1719) shows the interconnected life cycles of plants and insects. Many Europeans of this period believed that insects spontaneously generated from mud or rotten meat. How does Merian's illustration exemplify modern scientific method?

philosopher Francis Bacon articulated new scholarly methods that relied on personal observation, not just on libraries of ancient texts. He argued for a total reconstruction of science, the arts, and all human knowledge to found conclusions on the careful observation, cataloging, and analysis of natural phenomena. He also advocated inductive reasoning, that is, the method of arriving at a general hypothesis or theory regarding a phenomenon from careful observation of specific examples of that phenomenon. His effort to devise a systematic classification of human knowledge not based simply on received wisdom was instrumental to the development of modern thought.

The questioning of tradition spread outward from scientific inquiry, which at this time was little separated from philosophy and other branches of knowledge. In fact, scientists like Newton were known as ªnatural philosophers.º Their work reinforced a growing conviction that much new knowledge was yet to be discovered, not simply dug up from the past. Governments began to look to science for potential contributions to economic progress and military advantage. By the mid-1600s, European states became more interested in promoting the spirit of inquiry than in punishing it. In 1660 Charles II of England granted a charter to the Royal Society of London for the Promotion of Natural Knowledge. It began publishing a scientific periodical to disseminate new developments. The French government approved a Royal Academy of Sciences in 1666.

The Enlightenment: Rethinking Human Nature and Society

The Enlightenment was a wide-ranging, many-sided intellectual movement among thinkers centered in Europe to put all inherited descriptions of nature and society to the test of reason. The movement emerged from several strands of thought. Most important was the work of scientists, especially Isaac Newton. He argued that universal physical laws governed all God's creation, that these laws could be expressed in mathematical equations applicable in all times and places, and that humans could understand the workings of the universe through their God-given powers of reason. John Locke, an English physician, politician, and colleague of Isaac Newton, was among the first to contend that if scientists like Newton could discover and articulate the laws of nature, then humans could also reason their way to clearer understanding of the operations of both the individual human mind and collective social behavior. Like the scientific revolution, the Enlightenment also aimed to make sense of the blizzard of knowledge arriving from other parts of the world. Finally, it built on the Renaissance commitment to humanistic education and creative thought, the Protestant Christian idea that individuals must discover God and their relation to him through private study and prayer, and reform efforts within the Catholic Church to rid it of ignorance, corruption, and superstitions that had no base in scripture.

TABLE 19.2 Innovative Thinkers of the Seventeenth and Eighteenth Centuries

Individual	Country	Achievements
Baha' al-Din ibn Ḥusayn al-Amili 1547–1621	Persia	Prominent mathematician, astronomer, poet, and Sufi mystic in Persia's Safavid empire; revived the study of mathematics in Persia.
Francis Bacon 1561–1623	England	Proposed a system of inquiry founded on empirical and inductive reasoning, later called the scientific method.
Galileo Galilei 1564–1642	Italy	Drawing on evidence from telescopic observations, supported Copernicus's heliocentric theory; discovered the moons of Jupiter.
Johannes Kepler 1571–1630	Germany	Proposed, following Copernicus, that the earth revolves around the sun (heliocentrism) and postulated three planetary laws of motion.
Yoshida Mitsuyoshi (Yoshida Kōyū) 1598–1672	Japan	Known along with two other scholars as the Three Arithmeticians; wrote the oldest surviving Japanese mathematical text.
Gadadhara Bhattacharya 1604–1709	India	Wrote prolific volumes on language, mind, law, and the concept of "meaning"; analyzed the emotive power of language and expression.
Margaret Cavendish 1623–1673	England	Wrote voluminously on power, manners, science, philosophy, and gender; an early writer of science fiction who also advocated for animal rights.
John Locke 1632–1704	England	Wrote extensively on theories of both knowledge (epistemology) and natural rights, postulating the idea of a social contract between ruler and subjects.
Isaac Newton 1642–1727	England	Set forth three laws of motion and described the operation of gravity; developed the calculus as a branch of mathematics.
Maria Sibylla Merian 1647–1717	Germany	Created observational drawings of numerous insect species that contributed to the discovery of insect metamorphosis; a founder of the scientific field of entomology.
Juana Inés de la Cruz 1651–1695	Mexico	Self-taught nun, poet, and scholar; wrote extensively on Christian philosophy and theology and defended the right of women to education and intellectual inquiry.
Baron de Montesquieu 1689–1755	France	Powerfully influenced liberal political theory, notably the concept of the separation of powers in government.
Voltaire 1694–1778	France	Historian, philosopher, and social critic; attacked the intolerance, superstition, oppression, and authoritarianism of the European old regime.
Benjamin Franklin 1706–1790	United States	Pursued research on electricity, sea currents, meteorology, and the nature of atoms; a revolutionary leader and diplomat who also founded the first lending library in the United States.
Carl Linnaeus 1707–1778	Sweden	Invented the modern system of naming and classifying organisms.
Jean-Jacques Rousseau 1712–1778	Switzerland	Wrote three major works that explored questions of morality, equality, freedom, government, and education; asserted that humans are good by nature but have been corrupted by society.
Dai Zhen 1724–1777	China	Neo-Confucian philosopher; wrote on human nature and metaphysics and incisively criticized earlier Confucian thinkers.
Immanuel Kant 1724–1804	Germany	Moral philosopher; proposed that humans have knowledge of reality only through the exercise of their rational faculties; had a large impact on modern philosophical speculation.
Ivan Shuvalov 1727–1797	Russia	Powerful figure in the Russian imperial court; championed the arts and humanities; first minister of education and overseer of Moscow University.
David Rittenhouse 1732–1796	United States	Astronomer, mathematician, and inventor; wrote an account of the transit of Venus and calculated to near accuracy the distance between the earth and the sun.
William Jones 1746–1794	England	Proposed structural relationships between South Asian and European languages, a hypothesis that launched the field of Indo-European studies.
Mary Wollstonecraft 1759–1797	England	Argued in *A Vindication of the Rights of Woman* that females are naturally equal to men but are deprived of education and the opportunity to develop fully their intellectual faculties.

Challenges to the Old Regime. Enlightenment figures, known in France as *philosophes*, explored humankind's relation to God, nature, and the universe from nearly every conceivable angle, sometimes making their arguments with mathematical equations and geometrical proofs (see Table 19.2). Many of them expressed faith that if scientific methods and enlightened reasoning guided human action, then continuous material well-being and progress could be ensured. Few of them advocated radical action to dismantle religious institutions, governments, or even absolutist

old regime The political and social system in France and other European monarchies between the sixteenth and eighteenth centuries; characterized by a rigid class hierarchy and rulers' claims to absolute authority.

monarchies, but most were highly critical of what they saw as the irrational, arbitrary, fanatical, or cruel aspects of what later was called the **old regime.** This term refers to the prevailing European social pyramid, the hierarchy of ranks from the monarch and the nobility on down based not on talent, education, occupation, or even wealth, but fundamentally on privilege either inherited or awarded by the state.

According to Locke, higher reasoning power distinguished humans from animals. This entitled people to certain **natural rights,** which no government should be allowed to take away without just cause, namely, ªlife, liberty, and property.º Locke expressed his philosophy in many works, two of which particularly influenced political thought in England and eventually around the world. The first, *A Letter Concerning Toleration,* helped justify Parliament's passage of the English Toleration Act following the Glorious Revolution of 1688. That bill significantly lightened discrimination against religious dissenters. In 1690 Locke published *Two Treatises of Government* to justify England's emergence as a constitutional, limited monarchy. He attacked absolutism, contending that government must be a civil contract between citizens and government. Both parties operated under legal obligations that, if unfulfilled, released the other party from its obligations.

natural rights Universal and inherent rights of human beings bestowed by nature or divine power.

Innovative thinkers in France also spoke out against the excesses of the old regime. These *philosophes,* including mathematicians, poets, playwrights, novelists, and essayistsÐ argued that rationality, not faith, custom, superstition, or revelation, should guide human affairs. Their debates collectively made a case for religious toleration, natural rights, eradication of cruel and unusual punishments, and even abolition of slavery. For some Enlightenment thinkers, such as the French poet and playwright Voltaire, the Christian church obstructed rationality and progress because of its rigidity and hypocrisy and the ignorance and dogmatism of its clergy. But even the skeptical Voltaire accepted the existence of a supreme being. Most Enlightenment philosophers, including Locke, Immanuel Kant, and Georg Wilhelm Friedrich Hegel, found no incompatibility between reason and faith, believing that human reason reflected God's wisdom and benevolence.

Some *philosophes* defined man's rationality in ways that excluded women. Jean-Jacques Rousseau, a creative thinker and a popularizer of Enlightenment ideas, argued that the male of the species in his natural state was fully equipped to solve the thorny problems of existence, many of which were the fault of civilization. But women, he believed, did not possess the ability to reason and thus the capacity to advance society except as nurturers of their families. A woman's physical functions overwhelmed her intellectual ones. ªThe male is male only at certain moments; the female is female her whole life,º Rousseau wrote in *Emile* (1762), a treatise on education. Rousseau did not mean to degrade women by his statements but to exalt all that in his view was ªnaturalº in them. Some women echoed his sentiments. In *Letters on the Female Mind* (1792), British author Laetitia Hawkins concurred that ªthe feminine intellect has less strength and more acuteness. . . . [W]e show less perseverance and more vivacity.º[15] Writings of Hawkins and other women helped open a new debate about women's rights toward the end of the eighteenth century. In 1792 Mary Wollstonecraft, an English essayist, wrote history's first indisputably feminist tract, *A Vindication of the Rights of Woman.* She argued that the social training given to girls taught them to be frivolous, vain, and incapable. If educated equally, women would be the intellectual match of men.

Europe's new breed of natural philosophers filtered great amounts of data and used it to formulate new theories, both natural and social. One debate swirled around the idea that because people around the world looked and behaved so differently from one another, God must have created man and woman more than once, a theory that some said contradicted the Bible and therefore could not be true. Carl Linnaeus, the Swedish botanist who devised the modern system for classifying plants and animals, identified five races of humans having particular physical and mental tendencies. (He also believed some human groups had tails.) Enlightenment sages generated early theories of inherent racial qualities and differences that scientists demolished fully only in the late twentieth century. As information, whether accurate or not, regarding American Indians, Pacific Islanders, Chinese, and Africans reached Europe, Enlightenment writers ventured all sorts of social and cultural comparisons, sometimes to affirm European and Christian superiority but quite often to critique European habits and institutions. In 1721, for example, the Baron de Montesquieu published the *Persian Letters,* an imaginary account of two Persian gentlemen who visited France and commented critically on various aspects of society.

Several eighteenth-century European monarchs invited Enlightenment thinkers such as Voltaire to their courts or exchanged letters with them. These rulers, including Frederick II of Prussia, Catherine II of Russia, and the Habsburg emperor Joseph II (r. 1780±1790), saw no particular contradiction between their claims to absolute political authority and the thought of French *philosophes.* For them, Enlightenment rationality translated into programs to improve government efficiency, codify laws, eliminate senseless torture of prisoners, advance technical education, promote the arts, and reform agriculture and industry in ways that would improve the lives of peasants and workers at least marginally, thereby improving their productivity and raising their taxable incomes. These rulers could chat amiably about natural rights and enlightened government without thinking that such notions should in any way upset the existing old regime hierarchy.

Communicating the Enlightenment. Individuals engaged in scientific and philosophical inquiry collectively produced a huge body of writings. But the Enlightenment was not simply an elite phenomenon. Many outstanding contributors were individuals of modest origins and means. Diatribes against intolerance, bigotry, and the political status quo became commonplace in newspapers, novels, essays, and pamphlets, most of these contributions the work of authors now forgotten. The Enlightenment was in large part a middle-class phenomenon made possible by inexpensive printing technology, the spread of literacy, and the emergence of libraries and coffeehouses, all media of communication that reinforced one another. The educated class gathered in public literary societies, some of which admitted women, to read popular works of the day.

Encyclopedias and dictionaries became a pronounced expression of the Enlightenment, putting forth the doctrine that any person who aspired to self-improvement must have a comprehensive knowledge of science, technology, and the humanities. For people of relatively low social status, these volumes could be an entry into polite society. In England, Ephraim Chambers edited what is considered the first modern encyclopedia. It went through five editions between 1728 and 1744. A French publisher, recognizing good market potential, commissioned Denis Diderot and Jean le Rond d'Alembert to edit *Encyclopédie,* ᵃa systematic dictionary of the sciences, arts, and crafts° that reached twenty-eight volumes. Scottish and German encyclopedias soon followed. The renowned British author Samuel Johnson published the first edition of a *Dictionary of the English Language* in 1755. The work contains 42,773 word entries, some of them laced with humor: ᵃLexicographer. writer of dictionaries; a harmless drudge that busies himself in tracing the original, and detailing the signification of words;° and ᵃPolitician. 1. One versed in the arts of government; one skilled in politicks. 2. A man of artifice; one of deep contrivance.° [16]

Although the scientific revolution and the Enlightenment were predominantly western European movements, they diffused quickly to parts of the world where people spoke or read European languages. Eastern European states, notably Poland and Russia, had their own Enlightenment figures. In Moscow, Ivan Shuvalov, minister of education and Catherine II's lover, played a major role in founding both Moscow University and the Russian Academy of Arts. Far to the west in British North America, Benjamin Franklin's path-breaking experiments with electricity earned him admission to the French Royal Academy of Sciences. In Massachusetts, John Winthrop III at Harvard College measured the distance between the earth and the sun with near accuracy. The Enlightenment idea of the natural equality of all humans began in the mid-eighteenth century to inspire some colonial religious leaders and intellectuals to plead for the abolition of slavery. Simultaneously, the ideas that came

out of the English Civil War and Glorious Revolution, combined with Enlightenment political thought, stirred colonial leaders to protest British imperial injustices and, finally, to declare independence in defense of their ᵃinalienable rights° (see Chapter 20).

The Continuing Growth of Islam and Christianity

Modern science emerged in the seventeenth and eighteenth centuries as a particular way of describing nature and the cosmos based on practical observation of material phenomena and, from that evidence, formulation of general theories and principles. In other words, science evolved as a specific system of knowledge. Other complex systems of knowledge, however, also existed, notably, the major world religions. They too sought to explain universal truths. The scientific revolution and the Christian system of knowledge challenged each other on numerous points. But they also influenced each other's development, and both remained intact. In the same period that modern scientific thought took root in Europe, the major religions, especially Islam and Christianity, attracted growing numbers of adherents. The success of these religions rested fundamentally on the ways they explained existence, roused hopes, and guided human conduct. They also benefited, however, from the great world convergenceÐ the opportunities that worldwide communication and transport, as well as empire building, offered to introduce the faith to more people across greater distances.

Islam in Afroeurasia. Islam grew faster than any other major religion in the early modern centuries. Muslim merchants, artisans, and scholars carried the faith to new places, often taking passage on European ships. Muslim pilgrims traveled from all directions and in larger numbers to make the sacred pilgrimage to Mecca and Medina in Arabia. In the early modern period about fifteen thousand South Asians made the pilgrimage yearly, most of them by sea.[17] These devotees often returned home eager to share the message of the Quran with unbelievers.

Sufi saints and devotees contributed immensely to conversions in regions where Islam had previously been a minority faith or completely unknown. Sufism appealed to individuals seeking not only a community of fellow worshipers but also individual spiritual enlightenment. It represented the mystical side of Islam, the quest to achieve direct and personal communion with God. From the eleventh century, Sufi teachings and practices became progressively integrated into both Sunni and Shi'a Muslim life. Sufi practitioners typically followed a pious teacher, or ᵃfriend of God,° who guided them along a spiritual path. The journey might involve a wide range of devotions, including study of mystical texts, visits to the shrines of deceased Sufi divines, and participation in sessions of chanting or dancing aimed at achieving a transcendent state. Most Sufi disciples also joined one or more religious associations, or orders, whose members pursued a distinctive path to enlightenment. For Muslim women, who did not typically occupy public or religious offices, Sufi devotions and affiliation offered an arena for religious expression and leadership. By the sixteenth century, Sufi organizations numbered in the hundreds, and some had branches in several regions.

When Sufi missionaries advanced into new regions, they often adapted to local, non-Muslim religious practices, contending that sincere commitment to God was more important than conformity to details of Muslim law. **Syncretism** was not uncommon on the frontiers where Islam met Hinduism, Buddhism, Christianity, and local religions. Examples of such compromise included symbolic linking of Hindu gods and goddesses with venerated Muslim saints; transforming sacred trees, rocks, or ponds into Muslim shrines; and wearing charms containing written phrases from the Quran to ward off evil spirits.

> **syncretism** In religion, the blending of beliefs or practices from two or more different belief systems; also the incorporation of beliefs or practices of one belief system by another.

From the sixteenth to the early eighteenth century, the Muslim Mughal dynasty ruled much of South Asia, but the majority population followed a variety of devotions that collectively we call the Hindu tradition. Sufi believers converted significant numbers of South Asians, notably in Bengal, the region of the lower Ganges River. The Mughal rulers encouraged Muslim farmers to migrate to the Ganges valley to cut forests and plant rice, cotton, and other crops, thereby extending agricultural lands that could be taxed. These pioneers assumed a leading role in the wave of economic expansion that benefited Bengal starting in the later seventeenth century. Sufism, together with the economic success of many Muslim entrepreneurs and merchants, firmly established Islam in the region, eventually as the majority faith.

Merchants, traveling scholars, and holy preachers, many from South Asia, introduced Islam to island Southeast Asia beginning in the fourteenth century. By the 1500s the religion was established across the Indonesian archipelago. Advancing northeastward from there, Muslim traders and Sufis founded communities in the southern Philippine Islands in the sixteenth century, even as Spanish priests introduced Catholic Christianity around Manila in the north.

Islam spread briskly in Subsaharan Africa from the later 1600s. Muslim populations had dominated the commercial towns along the East African coast for several centuries. Conversion intensified from the end of the seventeenth century, when the sultans of Oman, a maritime state located at the southeastern end of the Arabian Peninsula, built a formidable navy and began to dominate the major East African ports. From that time, Muslim merchants began to introduce their religion along the trade routes that led into the East African interior. In South Africa, the VOC brought in Muslim slaves and political prisoners. Islam's message also proved attractive to non-Muslim slaves, offering them a focus of social and devotional life separate from their Christian masters. In West Africa in the seventeenth century, Muslims both ruled and dominated trade in the savanna lands just south of the Sahara, and Sufi brotherhoods carried the faith to rural herders and farmers. The extensive conversion of peoples of Sudanic West Africa, however, did not take place until the nineteenth century (see Chapter 22). A significant percentage of the slaves transported to the Americas from the sixteenth to the nineteenth century were West African Muslims. Christian masters, however, prohibited Muslim slaves in America from open communal worship. Practice could be preserved only in fragmentary ways or in secret.

Christianity around the world. The Roman Catholic Church enjoyed global reach in the sixteenth century because Portuguese, Spanish, and Italian sea captains, virtually all of them Catholics, opened the global sea routes and

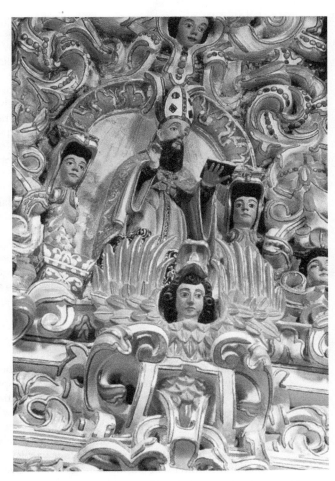

Christianity made local. Nahuatl artists decorated the church of Santa María de Tonantzintla starting in the early seventeenth century. This detail from an interior wall shows a Catholic bishop flanked by women wearing local headdresses. What other Native American influences do you see in this picture? What does this artwork suggest about local understandings of Christianity?

Individuals MATTER

Dona Beatriz Kimpa Vita: Visionary Christian of the Kongo

Dona Beatriz as portrayed in a letter written by Father Bernardo da Gallo, who interviewed her after her spirit possession in 1704.

In 1665, the once proud and powerful Kong kingdom, an African realm the size of England, descended into civil war, as rival lords fought over succession to the throne. This war was still raging four decades later, when Dona Beatriz Kimpa Vita (1684–1706), a twenty-year-old Christian woman, determined to intervene. As she lay wracked by illness, she dreamed that the Catholic saint Anthony of Padua had entered her body. When she recovered, she began traveling throughout Kongo, speaking out against both factional violence and enslavement and attracting followers to what became known as the Antonian Movement. St. Anthony instructed her, she preached, to heal the kingdom of civil strife.

She also preached a novel Christian theology, declaring the teachings of European clerics in the Kongo were incorrect in important particulars. Jesus Christ, she proclaimed, was not born in Bethlehem, but in São Salvador, the Kongo capital. Nazareth was a corruption of the name Nsundi, a northern province of Kongo where Christ had been baptized. Mary, his Kongolese mother, had been a slave when she and Joseph sought shelter on the night of the messiah's birth. Though Dona Beatriz and the Antonian Movement recognized the authority of the pope, they rejected the presence of Portuguese monks of the Capuchin order and wanted to spread their distinct Kongolese version of Christian truth.

Dona Beatriz's preaching exerted a powerful pull on the Kongolese population for both religious and political reasons. The Antonian Movement gained devoted adherents among both the nobility and the common people, many of them tired of civil conflict and rampant slave trading. Dona Beatriz and her followers, however, placed Pedro, the reigning king at the time, in an awkward and dangerous position. He resented the condescension of Capuchin missionaries, but he could not allow a charismatic young woman to undermine his authority. In 1706 the king ordered Dona Beatriz arrested and tried on charges of witchcraft and heresy. Convicted, she was burned on a flaming pyre.

Though the Antonian Movement continued after Dona Beatriz's death, thousands of her followers were rounded up and sold into slavery. Capuchin monks objected but only because these captives were shipped to Protestant countries. Many, in fact, may have ended up in South Carolina, which, after Haiti, had the second largest concentration of slaves from Kongo. In 1740, Catholic Kongolese slaves led a bloody though futile rebellion against their masters near the Stono River in South Carolina. Their battle cry was "*lukangu*," which in the Kongo language meant both "liberty" and "salvation."[19]

Thinking Critically

Would you characterize Dona Beatriz as an anti-European resistance leader? Why or why not?

---

began conquering the Americas. Missionaries who followed the conquistadors across the Atlantic began baptizing Indians. Priests and monks had the greatest initial success in Mesoamerica and Andean South America, where people had previously lived under Aztec or Inca rule and were therefore accustomed to an ªofficialº religion and a priesthood associated with the state. In other words, the institution and hierarchy of the Catholic Church moved into the place of the Aztec and Inca religions.

Though one Spanish priest reported baptizing up to fourteen thousand Indians in a single day,[18] such mass conversions did not typically run deep. Syncretism flourished as many local religious practices became intermeshed with Christian ones. Since Spanish clergy usually spent little time in rural villages, they appointed local people to run churches. The Spanish called these native helpers ªcantorsº and ªsacristans.º In Mexico, however, Nahuatl speakers persisted in calling them ª*teopantlaca*,º the name given to workers in the old Aztec temples. Spanish priests granted villagers their own patron saints, but Indians routinely melded these Christian figures with local deities that they believed watched over their communities. The Spanish required Indians to accept one God and the Holy Trinity but also shared with their imperial subjects popular Christian beliefs in the power of magical and supernatural forces in various manifestations. In short, Spanish missionaries and Mexican Indians shared some common religious ground even though they often assigned different meanings to the same rituals and beliefs.

In China and other parts of Asia, Christian conversion proceeded slowly. In contrast to the situation in the Americas, wherever the Portuguese seized coastal enclaves or entered ports to trade, they had to deal with local authorities and urban populations who could limit or prohibit missionary activity. The Jesuit priest Francis Xavier (1506±1552) preached in Japan, ordering priests under him to observe Japanese etiquette and conduct themselves in the manner of Zen Buddhist dignitaries. By 1600 the church counted 300,000 Japanese believers, most on the southern island of Kyusu. But the Buddhist Tokugawa shoguns, who consolidated their power in the early seventeenth century, clamped down on Christian conversion and worship and Catholic communities withered away (see Chapter 18). In China, Matteo Ricci (1552±1610) and other Jesuit priests secured permission to preach and build churches, and they tried to show parallels between Catholic doctrine and Chinese Confucian philosophy. Both the Ming and the early Qing royal courts made use of Jesuit knowledge of cartography, astronomy, mathematics, clock making, and firearms technology. The Catholic missions, however, reached few ordinary Chinese. After 1704, when an envoy from the pope insolently announced that Chinese Christians must be prohibited from venerating their family ancestors, the emperor had missionaries expelled. The church's hopes of large-scale conversion evaporated after that.

Wherever Portuguese, Dutch, British, or French merchants founded stations along the West and Central African coasts, they introduced their own Catholic or Protestant religion. But Europeans operated in most places as the guests of African rulers and usually huddled close to their posts. Christianity did not therefore spread far before the eighteenth century, though the ancient Christian church in Ethiopia, whose teachings differed significantly from either Catholic or Protestant churches, continued to flourish. In tropical Africa, Europeans achieved the most conversions in the Central African Kongo kingdom, whose royal family became Catholic early in the sixteenth century. Subsequent monarchs vigorously promoted the Christian gospel, and the religion became deeply ingrained in Kongolese life.

Jesuit missionaries in China. Jesuits combined assimilation of Chinese cultural forms, European scientific knowledge, and Christian theology to persuade potential Asian converts. What evidence does this engraving provide of their blending Christian and Chinese symbols?

This involved, however, significant syncretism, as Catholic and older Kongolese religious practices intermingled.

• • •

Conclusion

In the sixteenth and early seventeenth centuries, rulers of a number of Afroeurasian states demonstrated that by fielding gunpowder armies and more effectively taxing their populations to pay for huge military expenditures, they could build stronger, more highly centralized states and even territorial or seaborne empires. Large-scale state building continued in the period from 1650 to 1800, a process assisted by the increasing sophistication and deadliness of firearms technology.

The world map of powerful states, however, changed significantly. The Muslim-ruled Mughal, Persian, and Ottoman empires reached the end of their long expansionary phases in the seventeenth century and either shrank or, in the case of Safavid Persia, disappeared. In the same era, however, Russian and Chinese armies advanced across the immense spaces of Inner Eurasia in opposite directions, while avoiding prolonged conflict with each other. In Europe, France, England, the Netherlands, Prussia, and (for a time) Sweden became both politically and economically stronger, while the Habsburg empire expanded deeper into southeastern Europe at the expense of the Ottoman state. By contrast, Portugal and Spain dropped to a lower rank in the hierarchy of European power.

European empire building overseas succeeded spectacularly in the Americas. The Spanish crown, despite economic troubles at home, continued to exploit its great Latin American viceroyalties, and Portugal progressively subjugated more of Brazil's Native American population. Britain, France, and the Netherlands seized territories in the Caribbean and eastern North America. All five of these powers deployed naval power to either acquire or hang on to coastal enclaves and islands in Asia and tropical Africa, but in those regions the balance of territorial power remained firmly in the hands of local rulers.

In the seventeenth century, Europeans also undertook a new kind of long-distance expansion, founding colonies of settlers in eastern North America, Siberia, and the Cape region of South Africa. In these regions, populations of mainly European descent not only made themselves politically dominant, but with the help of infectious diseases and armed aggression gradually succeeded in displacing native indigenous communities to create neo-Europes, societies whose populations and cultural form were of largely European origin. Across much of the world's temperate zones, these societies would grow much larger in the nineteenth century, to the grim detriment of indigenous peoples.

In the seventeenth and eighteenth centuries, networks of both transoceanic and long-distance overland communication became increasingly complex. As that happened, all but the most isolated societies had to confront immense amounts of new information arriving from afar. This avalanche of knowledge, circulating from one part of the world to another, provoked new questions about the universe, nature, and human society, as well as growing distrust of old answers. Peoples around the world took part in generating knowledge and posing fresh ideas , though the intellectual hub of this phenomenon was the globally connected ports and capitals of western Europe. The resulting scientific revolution and cultural Enlightenment changed forever the premises and methods for discovering and knowing truth. The new ways of thinking challenged time-honored religious doctrines on many points. Nevertheless, the great missionary religions, especially Christianity and Islam, continued to grow apace as monks, priests, ministers, pious scholars, and Sufi devotees fanned out along land and sea routes to share their own solutions to the problem of being.

• • •

Key Terms

absolutism 547
creole 550
English Civil War 568
Enlightenment 563
Glorious Revolution 556
natural rights 567

neo-Europe 556
New Spain and the Viceroyalty of Peru 549
old regime 567
Peace of Westphalia 551
philosophes 566

Qing dynasty 545
regent 545
scientific revolution 563
syncretism 569
Treaty of Nerchinsk 546
War of the Spanish Succession 554

Change over Time

1582	Confucian scholars encounter Catholic Christian missionaries in China.
1632	Galileo Galilei offers proof of heliocentric theory of planetary motion.
1639	Russian explorers advancing across Siberia reach the Pacific.
1642–1660	The English Civil War involves temporary abolition of monarchy.
1643–1715	Louis XIV rules France, promoting absolutist principles.
1644	The Qing dynasty comes to power in China, replacing the Ming dynasty.
1648	The Peace of Westphalia proposes principles to guide international relations in Europe.
1652	Khoisan peoples of South Africa encounter Dutch East India Company (VOC) colonizers.
1654–1722	The Kangxi emperor expands China's land frontiers.
1675–1676	Native Americans unsuccessfully rebel against settlers in Massachusetts Bay Colony.
1682–1725	Peter the Great transforms Russia into a major European power.
1687	Isaac Newton publishes *The Principia,* detailing laws of gravity and motion.
1688	The Glorious Revolution in Britain limits the monarchy's power.
1689	China and Russia settle land frontier disputes with the Treaty of Nerchinsk.
1690	John Locke publishes *Two Treatises of Government,* criticizing absolutist government.
1690s	The Austrian Habsburg empire drives Ottoman forces out of Hungary.
1701–1714	The War of the Spanish Succession drains economies of western European states, especially France.
1713–1740	Frederick William I consolidates power in Prussia.
1792	Mary Wollstonecraft publishes *A Vindication of the Rights of Woman,* arguing for equal education for women.
Early 1800s	The Spanish American empire reaches its greatest territorial extent.

Please see end of chapter reference section for additional reading suggestions related to this chapter.

The Modern World Takes Shape 1750–1914

part 6

The Modern World Takes Shape

1750–1914

Thomas Edison's incandescent
bulb, invented in the 1880s.

In the middle decades of the eighteenth century, human life on earth began to change at an accelerating speed. The transformations of the past 250 years—in society, economy, and human interaction with the physical and natural environment—are comparable in their historical significance only with the invention of agriculture 12,000 years ago. In this book we associate these transformations, which are still under way, with the modern era or, simply, modernity. In Part 6 we survey the modern period from about 1750 to 1914, the year World War I broke out.

Scholars of history have long debated the factors that distinguish the modern age from all earlier times. In our view, the development on which all other transformations turned was the onset of what we call the "energy revolution." In the later 1700s, humans found ways to tap an immense stockpile of energy concentrated in fossil fuels—coal first, then petroleum and natural gas. Since then, exploitation of this underground energy bonanza has permitted levels of population growth, economic productivity, social complexity, military destructiveness, and human intervention in the environment inconceivable in any earlier era. Today the average individual uses something like 46,000 times more energy than our ancestors did 12,000 years ago, and most of that increase has occurred since 1750.

The modern era, however, also has several other characteristics, all interrelated in complex ways with the energy revolution and with one another:

■ Humans have for the first time acquired the technical power not only to adapt successfully to the earth's environment but, for good or ill, to *transform* it. In other words, our own species, rather than physical and natural forces, has since sometime in the nineteenth century become the chief instrument of change in the earth's ecology, geology, and atmosphere.

■ The growth rate of world population began to accelerate in the mid-eighteenth century far faster than in any earlier time. The world had about 770 million people in 1750 and more than 7 billion by 2012. About 28 percent of all humans who were ever alive have lived since 1750. This growth has carried with it much greater social complexity, seen, for example, in the rise of giant cities. Between 1000 and 1700 C.E., the world had no more than three cities with populations in excess of 1 million. In 2000, there were 299 such cities.[1]

■ Rates of technological and scientific advance have accelerated greatly since the eighteenth century, and no slowdown appears in sight. This rush of novelties began in connection with the energy revolution and the accompanying industrial revolution with its countless transformations in manufacturing, farming, and communication. Today, innovations in science and technology proliferate at breathtaking speed. Material advances, together with huge inputs of fossil fuel and to some extent nuclear energy, account for the accelerating rate of long-term global economic growth since the late eighteenth century.

■ Networks of world-girdling commercial, cultural, biological, and migratory exchange have become much denser and more complicated in the past 250 years. Global exchanges, especially messages transmitted instantaneously through electronic networks, have made possible a great acceleration of "collective learning." This is the ability that humans, unlike any other living species, possess to amass, store up, and transmit information, much of it useful to human well-being, some of it harmful.[2]

■ States, that is, territories whose inhabitants live under the authority of a central government of one type or another, have come to exercise both military power and command over the lives of their own citizens on a scale unknown in premodern times.

■ A new kind of political thought emerged in the eighteenth century centered on the twin ideas that God and nature have bestowed on human beings certain indisputable rights and that the source of any government's authority is rightfully the "people," not kings or high priests. This ideology gradually captured the whole world's imagination, provoking wars and revolutions but also animating both private capitalist enterprise and the political experiment to organize the world in sovereign nation-states, nearly two hundred of them.

In exploring the period from 1750 to 1914, we should keep in mind that the meaning and direction of the modern age are unknown to us because it is still in progress. Revolutions in economy, social organization, microbiology, or electronics may already be happening, though we cannot yet see their shape or significance. We should remember, for example, that the computerized and digitized world we live in today would have been unimaginable to the nineteenth-century scientists who first harnessed electrical energy and unknowingly made possible smartphones, genetic decoding, and Facebook.

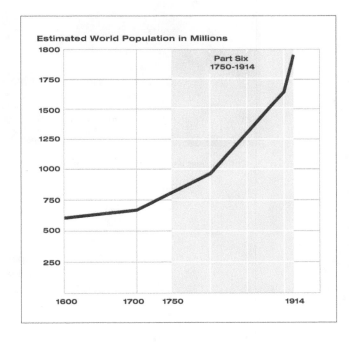

Estimated World Population in Millions

20 Waves of Revolution
1720–1830

Coffeehouses were important sites of political conversations in the eighteenth century.

free and lively newspaper culture has been a feature of democratic societies in modern times, but is this medium disappearing? Communication experts have been asking this question ever since the Internet emerged as a carrier of news, opinion, and advertising. In the United States, print editions of most major newspapers have been steadily losing circulation, and some have gone exclusively online. Futurists have predicted that newsprint will vanish entirely before the end of the current century.

If newspapers endure only in cyberspace, they will have had a relatively short history as a print medium. Daily or weekly broadsheets with small circulations first appeared in western Europe and British North America in the late 1600s and in other parts of the world barely two hundred years ago. Newspapers flourished in connection with the epic transformations that took place in human society in the eighteenth and nineteenth centuries. News writers could gather more information and put it in print faster as roads improved, ships got faster, postal services were set up, and, in the early nineteenth century, steamships, railroads, and the telegraph were invented. Newspapers helped meet the capitalist world's constant demand for quick information about political conditions, wars, prices, and the movement of commodities. The popular revolutions that erupted in North America and Europe in the late eighteenth century spawned many new broadsheets to inform the public of late-breaking events and to promote one political view or another. In the following century, steam-powered presses rolled out thousands of copies of news sheets. The handful of newspapers published worldwide in the 1700s grew to an estimated 3,168 by 1828 and to more than 31,000 by 1900.

The rise of the newspaper was one event in a large cluster of changes that we associate with modernity. This chapter spans the period from approximately 1720 to 1830 and focuses on the momentous political and social changes that occurred in the world in those 110 years. This was an era of accelerating global population growth, a nearly continuous surge in the volume and value of global commerce, a dramatic increase in the number of people using money to buy and sell goods in the market, and the creation of far more complex networks of transport and communication. These developments inspired radical new thinking about how to organize society and manage change, and they brought higher standards of living to millions in some parts of the world. They also, however, aggravated political and social stresses for many more millions and triggered conflict among classes, ethnic peoples, and rival states.

In the first part of the chapter we explore the relationship between rapid change in the world economy, especially the complex intermeshing of societies through commerce, and the mounting problems that the world's large states faced in financing bureaucracies, fielding armies, and keeping public order. In the middle decades of the eighteenth century, European states, especially Britain, France, Habsburg Austria, Prussia, and Russia, projected more military power relative to the large Asian empires than ever before. They also competed violently with one another for shares of accumulating global wealth. European states, North American Indians, and South Asians all clashed in the Seven Years' War from 1756 to 1763, a "world war" that helped set the stage for several popular revolts.

The second part of the chapter investigates the first wave of revolutionary movements that took place on both

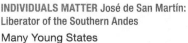
• • •

sides of the North Atlantic between 1775 and 1815. Political, economic, and cultural forces reverberating back and forth across the ocean intricately linked the rebellions that erupted in British North America, France, and Haiti. Those movements drew on new ideas about natural rights and the "sovereignty of the people" that had emerged from the Enlightenment (see Chapter 19), ideas that have shaped protest, revolution, and the organization of governments ever since.

The final part of the chapter explores the second wave of revolutions, which engulfed nearly all of Latin America. These insurgencies took place in social environments that differed greatly from British North America and Haiti, but as in the British colonies, they were led mainly by American-born, property-owning men of European descent. The wars of independence ended Portugal's rule of Brazil and nearly obliterated Spain's enormous American empire, replacing it with multiple states founded on modern patriotic ideas of self-government by and for the people.

A Panoramic View

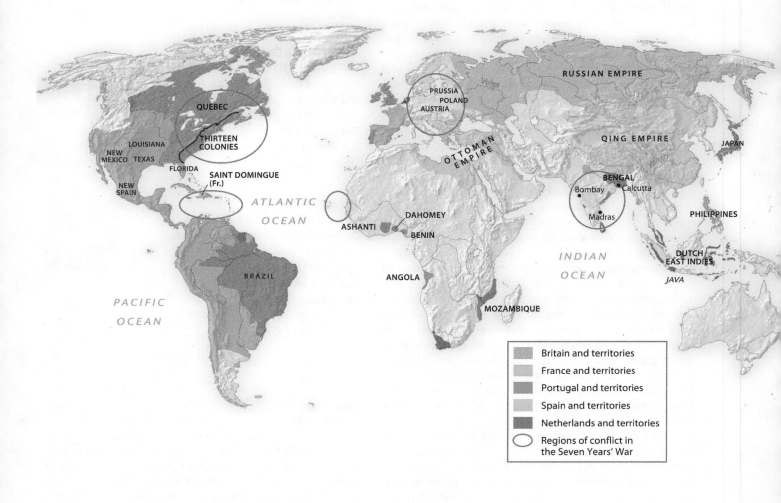

MAP 20.1 Major states and colonial territories after the Seven Years' War (1756–1763).

Empires claimed huge swaths of territory—some in contiguous stretches of land and others overseas. Desire for even more territory and wealth fueled rivalries among empires. What aspects of this political map of states after the Seven Years' War might explain the global nature of that conflict among European powers?

World Economy and Politics, 1720–1763

FOCUS To what extent was the growth of the world economy connected to changes in the relative power of large states during the eighteenth century?

Scholars have conventionally dated the political and social upheavals that enveloped much of the world in the later eighteenth and early nineteenth centuries to the outbreak of rebellion in Britain's thirteen North American colonies in 1775. More recently, however, historians have offered evidence that beginning about 1720 several of Afroeurasia's large and prosperous states experienced growing economic problems, political turbulence, and social stresses. In several place these troubles led to regional rebellions and new wars.

Observers of the world scene would not likely have foreseen the impending instability. Its early signs appeared against a background of intense and accelerating global economic activity. The world was rapidly commercializing. The buying and selling of raw commodities, manufactured products, and labor in response to changing prices and market conditions was surging upward both locally and between regions. The later seventeenth and the eighteenth centuries also witnessed a phenomenon in which families with relatively modest incomes began to purchase more material goods on the market and to pay for them by working harder and for longer hours than they ever had before.

Global commercialization raised the stakes for all states determined to stay in the competitive game and to acquire greater wealth. It put added pressure on them to control more farm land and mines, dominate trade routes, protect markets against foreign merchants, and grab new colonies before their rivals moved in ahead of them. These objectives, however, required rulers continually to expand bureaucracies, recruit new troops, and upgrade expensive military technology. The costs of government therefore mounted at an accelerating rate, especially where armies had to defend long frontiers or overseas colonies. The expense of simply *maintaining* a state's status as a major regional player, regardless of further expansion, obliged governments to impose heavier taxes on their populations of peasants, town dwellers, and money-making merchants. Heavier fiscal burdens, however, triggered rural uprisings, urban riots, or colonial protests that cost the state even more treasure to suppress. Signs that powerful states were losing the struggle to pay for their own centralizing and military success appeared first in Asia and then in Europe.

A Commercializing World

By the early eighteenth century, nearly every state in Afroeurasia, whether giant empire or tiny kingdom, was connected in some degree to the global commercial system that moved commodities, manufactured goods, and laboring men and women from one place to another. A combination of private profit-seeking and commercial competition between states motivated the emerging modern commercial system. The merchants who ran it relied increasingly on gold, silver, and other forms of money to make their transactions. Commercialization depended on an assortment of capitalist institutions and practicesÐ partnerships, joint-stock companies, banks, credit, currency conversion mechanisms, insurance policies, merchant information networks, and strategies to persuade consumers to buy new products.

The commercializing trend, however, was still at a primitive stage compared to today. Tens of millions of people lived by subsistence farming or herding and had no more than occasional contacts with the market. Others were shut out of the commercial system because their labor was controlled or owned by others. In eastern Europe and Russia, for example, millions of serfs had to turn over much of their farm production to estate-owning nobles, who then sold it for export to western Europe at profit only to themselves. The African slave trade was part of a highly commercialized system that benefited African rulers, American plantation owners, Atlantic merchants, and European manufacturers but not the slaves who brought in immensely profitable harvests of tropical sugar and tobacco.

Industrious revolutions. The demands and habits of consumers around the world began to change rapidly in the eighteenth century as many new and alluring products came on the market. For example, hardly any Europeans had ever tasted Chinese tea in 1664, when British East India Company officials presented two pounds of it to King Charles II. In the next few decades, however, tea caught on in Britain as an energy-supplying and mildly addictive beverage mixed with sugar. Imports from China rose from around 38,000 pounds in 1690 to 37.4 million by the 1750s.[6] As choices of new foods and other goods multiplied, consumers throughout the world became fussier about the wares they wanted to buy. In regions like southern China, Japan, India, western Europe, and the British North American colonies, where commercialization was proceeding fast, people who made money acquired more extravagant tastes for fine textiles, art, and home furnishings that only land-owning aristocrats had previously been able to afford. In West Africa, local merchants might refuse to sell captives to European slave shippers unless they could buy Indian calico cotton textiles with particular prints, not last year's outmoded fashions.

On a global scale, more rural farmers and artisans sold at market whatever surpluses they might manage to produce. More people abandoned their fields altogether and earned wages to buy food, clothing, and furnishings. In western Europe, for example, ordinary men and women purchased more goods from foreign places, including tobacco, sugar, tea, coffee, wine, Indian cottons, cheap porcelain tableware, and exotic furniture. Wherever people who were not

Indian fabrics influenced British fashion. A young woman's jacket and matching petticoat exemplify eighteenth-century European fashion. The fabric, which is hand-painted cotton chintz, came from the Coromandel coast in southeastern India. The flowers are a typical Indian design. An English tailor made the outfit around 1780. What might account for the popularity of exotic fabrics in England in that period?

wealthy aspired to consume more goods, they became participants in what historians have called industrious revolutions. This means that laboring men and women bought more goods rather than making them at home. They did this chiefly by working harder and more productively. Younger family members might toil longer hours on the farm, and adults might spend more working days earning wages. Families might fabricate a single specialized product at home but purchase rather than make their own candles, tables, or chairs. We have good evidence from western Europe, China, and Japan that men worked longer hours and more days of the year and that more women and children took up wage labor to satisfy hankerings for a wider selection of consumer

goods. This persistent industriousness and the resulting rise in demand for goods stimulated international commerce and gave more incentive to people to master complicated specializations or make technical improvements in farming or manufacturing.

Asia's economic weight. The center of gravity of global production and commerce remained in Asia until after 1750. Between the sixteenth and eighteenth centuries, remarkable demographic and economic growth took place in East and South Asia. China, India, and Japan together accounted for about 55 percent of the world's total population, compared to western Europe's 12 percent. China's population more than doubled in the eighteenth century, from about 160 million to 350 million. One measure of comparison between Asian and western European economies is farming productivity, the agricultural output of an average worker in a given time period. In 1750, productivity in the Yangzi River valley, China's richest agricultural region, was about the same as it was in England and the Netherlands, the two most productive countries in Europe. **Real wages** of agricultural workers were approximately the same in southern China and western Europe, as was life expectancy, at about forty years. China put out more than 30 percent of the world's manufactures, whereas India and Europe produced about 23 percent each (see table: Shares of world manufacturing output[2]). Knowledgeable Europeans recognized China's economic muscle. Adam Smith, the Scottish economic thinker, observed in 1776 that "China is a much richer country than any part of Europe." As for India, it was by far the world's largest exporter of hand-woven cotton textiles. As of 1750, weavers in southern India may well have enjoyed higher standards of living than their counterparts in Britain.[3]

> **real wages** Wages estimated in the amount of goods those wages will buy rather than in the face value of money paid.

Japan's economy achieved stunning growth in the seventeenth century under the government of the Tokugawa shogunate, though it slowed after about 1700. This probably happened in large part because the archipelago's population could no longer find much new arable soil or forests to exploit. Industrious Japanese peasants continued to increase their output but mainly by making small technical improvements or working longer hours to raise their productivity. Commercial fishermen also exploited the seas around Japan more intensively, catching fish that enriched supplies of food protein and fertilizer. Unlike western European countries, Japan had no overseas colonies from which to draw resources. Even so, the country remained highly commercialized, and it continued to trade with China, Korea, and Southeast Asia until the later eighteenth century. As of 1750, a larger percentage of Japan's population– about twenty-six million in all– lived in cities than did the populations of southern China or Britain. Edo (Tokyo) swelled to more than one million inhabitants, making it one of the largest cities in the world.

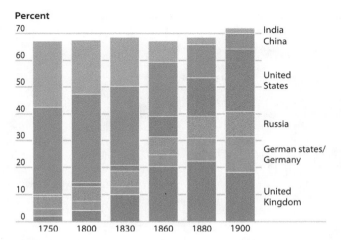

Percent

India
China

United
States

Russia

German states/
Germany

United
Kingdom

1750 1800 1830 1860 1880 1900

Shares of world manufacturing output, 1750–1900. In what countries did manufacturing increase during the late eighteenth and nineteenth centuries? Where did manufacturing stay relatively constant? Which regions lost significant shares of global production? What factors might help explain these changes?

Commercializing tropical Africa. In the early eighteenth century, peoples of Africa south of the Sahara Desert were already well entangled in the web of global commerce, though not in the same way that Chinese or South Asians were. The European capitalist entrepreneurs and merchants who developed the Atlantic economy bought gold, textiles, and numerous other commodities from African coastal merchants and the rulers of such monarchies as Ashanti, Dahomey, and Benin (see Chapter 18). Nevertheless, by the seventeenth century, Europeans visitors wanted slaves more than any material product, and as commercial plantations multiplied in the Americas, the demand for slave labor increased constantly. In the 1700s, more than six million men and women were forced to cross the Atlantic to work in bondage until they died. Traffic in captives also thrived from West Africa across the Sahara Desert to the Muslim Mediterranean and from the eastern side of the continent to the Arabian Peninsula, Persia, and India. In the mid-eighteenth century, the total number of Africans taken from their homelands may have numbered about seventy thousand annually.

The slave trade was not only a human tragedy but also a disaster for African economies. It deprived particular regions that were agriculturally rich of hundreds of thousands of productive farmers, artisans, and community leaders, as well as women of childbearing age. Just when the populations of China, Europe, and other parts of Eurasia were swelling, tropical Africa's population, which was about fifty million in the mid-eighteenth century, either held steady or declined slightly. Most regions from which slaves were taken would have gained economically from higher populations because arable land and pasture were

abundant. Furthermore, along the Atlantic coasts, European merchants sold shiploads of cotton cloth and iron goods in exchange for slaves. These imports gradually depressed once-flourishing African textile and iron-working industries. Rulers and merchants tried to meet the incessant demands European slave buyers made, and this led to more wars, population displacements, famines, and crime. In West and Central African coastal regions, slave trading significantly reduced male populations. This meant that the burden of agricultural labor fell more heavily on women than ever before. In short, in the mid-eighteenth century, economic output in East and South Asia remained strong and western Europe's economic star was rising. By contrast, violent trafficking in people weakened the commercial position many African societies may otherwise have had in the advancing wold economy.

Troubled Empires in Asia

Among the great Asian states, China under the Qing dynasty (1644±1911) remained prosperous and largely free of internal strife until nearly 1800. However, the three giant Muslim empires of the era experienced serious financial and governing problems in the early eighteenth century. The Safavid empire of Persia flourished under the talented ruler Shah Abbas (reigned 1587±1629) and for several decades thereafter (see Chapter 17). The costs of maintaining a larger gunpowder army continued to mount so relentlessly, however, that the government eventually allowed it to deteriorate. In 1722, a motley force of mounted rebels from Afghanistan overran Isfahan, the Safavid's fabled capital, and the dynasty collapsed. Until late in the century, Persia remained divided among competing military lords, none of whom managed to rebuild stable central authority.

To the east, the Mughal empire of South Asia, whose Muslim military elite ruled tens of millions of Hindu farmers and town dwellers, reached its greatest territorial extent under the rule of Aurangzeb (r. 1658±1707). The imperial regime had always negotiated the loyalty of locally powerful estate owners by generously awarding them rights to tax revenues from land. The government, however, found it increasingly difficult to make these grants as the costs of conquest and administration mounted. Aurangzeb kept restless local elites in line through great force of will, but his successors had few of his talents. After he died, local magnates and even provincial governors found they could defy central authority. Many of them also amassed wealth independently in South Asia's expanding commercial sphere, buying and selling crops of maize, tobacco, and chili peppers (all introduced earlier from the Americas) and doing business in cotton textiles.

As landlords accumulated new resources and the Mughal government creaked and sagged under its heavy financial burdens, regional rebellions multiplied. In 1739 the Persian warlord Nadir Shah invaded northern India and ferociously sacked Delhi before retreating. In the first half of

Sultan Selim III (r. 1789–1807) receiving dignitaries at the Topkapi Palace. The Ottoman court in Constantinople was the focal point of imperial administration. Here the Sultan is attended by courtiers, officials, and Janissaries.

the eighteenth century, the Mughal empire splintered into a number of regional power centers. Some of them offered ceremonial allegiance to the Mughal sultan in Delhi, others not even that. The Marathas, a confederation of Marathi-speaking clans based in central South Asia's Deccan Plateau, most vividly exposed Mughal weakness by creating a regional empire of their own that spanned nearly all of central India. In Mysore in the far southwest, Haider Ali and his son Tipu Sultan founded a state in the 1760s that fielded an army of sixty thousand and equipped it with artillery.

In contrast to the Safavids and the Mughals, the Ottoman empire, the third great Turkic-ruled state, remained a major Afroeurasian military power throughout the eighteenth century. After a long and losing war with Habsburg Austria, the empire had to cede several of its European provinces in 1699 (see Chapter 19). But it gained some of them back in the following decades and only began to suffer severe and permanent territorial losses in the war with Russia that ran from 1768 to 1774.

Nevertheless, growing fiscal difficulties and the rapidly changing world economy steadily wore down Ottoman

resources. The sultans installed in their fabulous Topkapi Palace in Constantinople became increasingly isolated from administrative affairs. Ministers of state who tried to make reforms repeatedly lost out to entrenched political and religious groups. The Janissaries, the slave army that had led the empire to military glory in earlier times, deteriorated from a highly disciplined fighting corps to a bloated assemblage of competing factions, each with business and commercial interests and an inclination to riot in the streets at the slightest challenge to their privileges. As in the Mughal empire, weakness at the top allowed elite landholders in the rural lands of both Anatolia (modern Turkey) and southeastern Europe to collect rents and taxes on their own account, rather than on behalf of the state. European governments and trading firms clamored for lower tariffs on imports, which deprived the Turkish state of an important source of revenue. Chronic price inflation, caused partly by the flow of American silver into the Ottoman economy, made life more expensive for thousands of bureaucrats and soldiers on fixed salaries and pensions. In addition, the land-owning elite demanded larger rents from local peasants. Many rural men and women fled the countryside for Constantinople and other cities, where they swelled the ranks of the underemployed.

Despite these numerous problems, the Ottoman empire continued in many ways to function as before. Uprisings and urban disturbances occurred with growing frequency, but dissenters hardly ever questioned the legitimacy of the Ottoman government. All kinds of institutions bound subjects of the sultan togetherÐ guilds, Muslim Sufi organizations, and local kinship groups. The Muslim legal system worked efficiently, and the Muslim, Christian, and Jewish communities within the empire regulated their own affairs. The main development was a process of decentralization in which power became more diffused through the empire to the advantage of local elite groups, clans, and estate magnates.

Global Sea Trade and the Eighteenth-Century "World War"

The major European states expended huge sums periodically fighting one another in the seventeenth and early eighteenth centuries and, in the case of Britain, France, the Netherlands, and Spain, expanding and defending their commercial and strategic interests. In the 1600s the Atlantic and Indian Oceans became theaters of intense competition among the main European naval powers. In the Atlantic, rivalry over the trade connecting Europe, Africa, and the Americas involved almost exclusively the western European states. The scene in the Indian Ocean and the China seas, however, was quite different. There, the chartered trading companies of Britain, France, and the Netherlands had the biggest ships and marine artillery, but the great majority of merchants and sailors operating in the southern seas were Chinese, Malays, South Asians, Arabs, and East Africans, including people who worked as crew members on European-owned vessels. In the ports of Southeast Asia, Chinese merchant and business communities grew steadily throughout the eighteenth century. For example, by 1800 the Chinese residents of Batavia, the Dutch East India Company's big port on Java in Indonesia, numbered nearly 100,000, far more than the population of Dutch company employees.

European belligerence in the southern seas. European competition for southern seas trade in cotton, silk, spices, porcelain, and tea intensified as the century progressed, in part because trading firm profits slumped gradually. Since the sixteenth century, Europe failed to offer many products other than silver that Asians wanted to buy. European merchants pumped more specie from American mines into the Asian economy. But as they did that the value of silver relative to gold began to decline so that a given unit of silver coinage bought fewer Asian goods. Moreover, the European East Indies companies learned early that despite their shipboard firepower, they could not come close to controlling the southern sea routes or the multitude of local traders and vessels that crowded into the network.

Europeans could monopolize direct sea commerce between the Indian Ocean and Europe, but they had to compete with Asians for the lucrative ªcarrying tradeº between one part of Asia or eastern Africa and another. And when it came to negotiating prices, Europeans had to depend on local rulers, entrepreneurs, and merchants who dominated the production of commodities and their transport from inland fields or mines to the ports where European ships awaited.

In response to shrinking profits, both the Dutch and British East India Companies took aggressive action. On Java, the Dutch sent armed bands from Batavia to the mountainous interior to seize direct control of more of the island's trade and to tax Javanese peasants. In 1725 they began to force highland farmers to grow coffee for export. In the same period the British firm strengthened the fortifications around its trading posts in South Asia, especially Bombay (Mumbai), which faced the Arabian Sea, and Madras (Chennai) and Calcutta (Kolkata) on the Bay of Bengal.

Calcutta emerged as the company's most profitable port, attracting a burgeoning trade in fine cotton and silk goods from the fertile and populous Ganges River delta. Local Indian merchants funneled textiles to the port, and Indian bankers supplied European traders with commercial capital. Calcutta and the company's other posts were formal dependencies of the Mughal emperor. But as imperial authority waned, the company began to defy the Delhi government, behaving much like Marathas and other rebellious South Asian power groups. In 1757, British East India Company accountant turned military leader Robert Clive took advantage of both Mughal weakness and divisions among local princes to seize Bengali territory using paid Indian troops supplied with British guns. This initiative gave the company control of inland markets, huge farm estates, and, more important for company finances, taxing rights. Clive himself became immensely rich.

In the following decades, company forces carrying up-to-date flintlock handguns advanced far up the Ganges valley. In 1799 troops invaded Mysore and killed Tipu Sultan after he tried and failed to get military help from France. The British Parliament fretted that by seizing territory rather than just trading from coastal stations the company was pulling the country into financial quicksand. But company shareholders were delighted, and company revenues helped pay for British naval operations around the world. Consequently, European colonization of India crept forward, partly by military action and partly by negotiations with local chiefs and princes who were badly outgunned.

The Seven Years' War. In its drive for territory and trade, the British East India Company faced opposition not only from South Asians but also from France, which had its own commercial stake in Indian Ocean commerce. Clashes between French and British naval vessels off the coast of India were among numerous episodes in a panoramic conflict among European states that lasted from 1756 to 1763. Because these states waged war in several far-flung places and because the combatants perceived it as a grim struggle for finite resources on a global scale, some historians have characterized it as the eighteenth century's ªworld war° (see Map 20.1).

The conflict had its prelude between 1754 and 1756 in the forests of the Ohio River valley, a region already under contention among France, Britain, Spain, and several Native American peoples. Fur traders operating from Britain's North American colonies wanted access to the Ohio and the Mississippi beyond. French troops began building forts to keep them out. When a British colonial militia under the leadership of an inexperienced, twenty-two-year-old colonel named George Washington marched into the Ohio country, a French force beat it badly, obliging the commander and his survivors to straggle back across the Appalachian Mountains. After a second French victory the following year, the exasperated British crown sent in a much larger force, setting off more fighting in North America, where the conflict became known as the French and Indian War.

In 1756, hostilities broke out in Europe, when Maria Theresa, the Empress of Austria, attacked Prussia to get back the rich province of Silesia, which Austria had lost fourteen years earlier. France and Russia joined the Austrian side, and in response England allied with Prussia. Under its king and brilliant military strategist Frederick the Great, Prussia held the advantage over Austria, though all the belligerents exhausted their war treasuries. The fighting stopped without significant change to Europe's political map.

Meanwhile, British and French forces clashed in North America, the Caribbean, the Mediterranean, West Africa, and South Asia. The British government spent lavish sums on the Royal Navy, which in the end outgunned and outlasted France, whose finances were in dire shape. By seizing Quebec City and Montreal on the St. Lawrence River in 1759±1760, Britain forced France to abandon Canada and to negotiate for peace. Under the terms of the Treaty of Paris of 1763, France ceded Canada and French Louisiana east of the Mississippi River to Britain. Britain's ally Spain was awarded the western part of Louisiana. In South Asia, France agreed to pull its warships back from the coast. It did not, however, lose its Caribbean island possessions. This outcome made a huge difference to France since the value of slave-grown sugar alone was much greater than all the wealth extracted from Canada. (The treaty also allowed France to retain sovereignty over St. Pierre and Miquelon, two tiny islands just off the coast of Canada's Newfoundland and Labrador province. These little fishing bases remain French overseas territories to this day.)

Both France and Britain emerged from the Seven Years' War strapped for cash, but Britain was now the world's top maritime power. The Royal Navy had sufficient ships and seaborne artillery to protect British merchants, plantation growers, and fur traders almost anywhere in the world these entrepreneurs cared to operate. Ships could also move raw commodities and manufactures in and out of British home ports with less risk than ever from foreign interlopers.

Revolutions on the North Atlantic Rim

FOCUS What major similarities and differences exist in the origins, development, and short-term consequences of revolutions in British North America, France, and Haiti?

In the four decades following the Seven Years' War, the political and social stresses attending global economic change exploded in violent popular uprisings. Britain's thirteen North American colonies revolted in 1775 and after six years of war achieved self-government as the Western Hemisphere's first **republic.** France burst into revolution in 1789, an event that not only turned French society inside out but also triggered war and political upheaval that gripped Europe for more than a quarter of a century. In the French Caribbean sugar island of Saint Domingue (Haiti), both slaves and free men and women of African descent banded together to fight colonial armies for thirteen years, finally achieving independence in 1804.

> **republic** A type of government in which sovereign power rests with a body of citizens possessing rights to vote to approve laws and to select public officials and representatives.

The Global Context of Popular Revolt

In the later decades of the eighteenth century, the world population, which had been rising since the fifteenth century, began to rise at a faster rate. But about the same time, economic growth appears to have ended a long upward cycle and leveled off. Wherever population advanced faster than food production, prices for the necessities of life spiraled upward. Squeezed financially more than ever, centralized states with armies and bureaucracies to support opted for the usual solution: They imposed heavier taxes on their populations and collected them more ruthlessly.

Faced with the twin burden of higher prices and heavier tax bills, rural farmers, urban workers, and enterprising businesspeople from North America to China expressed their discontent in petitions, demonstrations, riots, and insurrections. To suppress such unrest, states had to raise even more cash or risk loss of their authority. If they boosted tariffs and commercial fees, governments easily alienated entrepreneurs and merchants, whose importance to commerce gave them political influence. Literate and well-informed people were usually better positioned to protest state taxes and fees than peasants were. This was certainly the case in overseas colonies, where settlers of European descent gradually built their own power bases and distinctive cultural identities.

At the low end of the social scale, peasants, serfs, and slaves instigated numerous uprisings in the later eighteenth century against taxes and brutal labor. In Russia under the rule of Catherine II (r. 1762±1796), tax increases, relentless military conscription, and rising grain prices accompanied

Peasants attack nobles and clergy in the Battle of Kazan, 1774. Pugachev's Rebellion, like many other eighteenth-century uprisings, challenged political and social elites who exploited peasants. Russian artist Fyodor Antonovich painted this scene in 1847. He shows a priest trying to protect a nobleman from an armed crowd. How would you describe the artist's point of view regarding the rebellion?

her campaigns of imperial expansion. Consequently, thousands of Russian peasants in the Volga River region rebelled in 1773±1774 under the leadership of Emelian Pugachev, a onetime imperial army officer. Catherine crushed the insurgents, but only after they spent a year pillaging the countryside, burning towns, and killing estate lords. In China, late-eighteenth-century problems of rising population, faltering living standards, and imperial tax demands ignited several regional revolts. In 1796 the religious sect known as the White Lotus Society sparked a massive peasant rising north of the Yangzi River, preaching the imminent coming of a savior in the form of the Buddha. The rebellion endured for eight years, exposing unexpected frailty in the Qing dynasty's economic and political health.

The War of Independence in North America

The rebellion that broke out in Britain's thirteen North American colonies in 1775 followed directly on the Seven Years' War. France's withdrawal from almost its entire North American domain immediately affected relations between Britain and both Native Americans and white colonists. Indians living in the Ohio River region had preserved self-rule by astutely playing France and Britain off against each other. But this game ended in 1763. Fearing that France's retreat would encourage Britain to seize more land, the Ottawa chief Pontiac organized a multitribal military alliance, which attacked European settlers and captured several British forts. After British reinforcements and colonial militias intervened, the war ended in an uneasy truce. Not long after it started, the crown proclaimed that the lands west of the Appalachian mountain crest were to be off limits to colonial settlers. It did not want colonists starting new and expensive wars with Indians. Nor did it want them to trade or otherwise fraternize with the Spanish on the Mississippi or divert fur trade from licensed British companies.

Though the imperial army never seriously enforced this proclamation, its enactment nonetheless infuriated colonial leaders. They thought the whole point of victory over France had been to open trans-Appalachia to land-hungry farmers, including thousands of Europeans who migrated to North America every year. The colonial population of white settlers and their American-born offspring, plus African slaves and free blacks, swelled from about 150,000 in 1680 to more than one million by 1750. The colonies prospered from agriculture, craft and the export of timber, furs, fish, grain, and tobacco, and they all firmly supported Britain in its war with France. The rewards of loyalty, however, seemed meager. The economic boom that accompanied the war's early years dissipated, but colonial numbers continued to soar, causing serious price inflation and declining living standards for many ordinary men and women.

Cracking down on the colonies.

The Seven Years' War left Britain saddled with twice as much debt as it had had in the 1750s. Consequently, the young and eager King George III (r. 1760±1820) cooperated with Parliament to impose tighter political control over North America in order to extract more revenue from colonial property owners. George argued, not without reason, that the colonists had traditionally paid much lower taxes than people did in Britain and that they ought to carry a larger share of imperial costs, including the costs of their own military protection. King and Parliament resolved to end this ᵃbenign neglectº and rule the thirteen colonies as they did their Caribbean possessions and Bengal, that is, as territorial dependencies existing to serve the economic and political interests of the British empire. Between 1763 and 1774, Parliament imposed a series of mercantilist laws on the North AmericansÐ including the Sugar Act, the Stamp Act, and the Tea ActÐ intended to amass revenue and obstruct colonial merchants and manufacturers who competed with English businesses.

Until 1774 few colonists questioned Britain's political authority. But for a century and a half, they had been building neo-European colonies in North America, societies culturally derived from the Old World but possessing their own distinctive styles and much pride in managing their own local affairs. In the decades before the Seven Years' War, Britain had allowed colonial assemblies of elected, property-owning white males to initiate laws. Colonial leaders regarded these deliberative powers as consistent with the principles of limited monarchy that England's own civil conflict and Glorious Revolution in the previous century had affirmed (see Chapter 19). Like England, the colonies had lively public forumsÐ newspapers, urban coffee houses, political discussion societiesÐ that freely debated the issues of the day. After

1740 the ideas of the Enlightenment, the intellectual and cultural movement to replace irrational traditions and autocratic rulers with individual rights and reasoned government (see Chapter 19), became a popular subject of colonial debate. Consequently, political leaders nurtured deepening grievances over British ᵃtyrannyº and violation of both the rights of colonial Englishmen and the natural and universal ᵃrights of man.º

In 1774 the crown responded to growing public agitation by cracking down on the colonies harder than ever. As boycotts and street protests spiraled into armed clashes, some colonists began to think about the unthinkableÐ separation from Britain. Early in 1776, Thomas Paine, an English immigrant to Philadelphia, published *Common Sense,* a political pamphlet arguing brazenly that George III was a ᵃroyal bruteº and that monarchy was a ᵃridiculousº form of government. The booklet sold 500,000 copies in a few months.

British customs official John Malcolm tarred and feathered, 1774. This political cartoon was published in Portsmouth, New Hampshire, with the caption, "The Bostonians paying the Excise Man, or tarring and feathering." The artist also depicts colonists dumping tea into Boston Harbor, though the Boston Tea Party had occurred earlier. Why do you think colonial protesters singled out a port official for such harsh treatment?

The storm finally broke when the Continental Congress, an assembly of colonial delegates, announced that the king had committed such a variety of ᵃabuses and usurpations° that the territories had the right to detach themselves from royal authority altogether. This was the leading argument of the Declaration of Independence, a ringing statement of Enlightenment ideology: ᵃWe hold these truths to be self-evident, that all men are created equal, that they are endowed by their Creator with certain inalienable Rights, that among these are Life, Liberty, and the pursuit of Happiness.° It was not inevitable that all thirteen colonies would join the rebellion. But they had many complaints in common, as well as postal systems and newspapers that helped weld them into a single domain of cultural and political communication. A fledgling sense of distinctly American **patriotism** had also been building slowly, especially among creoles, that is, colonists born in America.

> **patriotism** An emotional or sentimental attachment to a place, an ethnic people, or a way of life; in modern times often to one's national homeland.

Revolutionary war and a new kind of state. Under the command of George Washington, the rebels battled imperial forces for six bloody years. At the same time, they contended with thousands of fellow colonials who for various reasons sided with the crown, many of them ultimately fleeing to Ontario or other parts of Canada. Eager for revenge over its humiliation in the Seven Years' War, France allied with the insurgents in 1778. Spain and the Netherlands soon joined the pact, which effectively ignited another ᵃworld war,° mainly on the sea, between Britain and several European powers. The Americans would likely have lost their struggle, at least in the short run, without generous European financial and military help. For example, at Yorktown, Virginia, where the war effectively ended in 1781, the British army surrendered to a rebel force whose ranks numbered more French and Spanish troops than colonists. Two years later, Britain agreed to a peace treaty that not only sealed the independence of the United States of America but also ceded to it crown territories as far west as the Mississippi.

After winning the war, the ex-colonies formed a loose union, but the central government first constituted under the Articles of Confederation had very limited authority. In 1787, delegates convened in Philadelphia to fashion a system that would yield one viable state on the world stage, rather than thirteen feeble ones. The result was a new constitution and its associated Bill of Rights. This document established a republic rather than a monarchy, defining the young state as a ᵃsocial contract° between government and people. That made it radically different from the eighteenth-century global norm of autocratic kingship. Like the Declaration of Independence, the Constitution explicitly affirmed Enlightenment principles, including the idea that sovereignty is a possession of the ᵃpeople° as citizens, not of a ruler commanding the obedience of subjects. The Constitution instituted three branches of government designed to check and balance one another. Also in stark contrast to European practice, the document's First Amendment stated simply that ᵃCongress shall make no law respecting an establishment of religion, or prohibiting the free exercise thereof.° The Constitution left much power to the thirteen former colonies, but it also erected a federal government with sufficient executive and lawmaking authority to convince the leading European states to take it seriously.

An astonishing global innovation in its time, the American governing charter announced that the new state aimed to ᵃsecure the Blessings of Liberty to ourselves and our Posterity.° This admirable goal, however, sternly qualified the definition of ᵃourselves.° The Constitution made no mention whatsoever of Native Americans as members of the new civic community, and the federal government encouraged settlers to move into Indian land west of the Appalachians. Nor did the Constitution's promise of liberty and prosperity extend to the enslaved. During the war, around eighty thousand African slaves fled to the British lines on the promise of freedom, though another five thousand, including free blacks, joined the rebellion. The founding fathers, however, put no restrictions on slavery in order to ensure that the southern states, whose economies depended on black labor, would accept the document. Colonial women were also excluded from civic life. They had contributed to the revolutionary cause in countless ways, boycotting British goods, making clothing for soldiers, and collecting money for the cause. But English political tradition, Enlightenment thought, and Christian teaching coalesced in support of the maxim that women belonged by the laws of God and nature in the ᵃprivate sphere° of home and hearth. No state enfranchised women, with the remarkable exception of New Jersey. There, unmarried women and widows who met certain property restrictions could vote, though only from 1776 to 1807. The same social class of propertied males that had dominated political and economic life before the revolution emerged at the end of it still in charge.

In 1797 George Washington retired to his Virginia plantation after serving two terms as president of the United States. This voluntary departure, so uncharacteristic of power holders in the eighteenth century, signaled that the new nation was indeed functioning as a republic. Even though non-whites and women were largely left out, moderate legal and political reforms favoring accountable government, individual rights, and legal equality continued to accumulate.

The French Revolution

France was another matter altogether. Its revolution and the American war shared the animating ideas of **popular sovereignty,** liberty, and equality that circulated on both sides of the Atlantic. In both cases, monarchies gave way to republics. But upheaval in France lasted for twenty-six years, counting the period under the rulership of

> **popular sovereignty** The doctrine that the sovereignty or independence of the state is vested in the people, and that the government is responsible to the will of the citizenry.

Napoleon Bonaparte, and it differed from the American experience in many ways. Fundamentally the North Americans sought to found a new sovereign state and a new government, separated from the one that had ruled it as a colony. French rebels aimed to keep the sovereign state of France but to change its government, initially attempting to reform it, then acting to replace it with a drastically different kind of regime. The American war was a harsh military struggle, but the French Revolution produced political and social mayhem, upending the established order of society and temporarily remodeling the map of Europe.

France and Europe on the eve of revolution. Europe in the middle decades of the eighteenth century was a region of multiple states whose royal dynasties claimed absolute authority over their subjects. Only in Britain and the United Netherlands did assemblies of elected, property-owning males formally participate in collective government. Nevertheless, the accelerating growth of capitalist enterprise and global trade, together with the spread of new ideas about sovereignty, rights, and government-by-reason, posed a challenge that hereditary rulers, land-owning aristocracies, and high officials of established Christian churchesÐ the guardians of what historians call the European Old RegimeÐ could hardly have foreseen.

France under the Bourbon dynasty had the largest population in Europe (about twenty-six million) and possessed great wealth in agriculture and manufacturing. Even after its territorial losses to England at the end of the Seven Years' War, it retained rich sugar colonies in the Caribbean, slave-buying ports in West Africa, and extensive international trade. But like so many other authoritarian states of that era, it faced deep debt, soaring public costs, and a population that continued to grow just as the global economy generally slowed. The monarchy hoped that by joining the rebellious North American colonies against Britain, it might reclaim at least some of the strategic influence it had exercised in the North Atlantic before 1763. The major consequence of the intervention, however, was a lot more debt.

France depended more than Britain did on millions of peasants to contribute to the state treasury. The central government, however, had no fair, uniform system for imposing taxes and collected them inefficiently nearly everywhere. Private entrepreneurs contracted with the government to collect public revenue but kept large percentages for themselves. Nobles and well-placed clergymen enjoyed

A faut esperer q'eu se jeu la finira bentot

The burdens of the Third Estate. This satirical cartoon represents the three estates—clergy, nobles, and commoners—as women. The French caption reads, "Let's hope this game finishes soon." The artist included several details that signaled class differences to eighteenth-century viewers. For example, compare the aristocrat's dainty slippers to the peasant's wooden shoes. What message might the nun's hand gesture or the aristocrat's decorated hat suggest?

exemptions from almost all taxes. Royal officials repeatedly proposed fiscal reforms but had little success. About 30 percent of peasants owned their own crop or grazing land, but rising grain prices in the 1770s and 1780s fell hard on the rest, as well as on the poor of Paris and other cities. In bad harvest years, failed farmers and destitute laborers clogged the roads seeking jobs or charity. France's silk and cotton handloom industries generally flourished, but they expanded and contracted from year to year and suffered a serious downturn in 1786. Despite these volatile economic conditions, the two Bourbon kings Louis XV (r. 1715±1774) and Louis XVI (r. 1774±1792) tried to solve their debt problems by saddling the common population with additional taxes that even the most fortunate peasants could barely pay. Meanwhile, big land-owners complained bitterly that inflation cramped their deluxe lifestyles.

Peasants grumbled, rioted, and turned to banditry. But France's urban bourgeoisie, or middle class of merchants, entrepreneurs, bankers, lawyers, bureaucrats, and intellectuals, had more influence with the monarchy. This class benefited from global commercialization, and it grew about threefold in the eighteenth century. Across Europe, educated middle classes, together with sympathetic members of the aristocracy, had for several decades been fashioning a new public style of culture centered on sociable discussion and debate on the great issues of the dayÐ science, social reform, religion, and the arts. In time, the public opinions of middle-class people who read popular newspapers and attended scientific and political meetings began to have an impact on the decisions of at least some of Europe's hereditary rulers. France had a knowledge-seeking, capitalist-minded middle classÐ indeed a much larger one than in North AmericaÐ ready to speak out on questions of rights, liberties, and good government. The royal household, which dwelled in splendor in the Paris suburb of Versailles, tried intermittently and with little success to refute the Old Regime's fundamental contradictionÐ the denial of legitimate political voice to society's economically most productive sector. The educated public relentlessly pressured government ministers to face up to severe fiscal problems. There was even a spirited underground press that viciously lampooned the royal family, blaming France's troubles on its depravity and greed.

Ships sailed constantly back and forth across the North Atlantic, and the North American rebellion seized the French public's imagination as soon as it began. Here was a new country putting the ᵃrights of manº into action. The Declaration of Independence circulated in French newspapers. Soldiers returning from the American war spread stories of patriotic heroism and the triumph of reason over despotism. Benjamin Franklin, who resided in Paris during part of the war, became a French celebrity. Moreover, French critics of autocratic government cheered Enlightenment-inspired uprisings in the United Netherlands, the Habsburg-ruled Netherlands, and Poland between 1787 and 1791, then watched in anger as royal armies crushed these movements. Poland, one of Europe's largest states in the seventeenth century, vanished from the political map as Russia, Prussia, and Austria violently partitioned it among them between 1772 and 1795.

France had a tradition extending back to medieval times of royal consultation with the three main divisions of society, called the **three estates.** But no king had bothered to call a meeting of the Estates-General, as this advisory body was known, since 1614. When Louis XVI, a man more interested in the workings of mechanical locks than the political system, failed to halt the country's slide toward fiscal bankruptcy, public pressure from the middle class and some noble families finally persuaded him to summon the Estates-General into session.

three estates The principal social classes or orders constituting societies in premodern Europe: the Roman Catholic clergy, the titled nobility, and everyone else.

Toward France's First Republic. By authorizing the Estates-General to elect deputies and convene in Paris, King Louis tacitly admitted its legitimacy as a representative body. Grasping this concession, leaders of the third estate, who were mainly professionals, intellectuals, and businesspeople, convened in June 1789 to form a National Assembly and to take the country's fate into their own hands. Some of the high clergy and nobility supported them. This upstart legislature proceeded to write the Declaration of the Rights of Man and the Citizen as preamble to a future constitution. Echoing the American Declaration of Independence, the document announced that the ᵃnation,º that is, the people of France, possessed sovereignty, not the king. Furthermore, all citizens had natural rights to ᵃliberty, property, security, and resistance to oppression.º This manifesto affirmed the principles of freedom of the press and religion and fair legal procedures. In the ensuing months, the National Assembly confiscated Catholic Church lands (to help pay down the public debt), made priests employees of the state (Civil Constitution of the Clergy), gave citizenship to Protestants and Jews, and thoroughly reorganized France's administrative and tax system. Millions of peasants were relieved of traditional customary fees, which landlords had collected for centuries. Buying and selling political offices was outlawed, and nearly all public officials, including judges and Catholic bishops, had to submit themselves to election. Under the Old Regime, France had 300,000 nobles with exclusive political and social privileges. The National Assembly abolished these privileges and in 1791 terminated noble titles altogether.

Meanwhile, French peasants and urban workers also mobilized themselves and entered the political fray. The country's common classes were bigger by many millions than they were in Britain's thirteen North American colonies, and they nursed profound social and economic grievances. Terrible harvests in 1788±1789 caused widespread hunger and more bitter complaints against the crown, while the meeting of the Estates-General excited zealous hopes. There, popular mobs pulled down the Bastille prison, a symbol of royal oppression, and in several cities mobs rioted over bread prices. In the countryside, farmers burned the chateaus of aristocrats. In October 1789 a small army of working-class women marched on the Palace of Versailles, compelling the king to move his court into the city.

Many women, however, came to the opinion that despite their political activism the revolution was quickly leaving them behind. In cities and towns across France, women expressed their dismay in newspaper articles and pamphlets, and some formed revolutionary associations that paralleled

Parisian women leading an armed crowd to Versailles, October 1789. Women's actions were important in many facets of the French Revolution, from mass protests like the march depicted here to publication of political treatises. The women pulling the cannon and others carrying pole weapons are wearing commoner's clothing. At the left of the scene, activists are encouraging an upper-class woman to join the march. What does this image suggest about the role of social class in the Revolution?

numerous male-dominated clubs. Olympe de Gouges, a writer and daughter of a butcher, railed against the failure of the Declaration of Rights to grant any to women explicitly. In 1791 she penned the Declaration of the Rights of Woman and the Female Citizen. This document emulated the language of the 1789 declaration but inserted women throughout. The first article of the National Assembly's pronouncement stated that ªmen are born and remain free and equal in rights.º De Gouges wrote, ªWoman is born free and lives equal to man in her rights.º For holding seditious beliefs, De Gouges was eventually executed, and French women waited another 151 years to get the right to vote.

In 1792 the revolution turned more radical, violent, and politically polarized. Leaders of a newly elected Legislative Assembly (constituted in the fall of 1791 and later renamed the National Convention) attempted to guide events but felt increasingly threatened by adversaries both at home and abroad. Many pious peasants turned against the revolution because of new restrictions on the Catholic Church. Thousands of aristocrats and army officers fled abroad to plot counterrevolution in league with Europe's deeply conservative Old Regime monarchs. To preempt an attack by its

hostile neighbors, the revolutionary government declared war on Austria in the spring of 1792. By the following year, France was also at war with Prussia, Britain, Spain, and the United Netherlands. In response, the legislature drafted a citizen's army, a remarkable development in itself in a global era of professional soldiers, mercenaries, and slave regiments. The prolonged fighting energized millions of men and women to defend the revolutionary cause by forging guns, sewing uniforms, eating less bread, and volunteering for the army, which grew to more than 700,000 combatants by late 1793. War with so much of the rest of Europe gave life to the abstract concept that all people of France, jointly possessing sovereignty and inalienable rights, therefore possessed a shared identity. Still, solidarity remained far from universal. Many young men shunned military service, peasants protected antirevolutionary priests and nuns, and in the spring of 1793 a full-scale rebellion broke out in rural western France in the name of king and church.

In the revolution's early days, the great majority of French people took the monarchy for granted as the natural foundation of the social order. They could not imagine doing away with it. Revolutionary leaders, however, soon became

King Louis XVI's execution, January 1793. The National Convention convicted Louis of treason after he attempted to flee from France. This public spectacle inaugurated the Reign of Terror—a particularly violent period in the Revolution. Notice the contrast between the gruesome display of the king's severed head and the calm order that appears to prevail among the military onlookers. Why would contemporary observers have regarded Louis's execution as a turning point in the Revolution?

constitutional monarchy A type of government in which a monarch, usually a member of a family that enjoys hereditary succession, serves as head of state. Under the terms of a constitution or body of laws, however, the monarch surrenders part or all of his or her governing power to a legislature and judiciary.

divided between those advocating a **constitutional monarchy** in which the king's power would be limited (the British model) and those pressing for a republic (the United States model). Radical republicans formed the Jacobin Club (named after a Parisian spot where the association first met), and its branch groups spread across France. From 1789 to 1792 the national legislature moved deeper into uncharted political waters, finally eliminating the monarchy altogether in the fall of 1792, instituting a republican constitution, and, in the following January, decapitating the hapless Louis along with his Austrian queen Marie Antoinette. Monarchs in the rest of Europe reacted to this spectacle in horror.

The year of the Terror. Civil rebellion and foreign wars, made worse by spiraling shortages of money and bread, deepened the mood of chronic crisis and helped push even more radical leaders to power. In 1793 the National Convention turned over much of its authority to a twelve-man Committee of Public Safety, which moved to eradicate all perceived opposition. Falling under the leadership of the lawyer Maximilien Robespierre (1758±1794), the committee set out to cleanse the nation of traitors and antirevolutionary opinions, replace Christianity with a Cult of Reason, and transform all citizens into eager republicans through cultural reeducation. To erect this ªRepublic of Virtue,º Robespierre and his agents demanded distinctly republican songs, festivals, art, plays, names, and dress. ªIf the mainspring of popular government in peacetime is virtue,º Robespierre declared, ªamid revolution it is at the same time [both] virtue and terror.º4 To its credit, the National Convention also abolished slavery in early 1794, conferring rights of citizenship to all black males in the French colonies.

Over a period of seventeen months, the committee's agents arrested more than 300,000 people and executed 17,000 of them. Eventually, however, the Terror devoured its own and burned itself out. In July 1794, Robespierre himself climbed the steps to the guillotine along with many of his supporters.

France under the Directory. In the next phase of the revolution, the National Convention managed to write a new constitution, restoring a wobbly stability under an executive council called the Directory. Meanwhile, republican armies continued to advance victoriously across Europe, and in the Netherlands, Italy, and Switzerland the invaders set up revolutionary ªsister republics.º The Directory reversed the most radical enactments of the Republic of Virtue and returned to the fundamental principles of the First Republic. The ªpeopleº remained sovereign, the principle of civil equality remained intact, elections were held, and women were allowed to exert influence through political writings and activism. The Directory, however, was also corrupt and politically inept.

Napoleon's European empire. In 1799 France retreated measurably from the trend toward civil freedom and democracy when Napoleon Bonaparte took power and launched sixteen years of empire building. Napoleon followed in the tradition of rulers, notably Charlemagne in the eighth century and the Habsburg monarch Charles V in the sixteenth, who envisioned Europe as a unitary imperial state comparable to other giant Afroeurasian empires. He also yearned to restore to France the global power the last two Bourbon kings had squandered. Indeed, at the height of his authority, Napoleon liked seeing himself depicted in art as a Roman emperor.

Born on the Mediterranean island of Corsica, Napoleon rose to power through the ranks of the revolutionary army. In 1795 he took command of French forces in Italy and made himself a national hero by displaying military genius and overrunning a large part of the peninsula. In 1798 the Directory dispatched him with a huge force of forty thousand troops to invade Egypt, which was then a self-governing province of the Ottoman empire. The Directory had several strategic aims. Conquest of both Egypt and Syria would help counterbalance the loss of Canada to England and provide a valuable source of grain for the home population. By occupying the northern end of the Red Sea, France could also challenge Britain's lines of communication with South Asia and revive maritime power in the Indian Ocean.

Ruled by a Turkish-speaking military elite that prized cavalry warfare, Egypt fell quickly in a barrage of withering French musket and cannon fire. The conquerors set quickly to work to reorganize Egypt's administration and finance along lines they regarded as modern. Napoleon also brought with him a large contingent of engineers, scientists, doctors, architects, and language experts to study Egypt and prepare to transform it. The experiment, however, was short-lived. The British navy destroyed Napoleon's fleet, Egyptians organized popular resistance, and French soldiers died of infectious diseases in large numbers. In 1801 the occupiers left. Among Egyptian officials and intellectuals, however, France's shocking display of military might triggered a long debate over the merits of modernizing Egypt along these lines.

Returning to Paris at a moment of domestic unrest, Napoleon engineered a *coup d'état* (koo day-TAH), abolished the Directory, and in 1799 assumed sweeping powers under a new constitution. During the ensuing decade, he made himself master of much of Europe, even restoring the principle of monarchy by crowning himself hereditary emperor of France in 1804 (see Map 20.2). By keeping public order and winning battles, he continued to enjoy broad popular support. He absorbed some neighboring territories into the French

> **coup d'état** The sudden overthrow of an existing government by a small group. A "stroke of state" in French.

Napoleon I on his Imperial Throne. This portrait by the French artist Jean-Auguste-Dominique Ingres shows Napoleon in his coronation regalia, holding the scepter of Charlemagne in his right hand and the hand of justice in his left. He also wears a golden wreath of laurels, invoking the emperors of Rome. Why do you think the artist portrayed Napoleon displaying symbols of past imperial glory so soon after the Revolution abolished the monarchy?

MAP 20.2 The Napoleonic empire.
What might you conclude about Napoleon's territorial ambitions from the location of major battle sites on this map?

state and created several new republics as French clients. The Austrian and Prussian monarchies retained their sovereignty but gave up territory.

In creating this empire, Napoleon built the largest army that Europe had ever known, drafting a total of about 2.3 million young men and selecting officers more for their military competency than their aristocratic pedigrees. This force had remarkable morale, the first in modern history to conceive of itself less as a professional, paid, or unwillingly conscripted force than as an instrument of the sovereign French people. In the occupied lands, men and women with republican sentiments at first welcomed the intruders, and Napoleon ordered economic and civil reforms, for example, abolishing serfdom wherever it existed in occupied areas. He also imposed heavy taxes and military conscription on dependent countries, however, and in most conquered territories the local welcome soon wore thin.

Napoleon was of two minds about the revolution. On one hand, he admired enlightened rationality, the idea of civil equality, and the principle of popular sovereignty. He endorsed modern scientific research and created a state-supported system of schools (*lycées*) for boys from well-to-do families. He had no reputation for Christian piety, but he made peace with the Roman Catholic Church, though insisting on freedom of worship. He declined to bring back the traditional French aristocracy but rather created a service nobility, that is, an elite of titled individuals whose status depended entirely on the pleasure of the state. In 1804 he instituted the Civil Code (Napoleonic Code), a rational, uniform legal system to replace a tangle of often inconsistent provincial laws. The Code embodied Enlightenment principles of private property and individual liberty, including equality before the law and freedom of contract. It also regulated numerous details of daily life, including the rights and responsibilities of employers, employees, husbands, wives, parents, and children. More generally, the Code contributed to France's social and cultural integration, and it eventually had a profound influence on European, French colonial, and Latin American legal systems.

Napoleon, however, was no radical republican. He loathed the idea of free speech if it permitted criticism of the state. He put stringent curbs on political expression, and his agents censored art, drama, and the press. The number of Parisian newspapers dropped from seventy-three in 1800 to four in 1811. He created a secret police and crushed all organized political opposition. The Civil Code reaffirmed the principle of men's intellectual and moral superiority over women, imposing new restrictions on divorce and prohibiting wives from bringing suits or disposing of property without their husbands' consent. For women of the revolution, this represented a discouraging backward step.

Napoleon's fall. In 1810 France loomed over Europe, but within six years the empire vanished. Napoleon conquered far and wide, but the imperial system was never stabilized. The emperor had no significant success against the British navy. Nor did his campaign to prohibit commerce between Britain and the rest of Europe, a policy called the Continental System, work well in the long run. As we shall see, Napoleon also lost control of Saint Domingue and its sugar exports. In 1800 he signed a treaty with Spain to recover the western part of the Louisiana Territory but then sold it to the United States three years later at a bargain price. And in Europe, people who turned against Napoleonic rule organized protest and resistance inspired by France's own revolutionary ideals. In Spain, for example, patriotic insurgents aided by Britain fought French occupying troops for six years. This was the first armed conflict to be called a *guerrilla* or ª little warº owing to Spanish tactics of hit-and-run, sabotage, and assassination.

In 1812 Napoleon made the disastrous decision to invade Russia, enraged that Tsar Alexander I had broken an existing alliance. The invading force of 650,000, the largest field army in European history, fought its way to Moscow only to face an evacuated and burned city, a dearth of supplies, and a long winter retreat to Germany, which reduced the army to barely 10,000 men fit for combat. This debacle heartened France's enemies and triggered more wars of liberation. Losing the support of his own ministers and generals, Napoleon abdicated in 1814 and was exiled to the island of Elba off the Italian coast. The following year the Napoleonic era had its famous coda, when the general eluded his minders on Elba and raised a new army, only to suffer terminal defeat at the Battle of Waterloo in Belgium. Taking no more chances, the victorious powers sent him to St. Helena, a tiny island in the South Atlantic, where he died in 1821.

When Napoleon was confined on Elba, Klemens von Metternich, the prime minister of Austria, called a meeting of European states in Vienna to negotiate the region's postwar political order. The Congress of Vienna did not restore borders and sovereignties exactly as they had existed before the French Revolution, but the heads of the most important states agreed on two things: first, to collaborate to stop any of their number from behaving aggressively in the future and, second, to suppress radical republicans and other extremists wherever they reared their heads. Louis XVIII, brother of the executed king, was placed on the French throne, though under a constitution that constrained his power somewhat. The principles of popular sovereignty, however, had already sunk deep roots in France. The new Louis and his royal successors never regained full popular acceptance, and more revolutions were shortly to follow.

The Idea of Nationalism

The Napoleonic regime may have run roughshod over individual liberties, but the founding of the French republic, the country's wars with its neighbors, and Napoleon's program to centralize and integrate political and legal institutions helped bring about a new popular consciousness of national identity. Today, virtually all sovereign states share a fundamentally nationalist ideology. And most people reflexively accept the idea that a world of sovereign nation-states is ª in the nature of things.º But in fact, the concepts of **nation-state** and **nationalism** did not exist two and a half centuries ago, and they took on life only gradually beginning in the late 1700s.

Where and when did the inhabitants of particular territories first conceive of themselves as possessing a common national identity? Historians have vigorous debates about this question, though many agree that wherever it happenedÐ England? the Spanish American empire? France?Ð literate political and cultural leaders were the first to acquire and consciously express the idea of the nation as a special kind of community. There is no doubt that the revolutions in both North America and France, and later in Latin America, activated the powerful Enlightenment principle that the legitimacy of the state, that is, its lawfulness, is derived from the will of the ª peopleºÐ not from the monarch or any individual claiming to act as an agent of God. Eighteenth-century republicans, as well as advocates of limited monarchy, came to conceive of the ª peopleº as a group of individuals sharing not only inalienable rights but also a common territory, historical experience, language, cultural distinctiveness, and hope for the future. This community constituted the ª nation.º National-*ism* took form as the doctrine that in order to preserve its rights and freedoms the national community is entitled to govern itself as a sovereign territory, to form a state. Corollary to that, the state and its government are legitimate only if they represent the nation's will.

Men and women naturally owed loyalty to a variety of different groupsÐ family, village, artisan guild, religious community, and so on. But nationalism announced that individuals owed their *highest* allegiance to their nation-state. Indeed, they should be prepared to die to defend it. These ideas, that the national community has the right both to

> **nation-state** A sovereign territorial state whose inhabitants share, or are ideally expected to share, common language, cultural traditions, history, and aspirations for the future.

> **nationalism** An ideology centered on the natural rights of a people or "nation" to constitute a sovereign state.

govern itself and to claim citizens' ultimate allegiance, separated modern nationalism from older forms of patriotism, for example, popular displays of loyalty to a monarch or emotional attachment to an ethnic homeland.

In 1789 the population ruled by the king of France spoke several different languages and had strong regional identities. The revolution sometimes aggravated those differences, but it also planted the idea that citizens should take pride in their common ᵃFrenchness.º The mobilization of a citizen army, achieved by a combination of conscription and emotional appeals to the French nation, strengthened this new kind of identity. As one young soldier from eastern France wrote to his parents, ᵃ Either you will see me return bathed in glory, or you will have a son who is a worthy citizen of France who knows how to die for the defense of his country.º⁵

Napoleon consistently represented himself as the supreme embodiment of the French nation. His conquests broadcast nationalist ideas across Europe, first by introducing revolutionary principles of citizen equality and access to justice, later by unintentionally rousing populations he had subjugated to put forward their own nationalist credos in opposition to French occupation. Guerrilla war in Spain, secret societies in occupied Italy, and dogged resistance in Russia were all incubators of nationalism, which in the nineteenth century gradually captured the imagination, not only of literate men and women, but also of urban workers, peasants, and colonized peoples.

A cockade from the French Revolution. Both men and women pinned ribbons like this one to their hats or lapels to show their support for the Revolution. The idea of a shared political commitment was an important building block of emerging nationalism. What symbols of shared identity have served to mobilize nationalist feeling in the United States or other countries?

The Birth of Haiti

While the French Revolution was playing itself out, another popular **insurgency,** intimately connected to events in France, took place between 1789 and 1804 in the colony of Saint Domingue, later renamed Haiti, in the Caribbean Sea (see Table 20.1). In contrast to the British North American colonies, Saint Domingue was not a European settler colony but a tropical plantation society whose inhabitants were overwhelmingly of African origin, most of them slaves. We may characterize the Haitian rebellion as the most revolutionary of all movements on the Atlantic

insurgency An organized, usually internal rebellion against a government or its policies, sometimes employing guerrilla or terror tactics.

rim because it abolished an entire social system founded on slavery. Nevertheless, the price of liberty ran high: thirteen years of brutal wars and a devastated economy.

Plantation society. In the eighteenth century, French planters exported sugar, coffee, tobacco, and cotton from Saint Domingue, which occupied the western third of the island Hispaniola. (The other two-thirds was the Spanish possession of Santo Domingo.) Together with Martinique and Guadalupe, France's two smaller Caribbean dependencies, Saint Domingue produced more exportable wealth in commercial crops than Spain's entire American empire. As in all plantation societies in the Americas, a small minority of Europeans and their descendants stood atop the political and social pyramid. But in 1790 this group numbered only about forty thousand, or around 7 percent of the colony's total numbers. It included plantation owners, colonial officers, and merchants, but also a larger group of relatively poor whites, who made their livings in farming, trade, or government. Beneath whites in rank order was the minority population of free people of African or mixed racial descent, known also as *affranchis* (freed people). This group embraced a range of economic statuses, from unskilled ex-slaves and female sex partners of white men to successful farmers with slaves of their own. The slave population, both people born on the island (creoles) and new arrivals from tropical Africa, occupied the society's bottom level. Living in a colony a little larger than Maryland, this population numbered close to 500,000Ð nearly twice as many slaves as in the entire United States in 1790. To meet world demand for sugar and coffee and to make up for the typically short lifespan of slaves, planters depended on steady labor imports. Between 1785 and 1790, for example, slave ships annually brought about thirty thousand slaves to the colony from West Africa.

Relations between and within these three broad social categories were tense in the late eighteenth century, the strains all related to Saint Domingue's prominent place in world trade. The poor white population included many people who had migrated from France to seek their fortunes but resented the planter elite, which controlled the bulk of wealth. The *affranchis*, despite their free status, suffered systematic social discrimination at the hands of all whites.

TABLE 20.1 Key Dates in the French and Haitian Revolutions

Year	France	Saint Domingue (Haiti)
1789	**May** Meeting of Estates-General **June** National Assembly formed **July** Fall of the Bastille **August** Declaration of the Right of Man	
1790	**July** National Assembly enacts Civil Constitution of the Clergy	
1791	**July** Louis XVI accepts constitutional monarchy but resists reforms **October** Legislative Assembly meets under Constitution of 1791	**May** French National Assembly grants full political rights to free blacks in Haiti **August** Slave uprising on Saint Domingue; Toussaint Louverture emerges as military leader
1792	**April** France declares war on Austria **September** France becomes a republic	
1793	**January** Louis XVI executed **April** Committee of Public Safety appointed and Terror begins	**September** British and Spanish troops invade Saint Domingue
1794	**February** Slavery abolished in French colonies **July** Radical leader Robespierre executed	
1795	**October** Directory government takes power	
1796	**March** Napoleon named commander of armies in Italy	
1798	**May** Napoleon invades Egypt	
1799	**December** Coup against Directory; Napoleon becomes First Consul	
1800		**August** Toussaint becomes commander-in-chief in Saint Domingue
1802		**February** French forces invade Saint Domingue to reestablish control **May** Napoleon reinstates slavery in French colonies **June** French forces arrest Toussaint and deport him to France
1803	**April** France cedes Louisiana to the United States	**November** French troops leave Saint Domingue
1804	**May** Napoleon crowned emperor of France	**January** Dessaline proclaims Haiti's independence
1805	**October** British navy defeats French at Battle of Trafalgar	
1812	**June** Napoleon invades Russia	
1814	**September** Congress of Vienna convenes	
1815	**June–October** Napoleon defeated and exiled to St. Helena	

They could not, for example, legally marry into white families. Talk in Europe of the rights of man resonated loudly with *affranchis* as soon as it reached the colony.

The grievances of the slave majority produced not merely resentment but dismay and fury. Planters and their henchmen struggled to contain those feelings by brutal repression. Creole slaves who caused no trouble might get jobs as household servants, work bosses, or petty enforcers. But most African-born slaves, who did not initially know Haitian Creole (the French-based, African-influenced language spoken in the colony), labored under the whip in the fields and mills. Slaves, however, did not lack for means of defiance. In the later eighteenth century, shippers brought in large numbers of captives from the lower Congo River region. Many of them, predominantly young males, had been soldiers in Africa and possessed military skills. Slaves on the plantations who spoke the same language or came from the same part of Africa created informal secret societies or

ᵃnationsº and elected their own ᵃkingsº and ᵃqueensº following African practice. When rebellion broke out, these societies served as cells for organizing resistance.

The long revolution. Like the French Revolution, the movement on Saint Domingue passed through several distinct phases, all of them closely interlocked with events in France. In the first phase, from 1789 to 1791, both white colonists and *affranchis*, receiving news of the National Assembly, held high hopes of benefiting from the new regime in Paris. Both groups sent delegations to France to try to influence politics, and Haitian whites set up elected regional assemblies. Planters, poor whites, and *affranchis*, however, saw the revolution from different angles of vision. The richest landowners talked much about liberty, meaning greater colonial self-rule or even independence in imitation of the United States, though on terms that left slavery intact. Poor whites wanted full equality with the planter class. The *affranchis*

Revolution in Saint Domingue. Slaves and French forces alike had to contend with rugged terrain, tropical climate, and infectious diseases in order to survive and fight. Toussaint Louverture stands in the center of this painting, fending off a French assault. How might Toussaint have used the island's geography to his military advantage?

wanted equality with all whites. In May 1791, in fact, the National Assembly granted legal equality to free blacks whose parents were also free, an action most colonial whites furiously opposed. In the meantime, these three groups fell to fighting with one another on the island, each one claiming to represent the true spirit of the French Revolution.

A sudden and massive slave insurrection announced the second phase of the rebellion. In the summer and fall of 1791, slaves looted plantations, burned cane fields, and murdered planter families. Armed white militias retaliated quickly, killing slaves in much greater numbers. Slaves may have responded to rumors that the king of France had already emancipated them. Secret societies appear to have kept alive African political ideas that kings should have limited powers and rule justly. These groups, together with creole slaves who had good knowledge of colonial society, helped organize fighters and provided commanders.

Saint Domingue remained in near anarchy from 1791 to 1794. French troops arrived to try to calm the situation, but soldiers died of yellow fever and other tropical diseases at an alarming rate. The scene became even more complicated in 1793, when Spain and Britain, both at war

with revolutionary France, invaded Saint Domingue to further their own strategic interests in the Caribbean.

Between 1794 and 1802, the third phase of the revolution, the ex-slave Toussaint Louverture (too-SAN loo-ver-CHURE) dominated the military and political scene. A creole slave who gained his freedom at the age of thirty, Toussaint rose to a commandership in the rebellion. A gifted guerrilla tactician who knew how to read, he successfully bridged the social divide between slaves and the other elements of society. When the French National Convention abolished slavery in all overseas colonies, Toussaint joined with French republican officials on the island to fight Spanish and British occupying forces. Yellow fever also served the resistance, killing 15,000 of 25,000 British soldiers. In 1800 the French government appointed Toussaint governor of Saint Domingue, though he founded no democratic regime. A newly written constitution concentrated nearly all power in his hands. Recognizing commodity exports as key to the island's economic viability, he also tried with mixed success to impose schemes of forced labor and sharecropping on liberated slaves to get them back to work on the plantations.

Toussaint Louverture Writes to the French Directory

After the French Revolution's most radical period ended and the more conservative Directory came to power, the Haitian revolutionary leader Toussaint Louverture feared that the government in Paris would reverse the National Convention's 1794 decree to abolish slavery in the colonies. Some political factions in Paris wanted to do exactly that. In November 1797, Toussaint wrote to the Directory, reassuring it of his loyalty to the republic and its high ideals but at the same time insisting that the freedom of his people must not be compromised.

The attempts on that liberty which the [French] colonists propose are all the more to be feared because it is with the veil of patriotism that they cover their detestable plans. We know that they seek to impose some of them on you by illusory and specious promises, in order to see renewed in this colony its former scenes of horror. Already perfidious emissaries have stepped in among us to ferment the destructive leaven prepared by the hand of liberticides. But they will not succeed. I swear by all that liberty holds most sacred. My attachment to France, my knowledge of the blacks, make it my duty not to leave you ignorant either of the crimes which they meditate or the oath that we renew, to bury ourselves under the ruins of a country revived by liberty rather than suffer the return of slavery.

It is for you, Citizens Directors, to turn from over our heads the storm which the eternal enemies of our liberty are preparing in the shades of silence. It is for you to enlighten the legislature, it is for you to prevent the enemies of the present system from spreading themselves on our unfortunate shores to sully it with new crimes. Do not allow our brothers, our friends, to be sacrificed to men who wish to reign over the ruins of the human species. . . .

I send you with this letter a declaration which will acquaint you with the unity that exists between the proprietors of Saint Domingue who are in France, those in the United States, and those who serve under the English banner. You will see there a resolution, unequivocal and carefully constructed, for the restoration of slavery; you will see there that their determination to succeed has led them to envelop themselves in the mantle of liberty in order to strike it more deadly blows. . . .

Do they think that men who have been able to enjoy the blessing of liberty will calmly see it snatched away? They supported their chains only so long as they did not know any condition of life more happy than that of slavery. But today when they have left it, if they had a thousand lives they would sacrifice them all rather than be forced into slavery again. But no, the same hand which has broken our chains will not enslave us anew. France will not revoke her principles, she will not withdraw from us the greatest of her benefits. . . . But if, to reestablish slavery in Saint Domingue, this was done, then I declare to you it would be to attempt the impossible; we have known how to face dangers to obtain our liberty, we shall know how to brave death to maintain it. . . .

It is sufficient to renew, my hand in yours, the oath that I have made, to cease to live before gratitude dies in my heart, before I cease to be faithful to France and to my duty, before the god of liberty is profaned and sullied by the liberticides, before they can snatch from my hands that sword, those arms, which France confided to me for the defense of its rights and those of humanity, for the triumph of liberty and equality.

Source: C. L. R. James, The Black Jacobins: Toussaint L'Ouverture and the San Domingo Revolution, 2nd ed. rev. (New York: Vintage Books, 1963), 195±197.

Thinking Critically

What evidence do you see in Toussaint's letter that he was familiar with ideas that inspired the American and French Revolutions? Along with appeals to the principles of the French republic, what argument does Toussaint make for not reinstating slavery? How would you interpret Toussaint's statement that the eagerness of some French factions to restore slavery "has led them to envelop themselves in the mantle of liberty in order to strike it more deadly blows"?

Saint Domingue fought its war of independence in the final revolutionary phase from 1802 to 1804. Napoleon, who wished to reinstate the slave regime, sent troops to invade the island. They seized all the ports and captured Toussaint, sending him to France, where he died in prison in 1803. Nevertheless, backcountry resistance continued, and French soldiers fell ill and died by the thousands. After France and Britain went to war in 1803, Napoleon decided to cut his losses and revise his priorities by selling Louisiana to the United States and pulling his army from Saint Domingue. The following year Haiti declared independence under the command of Jean-Jacques Dessalines, one of Toussaint's former officers. Unfortunately, the long revolution left both towns and plantations in desolation. The sovereign Haitian population, largely illiterate and abjectly poor, had to struggle on for decades in nearly total political isolation, its government a dictatorship in republican guise. France did not recognize Haiti's independence until 1825, the United States not until 1862.

Toussaint Louverture in command. This portrait presents the Haitian leader dressed as a European military officer. An aide waits with a saddled horse. Toussaint sits before a glass of wine. Behind him is a comfortable-looking house. How would you compare this scene with the depiction of the commander on page 597?

The Second Wave: Revolutions in Latin America

FOCUS What factors contributed to the success of revolutionary movements in overturning Spanish and Portuguese colonial rule in the Americas?

Independence movements started later and struggled for freedom longer in Spain's and Portugal's American colonies than in Britain's thirteen North American colonies or in Haiti. The prelude to Latin American revolutions was Napoleon's invasion of Spain and Portugal in 1807±1808, which forced the kings of both countries to flee. Lacking direction from Madrid, **juntas** took control of political affairs in several Spanish American

junta A committee or council that seizes control of a local or national government, especially following civil upheaval or revolution.

cities in defiance of local imperial officials. In 1810, armed rebellions broke out in Buenos Aires and Caracas. That same year Miguel Hidalgo, a Mexican parish priest, launched a peasant revolt against Spanish authority in the viceroyalty of New Spain (the imperial territories of North America and most of Central America).

After the Spanish king Ferdinand VII (r. 1808, 1814±1833) returned to his throne in Madrid, fifteen years of bloody fighting ensued between colonial rebels and Spanish troops. Only in 1828 did Spain finally abandon mainland America, leaving a cluster of new republics to replace the four colonial viceroyalties. The Spanish empire endured only on the islands of Cuba and Puerto Rico. As for Brazil, Napoleon's attack on Portugal in 1807 obliged the royal government to leave Lisbon, cross the Atlantic, and reconstitute itself in Rio de Janeiro. In 1822 Brazil achieved independence without a long revolutionary struggle, in large measure because the reform-minded Prince Dom Pedro refused to accompany his father King João VI (r. 1816±1826) back to Portugal at the end of the Napoleonic interlude. Instead, he cooperated with the Brazilian propertied elite to head a new constitutional monarchy.

Colonial Society on the Eve of Rebellion

In both Spanish America and the thirteen British colonies, revolts started when political and economic grievances against European imperial masters became intolerable. In both cases, property-owning white creoles led the movements after failing to gain relief from onerous taxes and mercantilist policies that choked business and trade. And in both cases, Enlightenment ideas about rights and liberties provided ideological fuel for insurgency. Latin American leaders also drew on the North American and French revolutions for models of resistance and republican government.

Nevertheless, the differences between the British and Spanish spheres of revolution were striking. First, the Spanish empire was much larger geographically and culturally more complex than Britain's thirteen colonies. Huge distances separated cities from one another, overland transport was rudimentary, and the empire's major regions, each with distinctive climate, ecology, and ethnolinguistic groups, maintained only irregular contacts with one another. The Spanish viceroyalties also differed from the British colonies in the makeup of their social hierarchy. In North America, people of European descent substantially outnumbered black slaves and Indians. In Spanish America as a whole it was the reverse. Of the seventeen million or so inhabitants, Indians accounted for about 44 percent, *castas* (people of mixed ancestry) 32 percent, whites 19 percent, and blacks 5 percent. These ratios varied from one part of the empire to another, but colonial law and cultural practice preserved a fairly uniform and inflexible social hierarchy: *Peninsulares* (whites born in Europe) stood at the apex of privilege and power, white creoles occupied the second level, and then *castas*, Indians, and blacks followed in descending order (see Chapter 18). Largely because of this combination of geographical and human factors, colonial rebels found themselves launching several uprisings rather than one.

The white creole property-owners at the forefront of the independence movements had distinctive aspirations. They harbored simmering resentments against *peninsulares,* who often lived in America temporarily but nonetheless cornered the high positions as officials, military men, and Catholic clerics. *Peninsulares* made up less than 5 percent of the white population, but they habitually touted their social superiority and sometimes accumulated great wealth before returning to Spain. The crown enacted political reforms in the eighteenth century, but like the British in North America, they did this, not to extend local liberties, but to keep order, control the flow of trade, and tax subjects more efficiently. In contrast to the thirteen colonies, Spanish America had never been allowed colonial legislatures where propertied creoles might exercise local authority or vent grievances. Creole leaders denounced these injustices, knowing that it was they, not *peninsulares,* who largely built the Spanish American economyÐ its haciendas, mines, plantations, and export trade.

Creoles and *peninsulares,* however, found common ground quickly enough when it came to complaints from the classes below *them* on the social scale. In most of Spanish America, the two white groups peered down on a mass of peasants, ranch hands, servants, and slaves whose numbers far exceeded theirs. They generally shared a determination to keep those classes in their ªproper place° as compliant laborers and social inferiors. As much as creoles chafed under Spanish authoritarianism, hardly any of them wanted a social revolution ªfrom the bottom.° In the 1790s most creoles recoiled at news of the French terror and of slaves burning Haitian plantations. When the insurgent priest Hidalgo raised Mexican Indians and *mestizos* (people of mixed white and Indian descent) against Spanish oppression and failed to stop killings of white property owners, many creoles turned against him. Spanish troops caught and executed Hidalgo in 1811, though the rural rebellion continued.

The Wars of Independence

Despite creole fears of losing control of events, the pace of change accelerated rapidly after 1810. Many leaders hesitated at first to renounce allegiance to King Ferdinand VII but finally despaired of his ever agreeing to negotiate over the political liberties they thought they deserved. In 1814,

Father Miguel Hidalgo and the Declaration of the War of Independence. This large mural shows two aspects of Mexico's fight for independence from Spain. On the left, Father Hidalgo proclaims "The Cry of Dolores" on September 16, 1810, voicing the resistance of Indians and other commoners to the rule of a small minority. On the right, members of the elite debate the terms of independence. Mexican artist Juan O'Gorman painted the mural in Chapultepec Castle, a former royal residence converted to a national history museum in 1939. What political or social purpose might O'Gorman have intended this mural to serve more than a century after the revolution?

José de San Martín: Liberator of the Southern Andes

José de San Martín (1778–1850) was born in Argentina, the son of an imperial lieutenant-governor. His *peninsular* parents took him to Spain when he was a child, and there he joined the army as a cadet at the age of eleven. He first saw action in 1791 in a fight against Muslim forces for control of the North African port of Oran. Later he won distinction in the Spanish struggle against Napoleon. Attracted to the political reform ideas swirling through Europe, he left the army in 1811 and sailed for Buenos Aires, where creole rebels had declared independence. He organized an army of resistance in far western Argentina and in January 1817 led a force of five thousand soldiers, a majority of whom were blacks and mulattoes, across frigid, 12,000-foot passes of the southern Andes to Chile. The Andes crossing severely weakened his army, but he nonetheless achieved an extraordinary logistical feat. In February his forces ousted Spanish and loyalist troops from Santiago, Chile's main city.

The Chilean land-owning class offered San Martín the country's presidency, but, declining political office, he planned an attack to liberate the viceroyalty of Peru. Because a thousand miles and the stark Atacama Desert separated Santiago from Lima, capital of Peru, he collaborated with the British navy in 1820 to transport his army up the coast. A cautious commander, he landed north of Lima, then waited a year hoping that because he was nearby the urban population would rise up against their Spanish masters. This did not happen, but when he finally advanced on the city, the viceroy and his forces fled. He entered Lima in July 1821, though only after the local creole leaders declared independence. "I have no ambition to be the conqueror of Peru," he protested. "The country has now become sensible of its true interests, and it is right the inhabitants should have the means of expressing what they think."

San Martín reluctantly agreed, however, to take command as Protector of Peru. In this office he immediately started making liberal reforms. He liberated Indians from tribute payments and forced labor, and he proclaimed that children born of slaves after independence must be free. In a decree foreshadowing the new era of nationalism, he declared, "The aborigines [indigenous population] shall not be called Indians or natives; they are children *and* citizens of Peru and they shall be known as Peruvians." Lima's conservative creole class, however, largely opposed the Protector's reforms, and his honeymoon with them ended quickly.

In mid-1822 San Martín went to northern Peru to meet with Simón Bolívar, whose army was moving south through Ecuador. No one knows what the two generals said to each other, but according to an eyewitness they emerged from the meeting "frowning gravely." They had conflicting visions of the ex-empire's political future. In any case Bolívar held the stronger military hand and was eager for political power. He carried through Peru's liberation, effectively concluding the Spanish American wars of independence, then took office as president of both Peru and Gran Colombia. San Martín, meanwhile, returned to Lima, resigned his office two months later, and eventually made his way back to Europe. Bolívar, after struggling to hold Gran Colombia together, died of tuberculosis in 1830. San Martín passed away quietly in his daughter's house near Paris in 1850, outliving Bolívar by twenty years.

General José de San Martin.

Thinking Critically

What factors do you think might have motivated San Martín to leave South America after the Spanish defeat rather than remain to play a political role in one of the new republics?

---

after the French withdrew from Spain and Ferdinand returned to Madrid, he sent a large force to smash the American insurrections.

At first, Spanish troops, in collaboration with *peninsulares* and creoles who remained loyal to the crown, went on the offensive. The rural revolt in Mexico became fragmented, and the Spanish administration suppressed creole demands for free elections. After 1816, however, the military situation began to change. Rebel leaders from Mexico to Argentina doggedly continued to fight, and the government in Spain, battling both serious debt problems and urban protesters demanding limited monarchy, could not afford to send more soldiers to America. In the far south, José de San Martín ousted the Spanish from Chile and much of Peru. In the northern viceroyalty of New Granada, Simón Bolívar, a creole land-owner, welded together a rebel army of creoles, *castas*, cowboy cavalry from the Venezuelan plains, and even slaves, who were promised emancipation.

By 1821 this force seized the regions that are now Venezuela and Colombia and in the next four years defeated royalist armies in Ecuador and Peru.

Leaders of Spanish American independence movements had a variety of ideas about the precise form that new sovereign governments should take. Simón Bolívar was a republican, an advocate of governance by the propertied creole class, a relentless political infighter, and for nearly a decade the authoritarian president of the short-lived republic of Gran Colombia. José de San Martín, by contrast, was a constitutional monarchist, a liberal reformer, and a gifted general who had little stomach for politics.

Mexico achieved independence following a chain of events closely intertwined with political developments in Europe, where a revolt in 1820 persuaded Ferdinand VII to accept a constitution that would limit his authority and establish a legislature. This turn of events, which the Mexican viceroy supported, revived creole hopes and impelled both them and the *peninsulares* to try to achieve political change without violent revolution. Augustín de Iturbide, a creole and a royalist military commander, came to the fore to broker a compromise among all social groups, aiming to safeguard the interests of *peninsulares*, creoles, the Catholic Church, and the army, though he also promised legal equality for all Mexicans except slaves. In effect, a conservative leadership maneuvered a sort of counter-revolution against the radical populist rebels that Hidalgo had represented. Indeed, Iturbide took power in 1821 as ªconstitutional emperorº of Mexico. Ten years of fighting, however, left the country in bad economic straits. Iturbide proved to be an inept decision maker, and in 1823 disgruntled army officers forced him out, replacing the short-lived monarchy with a republic.

Many Young States

Some independence leaders, notably Bolívar, had visions of leading Spanish America quickly to prosperity and world influence as a single super-federation in imitation of the United States. Creole property-owners throughout the former empire shared commercial interests, spoke Spanish, read the newspapers that sprang to life in the major cities, and, for the most part, thought of themselves as ªAmericanosº with a common history of discrimination at the hands of *peninsulares*. But union was not to be. Spanish America extended about eight thousand miles from California to Cape Horn, and regional cultural identities and political interests had hardened over three centuries of imperial rule. Creole elites in different regions had little experience working together. In any case they aimed first to substitute themselves for royal officials in the *existing* administrative units. Even partial federation plans failed. Bolívar's Gran Colombia quickly fragmented into Venezuela, Colombia, Ecuador, and eventually Panama. The viceroyalty of Rio de

Independent Latin American states in 1830

MAP 20.3 The Americas in 1830.

What geographical factors might help explain why Spain's American empire broke initially into eleven sovereign states rather than remaining united as one?

La Plata fractured into Argentina, Paraguay, Uruguay, and Bolivia (see Map 20.3). The United Provinces of Central America lasted as a unitary state until 1840 and then broke into five small republics. By contrast, enormous Brazil, despite deeply embedded regionalisms, managed to hold together, partly because of the astute leadership of the young king Dom Pedro and partly because the slave population numbered in the millions, persuading white elites that they had better stick together.

In both Spanish America and Brazil, property-owning males of European descent occupied the pinnacle of the social hierarchy both before and after the wars of independence.

Revolutionary leader Manuela Sáenz (1797–1856). A military strategist, soldier, politician, and activist, Sáenz played an important role in Latin American independence. As with many other politically engaged women, postindependence histories downplayed her participation. Historians have only recently begun to investigate her political and cultural significance, instead of focusing on the relationship she had with Simón Bolívar. How would you account for the changing perceptions of women's contributions to Latin American independence movements?

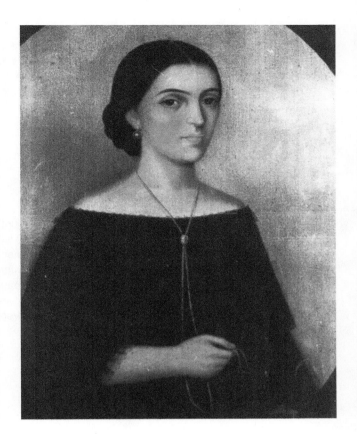

As in the young United States, profound social and economic inequalities remained to be addressed. In the first decades of independence, all the new states except Brazil and the remaining Spanish colonies of Cuba and Puerto Rico abolished slavery. Even so, Indians and free blacks participated little in public life, and castas climbed social and political ladders at a discouraging pace. Women of all classes fought valiantly in the wars, and several gained fame as patriots. Juana Azurduy, a Bolivian casta, led a cavalry charge against Spanish troops in 1816. Gertrudis Bocanegra served as a courier for Mexican rebels, as many women did, until the Spanish caught and executed her. Manuela Sáenz, the illegitimate daughter of an affluent *peninsular* and the mistress of Simón Bolívar, served the revolutionary movement as intelligence agent, fighter, nurse, and postindependence politician. The freedom movements, however, left male patriarchy largely intact. Nowhere in Latin America did women achieve voting rights or liberalization of restrictive marriage laws. Rather, their men folk expected them to observe the new age of independence from home.

• • •

Conclusion

The violent and sometimes chaotic revolutions that took place in Europe and the Western Hemisphere between 1775 to 1830 firmly planted in the human imagination the novel idea that a community of people welded together by shared rights and responsibilities could form a sovereign state. This idea clashed head on with the principle—conceived thousands of years earlier—that the state existed of, by, and for its ruling elite of kings, queens, aristocrats, generals, and priests. We should not conclude, however, that the modern revolutions spelled the triumph of democracy around the Atlantic rim or anywhere else. When Britain lost its thirteen North American colonies, it did not then proceed to prevent trouble in colonized Ireland, South Asia, or the Caribbean by granting popular rights and freedoms. Rather, the crown did its utmost to shore up its authoritarian power. At home, the British government gave the vote to more adult males in 1832 but continued to respond to popular political protests with police repression and restrictions on speech and assembly. In France, radical democratic revolution shifted to Napoleonic despotism, then in 1815 to the restoration of yet another King Louis and a constitution that rigidly limited voting rights. The Congress of Vienna either restored royal autocrats to their thrones or endorsed conservative constitutional monarchies. Haiti went quickly from a democracy of liberated slaves to a politically isolated dictatorship. In the new Latin American republics, propertied elites or rural warlords took full charge of affairs, leaving Indians, blacks, and castas nearly as politically marginalized as they had been under Spanish or Portuguese rule. The young United States not only kept 10 percent of its population in slavery but also launched its own imperial adventure to conquer and subjugate Native Americans. As of 1830, a large majority of the world's population continued to live as subjects of monarchs who suffered no formal limits on their power.

Nevertheless, 1830 represented a transitional moment in the modern era. In the following decades, the complexities and uncertainties of the rapidly changing world economy impelled more communities to demand rights, liberties, and national self-determination. More urban workers and country peasants mobilized themselves to take part in public life, more males gained voting and officeholding rights in particular countries, opponents of slavery and the slave trade gained strength, and the ideas that fueled the Atlantic revolutions began to arouse literate men and women in cities across Asia and Africa.

• • •

Key Terms

American Revolution 599
British East India Company 579
constitutional monarchy 591
coup d'état 592
French Revolution 587
Haitian Revolution 595
insurgency 595

junta 599
Mysore state 582
nation-state 594
nationalism 594
patriotism 587
popular sovereignty 587
Pugachev's Rebellion 585

real wages 580
republic 584
Seven Years' War 583
three estates 589
trans-Atlantic slave trade 579
U.S. Constitution 587
White Lotus Rebellion 585

Change over Time

1722	The Safavid empire in Persia collapses after allowing its gunpowder army to deteriorate.
1756–1763	England, France, and their allies clash in Europe and abroad during the Seven Years' War.
1757	The British East India Company begins to seize territory in India.
1761–1799	South Asia's Mughal empire breaks apart; the Mysore state is established in southern India.
1768–1774	The Ottoman empire loses significant territory in war with Russia.
1773–1774	The Pugachev peasant rebellion erupts in Russia during the reign of Catherine II.
1775–1781	British colonists fight for independence in the American Revolution.
1780s	The trans-Atlantic slave trade reaches its numerical peak.
1787	The U.S. Constitution is signed by state delegates meeting in Philadelphia.
1789–1799	French government and society is transformed by the French Revolution and a series of revolutionary councils.
1789–1804	The plantation colony of Saint Domingue wins independence from France and an end to the slave regime in the Haitian Revolution.
1796–1814	The White Lotus peasant rebellion weakens Qing China.
1798	French forces led by Napoleon capture the Ottoman province of Egypt.
1799–1814	France embarks on empire building under Napoleon Bonaparte.
1810–1828	Wars of independence erupt across Latin America.

Please see end of book reference section for additional reading suggestions related to this chapter.

21 Energy and Industrialization
1750-1850

George and Robert Stephenson's *Rocket* locomotive.

anny Kemble, a young London stage actress, had an exciting experience in the summer of 1830. She received an invitation to ride on a test run of the *Rocket,* a steam-driven locomotive engine built to carry passengers and freight between Liverpool, England's busy west coast port, and the cotton-textile-producing city of Manchester thirty miles to the east. Designed by George and Robert Stephenson, a father and son team, the *Rocket* could pull coaches and flatcars at speeds in excess of thirty miles per hour. "You cannot conceive what that sensation of cutting the air was," Fanny later wrote. "The wind, which was strong, or perhaps the force of our thrusting against it, absolutely weighted my eyelids down. . . . When I closed my eyes this sensation of flying was quite delightful, and strange beyond description; yet strange as it was, I had a perfect sense of security, and not the slightest fear."[1] Though Kemble thrilled at the locomotive's power, her confidence in the safety of rail transport was not entirely warranted. When the Liverpool and Manchester Railway formally opened on September 15 with eight locomotives pulling passengers between the two cities on parallel tracks, William Huskisson, a member of Parliament, died of injuries suffered after he slipped and fell into the path of an oncoming train.

Despite this disaster, the Liverpool and Manchester line, the world's first fully operational intercity railroad, proved an immediate success. Not only did it move passengers at unheard of speeds, but it soon supplanted the local canal network by reducing from days to hours the time it took to transport cotton bales from the Liverpool docks to Manchester. By 1838, Britain had 743 miles of track; by 1850, it had 6,088. By then, rail lines were stretching out across continental Europe, the United States, Canada, Russia, and, a few years later, India.

Early locomotives could burn wood or charcoal in their fireboxes to heat water for steam, but they also used coal or its more efficient chemical derivative, called coke. At the time the coke-burning *Rocket* went into service, humans had long known the potential of coal as a source of useful energy. The nineteenth-century development we call the energy revolution, however, began to transform humankind's relationship to the whole material world. The marriage of coal and pressurized steam enabled our species to smash through limits on economic growth that had been in place for 200,000 years. This breakthrough was a key characteristic of the industrial revolution, an unprecedented surge in human capacity to organize production, manufacture goods, innovate technologically, and manipulate the planet's natural and physical environment.

The first section of the chapter introduces the energy revolution, the development that began barely two centuries ago and soon enabled humans to exploit immense stores of energy concentrated in underground hydrocarbon deposits. Our species also began to master the technical means to convert this treasury into useful mechanical power. These developments transformed the earlier ecological system under which human society had invented agriculture, built cities, forged empires, and created complex systems of commercial and cultural interchange.

The second part of the chapter examines how the exploitation of coal and steam led to an immense increase in the scale of industry early in the nineteenth century. This investigation requires a close look at Britain and the remarkable technological and social changes that took place there. That relatively small country, however, had complex economic and political connections with other parts of the world. Large-scale industrialization would not have occurred in Britain when it did if those connections had not existed. From the start, therefore, the industrial revolution was a

• • •

global development, an event inseparable from multifaceted changes in the wider world economy.

In the final section of the chapter we explore how quickly steam-powered industrial production became a global phenomenon. Technical innovation and factory building continued apace in Britain in the first half of the nineteenth century, and industrialization began to take hold in eastern North America and continental Europe. Egypt emerged as a site of early experimentation with steam power, though its particular experience revealed the great pressures peoples in many parts of the world came under to supply raw materials rather than develop their own industrial economies. Britain took a commanding lead in world commerce, a status made possible by its unrivaled production of textiles and other exportable products and by an immensely powerful navy deployed to advance the state's interests around the world. Industrialists and international merchants became advocates of free trade, arguing that if countries lowered their barriers to foreign imports, especially British ones, everyone would ultimately benefit. In the realm of ideas, the tenets of free trade were woven into the more complex ideology of liberalism, a body of political and economic thought that guided the expansion of the capitalist world economy throughout the nineteenth century.

A Panoramic View

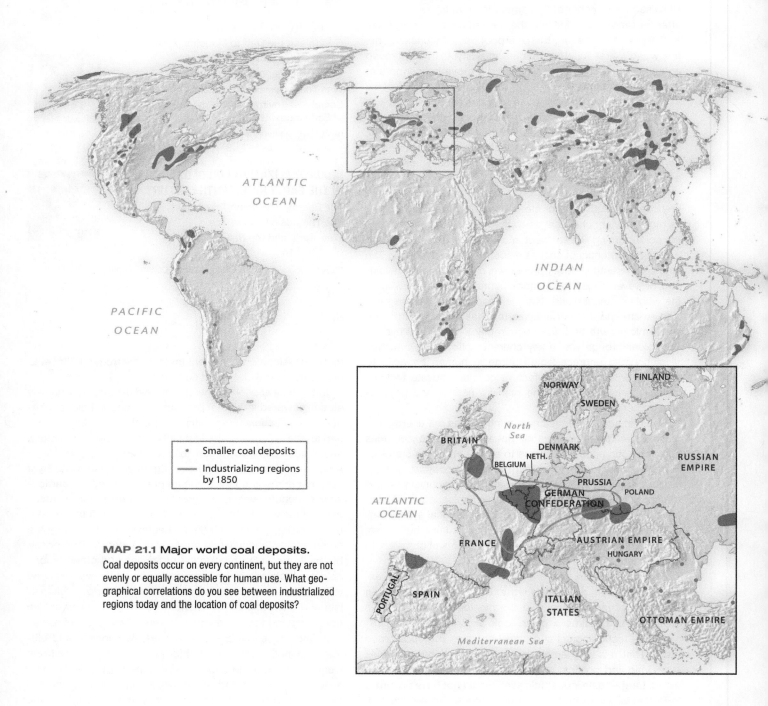

MAP 21.1 Major world coal deposits.

Coal deposits occur on every continent, but they are not evenly or equally accessible for human use. What geographical correlations do you see between industrialized regions today and the location of coal deposits?

Legend:
- Smaller coal deposits
- Industrializing regions by 1850

The Energy Revolution

FOCUS What were the basic features of the energy revolution, and why did it represent a critical turning point in human history?

During most of our history, humans have had access only to sources of energy concentrated on the surface of the earth, or barely below it. Solar rays blanket the face of the planet, where plants convert that radiation into chemical energy through photosynthesis. A thin film of arable soil and the uppermost layer of the seas have throughout most of our history provided the food that we and our domesticated animals consume, then transform into muscle and brain energy required for useful work. The earth's outer membrane has also supplied the biomass (wood and other plant material) that humans have burned to release heat energy for light, warmth, cooking, pot making, and metal forging. Within the past few thousand years, inventors began to construct sailing ships, windmills, and waterwheels, which harnessed a little of the mechanical (kinetic) energy produced by surface winds and flowing water. But less than two hundred years ago, people and draft animals were still the chief ªprime movers.º

The Fuel That Lies Beneath

In some parts of the world, immense stocks of untapped energy lay deep below the earth's surface. From thousands to hundreds of millions of years ago, plant matter became submerged under layers of water, mud, and rock. Consequently, some of the energy stored in this matter did not dissipate but remained intact and, under relentless heat and pressure, became fossilized and densely concentrated, producing coal, crude oil, and natural gas, also known as **fossil fuels.** As one historian has put it, deep coal deposits are energy-rich ªsubterranean forests,º biomass that once stood green and leafy in the sunshine (see Map 21.1).[2]

fossil fuels Hydrocarbon deposits, especially coal, crude oil, and natural gas, derived from the remains of once-living plant and animal organisms; these deposits are burned to produce heat energy.

Until the eighteenth century, people could get at deposits of burnable fossil matter only where they could find them quite near the ground. In China, Japan, Europe, and other regions, people have mined coal from surface outcrops, washouts, or open pits since ancient times, and they have known that coal burns hotter and slower than an equivalent weight of wood or charcoal. From at least the tenth century, artisans who built China's flourishing iron industry used large quantities of coal, along with wood and charcoal, to heat blast furnaces. This technology worked well in northern China for several hundred years because abundant deposits of iron ore and coal were close to each other. No premodern society, however, had the knowledge or skills to exploit coal's full potential. Coal gives off more harmful gases than wood does, and burning coal in an open fire or in an inefficient furnace captures little of its stored heat energy. Moreover, deep hard-rock coal mining was beyond any society's technical capacity before the eighteenth century. Extracting and concentrating the heat energy of petroleum or natural gas presented even bigger technical problems.

The **energy revolution** got under way only when people figured out how to mine coal on a much larger scale and then convert it more efficiently into heat energy and horsepower. This happened in connection with two nearly simultaneous developments. One was the invention of machines, initially driven by animals, windmills, or waterwheels, that could produce sustained, powerful repetitive motion in order to manufacture products in unprecedented quantities and at record speeds. These devices could replace muscle action, for example, to spin yarn or weave cloth. The use of mechanical devices for manufacturing or for lifting water has a long history. Individually operated machines for reeling and winding silk filaments came into use in China no later than the eleventh century. About the same time, innovators in Muslim Southwest Asia invented mechanical devices to twist silk thread. In other words, the pioneers of the **industrial revolution** did not invent mechanized manufacturing. Rather they invented more complex and efficient machines for performing repetitive tasks, and they put them into use on a much larger scale.

energy revolution The massive increase of useful heat energy made available to humans by extracting and burning fossil fuels.

industrial revolution The technological and economic processes whereby industrialization based on fossil-fuel energy, steam engines, and complex machines led to worldwide economic, social, and environmental transformations.

The second big development was the invention of the steam engine. Fundamentally, this is a mechanism that puts steam under pressure to drive a piston (or multiple pistons) up and down in a closed cylinder and to do it efficiently enough to generate repetitive force that humans, animals, or waterwheels could not match. Engineers first connected steam engines to pumps to lift groundwater from coal or other mines, but this innovation immediately suggested numerous other applications of pressurized steam. Thus, the power of steam engines and manufacturing machines became intertwined.

By the early nineteenth century, a process of self-sustaining innovation began to take hold. New energy sources, machines, production methods, technical ideas, and markets for goods interacted dynamically, stimulating more innovations, which fed back positively on one another. Economic thinkers began to talk of the possibility of unremitting, self-generating innovation, and with it continuous economic growth. ªFrom west to east, and from north to south,º an official of the Liverpool and Manchester Railway declared exuberantly in 1830, ªthe mechanical principle, the philosophy of the nineteenth century, will spread and extend itself. . . . The genius of the age, like a mighty river of the new world, flows onwards, full, rapid, and irresistible.°³

The End of the Biological Old Regime

In Chapter 20 we described the European Old Regime as the socially rigid and politically authoritarian system that existed in Europe before the French Revolution. More recently, scholars have introduced the concept of the **biological old regime.** This is the idea that for all of history up to the late eighteenth century, plants,

> **biological old regime** Human history before the nineteenth century, when economic production depended almost entirely on capturing flows of energy from the sun.

animals, and people all depended for survival on the day-to-day stream of energy from solar radiation. Humans cannot in any continuous way increase the amount of solar energy that reaches the surface of the earth and makes plants grow. Consequently, the resources of the land are finite. Exploiting them involves tradeoffs: Cutting forests to provide a source of heat means that less wood is available to build houses or ships; using land to pasture animals means that less is available for crops.

These constraints on land meant that not even the richest societies could break through thick ceilings on productive growth. In premodern times, if a society expanded its territories or achieved a burst of technical creativity, it might produce more food and manufactures for several decades or even centuries. The majority of its people might enjoy rising incomes and living standards. In such prosperous times, population typically increased. But that growth eventually outran the rate of economic advance. In other words, more people put pressure on the land's finite resources. Consequently, production of food and goods slowed down again, and living standards, except for the wealthiest and most powerful class, declined. Moreover, the biological old regime had a collection of pranks to play on a productive society. Droughts, floods, famines, epidemics, rebellions, or foreign invasions could easily sabotage growth. Agrarian abundance depended heavily on good harvests and reasonably stable social conditions. In the eighteenth century, scholars in both China and western Europe expressed vague fears that rapid population growth was putting too much strain on both crop and forest land and that economic crisis lay ahead.

Near the end of the century, however, humans began to challenge the biological old regime's limits on growth by exploiting not only solar energy available on the surface of the earth but also energy stored underground in the form of fossil fuels. *Input* of immense quantities of new energy to propel pistons, wheels, gears, lathes, and pulleys permitted *output* of far more goods than was possible when their manufacture depended on muscle, water, or wind. This development spelled the end of the biological old regime because the rate of world energy production, and with it the production of food and material goods, rose much faster than ever before. On a global scale, the world's gross domestic product (GDP) per capita (per person), or its total output of goods and services divided by total population, rose by nearly four times between 1500 (when the biological old regime was in full force) and 1900. On a global scale, this growth nearly kept up with the rate of population increase (see graph).⁴

Population in millions

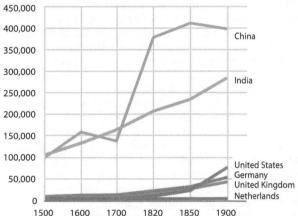

GDP per capita, 1990 international dollars

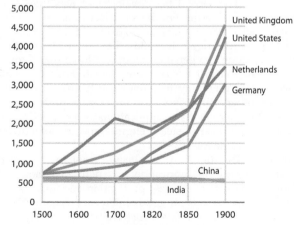

Population and GDP, 1500–1900. Which countries experienced the biggest change in population during these centuries? Which saw the largest per capita economic growth? Based on this data, what would you infer about regional differences in the relationship between population growth and change in per capita GDP?

Industry on a New Scale

FOCUS How did the interplay of events in England and other parts of the world in the late eighteenth and early nineteenth centuries contribute to industrialization?

Chinese traders in Malacca, Hindu bankers in Calcutta, and Swahili merchants in Zanzibar could recognize as easily as Europeans the potential wealth that might come from enlarging the scale of enterprises to produce and exchange goods. But in 1750, no one could have imagined any country's having the technology or capital to expand manufacturing output many times over and to continuously accelerate production in a range of industries. Over the next several decades, however, Britain, or more specifically the midlands and north of England, did accomplish this transformation. In 1815 Patrick Colquhoun, a Scottish merchant, marveled:

> It is impossible to contemplate the progress of manufactures in Great Britain within the last thirty years without wonder and astonishment. Its rapidity . . . exceeds all credibility. The improvement of the steam engines, but above all the facilities afforded to the great branches of the woolen and cotton manufactories by ingenious machinery, invigorated by capital and skill, are beyond all calculation.[5]

The ªprogress of manufacturesº in Britain was indeed an extraordinary development in world history. Generations of historians have debated the question of how and why large-scale industrialization took off first in England. In investigating these events, we should keep two factors in mind. One is that once inventors and entrepreneurs in Britain began to understand the economic potential of steam-driven, fossil-fueled machines, the idea spread rapidly to other parts of the world. An industrial revolution was unlikely to happen independently some place else, because it became a global event in a very short time. Peoples all around the world rapidly became enmeshed in it in one way or another. The second factor is that Britain's early industrialization took place in a global frame. Its domestic economy was embedded in the world economy. We must therefore look beyond England itself for explanations of how fossil-fueled industry got started.

Cotton and the Drift to Industrialization

At the start of the eighteenth century, Britain had a productive agricultural economy, having in the previous two centuries followed northern France and the Low Countries (the region centered on modern Belgium, the Netherlands, and Luxembourg) in adopting a range of innovative farming techniques. Britain also produced and exported copious amounts of wool and woolen fabric. Cotton, however, would not grow in the northern European climate. Britain relied chiefly on South Asia, the world's largest cotton exporter, for expertly dyed and printed cotton goods. Lightweight, low-priced, brightly colored Indian ªcalicosº imported by the East India Company became so popular that wool, linen, and silk manufacturers feared their industries might collapse. In the words of one dismayed English commentator writing in the early 1700s, ª[Cotton] crept into our houses, our

closets and bedchambers; curtains, cushions, chairs, and at last beds themselves were nothing but Callicoes or Indian stuffs. In short, almost everything that used to be made of wool or silk . . . was supplied by the Indian trade.º[6] English businesspeople complained that South Asia exported tons of cheap cotton because spinners and weavers there labored in poverty. In fact, real wages were probably higher for Indian textile workers than they were for English laborers because food prices in South Asia were relatively lower.

Shortly after 1700 the British Parliament tried to plug the Indian calico stream by raising port tariffs, thereby protecting the fledgling English industry. It is not clear whether this action stimulated English business directly, but it helped inspire some entrepreneurs to investigate new methods of manufacturing textiles at home that would cut both labor costs and the price of finished goods. They did this knowing they would still have to depend on imports of raw cotton from South Asia or other places where farmers could grow it.

Textile spinning and weaving traditionally took place in farmers' homes and village workshops. Crafts workers' dexterous fingers, even though assisted by spinning wheels and handlooms, did most of the work. Capitalist merchants, however, learned to accelerate production by introducing variations of the **putting-out system.** This

> **putting-out system** A production method in which employers distributed raw materials to individuals or families, who then made finished goods, typically woolen or cotton yarn or cloth, and returned these goods to the employer for payment.

Four women engaged in cottage textile production. This 1791 print shows Irish women spinning, reeling, and boiling yarn, working in the putting-out system. Notice the child helping tend the fire and the pets in the foreground—details that emphasize the domestic location of the work. How might this work have compared to household production intended for family consumption, rather than to fulfill a contract with a textile merchant?

economic practice, first used in the woolen industry, involved wholesalers distributing, or ᵃputting out° raw material to cottagers in a locality and paying them by the piece to spin yarn or weave cloth. The merchants then collected the finished work to be dyed, printed, sold domestically, or exported. This system was different from home handicraft industry because workers did not buy their own materials or sell their finished products at the local market.

About 1730, however, entrepreneurs began to introduce new machines. Here, the global network of knowledge exchange came into play. In small mills in central England, manufacturers produced silk thread from imported silkworm cocoons by drawing out the raw fiber and winding it evenly on reels using hand-operated machines. Designs for these devices came directly from Italy, though they almost certainly originated in China, where, as we have seen, the textile industry had invented various mechanical contrivances centuries earlier. When English reeling mills first opened, engineers studied the technology to see how it might apply to cotton spinning. In 1730 John Kay, the son of an English farmer, invented the flying shuttle, a device that significantly speeded up cotton handloom weaving.

A practical invention, however, may trigger the need for other inventions. Weavers using the flying shuttle could produce cloth faster, but workers who produced cotton yarn on traditional spinning wheels could not keep up with weavers' demand for it. James Hargreaves, a weaver with no formal education, solved the problem in 1765 by inventing the spinning jenny. According to the legend, his daughter, whose name was Jenny, accidentally knocked the family spinning wheel over one day, prompting Hargreaves to think about how he might design a machine that would draw out wool or cotton fiber and twist it into thread. The operator turned a crank that spun eight spindles at once, multiplying the work of a single spinning wheel by that many times.

Four years later, Richard Arkwright devised the water frame, a more efficient spinning machine powered by a waterwheel rather than a crank. Women and children with little technical skill managed water frames in return for humble wages. In 1779 Samuel Crompton invented the ᵃspinning mule,° a more complicated apparatus that produced yarn of South Asian quality. A power-assisted mule could spin one hundred pounds of cotton in about 300 hours, a feat that would have taken an Indian hand spinner about 50,000 hours, or five years and nine months of work! England had rivers and streams in abundance, and as the cloth industry grew, waterwheels became the chief source of power for the new machines.

These innovations in spinning now meant that yarn could be turned out *faster* than weaving machines could use it. In 1784, however, Edmund Cartwright, a minister of the Church of England, invented a power loom that could do the job of numerous handloom operators working manually. Other mechanisms and techniques came to England from the wider world. In 1785, for example, Claude Berthollet, a French chemist, demonstrated how to bleach

A worker using a Jacquard loom. The swags of punch cards at the top of the loom contained code that produced complicated woven patterns in cloth. These looms were among the many innovations that increased textile production in Britain and France. Emerging technology also meant that less-skilled workers could operate machinery that produced fine quality cloth. Why might workers have targeted these looms for destruction when they violently resisted changing working conditions?

textiles with chlorine. In 1804 Joseph Jacquard, also French, invented a loom that used punched cards to create a rudimentary binary coding technology for weaving complex patterns into cloth. Knowledge of dyes, notably a coveted bright red, passed from workshops in Ottoman Turkey to France, Switzerland, and England. Across the Atlantic, Eli Whitney invented the cotton gin in 1793. This startlingly simple cylindrical device drastically reduced the work hours required to clean green-seed cotton, triggering the opening of millions of acres in the American south to fiber production and African slave labor. In the early nineteenth century the United States surpassed the Caribbean and India as the largest supplier of raw cotton to the mills multiplying across England.

Mines and Machines

Wide, deep vaults of coal run underneath parts of England, Wales, and Scotland, and over the centuries people collected tons of it at the surface or from shallow mines (see Map 21.1). Coal consumption in Britain grew steadily in premodern times, mainly because the mineral was cheap relative to firewood and charcoal. In fact, as population grew and forests fell to the axe, wood became increasingly expensive. By the seventeenth century, coal substituted for wood in many urban homes and businesses in Britain and some parts of continental Europe. If British miners tried to dig deep for coal, however, groundwater inevitably flowed into shafts and tunnels. Mechanical pumps operated by workers or horses were too inefficient to keep up with seepage.

The union of steam and coal. English inventors, notably Thomas Newcomen, began in the early 1700s to tinker with ᵃatmospheric engines,° adapting ideas from scientific research on air pressure and vacuums. Miners put Newcomen's early steam machine to work both pumping water out of coal tunnels and forcing fresh air into them. This engine was not very efficient, but it suggested a new line of experimentation. Margaret Bryan, an English girls' school headmistress, explained in a science textbook she published in 1806: ᵃ But for this machine we could never have enjoyed the advantages of coal fuel in our time; as our forefathers had dug the pits as far as they could go: for the water rising in them from different fissures prevented working deeper;

but this machine enables us to drain all the water from the mine, as it rises to impede the miners in their progress.°⁷

In the 1760s James Watt, a Scottish instrument maker and businessman, built a much more efficient engine that transferred a piston's thrust to a rotating shaft, producing a circular motion that could be applied to many new mechanical tasks. About two decades later, Samuel Crompton successfully attached steam engines to his power looms. This meant that cotton mills did not have to be located next to streams but could be built anywhere near a wood or coal source. Though a general shift from water to steam power in the textile industry took several more decades to accomplish, manufacturers in both Britain and continental Europe used Watt engines to power cotton, paper, flour, and iron mills, which numbered in all around 2,500 by 1800.

British entrepreneurs also recognized the mutually reinforcing uses of coal and steam. Coal cost less than wood or charcoal to drive steam engines; engines powered by coal permitted deep extraction of even more coal; and expansion of coal mining increased the demand for more and better engines for a widening range of industries. In the second half of the eighteenth century, British coal production multiplied more than three times. By 1800 the country was producing an astonishing 90 percent of the world's total supply.

Iron: The third component. Until late in the eighteenth century, coal had limited potential for smelting iron. Because of coal's chemical impurities, it produced pig iron, a

Children working in a British coal mine, 1844. Their small size meant they could fit into tight workspaces, so children worked in particularly brutal conditions underground. Children often labored as hurriers, dragging wagons of coal from the mining face to the surface in tunnels as small as 18 inches tall—depicted here in the middle horizontal tunnel. How does the work underground differ from work above ground in this lithograph?

substance that was too brittle to refine into usable wrought iron. In the 1780s, however, Abraham Darby, an ironware maker, found a way to use coal much more efficiently in iron smelting by first coking it, that is, by heating it in air-tight ovens to drive off chemical residues. The resulting coke had a high carbon content and did not contaminate iron ore in the blast furnace. Coke was also more suitable than coal for cooking and many new industrial processes. Two other key innovations of the late century were steam pumps designed to shoot air into industrial furnaces and mechanical rollers that forced impurities out of iron much faster than numerous blacksmiths could do it.

Iron ore was plentiful in Britain, and metal production grew five times between 1720 and 1804. In turn, many new iron products supplied the mining and textile industries. The British navy had an insatiable appetite for iron for guns and ship fittings. The farms that supplied the country's growing population required iron wagon wheels, plowshares, horseshoes, and shovels. Thus, agriculture also became increasingly dependent on steam, coal, and iron.

Steam engines on tracks. Industrialization was under way in Britain for several decades before railway lines began to compete with canals, roads, and coastal shipping lanes to move commodities and people more than short distances. Well before the eighteenth century, miners in Britain and on the continent moved loads of ore short distances by setting carts with grooved wheels on rails to reduce friction. Workers or animals then pushed or pulled the wagons. A steam engine on wheels could make a coal cart go, but only if it could generate enough horsepower to move itself, the engine carriage, and the loaded carts.

In 1800 Richard Trevithick, the son of a miner, invented the earliest working locomotive by designing a compact engine that pressurized steam much more efficiently than James Watt's engine did. Because of skepticism among miners, Trevithick had to introduce his engine to the public as an amusement ride. Doubts dissolved, however, especially after 1820, when foundries began to turn out wrought iron rails that could support heavy loads without breaking. In 1830, the same year that the *Rocket* began pulling amazed passengers between Liverpool and Manchester, a passenger line opened in the United States between Baltimore and Elliott, Maryland. The railroad-building race was on.

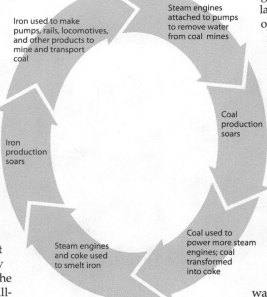

Iron used to make pumps, rails, locomotives, and other products to mine and transport coal

Steam engines attached to pumps to remove water from coal mines

Coal production soars

Coal used to power more steam engines; coal transformed into coke

Steam engines and coke used to smelt iron

Iron production soars

Steam, coal, and iron: a positive feedback loop. What conclusions can you draw from this diagram about the role of coal in the process of industrialization?

Working in Factories

Long before modern times and in several parts of the world, governments and private entrepreneurs learned the advantages of bringing groups of workers to central locations to manufacture weapons, build ships, or weave cloth under close supervision. The idea was to increase the scale and speed of production. Historians have also argued that tropical American sugar plantations were prototypes of the modern factory. Most of the African slaves on these plantations worked full time in the fields, but some operated the mills, which resembled modern factories in several respects. A sugar mill was a large central building that housed heavy crushing and boiling equipment. Managers imposed a division of labor, grouping workers by gradations of skill and dividing them into crews that performed different tasks. At harvest time, when the mills often operated around the clock, the sequence of cane cutting and milling had to be synchronized meticulously, requiring rigorous discipline and punctuality. Finally, workers toiled in conditions of continuous heat, noise, and danger. A planter on the Caribbean island of Barbados, writing in 1700, described mill operations: [a] 'Tis to live in a perpetual Noise and Hurry; . . . since the climate is so hot and the labor so constant, that the Servants [slaves] night and day stand in the great Boyling Houses, where there are Six or Seven large Coppers or Furnaces kept perpetually Boyling.[o 8]

The spinning, weaving, and iron-smelting factories that began to rise up in Britain in the late eighteenth century had regimens similar to slave plantations. Manufacturing operations used heavy, complicated machines that could not be [a] put out[o] to workers' shops or cottages but had to be concentrated in central buildings. Mill workers did not perform every phase of production but learned to carry out specialized, repetitive tasks, chiefly feeding and tending the machines. Since idle factories generated no return on investment, supervisors had to make sure that all phases of production ran smoothly and perhaps day and night. Regular work shifts had to be scheduled, clocks and whistles had to be installed, and slack workers had to be penalized appropriately.

Workers in early English mills were wage earners, not slaves. But from the point of view of owners, who invested large, often borrowed sums in buildings and equipment, the pace of production required a strict hierarchy of authority. Profit margins were usually narrow, so owners kept wages as low as possible, though pay rose slowly as factories multiplied. Much like slave plantation owners, English industrialists preoccupied with efficiency could easily think of their workers as impersonal components of the systemÐ units of muscle to be hired, fired, and disciplined as production schedules demanded. After 1820, when steam engines came into wider use in textile production, the pace and rigidity of work sped up even more.

Naturally enough, self-respecting farmers and artisans did not clamor for jobs in noisy, claustrophobic mills, and many complained bitterly about losing skilled occupations to machines. But despite the negatives of factory work, workers became available, notably owing to rapid population growth after 1750 and the steady transfer of farm land from smallholders and tenants to large agricultural estates. These big farmers paid even lower wages than workers might earn in industrial mills. Factory hands had little incentive to work hard, but the ever-looming threat of job or wage loss helped keep the machines humming. In central and northern England the population of urban workers rose spectacularly. For example, Manchester, a city at the center of the mill country, grew from 24,000 people in 1773 to 250,000 by 1850. Even so, factories did not appear everywhere in Britain, and in the early industrial decades the great majority of people continued to farm, do unskilled work, or make clothing, leather goods, nails, and many other products by hand.

Was There Something Special about Britain?

Britain cannot claim to be the birthplace of the factory, but it was the first country in the world where factories crammed with machines and powered by a new source of energy began to multiply on the landscape. It was also where factories became the central workplaces in a new economic system capable of turning out goods on scales previously unimaginable. It was in Britain that businesspeople began to see signs that human society might just be capable of self-sustaining, perpetually accelerating economic growth, an inconceivable notion under the biological old regime.

In the long perspective of history, large-scale industrialization might have gotten under way in some part of the world besides Britain. But it could not have happened just anywhere, because it required a location where society possessed a certain density and complexity of population, food production, knowledge, and skill, as well as access to wider networks of economic and cultural exchange. Between the fifteenth and eighteenth centuries, northern Italy, the Netherlands, southern China, and parts of South Asia all experienced periods of technical brilliance and economic flowering, only to fall back to more modest levels of growth. Britain might have met a comparable fate. Industrialization there advanced quite fitfully until about 1830, and the population continued to grow faster than domestic resources. In the world at large, the later eighteenth century was a period of economic slowing. In Britain both agricultural productivity and real wages slumped. Nevertheless, industrialization did not stall out, and sometime after 1830 Britain crossed the line from being an innovative society like others before it to one where steam power and fossil fuel set economic growth spiraling upward.

We also cannot explain early industrialization, as scholars used to do, by pointing to special cultural or social traits that British people, or Europeans in general, possessed. Historians have richly demonstrated that most types of values and attitudesÐ for example, individual desire to take initiative or to innovate to solve problemsÐ are likely to be found in all complex societies. We need, rather, to pay attention to the attitudes and practices that appear to have had the strongest influence on the directions a society has taken at a particular historical moment. We must explain industrial development in England by a convergence of factorsÐ food production, energy sources, technology, communication, government, social relations, intellectual tendencies, and interactions with other parts of the world. Also, we should recognize that Britain did not achieve a complete industrial revolution that only later spread to other parts of the world. Key processes got under way first in Britain, but many innovations in technology and the organization of industrial production and commerce originated in other parts of the world as the nineteenth century proceeded.

Food for workers. Industrialization could continue beyond a certain point only if the society could produce or import sufficient food to sustain growing numbers of men and women to work in industry rather than grow their own meals. In fact, England was an unusually productive agricultural society in the two centuries before industrialization began. Like farmers in southern China, South Asia, Japan, and the European Low CountriesÐ all regions where population was increasingÐ English cultivators found ways to squeeze higher crop yields from given acreages of land. English farmers at first borrowed a number of ideas from the Netherlands. These included ingenious techniques for draining marshes, new crop rotation strategies to enrich soil, more efficient use of animal manure for fertilizer, and construction of more windmills and watermills. One distinctively English innovation was the expansion of commercial agriculture, that is, the concentration of more crop and pasture land in the hands of wealthy land-owners attuned to the capitalist market. Historians continue to debate whether this ªenclosure movement,º which involved transferring land from peasant producers to commercial estate lords by legal or extralegal means, improved agricultural output very much. It certainly changed the way millions of ordinary men and women made their livings. Big land-owners collected rents from tenant farmers and hired day laborers who worked for modest wages. In the eighteenth century, England's landholding peasantry nearly disappeared, whereas in France, for example, it represented the vast majority of the population. Ex-farmers moved in

A critique of parliamentary politics. England's local political officials did not escape criticism. The property qualification meant that only a minority of men were eligible to vote for members of Parliament, so politicians did not necessarily represent the interests of the majority of their constituents. This oil painting, *Chairing the Member* (1755), is the final installment in a four-part series called *The Humours of an Election*. The artist William Hogarth was an English painter, printmaker, satirist, cartoonist, and social critic. The scene depicts a victorious candidate being carried through the streets in celebration, but Hogarth's critique of an electoral system marred by bribery and intimidation would have been clear to eighteenth-century viewers. What elements of the image suggest Hogarth was poking fun at the election, and its result?

growing numbers to towns and cities, where they worked for wages if they could find work at all. Eventually, much of this growing urban population drifted into the waiting arms of factory owners.

Agricultural productivity in Britain leveled off around 1750, just when population started growing faster and industrialization was getting under way. However, like other European states that possessed overseas colonies (mainly Spain, Portugal, France, and the Netherlands), Britain had access to extensive food and fiber resources from beyond its own shores. North America and the Caribbean supplied Britain with grain, sugar, cotton, coffee, timber, fish, and numerous other products, and these resources became increasingly important as industrialization moved into high gear. In effect, the Americas provided productive land that Britain would have had to possess (but did not) in order to sustain the high rate of economic growth that it achieved.

For example, by the late eighteenth century, English sheep farmers would have had to expand pasture land by many millions of acres, which was not possible, in order to produce the equivalent yardage of textiles, produced from wool, that could instead be made from cotton grown in America or other overseas regions. By around 1800, England would have required somewhere between one and two million acres of farm land (which it did not have) to produce the food calories that the population consumed by eating imported American sugar. As industrialization continued in the nineteenth century, imports accounted for an increasing percentage of the British population's diet.[9]

British government and industrialization. After enduring nearly a half-century of civil war and political crisis, which finally ended with the Glorious Revolution of 1688 (see Chapter 19), Britain entered the eighteenth century as a limited monarchy. The king or queen remained head of state, but Parliament, a legislature elected by a minority population of male, property-owning citizens, had prime authority to govern. For example, in contrast to rulers in most of continental Europe, the British crown could not seize property arbitrarily, unilaterally impose taxes, or arrest and imprison people simply by ordering a judge or police officer to do it. British common law specified that people accused of crimes must face a jury of their peers, not a crown-appointed judge who rendered a verdict. All these laws and institutions served the interestsÐ in fact they were *intended* to serve the interestsÐ of people more likely to invest in technical innovation and industrial growth if they knew their property would remain secure. Compared to the continental monarchies, Britain was also a more decentralized state. That is, much of the country's day-to-day government rested with locally elected officials rather than with governors, commandants, and tax agents sent out from the capital. Typically, these local magistrates were members of the land-owning and business class and therefore mostly stayed out of the way of entrepreneurs and artisans who experimented with new machines and commercial strategies.

The founding of the Bank of England in 1694 illustrates Parliament's business-oriented disposition shortly after the Glorious Revolution. The bank functioned to support Britain's commercial growth and international trade. It issued bonds, that is, it borrowed money from British subjects, guaranteeing those loans with the capital the bank steadily accumulated. This borrowed capital was Britain's ªnational debt,º but the bank made regular interest payments on that debt, thereby attracting more investment in it. A large part of the bank's assets went into expanding the Royal Navy, an investment that safeguarded Britain's catapulting income from global trade.

Parliamentary government, however, does not provide a sufficient explanation for industrialization. The Netherlands also had a collective government of capitalist-minded property owners but did not begin to build factories until well into the nineteenth century. Conversely, Germany after its unification in 1870 achieved spectacular industrial success under the direction, not of an elected legislature, but of a small authoritarian oligarchy. Nor did industry take root in Britain because Parliament kept taxes low. On the contrary, it taxed British subjects at a much higher rate than did France or other autocratic monarchies. Moreover, Parliament did not invest directly in industrialization. Early factory, canal, and railway builders had to depend on private startup capital, often from family and friends.

A final political factor is that Britain remained a relatively stable society throughout the early industrial decades. Although government and business achieved this tranquility partly by allying to repress sometimes adamant working-class protest over wages, factory conditions, and unemployment, Britain was a haven of peace compared to continental Europe. There, people who contributed new machines and technical processes had to carry on amid the turbulent conditions of the French Revolution, war between France and several other states, and Napoleon Bonaparte's imperial venture (see Chapter 20). Industrialization might have gotten under way on the continent somewhat earlier were it not for this protracted time of troubles.

Creative energy in science and technology. One of the hallmarks of modernity has been continuous technical and scientific innovation, rather than the temporary surges of it in one part of the world or another that characterized the agrarian age. In the seventeenth and eighteenth centuries, Europe's scientific revolution generated a torrent of new ideas about nature and the universe, though it drew on the accumulated wisdom of all of Afroeurasia and on vast new knowledge that poured in from America following the sixteenth-century global convergence (see Chapters 16 and 19). In Europe, thinkers probed the heart of nature by subjecting it to rational, mathematical analysis and to careful observation, rather than by fitting it, one way or another, into principles and dogmas inherited from the Bible, early Christian texts, or ancient Greek philosophy. Careful observation of the physical and natural world required inventions that allowed investigators to peer deeper into phenomena (microscopes and telescopes), to create special environmental conditions (electrostatic machines, vacuum pumps, prisms), and to precisely measure observed phenomena (micrometers, thermometers, and sextants). These devices had themselves to be accurately designed and tooled, as well as standardized to ensure consistency.

To give one instance, John Harrison, an eighteenth-century clockmaker, spent decades holed up in a workshop in Yorkshire trying to build a special clock so delicately balanced that it would keep accurate time on a pitching ship. He finally succeeded, producing a chronometer, as it was called, that allowed sea captains to keep track of the time difference between a given location and the port from which they debarked. Mariners needed that knowledge in order to accurately calculate longitude, that is, a vessel's position east or west of the port of departure. In Britain, scientific work and material instrumentation supported each other. Precise and powerful devices led to new scientific discoveries, which demanded more and better contrivances to expand and compound those discoveries. John Harrison's chronometer, for example, was a crucial aid to Captain James Cook in mapping Pacific islands in the 1770s.

Researchers used scientific instruments throughout Europe, in the colonies of Europe, and to some extent in the Ottoman empire and China. In Britain, however, interest in mechanisms, engines, and gadgets, and in the knowledge they might reveal, reached the dimensions of a popular craze. Scientific societies hosted talks and demonstrations that attracted men and women from all levels of society. Mechanical demonstrations became a form of public entertainment. Aristocratic scholars, craftspeople, and machinists communicated with one another through meetings and associations to discuss connections between scientific principles

John Harrison's marine chronometer. The British Parliament established a prize in 1714 to reward the first person to devise a method to measure accurately a ship's longitude at sea. Harrison's H4, a bit bigger than a pocket-watch, proved successful at keeping accurate time during an Atlantic crossing in 1761, despite the rolling and pitching of the ship, which disrupted the mechanism of standard eighteenth-century timekeepers. Harrison's work laid the groundwork for modern watches. Why might the government have encouraged this scientific research with a significant financial prize?

and down-to-earth technical problems. From the 1750s British secondary schools taught not only the classical curriculum centered on Latin, but also algebra, physics, surveying, and other subjects considered of practical use to ambitious young men. By the 1780s academies for girls taught science and mechanics. Margaret Bryan's 1806 textbook titled *Lectures on Natural Philosophy* combined genteel religious moralizing with rich expositions of the writings of Isaac Newton.

The career of James Watt vividly illustrates these eighteenth-century trends. The son of a Scottish builder, he studied in both England and Scotland to master the arts of instrument making. In 1765 he applied this experience, as well as knowledge of Newton's energy theories and Joseph Black's work on the properties of latent heat, to improve on the Newcomen steam engine. He regarded himself as a hardheaded businessman, but he also participated in the Lunar Society, an association of intellectuals dedicated to

scientific achievement. ªGeometry and algebra with the science of calculation in general,º he advised his son, ªare the foundation of all useful science, without a complete knowledge of them natural philosophy is but an amusement.º[10] Watt's wife Annie collaborated with him in both science and business and undertook research of her own in chemistry to explore practical applications of chlorine bleach.

Britain's partiality for empirical science, that is, inquiry grounded in observation, experiment, and practical application, cannot be generalized for all of Europe. It contrasted markedly with the deductive logic favored in France, whereby scientific thinkers attempted to explain the workings of nature by rational, mathematical analysis founded on established principles. Though French technologists made several key contributions to mechanical industry, highly educated scholars in France and other continental countries showed little interest until the nineteenth century in the gears, pulleys, clocks, and pumps that engrossed British innovators.

Social and Environmental Consequences of Early Industrialization

When industrialization first got under way, no one could have foreseen how railroads, massive coal burning, and regimented factory work might transform daily life. Nor could anyone have perceived what became a fundamental feature of modernity: the continuous acceleration of change, not just in Britain but eventually everywhere in the world.

The rapid rise of global population that we associate with modernity preceded the industrial revolution but continued to accompany it. In Britain, population growth, urbanization, and industrialization positively reinforced one another earlier than in other societies. England's population grew by a little less than 1 million in the seventeenth century but by nearly 8.7 million by 1801.[11] More abundant food supplies, a wider variety of foods, more wage jobs, and improved public hygiene combined to generate this startling acceleration. A trend toward earlier marriage may have contributed as well. In Britain and other northern European countries, people traditionally delayed marriage later than in many other parts of the world. But the opportunities for wage labor, including factory employment, encouraged young women and men to start their own households earlier than if they had to wait to inherit a farm or other family property. In the eighteenth century, London's population grew from about 550,000 to 860,000, making it the largest city in Europe and perhaps the second biggest in the world, after Beijing. In the English midlands, cities like Birmingham, Liverpool, Manchester, and Leeds mushroomed as well. By 1800 about 28 percent of England's people lived in cities, a far higher proportion than in any continental European country (see Map 21.2).

Discontents of the new industrial working class. The multitudes who moved from countryside to city faced

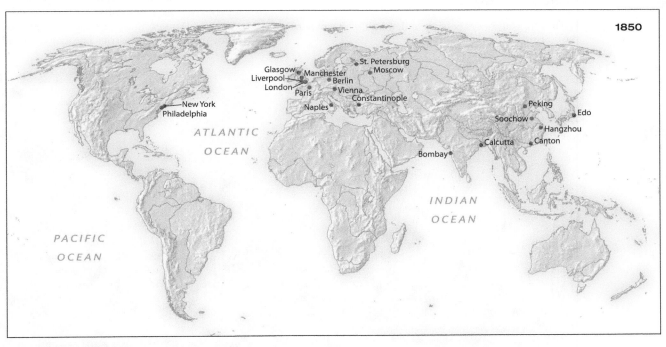

MAP 21.2 The world's twenty largest cities, 1750 (top) and 1850.

Which regions of the world gained more large cities during this one-hundred-year period? Which regions lost cities in the top twenty? May a general change in the geographical distribution of cities be inferred during that century? What factors might explain increased urbanization?

sprawling slums, jammed apartments, filthy groundwater, wretched sanitation, and contagious disease. Urban working conditions also contrasted sharply with rural routines. Both adults and children typically labored on the farm from dawn to dusk, but they worked at home, setting the pace and relying on the family for support in bad times. The putting-out system allowed women and children to spin yarn and weave cloth under the supervision of a husband or parent, not an impatient shift boss. In the new factories, this way of life changed dramatically. In fact, mill managers looked to English prisons and penal workhouses for models of how to keep workers alert and disciplined. Work days typically stretched from 6:00 a.m. to 7:00 p.m. Illiterate employees had to learn to keep track of time on factory floor clocks. Physical strain, repetitive motion, and industrial accidents crippled or deformed many. Industrial workers had a life expectancy of about seventeen years shorter than the moneyed owners of the plants and machines. In the early industrial decades, neither trade unions nor labor protection laws existed.

Elizabeth Bentley, a women from Leeds in the English midlands, typified a young, female linen-mill worker. She entered the factory when she was six years old, in about 1809. In 1832 she answered questions before the Sadler Committee, a parliamentary commission called to investigate British labor conditions:

What were your hours of labor in that mill? Ð F rom 5 in the morning till 9 at night. . . .

What time was allowed for your meals? Ð F orty minutes at noon.

Had you any time to get your breakfast or drinking? Ð N o, we got it as we could. . . .

Your labor is very excessive? Ð Yes; you have not time for any thing.

Suppose you flagged a little, or were too late, what would they do? Ð S trap [whip] us. . . . Girls as well as boys? Ð Y es.

Have you ever been strapped? Ð Y es.
Severely? Ð Y es.[12]

The British textile industry employed far more women and children than men until well into the nineteenth century. In London's silk industry in 1765, women and children outnumbered men fourteen to one. By contrast, males dominated occupations in mining, construction, and leather making. Business leaders appear to have assumed that women and girls were innately suited to work in industries incorporating new technologies. James Hargreaves, for example, configured the dimensions of his spinning jenny from the premise that a young girl would likely operate it.[13] In other words, machine textile manufacturing was °gendered° for women from the start. Entrepreneurs believed that females had superior motor skills for operating textile machines and naturally possessed the proper cooperative and submissive attitudes necessary for factory work. Women, industrialists argued, had ideal qualities for innovative industries because they did not have to

Women making pens. More than 50 women sit at individual grindstones finishing metal pen nibs at the Hank Wells & Co. factory in Birmingham, England. What differences in communal work do you notice between this image and the depiction of women engaged in cottage textile production on page 611?

Ned Ludd: Legendary Foe of Industry

The word *Luddite* is colloquial English for anyone who dislikes new technology or cannot get the hang of it. This expression originated with Ned Ludd, a character in the mold of Robin Hood, who robbed the rich to help the poor. In English tradition Ned Ludd rose through the ranks of the laboring poor to become a "general," and some of his followers wanted to make him king. In fact, he may have existed only in the imaginations of English workers. Perhaps a living person inspired his legendary personality, but as an actor of historical significance he was a composite individual, a symbolic embodiment of working-class anxieties brought on by bewildering economic change.

Political and economic developments combined in the early nineteenth century to spread misery among English workers. Britain had been fighting Napoleon since 1803, and the emperor impeded Britain's trade with the European continent. English warehouses were overstuffed with cloth intended for export. Excess supply led employers to cut their workforces, which were already reduced because of mechanization. One person operating a steam-powered loom could do the work of two hundred or three hundred people. Parliament supported speedy industrialization without much regard for the poorer classes, overturning legislation that limited the use of labor-saving devices. Although some wealthy landlords and factory barons sympathized with the plight of the poor, most agreed that economic progress came first.

In 1811, following a poor harvest season in parts of England, masked bands of laborers calling themselves Luddites began breaking into mills at night to demolish the newfangled machines that had taken over their jobs. In Nottinghamshire, insurgents sent threatening letters to factory owners ordering them to dismantle their equipment. When owners refused to comply, rioters took hammers to more than four hundred textile looms. The British government sent nearly two thousand soldiers to restore order, but saboteurs continued to destroy machines.

From Nottinghamshire, the insurgency spread rapidly to five other midlands counties. Numerous individuals invoked "General Ned" as their leader, signing his name to protest letters. In the spring and summer of 1812, food riots broke out. Some protesters claimed Lady Ludd, the legendary general's reputed wife, as their leader. At night, small bands roamed the countryside, stealing grain and demanding guns. Lead pipes, faucets, and fittings disappeared from churches and other buildings and were melted into bullets. The Luddites renounced violence toward persons, but at least one manufacturer was killed, and more than a dozen workers died in skirmishes with soldiers. Insurgents burned five factories and attacked dozens more. The movement had no coherent plan of action, but leaders demanded respect for skilled

Luddites wrecking carpet-weaving machinery.

craftsmanship, the valuing of workers as partners in production, and the outlawing of industrial machines. English authorities watched highways and taverns for Ned Ludd, but he never turned up. They tried until 1816 to arrest him for robbery, arson, and the destruction of private property, all offenses that carried the death penalty.

Mass arrests and harsh penalties finally brought the protests under control. Food rioters and machine breakers were convicted regardless of age. Twenty-four men, women, and children were hanged, one a sixteen-year-old whose crime was to stand guard outside a mill while his confederates attacked it. In addition to the people executed, eighteen Luddites were imprisoned in England, and fifty-one were transported in chains to Australia to serve terms of seven years or longer. Luddism withered away by 1816, and the general himself was never found. Nevertheless, the movement exposed worker discontent, and it foreshadowed the parliamentary worker reform and the organized labor movement that was shortly to come.

Thinking Critically

Do you think it would have made a difference to the temporary success of the Luddite movement if Ned Ludd had not existed as the primary leader or even as a real person?

shed traditions of craftsmanship that tied male artisans to old-fashioned ways of doing things.

Entrepreneurs also ªsold° factory mechanization to the public as a fine way to create jobs for poor women and girls. Indeed, male artisans commonly lost work both to machines and to the unskilled employees who tended them. In 1786, for example, textile craftsmen in the midlands formally protested the coming of factories that used scribbling machines, which were mechanical devices for preparing wool for spinning: ªOne machine will do as much work in one day as would otherwise employ twenty men. How are those men, thus thrown out of employ to provide for their families?° 14

As working conditions in mines and factories worsened, which they generally continued to do until the 1840s, shouts of protest became louder. In the early decades, workers expressed their discontent in petitions, walkouts, absenteeism, riots, and public rallies, but also in drunkenness, prostitution, mental collapse, and suicide. Since the new machines were the handiest targets of loathing, disgruntled workers sometimes destroyed them, or even attacked their inventors. In 1753, for example, workers assaulted the home of John Kay, the inventor of the flying shuttle, forcing him to flee to France, where he died in poverty. In 1806, workers in France organized a public ªexecution° of the Jacquard loom, ritually destroying one of the machines to protest job losses. In response to persistent protest and fear of disorder, the British Parliament voted in 1824 to permit workers to form trade unions to advocate for rights and better conditions and in certain circumstances to call strikes. The trade union movement, however, advanced slowly in Britain and got virtually nowhere in continental Europe until after midcentury.

ªAn evil and corrosive smoke.° Since ancient times, cities were incubators of ill health because they put large numbers of people in close quarters with diseased animals, the smoke of burning biomass, and bodily waste. In the eighteenth century, cities throughout the world suffered from these curses. In Britain, however, industrialization and the shift to coal energy released new toxins and pollutants into the environment. Manufacturing waste poured into rivers and lakes, and water runoff from cities contaminated the surrounding countryside. Air quality declined as well, especially in London. That city's high concentration of people, houses, and workshops generated a significant differential in air temperature between the city and the surrounding countryside. When this differential became too large for normal wind movements to dissipate, it transformed the city into a more or less permanent ªheat island° that trapped unhealthy gasses.

In the early industrial period, people had a poor grasp of the consequences of pollution. No one, for example, recognized the connection between urban typhus or cholera epidemics and contaminated water. But as early as the seventeenth century, Londoners complained bitterly about bad air and squarely blamed the growing use of coal for manufacturing and home heating. In 1664 John Evelyn, an English pamphleteer, deplored ªwith just Indignation° that ªthis Glorious and Ancient City . . . which commands the Proud Ocean to the Indies, and reaches to the farthest Antipodes, should wrap her stately head in Clowds of Smoake and Sulfur, so full of Stink and Darknesse.° According to Evelyn, coal smoke fouled the water supply, ate away buildings, spoiled laundry, killed bees, and made people sick: ª Is there under Heaven such Coughing and Snuffing to be heard, as in the London Churches and Assemblies of People, where the Barking and the Spitting is incessant and most importunate?° Those who profited from coal mining campaigned to muffle protest, arguing that coal fumes might even be beneficial because they cleansed the air of pests and poisonous humors. The physician Samuel Hahnemann wrote in 1787 that the high incidence of lung diseases in London had nothing to do with coal vapors but could to be attributed to ªnight life, excess of heating, drink and food, the enormous indulgence of tea . . . and the most horrifying and often unnatural passions.° 15 By the early 1800s coal burning began to have a significant effect on air quality in German cities that were close to coal sources. According to an official who visited the United States in the late 1830s, the young industrial city of Pittsburgh was already enshrouded in ªa dense, black smoke, which . . . falls in flakes of soot upon the dwellings and persons of the inhabitants.° 16

Industrialization and Global Trade in the Early Nineteenth Century

FOCUS What were the fundamental features of new doctrines of free trade and liberalism in the late eighteenth and early nineteenth centuries?

The foundational period of the industrial revolution overlapped in time with the popular revolutions that took place in Europe and the Americas. Few of the millions of people involved in the political upheavals of 1775±1815 knew anything about steam engines or power looms. The obscurity of these new contraptions, however, began to lift rapidly in the early 1800s, not only because machines and factories came into use beyond Britain, but also because producers around the globe needed to increase outputs of food and other commodities to supply the new manufacturing centers. Industrial growth also required that both rich and poor be induced to consume the merchandise that factories poured out. The industrial revolution evolved during the nineteenth century as a world event, occurring not only where steam engines, factories, and railroads appeared, but also where people produced raw commodities destined for mills and urban populations and where people consumed industrial goods. In other words, it occurred just about everywhere.

The Energy Revolution Takes Hold

In Britain, demand for wage workers in new factories and in all sorts of urban crafts and services accelerated rapidly after 1820. The real wages of workers, which had remained stagnant during the early decades of industrialization, began to rise. Between 1800 and 1850 the country's total population doubled from about nine to eighteen million. At midcentury half of Britain's population lived in cities, a far higher proportion than anywhere else in the world. London's population grew from about 860,000 in 1800 to about 4.2 million by 1875. Factories increased cotton production about elevenfold, a success that inspired entrepreneurs to apply steam power to many other types of manufacture. Industries that made bricks, pottery, paper, beer, and numerous other products became mechanized. In 1850 Britain's population was about 4.5 percent of China's, but Britain used fifty times more energy than China did, in large part because steam and coal drove so many machines.

The tentacles of transport reached out in all directions as private businesses undertook hundreds of road, canal, railroad, and iron bridge projects. Canal digging continued apace in the early nineteenth century because barges could move large tonnages of coal and iron ore from mine to factory. In the 1840s, however, steam locomotives proved they could pull heavy loads over long distances faster and at cheaper rates than barges, spelling the end of the canal boom. Rail lines, together with improved roads and coach routes, meant that people could exchange business and technical information more efficiently. The volume of letters and packages moving across Britain surged after 1840, when a talented modernizer named Rowland Hill inspired a project to standardize mail charges and introduce the adhesive postage stamp.

Industrialization on the European continent. After 1815, when the Napoleonic Wars ended, manufacturers on the continent cut back military-related production, triggering a serious economic slump that lasted nearly five years. In the four decades after 1820, however, steam industries spread rapidly in Belgium, France, the Netherlands, Germany, and the Austrian empire (see Map 21.3). In that period the major European powers stayed mostly at peace with one another, a condition that benefited industrialization, especially in areas well-endowed with raw materials, local labor, or natural transport corridors.

Large-scale industry advanced fastest in Belgium (which became a separate state from the Netherlands in 1831). Its

Open-cast mines at Blanzy, France. Industrialization transformed both cities and the countryside. This scene, painted in 1857 by Ignace François Bonhomme, shows the magnitude of changes to the landscape caused by large-scale resource extraction. Notice how small the human figures in the foreground are. What does this painting suggest about how people responded to these changes in the nineteenth century?

MAP 21.3 Urbanization and industrialization in Europe, 1850.
Urbanization accompanied industrial growth in the nineteenth century. What do you notice about railroads and industrial sites in Germany compared to France or Britain in 1850? What might account for Germany's less urbanized population?

plants specialized in producing coal, iron, textiles, glass, and armaments. German mine owners began to use steam engines in coal fields of the Ruhr Valley in the 1830s, though industrialization advanced slowly at first, in large part because Germany remained divided into numerous states and principalities until 1871. In France, novice industrialists drawing heavily on British technology made impressive headway in steam-driven textile and iron production in the 1830s and 1840s. French inventors also contributed numerous mechanical devices and processes, including looms, linen spinners, and gas lighting. Even so, the country did not come close to catching up with Britain in overall production, and it gradually fell behind Germany. France had a predominantly peasant population slow to consume manufactures or to move into cities to take mill and foundry jobs. In Portugal, Spain, Italy, and the Balkan lands, clusters of industry began to appear in later decades. For example, Milan, destined to become Italy's greatest manufacturing

The waterfront in Cincinnati, Ohio, 1848. Steamboats and other vessels are moored in front of a mix of commercial and residential buildings in an image captured by Charles Fontayne and William Porter applying an early photographic process called daguerreotype. They used this emerging technology to create a multiframe panorama that captured about two miles of Cincinnati's booming riverfront. Why might a growing industrial city have captured the attention of photographers experimenting with a new medium?

center in the twentieth century, had only two steam engines in 1841. Nevertheless, as industrialization in Britain and some continental regions became rooted, Europe's share of global GDP soared upward. According to one estimate, it grew from about 24 percent of total world GDP in 1820 to 34 percent in 1870.[17]

The United States. Close economic and cultural ties between Britain and the United States after the Napoleonic Wars increased the flow of industrial technology and financial capital westward across the Atlantic. British skill and investment helped build the textile mills that sprouted in New England in the 1820s. African slave laborers in the South spurred industrialization by supplying both northern mills and the much bigger British textile sector with cotton fiber. Raw cotton sales to Britain brought large infusions of foreign currency into the United States, capital that American banks then loaned to industrial, transport, and mining entrepreneurs to speed development.

The United States joined western Europe in developing a successful industrial sector before 1850. As in Britain, the first generation of textile mills in the northeastern states used flowing water to power spinning and weaving machines, and they also employed large numbers of girls and women. The workforce in factories in Lowell, Massachusetts, the leading U.S. textile town, was about 70 percent female. A surge of canal construction between 1820 and 1840 animated economic growth, reducing the transport

cost of bulk goods in and out of the deep American interior. By 1840, however, private companies had laid about three thousand miles of rail line in the Northeast. In the following decade the network spread west and south, bringing the canal boom to an end. Fossil-fuel energy also came to America in the 1840s, when abundant coal deposits were discovered in Pennsylvania. Industrialization moved into the Ohio River basin, and by 1840 Cincinnati, situated on the edge of the midwestern plains, was the country's third largest manufacturing city.

Egypt's early industrial experiment. Egypt was the first country outside of western Europe and the United States to introduce complex machines and house them in factories. It was the first place in the world where the state, rather than private individuals or firms, organized, directed, and chiefly profited from those enterprises, an approach to industrialization that other countries would later adopt. Egypt's program did not go well, however, owing in part to British efforts to undermine it.

Egypt was formally part of the Ottoman empire, but a small class of Turkish military men, or *mamluks* governed the country autonomously, extracting revenues from the Arabic-speaking masses. Four years after France's ill-fated invasion of the Nile valley, which ended in 1801 (see Chapter 20), Muhammad Ali, an Ottoman army officer of Albanian origin rose to power as Egypt's governor (r. 1805±1848). Impressed by the easy victory that Napoleon's forces achieved

Muhammad Ali. This 1840 portrait by a French artist depicts the Egyptian ruler as he presided over efforts to modernize the economy and expand territorially. How can you account for the British government's opposition to Egypt's industrialization?

over *mamluk* cavalry, he launched a crash program to modernize the army and government, revitalize the verdant Nile River valley's agrarian economy, and make Egypt a regional power to be reckoned with. He swept away the conservative *mamluk* elite, hired French and British military advisers, sent Egyptian officers to Europe for training, and opened institutes for future officers and bureaucrats to learn foreign languages, engineering, medicine, and chemistry. He reorganized government ministries and the tax system to channel more wealth to the state. He had no interest in constitutions or parliaments. Rather, he conceived of economic growth, as most contemporary autocrats did, as a strategy for transferring revenue from ordinary people to the state and its ruling class.

To finance these reforms, Muhammad Ali moved to increase the agrarian population's output of cotton, silk, wool, and flax (for linen). He drafted peasants into labor gangs to renovate the Nile valley's irrigation system. With European advice he introduced a new variety of long-staple cotton, which had strong fibers and held up well on mechanical looms. He also recognized the economic logic of manufacturing textiles at home in order to clothe both his army

and the general population at direct benefit to the state, not to foreign importers. The first textile workshop opened in Cairo about 1818, and by the 1830s that city and others had about thirty factories producing cotton, silk, linen, and woolen fabrics. Carding machines (for disentangling and aligning fibers), spinning mules, and power looms were put into service. Animal traction powered most of these devices, but a few used imported steam engines. Muhammad Ali also built weapons factories to turn out muskets.

In the later 1830s, however, new political and economic problems plagued Egypt's fledgling industrialization. Military costs rose astronomically as Muhammad Ali embarked on wars of conquest. Between 1811 and 1831, he invaded western Arabia, the Sudan (Upper Nile valley), and the Ottoman provinces of Syria to find resources that Egypt needed and to magnify his international reputation. Scarce investment capital, lack of coal, and a chronic shortage of wood also restricted energy supplies.

Muhammad Ali's attack on Syria provoked the wrath of Britain, which regarded an ascendant Egypt as a potential threat to its lines of communication with colonial India. In 1838, Britain signed an agreement with the Ottoman state, to which Egypt still officially belonged, which lowered import tariffs on European textiles and prohibited the commercial monopolies that Muhammad Ali had imposed. Two years later, British and Ottoman troops drove Egyptian forces out of Syria and compelled Muhammad Ali to drastically reduce his army, his biggest domestic market for clothing and guns.

British action and a dearth of energy resources sentenced Egypt's budding textile industry to failure. Gradually, the workshops fell idle, and after Muhammad Ali died in 1849, Britain kept up pressure on the Egyptian government to export more raw cotton. That strategy enriched Egyptian officials, merchants, and land-owners but did not produce broad-based economic development. Consequently, Egypt took part in the industrial revolution after 1840 mainly as a supplier of farm commodities to industrializing countries.

The Threads of Commerce

In the nineteenth century the volume of world trade grew nearly twenty times, a spectacular acceleration compared to any earlier era. Global exchanges of raw materials, manufactures, and migrating workers reached nearly everyone on the planet, and the capitalist industries, labor systems, and institutions that we associate today with ªeconomic globalization° largely took shape. This happened primarily because fossil-fuel industries in Britain, joined by new ones in continental Europe and the United States, churned out stupendous volumes of merchandise. This torrent, however, could have slowed if markets for these wares, raw materials for factories, and city populations had not grown as well.

Tracks, propellers, and copper wires. Commerce grew spectacularly because of continuing, multiple innovations

MAP 21.4 Railways in 1860.

In what regions of North America and Europe were the densest rail networks built by 1860? How would you account for relatively high density construction in those particular areas? Why do you think railway building started later in India than in Europe or the United States but earlier than, for example, in China or West Africa?

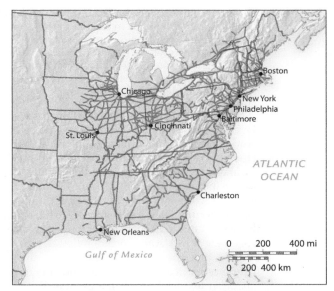

in steam-powered transport and electrical communication, which brought novel consumer goods to millions more people, opened up new sources of minerals and foodstuffs, and speeded the exchange of market information. Total world railway mileage grew nearly fifteenfold between 1840 and 1860, mainly in Europe and North America, though extensive track laying was shortly to follow in India, Latin America, and Australia (see Map 21.4). In 1807 the American entrepreneur Robert Fulton rigged a wood-fueled Watt engine to a paddlewheel on a river vessel, inventing the first commercially successful steamboat. In 1833 the *Royal William*, a vessel operating almost entirely under steam power, crossed the Atlantic from Canada to England. Three years later, John Ericcson, a Swedish inventor, patented the first successful screw propeller, a more efficient underwater drive mechanism than paddlewheels. Early steam vessels had advantages over sailing ships because they did not depend on changeable winds, though exquisitely engineered sail craft, notably clipper ships, made long oceanic voyages well into the second half of the century.

The telegraph, which transmitted a pattern of electrical impulses along a wire, was the first reliable, nearly instantaneous form of long-distance communication in history. In 1837, inventors in England and the United States separately built telegraph machines operated by inexpensive batteries. Samuel Morse, the American inventor, created the more efficient device. In 1844 he transmitted the phrase ᵃWhat hath God wrought!º from Baltimore to Washington, D.C. Seven years later, a convention of European states adopted Morse's telegraphic code as the international standard for transmitting messages. In this way, the world adapted its first universal language. Railroad builders commonly erected telegraph lines alongside tracks, so the two communication systems grew together. As workers strung copper wires across continents, telegraphy had a growing impact on production and commerce: It allowed high-velocity transmission of the sort of information about political conditions, weather, harvests, prices, and currency rates that businesspeople needed to make rational and timely economic decisions.

Britain, the trade colossus. In the *Communist Manifesto*, published in 1848, Karl Marx (see Chapter 22) characterized the rising power of the capitalist money-making class, which he called the bourgeoisie, as a worldwide, and in his view fateful, development:

The need of a constantly expanding market for its products chases the bourgeoisie over the whole surface of the globe.

It must nestle everywhere, settle everywhere, establish connections everywhere. . . . In place of the old wants, satisfied by the production of the country, we find new wants, requiring for their satisfaction the products of distant lands and climes. In place of the old local and national seclusion and self-sufficiency, we have intercourse in every direction, universal interdependence of nations.[18]

Marx's model for this globe-trotting bourgeoisie was no doubt an Englishman. When he wrote those words, Britain loomed over world commerce, finance, and shipping. This happened fundamentally because that country sprinted far out ahead of the rest of the world in applying fossil-fuel energy to industry. Between 1820 and 1870 the value of British exports increased nearly 1,000 percent. Consequently, the country accumulated a vast store of surplus capital. Some of this wealth funded expansion of the Royal Navy, which patrolled the world. And much of it flowed into domestic and overseas investments in railroads, mines, shipyards, banks, insurance services, and numerous other enterprises.

Cotton textiles became the premier British export. English mills turned out hundreds of millions of yards of fabric, and consumer markets in the rest of the world could not get enough of it. By the late 1850s, plantations in the southern United States exported about 600 million pounds of cotton a year. Planters also bought back some of this cotton, as it were, by importing cheap English fabric to clothe their enslaved black workers.

The consequences of British textile production for South Asia were catastrophic. For many centuries India had been the world's leading cloth producer, but from about 1820, spinners and weavers started losing even their own domestic market to British machine-made cottons. Thereafter, the region underwent a drastic economic shift from cloth manufacturer to grower of raw fiber for European factories. Several million Bengalese weavers lost their livelihoods, and many families turned from manufacturing to farming, just when the British workforce was moving in the opposite direction. The British East India Company, which by 1850 ruled most of South Asia and profited handsomely from cloth imports, had no interest in permitting Indian entrepreneurs to build their own textile factories. Between 1750 and 1860, Britain's share of world manufacturing output rose steadily, from 2 percent to 20 percent, while India's dropped from 25 percent to 9 percent (see graph).[19]

Free Trade and the New Doctrine of Liberalism

Between the sixteenth and eighteenth centuries, European commercial states generally subscribed to the economic doctrine of mercantilism, which held that the world's exploitable wealth could not expand and that the home country and its colonies should erect high barriers to exclude rival states from intruding into its circuits of trade. A state's chief mercantilist weapon was customs taxes on foreign imports, which raised their price to consumers and presumably limited markets for them (see Chapter 18). States such as China, Japan, and the Ottoman empire also traditionally imposed high customs duties or tightly restricted foreign trade. Although these protective policies worked only part of the time, mercantilism dominated European economic thought for decades after the hum of British textile machines suggested that world wealth might be expandable after all.

The age of mercantilism faded after 1820, when continuous improvements in steam-powered manufacturing steadily drove down the price of cotton goods. British industrialists began to question the logic of blocking foreign imports with high tariffs if those goods would not in any case compete with cheaper home-produced items. For example, why should Britain keep out Indian textiles now that British cottons not only supplied the home market but were flooding into India as well? If Britain unilaterally dropped customs barriers in favor of **free trade**, would not other countries do the same and world commerce boom for all?

> **free trade** An economic doctrine contending that trade among states should be unrestricted, principally by lowering or eliminating tariffs or duties on imported goods; factors of supply and demand should mainly determine price.

Britain would also disproportionately benefit because it was the top industrial and naval power.

In the first half of the nineteenth century, the free-trade movement slowly gathered momentum. In the decade and a half after 1846, when Parliament rescinded the Corn Laws, which had restricted imports of foreign wheat and other grains, Britain eliminated virtually all protectionist tariffs. Its global commerce thrived under this new regime, and by the 1860s, all the industrializing countries of continental Europe, even largely rural Russia, were scrambling to sign

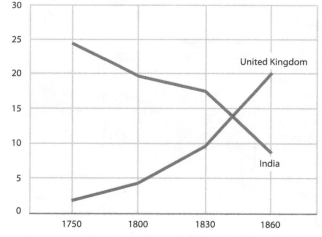

Percentage of global output

Manufacturing output in Britain and India, 1750 and 1860. How can you account for the relative change in British and Indian manufacturing output between 1750 and 1860?

tariff-busting treaties with one another in order to take advantage of new trade opportunities.

The high price of free trade. To dismantle protectionism everywhere, British free-traders saw no reason why the Royal Navy should not lend a hand. This flotilla, government leaders argued, must safeguard British commerce, especially the seaward approaches to colonial South Asia. The navy should not have to transport many ground troops but only capture key ports and coastal enclaves that could serve as operational and supply bases. Thus, in the early nineteenth century, British forces seized the formerly Dutch Cape Colony at the tip of South Africa (1806), the island of Malta in the Mediterranean (1814), Singapore on the Strait of Malacca (1819), and Aden at the entrance to the Red Sea (1839). Naval squadrons were then well positioned to pressure Asian and African states to lower trade barriers to British goods. Indeed, several states opted to negotiate what became known as ᵃunequal treaties.º In 1838, as we have seen, Britain persuaded the militarily weaker Ottoman empire to sign a free-trade pact, which worked overwhelmingly to the advantage of European importers.

Free trade by coercion played out dramatically in China. British textile producers wanted badly to split open the potentially huge East Asian market. The Qing imperial government, however, strictly regulated seaborne trade with foreigners and limited it exclusively to the port of Guangzhou (Canton). A hopeful British trade delegation visited the Qianlong emperor in Beijing in 1793 but failed to get restrictions loosened. Considering China's still healthy productivity, the emperor's rebuff was perfectly rational, if not very far-sighted regarding the direction of his country's economy: ª There is nothing we lack. . . . We have never set much store on strange or ingenious objects, nor do we need any more of your country's manufactures.º[20] British merchant capitalists found this response galling because their own compatriots were drinking millions of cups of imported Chinese tea. This habit grew steadily in the eighteenth century. Tea and sugar together made a marvelous and only mildly addictive ªdrug food,º and it gave tired urban workers quick jolts of caloric energy. East India Company merchants, however, had to pay for tea chiefly with silver because Asian markets did not want much of anything else Europe had to offer.

As tea consumption soared, the company discovered that China offered a promising market for opium, a more expensive and addictive drug food than tea or sugar. It also discovered that Indian farmers in Bengal could be induced to grow the poppies from which opium was made. Company merchants purchased opium at low cost from Bengali middlemen, then sold it at a huge markup to Chinese buyers. The Qing government forbade importation of opium, so Chinese wholesalers had to take delivery of it off the south China coast and smuggle it in. The trade grew fast after 1800, as a cheaper, more powerful opium compound became available and as more affluent, urban Chinese acquired a taste for it, despite its debilitating effects on health and livelihood. By the mid-1830s, British merchants were

Customers in a Chinese opium den. This late nineteenth-century engraving is based on a drawing by Thomas Allom, a British artist and architect who traveled to East Asia. The detailed representation inside a Chinese building shows opium smokers in various states of intoxication. What reasons did British merchants and officials give for promoting the opium trade when there was evidence of the drug's harmful effects?

On Legalizing Opium in China

In 1800 the Qing imperial government banned the importation and domestic production of opium, but not all officials agreed with the decision. Opponents of the ban generally agreed that opium addiction represented a serious social problem, but they also believed the state should manage the substance rather than criminalize it. If opium imports were legal, they argued, the government would be able to impose tariffs on the drug. It could also require that opium be paid for with merchandise such as tea in order to stem the outflow of silver resulting from persistent opium smuggling.

Xu Naiji, a Beijing scholar-official, favored legalization and in 1836 made an argument for it in a "memorial," or formal written communication, to the emperor Daoguang. Xu denounced opium use, but he recognized that addicts would do anything to get it and that smugglers were happy to oblige them. By banning imports, China created an illegal narcotics trade that in turn fed violence, corruption, and economic stagnation. Legalizing and regulating opium would help eliminate those problems. The passage below is taken from Xu's memorial.

The emperor also received memorials from officials who wanted even stricter prohibitions on both importation and use. Zhu Zun, an imperial bureaucrat like Xu, predicted that if opium were legalized, it would no longer carry a social stigma and addicts would overrun the country. The emperor sided with this man, not Xu, and in 1838 he ordered a vigorous campaign against opium, a policy that led to war with Britain the following year.

I would humbly represent that opium was originally ranked among medicines; its qualities are stimulant; it also checks excessive secretions; and prevents the evil effects of noxious vapors. . . . When any one is long habituated to inhaling it, it becomes necessary to resort to it at regular intervals, and the habit of using it, being inveterate, is destructive of time, injurious to property, and yet dear to one even as life. Of those who use it to great excess, the breath becomes feeble, the body wasted, the face sallow, the teeth black; the individuals themselves clearly see the evil effects of it, yet cannot refrain from it. . . .

In Qianlong's reign [1735–1796], as well as previously, opium was inserted in the tariff of Canton as a medicine, subject to a duty. . . . After this, it was prohibited. In the first year of Jiaqing [1796], those found guilty of smoking opium were subject only to the punishment of the pillory and bamboo. Now they have, in the course of time, become liable to the severest penalties. . . . Yet the smokers of the drug have increased in number, and the practice has spread throughout almost the whole empire. . . . Formerly, the barbarian [European] merchants brought foreign money to China; which, being paid in exchange for goods, was a source of pecuniary advantage to the people of all the seaboard provinces. But latterly, the barbarian merchants have clandestinely sold opium for money; which has rendered it unnecessary for them to import foreign silver. Thus foreign money has been going out of the country, while none comes into it. . . .

It is proposed entirely to cut off the foreign trade, and thus to remove the root to dam up the source of the evil? . . . While the dealers in opium are the English alone; it would be wrong, for the sake of cutting off the English trade, to cut off that of all the other nations. Besides, the hundreds of thousands of people living on the seacoast depend wholly on trade for their livelihood, and how are they to be disposed of? Moreover, the barbarian ships, being on the high seas, can repair to any island that may be selected as an entrepôt, and the native sea-going vessels can meet them there; it is then impossible to cut off the trade. . . .

Since then, it will not answer to close our ports against [all trade], and since the laws issued against opium are quite inoperative, the only method left is to revert to the former system, to permit the barbarian merchants to import opium paying duty thereon as a medicine, and to require that, after having passed the custom-house, it shall be delivered to the [Chinese] merchants only in exchange for merchandise, and that no money be paid for it. . . . Offenders when caught should be punished by the entire destruction of the opium they have, and the confiscation of the money that be found with them. With regard to officers, civil and military, and to the scholars and common soldiers, the first are called on to fulfill the duties of their rank and attend to the public good; the others, to cultivate their talent and become fit for public usefulness. None of these, therefore, must be permitted to contract a practice so bad, or to walk in a path which will lead only to the utter waste of their time and destruction of their property. . . . It becomes my duty, then, to request that it be enacted, that any officer, scholar, or soldier, found guilty of secretly smoking opium, shall be immediately dismissed from public employ, without being made liable to any other penalty.

Source: John Slade, *A Narrative of the Late Proceedings and Events in China* (Canton: Canton Register, 1839), 1±5; reproduced in Pei-kai Cheng and Michael Lestz, with Jonathan D. Spence, *The Search for Modern China: A Documentary Collection* (New York: Norton, 1999), 111±114.

Thinking Critically

How had the punishments for smoking opium changed between the late eighteenth century and Xu's day? Why did Xu not want to ban all foreign trade with China? How did he think the legalization of opium would benefit both Chinese people and foreign merchants? If you were the emperor of China, would you have favored legalization or banning of opium imports? Why? How might you compare this controversy with debates about drug trade and use today?

selling more than 1,800 tons of opium in the Chinese market every year.

Because of this demand, the international flow of silver between Europe and East Asia went into reverse: British traders could buy tea with Indian opium rather than coins, while their Chinese counterparts now had to export not only tea and manufactures but also their own country's silver reserves to satisfy drug appetites. For the first time in the Common Era, China experienced a foreign trade deficit, while revenues from tea and opium sales piled up in London banks.

In 1838 the Qing government, facing not only a weakening economy but also high social costs of addiction and drug-fueled crime, launched a campaign to eradicate the trade. When Chinese authorities seized 20,000 chests of opium in Guangzhou, the East India Company recognized a golden chance to force China to join the free-trade era. In 1839 the firm dispatched a squad of battleships and steamers, including one ironclad gunboat, to the Chinese coast, triggering the First Anglo-Chinese War, or Opium War. Company ships bombarded imperial shore defenses and a Qing fleet, while several vessels mounted with heavy guns sailed up the Yangzi River. The emperor had no choice but to sue for peace.

By the punitive terms that ended the conflict in 1842, Britain annexed the island of Hong Kong, forced down import tariff rates, and acquired the right to trade any and all manufactures in five Chinese ports. Trade in opium remained illegal until 1860, but it continued anyway. Once Britain demonstrated that ªgunboat diplomacyº was an effective way to open new markets to European goods, France, Russia, and the United States moved quickly to demand that the emperor grant them similar concessions. The industrial revolution thus reached China in a way that was distinctly detrimental to its own economy.

Liberalism: An ideology for the capitalist world economy. The First Anglo-Chinese War (a second one was fought between 1856 and 1860 to expand European privileges in China) was just one episode in the momentous transformations in global economic relations that took place in the nineteenth century. Political and economic leaders wanted to understand the meaning of these transformations and the social disturbances that seemed connected to them. Capitalist investors and governments also wanted to manage and forecast economic change in whatever measure they could.

liberalism A set of economic and political doctrines advocating individual freedom, unrestricted market competition, free trade, constitutional government, and confidence in human progress; sometimes called "classical liberalism."

Liberalism, which was both a political and an economic doctrine, emerged as a set of explanatory ideas that many leaders found persuasive.

Derived from the Latin word *liber,* meaning ªfree,º liberalism initially evoked the principle of limited government, whether practiced in a republic or a constitutional monarchy. Rooted intellectually in the eighteenth-century Enlightenment and slowly elaborated during the Atlantic revolutions, liberalism championed legal protection of private property, representative government, an independent judiciary, scientific and technological progress, economic decision-making based on rational calculation rather than static tradition, and international commerce unfettered by state tariff barriers. Many liberals also advocated free public education, religious toleration, secular government (no state religion), and reforms to improve social conditions of the poor.

All these ideas rested on the premise that the liberty of individuals to think and act as they like, especially to accumulate and dispose of property, should be constrained only to protect the public good. In the words of the English political philosopher John Stuart Mill (1806±1873), ª The sole end for which mankind are warranted, individually or collectively, in interfering with the liberty of action of any of their numbers, is self-protection. That the only purpose for which power can be rightfully exercised over any member of a civilized community, against his will, is to prevent harm to

Adam Smith portrayed as a man of letters and property in 1790.
This engraving by fellow Scotsman John Kay presents the influential political-economist with books and writing material, formally posed for a portrait. What liberal ideas does this image of Smith reinforce?

others.[°][21] The Scottish philosopher Adam Smith (1723±1790) had argued earlier in the *Wealth of Nations* that buyers and sellers in the capitalist market advance the welfare of all by simply attending to their own private interests. Governments should practice *laissez faire,* a French term meaning, loosely, ª non-intervention.° They should allow individuals to buy and sell property freely, abolish tariffs on imports, and otherwise refrain from regulating or interfering in the marketplace except to ensure public safety.

Witnessing the wonders of industry, liberal writers and politicians professed great confidence in the world's material progress. They wished to promote sensible reforms to improve society and to blaze a trail of moderation between two extreme forces. On one side, liberals saw political conservatives, who clung to dead customs, upper-class privileges, church dogma, and the economic status quo. On the other side, they saw radical republicans and other zealots, who would give power to the illiterate, propertyless, sometimes irrational masses, thus risking upheaval in the social order. Liberals who experienced political revolution in France and the Americas had widely ranging views about democracy, or ª rule by the people.° Some greatly feared that if democracy meant rule by ª interested and overbearing majorities,° as the American statesman James Madison referred to it, then society might end up in the hands of the ª mob° Ð common folk of the sort that perpetrated the worst excesses of the French Revolution. For other liberals, democracy should be society's goal, but with voting and officeholding rights extended to more citizens only by careful stages. Elected representatives and magistrates should be property-owning adult males. Such men would presumably guard legal rights and refrain from meddling in the operation of the free market.

Economic and political liberalism blended together, though some exponents accepted certain aspects of this ideology while rejecting others. For example, industrialists tended to stress the inviolability of private property and free trade, whereas the poor and unenfranchised warmed to the promise of political equality. Autocratic monarchs in Europe and dictatorial presidents of Latin American republics might also identify themselves as liberal in their dedication to rational economic policies, private wealth, and technological progress. But this type of liberal had no interest in redistributing wealth to ordinary men and women or allowing popularly elected legislatures free rein over the country's affairs. Though liberalism had many, sometimes conflicting tendencies, it emerged in the early nineteenth century as the creed that guided and informed the expansion of global capitalism. By the 1830s small circles of intellectuals and business leaders in places like India, Egypt, and the Ottoman empire were also discussing how liberal ideas might be applied in their own societies.

• • •

Conclusion

This book takes the view that the modern era, or modernity, got under way about 250 years ago and that it represented the sharpest turn in the human venture since the invention of farming 12,000 years earlier. At the top of our list of the characteristics of modernity (see the introduction to Part 6) is the human capacity for harvesting and using energy on a large enough scale to transform our species' fundamental relationship to the material world. This chapter has addressed the early decades of that transformation. According to one scholar, humans who lived about a thousand years ago used a per-capita average of about 26,000 calories of energy per day, mostly energy generated by human or animal muscle. Currently, the average individual uses at least 230,000 calories every day, thanks to a multitude of machines. The better part of that increase has taken place in the past 150 years.[22] Between 1750 and 1900, the efficiency of industrial labor grew about two hundred times. That is, a worker at the end of the nineteenth century could produce in a week's time what a worker in 1750 could produce in four years.[23]

The revolutionary scope of developments in Britain between 1750 and 1850 would not at the time have been noticed in most of the world. After all, in Europe as a whole in 1800, human and animal muscle still supplied about 80 percent of useful mechanical energy. Steam engines provided only about 4 percent.[24] As the midpoint of the nineteenth century approached, the highest levels of energy consumption for manufacturing were concentrated in Britain, parts of continental western Europe, and the United States. And in all those regions the consumption rate was soaring. By contrast, the relative share of energy use in China, South Asia, and the central Muslim lands was falling rapidly.

This development correlates to a large shift in the configuration of global power. For the first time in history, western Europeans and North Americans shot ahead of the rest of the world in their ability to mass-produce goods, develop new technologies and industrial processes, invent lethal weapons, create sophisticated commercial and banking systems, communicate across long distance, and move wage workers from countryside to city or from one part of the world to another. In the next few chapters we will see how humankind's success at breaking through the limits of the biological old regime served the economic and power interests of some societies and classes much more than others.

• • •

biological old regime 610
capitalism 632
energy revolution 609
First Anglo-Chinese War
(Opium War) 631

fossil fuels 609
free trade 628
industrial revolution 609
liberalism 631

Luddites 621
putting-out system 611

Change over Time

1694	Parliament founds the Bank of England to support Britain's commercial growth and international trade.
1765	James Hargreaves invents the spinning jenny.
1769	James Watt patents an improved steam engine.
1784	Edmund Cartwright designs the first power loom.
1793	Eli Whitney invents the cotton gin.
1804	Joseph Jacquard invents a loom for weaving patterns in cloth.
1805–1848	Muhammad Ali rules in Egypt, instituting industrializing reforms.
1811–1816	Luddites destroy industrial machinery in England.
1819	British forces seize Singapore in the Strait of Malacca.
1830	The Liverpool and Manchester Railway opens.
1833	A steamship crosses the Atlantic for the first time.
1838	The Ottoman empire signs a trade agreement with Britain.
1842	Britain annexes Hong Kong and secures trading rights as victors in the First Anglo-Chinese War (Opium War).
1844	Samuel Morse transmits telegraphic code from Baltimore to Washington, D.C.
1848	Karl Marx publishes the *Communist Manifesto*.

Please see end of book reference section for additional reading suggestions related to this chapter.

22 Coping with Change in the New Industrial Era

1830–1870

Queen Victoria and family (center left) admiring a display in the Crystal Palace.

I n the spring of 1851, thousands of exhibitors from around the world gathered in Hyde Park, London, for the opening of the Great Exhibition of the Industry of All Nations. On display within the colossal Crystal Palace, so named for its dazzling glass walls and ceilings, were the latest machines and manufactures, as well as handicrafts, artworks, and exotic plants, animals, minerals. Six million visitors flocked to the exposition to marvel at the goods and cultural artifacts of many lands. Organized by the Royal Society for the Encouragement of Arts, Manufactures and Commerce, the Great Exhibition aimed to educate the public, spur technological progress, and illustrate the marvelous potential of unfettered world trade.

Exploring this array of products, wonders, and amazing inventions (including a primitive ancestor of the fax machine), attentive visitors must have thought about the dizzying speed of change in the world, though no one could have understood how compellingly the fair displayed the arrival of the modern age. London's population of about 2.3 million in 1850 was more than one-third of what the entire world's population had been in 8000 B.C.E. Between 1830 and 1870, global population grew by about 130 million, about three and a half times as much as in the entire first millennium B.C.E. Industrialization continued to spread across Europe and the United States, and global industrial output in those four decades increased by around 50 percent. In 1800 a steam engine could put out more than 100,000 watts of power, by 1870 about 1 million. Also by that year, rail locomotives could go more than sixty miles per hour, faster than any horse. Looking back, we can see that in the middle decades of the nineteenth century, the world of machines, communication networks, urban living, and governing systems became much more like the one we live in today.

The Crystal Palace housed exhibits from overseas regions where British people and numerous other Europeans were settling in large numbers between 1830 and 1870. The first section of the chapter explores the global conditions that prompted a rapid acceleration of human migration from one part of the world to another in the nineteenth century. Tens of millions of men and women from both Europe and Asia traveled far from home to seek work, opportunity, and refuge, even as the forced transfer of African slaves across the Atlantic to American plantations finally came to an end. Mass global migration was multidirectional and complex, and it had profound, often disastrous consequences for the indigenous populations on whose lands newcomers encroached.

In the second part of the chapter we consider how societies in Europe, the Americas, and the Muslim lands attempted to reimagine government and the social order in the

Chapter Outline

WAVES OF MIGRANTS
The End of the Atlantic Slave Trade
The Outpouring from Europe
Neo-Europes and the Fates
of Indigenous Populations
Migrations of Asians and Africans
Oceania Connected

GROUNDSWELLS OF POLITICAL AND SOCIAL REFORM
Nationalism and the Power of the People
Varieties of Socialism
Movements for Women's Rights
Movements for Political Reform
and Unification in Europe
Modernizing Reforms in Muslim Lands
WEIGHING THE EVIDENCE A Moroccan Diplomat in France
The Limits of Liberalism in Latin America

RELIGION AND REFORM
Global Trends and Religious Change
Christian Evangelism
Jewish Reform
Religious Reform and Revolution
in the Muslim World
INDIVIDUALS MATTER Ram Mohan Roy: Hindu Reformer

GLOBAL CHANGE AND THE CALAMITOUS WARS OF MIDCENTURY
The Crimean War and the Industrialization
of Violence
Paraguay: A War of Annihilation
The Taiping Rebellion in China
The Great Indian Rebellion
The American Civil War

• • •

face of perplexing demographic and economic change. The Great Exhibition trumpeted not only liberalism, the doctrine that extolled free trade, private property, and limited government, but also nationalism, the principle that human beings naturally cluster together in distinct cultural communities, or nations, and that every genuine nation has an inherent right to govern itself. The mid-nineteenth century was the period when nationalism and liberalism as intertwined ideologies began in some measure to shape human thought and action through much of the world. Also in this era, thinkers who witnessed the social injustices and inequalities that

A Panoramic View

MAP 22.1 Global migrations, 1820–1913.

Large scale migrations affected every inhabited region of the world in the nineteenth century. Which migration routes were part of networks that operated within empires? Which routes linked independent states with one another?

accompanied industrialization began to frame the principles of socialism as a critique of liberal capitalist economics and an alternative path to the future.

The Great Exhibition did not neglect the representation of religious faith. Indeed, in midcentury, most people in the world looked to their religions and traditional moral codes as guides to bewildering change in the conditions of life. The third section of the chapter explores connections between modern technology and religion, religious reform, and the activism of missionaries.

In the final part of the chapter, we survey the surge of wars and revolutions that agitated the world in the middle decades of the century. The Great Exhibition was on some level an affirmation that in 1851 peace reigned in most of Europe and that civilized and orderly progress lay ahead. But for humankind as a whole, the 1850s and 1860s were decades of war and revolution on an unprecedented scale of violence. These conflagrations were all linked to the disruptions that attended the great transition to fossil-fuel industry and globe-embracing capitalism.

Waves of Migrants

FOCUS Why did many millions of people undertake long-distance migrations in the nineteenth century?

In the nineteenth century, roughly 150 million people worldwide left their homes to seek wealth, work, or a better chance of survival in foreign places (see Map 22.1). This migration represented a spectacular acceleration of human movement compared to any earlier century. It happened because the industrial revolution created colossal demands for labor, not only in rapidly growing manufacturing centers but everywhere that capitalist entrepreneurs oversaw production of raw materials for industry and food for urban workers. Railways, clipper ships, and steamer networks met the physical challenge of moving millions of people across continents and oceans. The anxieties of migration also diminished somewhat because telegraph lines and faster mail services allowed friends and family members to keep in regular contact with one another over longer distances.

Rapid global population growth in the nineteenth century provided businesses with a much larger potential labor force to meet the multitude of new job demands. Nineteenth-century capitalists argued that this force should earn cash wages and be liberated both from government restrictions on travel and from customary labor obligations to chiefs and landlords. Consequently, the forms of migration changed dramatically in the nineteenth century. The number of people who migrated long distances as slaves to toil entirely for someone else's benefit declined sharply, though forced labor systems by no means disappeared. Conversely, the numbers who migrated voluntarily, if often under economic or political pressures, increased by many millions.

The End of the Atlantic Slave Trade

From the sixteenth century to the early nineteenth, about eight million enslaved African men and women were transported across the Atlantic to the Americas. The slave trade produced the largest and most sustained transoceanic flow of peoples in those centuries. The number of Africans arriving in American ports exceeded the number of free Europeans by four to one. The trade reached its numerical peak in the 1780s. It declined gradually thereafter until about 1840, then dropped fast, ending altogether around 1870. But why *did* the slave trade end, considering that in the nineteenth century many societies in the world accepted slavery as customary and normal? The answers lie in the growth of social movements to end the slave trade and to emancipate slaves, as well as economic changes in the Atlantic region.

Antislavery movements. In eighteenth-century Europe, several leading Enlightenment thinkers denounced slavery as incompatible with the natural rights of human beings. Between 1761 and 1800, Portugal, Britain, and several northern states in the United States made slavery illegal on home

territory. In 1794 the French revolutionary government outlawed slavery both at home and in overseas possessions, though Napoleon restored the institution eight years later. An internationally linked antislavery movement was slow to develop, but abolitionist organizations, for example, the British Anti-Slavery Society, formed in countries on both sides of the Atlantic. In Britain evangelical Christians and small numbers of freed Africans agitated against both slavery and the slave trade, branding it manifestly inconsistent with both human rights and the moral responsibility to introduce Christian civilization to Africans. Economic liberals also joined the emancipation chorus, arguing for the benefits of a free and mobile work force.

Between 1803 and 1814 the pressure of antislavery movements pushed Britain, the United States, Denmark, and the Netherlands to outlaw slave trading, though abolition of the institution of slavery took decades longer. France, Spain, Portugal, and most of the new Latin American states outlawed the trade in the ensuing decades. However, it fell mainly to the British navy, with some help from French and American vessels, to enforce the new policy by intercepting slave ships when they left African ports. Beginning in the 1820s naval crews caught and arrested numerous shippers, releasing their human cargos mainly to the tiny British colony of Sierra Leone in West Africa. Owing to the immense length of the continental coast, however, the patrols seized only a fraction of outbound slave ships. Until 1850, plantation owners in Brazil continued to purchase an average of about thirty-seven thousand slaves a year, mainly from West Central Africa.

The changing economics of slave labor. On the American side, the demand for slave labor remained high in countries where the practice was legal and plantation agriculture profitable. Industries relying on slave laborÐ coffee in Brazil, sugar in Cuba, and cotton in the United StatesÐ continued to expand to meet world market demand. Although the United States outlawed slave imports in 1807, the American-born slave population reproduced itself, thereby making up for the loss of imported labor. In Brazil and Cuba, however, native-born slave numbers continued to show a net yearly decline, owing largely to the lethal conditions of work on tropical plantations. Consequently, both of those countries tried to keep the Atlantic trade going as long as they could.

Planters and merchants, however, had increasing trouble defending their labor system, which came under economic as well as social attack. The abolition of slavery in Haiti following the long revolutionary struggle there (see Chapter 20) inspired slave uprisings elsewhere, for example, the Nat Turner rebellion in Virginia in 1831 and a rising of Muslim slaves in Bahia, Brazil, in 1835. These and numerous other insurgencies forced planters and colonial governments to spend increasing sums on armed security. Liberal Britain eliminated tariffs on sugar imports in 1846, which slashed the world price and further reduced planters' profits. On the global scale, European capitalists found attractive

Freed slaves arriving in Sierra Leone. In its efforts to suppress the slave trade, the British navy relocated over 40,000 liberated Africans to Freetown, the capital of Sierra Leone, between 1808 and 1855. There they received land and Christian baptism. This influx created tensions with local residents, who resisted both British colonial rule and the status of the transplanted men and women, known as Krios. Why might British officials have decided to release freed slaves at Freetown rather than return them to their places of origin?

new investment opportunities besides American sugar. Consequently, international capital shifted toward mechanical industries, railway building, mining, and commercial farming in places like South Asia, South Africa, Latin America, Canada, and the United States, using legally free if not necessarily well-treated wage laborers.

Once most European states abolished slavery, they mounted pressure on other countries to follow suit. Britain outlawed the institution in its colonies in 1833, France (for a second time) in 1848, and the United States in 1865, following its civil war. Thereafter, the United States joined the European democracies in urging Brazil and Cuba (still a Spanish colony) to enact full emancipation, though politically dominant sugar and coffee interests prevented that from happening until the late 1880s.

The Outpouring from Europe

The transition from predominantly African to heavily European and Asian transoceanic migration took place in the decades after 1820. Somewhere between fifty and fifty-five million men and women emigrated from Europe up to 1939. In the nineteenth century most Europeans emigrated voluntarily and sold their labor freely, though poverty or misfortune could impose their own forms of servitude on settlers. In contrast to African slaves, European migrants had legal freedom to move from place to place. A minority of them returned permanently to Europe for one reason or another. Others traveled regularly back and forth between Europe and points abroad to do seasonal agricultural work,

for example, laborers who made repeated trips between Italy and Argentina or Brazil.

Beachheads and neo-Europes. The great majority of migrants went to regions where other Europeans in much smaller numbers had already established what we have called neo-European societies, places where the newcomers put down roots, worked the land, and attempted to recreate as best they could the European cultural and social environments they had left behind. In those places the population of European ancestry came to far outnumber indigenous populations (see Chapter 19). In 1800 the largest frontier of permanent European migration was the young United States, which then had about 4.3 million people of European descent, plus another 1 million African slaves, free blacks, and American Indians. Other, demographically smaller regions of settlement before 1800 included eastern Canada, Siberia, the Cape region of South Africa, and Australia. All those regions attracted much greater settlement in the nineteenth century.

Why did so many people leave Europe? In a sense the scattering of millions of European migrants to faraway lands represented a global extension of the even more complicated journeys of people from one part of Europe to another. In the first century of industrialization, Europe was a whirl of human movement, some of it one way and permanent, much of it round trip and temporary.

Three developments underlay this mobility. First, the continuing growth of capitalist industry and commercial agriculture required movable labor, that is, workers who could be shifted to places where factories and mines were opening and who could be hired and fired at will. Second, new canal, rail, and steamship networks meant that people could travel both faster and more reliably from one worksite to another. For example, Europe's rail network grew from 1,700 miles in 1840 to 63,300 miles by 1870. Third, Europe's population doubled between 1820 and 1913, from about 170 million to more than 340 million. With that growth came increased competition for land and employment. Although industrialization created many new jobs and prosperity in parts of Europe, uneven economic development between one region and another, plus fluctuations in prices and wages forced multitudes in poorer and more rural countries to relocate to find work.

Rural people left their lands by the millions to take urban or agricultural wage jobs. Many had lost their plots to capitalist landlords or simply hoped to escape chronic poverty. The elimination of serfdom in Poland, Prussia, Austria, and Russia between 1807 and 1861 propelled growing numbers of eastern European and Russian peasants into the migratory stream of wage seekers. Most of those migrants were men and teenage boys. Married men often sought seasonal or temporary work away from home, while wives and daughters continued to work the family plots. By 1850 half the population of most European cities had been born elsewhere.

Fewer people might have left Europe for new shores if more farm land had been available or industry had developed faster in the east and south. But this was not the case. Consequently, population movement within Europe spilled out across the world to New York, Chicago, Toronto, Buenos Aires, and Sydney, then onward to farming frontiers. Many people also fled Europe in the extremity of famine, revolution, or persecution. The Irish famine of 1845±1852, a catastrophe caused by loss of potato crops to a devastating fungus, washed the poorest of the poor onto foreign shores,

about 1.8 million people by 1855. In the aftermath of revolutionary movements that briefly upended Europe in 1848, a wave of migrants headed to America in fear of political reprisals. Jews deserted their homes by the hundreds of thousands to escape anti-Semitic persecution or violence. In the 1880s pogroms in Russia, that is, organized massacres or ethnic cleansing of Jews, triggered mass flight.

In short, several forces combined to ᵃpushº people out of Europe. Other forces worked to pull them overseas. Emigrants usually had high expectations that in places where neo-Europes were emerging they would find cheap land and a cultural and social life not too different from the one they were leaving behind. Moreover, getting there was not prohibitively expensive, because transport costs dropped steadily as railway and steamship routes multiplied. Before 1870, emigrants came principally from the northern European lands stretching from Ireland and Britain to Germany and Scandinavia. After that date, millions of Italians, Poles, and Russians gravitated to the industrial core regions of western Europe, then out again to overseas destinations. The proportion of women in emigrant groups varied widely among different nationalities. Most women traveled with families or followed fathers, husbands, and fiancés who had preceded them to find employment.

Neo-Europes and Indigenous Populations

For several millennia before the nineteenth century, peoples who foraged, herded animals, or practiced subsistence farming on the margins of densely agrarian and citied lands had been gradually losing their livings and habitats to invaders or immigrants who possessed superior numbers, technologies, and armed power. This process sped up after 1800. Neo-Europes formed where indigenous societies retreated, shrank in size, or died, despite their attempts to fight back.

Russian Jewish immigrants arriving in New York City with their belongings. Pogroms prompted a thirty-year migration of Jews out of Russia and eastern Europe. Why might some U.S. citizens have responded to this illustration with sympathy but others with hostility?

North America. In the thirteen British colonies of North America, European colonizers battled and expelled Native Americans whose numbers had already been depleted by diseases that the first waves of Europeans or African slaves introduced two or three centuries earlier (see Chapter 16). Conversely, the descendants of Europeans multiplied. In 1820 the United States (twenty-two states at that point) already had a population of 9.6 million, 82 percent of it of European descent. As migrants poured into the Southeast and Midwest, government authorities collaborated with them to subjugate, kill, or expel Indians still living east of the Mississippi. The largest southern groups, including the Cherokee, Choctaw, and Creek, cultivated and hunted lands that immigrant farmers and cotton planters wanted. President Andrew Jackson (1829±1837) ensured the availability of land to white Americans and their black slaves by pushing the great majority of Indians across the Mississippi River to stark reservations in the Oklahoma territory.

Nevertheless, Native Americans contested the immigrant intrusion. Fighting between Indians and settlers marked every phase of the westward advance. In Florida, for example, Seminole Indians rebelled in 1835 rather than relocate to Oklahoma. Fighting alongside runaway African slaves from strongholds in the Everglades, the insurgents held off U.S. soldiers for seven years. The federal government ended the war in 1842 without ever forcing all the Seminoles out of their swamps and forests.

South America. The temperate southern cone of South AmericaÐ Argentina, Uruguay, Chile, and southern BrazilÐ attracted a growing multitude of European migrants, especially in the later nineteenth century. Wheat, horses, cattle, and sheep flourished on the pampas, or prairies, west and south of the Plata River. Export of hides, wool, and grain grown on some of the richest soil in the world provided the economic foundation for the neo-European society that gradually took hold. Between 1870 and World War I, about six million Spanish, Italian, and other European workers moved to Argentina.

As for the native peoples, their numbers had been historically small compared to the societies of the Andean highlands. Alien diseases shrank them even more, and resistance that Indian cavalry put up on the southern pampas ultimately proved futile. Today the descendants of European immigrants make up 97 percent of Argentina's population of more than forty million.

Australia. Although Australia lies eight thousand miles from Europe, 92 percent of its current population claims European descent. Aborigines, the indigenous people who had Australia to themselves barely more than two hundred years ago, number just 1 percent. The settling of the continent by Europeans began in 1788, when a fleet of British naval vessels landed at Botany Bay in the far southeast to set up a penal settlement. Between 1788 and 1852 the British

crown condemned more than 160,000 men, women, and children to ᵃtransportation° to the Australian colony of New South Wales. Women accounted for about one-sixth of these involuntary travelers, and, like many of the men, they were often poor people found guilty of minor crimes. Above this penal class, which labored in slave-like and unhealthy conditions, stood a small hierarchy of British officials, military officers, merchants, and land-owners. In the 1830s free European farmers began to export wool and beef, linking New South Wales to the global economy. The settler population, however, grew slowly until 1851, when gold prospectors hit pay dirt. After that, voluntary migrants scrambled in, swelling the population from about 400,000 in 1850 to 1.4 million just ten years later.

Meanwhile, Aboriginal hunting and foraging bands slowly retreated and withered. Like the Americas, Australia had for thousands of years remained isolated from the teeming pool of infectious diseases endemic to Afroeurasia. When the early European settlers introduced influenza, smallpox, and other virulent ills, epidemics raged through indigenous communities. By the 1820s European settlers began pushing inland. Aborigines regarded land as communal property, but Europeans saw individual ownership as the natural form of land use. Since no one presumably ᵃowned° Aboriginal land, it was free for the taking. According to one British official, ᵃIt is in the order of nature that, as civilization advances, savage nations must be exterminated.°[1] Carving out commercial farms and huge stock ranches, European immigrants pushed native communities toward the arid interior or massacred those who refused to fall back. After 1850 the balance of population shifted steadily in favor of the immigrants.

Siberia. The enormous Inner Eurasian land of Siberia was different from other emerging neo-Europes because it was within Afroeurasia, not separated from it by a span of ocean. However, the indigenous population, which included Yakuts, Evenks (Tungus), and numerous other hunting, fishing, and horse-herding groups, lived far enough away from Afroeurasia's denser population centers that they fell easily to the same noxious diseases that killed Australian Aborigines and Native Americans (see Chapter 19). In the late eighteenth century, for example, a pestilence on the Pacific peninsula of Kamchatka carried off as much as three-quarters of the local inhabitants.

Between 1830 and 1914, Siberia became overwhelmingly European. Similarly to Australia, the discovery of gold in the 1830s brought a fresh wave of immigrants. In 1858±1860, one-sided treaties between Russia and the weakened Chinese empire opened new lands to farm settlement in the Amur River valley north of Mongolia. The emancipation of Russian serfs in 1861 propelled hundreds of thousands of men and women over the following decades to migrate eastward. After 1880, new mine, rail, and commercial farm enterprises in southern Siberia drew in five million more.

Europeans and Aborigines exchange goods—at a distance. The French writer and artist Jacques Arago drew this scene about 1820 during a visit to Australia. What features of the picture suggest that the meeting was probably tense and might easily have turned violent?

Migrations of Asians and Africans

Next to Europe, India and China were the largest suppliers of migrant workers to plantations, mines, factories, and railroads in distant lands. Between 1820 and 1914, approximately twelve million men and women left those lands on the promise of work or opportunity abroad. This number represented about one-fifth of the European exodus, and more Asians than Europeans eventually returned home. Nevertheless, in Southeast Asia, the Indian Ocean rim lands, and the Americas, Chinese and Indian migrants planted permanent minority communities.

Nineteenth-century Chinese migrants perpetuated on a growing scale a long tradition of settlement in Southeast Asian cities from the Philippines to Burma. Indian neighborhoods sprang up in almost every part of the British empire where employers needed labor, for example, in Malaya, South Africa, and British Guiana in South America. The great majority of Asian migrants went to areas where commercial export agriculture was expanding. For example, as the African slave trade shrank, European investors opened new sugar plantations in South Africa, Southeast Asia, and Oceania, employing Indian and Chinese contract workers.

The meaning of ᵃvoluntary migration.° Like Europeans, most Asians left home voluntarily, but that term had shades of meaning. Most traveled to ports and boarded ships because they had experienced economic stress or discontent. Beginning in the 1820s, for example, the British colonial authorities in India systematically organized labor

transport of poor people to other parts of the empire to do farm work. In China, land shortages arising from population growth, price inflation, rebellion, and periodic drought propelled tens of thousands out of the country every year, especially from the densely populated southern provinces. Labor recruiters, whether Europeans or Asians, often deceived illiterate men and women about the intended destination, the working conditions, or the promised wages. In Portuguese Macao, off China's coast, for example, unscrupulous recruiters sometimes snared poor Chinese into games of chance, then demanded that they or a family member pay losses by accepting an overseas labor contract requiring work over a specified period of time.

The great majority of emigrants from South and East Asia were boys and men, but women also left home, especially migrating to places where the labor importers wanted to encourage men to settle permanently. Also, the social conventions of Chinese and Indian societies restricted women from circulating in public as freely as European women could. For example, the midcentury gold rushes that happened in both California and Australia attracted tens of thousands of Chinese construction workers. Of the 65,000 Chinese in California in 1860, only 1,800 were women. Some single women went abroad voluntarily, but many were kidnapped or deceived and ended up as prostitutes or domestic servants.

Asian workers in tropical America. The decline and eventual end of slavery created a serious labor crisis for plantation owners in the Caribbean and South America.

Chinese immigrants working in a sugar factory in Cuba, 1872. Men and women from East and South Asia filled a labor void after the importation of African slaves declined. Working conditions, however, did not much improve for Asian laborers under contract. What factors might have motivated people to cross the Pacific to engage in ardous, dangerous work for little pay?

with 12 lashes; if he persists, with 18 more, and if even thus he should not enter on his course of duty, he may be put in irons, and made to sleep in the stocks.[o][2]

Continuing slave trade. Even though the trans-Atlantic slave trade shrank to insignificance between 1840 and 1870, human trafficking continued, whether legally or not, wherever people could be held in bondage. Commercial planters from the southern United States continued to buy and sell slaves and move them from one state to another until 1865. Between 1820 and 1860, Brazilian merchants moved about one million slaves from depleted sugar plantations in the northeast to expanding coffee-growing lands in the south. Slavery and slave trading remained a customary practice in many Asian lands and most of Africa throughout the nineteenth century. Industrialization in Europe increased demand for African commodities such as lumber, peanut oil, and palm oil. Consequently, slavery actually expanded in some parts of West and Central Africa in the mid-nineteenth century as rulers and proprietors responded to new opportunities in the global economy.

In northeastern Africa, the Egyptian ruler Muhammad Ali (see Chapter 21) invaded the upper Nile River valley (today the republics of Sudan and South Sudan) in 1820 to capture boys and young men to serve as military slaves. Thereafter, Sudanese merchant expeditions armed with modern guns raided far to the south, enslaving villagers and selling them downriver to Egypt. To the west, slave traffic across the Sahara declined steadily in the nineteenth century, though in the middle decades around four thousand slaves a year may have entered Morocco, most of them women. Along the Indian Ocean coast of Africa, the sultanate of Oman and Zanzibar tapped East Africa for ivory and slaves in exchange for imported textiles. At midcentury, armed convoys drove as many as fifty thousand slaves a year from the interior to the Indian Ocean coast. Some of them, predominantly women, were then shipped to Arabia and other Muslim lands for domestic or sexual service. Others were taken to Zanzibar Island, where they harvested cloves, a popular spice in the international market. Under British pressure the Omani sultan abolished the export slave trade in 1873, though effective enforcement came slowly.

Many freed slaves stayed on plantations, but others left to plow their own farms or work in towns. Consequently, colonial governments and private planters devised new schemes to replace slaves with contract workers. Historians have asked whether contract labor work might typically have been as harsh as slave labor. Asian workers bound for the Caribbean or South America usually suffered dreadful shipboard conditions, and their employers sometimes housed them in barracks originally built for slaves. Between 1853 and 1874, about 125,000 Chinese workers debarked in Cuba, where slavery was still legal. There, they sweated in the cane fields alongside black slaves, and they suffered numerous restrictions and punishments set forth in Cuban law: [a] The colonist disobeying the voice of the superior, whether it be refusing to work, or any other obligation, may be corrected

Oceania Connected

The peoples who inhabited the immense Pacific basin became permanently incorporated into the global network

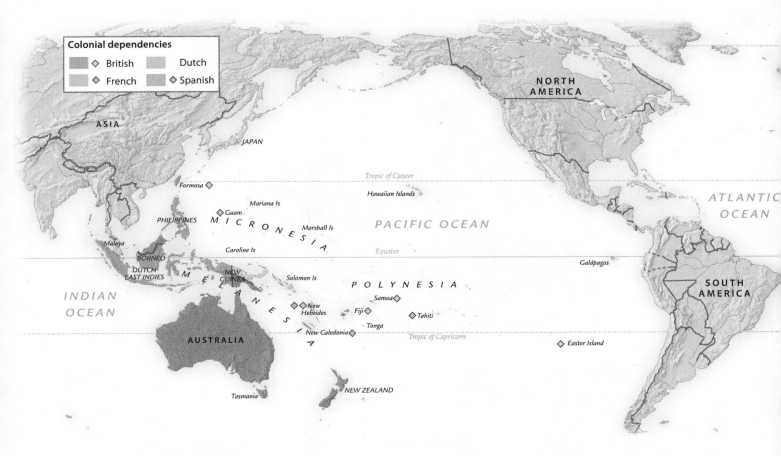

MAP 22.2 The Pacific basin, 1760–1880.
Considering that the Pacific is dotted with thousands of islands and the Atlantic is not, why did it take nearly three centuries longer to establish routine communications across the Pacific than it did across the Atlantic?

of migration and trade in the later eighteenth century (see Map 22.2). Over a period of about 2,600 years, migrants who spoke Polynesian languages had sailed outrigger canoes to explore and settle many of the ocean's twenty-five thousand islands. Those colonizers adapted ingeniously to a variety of climates and natural environments, building societies that ranged from hunter-forager bands in southern New Zealand to small kingdoms on Tonga and the Hawaiian Islands. But they maintained no sustained contact with Afroeurasia, the Americas, or Australia. Then, beginning in the 1760s, European mariners, notably the English explorer James Cook, crisscrossed the Pacific in growing numbers, landing on many islands, introducing new crops and animals, opening mines and plantations, and founding Christian missions.

The perils of contact. In the early nineteenth century, Oceania became a new zone of world commerce and migration, though the cost in lives and environmental degradation ran high. The thousands of Europeans and Asians who sailed into the Pacific brought with them a ªsuitcaseº of plants, domestic animals, pests, and microorganisms, many of them unknown to Polynesians. Like Australian Aborigines, Pacific Islanders initially suffered catastrophic die-off owing to exposure to unfamiliar infectious diseases, including smallpox, measles, and influenza. For example, when European settlers started arriving in New Zealand in 1840, the Maori population may have numbered 100,000 or more. By 1858 it declined to 56,000, owing mainly to imported infections.

Merchants and migrants swarmed into the Pacific to exploit resources of both land and sea. Russian, American, and Australian hunters profited handsomely from trade in seal fur, though by 1840 they nearly wiped out this species in the Pacific. Beginning in 1819 American and other whale hunters entered the ocean. Whale oil commanded a huge market for lighting, industrial lubrication, and cooking. The industry flourished at first, but hunters rapidly depleted several species, forcing this enterprise to shut down almost entirely for several decades after 1860.

Whalers in the port of Honolulu, Hawaii, 1849. Though ship owners were typically American or European, whaling crews included Pacific Islanders. Honolulu's buildings, too, reveal a blend of European and Hawaiian architecture. What elements of this nineteenth-century engraving might have seemed unusual or exotic to American viewers?

In the later century, thousands of Polynesians migrated from island to island to find jobs in commercial agriculture and shipping. A sugar industry in Fiji succeeded because planters attracted contract laborers from South Asia. Their descendants make up nearly 40 percent of the population today. Sometimes, however, migration was induced by brute force. In several parts of the Pacific, armed labor contractors made a business of kidnapping islanders, a practice called ᵃblackbirding.° In 1862±1863, Peruvian kidnappers carried off about 1,500 men and women from Rapa Nui (Easter Island) to work in South American mines and sugar fields.

The birth of the ᵃPacific world.° As trade grew across the Pacific, port cities multiplied. Oceania offered a variety of exotic commodities that East Asians wanted to buy, including sealskins, otter pelts, pearls, and ambergris, which is an intestinal secretion of sperm whales used as a spice, in perfume, and as an aphrodisiac. Honolulu, today the capital of Hawaii, emerged after 1820 as the key mid-ocean trans-shipment center. Vessels converged there from Guangzhou (Canton), Manila, Sydney, and several Latin American ports, as well as from small havens along the coasts of California and Canada, where Native Americans and European settlers sold furs, skins, and timber.

Gold rushes in California (1849), Australia (1851), and British Columbia (1858) added yellow metal to the Pacific exchange web. The gold bonanzas did not last long, but they revved the Pacific economy chiefly because European populations in the mining regions became permanently much bigger. California grew from about 15,000 inhabitants in 1848 (not counting American Indians) to more than 250,000 in 1852. Southeastern Australia experienced similarly explosive immigration. Fast clipper ships and then steamers progressively shortened Pacific crossing times.

Groundswells of Political and Social Reform

FOCUS What historical factors account for the rise of a variety of reformist and revolutionary political movements in the nineteenth century?

In every era of world history over the past five thousand years, prophets, reformers, and revolutionaries have stepped forward in times of change to offer solutions to problems of instability, economic stress, or social injustice. Beginning in the eighteenth century, however, the pace of global population growth, industrialization, and human migration accelerated at such a rapid pace that movements proposing better ways to manage or restructure society multiplied around the globe. Newspapers, telegraph lines, railways, and urban coffeehouses all permitted would-be reformers to spread their ideas much faster and farther than ever before. The nineteenth century, we might say, was the first age of ªismsºÐ liberalism, republicanism, conservatism, nationalism, socialism, and communism. All of these ideologies were imprecise, complicated, and prone to spin off in multiple directions. Nevertheless, they animated social movements that greatly affected the course of change as the century progressed.

Nationalism and the Power of the People

Public debates in Europe and the Americas over the ideas of nationalism and liberalism (see Chapters 20 and 21) were barely separable from each other. Both ideologies grew in the nineteenth century as political doctrines of great appeal to capitalists, governing elites, and affluent urbanites. But by midcentury, nationalism began to resonate deeply in the cultural and emotional lives of ordinary people, as liberalism did not. In the past hundred years, nationalism has been the most potent force in the world for mobilizing popular action.

According to nationalist thought, a group of people sharing a common language, cultural forms, history, and a sense of common destiny ought in the natural order of things to enjoy sovereign self-government. When the society achieved that aim, it constituted a nation-state. By appealing to such nationalist feeling, central governments could both shore up popular loyalty and organize citizens for public action more effectively than they had in any previous era. States could take advantage of new communication technologies to encourage people to ªimagine themselvesº as a single community, even though the sovereign territory embraced individuals, perhaps tens of millions of them, who were not culturally homogeneous and knew little or nothing about one another's daily lives.[3]

Modern states, especially the large ones, invariably included different social classes and political interest groups. Urban workers agitated for higher wages, ethnic communities demanded regional self-government, liberals pressed rulers for legal equality and economic freedoms, and radicals urged broader democracy. At the opposite end of the political spectrum, conservatives, including both aristocrats and many rural peasants, contended that traditional ways such as a strict social hierarchy and a state-sanctioned church should be preserved and honored as the social glue that held society together.

Because of these various pressures and conflicts, governments turned with growing enthusiasm to the idea of the national community as a way to soften social tensions. Governments also tended increasingly to claim legitimacyÐ their rightfulness and legality as managers of the stateÐ in secular rather than religious terms, that is, as advocates of the welfare and rights of national citizens rather than as agents of God. To be sure, the ingredients of a national community in the making often included a dominant religious culture, though priests and other clerics tended steadily to lose political power in favor of secular rulers and officials. Elements of a national society also typically included history, literature, music, folklore, and legend. Governments supported public education that would instill patriotic love and selfless service to the state. They promoted civic ceremonies, stirring anthems, a single vernacular language, and a set of founding leaders and patriotic heroes that everyone should revere. In the United States and the Latin American republics, for example, the wars of independence provided a wealth of narratives (George Washington at Valley Forge and the liberation exploits of Simón Bolívar) to feed sentiments of common nationality. In Europe the first half of the nineteenth century was the era of the Romantic Movement, when folkways and fables served as sources of inspiration for modern poetry, novels, and music seeking to capture the nation's ªsoul.º

French citizens defend the Republic. *The Departure of the Volunteers of 1792* by the sculptor François Rude adorns one of the four pillars of the Arc de Triomphe, which Napoleon erected in Paris in 1836 to celebrate the glory of France. A Winged Victory leads volunteers to battle in a scene so connected to French patriotism that the relief has become known as "The Marseillaise," after the revolutionary song that became the national anthem. How might an image like this one have served to galvanize shared national identity?

Varieties of Socialism

socialism A variety of ideologies that advocate social equality and justice and the community's collective control and management of economic institutions; in Marxist thought, socialism follows capitalism in society's transition to communism.

The word *socialism* originally evoked the idea of a society founded on cooperation and mutual concern rather than on individual self-interest. Among intellectuals and activists agitating for reform in the nineteenth century, socialists often championed the democratic and egalitarian ideals of nationalism, but they questioned liberalism's most cherished tenets. All socialists regarded liberalism as an inadequate and at least partially misguided response to the harsh realities of industrialization. Socialists did not share liberal confidence that the selfish pursuit of profit would benefit all levels of society. Rather, private ownership of industry, accumulation of capital in the hands of a few, and ruthless competition all made for appalling working conditions and nearly hopeless life prospects for wage earners and their families. Workers were ᵃwage slaves°Ð men and women at the mercy of capitalist owners. Low pay, unsafe mills, and urban squalor not only created misery for workers but also led inevitably to social conflict and disintegration. Society must therefore be reformed and restructured to achieve fairer distribution of expanding riches. Socialists generally supported the struggles of artisans, factory hands, and miners to improve their lot by marching, striking, organizing trade unions, and agitating for government action. And many socialist leaders doubled as theoreticians and public activists.

One of the earliest socialist pioneers was Claude Henri de Saint-Simon (1760±1825), a French nobleman who nevertheless despised aristocratic privilege and wealth. He was one of the first writers to argue that free-market competition would in fact benefit relatively few and that industrialization should be linked to society's general welfare. He advocated planned industrial communities in which politicians would relinquish power to entrepreneurs, engineers, and bankers. Those experts would advance economic and technological progress while scientists and artists took charge of civic and moral affairs. Saint-Simon influenced other socialist innovators in Europe and the United States who set up, or at least sketched out, small-scale utopian communities, where workers would share equally in the fruits of production or at least receive fair treatment from employers. For example, Robert Owen (1771±1858), a Welsh factory manager, founded a textile-producing community in Scotland in 1810 that catered to the security and comfort of workers. But like other utopian projects, this one did not outlast its founder.

The most elaborate statement of socialist principles, and the most pungent critique of capitalist economics, came from the pen of the German philosopher and activist Karl Marx (1818±1883). He and Friedrich Engels (1820±1995), his

Karl Marx. Though he championed the rights of working people, Marx came from a prosperous family. He studied philosophy in German universities, where his social activism began to bloom. In 1845 he famously wrote, "The philosophers have only interpreted the world in various ways—the point however is to change it."

longtime collaborator, emerged at midcentury as the leading proponents of what they called ᵃscientific socialism.° In 1848 Marx published the *Communist Manifesto,* which set forth his fundamental idea that the laboring masses could achieve economic and social justice only through revolutionary struggle. Moving to England the following year, he spent the rest of his life there, much of it reading and thinking in the British Library and elaborating his ideas in *Das Kapital* (ᵃCapital°).

Marx drew on earlier socialist ideas but also scorned the utopians for thinking that programs of kindly cooperation among employers, governments, and workers would ever produce a just society. He also thought that class distinctions

bourgeoisie The urban middle class; in Marxist thought, the property-owning class that oppresses the working class.

proletariat The working class; in Marxist theory, the class that must overthrow the capitalist bourgeoisie to achieve control of the means of production.

were much more important than national ones. He contended that the industrial elite, or **bourgeoisie,** merely fooled workers into thinking that it shared with them a national bond. To the contrary, wage workers everywhere, whom he called the **proletariat,** must unite against their bourgeois oppressors. Marx argued from what he called a ªmaterialistº standpoint that work, or ªproduction,º was central to all social organization and that history was fundamentally a class struggle between those who controlled the ªmeans of productionº and those who did not. In the modern era, industrial capitalists had replaced slave owners and estate lords as the dominant class. Now, Marx proclaimed, the proletariat must rise up to recover for itself the means of production, securing its interests by confiscating all productive property. Factories, farms, and businesses must be held in common for everyone's use and benefit.

For Marx, history was a process in which conflict over contrasting social systems would inevitably lead to a higher form of society. In the *Communist Manifesto,* he argued that the proletariat would ultimately triumph: ªWhat the bourgeoisie therefore produces, above all, are its own grave-diggers. Its fall and the victory of the proletariat are equally inevitable.º 4 Once workers overthrew the owners of capital,

communism A dimension of socialist thought that advocates revolution to eradicate capitalism and establish the universal triumph of the proletariat.

class struggle would end and **communism,** the existence of society without class or private property, would be established worldwide.

Socialists founded political parties and labor unions in most European states in the second half of the century, though some of them rejected or modified Marx's radical program. Marxian socialists also struggled with two developments they did not expect. One was that legal reforms and continuing economic growth progressively lifted workers' standards of living in the industrializing countries without proletarian revolution. The other was that nationalism proved a powerful tool for persuading ordinary people to identify with even their richest fellow citizens. Nevertheless, the power of Marxist ideas grew as the century proceeded and the gap between rich and poor continued to widen on a global scale.

Movements for Women's Rights

For some thinkers, both liberals and socialists, the logic of their doctrines demanded radical change in the civic rights and responsibilities of women. Around the world, women had long fought to loosen the control of men over such institutions as marriage, divorce, property ownership, and religious leadership. The new European ideologies, however, offered frameworks for thinking critically about the social relations between women and men. Several women, for example, rose to prominence in the socialist movement. The English activist Anna Wheeler campaigned tirelessly for women's rights and in 1825 coauthored the bluntly titled book *Appeal of One Half of the Human Race, Women, Against the Pretensions of the Other, Men.*

Many women educated in the United States and Britain saw a blatant inconsistency between slave emancipation and the web of legal inequalities that kept females out of public life. In 1840 the male organizers of the World Anti-Slavery Convention in London initially stopped female delegates at

Elizabeth Cady Stanton speaking at the first Woman's Rights Convention, 1848. Making bold political claims, Stanton addressed a mostly female audience in the Wesleyan Methodist Chapel in Seneca Falls, New York. What might you infer from this picture regarding the social class of Stanton's supporters?

the door, then compromised by allowing them to be seated behind a curtain. Eight years after she attended that conference, Elizabeth Cady Stanton joined with her fellow American Lucretia Mott to convene the first women's rights meeting in Seneca Falls, New York. The delegates' Declaration of Sentiments demanded women's enfranchisement. Slave abolitionism, however, tended to overshadow their budding movement. In 1870 the U.S. Congress passed the Fourteenth Amendment, which gave the vote to freed male slaves but not to the women of any race. In Britain, though bills introduced in Parliament to enfranchise women failed repeatedly throughout the nineteenth century, a movement for women's rights initiated in 1851 continued to grow. In that same decade, liberals in Mexico began to lobby for expanded female education, and the Argentine-born writer Paula Manso de Noronha launched a feminist magazine in Brazil.

Movements for Political Reform and Unification in Europe

Between 1815 and 1848, Europeans lived with a vexing and potentially explosive contradiction. An assortment of dynastic monarchies, their ruling houses almost all related to one another by blood, endeavored to limit as much as possible the effects of the French Revolution, especially any drift toward popular democracy or social revolution. Simultaneously, however, liberals, nationalists, and radical democratsÐ their ranks growing among the urban administrative and professional classesÐ pushed for reforms. In almost every European country, protest marches, strikes, or urban riots disturbed the relative peace that prevailed among the region's states.

Some of those popular actions succeeded in forcing change. In France, Parisian insurgents overthrew the deeply reactionary King Charles X (reigned 1824±1830) in the July Revolution of 1830, replacing him with Louis-Philippe (r. 1830±1848), a nobleman dubbed the ªCitizen Kingº because he accepted his mandate from the French National Assembly, not from God. The same year, rebels succeeded in splitting the Netherlands to create the new constitutional monarchy of Belgium. Greece achieved independence in 1830 after an alliance of middle-class merchants and mountain chieftains, with help from the British navy, drove out their Ottoman Turkish rulers. Britain also experienced industrial walkouts, protest rallies, and, in Ireland, rural insurrections. Liberal members of Parliament slowly pushed through political reforms. In 1832 Parliament voted to lower property requirements for male voters. This doubled the size of the electorate, though only to about 217,000 out of a population of 27 million.

Revolutionary movements of 1848.

Then, in 1848, popular uprisings burst forth across Europe, surprising not only liberals but also socialists and republicans who had longed for just such an event. Street fighting broke out in Paris, targeting King Louis-Philippe, whose liberalism did not go nearly far enough for many. When the army failed to quash the insurrection, the king abdicated. Telegraphs and trains carried the breaking news across Europe, triggering urban uprisings, first in several major German cities, then in the Habsburg empire and Italy. In several places, rural farmers rose up as well, seizing towns and burning down their landlords' stately houses. Within just a month, French insurgents proclaimed a republic, the Habsburg emperor lost control of several cities, and revolutionary leaders in some of the small states of Germany and Italy began to write new constitutions. In far-off Brazil, rebels briefly rose up against Emperor Pedro II.

Social and political discontent had clearly been building for three decades. Urban workers complained of bad wages and vile working conditions. Men objected to the loss of their jobs to wage-earning women. Peasants protested against chronic poverty and consolidation of land into big estates. Minority ethnic groups in the Austrian, Russian, and Ottoman empires began to hatch their own nationalist movements. In the three years before the uprisings, moreover, western Europe experienced two seasons of bad harvests, rising food prices, and a moderate drop-off in economic growth. Anxious governments either froze in panic or retaliated so ineptly that even more people joined the insurrections.

The revolutions of 1848, however, played themselves out within a year. Government forces regrouped, and the laborers and artisans who had taken to the streets did not succeed in coordinating their actions in different cities. In France, the army killed ten thousand street fighters. In Hungary, Russian troops helped the emperor crush a rising of Magyar (Hungarian) nationalists seeking independence from Austria. Reactionary governments returned to power, but the risings frightened them and caused them much expense. Not wanting to witness such a pan-European explosion again, most dynastic regimes moved gradually over the next two decades to concede at least moderate political reforms and to try to identify themselves more intimately with the national community.

European nation-building after 1848.

Liberal and nationalist ideologies were powerful enough in the two decades after the uprisings to inspire three successful nationalist movements, which reshaped Europe's political geography. In Hungary, Magyar nationalists did not stop agitating for independence from Austria. In 1867 the emperor Franz-Joseph agreed to a power-sharing arrangement called the Dual Monarchy. It retained him as head of state of both Austria and Hungary but granted each region its own parliament and control of internal affairs.

In the Italian peninsula, a nationalist movement to weld together a unified Italy took concrete shape in the first half of the century. In 1848 the region was a patchwork of territories variously ruled by Austria, the kingdom of Piedmont-Sardinia, the Spanish Bourbon dynasty, the pope, and several minor princes. However, secret independence associations multiplied in most of those territories. In Piedmont-Sardinia, Camillo di Cavour, prime minister to King Victor

Wilhelm I of Prussia proclaimed Kaiser of Germany following its unification, 1871. Anton von Werner's 1885 oil painting, *The Proclamation of the German Empire*, depicts Kaiser Wilhelm flanked by nobles, including Crown Prince Friedrich on his right. Otto von Bismarck, wearing a white tunic, stands facing the king. The royal family commissioned this painting to commemorate Bismarck's 70th birthday.

Emmanuel II (r. 1849±1878), worked doggedly to construct economic foundations for unification by modernizing industry, building rail lines, and expanding the army. He also played a skillful political game, negotiating with France's Napoleon III for support against Austria.

Modern Italy came quickly together between 1859 and 1870. With the help of French troops, Piedmont expelled Austrian forces from most of the northern peninsula and unified it under the banner of Italian nationalism. Giuseppe Garibaldi, a passionate revolutionary who had fought for democracy in Brazil and Uruguay, launched a private and brilliantly successful expedition to bring Sicily and the south into the Italian union. In 1861 a newly constituted parliament proclaimed Victor Emmanuel king of Italy. In the following nine years, the new state seized Venice from Austria and all of the pope's territories except the Vatican. Italy thus emerged as an independent constitutional monarchy that embraced most of Europe's Italian speakers.

Like Italy, Germany in midcentury was a collection of loosely confederated states. Prince Otto von Bismarck (1815±1898), the premier of the kingdom of Prussia under Wilhelm I, cared more for aristocratic privileges than for liberal principles. But he worked ceaselessly to expand Prussia's territorial reach and economic power, regarding military victories and rapid industrialization as potent ways to stimulate unity.

In a series of deft political and military maneuvers starting in 1864, Bismarck provoked successive wars with Denmark, Austria, and France, winning them all after short campaigns and then annexing additional German-speaking territories to Prussia. Victory in the Franco-Prussian War (1870±1871) brought down Emperor Napoleon III, cost France

its provinces of Alsace and Lorraine, and generated enduring antagonism between Germany and the Third Republic, the new French parliamentary government created in 1871. In the triumphant aftermath of victory in France, all remaining German-speaking states, except for Austria with its multitude of ethnic minorities, joined Prussia to form a unitary monarchy that same year. The new Germany, however, was no democracy. ªThe great questions of the day,º Bismarck declared, ªwill not be settled by speeches or majority votesÐ that was the great mistake of 1848 and 1849Ð but by blood and iron.º Power remained concentrated in the hands of the emperor and his central ministries, though Bismarck placated liberals by agreeing to a parliament (Reichstag) elected by property-owning males.

Modernizing Reforms in Muslim Lands

Since the fifteenth or sixteenth century, several Muslim monarchies, similarly to China, Russia, and western European states, had been occupied with projects to strengthen and extend central power by adopting both firearms technology and new, more efficient ways of governing and taxing their populations. As global commercial relations became more complex and European states projected more military and economic might, the political elites of most Muslim states considered new policies, which historians have called ªdefensive modernization.º These military, technical, and administrative reforms were intended to stave off European diplomatic and commercial pressures or even prevent foreign invasion.

In the early 1800s liberal and nationalist ideas began trickling into major Muslim cities, reaching small numbers of army officers, officials, and international traders, especially people with knowledge of European languages. Muslim rulers knew well that European states were outpacing them technologically. Austrian armies had overpowered Ottoman forces in southeastern Europe; the British were conquering South Asia; Napoleon had invaded Egypt in 1798; and Greece, with British help, successfully threw off Turkish rule in 1830. Urban intellectuals and educated officers speculated on possible connections between material power and new ideas and institutions like constitutions, legislatures, and civil rights. Many reform-minded Muslim leaders favored fundamental secular changes, or modernization unimpeded by established cultural ways and authority figures. The trick for Muslim governments was to select innovations from abroad without upsetting delicate agreements with various power groupsÐ religious leaders, land magnates, rural tribesÐ on which the stability of the state depended.

Reforms in the Ottoman empire. Among Muslim states, the Ottoman empire launched by far the most ambitious modernizing experiment, initiating military, administrative, educational, and political reforms. The Tanzimat, or ªReorganization,º as these reforms became known, began with Sultan Mahmud II (r. 1808±1839) and continued through several of his successors. In the military sphere the government hired French and Prussian advisers, translated French army manuals into Turkish, and imported up-to-date European weaponry. In 1826 Mahmud deployed a well-trained force to eradicate, amid great bloodshed, the janissary corps, the conservatively minded class of soldiers and artisans that had maintained a semi-independent army (see Chapter 17). To modernize education, the government sent young men to Europe to study, and it opened new schools to train future officers and civil servants in European languages, administration, and science. Tanzimat reformers gradually reorganized the state bureaucracy along French lines and, much to the dismay of the religious establishment, laced the Muslim legal system (*shari'a*) with language taken from the French Civil Code. Appropriately characterized as the ªFrench-Knowers,º reformist officers donned European-style uniforms, and bureaucrats traded their robes for western frockcoats.

The most audacious modernizers also pushed for new laws founded on liberal and nationalist principles. Before the Tanzimat, the major Christian and Jewish groups in the empire enjoyed autonomy over their internal affairs but also lived under legal restrictions that did not apply to Muslims. Between 1839 and 1869 a series of imperial edicts made all religious and ethnic communities equal citizens and subject to the same laws and reforms. Like European nationalists, Turkish leaders tried to infuse the culturally diverse population of thirty million with feelings of patriotic attachment to the Ottoman state. Reforms based on this essentially secular Ottomanist ideology culminated in a constitution (1876) that instituted a national elected assembly and put mild restrictions on the sultan's power.

Unfortunately for the modernizers, the Tanzimat era ended shortly after the new constitution appeared. The reformers themselves tended to be out of touch with peasants and urban workers and therefore lacked mass support. Moreover, the plan to cultivate a united Ottoman cultural identity ran up against local nationalisms that were awakening among Serbs, Bulgarians, Romanians, and several other ethnic communities within the empire. Finally, the government continued to sign ªunequal treatiesº with European powers (see Chapter 21) and contracted large loans with European banks. These policies sank the state ever deeper into

Students of the Ottoman Military Medical School. Western education was an important aspect of the Tanzimat reforms. The students wear Western-style military uniforms along with the modern Turkish headgear, or fez. Notice the skeletons and other bones posed in the photograph. Why might a formal group portrait like this one have been important to the reform movement?

A Moroccan Diplomat in France

Several Muslim states besides the Ottoman empire experimented with modernizing reforms in the mid-nineteenth century, though on a much smaller scale. These states included Iran, Egypt, Tunisia, and Morocco. The kingdom of Morocco ventured only the most cautious steps toward military and administrative modernization, though some members of the official class centered in the capital city of Fez took a serious interest in European affairs.

In early 1845 Mulay Abd al-Rahman, the reigning sultan, assembled a diplomatic embassy to visit France and the government of King Louis-Philippe. The sultan instructed the delegation to negotiate a solution to violence along Morocco's border with Algeria, which France had invaded fifteen years earlier. He also advised the mission to learn as much as possible about French society and come back with insights that might help explain its apparent military prowess. Muhammad al-Saffar, a young legal scholar and secretary in the employ of the embassy's diplomatic leader, kept notes during the group's stay in France and wrote an account of the adventure upon his return. In this selection, Al-Saffar offers his views on French economic values, military power, and religion.

The people of Paris, men and women alike, are tireless in their pursuit of wealth. They are never idle or lazy. The women are like the men in that regard, or perhaps even more so. . . . Even though they have all kinds of amusements and spectacles of the most marvelous kinds, they are not distracted from their work, and give every moment its due. . . . Nor do they excuse someone for being poor, for indeed death is easier for them than poverty, and the poor man there is seen as vile and contemptible. . . .

Their Sultan [King] summoned us to attend a review of the troops as an extravagant expression of his high esteem for us, . . . We were blinded by the flashing of their swords, the gleam of the horses' trappings, the shine of their helmets, and the radiance of the armor they wore both front and back. . . .

So it went until all had passed, leaving our hearts consumed with fire from what we had seen of their overwhelming power and mastery, their preparations and good training, their putting everything in its proper place. In comparison with the weakness of Islam, the dissipation of its strength, and the disrupted condition of its people, how confident they are, how impressive their state of readiness, how competent they are in matters of state, how firm their laws, how capable in war and successful in vanquishing their enemies—not because of their courage, bravery, or religious zeal, but because of their marvelous organization, their uncanny mastery over affairs, and their strict adherence to the law. . . .

In Aix [Aix-en-Provence] we saw a huge cross made of wood standing on one side of the town square. At its top was a smaller bit of wood made into the likeness of a crucified man, naked except for a cloth covering his maleness. What a sight it was! . . . They claim he is Jesus, that is to say, a likeness of him crucified. . . . May [God] preserve them from that, and may He be raised high above what the sinners say. The proof of our eyes only increased our insight into their unbelief, the falsity of their creed, and the stupidity of their reasoning. Thanks be to God who guided us to the true religion.

Source: Susan Gilson Miller, trans. and ed., *Disorienting Encounters: Travels of a Moroccan Scholar in France in 1845±46: The Voyage of Muhammad as-Saffar* (Berkeley: University of California Press, 1992), 108, 110, 153, 190, 193±194.

Thinking Critically

Which aspects of French society and culture impress Al-Saffar, and which do not? Why do you think his views are ambivalent? What inferences might you make about Moroccan society in the 1840s, based on Al-Saffar's observations about France?

debt. Sultan Abdul Hamid II, who came to power in 1876, had no sympathy for European-style reforms. He halted the Tanzimat, suspended the new constitution, and ruled in the old autocratic manner until 1909.

The fate of Muslim Algeria. In the territory that is today the Republic of Algeria, Muslims witnessed a demonstration of Europe's raw military power when in 1830 French forces crossed the Mediterranean to seize the port of Algiers. Before then, an elite of Turkish military men owing formal loyalty to the Ottoman sultan ruled the cities and towns along Algeria's Mediterranean coast. Self-governing Arabic- and Berber-speaking tribes held sway in the interior plains and mountains. France's Charles X, motivated more by hunger for political prestige than by any clear strategic aim, exploited a minor diplomatic incident to occupy Algiers. When local resistance erupted, the intruders found themselves fighting for more territory than they had planned. The French quickly eliminated the Turkish regime, but rural populations led by Abd al-Qadir battled French forces for nearly fifteen years. An Arab cavalry warrior esteemed for his Muslim learning, Abd al-Qadir founded a centralized Algerian state in interior areas beyond French reach. He also modernized his struggle by acquiring up-to-date weaponry and arguing his cause to European newspaper reporters. In 1840, however, France unleashed a scorched-earth campaign to make Algeria's Mediterranean hinterlands safe for land-hungry European settlers, who were beginning to pour in. In 1847 Abd al-Qadir was caught and deported, though popular risings continued to shake the country for another quarter-century.

The Limits of Liberalism in Latin America

Liberal ideas spread widely among educated city dwellers in the Latin American states that gained independence from Spain in the 1820s. The sixteen states created in the aftermath of the liberation wars became constitutional republics. Only Brazil remained a monarchy after Portugal withdrew. Land-owners, professionals, and government functionaries who admired the European and North American models of popular sovereignty formed liberal blocs in almost every country to press for continuing reforms. Liberals had no desire to perpetuate the authoritarianism and restricted commerce that had characterized the Spanish and Portuguese colonial empires, and they yearned to reduce the power of the Roman Catholic Church over social life and education.

During the first few decades after independence, however, liberal hopes wilted. Activist political groups remained small, and liberals quarreled incessantly with conservatives; each group promoted its own political and economic agenda. Like their counterparts in Catholic European countries, conservatives argued for strict social ranking between land-owning elites and ordinary people, and they honored the church as the preserver of tradition. Liberals contended that a combination of modern technology, property rights, and free trade would push their countries along Europe's path of material progress. But in fact, most of Latin America remained economically stagnant until after 1850. The wars of independence had wrecked economic infrastructures, and most of the urban educated class, including liberals proclaiming universal equality, held deep cultural prejudices against the Indians, *mestizos*, and black workers that inhabited the rural backlands.

Dictators on horseback. When postindependence governments achieved little economic change, military officers seized power, sometimes in rural regions, sometimes in whole countries. Across Latin America, the period from 1830 to 1860 was the age of the **caudillos** (kahw-DEE-yohs), political strongmen who led their own Indian

caudillos Autocratic political bosses or dictators, especially in the postindependence period in Latin America.

and *mestizo* cavalry and who typically ruled with clenched fists. In several countries these warlords competed ruthlessly with one another for power and land, inflicting prolonged political and economic turmoil in the process. Those who fought their way to national ascendancy retained republican institutions and symbols but routinely stuffed ballot boxes and suspended representative assemblies.

Two larger-than-life caudillos were Juan Manuel de Rosas and Antonio López de Santa Anna. Rosas dominated Argentina from 1829 to 1852. He personified the caudillo ideal, galloping with gauchos (cowboys), proclaiming himself champion of the poor, and having his own portrait placed on church altars. Simultaneously, he protected the wealth of the land magnates. He finally fell to an enemy alliance of exiled liberals and rival caudillos.

In Mexico, Santa Anna served as caudillo-president of the republic nine different times between 1833 and 1855. Like Rosas, he had the support of rich patrons, who locked up huge acreages of land while the economy stagnated. As one midcentury liberal wrote, "There are Mexican landowners who occupy (if one can apply the word "occupation" to a purely imaginary thing) a greater extent of land . . . even than one or more European countries. Over this vast expanse of land, much of which lies idle, . . . live scattered four to five million Mexicans who have no other means of subsistence than agriculture yet are forbidden the use of the land."[5] Mexico's still rudimentary communication system made sustained central management of the state, which extended from tropical forests to northern California, nearly impossible. In the north, settlers from the United States penetrated Texas and in 1836 declared independence from Mexico. They also legalized slavery again. In the Yucatan Peninsula, a rebellion of Maya farmers simmered well into the second half of the century.

The Santa Anna era ended in the traumatic aftermath of war with the United States from 1846 to 1848, an episode that cost Mexico half its territory. The United States was industrializing, settlers were pouring across the Mississippi, and President James Polk aimed to annex territory all the way to the Pacific. The Mexican government lacked comparable economic resources and suffered from chronic political factionalism. U.S. forces occupied Mexico City briefly but did not pursue annexation south of the Rio Grande. The federal government was more interested in settling American and European migrants on western Indian lands than in ruling millions of Mexican farmers.

Liberal revival. After 1850, liberal elites took back the presidential palaces in several Latin American countries, including Mexico, Argentina, Colombia, and Chile. Those states wrote new constitutions, trimmed the power of the church, and dropped tariffs in order to export more minerals and farm commodities. In many countries, *mestizos* and Indians began to take a freer part in civic life. Liberal regimes abolished slavery in most countries by 1854, though

Mexican cavalry charge a U.S. artillery position. Mexican artist Julio Michaud y Thomas depicts the 1847 Battle of Sacramento near the city of Chihuahua. Mexican troops outnumbered the Americans three to one, but U.S. artillery power forced them to retreat with "great confusion in their ranks." How does Michaud's lithograph express a Mexican nationalist perspective on the Mexican-American War?

especially in the later nineteenth century, typically defined the national community partly in terms of its religious culture. For example, Polish nationalism identified with the Roman Catholic Church and Serbian nationalism with the Serbian Orthodox Church. Secular liberals critiqued conservative church hierarchies but religious beliefs not so often. Under liberal pressures, monarchs associated with an official state religion came slowly to accept wider religious liberties. The Protestant constitutional monarchies of northern Europe, for example, progressively abolished discriminatory laws against Roman Catholics.

For hundreds of millions of farmers and urban workers, who, like educated men and women, worried about the directions the world might be taking, religion provided a fundamental moral foundation for coping with rural impoverishment, job insecurities, price fluctuations, and taxes. Spiritual teachings provided ideological frameworks for thinking about the world, finding meaning in it, and perhaps making it better.

nowhere did women gain rights to active citizenship. In Mexico, liberal reformers under Benito Juárez, an Indian and two-time president, achieved stability and conditions for economic growth in the late 1860s.

Nationalism gelled slowly in Latin American countries. In the decades after independence, popular identification with Mexico, Venezuela, Chile, or any of the new republics as distinct national communities barely existed. Even so, newspapers and café talk in the larger towns helped broadcast economic and political news along with a rising national consciousness. Such sentiment took longer to spread to the countryside, but in the late nineteenth century, rising literacy rates together with patriotic expressions in art and literature broadened the base of the imagined community in all Latin American countries.

Religion and Reform

FOCUS How did established religions and new religious movements address popular concerns about rapid economic and social change in the nineteenth century?

Liberalism and nationalism were secular ideologies, but they did not disdain all religion. Emerging nationalist movements,

Global Trends and Religious Change

Two broad developments presented the world's religions with both dangers and opportunities. First, religious leaders saw their political power eroded in several parts of the world. This happened partly because republics in Europe and the Americas whittled away the independent authority of churches. Or they ªdisestablished° religious organization, as the United States Bill of Rights did in prohibiting Congress from making laws ªrespecting an establishment of religion.° Clerics also lost power because some states, for example, the Ottoman empire in the Tanzimat period, gave government officials tighter management over religious affairs and protected freedom of worship for minority groups.

The second development was the revolution of steam-powered travel and mechanical printing, which allowed religious ideas to circulate wider and faster. In the nineteenth century, pilgrims traveled in larger numbers than ever before to holy sitesÐ Roman Catholics to Rome, Muslims to Mecca, Hindus to the banks of the GangesÐ where they identified intellectually and emotionally with a larger community of co-believers. Modern transport carried missionaries to previously inaccessible countries. Printing presses cranked out Bibles, Qurans, Buddhist texts, and the literature of new sects and reform movements.

These two trends contributed in turn to important changes in religious life. The adherents of the major traditions, particularly Buddhism, Christianity, Islam, and Hinduism, became more acutely aware that they belonged to a ªworld religion.º This happened as leaders disseminated authoritative versions of sacred texts and worked to standardize and purify doctrines. In 1864, for example, the Roman Catholic pope Pius IX published the ªSyllabus of the Most Important Errors of Our Time,º which clarified and reaffirmed the church's position on numerous issues ranging from state±church relations to marriage. In Muslim lands, the Ottomans and other rulers regularized the curriculum taught in universities and strengthened their supervision of religious law courts. In India, intellectual and moral leaders worked together to make Hindu belief and practice more coherent, knowing that from ancient times this tradition had embraced a multitude of ideas and devotions. The idea of Hinduism as a unitary tradition entered the popular imagination of millions of Indians only in the nineteenth century.

Christian Evangelism

evangelism The practice of propagating the Christian gospel by preaching, personal witnessing, and missionary work.

A new spirit of **evangelism** permeated both Protestant and Catholic communities. The term *evangelism*, derived from Greek, refers to the sharing of the Christian Gospels. Protestants had traditionally been less zealous than Roman Catholics about leading strangers to Christ. But this changed in the nineteenth century as Protestants realized the power of print to spread the holy word, as well as the urgency of ministering to those who endured urban poverty. Church organizations became more deeply engaged in modern social issues, taking up causes like slave abolition, alcohol addiction, education, and poor relief. For example, political groups broadly described as Christian socialists argued that social compassion and justice lay at the heart of the Gospels. In 1865 the English preacher William Booth founded the Salvation Army, a new denomination with military ranks and uniforms that waged war for Christ among the working classes of London.

In the middle decades of the century, Protestant migrants from northern Europe carried evangelical zeal to the growing neo-Europes, transforming Australia, New Zealand, and Canada into mainly Protestant lands (though French-speaking Canada remained predominantly Catholic). By 1870 the United States was the largest Protestant country in the world. Traveling pastors fanned out across the country, holding gospel meetings and saving souls. America was also fertile ground for new faiths. The Church of Jesus Christ of Latter-day Saints (Mormonism), which grew as migrants poured westward, established a powerful base among new settlers in Utah. In Massachusetts, Mary Baker Eddy (1821±1910) founded the Christian Science

Catherine Booth, mother of the Salvation Army. An impressive speaker, she partnered with her husband William to reach out to the urban poor. She also advocated eloquently for women's ministry in a time when females were excluded from speaking in most Christian churches. What might account for Catherine Booth's popularity as a preacher among middle-class British Christians, when the focus of her evangelical work was criminals, addicts, and other outcasts?

church, which taught that redemption and healing were to be found through self-surrender to rational spiritual laws. In Africa, Asia, and the Island Pacific, Protestant missionary organizations competed with Catholic priests and nuns who had been proselytizing abroad since the sixteenth century. Wherever British forces seized new territory, missionaries from the Church of England and other Protestant denominations invariably turned up. Catholic missions similarly followed the French flag. Wherever they went, Christian missions included teachers and medical personnel, many of them women.

Jewish Reform

Within the world's dispersed Jewish communities, new movements arose to adapt religious practice to ideals of

Ram Mohan Roy: Hindu Reformer

In the commercial ports of South Asia, European liberal ideas circulated among young Hindu and Muslim intellectuals, who fiercely debated the challenges of British East India Company rule and the rapid commercialization buffeting the subcontinent. Among these thinkers was Ram Mohan Roy (1772–1833), who rose to public prominence as an advocate of modernization and a tireless reformer of traditional Hindu beliefs and practices.

Roy belonged to a small elite of well-educated Hindus determined to fathom Europe's swelling economic and military power by grappling seriously with European ideas. These scholars learned English and studied the European Enlightenment alongside the classics of Indian religion and philosophy. A man of high caste from the region of Bengal, Roy received a thorough classical education, including studies in Bengali, Hindi, Sanskrit, Persian, and Arabic. A young man of boundless intellectual energy, he went on to master English and even learned some Greek, Latin, and Hebrew.

In his thirties Roy took a post with the East India Company, as other literate men did, and he rose as high in the giant British firm as a native Indian was allowed to go. In 1814, however, he left the company to join other Hindu intellectuals in Calcutta to talk and write about religion, philosophy, and politics. His studies led him to conclude that over the centuries layers of false belief, deadening ritual, and baneful superstition had concealed the original Hindu faith. The pure teachings of ancient India, he argued, attested to a universal monotheism; to a religion founded on reason, not on the personal authority of priests; to social equality, not caste hierarchy; and to egalitarian relations between men and women. Despite his own family's attachment to traditions that subordinated women to male relatives, he denounced polygamy, child marriage, and male exploitation of women's labor. He also denounced *sati*, the custom of high-caste women throwing themselves on their husband's funeral pyre as proof of their fidelity. This stance pleased English liberals, who looked down on most Hindu practices as antiquated and barbarous, even though there is little evidence of *sati* being widely practiced.

Roy believed that Indian spirituality, washed of unreasonable customs, was readily adaptable to the modern world and had much to give to it. Fundamentally a moral reformer, he also aimed to harmonize religious belief with the new doctrines of secular liberalism, which were just beginning to reach the elites of Asian cities. For example, as much as he loved Sanskrit learning, he advocated a modern system of education that would employ "European gentlemen of talent and education to instruct the natives of India in mathematics, natural philosophy, chemistry, anatomy, and other useful sciences."[6]

Roy was well versed on the French Revolution, sympathized with popular uprisings in places like Ireland, and imagined the day when South Asians would again take charge of their own affairs. In his time, nationalist ideology was still in its formative phase. Nevertheless, he and his fellow activists were the first to express the idea of South Asia, not just as the land of Bengalis, Punjabis, Sikhs, and numerous other ethnic and religious groups, but as India, a distinct cultural community whose members deserved modern rights to equality and justice. On this idea Roy's intellectual successors founded the Indian nationalist movement in the decades after his passing. He died of meningitis in 1833 during a visit to England.

Ram Mohan Roy

Thinking Critically

Why do you think that Ram Mohan Roy's proposals for change in South Asian society did not include a demand that Britain and its East India Company immediately restore the region's political independence?

---

modernity and national citizenship. The German thinker Moses Mendelssohn (1729±1786), a leader of the reform movement known as the Jewish Enlightenment, translated the Hebrew Bible (Old Testament) into German and urged Jews to strive for integration into the social and cultural mainstreams of the countries where they lived. In the early nineteenth century, German Jewish intellectuals established schools to teach modern subjects in addition to religious texts. Mendelssohn and others argued that Judaism must change with the times rather than cling to laws belonging to ancient Jewish kingdoms long vanished.

Pushed by liberal opinion, many European governments, though not all, gradually lifted limitations on Jewish civil and cultural rights. Where Jews became more successfully linked into national life, notably in Germany, Austria, Britain, and the United States, growing numbers embraced what became known as Reform Judaism. Its adherents simplified rituals, ended sexual segregation in worship, and introduced sermons in vernacular languages.

Religious Reform and Revolution in the Muslim World

Like Christians and Jews, devout Muslims responded to the acceleration of global change in a variety of ways. In urban intellectual circles, Muslims talked of ways to join Islamic beliefs and traditions with modern science and liberal ideology. The Iranian-born writer and activist Jamal al-Din al-Afghani (1839±1897) sparked the imagination of young Muslims in the early 1870s by insisting that Muslims must stand up to European material power. This would require reviving feelings of unity among all Muslims as members of the universal *umma*, or ªcommunity of believers.º Al-Afghani was the first Muslim thinker to put forward the idea of pan-Islamic solidarity as a modern political ideology.

The Wahhabi movement. In the Arabian Peninsula, tarnished faith and gross materialism, though not anything that Europeans in particular were doing, troubled the pious scholar Muhammad ibn Abd al-Wahhab (1703±1792). He urged Muslims to renew their spiritual commitment by dedicating themselves to the Quran and to the authentic traditions of the Prophet Muhammad as the foundation of law and daily life. He rigorously criticized local popular beliefs that had seeped into Islamic culture, as well as Sufi

mystical practices, which included veneration of living or deceased holy men. His school of thought, which became known as Wahhabism, demanded reverence for God alone. He also argued that Muslims must fulfill the Quranic requirement to respect women and their legal rights, though later Wahhabi leaders largely failed him on this point.

Ibn Abd al-Wahhab allied with Muhammad ibn Sa'ud, an Arabian warrior chief, who in 1808 conquered Mecca and a large part of Arabia. That success ended the relatively loose rule that the Ottoman empire exercised in the region and replaced it with a new state based on Wahhabi teachings. This kingdom, however, flourished only a few years before an Egyptian army invaded the peninsula and reduced it (at least for the time being) to a small desert principality. Nevertheless, the Wahhabi call to return to belief and worship presumably as practiced in the early Muslim centuries continued to influence Islamic reform movements, especially in West Africa, India, and Indonesia. Wahhabism is the religious ideology of the modern kingdom of Saudi Arabia founded in 1932, and in the past few decades its precepts have inspired radical Muslim political movements, including al-Qaida.

Religious revolution in West Africa. The impulse to reform also inflamed popular uprisings in West Africa. Islam had been established for centuries in the Sudanic region, that is, the savanna lands south of the Sahara Desert, though mainly among urban merchants, scholars, and ruling families. In the eighteenth century Muslim reformers

Warriors of the Sokoto Caliphate. This American engraving from 1857 shows Sokoto horsemen and infantry raiding for slaves. Why might the artist have focused on slavery rather than depicting the Muslim religious reform that also contributed to Sokoto's imperial success?

THE SLAVE HUNT.

in the area that is today Senegal, Gambia, and Guinea overthrew chiefs and land-owning nobles that they believed violated the Muslim ideals of good governance. At the center of those movements were the Fula (or Fulani), a predominantly cattle-herding people who increasingly identified with Islam.

In the early nineteenth century Usuman dan Fodio (1754±1817), a town-dwelling Fula and respected Muslim scholar, led a rebellion that changed the political and religious map of West Africa. His targets were the rulers of the large and prosperous city-states that are today part of Nigeria and Niger. The rulers of those walled cities, the largest of which was Kano, spoke the Hausa language and identified themselves as Muslims, but they gave little attention to religious duties or law. Dan Fodio called upon Muslim Fula and non-Muslim Hausa peasants (the majority of the population) to join together to overthrow their tyrannical rulers, whom he accused of a multitude of transgressions, including the enslavement of fellow Muslims. Like Abd al-Wahhab in Arabia, dan Fodio aimed to strengthen the Muslim community by cleansing it of local folk beliefs. But in contrast to the Wahhabis, he embraced the Sufi tradition and indeed propagated his movement through the Qadiriyya, a large mystical fraternity. Among family members who helped lead the revolution, dan Fodio's daughter Nana Asma'u played a key part as an essayist and poet who called upon women to educate their children in orthodox Muslim practice.

Between 1803 and 1808 dan Fodio's force of mounted archers and spearmen swept several Hausa dynasties out of power. He united the city-states under his rule, taking the title of *khalifa* (caliph), a rank that combined religious and political authority. Under Muhammad Bello, his son and successor, the Sokoto caliphate continued to conquer territories east, west, and south until it eventually became one of the largest empires in Africa. The successors of dan Fodio, however, failed to sustain his reformist zeal. Within a short time, they came to resemble the Hausa princes they had replaced, amassing property, trading slaves, and imposing burdensome taxes. Nevertheless, dan Fodio's example inspired similar Muslim revolutions in other parts of West Africa. Because of those movements and the continuing work of the Sufi fraternities, Islam became the predominant religion across Sudanic Africa by the end of the century.

Global Change and the Calamitous Wars of Midcentury

FOCUS Why did so many wars break out in the middle decades of the nineteenth century, and why did these wars produce death and destruction on such a large scale?

On a world scale the 1850s and 1860s were decades of extraordinary violence. Each of the disastrous conflicts of the period had its distinctive causes, but all of them were bound up with the explosive growth of the capitalist world economy, advances in military technology linked to mass production, and the social stresses of rapid change. One historical estimate suggests that more people died in war and rebellion during those decades than in any comparable period earlier in history. Such mortality was not to be exceeded until the catastrophe of World War I.[7] Two of the most destructive clashes of the period, the Crimean War (1853±1856) in the Crimean Peninsula (today part of Ukraine) and the War of the Triple Alliance (1864±1870) in South America, pitted one sovereign state against others. Three of the conflicts, the Taiping Rebellion in China (1851±1864), the Great Indian Rebellion in South Asia (1857±1859), and the American Civil War (1861±1865), were internal revolts against central state authority (see Map 22.3).

The Crimean War and the Industrialization of Violence

Imperial Russia in the nineteenth century deployed its huge land army to expand its borders, pushing in the west against the Ottoman empire. Conflict between Russia and the Ottoman empire over territory in what is today Romania triggered the war in October 1853. The following year Britain and France joined with the Ottomans to blunt Russia's advance by invading the Crimean Peninsula, Russian-ruled territory on the northern rim of the Black Sea. The European powers had no urgent interest in the Crimea, but their political and commercial strategies required that Russia be prevented from controlling Black Sea shipping, invading southeastern Europe, or seizing Ottoman Constantinople, which guarded the vital Bosporus strait that gave access to the Mediterranean.

The war lasted barely more than two years, but it cost the lives of an estimated 264,000 soldiers in combat and an even greater number from diseases such as dysentery and cholera. Historians generally agree that generals on both sides hopelessly mismanaged the fighting, but the belligerents also introduced new technologies and tactics that foreshadowed the American Civil War and even World War I. These included field communication by telegraph, steam-powered supply vessels, massive artillery barrages, and, in the British and French forces, new rifles that could shoot accurately eight hundred yards farther than older muskets. This was the first modern war in which military machines of the industrial era wreaked serious havoc. It was also the first war recorded by photographers. Primarily because Britain and France could easily resupply their forces by sea, they eventually forced Russia to sue for peace. The struggle checked Russian ambitions in the region, at least for a time, though it also signaled growing volatility in relations among the European powers.

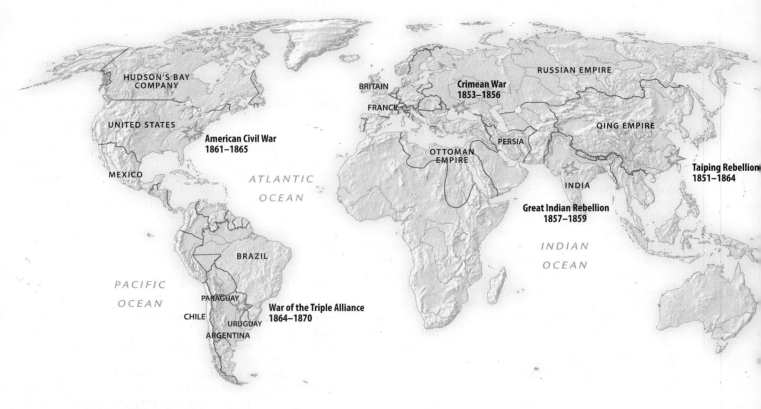

MAP 22.3 Wars of the mid-nineteenth century.
Which of these wars, if any, might be described as a colonial resistance movement?

Paraguay: A War of Annihilation

In South America the waning of the era of caudillo strongmen and the revival of liberal-minded governments restored political calm to most countries and spurred economic growth, especially in exports of raw commodities. Tensions grew, however, among countries over control of regional resources and the ports and transport routes that afforded access to world markets. Such pressures led the land-locked republic of Paraguay to war against its three neighbors.

In 1860 Paraguay had a remarkably prosperous economy based on crops that the Guaraní Indian population grew. Between 1840 and 1870 Carlos Antonio López, followed by his son Francisco Solano, ran Paraguay as a dictatorship with republican trappings. Still, they had a modernizing agenda that included abolishing slavery, promoting literacy, building industries on a small scale, and creating a well-equipped military. Francisco López even visited the Crimean War front to get military ideas, and he modeled his force on the French army.

The War of the Triple Alliance broke out in 1864, when Brazil invaded Uruguay, inciting López's fears that those two countries in collaboration with Argentina would restrict Paraguay's access to the Atlantic ports of Buenos Aires and Montevideo. When López declared war on Brazil, all three of his neighbors did indeed gang up on him. Though Paraguay had an army of seventy thousand soldiers, by far the largest in the region, the alliance gradually wore down the country amid ghastly carnage. In five years of fighting, more than 300,000 combatants died on both sides, and in Paraguay invading armies slaughtered people indiscriminately, reducing the population by 20 percent, including the great majority of adult males. In the peace that finally came in 1870, the country lost large chunks of territory to the victors, as well as most of the economic gains it had made earlier. Thereafter, the economy became increasingly tied to foreign merchants, land speculators, and banks.

The Taiping Rebellion in China

By far the bloodiest conflict of midcentury was not a war between states but a volcanic protest of a people against its own government. Historians have estimated that the Taiping (TEYE-pihng) Rebellion of 1851±1864 cost between ten and thirty million Chinese lives, either in combat or from the disease and hunger that accompanied the destruction.

The Taiping revolt was the biggest of several popular risings that challenged the authority of the Qing dynasty in the nineteenth century. All of these movements grew out of peasant grievances over land shortages linked to growing population, price inflation, government negligence, and, in some areas, floods and famines. China's humiliating defeat by Britain in the Anglo-Chinese wars of 1839±1842 and 1856±1860 (see Chapter 21) exposed the empire's military weakness. Chinese of all classes also saw weakness in the growing numbers of foreigners doing business in the ports, in the degrading unequal treaties the Qing government had to accept, and in the opium trade, which debilitated millions of men and women while enriching European merchants.

Hong Xiuquan (hoong shee-OH-chew-an, 1814±1864), the leader of the Taiping movement, was a poor schoolteacher from southern China who had failed the Confucian civil service exams and could not get a place in the imperial bureaucracy. After reading bits of Christian literature, he had a vision instructing him that he was the younger brother of Jesus sent by God to right the wrongs of the world. He had only minimal contact with European missionaries in China, but he preached to aggrieved peasants an austere doctrine that, vaguely echoing European socialism, proclaimed the equality of men and women and the eradication of private property. He denounced female foot-binding, opium use, prostitution, and gambling, and he promised to stock public granaries for famine relief, which the Qing government had neglected to do.

In 1851 Hong declared himself leader of the Kingdom of Heavenly Peace (Taiping), which would soon embrace the world. Amassing a following of hundreds of thousands of Chinese farmers and workers, he and his poorly equipped army overran several cities in southern and central China, flattened opposing militias, and executed rich land-owners. In 1853 the rebels captured the northern metropolis of Nanjing and killed most of its inhabitants. Although government forces repulsed an attack on Beijing, Hong's army grew to about a million men and women and took control of seventeen provinces.

Hong ruled from Nanjing for a decade, but his lieutenants frequently quarreled. Little came of his radical reform plans. In the meantime, wealthy families and bureaucrats gradually organized opposition. In 1864 a Qing army retook Nanjing,

Qing troops attack a rebel stronghold at Tientsin. This image conveys the magnitude of the Taiping Rebellion, which resulted in huge casualties on both sides of the civil war. What elements of the painting suggest it commemorates a Qing victory?

killing about 100,000 beleaguered rebels. Hong soon died in mysterious circumstances. The end of the rebellion left China economically depleted and more vulnerable than ever to European political pressures. The imperial government had to defer to regional lords and officers to quell the rebellion and try to revive farms and cities. Consequently, the regime lost more of its authority over provincial leaders, a process that worked to the benefit of foreign merchants, who wished to be regulated as little as possible. Nevertheless, the revolt roused small bands of Chinese modernizers to search for new ways to strengthen the empire's defenses against European power and the gales of economic change.

The Great Indian Rebellion

In contrast to China, most of South Asia in midcentury was already a European colonial possession. It was therefore bound more tightly to the capitalist world economy than China was, a fact visible to anyone who watched raw cotton, opium, and migrant labor flowing out of Indian Ocean ports in return for growing volumes of European manufactures.

In 1857 local soldiers in the pay of the East India Company mutinied against their European officers, triggering a popular revolt that within a few months engulfed northern and central India. Mutinies flared in several towns after Indian garrison troops, or *sepoys*, refused to load rifles that officers had issued them because the cartridges were smeared with either pig fat, which Muslim soldiers would not touch, or beef tallow, which repelled Hindus. Behind this cultural complaint, however, lay numerous grievances over inadequate salaries, bad living conditions, use of Indian troops to support British conquests in Burma, and racist policies that permitted only Europeans to hold officer ranks. More broadly, millions of South Asians seethed over the company's rapacious taxation and its refusal to seriously consult Indians on any aspect of colonial policy. The revolt had no central direction, but rebel forces marched on Delhi and several other large cities, amid much burning of villages, executions, and other horrific violence. The company spent a full year suppressing insurgencies in several different regions.

The rebellion had long-term consequences for both India and Britain. Parliament in London dissolved the East India Company and assumed direct control over the colony, henceforth known as the British Raj, or ªRule.º The new British governors, or viceroys, initiated many reforms to strengthen colonial authority and internal communication, though not to widen Indian political participation. Reforms also encouraged more systematic exploitation of the country's resources for the benefit of European firms and a small sector of wealthy Indian land-owners and investors. The rebellion cost the British government millions of pounds and therefore hardened colonial resolve to crush any new insurgency.

The American Civil War

More blood ran in the American Civil War than in any other conflict of the era except for the Taiping catastrophe. Similarly to the situation in Germany and Italy before their unifications, the United States suffered tensions between those who believed concentrated power was the key to material progress and those who defended regional autonomy. In the first half of the nineteenth century the country had a relatively weak central government. The federal bureaucracy in Washington, D.C., was tiny, especially compared to those in countries like France or the Ottoman empire. The country had no integrated communication or transport system, not even a single national currency. Although Americans envisioned their land as a cultural community dedicated to republican principles, there were deep economic and political divisions. The most toxic of these centered on slavery.

On this issue the United States swam against the Atlantic current. All European states except Spain abolished slavery in their American colonies by midcentury, as did all Latin American countries except Brazil. In the southern United States, by contrast, slavery grew and spread. The plantation-owning class and its political allies played a key part in the industrial revolutionÐ not by industrializing, but by making themselves the world's chief supplier of raw cotton to both Britain and the northern states. Although abolitionism gained strong support in the North, southern leaders insisted that slavery was essential to economic growth.

The dispute became aggravated every time the United States acquired new land. In the space of fifty years the country more than tripled in size, acquiring the huge Louisiana Territory from Napoleon in 1803, adding Florida and land in the Pacific Northwest in 1819, and seizing millions more square miles, including California, in the settlement of the Mexican War of 1848. All these acquisitions raised the thorny question of where slavery should be allowed. Capitalist and political interests in the North perceived the west as wide open space for the throngs of new settlers from Europe. The army would deal with obstinate Indians, and towns and railways would rise up everywhere. This vision had no room for planters bent on locking up huge tracts of land to produce crops with slave gangs. Southern slave owners also feared that their workers would try to run away to new free states with abundant land. Between 1820 and 1854, Congress enacted a series of compromises that treated each phase of westward expansion as a matter of balancing northern and southern interestsÐ permitting slavery in one new state but not another. In the 1850s, political relations between North and South deteriorated steadily.

Opposing the extension of slavery, northern leaders founded the Republican Party. When its candidate, Abraham Lincoln, won the presidency in 1860, eleven southern states seceded from the union, joining together to form the Confederate States of America. In stark contrast to the 1848 revolutions in Europe or even the Taiping Rebellion, this revolt did not aim to broaden democracy or win social justice but to perpetuate black bondage.

To Lincoln, who had written that ªthat portion of the earth's surface which is owned and inhabited by the people of the United States, is well adapted to be the home of one national family,º the secession was unacceptable.[8] The war that followed, mostly a protracted Union invasion of the South, lasted almost four years and caused nearly a million casualties, including about 620,000 combat deaths. At first, Lincoln justified the war as a mission to save the union, not end slavery, but in early 1863 he proclaimed the emancipation of slaves in all the rebellious states, though not in slave

Freed slaves travel north. Copies of Lincoln's Emancipation Proclamation decorate the coach and serve as flags. This illustration appeared in a French magazine, suggesting that the proclamation attracted international interest. What events in French history might this image have brought to mind?

states that remained in the union. The proclamation encouraged slaves to flee to the North, permitted blacks to join the Union army, and roused livelier sympathy in Europe, especially in Britain, for the northern cause.

The Civil War showed on a far larger scale than the Crimean conflict the power of mechanized industry to wear down an economically weaker enemy, if not win every battle. The Union pumped vast amounts of capital into factories in order to produce arms, ammunition, food, uniforms, locomotives, and steel rails. The accurate, long-range rifles introduced in the Crimea were further improved, and inventors made early experiments with machine guns. The war produced great butchery on both sides, but it eventually exhausted the Confederacy, which depended heavily on European imports to sustain its fight.

Near the end of the war, Congress passed the Thirteenth Amendment to the Constitution, which ended slavery everywhere in the United States. Subsequent amendments granted rights of citizenship to all African Americans and the vote to black males, though another century would pass before these rights were seriously enforced in the South. The war also propelled the United States to the rank of a major industrial state. By 1873 only Britain exceeded it in industrial output. Finally, the conflict shifted the balance of power in the United States in favor of the central government. For the first time, it became a proactive maker of national policy, sponsoring a national bank, a common currency, a homestead policy for the West, broader education for the young, and a transcontinental railway.

• • •

Conclusion

In the middle decades of the nineteenth century, the transition from the agrarian era in human history, which lasted 10,000 years, to the fossil-fuel age, in which we now live, went into full swing. In the half-century this chapter has explored, world population grew by more than 20 percent, global GDP increased by more than 60 percent, and the value of British exports alone grew by nearly 1,000 percent. Changes like these inevitably had a radical reordering effect on the way millions of people worked, thought, and organized themselves. This was the first period in which mass, long-distance migration took place to supply the global economy with infusions of wage labor for thousands of new enterprises around the world. Also in this period, reformers worked out elaborate new secular ideologies to try to explain and manage a world profoundly different from the one into which they were born. Religious leaders brought their spiritual and ethical systems to bear on the same problem.

Throughout those fifty years, western Europe, the first region to harness the energy of coal on a large scale, accumulated scientific knowledge, technical power, and disposable capital much faster than any other region of the world, with the exception of the United States. After 1870, as we will see in Chapter 23, European states deployed their armies, engineers, entrepreneurs, and migrant settlers to dominate by one means or another a large part of the planet.

• • •

Key Terms

American Civil War 638
bourgeoisie 647
British Raj 660
caudillos 652
communism 647
Crimean War 657
evangelism 654

Great Indian Rebellion 657
Mexican-American War 652
neo-Europe 638
pogrom 639
potato famine 639
proletariat 647
revolutions of 1848 639

secular 645
socialism 646
Taiping Rebellion 657
Tanzimat 650
War of the Triple Alliance 657

Change over Time

1788	First European settlers reach Australia.
1803	Usuman dan Fodio launches Muslim revolution in West African Sudan.
1808	Wahhabi forces seize Mecca in Arabia.
1829–1852	Caudillo Juan Manuel de Rosas rules in Argentina.
1830	French forces undertake invasion of Algeria. Greece wins independence from the Ottoman empire.
1832	The British political reform act expands voting rights.
1839–1876	The Ottoman state institutes modernizing reforms known as the Tanzimat.
1840s	The trans-Atlantic slave trade begins a rapid decline.
1846–1848	Mexico under Santa Anna loses half of its territory to the United States in the Mexican-American War.
1848	Insurrections rock Europe in the revolutions of 1848.
1845–1852	A potato famine propels massive migrations from Ireland.
1848	Karl Marx publishes the *Communist Manifesto.*
1851–1864	Millions die as a result of the Taiping Rebellion against Qing rule in China.
1854–1856	The French, British, and Ottomans ally to thwart Russian expansion in the Crimean War.
1857–1859	Indian Rebellion against the British East India Company spreads across South Asia; Parliament creates the British Raj.
1861–1865	North and South fight over slavery and secession in the American Civil War.
1864–1870	The War of the Triple Alliance pits Paraguay against its neighbors in South America.
1870–1871	Italy and also Germany complete the process of unification.

Please see end of book reference section for additional reading suggestions related to this chapter.

23 Capital, Technology, and the Changing Balance of Global Power

1860-1914

The Ueno railway station in Tokyo, Japan, 1885.

Satellite photo technology has given us striking images of the earth at night. On a world projection, we can see the brilliantly lighted megalopolis that runs from Boston to Washington, D.C., and the gas flares burning in Saudi Arabian oil fields. If we look carefully, we can also see a single thread of light running almost continuously from northeastern China westward across Eurasia to the bright star that represents the city of Moscow. This long filament traces the line of the trans-Siberian railroad. It is visible from space because of the numerous cities and industrial centers that have grown up along it since it opened in 1903.

Steam locomotives, majestic train stations, and steel tracks running across continents are vivid symbols of the capitalist world economy in the second half of the nineteenth century. Railroads connected factory cities to one another and opened the deepest interiors of Eurasia and the Americas to mining and commercial farming. They carried peasant families by the millions away from ancestral villages to jobs in cities and on tropical plantations. Locomotives and steamships transported European soldiers to new conquests in Africa, Asia, and the Pacific basin. Almost everywhere that railways were laid, Europeans or Americans arrived to invest capital, introduce steam technology, and provide engineering and scientific skill. For a period of about seventy years, western

Europe, together with Japan and the United States, dominated the globe—militarily and economically—to an extent no empire of the previous five thousand years had ever come close to doing. These decades were, we might say, the "European moment" in human history.

In the first section of the chapter we examine the pattern of events that transformed fossil-fueled industry into a world-scale phenomenon. Between 1860 and 1914, factories multiplied in western Europe and the United States, and new clusters of industry sprang up in Russia and Japan. In those same decades, entrepreneurs in many other countries experimented with steam-powered machinery, though on more limited scales. According to one estimate, per-capita gross domestic product (GDP), that is, the world's total output of goods and services divided by total population, rose by about 18 percent between 1500 and 1820 B.C.E. but by more than 100 percent between 1820 and the outbreak of World War I in 1914.[1] Population growth worldwide continued to soar, a phenomenon made possible by continuous innovations in medicine, public health, and agricultural technology. Simultaneously, however, humans and their machines continued to alter and degrade the globe's natural and physical environment at a quickening pace.

The second part of the chapter explores the increasingly complex global network of communication and exchange associated with modern industrialization. Manufacturers depended on constant in-flows of food, raw materials, and labor from other regions. In turn, they searched around the world for buyers of their finished goods. The gap between rich and poor regions opened wider, and radical changes occurred in the way both city dwellers and rural people lived and worked.

In the third section we recount the era's most dramatic story, the armed assaults by several European countries, as well as Japan and the United States, on technically weaker societies, mainly in the tropical latitudes of Africa and Asia. This wave of warfare resulted directly from power rivalries among European states themselves, a competitive imperialism that began to accelerate after the unification of Germany in 1871. As military aggressions mounted, African and Asian peoples devised various strategies to cope with the invaders, some organizing armed resistance movements, others negotiating terms of submission. A few states managed to preserve their independence, but tens of millions of people had to accept new colonial masters.

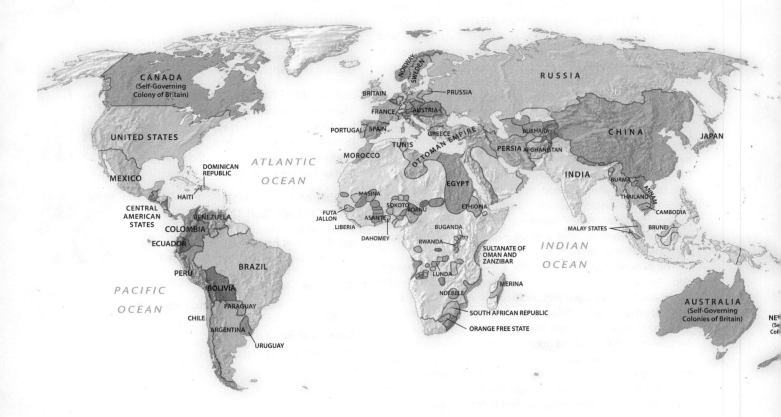

MAP 23.1 Major states, 1860.

From small kingdoms to huge empires, independent states provided the basis of political organization across most of the world in the mid-nineteenth century. What factors might help explain why in some regions several small states existed in clusters but in other regions single states spanned extensive territories?

The Spread of Steam-Powered Industry

FOCUS Why did industrialization projects have more success in some regions than in others?

Britain emerged in the early nineteenth century as the world's leader in steam engine technology. By midcentury the marriage of steam and coal transformed the country into an economic powerhouse. On the European continent, industrial hubs continued to grow and multiply. By the 1880s the United States became a major exporter of goods, and by the 1890s Russia and Japan joined the club of countries whose technical modernization produced strong economic growth. In fact in nearly every society with an agricultural economy and a relatively dense population, groups of merchants, officials, and intellectuals advocated for industrialization, even if circumstances prevented them from having much success anytime before World War I.

Wealthy Britain

By 1870 more than half the population of England worked in industry, though mainly in shops employing fewer than two dozen men or women, not in big factories. Late in the century, England remained the most densely industrialized region in the world, though its share of world GDP declined gradually relative to that of other, newer manufacturing countries. British business leaders, accustomed to the spectacular success of the century's first half, tended to resist risky new technologies. Consequently, the rate of growth slowed. Because of urbanization, the country also imported increasing amounts of food, which resulted in trade deficits with both continental Europe and big grain-growing countries like the United States.

British capitalists, however, did not worry too much about industrial productivity at home. Many of them made huge profits from worldwide banking and insurance services and from global investments in railroads, mines, shipbuilding, and other modernization projects. Industrialists also enjoyed special trade advantages. British factories exported massive quantities of cheap goods to India, an imperial possession. Like all conquering powers in history, Britain ran its colonies mainly to benefit itself. Official policies protected British manufacturers while inhibiting Indian entrepreneurs, of whom there were many, from building home industries that could compete with European products. After the first Anglo-Chinese War (1839±1842), British merchants also gained handsomely from the sale of Indian opium in China (see Chapter 21). Consequently, Britain enjoyed large trade surpluses with both India and China. This arrangement kept investors awash in capital and went far to compensate for the country's industrial lag relative to states like Germany or the United States.

Industrial Hubs in Europe and the United States

On the European continent, steam-powered industry developed mainly along an arc of coal- and iron-rich territory that extended from northeastern France through Belgium to Germany (see Map 23.2). Belgium was a densely industrialized country by 1850. France, which had a much larger peasant population and fewer coal resources than Britain, moved

The Krupp Steelworks, 1880. Companies specializing in heavy industry flourished in Germany after 1871. Why do you think Germany was able to excel at steel production in the late nineteenth century?

MAP 23.2 Industrialized and industrializing regions, 1900.
How does this map show that industrialization was uncommon but not unknown in colonial dependencies by the end of the nineteenth century?

at a slower pace than its northern neighbors. In 1870 it took a serious economic blow when it lost the Franco-Prussian War and had to transfer its iron-rich Alsace-Lorraine region to Germany. Nevertheless, new manufacturing enterprises continued to multiply, including a profusion of workshops that made furniture for export and, in eastern France, thriving silk-weaving centers. By 1870 the country had a national steam railway network that expanded to 25,000 miles of track in the following forty years.

German industry advanced rapidly after 1870, when political unification transformed a region of competing monarchies and dukedoms into a single state with an integrated economy. Exploiting deep coal and iron reserves, German capitalists invested heavily in steel plants. Their innovative technology steadily reduced the cost to mass-produce high-quality metal for rails, industrial equipment, and armaments. Germans also pioneered chemical industries, which fabricated synthetic dyes, chemical fertilizers, and dynamite. And they innovated in electrical technology, inventing the first industrially useful electric generator, or dynamo, in 1870.

The Netherlands, the Scandinavian countries, and some areas within the Austro-Hungarian empire industrialized

vigorously in the later nineteenth century. By the 1890s smokestacks also began to appear on the horizons of northern Italy and northeastern Spain. By contrast, western France, most of Spain, southern Italy, Poland, and the Balkan countries built few factories or rail lines. These were all regions having relatively few cities, small entrepreneurial classes, low levels of investment capital, and strong land-owning elites that depended on masses of rural peasant labor. Nevertheless, those areas participated in the world economy by continuing to produce primary commodities such as grain, wool, timber, and minerals for export to Europe's industrial core zones. They also contributed labor, sending millions of poor farmers and workers into the migrant streams to European cities or to points abroad.

More than twenty-five million able-bodied women and men streamed into the United States between 1865 and 1915, from China as well as from Europe, contributing to America's tremendous economic expansion in the decades following the Civil War. Northern manufacturers of textiles, steel products, and weapons rapidly expanded production during the war years. In 1860 the northeastern states provided jobs to more than 70 percent of manufacturing workers. But new railroads and river steamers carried job seekers west and south to Buffalo, Pittsburgh, Cincinnati, St. Louis, and Chicago, where workshops, factories, and processing plants turned out clothing, ironware, steel, furniture, lumber, meat, and hides (see Map 23.2). Fossil-fuel industry grew at an exhausting pace. For example, a huge plant that efficiently transformed iron into steel using the recently invented Bessemer process opened in Pittsburgh in 1881. It employed four hundred men working twelve-hour shifts without rest or meals. The owners of such mills maintained strong economic ties with European bankers and industrialists, who loaned them venture capital and helped keep them up to date on technology. The United States had plenty of coal and iron ore, and by the mid-1880s, it generated about 30 percent of total global industrial output, as much as Britain.

Smokestacks in Russia

Like the United States, Russia was a giant state that sprawled across a continental land mass. In 1870 its population, though overwhelmingly rural and mostly illiterate, was more than twice that of the United States. The government of the tsar (emperor) was rigidly authoritarian, permitting no national representative institutions. The small merchant class had industrial ambitions but remained politically weak. In these respects Russia resembled much of eastern Europe.

Russian rulers had long encouraged commercial ties with western Europe, and they supported military industries both to bolster the empire's international standing and to speed the conquest of Inner Eurasia. The government, however, kept a short leash on would-be industrialists, fearing that a strong private business class might challenge the aristocratic land-owners, who were the tsar's chief allies. Nor did the regime want a large urban labor force that might press for political rights or socialist labor unions, as workers were doing in western Europe.

In midcentury, however, Moscow's policies began to change. Russia's defeat at the hands of Britain, France, and the Ottoman Turks in the midcentury Crimean War (see Chapter 22) brought home the sad inadequacies of the empire's technology and internal communications. This realization triggered economic reforms. The government subsequently removed barriers to foreign investment, streamlined commercial laws, founded state banks, and began building railroads. Tsar Alexander II (reigned 1855±1881) abolished serfdom in 1861, but the state did little to help freed serfs acquire land of their own rather than work for low wages on large farm estates.

In the early 1890s the Russian government, not private entrepreneurs, initiated a comprehensive industrialization plan, imitating Egypt's state-directed though unsuccessful industrializing scheme earlier in the century. The tsar's economic architect was Sergei Witte, a man of merchant roots who took over the ministry of finance. Witte feared that Russia, an important grain exporter to western Europe, might slide into economic dependence on the big industrialized countries rather than imitate them. In 1899, he lamented, ª The economic relations of Russia with Western Europe are fully comparable to the relations of colonial countries with their metropolises. . . .º Russia, he declared, must not be ªthe eternal handmaiden of states which are more developed economically.º[2]

Under Witte's direction, Russia encouraged foreign investment and technical advice, and it poured tax revenues into steam power, mining, iron metallurgy, and mechanized farming. The trans-Siberian railway, Witte's favorite project, opened Siberia to large-scale farm and mineral exploitation. Russia's economic growth managed to keep pace with population, and by 1914, three million men and women worked in factories. Even so, the country could not easily catch up to western Europe or the United States because industrialization started later and from a lower economic baseline. In

Peasants in a Russian village. This photo from the later nineteenth century records the unpaved streets, rough-hewn timber houses, and poorly clothed residents of a rural settlement. Why might an image like this one have encouraged the Russian government to pursue industrialization?

1913 Russia's per-capita GDP was only a little more than a quarter that of the United States.[3]

The Meiji Restoration and Japanese Industry

As in Russia, Japan's governing elite looked warily at the economic power of western Europe and the United States. Its members fiercely debated the merits of a state-led industrialization campaign. The proponents squarely won the argument, but only after three decades of political struggle.

Since 1603 the Tokugawa shogunate (Chapter 20) had worked remarkably well as a semicentralized government carefully juggling the particular interests of several groups: the imperial court of the emperor (a ceremonial figure without governing power), the central administration headed by the shogun, the land-owning daimyo (aristocrats), the elite samurai warrior class, the town-based merchants, and the village authorities who spoke for the rural masses. By the early 1800s, however, the country faced grim financial problems. The remarkable expansion of farming that had characterized the seventeenth century leveled out in the eighteenth because the three big rice-producing islands had little virgin land left. The population of about twenty-seven million remained stable in numbers and highly productive, so living standards did not decline severely. Nevertheless, bad harvests occurred repeatedly, erosion and flooding took a toll, and silver mines and forests became depleted. The shoguns faced shrinking tax revenues, violent feuds among daimyo landlords, and recurring protests by land-hungry peasants. The Tokugawa also enforced a ᵃclosed countryº policy to restrict foreign trade and cultural contact. This strategy deprived Japan of profitable commerce with other parts of Afroeurasia. But it also shielded Japanese producers from foreign competition, and it kept European merchants from selling guns to potentially rebellious daimyo or peasants.

Foreign merchants and the end of the Tokugawa. By the 1840s the shogunate could no longer disregard Europe's expanding power in East Asia. When British naval steamers defeated China in the Anglo-Chinese War, Japanese officialdom reacted in alarm. Would their island kingdom be the next target? Just as defeat in the Crimean War stunned Russia's rulers, so the Anglo-Chinese conflict jolted the Japanese elite into intense arguments over the meaning of European seaborne power. Debate turned into national crisis in 1853, when the American commander Matthew Perry barged uninvited into Tokyo (Edo) harbor at the head of eight heavily armed naval ships. The shogun had little choice but to accept a ᵃconvention of peace and amity,º an agreement requiring Japan to open several ports to trade with Americans. Britain, France, Russia, and other European powers soon negotiated their own pacts.

The collapse of the closed country policy, coupled with continuing economic distress, exploded into civil war in the mid-1860s. A rebel coalition of daimyo and samurai warriors captured Tokyo, abolished the shogunate, and restored supreme executive authority to the young emperor, who had ascended the throne in 1867. This turning point became known as the Meiji (MAY-jee) Restoration after the emperor's reign name. However, the aristocratic faction that seized power, not the emperor alone, exercised political authority.

From 1868 to 1882 the Meiji rulers struggled to create an efficient centralized state. They terminated all independent authority of daimyo land-owners, and they sent legions of civil officials, many of them ex-samurai knights, to the provinces to regulate taxes and draft young men into a new national army. The leaders who favored adoption of European industrial technology and models of government gained full political control with the emperor's blessing. Japanese diplomats, engineers, and students began traveling to Europe and North America. As of 1875, more than five hundred foreigners, most of them Europeans, held advisory jobs in the Japanese government. By 1890 a large majority of young boys were enrolled in new public elementary schools, where they studied modern math and science. About 35 percent of girls went to school, too, raising female literacy rates much higher than in most countries outside of Europe and North America.

Factories and prime ministers. Meiji Japan soon joined the modern energy revolution (see Map 23.2). Engineers harnessed steam power to coal, iron, and copper mining. They built factories, mechanized the silk industry, laid rail lines, and churned out handguns, cannons, and naval vessels. As in Russia, the government invested in new technology, railroads, and iron manufacturing. However, private businesses, such as the rapidly growing Mitsubishi firm, also invested enormous sums in an array of industries. Agricultural production rose once again as the government streamlined land-use rights for peasants and introduced new machinery and fertilizers.

Japan went much further than Russia in experimenting with European-style governing institutions. In 1889 the emperor promulgated a national constitution that provided for a prime minister, a cabinet, and a two-house legislature comprised of an elective body called the Diet and an assembly of hereditary peers, like the House of Lords in Britain. The democratic base, however, was narrow. Only males who met strict property qualificationsÐ about 2 percent of the populationÐ could vote. Moreover, a tight oligarchy of wealthy men continued to dominate the Meiji regime. Even so, the government correctly guessed that a radical break with the past would encourage the European powers to respect Japanese sovereignty, rather than challenge it, as they were doing in China.

Between 1890 and World War I, Japan evolved an industrial economy that exported silks and other finished goods and that, like Britain and Germany, imported increasing amounts of foodstuffs and raw materials. Several factors encouraged Japan's sudden ascent into the fossil-fuel era.

Japanese school girls, 1905.
Both girls and boys benefited from educational reforms begun during the Meiji Restoration. What conditions in Japan in the late nineteenth century might have convinced the government to invest in popular education?

First, in contrast to Russia or the Ottoman empire, Japan was nearly homogeneous in language and culture, free of the ethnic tensions that might have stalled popular support for change. Japanese people almost universally revered the emperor, who gave his royal blessing to the modernizing program. Second, the population remained quite stable straight through the Tokugawa and early Meiji periods. Numbers began to rise after 1875, but so did economic expansion, which kept living standards up during the early industrial decades. Third, the samurai warrior class played a special role. For the most part, these nobles, most of them literate, had a value system that encouraged loyal service to people above them on the social ladder. Many samurai moved easily into salaried managerial jobs in the Meiji administration, national army, and industry. Finally, the American and European intrusion happened so abruptly, in contrast to the more prolonged commercial penetration of China or the Ottoman empire, that Japanese leaders had to make drastic choices with little hesitation. Thanks to deft policy decisions and large helpings of luck, the country transformed itself in barely three decades into a new center of fossil-fuel industry.

Industrialization on Smaller Scales: Gains and Disappointments

Elsewhere in the world, entrepreneurs and political leaders launched new industrial experiments, at least on a modest scale. The worthy but limited successes of these initiatives revealed the problems that could thwart eager capitalists in countries with relatively weak technological bases.

Internal and external obstacles to industrialization. In some countries, those in power failed to see any special benefit in encouraging mechanical industries as long as peasants or slaves provided cheap labor and the landowning elite made money exporting raw commodities and food. Also, potential capital for investment tended to pile up exponentially in the leading industrial countries but remained chronically scarce almost everywhere else. Another obstacle was unequal treaty signing: Militarily and economically strong states pressured weaker ones to open ports to trade, set low import duties, grant special privileges to foreign merchants, and in some places to give up territory, all without offering the disadvantaged partner much in return other than potential wealth for merchants and officials.

In this way strong states erected what historians have labeled **informal empires.** That is, Britain, France, Germany, the United States, and Japan used inequitable tariffs, large bank loans, and displays of naval power to compromise the independence of other states in order to serve their own strategic and commercial interests. By imposing such controls the industrial giants stood to dominate global commerce without having to take on the inevitably huge costs of invading and ruling countries whose economies they wished to manipulate. Although Britain conquered South Asia and France subjugated Algeria by stages, European governments generally preferred to exercise less expensive, informal influences on

> **informal empire** A situation in which a powerful state protects its interests in a foreign society by exerting political and economic influence but without assuming the costs of territorial control.

Turkish carpet production, 1910. Despite the introduction of some steam-powered textile factories, artisanal carpet production on large hand looms remained important to the Turkish economy. In this scene, workers prepare wool and tie knots of colored fabric. The finished part of the carpet is rolled up at the base of the loom. What might you infer from this photograph about the division of labor by age and gender?

weaker countries, at least until the 1880s, as we see later in the chapter.

Despite relentless big-power pressures, several societies with largely agricultural economies created small islands of industry. In some cases these experiments provided models for later development. Experiments in the Ottoman empire and British-ruled South Asia are two examples.

Turkish carpets. Even though Egypt's ambitious industrialization program withered, hopeful capitalists in the Ottoman empire started up new textile enterprises after 1875. Economic and political conditions were not especially favorable. Between 80 percent and 90 percent of the empire's population of nearly twenty-six million lived by farming or craftwork. Surplus capital was meager, and unequal treaties with European states allowed mass imports of cheap fabrics and other goods that the empire's artisans had once produced themselves. The state also had to pay interest on growing debts to European banks, expenditure that forced higher taxes on people who might otherwise have put capital into new businesses.

Nevertheless, small groups of entrepreneursĐ including Muslims, Christians, and JewsĐ imported European textile machinery, mainly to produce patterned, multicolored carpets that Europeans called ªoriental rugs.º These carpets had a large market in Muslim lands and a growing one among prosperous middle-class families in Europe and the United States. Ottoman manufacturers combined traditional hand-weaving methods with small steam-powered factories to spin cotton, reel silk, and weave carpets. They introduced new synthetic dyes from Europe and supplied weavers with ªcartoons,º that is, preset templates of rug designs that merchants knew would sell. Shop owners kept wages down by employing mostly rural women of little education. But even though this industry flourished, it remained dependent on European merchants for machinery and for carpet sales abroad. Moreover, it did not generate nearly enough surplus capital to trigger industrial production of numerous other goods. Finally, no energy revolution could have taken off in that period without huge supplies of coal, which the Ottoman empire did not have. At the end of the nineteenth century the Turkish economy remained overwhelmingly agrarian.

South Asian industrialists. Entrepreneurs in South Asia undertook some remarkable factory-building projects despite major obstacles. Unlike the Ottoman empire or China, India was not a sovereign state in the later century but a British imperial possession. In the eyes of British industrialists, the subcontinent's population of more than 250 million (compared to about 31 million in Britain itself) offered a huge captive market. India's handloom weaving industry, which had exported cotton fabrics far and wide for centuries, declined steadily as European merchants bought raw fiber instead, shipped it to home factories, then sold machine-made cloth back to South Asians at prices lower than locally made cloth. In short, South Asia experienced serious **deindustrialization** in the nineteenth century, trending from high to much lower textile manufacturing.

deindustrialization An economic process in which a state or region loses at least part of the capability it previously had to manufacture goods, especially owing to foreign competition or intervention.

Even so, Indian business-people continued to finance internal trade, invest in commercial land, and explore industrial possibilities. In the late 1850s, groups of South Asian and European entrepreneurs collaborated to start up steam-powered mills to make products that did not compete with British textiles, notably bags, mats, rope, and other coarsely woven products fashioned from jute, a tropical fiber. J. N. Tata, a Bombay (Mumbai) merchant who first made money with a cotton mill, founded India's first modern iron and steel plants. He traveled to Europe and the United States to study metallurgy, and after he died his sons and other family members sold shares of stock, mainly to Indians, to build a steel complex near Calcutta. The enterprise succeeded, and at the start of World War I, the Tata company was supplying tons of rail stock to the colonial transport authority. Today, Tata is a conglomerate of corporations and one of the world's largest steel producers.

Capitalism's Global Reach

FOCUS In what ways was the global economy changing in the later nineteenth century?

Few countries built large factory complexes in the nineteenth century. Rather, people took part in the industrial revolution in many different ways, producing food and fiber, working for capitalist firms, and consuming imported manufactures. Millions of people worked in steel and textile mills, but many millions more harvested grain, picked cotton, cut timber, or tapped wild rubber.

The Worldwide Communication Grid

In the first half of the nineteenth century, some economic thinkers in Europe feared that industrialization could sputter out because markets for manufactures would not grow nearly fast enough to keep up with factory output. Industrial overproduction had already contributed to short-term economic downtowns. The problem did not, however, reach crisis proportions in the middle decades of the century in large part because producers were able to cultivate new markets farther from home. Modern rail and steamship lines allowed cargos to move on regular timetables. This gave merchants and manufacturers more confidence to plan operations and estimate prices. Long-distance telegraph lines hummed with orders for raw materials, price quotes, and money transfers.

The United States, Britain, Germany, France, and Russia led the world in railway construction (see Table 23.1). Canada, Australia, and Argentina also built impressive systems, benefiting from European capital and expertise. In the United States, rail engineers joined the Atlantic to the Pacific in 1869; Canada did it sixteen years later. Private companies developed India's rail network, partly to strengthen British military control over the subcontinent following the Great Indian Rebellion of 1857±1858 (see Chapter 22). Rails were also laid in Egypt, the Ottoman empire, Japan, Algeria, South Africa, and almost all Latin American countries. By 1880 a person could travel by rail directly from Mexico City to New York. The opening of the Suez Canal to steamships in 1869 slashed trade costs by shrinking the travel time between Asian and European ports. In 1800 it took two years to exchange a set of business letters between London and Calcutta. By 1914 it took four weeks.

The age of undersea cable communication opened in 1851 when technicians sent messages over a line strung across the English Channel. After engineers completed a cable line

TABLE 23.1 **Lengths of Railway Networks in Seven Countries (in kilometers)**[4]

| Year | Country | | | | | | |
	United States	Britain	Germany	Russia	India	Japan	Argentina
1860	49,286	14,603	11,089	1,626	1,542	—	9.8
1880	186,111	25,060	33,838	22,865	15,764	—	6,500 (1885)
1900	416,461	30,079	51,678	53,234	40,396	5,720 (1899)	8,138
1910	566,099	32,184	61,209	66,581	52,767	11,479 (1914)	28,574

Inauguration of the Suez Canal, November 17, 1869. Ships powered by a combination of sail and steam—along with a typical Egyptian felucca with white sails—traverse the canal as spectators watch. What causal connection might you make between the advent of steamships and the building of the canal?

between Britain and Canada in 1858, New Yorkers held a public celebration. One banner proclaimed:

> MARRIED,
> On Thursday, August 5, 1958,
> In the Church of Progress,
> At the altar of Commerce,
> The Old to the New World.
> May they never be divorced![5]

This marriage, however, had a rough start because the line quickly went dead. Nevertheless, workers tried again, pumping in more powerful electrical current and inventing materials that protected underwater lines from corrosion and breakage. A new trans-Atlantic line laid in 1866 kept working. Four years later, British technicians connected London to the west coast of India, making it possible for an English mill operator to telegraph a cotton order to India in minutes.

Feeding Industrial Societies

As millions of people poured into cities in the later nineteenth century to work in manufacturing, service, and export±import industries, other people had to supply them with nutriment, including foodstuffs that offered simply caloric energy or a bit of pleasure. Farmers who lived close to burgeoning cities could not come close to meeting the demand, so food had to be shipped in from afar. Fortunately for hungry workers, the new steam-powered transport systems increased the speed and lowered the cost of moving grain and other foods from one part of the world to another.

Food from the neo-Europes. Urban workers in industrialized Europe wanted to eat wheat, beef, pork, and mutton, but increasingly these staples had to come from other temperate regions of the world. In the 1880s the United States became a major exporter of wheat and other crops. The grassy plains that stretched 1,200 miles from the Appalachians to the Rockies invited experiments in super-scale farming. Once the army drove Native American peoples out of the way and private companies built railroads to haul grain and livestock from prairie to city, commercial farmers moved in with the McCormick reaper and other mechanical devices. Flush with British capital, Canada followed the United States in mechanizing farming, mining, and transport. In the late century, investors began to exploit the grain, timber, and mineral riches of Canada's western territories from Manitoba to British Columbia. In Australia, stock ranchers pushed deeper into the arid Outback, displacing Aboriginal hunter-foragers to make room for millions of sheep. Climates friendly to wheat, sheep, and cattle spurred economic growth in the southern cone of South America. Between 1871 and 1915 about 2.5 million Europeans settled permanently in Argentina, many of them making their livings exporting wheat and beef from the fertile pampas.

Tropical groceries and drug foods. Foods that flourished in tropical latitudes, including seed oils, nuts, fruits, and spices also commanded growing urban markets. Most desirable of all were the ªdrug foods,º that is, pleasurable, in some cases addictive stimulants and narcotics, especially sugar, tea, coffee, cocoa, tobacco, and opium. Shipped in bulk from tropical plantations, these substances altered the dietary habits of men and women in every country where urban classes could afford them. A chronicler of nineteenth-century English cooking describes the popular new taste for sugar-loaded desserts: ªEven the plainest dinner served above

The benefits of sugar. In the late nineteenth century the Glebe refinery in Plaistow, a London suburb, manufactured golden syrup from imported cane sugar. How does this Glebe advertisement illustrate the importance of sugar as a product of mass consumption?

the poverty line was not complete without its pudding. Hot puddings, cold puddings, steamed puddings, baked puddings, pies, tarts, creams, . . . milk puddings, suet puddings."[6]

Tea and coffee mixed with sugar energized tired workers and helped restrain their thirst for rum or gin. Coffee houses and tea shops multiplied as gathering places for the middle and working classes. Consumption of tobacco and opiumÐ to relax the body, sedate the mind, or relieve painÐ also rose dramatically. British merchants gladly helped addict millions of Chinese to opium, a powerful morphine alkaloid that financed purchases of tea, Britain's favorite but much milder drug.

Capitalist farming. Merchants could meet soaring demand for tropical goods only because investors opened millions of acres of land to commercial farming. European and American entrepreneurs, often in collaboration with

Asian, African, and Latin American rulers and landlords, cleared great swaths of tropical forest and grassland for cash-crop production. To consolidate small properties into big plantations, entrepreneurs, often in collaboration with governments, bought up or confiscated peasant plots and required cultivators to pay taxes in money rather than goods to force them into wage jobs. For example, the government in Argentina and other South American countries allowed wealthy investors to buy up large tracts of prairie to produce food and wool for overseas markets. In South Asia, British colonial authorities encouraged wealthy individuals to consolidate land into big estates, which paid scant wages to men and women who had previously owned their own spinning wheels and looms. In 1869 the British cotton commissioner explained in blunt terms the objective of colonial commercial policy in one part of India:

> Now it is not too much to hope, that, with a branch railway to this tract, European piece goods might be imported so as to undersell the native cloth. The effect would be, that, not only would a larger supply of the raw material be obtainedÐ for what is now worked up into yarn would be exportedÐ but the larger population now employed in spinning and weaving would be made available for agricultural labor.[7]

Commercial crop enterprises expanded in many regions in the later nineteenth century, including coffee in Brazil, sugar in Cuba, cocoa in the Gold Coast (Ghana), palm oil in Nigeria, rubber in Malaya, and rice in Southeast Asia. Large-scale cotton growing spread from the United States to India, Egypt, Brazil, and eastern Russia. Land-owners recruited local peasant workers at the lowest possible wages or brought in foreign contract labor, sometimes from great distances (see Chapter 22).

European and American capitalists, supervising unskilled work gangs, built rail lines in countries that produced tropical exports, though mainly to siphon commodities to seaports and waiting ships, not to help the countries integrate economically. Profits from these lines went to investors and local elites. This happened, for example, in Mexico, where the authoritarian president Porfirio Díaz (who ruled most of the time from 1876 to 1910) extended the country's rail network to 15,000 miles by 1911. Diaz talked of unifying the Mexican nation, but in league with foreign bankers and engineers, he aimed first to streamline the export of copper, lead, zinc, and a range of tropical crops to the benefit of investors, wealthy Mexican families, and the state.

Farmers in debt. The movement of once self-sufficient farmers into agricultural wage work often led to impoverishment. This happened notably in the world's cotton fields. The American Civil War (1861±1865) drastically disrupted the southern states' export of slave-grown cotton. This development drove raw cotton prices rapidly upward. In India, Egypt, Brazil, and a few other regions where land-owning or rent-paying peasants grew cotton for the market, entrepreneurs with capital saw this price trend as an excellent business opportunity. They pressed independent farmers to grow less food for themselves and more cotton for the market. Indeed, millions of peasants took the plunge and initially enjoyed good returns. Between 1860 and 1866, cotton exports doubled in India and tripled in Brazil.

Families that grew less food, however, typically had to borrow from landlords or local moneylenders to pay taxes, buy seed and tools, and make ends meet while their cotton crops ripened. After the Civil War ended, American cotton production revived quickly and world prices plummeted. Small cotton farmers everywhere found themselves spiraling into debt. If they could not meet their obligations year after year, they became **debt peons,** men and women destined to perform agricultural or other wage work and make regular debt payments for the rest of their lives. In the later nineteenth century, millions of farmers in India, Egypt, Latin America, and the southern United States harvested cotton or other crops for the global market whether they wanted to or not.

debt peon A laborer, usually on a farm or plantation, who works under obligation to repay a loan.

Rich Regions, Poor Regions

From the dawn of complex societies six thousand years ago to the industrial revolution, all agrarian societies had richer and poorer social classes. Typically, aristocratic classes enjoyed generous access to surplus riches, while farmers and workers had much humbler standards of living, whether they lived in China, West Africa, or Spain. By the late nineteenth century, however, disparities in living standards correlated with social rank not only *within* a society but also *between* societies in different parts of the world. Most notably, average individual incomes and life expectancies improved in the major industrializing regions faster than in countries producing only primary commodities. Near the end of the century, for example, an industrial worker in Berlin might expect to live around forty-two years, but a laborer in Bombay only twenty-eight years.[8] Farm families in India, China, and Peru were generally getting poorer, whereas farm families in France, Germany, and Canada were bettering their lot, at least a little. This widening gap between ᵃhaveº and ᵃhave-notº societies has confounded humankind ever since. Several factors contributed to it, some of them local but others of global scope.

World population growth. First, the world's population grew from about 1.27 billion to nearly 1.8 billion between 1870 and 1914. On a global scale, cropland expanded greatly as well. However, in many predominantly rural regions, notably in Latin America, poverty intensified because population growth accelerated but neither new land nor many labor-saving technological improvements became available. Consequently, living standards declined. Even so, chronic impoverishment cannot be attributed simply to

ᵃoverpopulation.º In China, for example, living standards generally fell even though the country's overall population grew only moderately between 1870 and 1913.

An uneven playing field. The buildup of investment capital, technical skill, and military power in the industrializing countries gave them a powerful advantage over nonindustrialized countries. They could drive out local industries by importing their own cheap goods, depress local wages by introducing foreign migrant workers, or apply political pressure to force down tariffsÐ all of which hurt the weaker country's economy. These arrangements rigged the system, as it were, making it profoundly difficult for nonindustrializing states to diversify their economies, especially when their own affluent class colluded with Western capitalists to accumulate wealth. In Mexico, for example, the real wages of ordinary men and women fell throughout the thirty-four years that Díaz ruled, whereas foreign investors and two hundred elite families amassed about 50 percent of the land.

Ups and downs in the global economy. Under the biological old regime, that is, the world before the modern energy revolution, economic well-being in all agrarian lands depended on the quality of annual harvests, which depended on natural and social conditionsÐ weather, natural disasters, social stability, foreign invasion, and so on. However, as countries industrialized and global trade surged, world economic conditions became more vulnerable to what economists began to call **business cycles.** These fluctuations in production, consumption, and trade were related to changing balances between industrial output of goods and consumer demand for them. They might last anywhere from a few months to several years. Also, the greater global economic integration ensured that a downturn in one part of the world might affect growth in other regions as well.

business cycle A sequence of economic activity typically characterized by recession, recovery, growth, and repeated recession.

In 1873, for example, a severe depression spread around the world, and commodity prices plunged. Company financial shares plummeted, railroads went bankrupt, and iron mills shut down. To reduce costs, both factory owners and commodity producers cut wages. Landholding peasants lost income when prices fell. Indeed, prices for cotton, sugar, tea, and other tropical merchandise remained depressed for nearly a quarter-century. The world economy shifted into a new expansive phase only in 1896, but by then more of the world's population than ever had become locked into long-term poverty.

Deforestation and drought. A final factor in the growing gap between rich and poor regions was environmental change. In the nineteenth century, humans dramatically accelerated their efforts to burn and clear forests to supply

A family starving during an El Niño famine in India. In periods of drought, people suffered especially badly in regions where commercial crops had replaced local food production.

lumber and grow more food and fiber. In Brazil, coffee fields consumed immense tracts of tropical forest. In equatorial Indonesia, Dutch and other European planters and loggers eradicated millions of acres of natural growth. Deforestation profited some, but it also led quickly to soil erosion and exhaustion, which could mean diminishing returns on intense labor on both large plantations and small family farms. Governments and land-owners could have retarded deforestation if they had tried harder, and a few regimes, notably Japan, implemented serious conservation programs.

Global ªweather eventsº were another matter. At three different periods in the later nineteenth centuryÐ 1876±1877, 1889±1891, and 1896±1902Ð severe droughts followed by ghastly famines afflicted large areas of Asia, Africa, Latin America, and to some extent North America and Europe. These natural crises were associated with successive El Niño Southern Oscillations, the periodic atmospheric phenomenon related to a rise in surface temperatures in the South Pacific Ocean. A journalist described the consequences of the 1878 drought in Mogador (Essaouira), a city on the Atlantic coast of Morocco: ªThe pauper population of Mogador, always disproportionately large . . . is being rapidly increased by numerous famished Jewish and [Muslim] families from the adjacent districts. It is a fearful sight to see some of themÐ mere living skeletons. . . . They are selling their clothes and furniture to obtain food.º[9]

El Niño episodes were nothing new in history, but these droughts happened to coincide with decades when capitalists extracted larger and larger amounts of foodstuffs from rural lands. In South Asia, for example, the British colonial regime took the view that help for the poor was admirable but that nothing should interfere with commodity exports. Indeed, rail cars and steamships continued to load wheat destined for England as starving Indians stood watching. In Asia alone, the death toll from the three El Niño events reached twenty to twenty-five million. The famines also debilitated sovereign states, especially in tropical Africa and Southeast Asia, making them more vulnerable to the European invasions that, as we shall see, came in the late century.

The Lot of the Urban Working Classes

Laboring men and women around the world devised numerous creative strategies to improve their economic conditions. The later nineteenth century, especially following the crash of 1873, witnessed a rising tide of protest against low wages, urban squalor, and limited rights. In the major industrializing countries, workers marched and rallied with some success. Men in skilled trades like carpentry or masonry formed unions, and sometimes skilled and unskilled laborers joined together in the same associations. These organizations engaged in strikes, demonstrations, and political lobbying to get pay raises, reduce the workday, abolish child labor, and protect product standards. Many unions adopted Marxist or other socialist ideologies and bonded with socialist political parties. Others, like the American Federation of Labor in the United States, sought to improve labor conditions within the liberal capitalist framework. In Germany, the conservative chancellor Otto von Bismarck repressed socialist unions but at the same time lured popular support by giving workers benefits such as disability insurance and old age allowances. Nevertheless, the Marxist

Domestic servants at Pembroke College, Oxford University. Both households and institutional employers hired servants to clean, cook, serve at table, wash laundry, and care for children. What would you infer about the gender, age, or racial profile of staff members of this Oxford residential college in the late nineteenth century?

labor and political movement grew larger in Germany than in any other European country.

Women in the labor force. The number of women worldwide who worked in the wage economy increased dramatically in the later nineteenth century. In places where indenture, share cropping, or debt peonage were common, women often toiled alongside men in the fields, while also keeping homes, cooking, and rearing children. Men and boys predominated in plantation and mine labor, especially when workers had to migrate long distances from their homes. Women remained in rural areas, often on poor land, to manage small farms.

In Japan in the late nineteenth century, large numbers of young, unmarried village women went to urban factories to work long hours for modest wages. At that time women constituted a larger percentage of the industrial workforce in Japan than in most industrializing countries. In western Europe, by contrast, the proportion of females in factory work actually declined in the later nineteenth century. Women who went to the mills, the patriarchal argument ran, drove down men's wages, tempted men to transgress their Christian morals, and loosened traditional male control over wives and daughters.

In western Europe, male cultural and social leaders formulated moral standards generally characterized as ᵃVictorian,° after Britain's Queen Victoria (r. 1837±1901). Advanced technical and scientific educations, as well as most skilled and managerial jobs, were considered inappropriate for women, whom God presumably made intellectually and emotionally weaker than men. By contrast, nationalist ideology awarded high cultural status to motherhood because women had the sacred responsibility to produce and educate future citizens. Western employers who hired women in skilled jobs sometimes simply redefined those positions as ᵃunskilled° in order to reduce wages. An array of occupations were socially ᵃgendered° to permit women to take them: primary school teaching, domestic service, sewing machine operation, and retail work as ᵃshop girls.° Thousands of other jobs were gendered ᵃmen only° irrespective of the physical demands.

Outlines of a global middle class. In today's world, the vast majority of people in industrialized countries identify themselves as members of the ᵃmiddle class.° In general terms, this means that they have, or aspire to have, sufficient income to enjoy the basic benefits of consumer societyÐ comfortable homes, automobiles, electronic gear, access to education, and so on. In less economically developed countries, the self-defining middle class may be much smaller but typically has similar expectations. This class has generally defined itself socially as occupying a rung *below* both the aristocratic land-owning class and the ᵃhigh bourgeoisie° that made fortunes in commerce and industry. It ranked itself *above* those who worked with their hands, had little education, or occupied the margins of society. In Britain, one informal standard of middle-class membership was having the resources to employ servants rather than to be one. Typically, the middle class embraced lawyers, doctors, scientists, engineers, teachers, journalists, civil servants, midlevel managers, and business owners. In nonindustrialized countries, merchants, professionals, educators, intellectuals, and government employees defined relatively small middle classes.

Certain characteristics of the nineteenth-century global middle class stand out. First, the industrial revolution required many more people with specialized skills and advanced education, far more than the world had ever needed before relative to total population. Second, middle-class men and women lived mostly in cities because that is where the businesses, legal offices, schools, and newspapers were. This was as true of Bombay, Constantinople (Istanbul), and Mexico City as it was of London or New York. City-dwelling middle classes around the world began to think of themselves as ᵃmodern,° that is, as the sector of society that aspired to particular standards of material ownership, dress, cuisine, and leisure activity. Third, the global balance of wealth and power tipped so far to the side of western Europe in the later nineteenth century that Europeans won the privilege, at least for a time, of setting the rules of how ᵃmodern° people should look, act, and think. Wherever Europeans traveled outside Europe, they took with them their Victorian values,

liberal or socialist ideas, and distinctive wardrobes. At the same time, more Japanese, Turks, Indians, and Mexicans from moneyed families journeyed to European or American cities, which showed them models for modern living.

Middle groups everywhere tended to accept the symbols and badges of modernity that Europeans set. Men in Buenos Aires, Alexandria, Tokyo, and Chicago all sported the same suits and top hats as Londoners and Parisians. Designed to express the wearer's industriousness and self-discipline, these were drab, functional garments. Middle-class men and women from Caracas to Hong Kong gathered in coffee houses and tea shops to talk art and politics; they took up sports like lawn tennis and cricket; and they made an effort to learn French or English, the languages of international prestige. Women of affluent modernizing families, notably in Japan and Latin America, hung European paintings on their walls, accompanied their husbands to the opera, and wedged themselves into whalebone corsets. Middle classes everywhere read newspapers to keep up with national and global events.

Urban middle classes around the world, though still a small minority of global population, acquired a certain uniformity of outlook and style. This cultural conversion, however, had limits. Witnessing Europe's mounting economic

The Monkey Show. The artist Kinkichiro Honda published cartoons in influential Japanese newspapers. This one is captioned, "All the monkeys dressed in European style, and in every respect trying to ape Foreigners." What broad developments in Japan might account for Honda's lampooning of the Japanese adoption of Western dress?

and military aggression in the world, many young modernizers sought a middle road between overt cultural ᵃwesternization° and reaffirmation of their native country's values and customs. In Japan, for example, young urban sophisticates indulged in a ᵃWestern craze° in the 1880s, reading European literature and sporting European waistcoats and hoop skirts. Within a decade, however, the cultural pendulum swung part way back toward traditional Japanese styles as people gained confidence in modifying Western ways to suit Japanese life. In the Ottoman empire, many modern-minded men adopted European dress, but they exchanged their traditional turbans for the conical, flat-topped North African fez, not the European top hat.

Globalizing Business, Technology, and Science

The global middle class rose in sync with both big business and highly organized scientific research. Modern industries required larger and more complex business organizations than the international trading firms of earlier centuries. Companies hoping to become major players had to structure themselves to handle complicated technologies, mass output, huge fixed expenses, and simultaneous manufacture of several different product lines. Investments, especially in heavy industries like steel or chemicals, also grew to unprecedented levels.

The managers of companies were less likely to be the owners along with their sons, brothers, and uncles than salaried executives directing a hierarchy of accountants, engineers, and laborers. Many successful family-owned businesses were incorporated and thereafter dominated by wealthy shareholders. Companies sometimes combined their businesses to form cartels or trusts, organizations that pooled huge amounts of capital and sometimes colluded to keep prices high and discourage newcomers from entering the competition. This trend toward greater economic concentration continued into the twentieth century, although some governments, such as the United States under President Theodore Roosevelt, took action to stop monopolistic abuses that artificially jacked up prices.

Some corporations moved to control all stages of production from extraction of raw materials through manufacturing to marketing. To do this, they had to control operations in multiple locations, sometimes in several different countries. For example, the firm founded by Friedrich Krupp in 1811 and passed on to his son Alfred (who started running it in 1826 at the tender age of fourteen) rose to loom over the German metallurgical industry, producing guns, naval ships, and numerous consumer products. At the time of Alfred Krupp's death in 1887, the company employed twenty-one thousand people and had sold military wares to forty-six countries.

Scientists in Europe and the United States made startling advances in both theoretical and applied fields in the later nineteenth century. Physics emerged as a distinct modern discipline in the 1840s with the discovery of the laws of thermodynamics, which describe the behavior of energy. In chemistry, scholars widely accepted the theory that atoms were primary chemical units and cells the basic building blocks of organic life. The Russian chemist Dmitri Mendeleev arranged the sixty-three known elements into the periodic table while also predicting that more elements would be discovered. In biology the germ theory of disease, associated notably with the French scientist Louis Pasteur, produced many beneficial applications to public health. In *The Origin of Species*, published in 1859, Charles Darwin proposed that life-forms are not fixed but evolving and that evolution occurs through the process of natural selection. Darwin argued that animal and plant species exhibit subtle

Darwin's theory of evolution sparked great controversy. This Parisian satirical magazine was not alone in depicting Charles Darwin as a monkey. What point do you think the artist intended to make by showing Darwin hanging from "the tree of science"?

differences and that competition for survival among species selects for any small genetic advantage. That advantage is then passed on to offspring. This revolutionary idea sent tremors through the scientific world and triggered intense public controversy over the notion that human beings share a common natural history with all animals, from apes to the simplest organisms.

More than ever, scientific discoveries depended not only on ingenious minds but also on systematic organization and partnership. In the early industrial era, technical entrepreneurs and scientists exchanged ideas, but their networks were informal and scattered. Practical inventors and engineers rarely had much formal education. Consequently, steam-powered machines were churning out finished goods decades before any theoretical scientist figured out why those contrivances actually worked. After 1850, however, scientists and practical technologists began to work together more methodically, setting up organizations dedicated to scientific research and its applications. German universities, which were government-supported institutions, took the lead in founding academic departments specifically for new scientific disciplines. Young scholars had to acquire formal Ph.D. degrees, and scientific knowledge was for the first time consolidated in textbooks. In Japan, modernizing educators founded the first universities in Tokyo in the 1880s, institutions that taught science, engineering, and medicine.

In countries where broad industrialization did not take place, modern-minded intellectuals nonetheless banded together to advance scientific and technical knowledge. In the Ottoman empire, for example, scholars translated hundreds of European scientific and technical works into Turkish or Arabic. New European-style schools and technical institutes adopted Turkish editions of textbooks in medicine, mathematics, chemistry, and other disciplines. In China, scholar-bureaucrats of the Confucian tradition resisted newfangled scientific theories, but independent Chinese thinkers collaborated with Protestant missionaries from Europe and the United States to translate scientific texts and promote modern curriculum in mission schools.

Starting about 1850, European governments and big businesses discovered the benefits of putting scientific minds to work in the service of economic growth. German universities were the first to collaborate with private industries to found research laboratories. Big companies also created their own research centers. In 1874, for example, the Friedrich Bayer Company, a German manufacturer of chemicals, dyes, and pharmaceuticals (including Bayer Aspirin), established a research division that eventually employed more than one hundred scientists. Two years later, Thomas Edison, a prodigious inventor, opened an industrial research laboratory in Menlo Park, New Jersey. Formal collaborative research also took root in Russia and Japan. In 1882 Russian scientists founded the world's first laboratory to improve the performance of railway locomotives.

European Imperialism and Popular Resistance

FOCUS Why did numerous societies in Africa, Asia, the Americas, and Oceania lose their political independence to European, Japanese, or American invaders in the late nineteenth and early twentieth centuries?

Over the course of four decades, beginning about 1870, the leading European powers undertook the conquest of most of tropical Africa, Southeast Asia, and the Island Pacific. Military forces under the command of European officers invaded and occupied about 18.6 million square miles, or 20 percent of the earth's total land area. The British empire alone grew from about 9.5 million square miles in 1860 to 12.7 million by 1909. On the eve of World War I, its colonial population numbered something like 444 million.[10] France, Germany, the Netherlands, Italy, and Portugal also waged wars abroad, either to build new empires or to enlarge colonies they already had. King Leopold II (r. 1865±1909) of Belgium carved out a private empire in the Congo River region. Near the end of the century, Japan seized Taiwan and other western Pacific islands; U.S. forces occupied the Philippines and Guam, as well as Cuba and Puerto Rico in the Caribbean (see Map 23.3).

Historians have conventionally labeled these aggressions the **new imperialism** to distinguish this late nineteenth-century surge of overseas conquests from those that took place sporadically in the 350 years after 1492. States that possessed the most advanced technologies and largest stores of capital assaulted and, in almost every case, overpowered societies that lacked comparable wealth or military tools. The states and ethnic peoples subjected to invasion, however, devised a variety of strategies to defend themselves and fight back. These ranged from pitched counterattacks and protracted guerrilla wars to mass flight and negotiated surrender. Whatever the indigenous response, the invading forces had by 1900 gained sufficient military control in Africa and Southeast Asia to start organizing colonial governments and extracting exportable resources.

> **new imperialism** The campaigns of colonial empire building that several European powers plus Japan and the United States undertook in the late nineteenth and early twentieth centuries against other societies, especially in Africa and Southeast Asia.

The Road to Colonialism in Africa and Southeast Asia

Scholars have dubbed the European partition of most of Africa a ᵃscramble° for new colonies. These assaults were indeed something of a free-for-all in the sense that seven different European states launched campaigns on multiple fronts in the space of five years (1879±1884). But the conquest

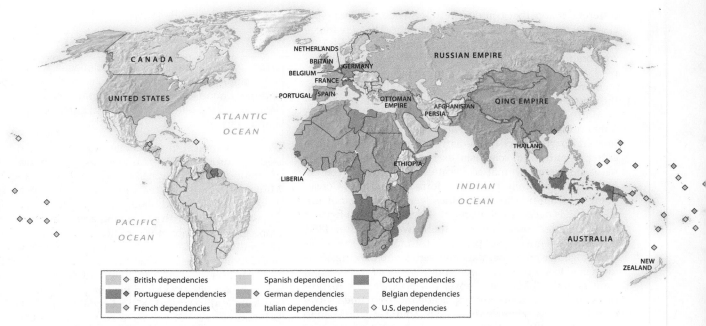

MAP 23.3 Imperial states and their empires, 1913.
Which empires had the largest territorial claims on the eve of World War I? Which states in Africa and Asia did not become colonial dependencies in that period? What geographical elements might help account for their success at preserving their independence?

period lasted into the twentieth century. The invasions typically involved fitful military advances in the face of resistance, uncertainty over strategic objectives, shortages of soldiers and supplies, criticism from the European home front, and gross ignorance of the people and geography of the territories being seized.

Tensions in Europe.

The multiple European invasions of immense territories in Africa and Southeast Asia had much more to do with international political relations than with well-organized plans to grab and exploit particular foreign lands. Those relations remained fluid and tense throughout the later century. The unifications of Italy and Germany in 1870±1871 put two large new centralized states on the chessboard of European power relations. Under Chancellor Bismarck, Germany expanded its industries faster than Britain, mass-producing armaments and building a steel-hulled navy. After losing coal-rich Alsace-Lorraine to Germany in the Franco-Prussian War of 1870, France under the regime known as the Third Republic (1871±1940) continued to industrialize and produce armaments in anticipation of taking back those territories. However, some French politicians, officials, journalists, and businesspeople, if not the public at large, thought new territorial acquisitions abroad might in the meantime shore up the country's prestige as a great power. As much as Britain contested Germany's armament, it also worried about French imperial ambitions. Britain and France remained suspicious of one another's intentions, and the absence of a formal alliance between them

served Bismarck's interests well. Britain also had strained relations with Russia owing to the tsar's expansionary drive up to the northern frontiers of Persia and Afghanistan. Britain regarded those countries as critical buffers against a possible Russian attack on India.

The economic depression that started in 1873 further aggravated European anxieties. It drove all the industrializing countries except Britain to raise tariffs, which helped domestic businesses but soured friendly international exchange. The economic slump also provoked the major powers to think about new outlets for capital investment, even though they had little idea what opportunities for it they might find in tropical Africa or Southeast Asia. Belgium's parliamentary government had no interest in overseas expansion, but Leopold II, the constitutional monarch, thought foreign conquest might be a good way to enrich himself and his royal house. He concocted the idea of identifying a vulnerable tropical territory, then sending a mercenary force to seize it and put the population to work to his profit. When he targeted the Congo River valley and its ivory and rubber resources without notifying the other powers of precisely what he was up to, he strained Europe's international relations even more.

Numerous individuals and private groups also complicated the political picture by launching their own projects in tropical lands and lobbying their governments to support them. These newcomers included trading companies, Christian missionaries, geographical expeditions, and a variety of adventurers looking for exotic encounters that might make for a best-selling book. For example, the Welsh-born American Henry Morton Stanley trekked through the central African rainforest with armed caravans paid for by European or American newspapers.

Annexation fever in Africa.

Political stresses in Europe probably made it inevitable that armies would be deployed. Between 1879 and 1884, the pace of events accelerated on several fronts. From enclaves founded in the time of the Atlantic slave trade on the West African coast near the mouth of the Senegal River, French marines advanced far up the Senegal valley, making commercial treaties with local African authorities as they went and without necessarily getting advance approval from the government in Paris. In North Africa, France invaded Tunisia in 1881, having already gained domination of that country's finances. Tunisia became a **protectorate,** that is, it remained a legally sovereign Muslim state but under French political control. In Egypt the government of Ismail Pasha (r. 1863±1879) tried to fend off European economic pressures by taking on modernization projects, notably the Suez Canal. But those expensive schemes resulted in huge debts to European banks. When Egypt went bankrupt in 1876, Britain and France took partial control of the state's fiscal affairs. Five years later, rebels under the command of Ahmad Urabi, an Egyptian army officer, tried to wrest power from Ismail Pasha's beleaguered government. In response, British forces moved in to restore order and defend the canal. As for Germany, its government had shown no interest in overseas colonies before France and Britain started making moves. In 1884, however, it sent armed expeditions to annex colonial beachheads in four different parts of Africa and in Oceania.

protectorate A type of colonial relationship in which a foreign power takes control of the top levels of government in the colonized territory but permits it to retain formal, if largely fictional sovereignty.

Because the European powers threatened to clash with one another over their new tropical conquests and claims, Bismarck called an urgent international conference in Berlin in 1884. The conferees managed to resolve a tangle of disputes over rights to territory, especially in the Niger and Congo River valleys, and to set rules, not necessarily followed later, for parceling out territories not yet occupied. A key agreement recognized King Leopold's right to penetrate the Congo region, his piece of what he called the ªmagnificent African cake.º No African rulers, however, were invited to the table. The conference mainly signaled to the world that the colonial starting gun had already sounded, though at that point Europeans ruled only a small part of the African land mass.

In hatching their invasion plans, the European powers had faint knowledge of the African interior or the commodities and markets they might find there. None of them, however, wanted any of their rivals to seize a disproportionate share of whatever riches might be discovered. Many European merchants and industrialists pressured their governments to undertake military campaigns, dreaming that precious metals and other bonanzas might turn up. Neither in tropical Africa nor in Southeast Asia, however, did much European businesses investment materialize relative to the huge ventures in Latin America or the United States.

After 1890, European military assaults on African societies intensified. None of the aggressors committed large numbers of their own troops to the campaigns. Rather, European officers usually led soldiers brought in from other colonies, fighters who had no fellow feelings for the people they were attacking. France dispatched Muslim Algerian contingents to fight in West Africa, and Britain sent Indian infantry to East Africa. In the Congo, mercenaries from several European states hired on as officers in King Leopold's private army. These soldiers-for-hire conscripted African men and boys into what was bizarrely called the Public Force, a virtual slave army charged with suppressing resistance and forcing Congolese to deliver quotas of ivory and wild rubber to the king's commercial agents. These operations involved sustained and horrifying violence.

Children mutilated by King Leopold II's employees in Congo. This photograph, taken about 1905, shows villagers who were brutally punished for not meeting their quotas collecting ivory or wild rubber. Mola (seated) lost both hands to gangrene after Leopold's henchmen bound them too tightly. Yoka's right hand was cut off to encourage others to work harder. Who do you think might have recorded these atrocities and for what reason?

Displaying unbounded hypocrisy, Leopold named his new colony the Congo Free State.

Conquests in Southeast Asia. European-led armies advanced into the interior of mainland Southeast Asia by fits and starts. In 1852 British troops invaded part of the kingdom of Myanmar (Burma) in order to shield India's border on the east. In the following three decades, Indian columns under British command penetrated the fertile Irrawaddy River valley and the neighboring highlands, finally destroying the Myanmar state in 1886. As long as it had Myanmar as a buffer, Britain made no serious objection to France's advances against Annam (Vietnam) and Cambodia, where it had long-standing commercial interests. The attack on Annam got under way in 1859. Despite military help from Chinese troops, the Annamese Nguyen dynasty had to accept a French protectorate in 1885, though local resistance continued for another fifteen years. In island Southeast Asia, the Netherlands had ruled densely populated Java since the early seventeenth century but secured control over most of the Indonesian archipelago after 1860. By 1914, Thailand was the only large state in Southeast Asia not under European control.

Japan and the United States join in. Japan confirmed its membership in the fraternity of industrial powers by seizing the island of Taiwan, a part of China, in the Sino-Japanese War of 1894±1895. In 1905 it fought a war with Russia, which we discuss in Chapter 24 in the context of events leading to World War I. In 1910 Japan invaded Korea. The United States joined the imperial club in East Asia because of the Spanish-American War of 1898. Rather like Germany, the United States seized territories abroad less to meet clear economic or security objectives than to enhance national prestige. It went to war with Spain in declared solidarity with Cuban nationalists, who had launched an insurrection against their Spanish rulers in 1895. The United States intervened, easily ejected Spain, then set up a military occupation and disbanded the rebel forces. Cuba became formally independent, but Washington exercised an informal protectorate over the country for several decades and permanently annexed Guantánamo Bay as a naval base. American forces seized most of the other territories that remained of Spain's five-hundred-year-old empire, including Puerto Rico, the Philippines, and the Pacific island of Guam. The war lasted just 123 days.

Imperialism in the Pacific. Although an interconnected Pacific world of commerce, migration, and cultural exchange emerged early in the nineteenth century (see Chapter 22), European powers showed little interest in seizing islands. There were a few exceptions. New Zealand, a destination of European settlers since the early century, became a British crown colony in 1841. Thirty-three years later Britain occupied Fiji, though many observers back home failed to see

what the benefit might be. Prodded by Catholic missionaries, France took Tahiti in 1842.

Wary of one another's potential strategic advantages, however, the major powers finally succumbed to annexation fever in the 1880s, hoping, as they did in tropical Africa, that the economic payoffs might be worth the great transport and administrative expense. Most Polynesian islanders lost their freedom sometime between 1870 and 1914 to invaders from Britain, France, Germany, or the United States. A few islands went to Chile, Australia, and New Zealand by international agreements, though no one asked Polynesians for their approval.

States that grew bigger. Because the story of late-nineteenth-century imperialism usually focuses on encounters between Europeans and Africans or Asians, we may forget that some powers simply extended their land borders and subjugated neighboring societies. Between 1864 and 1880, Russian imperial forces terminated the last independent Muslim states in Central Asia, the region of steppes and mountains east of the Caspian Sea. Russian engineers followed with railway and irrigation projects, and by 1900 Muslim laborers under Russian rule were harvesting large volumes of cotton for the world market.

In South America, Brazil claimed sovereignty over most of the huge Amazon rainforest. But the government largely left its Indian hunters and farmers to themselves until the early 1880s, when global demand for rubber propelled thousands of European fortune-seekers, along with the Brazilian army, much deeper into the river basin to collect wild sap. Nine hundred miles up the Amazon, the city of Manaus became the center of a widening circle of Brazilian state power and trade, at little advantage to Amazonian Indians.

In North America, Indian societies of the Great Plains began to confront wagon trains of white settlers moving into the region or through it to reach California and Oregon. Some plains tribes, such as the Omaha and Pawnee, farmed the land; others, including the Cheyenne, Oglala Sioux, and Shoshone, had nomadic economies centered on hunting buffalo from horseback. As white immigrants occupied more land west of the Mississippi and joined the hunt for buffalo (sometimes for pure sport), Native American groups had to compete more ruthlessly with one another for diminishing resources. As buffalo herds dwindled, relations deteriorated and violence worsened both among Indian tribes and between them and intrusive white settlers. In 1851 the U.S. government, aspiring to extend neo-European settler society into the plains, persuaded Indian leaders to agree to the first of many treaties that restricted particular tribes to defined areas apart from where whites intended to settle. Herding and buffalo-hunting peoples regarded such confinement as economically disastrous.

Sioux, Apache, and other tribes, however, resented this confinement and fiercely resisted it. In the decade after the Civil War, fighting raged between U.S. Army cavalry and

Chief Geronimo and other Apache warriors. Geronimo fought the U.S. army for forcing Native Americans on to reservations. This photo was taken shortly before his surrender in 1886. How do you think non-Indian Americans might have responded to this picture?

Cheyenne, Sioux, and other mobile warrior bands sometimes armed with guns. The army, however, advanced relentlessly, much of the time driven by General William T. Sherman's dictum that ªthe more we can kill this year, the less will have to be killed the next war, for the more I see of these Indians the more convinced I am that they all have to be killed or maintained as a species of paupers.°[11] By the late 1890s all but the most remote Native American societies submitted to the U.S. government and to life on reservations of marginal economic value.

Why Did European Invasions Succeed?

Whatever ambitions they might have had, European states would have had a hard struggle founding large empires in the world's tropical latitudes before about 1850. Dangerous disease environments were one obstacle. The lack of clear European military superiority over African or Asian societies was another. Both of these impediments were overcome in the second half of the century.

European health in tropical lands. Before the mid-nineteenth century, any European army that ventured into the tropics risked serious losses to malaria, yellow fever, or other diseases, as Napoleon Bonaparte's generals discovered when they tried to reconquer Haiti in 1802±1803 (see Chapter 20). Most Africans or Southeast Asians, on the other hand, did not suffer catastrophic mortality following contact with Europeans, as American Indians had in the sixteenth century. Over the millennia, most peoples of Afroeurasia had acquired the same biological defenses Europeans possessed for fighting major infections like measles, smallpox, and influenza. Only the most isolated groups, for example, hunters of eastern Siberia or Khoisan

herders of the South African Cape region, lacked those partial protections.

Starting in the 1840s, however, Europeans who went to the tropics began to live longer because of the availability of quinine. This medication, a substance extracted from the bark of the South American cinchona tree, offered significant defense against malaria. From that point, mortality from this parasite declined everywhere in the world where soldiers took quinine in proper doses. Also, tropical medicine emerged as a research field in Europe in the late 1800s, leading to advances that showed a link between certain species of mosquitoes and the microorganisms that cause both malaria and yellow fever. This discovery spurred campaigns to eradicate mosquitoes near military camps and garrisons, which drastically reduced troop death rates. Together, new drugs and public health measures permitted Europeans to penetrate and rule tropical lands without suffering disastrous disease mortality.

The military technology gap. European states dominated the world's sea lanes throughout the nineteenth century, but only after 1870 did they gain decisive technical superiority on land. Handheld guns of earlier generations had to be loaded through the barrel and fired one shot at a time. Tight discipline and synchronized firing maneuvers gave some advantage, but resisting populations had ploys of their own such as guerrilla tactics in forest or mountain terrain or skillful cavalry operations. For example, France invaded Algeria in 1830, but it took the army nearly fifteen years and tens of thousands of troops to break Muslim resistance.

In the late nineteenth century, however, advances in firearms technology multiplied. New handgun types had rifled, or grooved, barrels that made the bullet spin, a trick

The power of the Maxim gun. British arms manufacturers demonstrate the destructive power of a machine gun to Chinese ambassador Li Hung Chang outside London in 1896. Why would gun makers want to give this demonstration, and why would the ambassador be interested in seeing it?

of physics that greatly increased range and accuracy. Rifles that fired cartridges loaded at the breech, that is, the rear part of the barrel, came into wide use in the American Civil War and in European colonial campaigns thereafter. Single-shot breech-loaders could be reloaded in seconds. In the 1870s gunsmiths reduced firing time even more by inventing repeating rifles, such as the American sixteen-shot Winchester, which accommodated magazines, or detachable containers loaded with bullets.

The Maxim gun, the first truly effective machine gun, arrived in the early 1880s and thereafter served as the decisive weapon in many colonial encounters. In 1893, for example, forces under the British South Africa Company destroyed the powerful Ndebele (uhn-duh-BEE-lee) kingdom in the territory that is today Zimbabwe. One eyewitness described the effect of the company's machine gun on African resisters: "The Maxim gun far exceeded all expectations and mowed them down literally like grass. . . . The natives told the king that they did not fear us or our rifles, but they could not kill the beast that went pooh! pooh! by which they mean the Maxim."[12] In 1898 British-led forces invaded the Muslim state known as the Mahdiyya in what is today the Sudan. Sailing up the Nile on steamboats, British and Egyptian troops leveled repeaters, Maxim guns, and field artillery against a huge but poorly armed defending force. At the end of the key battle, fewer than forty soldiers on the British side lay dead. The Mahdiyya army lost 11,000.

In many battles in both Africa and Southeast Asia, defending forces had guns, often bought from European traders or sometimes manufactured locally. The problem was technological lag: Resisting forces could rarely acquire the most advanced generation of weapons that European factories mass produced and supplied to colonial regiments. Consequently, the imperialist powers enjoyed a large comparative advantage in military technology from about 1870 until well into the twentieth century.

European confidence and ideas of race. European states had the technical power to violently seize other peoples' lands. But since they regarded themselves as modern, civilized nations, they had to invent intellectual and moral justifications for doing it. The rationale for late-nineteenth-century imperialism, elaborated by scholars, journalists, religious leaders, and politicians, centered on the idea that Europeans possessed not only cultural but also biological superiority to the societies they were subjugating. The colonized, so the argument ran, were both culturally backward, requiring a higher civilization to lead them forward, and mentally deficient, requiring wise and intelligent caretakers to help them struggle into the modern world.

Historically, most societies have indulged in ethnocentric arrogance, regarding themselves as smarter or morally better than the folk living over the mountain or across the river. European cultural conceit was fundamentally no different. In the later nineteenth century, however, the language and methods of science were invoked to validate a claim that Europeans were innately superior to people who looked physically different from them. In the mid-1800s, some European writers pursued the notion that humankind might be subdivided into different biological varieties. These distinct ªraces,º they insisted, could be ranked on a scale of mental capability. Naturally enough, the people who proposed such a biological hierarchy placed themselves on the highest rung. Skin color, plus some other easily observable physical characteristic like nose width or head shape, became the primary determinant of a group's place on the spectrumÐ the darker the skin color, the lower the position on the chart of intellectual skill, moral responsibility, and cultural potential.

The intellectual movement to categorize human groups in this way is known historically as pseudo-scientific racism, that is, a view of human differences founded on misleading and phony applications of science. It was one aspect of social Darwinism, a wider European movement that played off, and distorted, Charles Darwin's theory of natural selection. Social Darwinists contended that dependent and debased elements of societyÐ poor people, illiterates, criminals, womenÐ occupy their inferior positions because over time they have exhibited less biological fitness than those who have had greater success in life, notably respectable, property-owning, white males. Pseudo-scientific racism thoroughly confused genetically inherited characteristics with culturally learned ones, contending, for example, that natural criminals could be identified by their low foreheads.

For European imperialists, dark-skinned peoples in places like tropical Africa had failed to create complex and dazzling technologies because their biological deficiencies trapped them at one level or another of barbarism. In the later nineteenth century, pseudo-scientific racist doctrine achieved nearly universal acceptance among educated people in Western societies. It enjoyed its widest acceptance in Europe just when the new imperialism was getting under way. In Africa and Southeast Asia, all victories reinforced European confidence in their biological qualifications for ruling the ªlesser races.º Only in the second half of the twentieth century did the absurdity of pseudo-scientific racism become fully exposed.

Resistance Movements and Their Consequences

Despite their lethal weaponry, European invaders tended to advance slowly enough to allow local African and Southeast Asian authorities time to organize armed resistance if they chose to do it. States that already had military forces and strong governing institutions stood the best chance of mobilizing resistance. Peoples having no central state organization, however, were also capable of rallying popular opposition to European intrusion. Even when combat failed, leaders could usually strike political bargains with their new rulers, who more often than not had fewer troops, weapons, supplies, and administrative personnel than they would have liked. African leaders sometimes negotiated political deals that allowed them to retain at least some of their traditional power and economic resources.

The East African empire of Tippu Tip. In the decades leading to the European conquests, many societies in Africa and Southeast Asia stepped up their involvement in international trade. This developments inevitably raised the stakes for political power. One manifestation of this competition was the emergence of new regional empires, states that used European technology, especially imported guns, to strengthen their rule and their access to commercial resources. In some places, therefore, fighting between regional rulers and Europeans took the form of rival empire building.

Hamid bin Muhammad, a Swahili-speaking ivory and slave merchant known popularly as Tippu Tip (ca. 1840±1905), carved out a large empire in the East African interior. Deploying soldiers, ivory hunters, and slave raiders armed with imported guns, he emerged as a potent political figure in the upper Congo River region in 1874. Swahili merchants and regional commanders reported to him in the framework of a loosely organized federation. From his capital at Kasongo, west of Lake Tanganyika, Tippu Tip fashioned a political administration, laid out roads and plantations, and monopolized the sale of ivory, which porters hauled to the Indian Ocean coast for export. He put thousands of captives to work as slave soldiers and farm laborers. Captive women grew food for his fighters. In 1887 King Leopold, whose mercenary army was just then penetrating the eastern Congo, tried to legitimize his Congo Free State by appointing Tippu Tip as a provincial governor, a position he held until 1891. He spent his last years in comfortable retirement in a coastal town.

Samori Ture and the French. In the West African savanna region, Samori Ture (ca. 1830±1900), built another sprawling empire. A member of the Muslim merchant class that dominated regional trade, he founded a state in the early 1870s in the region of modern Guinea near the headwaters of the Senegal and Niger Rivers. At first, this state was just one of several kingdoms that Muslim merchants organized to consolidate their domination of agriculture and trade. Samori, however, succeeded in seizing important gold fields and then used this mineral wealth to defeat competing rulers and incorporate tens of thousands of farming and herding peoples into his realm. He invoked Islam, still a minority religion in the region, as an ideology of imperial unity.

When Samori first emerged as a state builder, France controlled Atlantic coastal enclaves and a stretch of the Senegal valley. As French officers leading Senegalese troops pushed farther up the valley, military columns soon came face to face with Samori's cavalry. From 1882 to 1886 the two forces skirmished repeatedly. A master of mounted hit-and-run warfare, Samori harassed French troops and avoided head-on battles. Eventually, however, he diverted his army eastward away from the French to conquer new territory in what is today the northern Ivory Coast and Ghana, subjecting local rulers to tribute payments as he went.

Samori continually improved his arsenal of modern weapons, buying single-shot and repeating rifles from British

French troops capture Samori Ture, 1898. Samori (at the left of the photograph, facing the camera) resisted French colonial expansion in West Africa for more than a decade. After his capture, the French exiled him to Gabon, where he died within two years. Notice the presence of African soldiers serving in the French colonial forces. Compare the tone and character of this photograph with the one of Geronimo on page 685.

merchants based in Sierra Leone to the south. He also employed several hundred blacksmiths to make copies of French repeaters, while village women manufactured gunpowder. However, as French and British forces raced each other to seize more West African territory, Samori had to retreat even farther east. He had no time to consolidate a strong state, and his modern weaponry finally proved no match for French artillery and machine guns. His thirty-year imperial adventure ended in 1898 when he was captured and sent into exile. Where he had ruled, French administrators began to move in.

Resistance movements without states. In both Africa and Southeast Asia, societies that lacked central governments nonetheless found ways to organize popular resistance, often drawing on religious ideas. One example is the Maji Maji Rebellion in Tanganyika (modern Tanzania) in East Africa. There, German-led forces had barely established a colony when, in 1905, Africans representing diverse ethnic groups rose together in resistance. Priestly leaders of local religions inspired this mass movement by instructing people to drink sanctified water, which they claimed had the power to bind fighters together in unity and to make European bullets harmless. German commanders suppressed the rebellion with great brutality, but it took a year.

In Zimbabwe, known in the colonial era as Southern Rhodesia, an explosive revolt broke out in 1896. The Shona-speaking peoples were the largest language group in the region, but they were organized in numerous local chiefdoms,

not a centralized state. By contrast, the Ndebele, who spoke a different language, maintained a cohesive military kingdom in the west of the country. In 1890 Cecil Rhodes, the British mining magnate, founded the British South Africa Company to penetrate Zimbabwe. He aimed to search for gold and to keep that region out of the hands of Germany. Company troops defeated the Ndebele state, then levied taxes on the African population, recruited forced labor, and allowed European farm settlers to confiscate land and cattle.

Under those stresses, both the Ndebele and the Shona rose in rebellion. In a speech before Cecil Rhodes, a senior Ndebele chief offered his explanation of why this happened: ᵃI myself once visited Bulawayo [the British South Africa Company's principal town], . . . and I sat down before the Court House, sending messages to the Chief Magistrate that I waited to pay my respects to him.° The nobleman and his entourage waited throughout the day, finally sending word that his people were getting hungry. ᵃThe answer from the Chief Magistrate . . . was that the town was full of stray dogs; dog to dog; we might kill those and eat them if we could catch them. So I left Bulawayo that night; and when next I tried to visit the Chief Magistrate it was with my [warriors] behind me. . . . Who blames me?°[13]

Local prophets, who served as mediums for divine instruction from the high god known as Mwari, stepped forward to lead the uprising. These spirit mediums assured people that a new day of freedom would soon dawn. A network of mediums woven through both Ndebele and Shona

Contrasting Perspectives on War in East Africa

Between 1884 and 1907 the German invasion of Tanganyika in East Africa set off numerous violent encounters between the African population and the combined force of Europeans and conscripted local soldiers. Karl Peters, a fervent German imperialist, played a key part in the early conquering campaign, leading two armed expeditions to persuade African authorities, by whatever means necessary, to transfer their territories to German sovereignty. The first selection here is from a book titled New Light on Dark Africa, *which Peters published in 1890. He describes his dealings with the Wagogo people of central Tanzania and his methods for stifling their opposition.*

In some parts of East Africa, popular resistance to German rule continued for years. For example, the Yao, a people who specialized in long-distance ivory trade, fought for nearly a decade, village by village. In 1890 Machemba, a Yao leader, wrote a letter to the German commander who had demanded his surrender. The second passage is an English translation of part of the German version of the letter, which Machemba wrote in the Swahili language.

DOCUMENT 1 Karl Peters on the Wagogo

I had made up my mind to practice patience in this country to the utmost possible extent, to get through peacefully; but practically I could not help seeing how impossible it is to get on with natures like these negroes without recourse to corporal punishment. . . . For these people themselves it is much better, if they are made clearly to understand that lying, thieving, and cheating are not exactly the things that ought to be in this world, but that human society rests upon a certain reciprocity of responsibility and service. Beyond all question, that is the manner in which the way will be best and most safely prepared for the opening up of Africa. To make oneself the object of insolence of the natives is the very way to confirm the blacks in the lowest qualities of their characters, and especially to degrade our race in their eyes. . . . We were still sitting at breakfast, when some rascally Wagogo began to crowd round our tent, and one of them placed himself rudely in front of the entrance. On my requesting him to be off, he grinned impudently, but remained where he was. Hereupon Herr von Tiedemann, who sat nearest to the door, sprang from his seat, seized the fellow, and flung him on one side. I too jumped up, and called out to Hussein to lay hold of him, and to teach him a lesson with the hippopotamus-hide whip.

DOCUMENT 2 Machemba on the Germans

I have listened to your words but can find no reason why I should obey you—I would rather die first. I have no relations with you and cannot bring it to my mind that you have given me so much as a *pesa* [fraction of a rupee] or the quarter of a *pesa* or a needle or a thread. I look for some reason why I should obey you and find not the smallest. If it should be friendship that you desire, then I am ready for it, today and always; but to be your subject, that I cannot be. . . . If it should be war you desire, then I am ready but never to be your subject. . . . I do not fall at your feet, for you are God's creature just as I am. . . . I am sultan here in my land. You are sultan there in yours. Yet listen, I do not say to you that you should obey me; for I know that you are a free man. . . . As for me, I will not come to you, and if you are strong enough, then come and fetch me.

Sources: Karl Peters, *New Light on Dark Africa*, trans. H. W. Dulcken (London: Ward, Lock, and Co., 1891), 192, 215; ᵃ Macemba: Facing Invasion,° i n Basil Davidson, ed., *The African Past: Chronicles from Antiquity to Modern Times* (New York: Grosset and Dunlap, 1967), 357±358.

Thinking Critically

How do these two accounts differ in the way they represent hostilities between Europeans and Africans? How do they differ in the way the writer portrays his opponent? How might you explain these differences in attitude and choice of language?

---

society coordinated resistance. The rebellion shocked the company, which nearly went bankrupt putting it down. Reinforcements from South Africa and tons of weaponry finally exhausted the rebels, though fighting continued until 1903 at a cost of about 450 European and 8,000 African dead.

States That Survived

The major European states had the technical potential to take over any African or Asian country they liked. Pragmatically, however, they preferred in certain regions to exercise informal imperialism in order to restrain both colonial budgets and great power rivalries. China, whose internal

Chulalongkorn: Modernizing Monarch

King Chulalongkorn and the Thai royal family.

In 1868 King Mongkut of Thailand (r. 1851–1868), a man of broad scientific interests, traveled from the royal capital of Bangkok to the Malay Peninsula to witness a total eclipse of the sun. Among his entourage was Prince Chulalongkorn (Rama V, r. 1868–1910), his fifteen-year-old son and presumed heir to the throne. During the journey, both father and son contracted malaria, and shortly after returning to Bangkok, Mongkut fell ill and died. Chulalongkorn recovered, however, and the royal councilors ratified his accession to the throne.

During the first four years of his reign, Chulalongkorn deferred to his ministers for day-to-day government while he gradually recovered his health. He also continued his education in both traditional Buddhist learning and modern sciences, which his father had insisted he and his numerous royal brothers receive. The memoirs of Anna Leonowens, an Englishwoman who tutored the young princes in the 1860s, inspired the Broadway musical *The King and I,* plus three Hollywood movies.

In 1873 Chulalongkorn took direct command of his realm, determined, as Mongkut had been, to save Thailand from a European invasion. Mongkut had appeased Britain and France with commercial concessions and a cautious program to modernize administration and technology. Chulalongkorn understood as well as his father the political dilemmas the monarchy faced. If he moved too aggressively to modernize, he risked inciting entrenched elites and conservative Buddhist leaders to open rebellion. That might in turn provoke a British or French assault. On the other hand, if he did not modernize to the extent that those powers demanded, he might still come under attack.

For nearly a quarter of a century, the king and his ministers maneuvered the state through this political minefield. Gradually the king replaced the "old guard" among his officials with eager young modernizers, many of them members of the royal lineage. In 1897 he visited Europe. Observing that even industrialized England accommodated time-honored traditions, he gained confidence that Thailand could find a middle road between modern reform and its distinct Buddhist culture. "I am convinced," he declared in 1898, "that there exists no incompatibility between such acquisition [of European science] and the maintenance of our individuality as an independent Asiatic nation."[14]

In his final two decades, he stepped up the pace of reform, reorganizing finance, adopting a legal system based partly on French law, and strengthening central authority over vassal princes and provincial estate lords. He also built railroads, improved rice irrigation, abolished slavery, and organized a small but efficient army, all measures that stimulated the country's market economy. In addition, he used his diplomatic skills to play on the continuing colonial rivalry between France and Britain and to convince all the European powers that he ruled a progressive state worthy of international respect.

Chulalongkorn reigned until 1910, straight through the era of European colonial expansion in Southeast Asia. He avoided indebtedness to European financial interests, and at the start of the new century, Thailand had an economy strong enough to generate huge annual exports of rice, as well as an emerging national culture centered on reverence for the monarchy. Nevertheless, he achieved these successes at a price. Under British and French pressure, he agreed to transfer more than 175,000 square miles of border territories to colonized Vietnam, Laos, Malaya, and Burma. He also had to accept one-sided tariff agreements and privileges for European companies. In contrast to Japan, Thailand did not manage to ignite large-scale industrialization. Rather, it remained a commodity-producing country, its people's well-being dependent on fluctuations in the global market.

Thinking Critically

What factor do you think was most important in Thailand's success at remaining free of European colonial rule?

The Battle of Adwa, 1896. King Menelik II (bottom center, on horseback) is depicted leading well-armed Ethiopian troops, are firing both machine guns and rifles as Christian clergy look on. How are the Italians represented in this painting?

politics became increasingly tumultuous in the late nineteenth century, remained sovereign under the Qing dynasty as it had since 1644. However, the western European powers, plus Russia and Japan, held China in economic bondage through foreign-ruled ªtreaty portsº and outright annexations of Hong Kong and Taiwan. Similarly, the Ottoman empire preserved its membership in the European club of states through modernizing reforms and agile diplomatic footwork. Moreover, no European government wanted to see the monarchy that straddled the shipping lanes between the Mediterranean and the Black Seas become the possession of any single colonial power.

Ethiopia under the Solomonid dynasty was the only large African polity to keep its independence by defeating a European invader on the field of battle. King Menelik II (r. 1889±1913) ascended the throne determined to modernize his army and to expand the royal territory outward from the Ethiopian highlands, whose population was predominantly Christian. Acquiring breech-loading rifles, artillery, and machine guns from European merchants, Menelik built

a secondary empire, subordinating millions of previously autonomous farming and herding peoples to the status of Ethiopian taxpayers. But at the same time, Italy, anxious to join the ªscrambleº alongside the bigger European players, seized ports on the Red Sea and in 1896 sent an army ten thousand strong into the mountainous interior. Ignoring the fact that Italian traders had already sold Menelik thousands of guns, the invaders suffered defeat at the battle of Adwa (Adowa) at a cost of seven thousand dead, wounded, or captured. The Italians retreated to their coastal holdings, and Ethiopia, having proved its mettle to the other European powers, remained independent for another thirty-seven years.

In Southeast Asia, Thailand survived as a sovereign state by modernizing reforms and a series of commercial and territorial compromises with Britain and France. It also had the luck of being recognized by those two powers as a convenient cushion between Burma, a formal British possession after 1886, and Annam and Cambodia, which France made into colonial protectorates.

• • •

Conclusion

In 1800 the world supported at least several hundred sovereign empires, kingdoms, republics, and city-states. One hundred and ten years later, independent polities numbered fewer than sixty. This consolidation happened because so many states, both large and small, were enfolded into one European colonial empire or another. In 1914 Europeans or their descendants occupied, ruled, or economically dominated as much as 88 percent of the earth's inhabited land area. Moreover, Europeans continued to emigrate by the millions to temperate North and South America, Southern Africa, Siberia, Australia, and New Zealand, further marginalizing what remained of indigenous populations.

In contrast to states in Africa and Southeast Asia, three neo-European countries made strides toward political freedom rather than losing it. Canada, once a collection of British holdings, won its own constitution and full self-government in 1867. Australia devolved into an independent federated union of states in 1901, and New Zealand achieved self-rule in 1907. All three countries retained the British monarch as their head of state. In 1910 Britain granted South Africa self-governing dominion status, acceding power to a white minority population that progressively locked the African majority out of political participation.

The new tropical colonies, on the other hand, followed the pattern of India, where a small corps of alien administrators and military officers ruled millions with the help of European soldiers, technicians, civil servants, doctors, nurses, and missionaries. Once the conquerors quelled resistance, they governed, not through numbers, but through control of communications, cooperation from local leaders, and the abiding threat of violent repression.

On the eve of World War I, therefore, a thin layer of Europeans (plus lesser numbers of Japanese and Americans) claimed autocratic authority over more than 500 million Africans, Asians, and Pacific Islanders. In China, the Ottoman empire, Persia, and a few other places, Europeans did not rule but pulled the strings of international trade and finance. Even so, this global hegemony was more brittle than either colonizers or colonized could have seen in 1914. The acute tensions among the European powers, which colonial adventures abroad aggravated, burst into all-out war in the summer of 1914. World War I did not immediately bring down any overseas empire except Germany's. But it weakened colonial confidence and emboldened the colonized to mount new forms of resistance. In other words, not only was European world domination short lived, but it was never for a moment uncontested.

• • •

Key Terms

business cycle 676	Meiji Restoration 670	Spanish-American War 684
debt peon 676	new imperialism 681	Suez Canal 673
deindustrialization 673	*The Origin of Species* 680	trans-Siberian railway 669
informal empire 671	protectorate 683	
Maji Maji Rebellion 688	Social Darwinism 687	

Change over Time

1861	Tsar Alexander II abolishes serfdom in Russia.
1862–1890	Otto von Bismarck serves as chancellor of Germany.
1866	A trans-Atlantic cable line is successfully completed.
1867	Canada achieves self-government.
1868	Civil war in Japan ends under the Meiji Restoration.
1868–1910	Chulalongkorn (Rama V) reigns in Thailand, successfully maintaining independence from European powers.
1869	A transcontinental railroad is completed in the United States, connecting Atlantic to Pacific. The Suez Canal opens, shortening travel time between Asian and European ports.
ca. 1870–1898	Samori Ture builds an empire in West Africa, clashing with French forces.
1873	A global economic depression begins.
1874–1891	Tippu Tip rules in the East African interior.
1876–1910	Porfirio Díaz rules in Mexico, extending the rail network to boost exports.
1881	British military occupies Egypt.
1885	France imposes a protectorate on Vietnam.
1885–1908	Belgian king Leopold II controls the Congo Free State.
1895	Japan takes Taiwan from China in the Sino-Japanese War.
1896	Ethiopian troops defeat an invading Italian army.
1896–1903	The Shona and Ndebele rebel against British control in Zimbabwe (Southern Rhodesia).
1898	Mexico loses half of its territory to the United States in the Spanish-American War.
1903	The trans-Siberian railroad opens.
1905–1907	The Maji Maji Rebellion in East Africa pits a coalition of African groups against German-led forces.
1914	World War I begins.

Please see end of book reference section for additional reading suggestions related to this chapter.

The Promise and the Perils of Accelerating Change 1890 to the Present

part 7

The Promise and the Perils of Accelerating Change

1890-Present

Dubai's Burj Khalifa, completed in 2010, is the tallest building in the world.

We have taken the view in this book that human history is a story of growing complexity, both in the nature of interconnections among individuals and groups and in relations between people and their natural and physical environments. The pace at which humans have created and become enmeshed in new forms of complexity began accelerating faster with the fossil-fuel revolution of the eighteenth century. Today, the rapidity of global change sometimes astounds and bewilders us. The term *globalization* has entered the language to capture the idea that human society is continuously restructuring itself in all sorts of ways and that human interconnections are becoming continuously more elaborate and intense.

In the introduction to Part 6, we identified several complex historical trends that gave shape to the modern era and that have sharply distinguished it from the preceding twelve thousand years of the agrarian age. These trends of accelerating energy exploitation, population growth, technological innovation, human intercommunication, state power, popular political participation, and environmental change have continued into the twentieth and early twenty-first centuries. On the global scale these developments represent strong historical continuities—consistent patterns—from the eighteenth century to the present. At somewhat lower scales of change, turning points and indeed jarring breaks have been evident, especially in matters of political power, war, and economy. Among the globally dramatic *discontinuities,* we may count World War I, the Great Depression, World War II, the Cold War, the emergence of dozens of new sovereign states from former colonial empires, the collapse of the Soviet Union, and the Great Recession of 2007–2009.

Events like those turned the world in new directions and reverberated across the years. We should not, however, allow the momentous events and startling disruptions of the past 125 years to distract us too much from the deeper structural trends that have characterized the modern world so far and that shape our daily lives in ways that we may rarely think about.

■ Since the eighteenth century, humans have acquired an astonishing and growing capacity to control energy for useful work. The rate of energy consumption from fossil fuels and nuclear power soared in the twentieth century. According to one estimate, humans probably used more energy in that period than in all earlier history, and the rate of consumption continues to accelerate.[1]

■ The rate of world population growth accelerated in tandem with the energy revolution, reaching a historic peak rate between 1950 and 2000. In the new century, however, the growth rate has slowed, a change linked to declining birth rates in many parts of the world. In absolute numbers, population will continue to climb through at least the next century. However, if the growth rate keeps dropping, a major turning point in modern demographic history may be taking place, allowing humankind to remove population explosion, if nothing else, from the long list of ecological challenges it faces. The rate of global urbanization has dropped somewhat, as well, but people have continued to pour into cities. In the twentieth century the world's urban population rose from 14 percent to more than 50 percent.[2]

■ Technological and scientific innovations, including the new energy technologies, have continued to multiply in peace and war, good times and bad, since the 1700s. In the past century both scientific advances and useful inventions have come one after another. In the past thirty years the electronics revolution has reinforced and accelerated innovation in virtually all other technical and scientific fields. Human capacity to generate, transmit, analyze, and store information has been growing exponentially since the birth of the Internet in the 1970s. Is the world transforming itself into a single, immeasurably complex "brain" in which everyone and everything is networked together electronically?

■ Since the start of the modern era, the sovereign state has remained the primary structure for organizing and interlinking humans in large and permanent groups. Because of the power of nationalist ideology, people living together in states have, at least in some measure, come to think of themselves as sharing common cultural and social identity. The state system has remained fundamentally intact in the past century, but its character has been changing quickly since the end of World War II. The number of states in the world has grown by several dozen, and large overseas empires of earlier centuries have disappeared. Sovereign states continue to insist on freedom from external interference. But the international operations of corporations, banks, and nongovernmental organizations; the flow of information and money across borders; and the actions of ethnic nationalists, religious revolutionaries, and warlords within states have all contributed to erosion of sovereignty as people

a hundred years ago would no doubt have understood it. The number and variety of "political actors" on the world scene has swelled, and the state system is in great flux. In the past century, for example, states have taken on much greater legal responsibility for implementing and enforcing human rights.

■ Finally, the energy revolution, plus soaring population growth, economic productivity, and technical advance, have had the unintended consequence of seriously altering, in fact despoiling, the earth's geological, ecological, and atmospheric systems. The evidence of global environmental degradation became so apparent by the 1960s that people in a position to influence government policy and business practice began to sound alarms. An environmental movement took hold, and governments, corporations, and a variety of public interest organizations have taken steps to slow or reverse some forms of environmental damage to forest, soil, sea, atmosphere, and other living species. However, political and corporate resistance, as well as human tendencies to evade environmental challenges, have hindered progress. Furthermore, the world became environmentally conscious just when big developing states such as China, Brazil, India, and Nigeria started ramping up their energy use to compete economically with the older industrial powers of Europe and North America. Consequently, the natural and physical systems on which life depends have continued to deteriorate. Our species is faced with either restoring an ecological balance between human action and the earth's fundamental systems, primarily by developing new energy sources, or else retreating to lower levels of population and social complexity.

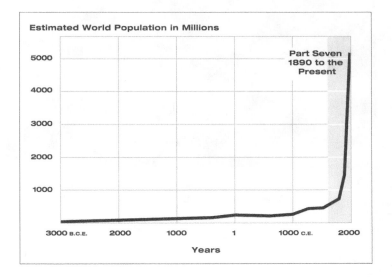

Estimated World Population in Millions

Part Seven
1890 to the
Present

Years

24 Innovation, Revolution, and Global Crisis

1890–1920

Telephone operators work the switchboard at the American military headquarters in St.-Mihiel, France during World War I. Gas masks and helmets hang at the ready in case of a German attack.

Most of us have become accustomed to communicating with disembodied computer voices on the telephone, often telling us to "hold." In the early decades of telephone communication, however, customers had to speak to a switchboard operator, who manually connected the lines between the caller and the other party. Operators wearing earphones sat at banks of switchboards plugging wires into jacks to connect calls.

When the first telephone exchanges were set up in the late 1870s, companies hired teenage boys as operators. Many of these lads, however, were not up to the job. They jostled each other, yelled into the receiver, insulted customers, and caused general havoc in the switchboard office. Firms then began to hire young, unmarried, reasonably educated women, and the job of telephonist soon became thoroughly gendered. Society came to define this occupation as naturally suited to women, or, more precisely, to middle-class white women without foreign accents. Females, or so late-nineteenth-century male managers argued, possessed certain "natural" traits that men were less likely to have: maternal patience, cooperative natures, devotion to details, and soft voices. Furthermore, phone companies, like most wage-paying firms, could get away with paying women lower salaries than men for comparable work. Switchboard skills became so closely identified with young women that the United States sent more than two hundred operators to Europe during World War I to handle military phone communications. Some of them worked near the front lines, where there were almost no other women except for nurses. In addition to the standard qualifications, these "hello girls," as they were known, had to speak both English and French.

The telephone contributed along with several other new machines to a huge advance in the speed and density of worldwide communication in the quarter-century before World War I. In the first part of this chapter, we situate this new communication and transport technology in the context of the sharp upswing that took place in the world economy in the mid-1890s, after more than twenty years of modest growth punctuated by recurrent recessions. Good times for well-employed and educated men and women, especially in industrializing countries and big commercial cities, inspired renewed faith in the power of science, technology, and capitalist enterprise to drive limitless material progress. On the whole, the gross domestic product of countries and regions worldwide grew spectacularly between 1896 and 1914, compared to any earlier era.

Chapter Outline

• • •

This boom, however, was severely lopsided. As growth *in general* ascended, the income gaps between the prosperous and the poor became wider. The second section of this chapter looks at the underside of prosperity and progress in the quarter-century before the global war broke out. Epidemics, famines, colonial exploitation, worker protest, and, in the first years of the twentieth century, armed popular rebellions counted among the distresses and upheavals of that period. Here, we survey revolutionary movements in Russia, Iran, Ottoman Turkey, China, and Mexico.

At the turn of the century, many educated observers predicted a long run of global progress and prosperity despite intense competition among Europe's Great Powers, plus Japan and the United States, to accumulate overseas territories and material resources. In fact, world economic growth aggravated rather than defused those rivalries, which after 1900 became increasingly toxic, rigid, and emotional. The last section of the chapter investigates the Great War, as people commonly called World War I. In the early summer of 1914, Europe's monarchs, prime ministers, and generals thought that if a general clash occurred it would be like wars of the previous half-century—localized, short, and not

A Panoramic View

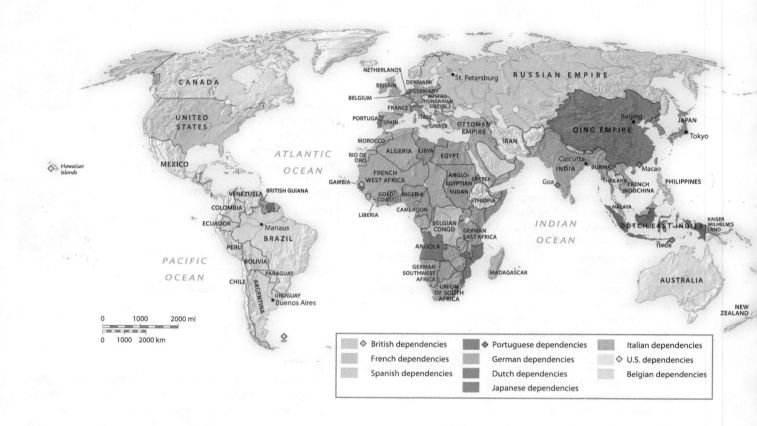

MAP 24.1 States and colonial dependencies, 1910.
On the eve of World War I, western European countries, the United States, and Japan claimed or administered large parts of Africa, Asia, and the Island Pacific. Which countries claimed the largest overseas empires?

unbearably expensive. Instead, the struggle lasted more than four years, took close to sixteen million military and civilian lives, aborted global economic growth, and spilled from Europe into Africa, Asia, the Americas, and the Island Pacific. In this chapter, we focus on the conflict's global dimensions, its relationship to industry and technology, and its immediate, largely disastrous consequences.

Turn-of-the-Century Prosperity, 1890–1914

FOCUS What factors might have accounted for accelerating global economic growth in the period from 1890 to 1914?

One of the ironies of the Great War is that the twenty years leading up to it witnessed unprecedented economic growth and a better quality of life for many millions of people. Accelerating economic growth has been the very *long-term* global trend during the past thousand years. But this general upward drift has been uneven. Since fossil-fuel-powered industrialization got under way, fluctuations of growth and recessionÐ what economists call ªbusiness cycles°Ð have followed one another every few decades. As we saw in Chapter 23, a severe recession in agricultural production and industry overtook the world in 1873 and lasted several years. In 1896, by contrast, a vigorous expansive phase commenced, and it continued without a significant break until 1914. Fossil-fuel industries in western Europe and the United States flourished and multiplied, corporate enterprises grew much bigger, and serious industrialization took root for the first time in the Netherlands, Scandinavia, Italy, Russia, and Japan (see Chapter 23). Urban workers in most industrializing countries enjoyed real wage increases and access to more consumer products from around the globe. In big cities from Chicago to Shanghai, new sanitation systems, wide boulevards, and mechanized transport improved urban living for many. Ornate railway terminals buzzed with activity, and affluent leisure-seekers escaped to distant spas and resorts. In Europe and North America the money-making classes fared so well that they came to think of the period as *la belle époque*, ªthe beautiful era° (see Map 24.1).

Commerce and Gold

The volume of world trade more than doubled between 1896 and 1913, increasing in value from about $8 billion to $18 billion. Western European investors moved mountains of capital overseas, some to tropical colonies but even more to Neo-European countries (the United States, Canada, Australia, and the southern cone of South America) to finance railways, harbors, mining operations, lumber mills, and factories. Companies could transport goods by ship and rail faster and at lower cost than ever before, partly because cheap coal fueled steam engines. Capitalist entrepreneurs and investors traveled the world seeking opportunities, and advances in telegraph, telephone, and undersea cable technology allowed them to transmit financial information from one continent to another almost instantaneously. The British economist John Maynard Keynes (1883±1946) recalled that in the years before World War I a well-off resident of London ªcould secure forthwith, if he wished it, cheap and comfortable means of transport to any country or climate without passport or other formality, and then proceed abroad to foreign quarters . . . bearing coined wealth upon his person, and would consider himself greatly aggrieved and much surprised at the least interferenceÐ He regarded this state of affairs as normal, certain, and permanent.°[1]

To smooth the flow of goods and money, the industrializing states took steps after 1870 to join Britain in pegging the value of their national currencies to a gold standard, that is, to a fixed price for an ounce of gold. Once the value of a currency was set relative to gold, it also became fixed relative to other currencies already on the gold standard. This system stabilized exchange rates among currencies. Consequently, prices for goods fluctuated less from one region to another, and businesspeople could conduct commercial transactions with fewer complications. The world's gold supply was ample owing to nineteenth-century mining rushes in California, Australia, Canada, Alaska, and especially South Africa. Britain, the dominant world financial power in the late century, largely set the gold standard rules, and other states wanting to carry weight in the international economy had to play by them. If a country subscribed to the gold standard, however, it could not unilaterally lower the value of its currency as a way to reduce the price of its exports and thereby increase their sale. This could present a disadvantage to poorer states dependent on exports of primary commodities.

Urbanization and Migration

Wherever populations became more involved in international exchange, towns and cities grew bigger. In 1900 the world had at least sixteen cities with more than one million people, compared to only four cities of that size a century earlier. Twelve of these cities were in western Europe or North America, the other four were Tokyo, Beijing, Calcutta, and St. Petersburg.[2] Cities that mainly channeled exports and imports through the markets and warehouses might grow as fast as industrial centers. Buenos Aires, which exported beef and wheat from Argentina and neighboring countries, attracted thousands of European immigrants annually. By 1909 it had 1.2 million inhabitants, a growth of 250 percent in twenty years. Some metropolises appeared out of nowhere. In South Africa, where prospectors discovered gold in 1886, the lonely prairie settlement of Johannesburg exploded into a city of 100,000 peopleÐ and five hundred saloonsÐ in a single decade. In the 1880s rising demand in industrial countries for rubber for insulation and auto and bicycle tires triggered a rush in the Amazon River basin to collect and export wild rubber. This bonanza converted Manaus, a sleepy Brazilian provincial capital in the depths of the rainforest, into a thriving urban center with a river port complex and a grand opera house.

The number of people who migrated long distances from home grew throughout the 1800s, peaking on the eve of the Great War. In the late decades of the nineteenth century, the great majority of migrants started from southern and eastern

Teatro Amazonas in Manaus, Brazil. This elaborate opera house was built in the heart of Amazonia between 1884 and 1896. Financed in part by the rubber boom, the building includes French roof tiles, English steel, and Italian marble. Why do you think Brazilians constructed an extravagant theater in such an isolated town?

Chinese and Russians transplanted themselves to farm lands and mines in northeastern Asia (Siberia and Manchuria). An equal number of people, mostly Chinese and Indians, migrated to tropical Southeast Asia.

Scientific and Technological Advances

International collaboration among private firms, research labs, governments, and universities continued to get more complex and to raise the scale of business enterprises. Scientists made new discoveries whose theoretical significance and practical applications would become fully realized only decades later. These advances included the discovery of X-rays, scientific proof that matter consists of atoms, and the early formulation of quantum mechanics by the European researchers Max Planck, Albert Einstein, and Niels Bohr. In 1909±1910 the German scientists Fritz Haber and Carl Bosch made one of the twentieth century's most momentous breakthroughs in chemical engineering by synthesizing ammonia on an industrial scale. This allowed nitrogen from the air to be converted into liquid form and processed into solid nitrates. This compound was used to make gunpowder and dynamite but also the nitrate fertilizers that hugely enhanced crop production and eventually revolutionized agricultural output in much of the world.

In the immediate prewar decades, communication and transport systemsÐ railways, scheduled steamship lines, telegraphy, and newspapers with mass readershipÐ became steadily more efficient. The invention of refrigerated steamships in the 1870s allowed plantation capitalists to ship tropical fruits and vegetables by sea, which opened year-round markets for such exotic fare in regions of temperate climate. Australia and New Zealand offered employment opportunities to immigrants to raise sheep and ship refrigerated mutton to English tables eight thousand miles

Europe, Russia, India, and China. Steadily falling transportation rates helped persuade people to seek better paying jobs abroad or simply to escape prosecution for crimes, political harassment by repressive governments, or, especially in the case of eastern European Jews, religious persecution. The United States and other neo-European lands continued to attract large numbers to work in expanding manufacturing industries. In tropic latitudes, plantation and mine managers needed continuous inflows of workers. Between 1900 and 1911, fourteen million Europeans migrated to the Americas, Australia, and New Zealand. In 1913 alone, 1.1 million

away. Between 1890 and 1910, for example, Britain, France, Germany, and the United States extended their combined rail systems by about 162,000 miles. Engineers laid an undersea cable from San Francisco to Sydney by way of Hawaii, spanning the Pacific with telegraphic communication. By 1911 Britain had a telegraph system that linked London with major colonial territories without having to use the wires of any rival states, thus ensuring the security of political and military signals. The Panama Canal, which opened under American authority in 1914 after ten years of continuous work, shortened steamship travel between the Pacific and the Atlantic by thousands of miles. Other technological innovations permitted both humans and their messages to transcend the limits of rails and copper wire and literally fly through the air.

Transmitting speech.

The telephone that Alexander Graham Bell invented in 1876 carried the human voice over a wire by converting it into electrical impulses. Early telephone networks linked offices, businesses, and homes in a number of urban areas. Phone sets sold fast in the United States, partly because people who did not have these gadgets began to feel disconnected from friends and associates who did. In the late 1890s the Italian physicist Guglielmo Marconi freed electrical communication from any dependence on wire by broadcasting signals on radio waves, a form of electromagnetic radiation. Marconi's work represented a fruitful marriage between science and technology. In 1887 the German scientist Heinrich Hertz demonstrated the existence of radio waves. Marconi built on Hertz's research to invent a practical wireless technology. In 1901 he transmitted a radio signal, the letter *S* in Morse code, from England to the coast of Canada. Within a few years, radio operators were routinely transmitting signals from ship to shore. On April 14, 1912, the British luxury liner *Titanic* struck a massive iceberg in the North Atlantic, but as it sank, its crew radioed distress signals to nearby vessels, bringing rescuers to the scene and saving lives. By 1915 scientists devised a way for electromagnetic waves to carry human speech. European states with overseas territories began to supplement their telegraph networks with chains of transmitting towers to link their imperial capitals with their colonies.

Preserving sound and motion.

While experimenting with telephone technology in 1877, Thomas Edison (1847±1931) inadvertently invented the first primitive phonograph, a machine that used a carbon stylus, or needle, to store replicas of sound waves in grooves on the surface of a rotating cylinder. Another stylus could then ªplay backº these tiny undulations by transmitting them through a sound box. A decade later, Emile Berliner (1851±1929), a German immigrant to the United States, invented a system for storing and reproducing sounds on flat discs, or ªrecords.º By 1915 the 78 revolution per minute (rpm) disc became the standard phonographic medium. It permitted complex and extended sound patternsÐ stories, lectures, political speeches, musical performancesÐ to be recorded, saved, and sent from one listener to another.

Like phonograph records, photographs captured immediate realityÐ a pretty landscape, the portrait of a monarch, a dead soldier on a battlefieldÐ and then preserved it for others to see. Photography was already a sophisticated technology in the 1880s when Étienne-Jules Marey (1830±1904), a French physician, invented a camera capable of taking multiple still photos at the rate of one per second. When these images were projected at the same speed, they created the illusion of reality in motion. Edison invented a similar camera

and soon thereafter the Kinetoscope, a projection box with a peephole that showed a short motion picture set to music. The first commercial Kinetoscope parlor opened in New York City in 1894.

The following year, the French inventors Auguste and Louis Lumière built the first lightweight movie camera and projector. The brothers recorded French daily life, filmed comedy shorts, made newsreels, and sent a team of camera operators around the world to show movies and shoot new material. In India, director-producer Dadasaheb Phalke made a full-length dramatic film in 1913, foreshadowing the ªBollywoodº industry that was to come.

The new communication media, together with the telegraph and popular newspapers, made it possible for humans to mentally encompass their planet on a scale never known before. The volume of information available even to people having only marginal connections to communication networks grew exponentially. Dissemination of sounds, photos, and moving images made access to information more open and democratic, first in the wealthiest countries, but soon in parts of the world where low literacy rates did not prevent people from listening and watching. Filmmakers also learned that sequences of filmed images could be edited in a way that stirred emotions, aroused indignation, or sold products. Political leaders used the new media to connect with citizens but also doctored speech and imagery to amplify nationalist feeling or ªspinº the news in their favor. In addition, governments had a harder time hiding wars, atrocities, and disasters from public view. In the late nineteenth century, for example, Christian missionaries

A scene from *Raja Harischandra*. Dadasaheb Phalke directed the first full-length Indian film in 1913, bringing to life a legendary Indian king whose story is recounted in the *Ramayana*, one of the great Indian epics.

Global influences in modern art. Pablo Picasso's large and daring oil painting, *Les Demoiselles d'Avignon* (1907), shows five prostitutes in intimidating poses not characteristically feminine for that period. Two of the women wear masks that evoke African art. Picasso's painting was controversial when he first unveiled it in Paris. Why might African imagery have contributed to emerging ideas of what was modern in the early twentieth century? © The Gallery Collection/Corbis © 2013 Estate of Pablo Picasso/Artists Rights Society (ARS), New York.

Motorcars and airplanes. Electrical communications permitted people to interact in real time over long distances without anyone having to go anywhere. The automobile and the airplane (along with the chain-driven bicycle invented in the 1880s), by contrast, allowed people to travel great distances even for work or leisure. Nineteenth-century coal-burning steam engines took up a lot of room on a locomotive or steamship. By contrast, the gas-powered internal combustion engine, developed mainly by German engineers beginning in the 1860s, could be made smaller, cheaper, and more efficient than conventional steam machines.

Just the names alone of technological pioneers like Gottlieb Daimler, Carl Benz, Rudolf Diesel, and Henry Ford signal their contributions to the manufacture of ª horseless carriages° with internal combustion engines. Cars and trucks, which most adults could readily learn to drive, liberated overland transport from both rails and timetables. Advances in petroleum chemistry, plus large oil strikes in the United States, Latin America, and the Middle East, sent the price of gasoline plummeting early in the twentieth century, making automobiles more affordable. Starting in 1913, Henry Ford deftly combined two nineteenth-century industrial ideas, the assembly line and the use of interchangeable parts, to mass-produce black Model T automobiles. Proclaiming that he would ª build a motorcar for the great multitudes,° Ford raised his workers' wages to enable them to buy a Model T, thereby creating a mass consumer market. **Fordism,** as it became known, involved hiring workers to perform the same specialized task over and over again. These men and women traded job flexibility and satisfaction for higher pay and

> **Fordism** A system of technology and organization, named after Henry Ford, which aims both to produce goods at minimal cost through standardization and mass production and to pay wage workers rates that allow them to consume the products they make.

the means to buy more manufactured products. Critics disparaged Fordism for chaining men and women to boring, alienating work. Nevertheless, motorcar sales in the United States, by far the biggest market before World War I, grew from 4,000 in 1900 to 895,000 by 1915.

Lightweight internal combustion engines also made mechanical flight possible. A petroleum distillate called benzine drove the propeller that lifted Orville and Wilbur Wright's heavier-than-air machine off the ground in North Carolina in 1903. It flew for twelve seconds the first time, then for longer intervals. Within six years of the Wright

serving in India used cheap Kodak cameras to photograph the ravages of famine, exposing the fact that the colonial government was doing little to relieve the suffering.

As speech, music, and imagery ricocheted around the world, people had increasingly to confront ideas and life ways different from their own. News photos, recordings, and movies amplified the trend toward cultural uniformity among the wealthy and middle classes, who adopted the fashions, music, and leisure activities they saw and heard about. New media tended to favor ideas emanating from Europe or North America because those regions led the technological advance. But cultural flows moved in all directions. West African sculpture informed the art of the young Pablo Picasso, for example, because he saw it at an exhibition in Paris, public museums being yet another growing medium of communication. In short, the cultural globalization that characterized the twentieth century got seriously under way when people thousands of miles apart could see, hear, and experience the same things nearly simultaneously.

Brothers' experiment, the French aviator Louis Blériot piloted an aircraft across the English Channel. By 1911 airmail services were established in North America, Britain, and India. Like wireless radio, the airplane eliminated an earthbound obstacle to communication.

Global Inequities and Their Consequences

FOCUS What social, economic, and environmental circumstances contributed to large protest and revolutionary movements at the dawn of the twentieth century?

The quarter-century before World War I was a period of global contradictions. The global economy became much larger and far more complex and integrated than it had ever been before. Tens of millions of people benefited from this growth, enjoying resurgent prosperity and new material wonders. But rapid economic growth and complexity also aggravated social stress and dislocation, and through these decades hundreds of millions remained poor or got poorer. The beneficiaries of good times lived disproportionately in the cities of industrializing regions in Europe, North America, and Japan. Elsewhere, the new affluence favored mainly elite property-owning classes who put themselves in positions to profit from commercial farming, import± export business, or compensation for services to European colonial masters. In some places, growing global trade benefited landholding peasants who sold surplus crops at prices higher than what they needed for food, rents, and taxes. More typically, however, farmers drawn into the world market found themselves prisoners to landlord exploitation, debt, price fluctuations, and cycles of bad weather.

Drought and Plague

An irony of late-nineteenth-century economic expansion is its correlation to natural disasters that took millions of lives and worsened poverty in many lands (see Map 24.2). The last of three major clusters of El Niño climatic disturbances took place between 1896 and 1902 (see Chapter 23). In several parts of the world, reduced rainfall caused successive years of bad harvests. When industrialized states suffered serious crop losses, as Britain did in 1895, they could reduce shortages by importing more grain from abroad. Most countries, however, did not have the global commercial power, railways, or government capital to keep subsistence farmers and wage earners fed during repeated food crises. European colonial officials consistently argued that famines, which hit dependent territories in Africa and in South and Southeast Asia, should not interfere with the operation of export markets, even for grain, because these shipments

MAP 24.2 Regions of drought and plague in the late nineteenth century.
What geographical aspects did the sites of plague outbreak have in common? To what extent did regions of drought overlap with European colonial territories?

benefited the colonial homeland. For example, in northern India, which experienced terrible dearth in 1896, European merchants continued to export wheat to compensate for Britain's own crop deficits. Meanwhile, the Indian colonial government rejected vigorous famine relief as too expensive. Reporting from India in 1896, an American missionary described the desperation of people who had no money to buy grain at the soaring market price:

> Already grain riots are common. Grain merchants will not sell grain, largely because they know the price will greatly increase. . . . So people break open grain shops and granaries, and threaten to kill the merchants if they interfere. . . . These people say to the police and courts: ªArrest us for stealing and support us in jail. There we shall not die from starvation.º 3

In 1896±1897, perhaps as many as eighteen million Indians perished from malnutrition, starvation, or infectious diseases. Consequently, India entered the twentieth century in conditions of deteriorating economic conditions and falling standards of living for much of the population.

Hunger and malnutrition made people more susceptible to cholera, diphtheria, or other contagious diseases. In the late nineteenth century, famines worsened mortality from epidemics of bubonic plague. This disease, associated with the bacterium *Yersinia pestis,* had killed millions of people in several parts of Afroeurasia in the mid-fourteenth century, the great pandemic known as the Black Death. Humans could become infected by the bite of fleas that lived on rodents and that carried the plague bacterium.

Like the Black Death five and a half centuries earlier, plague spread in the 1800s along routes of travel. Originating in the highlands of western China about midcentury, an epidemic struck the ports of Guangzhou (Canton) and Hong Kong in 1894. Commercial steamships whose nonpaying passengers included infected rats and fleas then transmitted the disease to other seaports. By 1901 eruptions had occurred in cities as distant from one another as Singapore, Cape Town, Sydney, Glasgow, Rio de Janeiro, Honolulu, and San Francisco. In South Asia something like ten to twelve million people died of plague by the 1920s. The disease continued to attack urban populations here and there until about 1950, when mortality dropped off owing to effective antibiotic treatment.

Africa and Southeast Asia under New Colonial Rulers

Map 24.1, at the beginning of this chapter, shows either a European power or the United States claiming

Anticolonial heroine Yaa Asantewaa. The Queen Mother served a politically important role in the Asante kingdom, in which women held offices parallel to those of male chiefs. Yaa Asantewaa used her influential position to mobilize an uprising against British colonizers in 1900. When Asante chiefs hesitated to act, Yaa Asantewaa responded, "If you the chiefs of Asante are going to behave like cowards and not fight, you should exchange your loincloths for my undergarments."

authority over most of Africa and Southeast Asia. The invasions of the previous thirty years (see Chapter 23) awarded foreign conquerors the right to decide among themselves the boundary lines between those units. Of the thirty-nine territories superimposed on Africa, thirty-seven were new European dependencies; the remaining two were the sovereign states of Ethiopia and Liberia (the latter a country where the United States exerted strong diplomatic and economic influence). In Southeast Asia, Thailand retained its independence, but together five European powers and the United States claimed authority over the rest of the region.

As of 1914, however, invading forces still did not fully control, or even occupy, all the territories they had assigned themselves on the map. In several parts of Africa and Southeast Asia, guerrilla bands continued to fight, while local rebellions frequently interrupted development of colonial administrations. In maritime Southeast Asia, for example, the Dutch ruled Java and other islands in the late nineteenth century but continued to mount operations to control large areas of the vast Indonesian archipelago. In West Africa, British forces thought in 1896 that they had conquered the once powerful Asante empire, but four years later its leaders instigated a revolt that took colonial soldiers nine months to put down.

Colonial objectives. In the areas of Africa and Southeast Asia where imperial governors had firm control at the start of the new century, they typically aimed to achieve three principal goals. One was to create an administrative system and keep the peace, which inevitably required the cooperation of local monarchs and notables. The second was to collect enough revenues from the colonized population so that it, rather than taxpayers back in Europe, would pay the costs of government. The third was to encourage export of whatever valuable commodities might be funneled from the colony into the world marketÐ rubber from Malaysia, palm oil from West Africa, copper from the Belgian Congo. These enterprises brought additional revenue to the colonial regime and business profits to European import±export companies. No early colonial administration in Africa or Southeast Asia made serious plans to offer mass education, advanced technical skills, or paths to political participation to subject populations.

Neither imperial governments nor foreign businesses invested much wealth in the economies of the new African or Southeast Asian dependencies, especially compared to European capital investments in North America, Australia, or Latin America. Mining and commercial agriculture offered low-wage employment in some regions, but these European-owned enterprises drained wealth from the colony rather than circulating it back into colonial development that would raise living standards for all. We look more closely at twentieth-century colonial systems in Chapter 25.

Gold and poverty in South Africa. South Africa illustrates how the economic lot of the majority population generally worsened in the late nineteenth century even as wealth grew at an astonishing rate. As of 1890, descendants of European settlers made up less than 10 percent of what is today the Republic of South Africa, but whites controlled all but small pockets of territory. Britain held the regions known as Cape Colony and Natal, while Afrikaners, the descendants of earlier Dutch and other European immigrants, ruled two republicsÐ the Transvaal and the Orange Free State. Afrikaners governed both states as a racially superior social caste. For them, the idea of equality for Africans, the overwhelming majority, was ªcontrary to the laws of God and the natural distinction of race and religion.º4

South Africa had exported diamonds since the 1860s, but after prospectors discovered gold in the Transvaal in 1886, the economic value of the region escalated. By the late nineteenth century, South Africa was supplying fully 25 percent of the world's gold, more Europeans were arriving to take skilled and semiskilled jobs, and men and women from greater southern Africa were streaming to mushrooming cities to seek low-wage work in the mines.

African hopes for greater rights rose during the South African War (Boer War), when Britain attacked the two Afrikaner republics in 1899, intending to annex them. British business magnates, notably Cecil Rhodes, despised the Afrikaner governments for heavily taxing the mining companies and refusing to grant full political rights even to English-speaking immigrants. To Britain's surprise, Afrikaner commandos mounted a tenacious guerrilla insurgency. In response, British troops burned Afrikaner farms, poisoned wells, and herded women and children into the twentieth century's first concentration camps, where thousands died of malnutrition and disease. Many Europeans reacted in dismay to these tactics, and when the Afrikaner leaders finally surrendered in 1902, the British moved quickly to reconcile with them. Both sides wanted to ensure that whites would continue to dominate society and have access to the subordinate African labor they needed to operate the mines and big farms. During the fighting, neither side wanted to recruit Africans for combat, fearing that if they contributed significantly to the outcome, they might feel justified in making social and economic demands. In fact, Africans materially supported both Afrikaner and British operations as construction and transport workers, couriers, scouts, and food producers. Military devastation also caused them much suffering. Nevertheless, the treaty

Miners travel to the rock face on a cable car, 1888. South Africa's nascent mining industry depended on both heavy machinery and intense manual labor. Higher-paid skilled work was reserved for white workers, many of whom were recent immigrants. What does this photo suggest about the hazards of mine work?

that ended the war omitted any mention of African rights. In 1910 Britain went further, awarding a unified South Africa self-rule under Afrikaner domination, leaving Africans subject to increasing repression and impoverishment.

Worker Protest and Nationalist Ferment in Europe

Even as economic growth accelerated in the first decade of the twentieth century, Europe seethed with protest and rebellion. In the western European democracies, socialists and other reformers kept up a steady barrage of strikes and marches to demand higher wages and better job conditions. Notably in Britain and the United States, urban women agitated for equal rights and enfranchisement, sometimes at risk of imprisonment. Also in the United States, the progressive movement, which bloomed in the aftermath of the economic

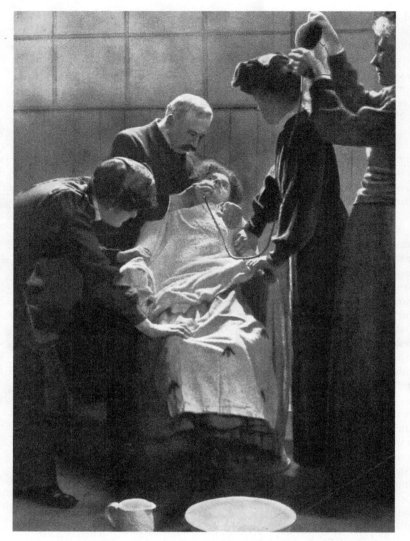

Suffragette on a hunger strike being force-fed by a nasal tube. After 1903 Holloway Prison in London housed many women arrested for political activism. What factors account for violent exchanges between police and women's rights advocates?

1878 the Great Powers of Europe responded to rising nationalist tensions by agreeing to support the independence of Serbia, Montenegro, Bulgaria, and Romania, though in fact none of those new states was ethnically homogeneous.

The pseudo-scientific racist ideas that emerged in the mid-nineteenth century (see Chapter 23) incited leaders advocating exclusive, us-versus-them forms of nationalism. Race theorists argued that people who shared the same language and cultural background also shared an exclusive biological inheritance that made them innately different from their neighbors and perhaps genetically superior to them as well. Self-styled ᵃsocial psychologists,° perverting Darwin's ideas about natural selection and recklessly confusing genetically inherited traits with culturally learned characteristics, claimed biological connections between the way people looked (skin color, skull shape) and their innate mental capacities. These caricatures of experimental science not only ranked all Europeans far above all Asians and Africans in the racial pecking order. Some theorists partitioned Europeans themselves into higher and lower races, arguing for example that the superior traits of northern Europeans included ᵃbeing Protestant,° whereas southern Europeans exposed their genetic shortcomings by being darker skinned and Roman Catholic.

Five Revolutions

In the first eleven years of the twentieth century, violent revolutionary movements erupted in Russia, Iran, Ottoman Turkey, China, and Mexico. In all of them, insurrectionists rose against their own governments, not foreign colonial overlords. But like Africans and Asians who resisted colonial rule, these rebels demanded democratic government, civil liberties, and greater economic security. In all five countries, ordinary men and women perceived themselves as benefiting little from the industrial and commercial boom of 1896±1914. Political activists regarded the existing regime as an unresponsive dynastic relic (Russia, Iran, Turkey, and China) or a republic-in-name-only that answered to wealthy elites and foreign companies (Mexico). In all cases except Russia, the rebels brought down the existing government, though without restoring political calm in the short run.

The 1905 Revolution in Russia. A colossal pan-Eurasian empire and, owing to its huge army, a European Great Power, Russia experienced energetic industrialization and rapid economic growth in the 1890s (see Chapter 23). Most Russians remained rural, poor, and ill-educated, but the

recession of 1893, brought together many reform societies to fight for labor legislation, universal education, improved housing, healthier cities, and corruption-free government.

Nationalism had been a potent public ideology in Europe through most of the nineteenth century. But Europeans increasingly venerated the nation, not so much as a community of citizens dedicated to sovereignty and universal rights, than as a defined ethnoracial group sharing a common language, culture, history, and destiny to the exclusion of outsiders. In southeastern Europe, where spiraling population growth in the nineteenth century aggravated unemployment and landlessness, radical young nationalists proclaimed their Serbian, Hungarian, Bulgarian, Albanian, or other ethnic identity in opposition to the oppression of the Austrian, Russian, or Ottoman Turkish regimes that ruled them. In urbanized and industrial worker population expanded fast, as did a money-making, reform-minded middle class of entrepreneurs, merchants, and intellectuals. On the other hand, Russia's manufacturing cities had unhealthy environments, workers suffered wretched working conditions, peasants paid crushing taxes, and the middle class fumed over its exclusion from the authoritarian government of Tsar Nicholas II (reigned 1894±1917).

In those conditions, urban laborers organized secret unions and staged regular strikes. Intellectual and business leaders in St. Petersburg, Moscow, and other industrial cities founded political associations and newspapers to demand reforms. They differed, however, on the best way to achieve change. Liberal democrats wanted a limited, constitutional monarchy. Many socialists thought the peasantry should lead a revolution. Communists, including the up-and-coming Marxist theoretician Vladimir Ilyich Lenin, contended that only the proletariat, that is, the urban working class, could overthrow the tsar's regime. The tsar responded to all talk of reform with more repression, dismissing the idea of a constitution for Russia as ªsenseless dreams.º

A series of crises at the turn of the century, however, undermined the tsar's authority. In 1898±1899 bad harvests followed one another and industrial growth nearly stagnated. Then in February 1904 Russia and Japan, both countries coveting new territories in East Asia in conditions of spreading political ferment in China, went to war over competing interests in Manchuria, Korea, and the Liaodong Peninsula (east of Beijing). The fighting went badly for Russia, and in May 1905 Japan's technically superior navy sank most of a Russian flotilla in the Tsushima Strait between Japan and Korea. This victory ended the war and ensured Japan's paramount interests in Korea and Manchuria.

Russia's successive military defeats in East Asia precipitated waves of popular protest in Moscow and other cities. In January 1905, 150,000 workers demonstrated in front of the tsar's Winter Palace in St. Petersburg, petitioning their sovereign to ªbreak down the wall between yourself and your people.º[5] In response, imperial troops killed several hundred men and women. This massacre triggered several months of strikes, peasant uprisings, assassinations, and military mutinies. In the industrial cities, workers organized their own elected political action councils known as **soviets,** an institution that would take on new meaning in the following decade. The tsar finally agreed to voting rights for adult males and an elected parliament (duma). But he refused to respect the new assembly's authority, and protests and insurgencies continued. The regime probably

> **soviet** Revolutionary workers' councils that served during the Russian Revolution as local units of government and civil order. The term was applied later to legislative bodies within the communist regime.

Russian crowds demand social reform, 1905. The first Russian Revolution brought thousands of demonstrators into the streets of St. Petersburg. The resulting massacre became known as Bloody Sunday. What might have prompted government troops to fire on this apparently peaceful crowd?

survived the 1905 revolt only because competing ideological factions could not unite and because most middle-class Russians could not bring themselves to identify with the interests of the rural masses.

Iran's fight for a constitution.

Throughout the nineteenth century, both Russia and Britain put heavy diplomatic and military pressure on the Qajar dynasty (1794±1925), which ruled Iran. Britain insisted that the governments of Afghanistan and Iran entertain no policy that might encourage Russia to threaten or attack India. For its part, Russia yearned for a warm-water naval port in the Persian Gulf, which bordered Iran on the southwest. Muzzafir al-Din Shah, Iran's autocratic monarch (r. 1896±1906) lacked an effective tax-gathering bureaucracy. Desperate for money to maintain his lavish court, he borrowed large sums from Russian, British, and French banks. In 1901 he sold oil-drilling rights in a large part of Iran to a British entrepreneur.

In response to such foreign intrusions, reform societies sprouted in several cities. In December 1905, demonstrators massed in the capital of Tehran to demand a constitutional monarchy. Muzzafir al-Din faced mounting protests from varied groups: artisans and merchants who chafed over cheap European imports, Shi'ite Muslim leaders who condemned foreign influence as an offense against Islam, and educated liberals who demanded a European-style constitution. The king finally called a constituent assembly, which enacted laws that transformed Iran into a limited monarchy.

Muzzafir al-Din died in late 1906, however, and his successor moved violently to restore autocracy. The country then descended into a civil war that dragged on for four years. In those chaotic conditions, Russia and Britain agreed to partition Iran into two spheres of influence. In 1911 they invaded the northern and southern provinces, respectively, not to create formal colonies but to ensure informal domination. The civil war ended with Iran a constitutional monarchy but its import±export economy in the hands of foreign companies and their wealthy Iranian collaborators.

Young Turks in revolt.

Japan's victory over Russia, the Russian Revolution of 1905, and the Iranian revolt all energized popular opposition to Sultan Abdul Hamid II, the Ottoman Turkish empire's ruler (r. 1876±1909). He believed in material modernization, including new military technology, advanced technical education, and telegraph and rail construction. But drawing support from the empire's most conservative land-owning families and Muslim leaders, he successfully suppressed a budding liberal reform movement early in his reign (see Chapter 22). He suspended a new liberal constitution within two years of its adoption and reinstated an autocratic and increasingly repressive government. Liberal opponents of this regime, mainly low-level officials, university students, and young military officers, continued to agitate for reform from underground or exile. As in

Iran, these activists formed secret societies. The Committee of Union and Progress (CUP), whose members became popularly known as Young Turks, emerged as the umbrella organization for groups demanding restoration of the constitution, military modernization, and an end to economic dependence on foreign companies and banks. In 1908 a band of officers, fed up with Abdul Hamid's neglect of the army, staged an uprising in league with the CUP. Alarmed by this turn of events, the sultan reinstituted the constitution and announced elections to a new parliament. When Abdul Hamid's conservative supporters tried to raise a counterrevolution, however, army units marched on Constantinople (modern Istanbul) and forced the sultan to abdicate in favor of a younger brother who had no power base.

This power seizure triggered five years of disruptive wrangling among political factions, though CUP leaders finally established their authority. This constitutional regime, however, became increasingly dictatorial. The Young Turks adopted an ideology that idealized the empire as a multicultural state in which all ethnic and religious communities should enjoy civil toleration and equality. But in fact the Turkish-speaking urban population moved toward a more exclusive ethnic nationalism similar to the trend across much of Europe.

The end of the Chinese empire.

The steep tilt of economic and military power toward Europe, the United States, and Japan in the later nineteenth century profoundly affected China. That state's political turmoil, moreover, was all the more dramatic because the country numbered nearly half a billion people, twenty-three times the population of the Ottoman empire. Relentless European pressures, a steady hemorrhage of silver to pay for imports, the catastrophic Taiping Rebellion, and recurring famines combined to undermine the Qing dynasty's political authority and financial solvency (see Chapter 22). As in Russia, Iran, and Turkey, young liberal modernizers railed against autocratic monarchy and its apparent helplessness in the face of foreign penetration and dizzying economic change. In 1894±1895, Japan's modern army readily defeated China's larger but poorly equipped forces in the Sino-Japanese War. The conflict started over rivalry for influence in Korea. It ended with Japan dominant there and in control of the big island of Taiwan, which had been part of the Chinese empire since the seventeenth century. In the aftermath of the Japanese victory, Britain, France, and Russia pressured the Qing government into approving their control over large chunks of Chinese territory where they would have preeminent trade rights and merchant exemptions from Chinese law. Consequently, the Qing gave up full political control of dozens of **treaty ports**. In those places, European merchants and their Chinese associates did business free of import taxes.

treaty ports Sea or river ports in China where, as a consequence of diplomatic and military pressure, foreigners gained special privileges to engage in trade and enjoy exemptions from Chinese laws and courts.

The imperial court proved helpless to resist this informal empire building. The Empress Dowager Cixi (r. 1861±1908), a tenacious autocrat, had ruled China as regent, or guardian and substitute, for two emperors, first a young son and after 1875 Guangxu (wang-soo), a nephew. She and the Confucian scholar-bureaucrats who served her professed little interest in technical modernization and much contempt for both Europeans and reform-minded Chinese.

Simultaneously, the cluster of El Niño disturbances of 1896±1902 hit the northern provinces furiously, setting off popular rebellion. Severe droughts alternated with massive monsoon floods, causing the death or displacement of millions of peasants. Seeking a cosmic explanation for such disaster, the Harmonious Fists, or Boxers—a secret society devoted to martial arts and rituals believed to convey special powers—targeted foreigners as the source of China's misfortunes. The Boxers preached eradication of European and American missionaries, who were at that time founding many churches in China. In 1899±1900 the Boxers appealed to impoverished young men, as well as rural women known as Red Lanterns, to seize foreign property, pull down telegraph lines, demolish churches, and kill both missionaries and their Chinese converts. Some Qing governors tried to quell the insurrection, but the Empress Dowager urged it on.

In response to Boxer provocations, Japan, Russia, Germany, France, Britain, and the United States organized a multinational army in the summer of 1900. Armed with

Empress Dowager Cixi after her 1902 return to Beijing. The Qing court tried to improve foreign diplomatic relations after the Boxer uprising. The Empress reached out in particular to wives of diplomats, thinking they might be open to appeals of friendship. In this photograph the Empress holds hands with Sarah Pike Conger, the wife of the U.S. envoy. The child is the daughter of the photographer. How might an image like this have changed both Chinese and foreign perceptions of the Qing rulers?

Qiu Jin: Social Reformer

Poet Qin Jin in a man's attire.

Most Chinese reformers of the early twentieth century recognized that the country's modern self-strengthening must include drastic changes in the social status and public roles of women. Criticism was particularly leveled at female seclusion in the home, lack of educational opportunity, and the traditional custom of foot binding. If women were hobbled in so many ways, especially members of the best educated and most affluent families, how could they help modernize society and expel alien occupiers? Amid the deterioration of Qing authority, literate young women began to join the blooming nationalist movement and to speak out for the social emancipation of their sex.

After the foreign seizure of Beijing in 1900, Qiu Jin (1875–1907), a women raised in a moderately well-off family in the eastern coastal province of Zhejiang, vowed to devote herself to China's transformation. Her parents allowed her to get an education, but she nonetheless found herself trapped in an arranged marriage to an older man with typically conservative ideas about wifely behavior. In 1904, at the age of twenty-nine, she broke with her husband and boarded a ship for Japan. While at sea, she wrote "Preoccupation (Written while in Japan)," a poem that later became famous:

> A lusterless sun and a wan moon have cast heaven and earth
> in obscurity—
> Sinking with help,
> more imperiled than anyone else,
> are the women of my race.
> Searching for a remedy,

> I pawned my jewelry, left behind my children,
> And sailed across the ocean
> to this foreign land.
> Unbinding my feet, I washed away
> a thousand years of poison.
> My heart fired with excitement, I awoke
> one hundred slumbering flower-spirits.
> But pity my shagreen [leather] handkerchief—
> Half stained with tears
> and half with blood.[6]

In Japan, Qiu Jin entered a women's vocational school but also joined the Revolutionary Alliance, a coalition formed by Sun Zhongshan to unite fragmented anti-Qing organizations. She prepared herself for revolution by practicing marksmanship and bomb-making. Like many young Chinese, she witnessed Japan's military triumph over Russia in 1905 with a mixture of admiration and anxiety. The victory vindicated Japan's program of rapid modernization but also put into relief that state's continuing threat to China.

In 1906 Qiu Jin returned to China, where she took a job directing a girls' school in the coastal city of Shaoxing. There she developed a sports program that included martial arts and military drills, in effect, revolutionary military training. She also founded the *Chinese Women's Journal,* a feminist periodical that exposed the evils of foot binding, arranged marriages, female infanticide, and wife-beating. She became notorious for her eccentricities, leading her sports class in a man's long gown and black leather shoes and riding a horse astride rather than sidesaddle as a decent woman was expected to do.

In 1907, she joined a cousin in a plot to stage an anti-Qing uprising. Imperial police seized her at her school along with compromising documents. Her captors tortured her for information, and when she refused to cooperate, they led her to the school parade ground, where they decapitated her. News of her courage spread rapidly, and nationalists hailed her as a martyr, an icon of women's freedom, and a beacon to young revolutionaries, who, four years later, brought down the Qing regime.

Thinking Critically

What relationship, if any, do you see between Qiu Jin's family background and early life and her career as a social reformer?

up-to-date rifles, machine guns, and artillery, this force advanced inland, killing tens of thousands of Chinese peasants, whether they were Boxers or not. The invaders seized Beijing, forcing the Empress Dowager to flee. The suppression of the insurrection left China vulnerable to full-scale foreign invasion. But international quarreling and the enormous potential costs of conquering China persuaded the Great Powers to hold back.

Military humiliation helped convince the Qing government to initiate at least moderate reforms, including military and administrative modernization, improved communication networks, and investment in education. In 1908 both the Empress Dowager and Guangxu died, leaving the succession to Puyi, who climbed onto the throne at age two. The following year a small electorate of males chose provincial assemblies, which were to select members of a national parliament.

For the growing class of radicalized reformers, however, the modern [a]self-strengthening[o] that China required could not be left to traditional Confucian palace officials. Like Young Turks, many Chinese reformers operated from exile. They published radical magazines, wrote letters to compatriots in China, and raised money. Sun Zhongshan (Sun Yat-sen, 1866±1925), the most famous liberal reformer of the early twentieth century, studied medicine in British-ruled Hong Kong and became a Christian. He allied with secret societies opposed to Qing rule, advocated a constitutional republic, and traveled to Europe and the United States to find funds and political backers.

The 268-year-old Qing dynasty collapsed in 1911, faster than its revolutionary opponents expected. Rebellious army officers seized power in part of the Yangzi River valley and declared the region independent of imperial authority. The news spread by telegraph to other officers and to new provincial assemblies. Within several weeks, more than a dozen provinces seceded. The court guardians of the child emperor Puyi had no choice but to agree to a constitutional republic. Sun Zhongshan quickly returned from abroad, but the former Qing general who assumed the presidency had no tolerance for democracy. This left the revolutionary government in turmoil, and in 1913 military men took over most of China's provinces, reorganizing them into personal fiefdoms defended by private armies. The foreign concession holders trafficked directly with these warlords, and the new central government proved impotent. China's postrevolutionary fate was to be thirty-six more years of division and war.

The Mexican Revolution. In contrast to the four movements discussed so far, the Mexican Revolution, which broke out in 1910, aimed initially to replace not a dynastic monarch, but the government of a long-established republic. At the end of the nineteenth century, the Western Hemisphere was a world zone of republicsÐ nineteen of them. There was also Canada, a constitutional monarchy, and an assortment of small colonial possessions. The republics ranged from popular though partially restricted democracies (the United States), to liberal regimes dominated by business and land-owning elites (Argentina), to dictatorships that made sure that elections were decided in advance. Mexico, headed by Porfirio Díaz from 1876 to 1911, falls into the last category.

The Porfiriato, as the Díaz regime was known, promoted liberal policies only in the material sphere. That is, he and a group of intellectual collaborators known as *cientificos* aimed to achieve modernization and progress, not by broadening rights and civic participation, but by strengthening the power and wealth of the state by expanding rail lines, mine operations, and textile production. The country's track network grew from about 400 miles in 1876 to nearly 12,000 miles by 1910. Its main functions, however, were to transport soldiers around the country and to channel minerals and commercial farm products out of Mexico in exchange for foreign manufactures. Díaz opened the country to European and U.S. investors, who formed a tightly knit capitalist fraternity with Mexican mine owners, land barons, and officeholders.

On the underside of economic growth were the Mexican masses whose labor produced everything the country exported. Only a small part of the overwhelmingly rural Indian and *mestizo* population owned land, and the Porfiriato aimed by legal means or otherwise to accelerate transfers of communal village lands to privately owned estates worked by low-wage tenants and day laborers. While agricultural exports boomed, harvests of maize, the country's basic food staple, languished. The elite class of mainly creole families (Mexicans of European descent) tended to regard *mestizos* and Indians through a racialist lens, dismissing them as genetically incapable of rising out of poverty.

Mexico's economic growth, however, also produced a new breed of urban, educated men and womenÐ lawyers, engineers, teachers, merchants, and business ownersÐ who abhorred the concentration of wealth in a few hundred families. These liberals founded associations pledged to individual rights, fair elections, freedom from foreign domination, and fairer distribution of the country's riches.

Grievance and protest exploded into revolution in 1910, when the octogenarian Díaz, after first proclaiming his retirement and a new era of free elections, presented himself for office once again. He also had Francisco Madero (1873±1913), a liberal reformer who ran against him, thrown into jail on the eve of the election. Madero subsequently fled to the United States, where he appealed to the Mexican people to rise up. Soon enough, local insurrections broke out in several regions. Emiliano Zapata, a former horse trainer who demanded restoration of expropriated peasant lands, led one uprising in the south. Pancho Villa, an ex-rustler, commanded another insurgency in the far north. Faced with rebellion on all sides, Díaz gave up and fled to Paris in 1911. Madero entered Mexico City in triumph.

During the next nine years, however, the country fragmented into rival and often warring ideological factions,

Rebel leader Emiliano Zapata (1879–1914). What features of this undated photo emphasize Zapata's role as a revolutionary general?

including middle-class liberals who wanted moderate changes, populist revolutionaries like Zapata, and counter-revolutionary peasants who supported the conservative Roman Catholic Church leadership. U.S. forces intervened in the revolution twice, once to pursue Pancho Villa south of the Rio Grande and once to occupy the port of Veracruz to blockade arms imports. Madero was assassinated in 1913, and though liberal leaders wrote a new constitution four years later, stable central authority was restored only in 1920 under the leadership of liberal property owners. In 1929, representatives of this group formed the National

Revolutionary Party (later the Party of Revolutionary Institutions, or PRI). The organization clothed itself in revolutionary and nationalist rhetoric, but Mexico nonetheless devolved into a rigid one-party state that restricted the operations of unions, the press, or rival political groups.

The Great War, 1914–1918

FOCUS Why did warfare between 1914 and 1918 reach such extreme levels of violence and destruction?

As grim as it was, revolutionary violence in the early twentieth century was restrained compared to World War I, in which something close to ten million military personnel died. Over four years the war's average *daily* death toll was 1,459 Russians, 1,303 Germans, 890 French, and 457 British combatants.[7] All but six European states were involved in the fighting. British soldiers warred against Germans in East Africa and against Turks in Iraq. Australians, New Zealanders, Canadians, South Asians, Africans, and eventually Americans fought in Europe. British and German ships and submarines pursued one another in the Baltic, the North Sea, and the South Atlantic. The struggle devastated large areas of Europe, sent world trade plummeting, and buried both winners and losers under mountains of debt.

In the perspective of any time after 1918, the war looks so irrational and horrifying that it nearly defies historical explanation. We cannot simply tote up a list of causes that made the catastrophe inevitable. There was no unstoppable march toward war in the previous years but rather a conjuncture of events in 1914 that, if rearranged even slightly, might have prevented the conflict, at least at that moment. Right up to that year, middle-class Europeans who gathered in opera houses and stylish cafés had stout hopes that peace and economic good times would continue indefinitely.

Nevertheless, political anxieties clouded Europe's splendid cityscapes of iron and glass. Competing nationalist, socialist, racist, and other provocative ideologies fueled social-class and ethnolinguistic tensions. The incessant rivalry among Britain, France, Germany, and Russia for shares of expanding world wealth gradually eroded the previously accepted rules for getting along together. In defiance of free-trade principles, all the major states except Britain raised tariff walls higher to protect home industries. International strains became so acute by the summer of 1914 that war, when it erupted, did not come as a great surprise to many European leaders. But they assured the public nonetheless that the conflict would be ᵃover by Christmas.º They did not imagine fifty-two months of savage, relentless fighting.

Lighting the Fuse

War broke out in 1914 under circumstances in which pacts and agreements that had once been fluid and pragmatic had become progressively unyielding. Europe hardened into two blocs of alliances in conditions of mounting suspicion and menace. Germany, Austria-Hungary, and the Ottoman empire joined forces as the Central Powers. France, Britain, and Russia formed the opposing Allied Powers.

Britain, France, and Germany. These alliances involved two fundamentally different kinds of states. Britain, France, and Germany were Europe's richest industrial powers. They had the largest overseas empires and the biggest stakes in world trade. They were also established national states. In other words, their populations, especially the urban middle classes, had largely accepted the nationalist ideology that the state and the national cultural community were, or should ideally be identical. Popular allegiance to the state must therefore take precedence over loyalties to local ethnic communities or religions. In those countries, nationalism expressed itself in representative assemblies (though in Germany the voting electorate was small) and in anthems, flags, a national language, and often zealously nationalistic newspapers. Public schools and army service were also crucial institutions for teaching patriotic love and duty.

On the chessboard of power in western Europe, Germany gradually crept ahead of its two rivals. In 1900 its population exceeded that of both Britain and France by many millions. It had higher production in key industries like coal and steel. It led the way in electrical and chemical technologies and fielded Europe's largest land army next to Russia. Kaiser Wilhelm II, Germany's militaristic head of state, clamored for more overseas colonies, ordered construction of a world-class navy, and competed with France for diplomatic influence in Morocco, a sovereign monarchy.

In response to these expansionist signals, France, which had already lost its eastern provinces to Germany in the Franco-Prussian War of 1870, stepped up arms production and strengthened the alliance it had made with Russia in 1892. Britain concluded that the kaiser could have no reason to build a sea force other than to challenge the Royal Navy. In 1904 Britain and France signed the Entente (ahn-TAHNT) Cordial, which settled outstanding colonial disputes. Three years later, Russia joined those two powers in the Triple Entente.

Germany, France, and Britain all poured national wealth into armaments, manufacturing far more guns, shells, and ships than what they would need if they remained at peace with one another. This feverish race suggested to the competitors that if war was on the way, it might be better to fight a short, conclusive one sooner rather than later. German leaders also perceived the Triple Entente as dangerous encirclement.

Already allied with the Austro-Hungarian empire, they nurtured close relations with Ottoman Turkey as preparation for a day of reckoning.

The three multiethnic empires. The political and social profiles of Austria-Hungary, Russia, and the Ottoman empire were rather different from the western European powers. All three had autocratic imperial governments. None of the three could be described as a national state. Rather, they embraced diverse ethnolinguistic groups that in many cases formed their own nationalist movements to agitate for one measure or another of self-government. The populations of these empires were overwhelmingly rural, and though industries were growing in Russia and Austria, both states lagged far behind Germany and Britain.

THE BOILING POINT.

Imperial politics in the Balkans reach the boiling point. This 1912 cartoon from the British humor magazine *Punch* depicts France, Britain, Germany, Russia, and Austria-Hungary grappling with challenges to European stability. What problems were these great powers trying to contain?

The shatter zone for these empires was the Balkan Peninsula. As we have seen, Serbia, Montenegro, Romania, and Bulgaria broke free of Ottoman rule in the last quarter of the nineteenth century. Austria and Russia ratified the independence of these states but then competed fiercely with each other for influence over them. The Balkans thus remained a boiling political cauldron. Russia, a predominantly Slavic-speaking power, projected itself into the Balkans as the champion of Serbs, Bulgarians, Macedonians, and all other peoples who spoke Slavic languages. This patronage encouraged Serbian nationalists to dream of a ªGreater Serbia° that would one day dominate southeastern Europe. Austria-Hungary, however, could not abide this prospect. In 1908 Austria annexed the Slavic region of Bosnia-Herzegovina, which poisoned its relations with Russia. In 1912 and 1913 two Balkan Wars involving several small regional powers resulted in the Turks losing nearly all their remaining European territory and Serbia doubling its own. In response to that development, Austrian officials talked of invading and dismantling Serbia altogether.

A World at War

In all of Europe's major rival states, generals made contingency plans for war because that was part of their job. In Germany the high command devised the Schlieffen (SHLEE-fn) Plan in 1905. This strategy projected a rapid and massive assault across Belgium to quickly overpower France. Quick success there would free troops to invade and defeat Russia before it had time to fully mobilize its presumably lumbering army. Austria-Hungary would force Russia to spread its forces by launching its own invasion. Kaiser Wilhelm assured himself with more hope than realism that Britain would stay out of the fight because ªshe will have to.° After 1905 the Schlieffen strategy became so congealed in German military minds that once it was activated, political leaders with second thoughts about war would not be able to stop it.

Some historians have labeled World War I the ªThird Balkan War° because it looked for a short time as if it might be just one more dreary but short-lived conflict in southeastern Europe. On June 28, 1914, Serbian nationalists assassinated Archduke Franz Ferdinand, the heir to the Austro-Hungarian throne, when he visited Bosnia-Herzegovina. Austria immediately made heavy demands on Serbia to atone for the murder, then, failing to receive satisfaction, declared war. Germany backed Austria to the full. This was perhaps the key moment. If the kaiser had restrained Austria, Russia would likely have held back as well. But the German government, fearing a large Slavic state to its south, let militarist sentiment have the upper hand. In a complicated sequence of events that historians have been interpreting ever since, the regional war escalated quickly. As Austria prepared to invade Serbia, the tsar commanded his army to mobilize to aid Russia's Slavic friend. When that happened, Germany declared war on both Russia and France without any immediate

provocation from them. On August 3, German troops penetrated Belgium. The next day, Britain, which had earlier guaranteed that little country's neutrality and believed it had to aid France, declared war on Germany. German units got within thirty miles of Paris, but the Schlieffen Plan failed. French forces counterattacked. One general commandeered taxicabs to rush reinforcements from Paris train stations to the front. At that point, both sides started digging in to hold their ground, and rapid troop advances skidded to a halt. This meant that Germany and Austria-Hungary would have to fight a war on two fronts (see Map 24.3).

The Western Front. Along the battle lines that extended across Belgium and northeastern France, soldiers on both sides excavated labyrinthine networks of deep trenches and bunkers. Concrete fortifications and tangles of barbed wire protected the trench lines, and hundreds of thousands of troops burrowed in so well that massive artillery barrages consistently failed to prepare the ground for successful attacks. Rather, as European armies had already learned in colonial wars, the machine gun proved to be a marvelous apparatus for mowing down wave after wave of advancing infantry. In the Battle of Verdun in February 1916, 420,000 French and German soldiers died. At the Battle of the Somme River, fought between July and November of that year, the German, French, and British armies together sustained more than 1.1 million casualties, including 58,000 British losses on the first day of the fight.

For the generals on both sides, every murderous offensive was to be the ªfinal push,° but none of those drives went far until August 1918, when Allied forces started advancing against exhausted German soldiers. Four years of trench warfare caused indescribable suffering. The deep ditches and bunkers filled with water, mud, rats, excrement, and corpses. Soldiers became malnourished and contracted infections such as trench mouth. Others developed neurological disorders, including facial ticks and severe depressionÐ a bundle of maladies that doctors summed up as ªshellshock,° or, in today's language, posttraumatic stress disorder. The English poet Siegfried Sassoon, who fought at the Battle of the Somme, caught the psychological terror of combat in his poem ªAttack°:

Men jostle and climb to meet the bristling fire.
Lines of grey, muttering faces, masked with fear,
They leave their trenches, going over the top,
While time ticks blank and busy on their wrists,
And hope, with furtive eyes and grappling fists,
Flounders in mud. O Jesus, make it stop![8]

The Eastern Front. Russian forces advanced fast enough at the start of the war to advance across Poland into northeastern Germany. But German divisions then forced them back. On the Eastern Front, fighting was somewhat more mobile than in the west owing to larger distances, wider dispersion of troops (from the Baltic Sea to Serbia), and shortages of guns. Nevertheless, neither side achieved a

MAP 24.3 World War I.

In what ways might the great geographical extent of the war have complicated military operations for both the Central Powers and the Allies?

decisive advance. When the fighting on the Western Front bogged down, the Allies tried to open new offensive lines in southeastern Europe. One was an assault on the Gallipoli Peninsula on the Dardanelles Straits (1915±1916) to capture Constantinople, the Ottoman capital. This campaign failed at deadly cost. Italy remained neutral until 1915 but then entered the war on the Allied side to only minor effect.

The war's global scope. The conflict might have remained confined to Europe if France, Germany, and especially Britain had not had colonies and vital commercial interests around the world. The German alliance recruited Bulgaria to its side, but thirty-six states joined the Allies, if only near the war's end. These countries included the United States, Australia, New Zealand, Canada, and South Africa. Approximately 331,000 Australians and 365,000 Canadians served overseas, many of them on the Western Front. Japan joined the Allies at the outset of the war, though largely to advance its own expansionist aims in East Asia. Its forces attacked German shipping and seized both its territorial concession in China and several of its Pacific island colonies. Britain recruited soldiers from its African, Asian, and

Infantry troops from Senegal head toward the front. Colonial subjects made significant contributions during World War I as soldiers and laborers. How might the war have encouraged changes in the ways colonized peoples and their colonizers perceived each other?

Caribbean colonies. Indian troops made by far the largest contribution, with more than 825,000 of them fighting in the British army. Nearly 7 percent of France's army comprised volunteers or draftees from Algeria, Morocco, Senegal, Niger, and other dependencies. As many as 71,000 of them died in service. Britain and France also recruited hundreds of thousands of colonials to perform labor in war zones and behind the lines on railroads and in factories.

The war also extended to East Africa, a region divided into British, German, and Portuguese colonial territories. German commanders and their African conscripts advanced from Tanganyika (modern Tanzania) deep into neighboring British and Portuguese colonies. Nearly fifteen thousand African soldiers died in German service, and scorched-earth tactics caused food shortages that ravaged village populations. On the British side, losses of African soldiers and carriers exceeded 100,000, compared to a little over 3,000 Europeans and white South Africans. Germany's East African forces did not finally surrender until mid-November 1918, two weeks after the war ended in Europe.

In the Middle East, the Young Turk modernizers who ruled the Ottoman state in 1914 debated passionately whether to enter the war and on whose side. They finally joined the Central Powers, hoping to regain lost territory in the Balkans and to fend off a potential Russian invasion. This decision impelled the Allies to attack the empire's Arabic-speaking provinces. British forces operating from both Egypt and India gradually advanced into the Arabic-speaking lands under Turkish rule, encouraged by young

Arab activists who were just then forming anti-Ottoman nationalist societies. In the summer of 1916, Prince Faysal, a son of Sharif Husayn ibn Ali, who governed the holy cities of Mecca and Medina under Ottoman authority, took charge of a revolt of western Arabian tribes against the Turks. In collaboration with a British army advancing from Egypt and the advice of British liaison officers such as T. E. Lawrence (Lawrence of Arabia), the Arab insurgents helped drive the Turkish army from Palestine, Syria, and Iraq.

The fight at sea and the entry of the United States. The economies of the opposing industrial powers relied on world trade for minerals, food, and other commodities to sustain both troops in the field and people at home. Britain depended on the Royal Navy to protect its shipping lanes to its colonies and to important trade partners like the United States. Germany, on the other hand, failed to break a British blockade of the North Sea, which prevented even neutral ships from moving between northern German ports and the Atlantic and causing appalling food shortages in German cities. To fight back on the seas, German engineers pioneered diesel-powered submarines, or U-boats, which torpedoed Allied ships. In April 1917, for example, U-boats sank about 25 percent of the ships leaving British ports. In effect, both sides aimed to use naval technology to weaken each other's civilian populations, if possible, by starvation.

The war at sea triggered the United States to enter the fight. Germany at first avoided submarine attacks on American vessels but decided early in 1917 that it could no longer

On patrol during the Arab Revolt. Arab rebels waged guerrilla warfare against Ottoman forces as British units advanced against the empire from Egypt. What geographical factors might have encouraged Arab nationalists to raise an insurrection during the war (see Map 24.3)?

afford such restraint. Though many Americans loathed the idea of plunging into Europe's incomprehensible ªcivil war,º President Woodrow Wilson (in office, 1913±1921) concluded that German militarism represented a global threat. In April 1917 he persuaded Congress to join the Allies.

Largely because Russia pulled out of the war in the fall of that year amid revolution at home, Germany attempted to break through the Western Front before American troops could get there. The gambit did not work, and in 1918 U.S. soldiers and supplies poured into France. Those fresh forces tipped the balance in the Allies' favor, even though the fighting went on until November. About two million U.S. troops served in western Europe, 126,000 of them never to return home.

Total War

World War I differed from any earlier war, not only because of its global scope and enormous cost in lives, but also because entire societies, not just armies and governments, were mobilized to fight it. The major opposing states mustered numerous public institutions, private businesses, the entire economic infrastructure, and men and women of all classes and occupations to win the struggle, waging what historians call **total war.** Because the fighting dragged on and on, both the Western and Eastern Fronts became gaping ª black holesº for soldiers, arms, and supplies. The adversaries thought they had no choice except to transform their societies into war-making machines, diverting their economies from consumer to military production and placing millions of civilians in war-related jobs. Governments began to stage-manage social and economic life on a far larger scale than ever before.

total war Warfare, especially characteristic of World Wars I and II, in which the opposing states mobilize their civilian populations and all available resources to achieve victory; also a wartime policy intended to damage or destroy both the enemy's military forces and its economic infrastructure and social fabric.

Mobilizing the people. When hostilities broke out, hundreds of thousands of patriotic young people flocked to the flag. In the warring countries, peace activists became scarce, and the vast majority of rank-and-file socialist and communist party members suspended their international workers' struggle against capitalist subjugation in order

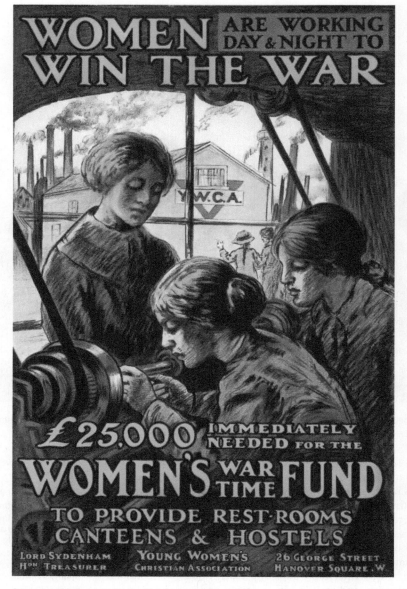

A war waged on many fronts. The increased demand for mostly young, single women to work in war industries strained available housing and support services. What strategies does this poster use to encourage public donations to funds for women workers?

nurses. Others served and sometimes gave up their lives as intelligence agents, reporting on enemy troop movements or spying in other ways. In Belgium, women served in the White Lady network, which spied on the German occupiers. On the home fronts, middle- and upper-class women formed various auxiliary organizations to recruit soldiers, patrol around army bases, sew uniforms, drive trucks, run public transport, and care for the wounded. In Britain, France, Germany, and the United States, millions of women took jobs in munitions factories and other industrial plants to replace men in service. In the Krupp armaments industry in one German city, for example, the female workforce went from zero in 1914 to thirty thousand in 1918. On both sides, rural women and their children managed farms in the absence of menfolk.

Pumping up production. When neither side achieved a quick knockout blow, both adopted strategies to deploy forces of destruction on a massive scale. This required rallying the society's total store of scientific, technological, and industrial skill. Indeed, Britain, France, and Germany generated new technologies and raised industrial output to levels that left the early industrial era in the dust. Because armies on both sides were so big, weapons manufacturers faced the critical challenge of devising machines that would kill large numbers of enemy combatants impersonally and fast. Machine guns were mass produced and continually improved, and munitions plants geared up to produce tens of thousands of artillery shells every day. German chemists pioneered different types of poison gas. Allied scientists made their own recipes in response, and both started firing gas canisters over enemy trenches. Engineers invented more effective masks and respirators, but even so, gas attacks caused great fear among troops and probably accounted for about 1.2 million total casualties.[9]

The warring powers also put new communication and transport technologies to effective use. The internal combustion engine powered supply trucks, troop vehicles, and ambulances. Early farm tractors with caterpillar tracks inspired the first battlefield tanks, which British generals put into service in 1916 to only limited effect. To combat German U-boats, the Allies grouped vessels in dense, destroyer-protected convoys, and their factories turned out ships faster than subs could sink them. Aircraft served in the war mainly for reconnaissance and modestly effective bombing and strafing. At war's end Britain had fifty thousand planes.

help the nation meet its emergency. Most of the adversaries already had large armies of conscripts when the war started. Britain did not, but 750,000 men volunteered for military service in the first two months of the fight.

Laws and deep-rooted traditions prevented women from volunteering for regular military service in any country. The one exception was Russia, where several thousand women served, notably in a unit called the Battalion of Death, which sent some female combatants to the front late in the war. Armies did, however, employ thousands of women as field

Total war and big government. Governments of the major opposing states amassed more authority than they had ever had in the nineteenth century. Central administrations were indeed the only bodies that could manage mobilization of whole societies. Government ministries, departments, and agencies proliferated to undertake specific war-related tasks. The number of people employed by government increased dramatically. Public officials took control of railroads, strategic industries, and research laboratories. Some states greatly expanded their roles in social welfare, supplementing or replacing activities that voluntary organizations had provided previously. These new activities included day nurseries, public housing, soup kitchens, refugee services, health clinics, food rationing, and workers' compensation plans.

All governments restricted civil liberties to one degree or another, suspending elections, curtailing press freedom, censoring mail, and sometimes either ignoring or encouraging persecution of citizens whose families originated in enemy countries. In the United States, laws in nearly half the states prohibited teaching and speaking German. Throughout the later nineteenth century, exclusive ethnic nationalisms had aggravated anti-Semitic prejudices. During the war, anti-Semites in eastern Europe and in some measure in the western European democracies harassed Jews as an imagined ᵃenemy within.º In 1915 the Ottoman government dealt with rising Christian Armenian nationalism in eastern Turkey by systematically massacring villagers and summarily evacuating hundreds of thousands more southward into the Syrian Desert. This proved to be a death march, and all told perhaps one million Armenians died in this horror of ethnic cleansing. When the war ended, democratically elected governments in Europe suspended many regulations and controls. But the model of vigorous state intervention was there to be applied again when the world faced new crises in the following decades.

Russia: From War to Revolution

Although the Russian imperial government enacted modest political and social reforms following the abortive 1905 revolution, Tsar Nicholas and his aristocratic inner circle remained blind to the need for far-reaching change. Even so, the Russian working and middle classes in the cities endorsed the national war cause as enthusiastically as their counterparts in western Europe. For the most part, labor unions and socialist parties, typically suspicious of tsarist appeals for popular unity, joined the march to battle.

The end of the Romanov empire. By 1917, however, extreme war weariness was setting in on both sides of the conflict. In western Europe, it was manifested in labor strikes, food riots, soldier mutinies, and covert diplomatic initiatives to end the carnage. For Russia, the fighting took 1.7 million lives by 1917, and German forces continued to advance across Poland. With no victories and little reform,

popular discontent transmuted into rage. On the Eastern Front, mutinies and mass surrenders multiplied. By 1917, Russians suffered grave food shortages, and peasants refused to sell grain to the government at fixed low prices. The army had to replace legions of dead and wounded soldiers with both urban middle-class men, who often had liberal or socialist sympathies, and poorly trained farmers, whose love for the tsar had long faded. In February 1917 bread rationing in St. Petersburg incited ten thousand women to march against the government. The violent repression that followed only incited more protests, labor strikes, and army disaffection.

As turmoil spread to more cities and into the countryside in the following month, pragmatic leaders finally persuaded Nicholas to abdicate. This act terminated the three-hundred-year-old Romanov dynasty and left the *duma,* the weak parliamentary assembly created in 1905, to form a new provisional government and restore public order. But as in Mexico and China about the same time, it proved easier to pull down the old system than to set up a new one. Dominated by moderate conservatives and constitutional liberals, the provisional regime watched helplessly as urban activists, many of them communists, organized soviets, or social workers' councils, in Moscow, St. Petersburg, and other cities. Meanwhile, peasants seized aristocratic estates, while non-Russian ethnic groups in places such as Ukraine and Latvia laid plans to secede from the empire. When tsarist authority collapsed, so did army discipline. Soldiers deserted en masse or assaulted officers who tried to force them to fight.

The October Revolution. The provisional government became mired in factionalism, while the most radical socialist and communist groups amassed popular support. Some socialist parties focused on rural land reform, but Marxist leaders like Lenin and Lev Trotsky looked to the urban working class, or proletariat, to foment revolution. After 1903 Lenin rose to leadership of the Bolsheviks (BOHL-shih-vehkz), or Majoritarians, a communist faction that demanded strict party discipline, dedicated activism, and unbending commitment to a proletarian government that would exclude the capitalist bourgeoisie, including constitutionalist liberals. In October 1917 Bolshevik militants, aided by army elements and good luck, seized power in St. Petersburg (renamed Petrograd) and disbanded the provisional regime. This audacious coup brought more socialist groups into Lenin's camp. The rapidly assembled Congress of Soviets under Bolshevik leadership claimed supreme political authority in the name of all workers' soviets. This sudden turnover of power amazed even Lenin himself: ᵃYou know, from persecution and a life underground,º he remarked to Trotsky, ᵃ to come so suddenly into power, . . . it makes you giddy.º[10]

In addition to abolishing private ownership of land, giving workers' committees management of factories, and replacing the tsarist legal system with ᵃpeople's courts,º the new Soviet government moved immediately to take Russia out of the war. By that time, German units were advancing

Lenin and Trotsky celebrate the second anniversary of the Bolshevik Revolution. This photograph from 1919 shows both revolutionary leaders at a ceremony in Red Square. Lenin stands at the top of the steps; Trotsky is next to him, wearing a military uniform, arm raised in a salute. Trotsky later lost a power struggle with Stalin and was assassinated in Mexico on Stalin's orders. When this photo was used in a 1967 Soviet book about Lenin, Trotsky was airbrushed out of it.

unchecked into Russian territory. Consequently, Lenin agreed to harsh terms. In the Treaty of Brest-Litovsk of March 1918, Russia ceded to Germany all the old empire's western borderlands, including Finland, the Baltic lands, Poland, and part of Ukraine. Though the new regime later retrieved some of that territory, it permanently lost authority over millions of people and much agricultural land. For their part, the Allied Powers, dismayed at both Russia's betrayal and the shocking communist takeover, now eyed their former partner with hostility.

Lenin's October Revolution led quickly to Soviet control over many Russian cities but only a small part of the boundless rural lands that stretched to the Pacific. At the end of 1917 the Bolsheviks had nothing close to majority popular support and no effective army of their own. Opponents of the new government recovered quickly, leading to two years of bloody civil war before the new communist ruling elite made itself secure.

Peace and Consequences

With Russia out of the war, Germany shifted forces to the Western Front for a big push. Britain and France, however, had access to global sources of food and materials, notably from the United States, that Germany and Austria did

THE GREAT WAR	
1914	Assassination of Archduke Franz Ferdinand in Sarajevo. German forces invade Belgium and France but fail to seize Paris. Western and Eastern Front lines form.
1915	Allied assault on Turkish peninsula of Gallipoli.
1916	Battle of Verdun and Battle of the Somme River.
1917	The United States declares war on Germany and sends troops to Europe. The Russian Revolution begins. Russia signs an armistice with Germany.
1918	Treaty of Brest-Litovsk. German forces fail to break through on the Western Front. Armistice ends hostilities.
1919	Paris Peace Conference.

not. By early 1918, Germany's economy was stretched thin and its population exhausted and malnourished. Worker strikes erupted and socialist parties gained strength, giving the kaiser good reason to fear a Russian-style revolution. When the western offensive met a wall of fresh American troops, an ordered retreat followed quickly. The armistice of November 11, 1918, ended the fighting, though the Allies achieved no crushing victory on the field; nor did they

Devastation on the Western Front. Human casualties were compounded by environmental damage during World War I. What does this photograph of soldiers posing in the charred remains of a forest tell us about the conditions and consequences of modern warfare?

invade and occupy Germany. Nevertheless, the kaiser abdicated amid a flurry of urban uprisings spearheaded by communists and other radicals. Russian Bolsheviks had high hopes of a German workers' revolution, but moderate socialists and anticommunists crushed the insurrections and proclaimed a new liberal republic.

The grim aftermath. The roughly sixteen million people who died as a result of the Great War numbered only about three million less those who died in all wars worldwide in the entire nineteenth century.[11] Those losses washed over countless more millionsÐ the families, friends, and communities of the dead. France, for example, lost half its male population between the ages of fifteen and thirty. Another twenty-one million or so returned from the war blinded, crippled, or otherwise injured. The war zones produced countless refugees, 600,000 from Belgium alone. Surviving African and Asian soldiers who fought on one side or the other returned home to find jobs in short supply and the same thoroughly authoritarian imperial systems in place as before the war.

Most of the conflict's physical devastation afflicted Poland, Serbia, Belgium, and northeastern France, where the heaviest fighting took place. Trenches, shell craters, and fires turned hundreds of thousands of acres of farm and forest into smoking wilderness. Although much of this land was eventually restored, entire villages disappeared forever. There is no doubt that atmospheric pollution from soot, smoke, and sulfur dioxide increased hugely during the war, especially in industrial zones like the English midlands or Germany's Ruhr Valley, where factories operated day and night. Total costs of the war in public expenditure reached nearly $150 billion on the Allied side, and all the European states involved in it found themselves swamped in debt. Only the United States and Japan emerged as financial winners. Japan's wartime exports nearly tripled, and the United States became a creditor rather than a debtor state for the first time in its history.

The influenza pandemic. Amid the violence of the war's final year, an infectious disease pandemic visited nearly every part of the world, wreaking more misery and death. The war itself helped empower this particularly virulent strain of influenza, for which no vaccination existed. A severe outbreak occurred at an army base in Kansas in March 1918. Infected soldiers then transmitted the virus along the military transport network to other bases and from there to Britain and France. In 1918 and early 1919 the flu killed upwards of forty million people worldwide, that is, millions more than died in the fighting. Although the pathological explanation is unclear, this particular virus sickened or killed more men and women in their twenties than the older age groups typically at risk.

Like the plague outbreak of the 1890s, the flu pandemic spread around the world by steamship. In the port of Cape Town, South Africa, for example, 4 percent of the population perished within a month. From ports the virus moved inland. In the Americas the contagion ripped through

Arab Independence That Was Not to Be

Starting in July 1915, Sharif Husayn ibn Ali, the governor of Mecca and Medina, exchanged a series of letters with the British High Commissioner in Egypt regarding political independence for Arabic-speaking peoples. Husayn vowed to raise a revolt against Ottoman authority in return for assurances of British support for a sovereign Arab state following victory over Turkey. Britain appeared to make promises to that effect, despite several qualifications. Instead, Britain and France safeguarded their own alliance by settling in advance potential disputes over the postwar Middle East. France had long-standing interests in Syria but worried that Britain, which was leading the Allied campaign against the Turks, might move to dominate the entire region. Accordingly, in May 1916, Mark Sykes, a British civil servant, and François Picot, a French one, negotiated a secret treaty to partition the Middle East, betraying assurances of Arab self-determination. This partition, as shown in Document 3, took place in 1919.

DOCUMENT 1 Sharif Husayn to the British High Commissioner, July 1915

Whereas the whole of the Arab nation without any exception have decided in these last years to accomplish their freedom, and grasp the reins of their administration both in theory and practice; and whereas they have found and felt that it is in the interest of the Government of Great Britain to support them and aid them in the attainment of their firm and lawful intentions.

Firstly—England will acknowledge the independence of the Arab countries, bounded on the north by Mersina and Adana [in modern Turkey] up to the 37th degree of latitude, . . . up to the border of Persia [Iran]; on the east by the borders of Persia up to the Gulf of Basra; on the south by the Indian Ocean, with the exception of the position of Aden to remain as it is; on

the west by the Red Sea, the Mediterranean Sea up to Mersina. England to approve the proclamation of an Arab Khalifate of Islam.

Secondly—The Arab Government of the Sharif will acknowledge that England shall have the preference in all economic enterprises in the Arab countries whenever conditions of enterprises are otherwise equal. . . .

Consequently, and as the whole of the Arab nation have (praise be to God) agreed and united for the attainment, at all costs and finally, of this noble object, they beg the Government of Great Britain to answer them positively or negatively in a period of thirty days after receiving this intimation.

DOCUMENT 2 British Foreign Office to French Embassy in London, May 1916

It is accordingly understood between the French and British governments:

That France and Great Britain are prepared to recognize and protect an independent Arab state or a confederation of Arab states (a) and (b) marked on the annexed map [see Document 3], under the suzerainty of an Arab chief. That in area (a) France, and in area (b) Great Britain, shall have priority of right of enterprise and local loans. That in area (a) France, and in area (b) Great Britain, shall alone supply advisers or foreign functionaries at the request of the Arab state or confederation of Arab states.

That in the blue area France, and in the red area Great Britain, shall be allowed to establish such direct or indirect

administration or control as they desire and as they may think fit to arrange with the Arab state or confederation of Arab states.

That in the brown area [appears yellow on map] there shall be established an international administration, the form of which is to be decided upon after consultation with Russia, and subsequently in consultation with the other allies, and the representatives of the sheriff [Sharif] of Mecca.

Sources: Husayn Letter: Quoted in Marvin Gettleman and Stuart Schaar, eds., *The Middle East and Islamic World Reader* (New York: Grove Press, 2003), 114±115. Sykes-Picot Agreement: Mideast Gateway, http://www.mideastweb.org.

Thinking Critically

What specific words and phrases in these two texts indicate a divergence between Arab and European aims in the Middle East? The Sykes-Picot Agreement refers to recognition of "an independent Arab state or a confederation of Arab states." But what other language in that text qualifies the French and British understanding of Arab independence? According to Sharif Husayn's specifications, how would the Arab state he proposed look on a map of the Middle East? Has a state with those approximate boundaries ever existed since World War I? How did Husayn's expectations differ from the territorial division agreed upon by France and Great Britain shown in Document 3?

The map of the Sykes-Picot Agreement partitions a large swath of the Ottoman Empire into territory directly administered by France (in blue), France's region of exclusive influence (labeled A), territory directly controlled by Britain (in red), and Britain's sphere of exclusive influence (labeled B).

Mexico, Chile, Brazil, and Argentina. South Asian ports, important nodes in the British wartime shipping web, were hit hard, and the affliction then crossed the subcontinent, inflicting perhaps half the total of global deaths. In Australia, two epidemic waves killed about twelve thousand. In the United States no major city escaped, and about 675,000 Americans died.

The death toll dropped in the spring of 1919, and the particular virus that caused the pandemic disappeared eventually. Those who survived exposure acquired immunity to that particular strain. Nevertheless, the flu outbreak inflicted on the world great anxiety, tragedy, and loss of human productivity just as it was striving to pull itself from the muck of war.

The peace treaties. The monumental task of restoring political stability to a depleted world fell in the short term on the diplomats who met at a series of international conferences held between 1919 and 1924, starting with the Paris Peace Conference. The victorious powers dominated these meetings and took it upon themselves to deal with the wreckage of four huge monarchiesÐ Germany, Austria-Hungary, Ottoman Turkey, and Russia. Three of those empires were the war's big losers. The forth was transforming itself into a communist state pledging global socialist revolution. The several conferences produced treaties that redrew political boundaries, created brand new states, and pronounced sentence on the defeated countries.

When leaders of the principal Allied powersÐ Britain, France, Italy, the United States, and JapanÐ initiated the treaty-making process at Versailles in January 1919, they first put forth high-minded visions of a safe, peaceful, and democratic world. Then, they got down to their hard-nosed plan to gather the spoils of victory, enfeeble Germany indefinitely, politically isolate the Russian communists, and get back to the business of ruling much of Africa and Asia. British and French leaders could not go along with Woodrow Wilson's ideal of ᵃpeace without victory,° if they hoped to retain public support at home. The French prime minister Georges Clemenceau summed up European leaders' skepticism and wariness about Wilson: ᵃNever before has any political assembly heard so fine a sermon on what humans might be capable of if only they weren't human.°

Wilson brought to Versailles his Fourteen Points, a set of goals for a new world order that emphasized the commitment of sovereign states to collective security (as opposed to secret bilateral deals) and the rights of ethnically based national communities to political **self-determination.** The European Allies, however, knew all too well that the war ended without seriously damaging Germany's future military and industrial potential. They insisted, therefore, that it be stripped of large chunks of territory,

self-determination The idea put forth during and after World War I that a society sharing common language, history, and cultural traditions should have the right to decide its own political future and govern its own affairs.

prohibited from recovering its overseas colonies, permitted only a small defensive army, and obligated to accept responsibility for starting the war. This ᵃwar guilt clause° served as justification for imposing on Germany more than $330 billion in **reparations** to the victorious states. This punishment served the domestic interests of French and British leaders, who desperately needed money to repay their own war debts, principally to American banks. German diplomats were not allowed to take part in the Versailles conference but nonetheless had to sign the treaty. The kaiser's empire was transformed into a militarily frail republic, and Germans nearly universally felt humiliated and aggrieved. In the aftermath of Versailles, radical German parties on the left and right struggled to dominate the country and to undo the treaties.

reparations The act of making amends or giving satisfaction for an injustice or injury; payment of compensation by a defeated state for presumed damages inflicted on another state as a result of war between them.

The last of Wilson's Fourteen Points declared that ᵃa general association of nations must be formed under specific covenants for the purpose of affording mutual guarantees of political independence and territorial integrity to great and small states alike.° The Versailles treaty duly established the League of Nations, the first formal organization of sovereign states dedicated to worldwide collective security through open negotiations. The League started out providing an institutional forum for communication among states and for international humanitarian, educational, and statistical work. Germany, Russia, and the United States, however, were not charter members. The Allied victors refused to allow the first two countries to join, and the U.S. Senate, averse to further European entanglements, kept America out.

The complexities of self-determination. The postwar agreements made a shambles of Wilson's principle of self-determination, which would ideally have provided a democratic nation-state to every significant ethnolinguistic group that had formerly been enclosed in one of the four defunct empires. The proposal was hopelessly unworkable. On the ground, most of eastern and southern Europe's numerous ethnic peoples were jumbled together, not territorially separate. Consequently, a nation-state created for one group within the former Austro-Hungarian or Ottoman empire would almost inevitably have its own minorities clamoring for *their* nation-states. Insofar as self-determination became a reality, it favored groups that had supported the Allies, notably Poles, Romanians, Serbians, and Italians. By contrast, it penalized groups that had joined the other sideÐ Germans, German-speaking Austrians, Hungarians, Bulgarians, and Turks.

In Russia in 1919, Lenin had not yet consolidated Communist Party authority, but that year his regime sponsored a congress of the Comintern, or Communist International, to support socialist revolutionary parties around the globe.

From the Allied perspective, such subversive provocation offered a persuasive rationale for quarantining the ᵃdisease° of Bolshevik communism behind a line of seven new sovereign states with governments guaranteed to be anti-Russian. Four of themÐ Lithuania, Poland, Hungary, and RomaniaÐ had historical precedents as sovereign states; the othersÐ Finland, Latvia, and EstoniaÐ were creations of the Allied treaty makers. Serbian nationalists got to dominate Yugoslavia, a new multiethnic state of Slavic-speaking peoples previously enfolded within the Austro-Hungarian or Turkish empires. Czechoslovakia was similarly set up as an assemblage of ethnolinguistic groups.

When Wilson proclaimed his Fourteen Points, nationalist groups throughout the colonized world experienced what historians have called the ᵃWilsonian Moment.°¹² For a few brief months, they anticipated that the American leader would use his considerable moral authority to convince the European imperial powers to grant genuine democratic self-determination to all subjugated peoples, not just in Europe but throughout the world. Wilson, however, failed to challenge European colonial authority with any vigor on this point, and the Wilsonian Moment evaporated. The victorious powers, despite their massive postwar debts and the war's blatant exposure of the myth of innate European moral superiority, expected to return to business as usual in ruling most of Africa and a good part of Asia. In the peace accords, the populations of Germany's African colonies were not invited to discuss their future self-determination. Rather, these dependencies were arbitrarily transferred to Britain, France, or South Africa (and its white government) under League of Nations supervision. Britain and France took over the defeated Ottoman empire's former Arabic-speaking provinces under a similar arrangement, despite promises to the contrary to Arab leaders. Young nationalists in colonized territories profoundly resented these actions, prompting them in the postwar decades to organize political movements, first to petition for reforms in imperial regimes and, when that process moved too slowly, to demand their sovereign freedom, as we will see in the coming chapters.

• • •

Conclusion

We have no way of knowing how the world would have changed during the twentieth century's second decade if World War I had not happened. There is no doubt, however, that the conflict not only caused far more death and devastation than any previous war but that it begat numerous long-term problems. Despite capitalist hopes, the global economy did not bounce back to prewar levels. Britain and France slowed European recovery generally by refusing to help reintegrate industrialized, heavily populated Germany. Germans, knowing that the Allies never decisively crushed their army on the battlefield, fumed over their country's degradation and dishonor. In eastern and southeastern Europe, nationalists complained that the settlements gave other ethnic groups too much territory and power or their own not enough. In Europe's Asian and African colonial territories, nationalist leaders gained popular support as soon as people discovered that self-determination was meant to apply to Europeans, but not to them. The war aggravated problems of air pollution, water contamination, and deforestation already under way in industrialized countries. Wartime scientists and engineers made numerous useful discoveries and innovations, but these included weapons of unprecedented power. The bluntest assessment of how well diplomats in tailcoats and top hats restored global stability is that within twenty short years another great war broke, a calamity more brutal and destructive than the first.

• • •

Key Terms

Bolshevik 719	Great War (World War I) 699	Russian Revolution of 1905 708
Boxers 709	League of Nations 724	self-determination 724
Comintern 724	Mexican Revolution 711	soviet 707
Fordism 702	October Revolution (Bolshevik Revolution) 719	total war 717
Fourteen Points 724	reparations 724	treaty ports 708
gold standard 699		Young Turks 708

Change over Time

1886	Gold is discovered in South Africa.
1896–1902	A series of El Niño–related floods and droughts affects harvests and triggers widespread famine.
1896–1914	The global economy experiences strong growth.
1899–1902	Britain makes war on Afrikaner governments in South Africa in the Boer War.
1901	The first trans-Atlantic wireless transmission strengthens the global communication network.
1905	Waves of popular protest challenge the tsar's authority in the Russian Revolution. Japan defeats Russia in the Russo-Japanese War.
1906	Iran adopts a constitution; civil war breaks out after the death of the shah.
1908	Young Turks force the sultan to abdicate in the Ottoman empire.
1910	The Mexican Revolution begins, with the goal of overthrowing the Díaz regime (Porfiriato). German scientists discover how to make solid nitrates, a key component of gunpowder, dynamite, and fertilizer.
1911	The Qing dynasty collapses in the wake of the Chinese Revolution.
1914	The Panama Canal opens, speeding steamship traffic between the Atlantic and Pacific.
1914–1918	The Allied and Central Powers and their colonies clash in World War I.
1916	The Arab Revolt against Ottoman rule begins.
1917	Russia withdrawals from World War I; the Russian Revolution begins.
1918–1919	An influenza pandemic strikes around the globe.
1919	Nationalist groups throughout the colonized world experience the "Wilsonian Moment." The Paris Peace Conference sets the terms of German reparations and ignores colonial requests for self-determination.

Please see end of book reference section for additional reading suggestions related to this chapter.

25 Turbulent Decades
1918–1935

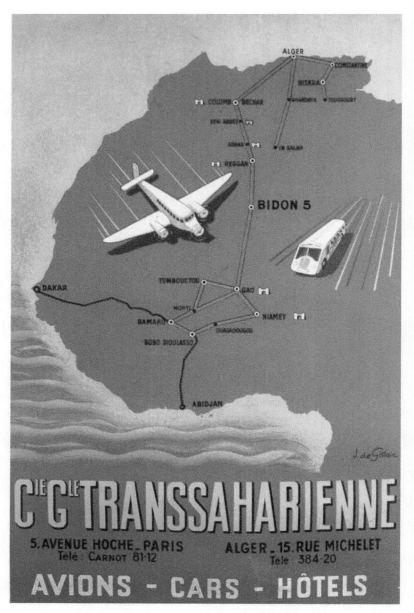

The General Trans-Saharan Company connected North and West Africa with motor vehicle and air services, though unpaved tracks across the desert could not accommodate sleek busses like the one shown in this poster.

idon 5, or Gas Can 5 in English, is a spot in a particularly desolate part of the Sahara Desert where in 1926 employees of the General Trans-Saharan Company set up a refueling depot for automobiles and airplanes. During the previous quarter-century, French colonial forces had seized control of the central Sahara's major oases and their Berber and Arab populations. In the 1920s the company began building numerous gas and water stations like Bidon 5 to facilitate travel and eventual mining operations in landscapes friendly in earlier times only to camel caravans. In 1920 French military pilots made the first flight across the Sahara, though it included many fuel stops. Four planes started the journey. Two did not get far, and a third crashed in a waterless tract, where one of the three crew members died. The fourth plane made it to the Niger River in what is today Mali. In 1922–1923 a French team in Citroën automobiles drove from northern Algeria to Timbuktu on the Niger in twenty-two days. Four years later, another Frenchman crossed the great void on a motorcycle. Trans-Saharan airmail and trucking services soon followed. French visionaries laid plans to crisscross the desert with rail lines, though that project never came to reality.

To the world's entrepreneurs, engineers, and scientists, the internal combustion engine's conquest of the Sahara was just one sign that a new age of technological innovation was at hand. Perhaps World War I, they surmised, had been only a brief, unfortunate interruption of modernity's exhilarating progressive march. The first part of this chapter examines some key developments of the

1920s that on the whole bolstered faith in humankind's dynamism and progress. The Great War turned out to have no lasting negative effect on global population growth or urbanization. The war itself also stimulated new technical and scientific research, including revolutionary theories about the workings of the universe.

In the economic and political spheres, however, expectations of a new era of prosperity and calm gradually faded. The global economy did not resume a heady upward spiral. Rather, the gross domestic product of the major European industrialized countries grew at half the rate of the boom that had preceded the war.[1] Most countries continued to struggle with inflation, chronic unemployment, or both. The second section of the chapter connects the economic insecurities of the 1920s and early 1930s to the spread of ultranationalist and authoritarian political regimes. Liberal democratic governments survived in western Europe and the Americas, but authoritarian leaders having no patience for multiparty legislatures and individual rights seized power, sometimes to popular acclaim, in much of Europe and in some countries of Latin America and Asia.

As of 1920, about one-third of the world's population lived under governments imposed by foreign invaders from across the seas. In the chapter's third part we explore interwar developments in the colonial dependencies of several European powers, plus Japan and the United States. Postwar treaty-making led to national independence for some groups previously enclosed within the Russian, German, Austro-Hungarian, or Ottoman empires. But on the global scale, colonial empires got bigger after the war, not smaller. In the early 1920s, all the states that held colonies were republics or constitutional monarchies, but they ruled their possessions by force, not by the consent of the governed. The very condition of imperial repression, however, accelerated social and economic change in the colonies and strengthened nationalist movements for self-rule.

The final section of the chapter surveys the Great Depression. Striking just eleven years after World War I, it represented the twentieth century's second globe-encompassing crisis. If some economic thinkers saw a business downturn coming in 1929, no one expected it to mutate into a financial and commercial catastrophe for much of the world. The depression caused great misery. It also propelled many states to amass even more central power than they had during World War I in order to grapple with the economic crisis. The most economically developed states also initiated public programs aimed at protecting citizens from the worst effects of economic downswings. Unfortunately, popular frustration and despair also played into the hands of popular demagogues and dictators even more ruthless than the ones who had seized power in the 1920s.

MAP 25.1 States, colonial dependencies, and League of Nations Mandates, 1925.

Which states had large territorial claims overseas in 1925? Where were most of those colonies located? What factors can explain changes in imperial land claims between 1910 and 1925 (see Map 24.1)?

Postwar Trends in Society and Culture

FOCUS What were key social, cultural, and scientific trends in the decade after World War I?

In the 1920s the pace of change in global population, urbanization, technology, and science continued at high speed. Unlike earlier generations, educated classes even warmed to the idea that the faster the world changed, the better off everyone would be. Philosophers, writers, and artists argued that continuous change is a fundamental condition of human life that should be embraced with enthusiasm, an idea summed up by the term **modernism.**

> **modernism** The movement in the arts and humanities that embraces innovation and experimentation and rejects adherence to traditional forms and values.

Population Trends

World War I and the influenza pandemic of 1918±1919 together took around fifty-six million lives, a number representing about 3.2 percent of the world's population in 1910. That many deaths from combat, bombs, hunger, and disease in just five years was ghastly, but it had no effect on the global population surge under way since the 1700s. Population worldwide *rose* by about 3 percent between 1910 and 1920, canceling the loss. Between 1920 and 1940, the earth accommodated about 410 million more people, a trend inseparable from issues of worldwide food production and economic inequality.

Demographic transition, or not. After the Great War, regional shares of world population began to shift decidedly away from Europe and toward other densely populated regions. In the early decades of the twentieth century, Europe as a whole experienced what social scientists call **demographic transition.** Since the eighteenth century, accelerating population growth had been associated primarily with declining death rates, a phenomenon linked to improved food supplies and nutrition and to lower mortality from infectious diseases (despite recurrent epidemics of maladies such as influenza). But in Europe sometime after 1900, *both* the death rate and the fertility rate, the average number of children a woman bore in her lifetime, declined. Lower fertility rates partially counteracted growth spurred by lower death rates, thereby lowering the *rate* of annual population increase. Declining births were associated with a complex combination of factors, including rising living standards, relatively late marriage, and improved birth control methods.

> **demographic transition** The stabilization of population level in a society resulting from the decline of both fertility rates and death rates.

By contrast, in Latin America, South Asia, Subsaharan Africa, and (after World War II) China, death rates declined

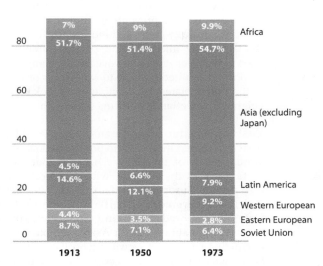

Percentage of world total

Changing shares of world population by region, 1913–1973. Shares of total world population increased in Africa, Asia, and Latin America during those sixty years because population growth rates remained relatively high. Regions with lower growth rates had declining shares.

but fertility rates remained high. In other words, people gained longer average life expectancies, as clean water, hygiene measures, and vaccinations against infectious diseases became more widely available. At the same time, however, women continued on average to bear the same number of children they had in the nineteenth century, or even more. This was a sure formula for swelling population growth rates.[2]

In regions of high growth rates, the long-term consequences included increased pressure on farm land, declining standards of living, stepped up migration from countryside to city, and accelerating deforestation owing to heavier demand for firewood, timber, and cleared fields. For example, the rate of forest depletion worldwide rose from an average of about 7.4 million acres per year between 1850 and 1919 to 28.4 million between 1920 and 1949.[3]

Postwar urbanization. In the first half of the twentieth century, the great majority of humans still tended crops or herded animals. As of 1930, only about 17 percent of the population of Latin America lived in cities. In South Asia it was 12 percent and in Africa, 7 percent. Nevertheless, cities became bigger and more numerous on every inhabited continent after World War I. By 1920 half the population of the United States lived in cities; Japan reached that benchmark about 1935.

Throughout most of history, cities had been incubators of infectious and lethal diseases. Populations grew only because in-migration exceeded the mortality rate. By World War I, however, cities were becoming safer places to live, especially in richer countries, owing to advances in public health and disease prevention. Higher, denser urban populations naturally generated more waste, air pollution, and the unhealthy microbes and particles that accompanied them. Wealthier cities, however, built complex sewer networks and shunted garbage to waterways or rural landfills. In the United States, for example, cities took to ᵃreclaiming° neighboring wetlands by filling them with garbage and ash.

Postwar migration patterns. After World War I, Chinese and Indian migration to Southeast Asia surged to the annual levels of the prewar decades. But westward migration across the Atlantic, which had carried nearly fifteen million Europeans to the United States between 1900 and 1914, recovered only partially. In the 1920s the United States had imposed strict immigration quotas on certain European nationalities and on Asians, a policy that reflected narrowing nationalist views of who should and should not be invited in. Brazil also introduced restrictive immigration laws in the 1920s.

On the regional and national levels, numerous complex population shifts took place after World War I. In the war's immediate aftermath, millions of refugees and people seeking to leave one ethnic region for another crisscrossed Europe. Christian Armenians who faced persecution and death during the Ottoman state's wartime ethnic cleansing of 1915 (see Chapter 24) fled to Syria, Lebanon, and various other lands around the world. In 1922 Greece and Turkey, after years of hostilities, agreed to a compulsory exchange that sent about 1.2 million Eastern Orthodox Christians from Turkey to Greece and half a million Muslims from Greece to Turkey. In North America, where the United States exempted Latin Americans from immigration restrictions, almost 500,000 Mexicans moved to the southwestern states in the 1920s in search of work.

New Ways of Living in the Industrialized World

Numerous new inventions and mass production techniques materialized during the Great War because governments instructed scientists and engineers to find technical solutions to particular military and industrial problems. In the interwar years, both governments and corporations continued to support research on larger, more efficient scales by organizing teams of scientists, engineers, managers, government bureaucrats, and university professors to work collaboratively.

Research and development labs dedicated to deliberate innovation proliferated after the war. Professional teams either invented or greatly improved upon such marvels as

nylon, synthetic rubber, and the affordable fluorescent lamp. Of course, individuals continued to come up with bright ideas. Talented loners invented the helicopter, the ballpoint pen, the vacuum tube, insulin, penicillin, and cellophane. In 1907 Leo Baekeland, a Belgian scientist, invented Bakelite, one of the earliest plastic materials, by synthesizing large molecules of the type found in many natural vegetables. Following the lead of North Americans, western Europeans started laying out hard-earned cash for cars, record players, radios, and movie tickets. By 1927, assembly lines of the Ford Motor Company boosted production of Model Ts to fifteen million. In the same decade, Brazilian entrepreneurs began to import ᵃautomobile kits° from abroad for local assembly and sale.

The torrent of new things transformed work and family life in countless ways. First in the United States and by the 1920s in western Europe, radios and phonographs transmitted jazz and other popular music that celebrated personal and sexual freedom. Evenings at the local picture house increasingly crowded out family conversations and reading sessions. Hollywood films exalted urban glamour, enticing young men and women to escape the farm and head to the city. The automobile gave people more personal and occupational mobility, accelerating the spread of residential suburbs. Intercity roads, parking lots, and new suburbs altered, indeed scarred, physical and natural landscapes, displacing farms, villages, and wild habitats. In the United States the network of intercity highways grew from 387,000 miles in 1921 to 1.3 million by 1940. First in the industrialized countries and then around the world, cities and industries became electrified. Nighttime lighting allowed factories to run work shifts around the clock, and it pushed women's domestic work deeper into the evening.

Scientific Challenges to the Knowable Universe

The pace of scientific discovery, which quickened in the late nineteenth century, moved even faster after World War I. Progress in physical, chemical, and biological theories tended to be incrementalÐ a small breakthrough here, another one there. In physics, however, scientists working in Europe between 1900 and 1930 made theoretical leaps that began to transform humankind's conception of reality. Isaac Newton and other geniuses of the seventeenth and eighteenth centuries had conceived of an orderly, stable, and predictable

Art Deco radio, 1930. The development of plastics made mass-produced decorative objects and useful goods more affordable for ordinary consumers. Art Deco used the same basic geometric shapes—circles and squares—and sharp angles of modern machines, arranged in attractive designs.

cosmos governed by laws expressible in exact mathematical terms. In the late nineteenth century, however, a small band of gifted thinkers, including the German physicist Albert Einstein, began to deconstruct this universe. In 1905 Einstein presented his theory of relativity, which demonstrated mathematically that there is no single spatial and chronological framework within the universe. Rather, time and space are relative to the individual or object measuring them. For example, gravity affects the passage of time so that clocks in space, distant from the planet's gravitational pull, would run faster than earthbound timekeepers. Einstein also helped redefine matter itself by showing that matter and energy are not distinct phenomena but instead are equivalent to each other, that is, $E = mc^2$. These ideas were bewilderingly at odds with both human sense perception and modern science up to that point. At first, most of the world rejected or ignored them.

Einstein believed that the new relativity would somehow be reconciled with the old physics. However, Werner Heisenberg, another German scientist, challenged even this premise. A pioneer in quantum mechanics, which describes the wave properties of submicroscopic particles, Heisenberg contended in 1927 that if one probes deeply enough into the tiniest elements that constitute matter, the ᵃknowabilityº of the universe evaporates. According to his ᵃuncertainty principle,º it is not possible to determine simultaneously the exact position and speed of a particle such as an electron orbiting the nucleus of an atom. The more precisely we measure the position, the less we can know of the speed. If we look at where the particle is, we cannot know where it is going, and vice versa. The very act of measuring the particle alters its behavior. Or more broadly, the physical universe simply cannot be described fully. And if it cannot, its fundamental laws can never be entirely known. In the ensuing decades, scientists adjusted to the ᵃuncertainty principleº as a working hypothesis, and the new physics stimulated many avenues of research that had long-term practical applications, such as radar, electronics, atom splitting, and the nuclear bomb.

Modernity and Modernism

In the late nineteenth century the reality of modernityÐ the rapid acceleration of change in nearly every sphere of lifeÐ began to impose itself on human consciousness, at least in industrialized and densely urbanized parts of the world. In the cities of western Europe, intellectuals argued that change should be understood as both continuous and invigorating and that no time-honored tradition of how to observe and interpret the world should be considered safe from challenge. A corps of writers, artists, scholars, and cultural critics took on the special mission of questioning conventional views of the world and prevailing standards of morality, taste, and respectability. To this end they experimented with fresh forms of literature, architecture, painting, dance, music, and film.

Very broadly, modernism as a cultural ideology signified an attitude of welcome and acclaim for the modern age and for any creative act that might evoke or illuminate modern life. Modernists zealously embraced the new, the here-and-now, rather than striving to resist and control change as entrenched political and religious elites tended to do. World War I strengthened the modernist critique. To unorthodox thinkers, the war's horrors and sheer mindlessness discredited traditional values, smug faith in rationality, and entrenched hierarchies (even in presumed democratic countries). Writers and artists expressed great cultural disillusionment but also resolved to reshape the world.

Heisenberg's uncertainty principle seemed to play into the modernist idea that rational thought cannot reveal the whole of reality. So did the ideas of the Austrian physician Sigmund Freud. He argued that the survival of organized society depended on people behaving rationally but that this required a mighty struggle against irrational and instinctual impulses. In 1900 he published *The Interpretation of Dreams*, which hypothesized that desire, self-delusion, and aggression ruled the deep structures of the brain, the ᵃunconscious mind.º People suffer guilt as a result of habitually repressing primal drives, especially sexual ones. This subconscious turmoil may then produce emotional disturbances, psychoses, or even physical illnesses. Freud contended that civilization's standards and laws serve to control base instincts. He also insisted, however, that the scientific method of therapy he called psychoanalysis could draw the mind's deepest, darkest operations to the surface

A famous piece of Surrealist art. Swiss artist Méret Oppenheim's teacup, saucer, and spoon are covered in the fur of a Chinese gazelle. She made the work in 1936. Why is this creation considered a statement of modernism? © UPPA/Photoshot © 2013 Artists Rights Society (ARS), New York/ProLitteris, Zurich.

Diego Rivera: Mexican Modernist

Diego Rivera and Frida Kahlo at an art exhibition in New York, 1930s.

The fact that modernism warmly embraced all things new practically ensured that its artistic movements would take off in many different directions. Early modernist painters like Picasso disputed the conventional idea that paintings should depict human figures and their world realistically. Diego Rivera (1886–1957), a graduate of a traditional art school in Mexico City, joined this modernist cause in his youth as an aspiring Cubist painter. But he soon followed other modernist impulses, painting murals in which naturalistically proportioned figures bore witness to Mexico's history and culture, including the Revolution of 1910. Rivera's modernism was expressed in his commitment to art that portrayed the lives of ordinary people, evoked Mexico's ethnic heritage, and served nationalist and revolutionary aims.

A son of urban middle-class parents, Rivera lived in Europe from 1911 to 1921, immersing himself in the heady art scene there and gradually refining his own vision. Distancing himself from Cubism, he left Paris for Italy in 1920, where he studied, among other things, fresco construction, that is, the labor-intensive art of painting on wet plaster. Rivera believed that art should be accessible to all, not just the affluent classes, and he came to regard the fresco technique, applied to enormous murals on the walls of public buildings, as an ideal form of public art.

In 1921 Rivera returned to Mexico to. participate in a government-sponsored program to create public murals with national and revolutionary themes. A leading figure in the Mexican Muralism movement, Rivera painted colorful epic scenes that depicted the country's Aztec past, the suffering of its people under Spanish rule, and the stirring events of the revolution. Rivera's art also commented harshly on Mexico's vulnerability to foreign and particularly capitalist interference. Both a nationalist and a Marxist, Rivera joined the Mexican Communist Party in 1922 and spent time in the Soviet Union in 1927–1928. He was expelled from the party in 1929, however, for criticizing Joseph Stalin's iron-handed rule. Nevertheless, he remained dedicated to socialist revolutionary ideals.

Though he married multiple times and had a notorious reputation as a womanizer, Rivera formed an enduring if stormy partnership with the painter Frida Kahlo, a woman eventually recognized as one of the early twentieth century's great artists. Rivera and Kahlo married in 1929 and, except for a brief divorce in 1939–1940, remained together until her death in 1954. Rivera's Marxist politics did not stop him from accepting commissions from some of the world's leading capitalists. Accompanied by Kahlo, Rivera traveled to the United States in 1930. He first painted murals in San Francisco, then moved at the invitation of Henry Ford to the Detroit Institute, where he undertook *Detroit Industry,* a monumental series of twenty-seven panels depicting both people at work in the Ford Motor Company and general themes of scientific and technological progress. Owing to his left-wing sentiments, which showed frequently in his art, his work in the United States caused considerable public commotion. In 1933 he inserted an image of the Russian communist revolutionary V. I. Lenin into a mural he painted at Rockefeller Center in New York. After he refused requests to erase Lenin from the mural, Rivera's sponsors had it destroyed.

In 1933 Rivera returned to Mexico, where he continued to produce murals as well as more commercial paintings of scenes from Mexican culture. He made a last, brief trip to the United States in 1940 to paint a series of murals for San Francisco's Golden Gate Exposition. He continued to paint in his later years, adding art to public spaces nearly until his death in 1957.

Thinking Critically

In what ways do you think Diego Rivera's career exemplified modernist cultural trends?

and effectively treat mental disease. Although Freud quickly provoked innumerable criticisms and countertheories, he, more powerfully than any other scientist of the early century, revealed mind and personality as an immense inner universe.

First in Europe, but soon in other parts of the world, numerous modernist movements succeeded one anotherÐ

Impressionism, Post-Impressionism, Symbolism, Expressionism, Cubism, Futurism, Dadaism, Art Deco, Surrealism, Constructivism, and musical atonality. Claude Monet and other artists of the Impressionist school, already at work in the 1870s, contended that painters should probe the pure sensations of nature and daily life by experimenting with color, light, form, and motion. In 1890 the French artist Maurice

Denis wrote, "It is well to remember that a pictureĐ before being a battle horse, a nude woman, or some anecdoteĐ is essentially a flat surface covered with colors assembled in a certain order."[4] That observation evoked the modernist urge to demolish illusions and penetrate to the honest heart of things. In the first decade of the twentieth century, Pablo Picasso (1881±1973) and his fellow Cubists reveled in distorting objective reality, disassembling objects, including the human figure, then putting them back together on canvas in jumbled bits and pieces that might baffle the viewer but also uncover some deeper reality (see Picasso's *Les Demoiselles d'Avignon* in Chapter 24). The Surrealists drew on Freud's psychoanalytical technique to paint disturbing, illogical images of the sort we see in dreams. Writers such as James Joyce and Gertrude Stein produced novels and poems that recorded private "streams of consciousness" or that abandoned standard rules of grammar and word order. The Russian composer Igor Stravinsky wrote music that substituted ambiguous chords, clashing sounds, and haunting rhythms for the harmonic melodies of the European classical tradition. Audiences tended to react to modernist experimentation with confusion, if not ridicule and shock. For modernists, however, this was precisely the point. If too many people found what they created easy to digest, then they were not pursuing their mission radically enough.

Modernist movements found eager disciples in places like Buenos Aires, Shanghai, and Tokyo, and artists and writers merged Western materials and styles with local traditions. Chinese painters applied European techniques to traditional visual themes. In several Muslim countries, writers experimented with Western poetry and prose fiction, and musicians combined local with European composition and instrumentation. The Iranian artist Muhammad Ghaffari (1848±1940) exemplified the small number of Muslim artists who traveled to Europe to study modernist painting. He returned home to open an art school in Tehran in 1911 to teach European techniques and styles. Modernists prided themselves on openness to unfamiliar art forms. For example, Japanese woodblock prints, a long-established art in that country, attracted a booming European market. They profoundly influenced the work of Western artists such as Henri Toulouse-Lautrec and the American painter Mary Cassatt. According to the French art critic Theodore Duret, "As soon as people looked at Japanese pictures, where the most glaring, piercing colors were placed side by side, they finally understood that there were new methods for reproducing certain effects of nature."[5]

Clashing Ideologies in the Political Arena

FOCUS Why did a number of authoritarian states emerge in the interwar years?

By the close of World War I, the modern idea that governments ought to exercise authority only with the consent of the "people" achieved nearly universal acceptance among sovereign states as a political ideal. Autocracy, defined here as the doctrine that rulers acquire legitimacy through tradition and inheritance, and usually with the endorsement of God, nearly disappeared. This happened in the wake of events that destroyed deep-rooted imperial dynasties in China, Iran, Russia, Germany, Austria-Hungary, and Ottoman Turkey in the early twentieth century. All the governments that replaced those empires claimed legitimacy as the rightful agents of the "will of the people."

States presumably founded on this principle, however, did not necessarily subscribe to the ideals of liberal democracy, in other words, to a political system characterized by contested legislative elections, independent judicial institutions, guaranteed liberties, and few legal restrictions on capitalist enterprise. In the decade after the war, many political activists took the view that the world needed governments with stronger executive authority to fire up patriotic pride, unify the masses, and get things done. For them, parliamentary debates and private freedoms frustrated decisive action in uncertain and dangerous times. In numerous states, authoritarian leaders found they could woo mass support by promising to act for the "nation."

Democratic Hopes

The western European and American leaders who signed the treaties ending World War I hoped that liberal democracy would soon sweep the world whether in the form of republics (like France and the United States) or constitutional monarchies (like Britain, Sweden, and the Netherlands). The signs looked quite good. Within two years of the war, the number of republics in Europe multiplied from three to thirteen. In the nine new national states that replaced Russian, German, Austrian, or Ottoman territories in eastern and central Europe, elected officials governed under the terms of a constitution in which "the people" held supreme authority. The defunct German empire became the somewhat smaller Weimar Republic, named after the city where its constitution was enacted. The core area of the former Ottoman empire became the Republic of Turkey.

The number of voting citizens in the world also swelled, as states both new and old broadened the franchise to include women, as well as males formerly excluded because of low social status or income. The Great War, which mobilized women to serve their nations in unprecedented ways, roused feminists to step up their demands for full civic rights and responsibilities. Between 1915 and 1920, women gained voting rights in Iceland, Denmark, the Netherlands, England, Germany, Russia, the new eastern European states, all forty-eight of the United States, and six provinces of China. Many more states, including most of the Latin American republics, enfranchised women during the following thirty years. In the postwar decades, many new organizations and publications called for women's full legal, social, and sexual equality. In the United States, for example, Margaret Sanger wrote voluminously in support

Margaret Sanger, champion of birth control. Sanger and her supporters endured heckling when they advocated publicly for women having greater control over their reproductive function. When challenged by a passerby, "Have you never heard God's word to 'be fruitful and multiply and replenish the earth'?", one of Sanger's fellow activists replied, "They've already done that."

of birth control as essential to women's social liberation. In Egypt, Huda Sha'rawi, a dedicated nationalist, founded the Egyptian Feminist Union in 1923. Sha'rawi and her associates gained public attention by arguing that traditional practices such as veiling, arranged marriages, and male control over divorce were distortions of Islamic teaching.

By the mid-1920s, however, the champions of liberal democracy had to reassess their hopes. In none of the major industrialized countries did elected governments succeed in meeting popular expectations for economic growth, employment, and social welfare. Consequently, those states, including Britain, France, Germany, and the United States, faced recurrent strikes, walkouts, and street demonstrations. Urban working classes rightly perceived that despite

regular elections the same bureaucratic and business elites that had dominated national affairs before World War I, and that had disastrously failed to prevent it, largely remained at the top of the political heap. Victorious France, whose Third Republic featured weak executive authority and a National Assembly often immobilized by quarreling political parties, offered a poor model of progressive, efficient postwar democracy.

The Soviet Union: Communist Authoritarianism

In Russia the abdication of Tsar Nicholas II in 1917 led, not to a new liberal era, but to the triumph of Bolshevik revolutionaries under the leadership of V. I. Lenin (see Chapter 24). For two years, the ^aWhites,^o a shaky coalition of liberals, monarchists, moderate socialists, and peasants, fought the communist ^aReds^o and their mostly urban supporters for political dominance. The Bolshevik ascent horrified the capitalist leaders of Britain, France, the United States, and Japan. Hoping to prevent the communists from consolidating power, those states materially aided various White groups and between 1918 and 1920 sent military expeditions to occupy several points of Russian territory in the north, south, and east. Those foreign incursions were halfhearted, however, and served only to rouse Russian nationalist feeling to Lenin's advantage. By late 1920 the unity and discipline of the communist forces won out. Within another two years, the new regime founded the Union of Soviet Socialist Republics, ^asoviet^o referring to communist workers' councils formed during the revolution. Against heavy odds, the Bolshevik regime effectively held together the greater part of the old tsarist empire.

The early communist state. The communist revolutionary leadership aimed to transform society primarily to the benefit of the urban working class, or proletariat, that is, to establish social democracy as opposed to capitalist-friendly liberal democracy. Guided by the writings of Karl Marx (see Chapter 22), leaders of the communist variant of socialism constituted a ^avanguard^o of professional revolutionaries to bring about worker supremacy. They intended to sweep away bourgeois capitalism, abolish private property, eliminate class divisions, and achieve social justice. In Lenin's view, however, this grand project required the party to take charge of the means of production and distributionÐ from factories and banks to apartments and retail stores. Under the Soviet constitution, men and women went to the polls to elect representatives to local and regional soviets. Even though the Communist Party selected all candidates in advance, many socialists and social democrats (members of the political ^aleft^o) in western Europe and the United States admired the Bolshevik design for improving the lot and ensuring the dignity of laboring men and women.

In 1921 Lenin initiated the New Economic Policy (NEP), a plan to fulfill socialist goals by stages. It allowed Russian peasants to sell surplus crops privately at local markets, that is, to behave like rural capitalists, as long as they paid the Soviet government a fixed percentage of harvest yields. Under the NEP, farm production rose rapidly. However, after 1924, when Lenin died, Joseph Stalin, the son of a poor villager from Georgia in the Caucasus Mountains, came gradually to power promoting a different economic agenda. Stalin wished to transform Russia into a first-rank industrial power. In his mind, profit-minded peasants had to be suppressed in order to transfer more wealth from the land to the industrial proletariat. Fast industrialization would not only restore national purpose, he insisted, but also forestall any foreign state from invading Russian territory, as Germany had done in the Great War. Stalin infused communist ideology with Russian nationalism, declaring that ªsocialism in one countryº rather than immediate international worker revolution must be the near-term goal.

Industrialization by decree. Stalin launched his industrializing drive by waging war against his own rural population. In 1928 he renounced the NEP and instituted a Five Year Plan, which involved creating huge, mechanized, state-run collective farms where peasants had to live communally to produce food for the growing industrial labor force. Peasants who resisted relocation to collectives typically found themselves being herded to factories, mines, Siberian concentration camps, or execution grounds. As one party official observed, ªA ruthless struggle is going on between the peasantry and our regime. . . . It has cost millions of lives, but the collective farm system is here to stay.º[6] By 1933, 83 percent of Soviet farm land was under state control.

Between 1928 and 1939 the country brought off an astonishing industrial expansion, especially in heavy industries, such as coal, oil, iron, electricity, and chemicals. Giant hydroelectric dams spanned rivers, factory cities arose out of nowhere, state-employed engineers and scientists labored feverishly to advance Russia's technological modernization, and factory managers competed to meet grueling production targets. The national literacy rate climbed rapidly, and the government offered advanced education to thousands of young Soviet men and women. Russia's gross domestic product nearly tripled, reaching a level second only to that of the United States.

Many intellectuals in Western countries continued to praise Soviet economic gains, not seeing, or not wishing to see, the terrible social costs of such spectacular growth.

By collectivizing, coercing, and terrorizing the rural population, the communist state procured bigger grain shipments to cities. But in the 1930s the great majority of peasants became profoundly disaffected and overall farm yields declined steadily. A horrendous famine in 1932±1933 took several million lives partly because of government ruthlessness and inefficiency. The Soviet state poured resources into heavy industries like steel and concrete, telling ordinary men and women that they would have to go without the automobiles, phonographs, and numerous imported goods that western Europeans and Americans were

Stalin promotes the Five Year Plan. This 1931 poster proclaims, "The Victory of the Five Year Plan Is a Strike Against Capitalism." Stalin was willing to kill millions of people to achieve the plan's vision of a modern, collective economy. Which social groups is the plan crushing in this poster?

coming to take for granted. Stalin aimed to make the Soviet state **autarkic,** free of all dependence on foreign commerce.

Nationalists and Communists in China

To Soviet Bolsheviks in the early 1920s, China, formally a republic since 1912, looked like a field where seeds of proletarian revolution might sprout. China, however, remained in political tumult throughout the interwar decades. Beijing, the formal capital, became the headquarters of a regional warlord who jockeyed for power with other strongmen, crime rings, and bandit gangs. In the far south, the revolutionary leader Sun Zhongshan organized the Nationalist People's Party (Guomindang) and laid plans to restore national unity. He advocated parliamentary government but also championed a social democratic program to improve workers' lives and redistribute land to impoverished peasants. He enjoyed keen support among China's young city dwellers, some of them schooled abroad or by Western missionaries. These youths demanded both material modernization and thorough renovation of the country's antimodern cultural identity. In 1919 *New Youth,* a radical magazine founded at Beijing University, proclaimed: ª To promote social progress, we have to destroy prejudices camouflaged as `law of Heaven and Earth' or `eternal practice of all times.' We, on our part, have decided not only to discard all these traditional or conventional concepts but also to create new ideas that synthesize old and contemporary philosophies in addition to those of our own. We wish to cultivate a new spirit for our times.°⁷

China had entered the war on the Allied side, but the victorious powers nonetheless clung to the territorial and commercial controls they had imposed on China in the previous century. The consequence in 1919 in several Chinese cities was the May Fourth Movement, an outburst of student protests and worker strikes that forced the hapless warlord government in Beijing to refuse to sign the Treaty of Versailles.

Needing support wherever he could find it, Sun Zhongshan accepted organizational aid from both the Soviet government and the Comintern, the international revolutionary arm of the communist movement. Some young Chinese took up the study of Marxism, and by 1925, the year Sun Zhongshan died, the new Chinese Communist Party was strong enough to convince the leaders of his Nationalist People's Party to accept a pragmatic alliance. The following year nationalist and communist military forces launched a combined expedition under the command of Jieshi (Chiang Kai-shek), a son of a wealthy land-owner, to overpower the northern warlords and reunify the country. Jiang proclaimed his support for a republic but fervently opposed any communist role in it. As the military operation proceeded, he abruptly terminated the pact with the Communist Party and ordered

Jiang Jieshi and Madam Jiang in Nanjing, 1930. In 1927, Jiang married Song Meiling, a member of a Chinese Christian business family and a graduate of Wellesley College in Massachusetts. As Madame Jiang, she threw herself into Chinese politics, partnering with her husband to strengthen his grip on power. She died in 2003 in New York at the age of 105.

mass arrests and summary executions of both communists and socialists. Between 1927 and 1930 Jiang hounded communists throughout the country and suppressed or won over most of the remaining warlords. Much preferring Jiang to the communists, the European powers and the United States recognized the nationalist government and gradually gave up their long-standing territorial privileges.

Fundamental economic and social troubles remained. Jiang made no move to limit the operations of industrialists, bankers, and estate owners, whether Chinese or foreign. The lot of the rural poor did not improve much. And despite the republican governing structure, Jiang and his army erected a transparently authoritarian regime. The common population became increasingly dissatisfied. In the southern interior, Mao Zedong (Tse-tung, 1893±1976), a communist leader who had eluded Jiang's roundup, began building a power base of his own (see Chapter 26).

New Governments on the Political Right

Jiang Jieshi's success in China was a victory for the ideological ᵃright.° Political groups of the left generally advocated change in society primarily to improve the lot of ordinary men and women, recognizing the injustices embedded in traditional social and economic class divisions. Parties of the right, by contrast, championed the maintenance of political order, respect for traditional authority, and the preservation of established national culture and moral values. On both the left and right sides of the political spectrum, ideals and programs varied from one political group to another. In predominantly rural countries, rightists typically endorsed a stable hierarchy of social classes, the leadership of land-owning magnates and conservative religious authorities, and government policies that kept urban worker activism under careful control. The more extreme right-wing parties almost always scorned liberal democratic institutions as faction ridden, indecisive, and poorly equipped to counteract communist or other left-wing subversion.

Right-wing sympathies in Europe. Rightist political groups gained strength in many European countries in the decade after World War I. Seventeen states that had liberal parliaments as of 1920 either abolished or hobbled those bodies sometime in the following twenty years. Instead, a mix of rightist one-party states, royal despots, and military dictators took power, notably in Italy, Spain, Hungary, Portugal, Poland, Yugoslavia, and Romania.

Right-wing authoritarianism appealed to citizens for a number of reasons. One was postwar fear among governing elites, urban middle classes, and many peasant farmers that communist revolution might spread beyond Russia. Worker uprisings in Germany, Hungary, and Austria amplified these anxieties. Another issue was the failure of liberal governments to address slow industrial recovery and chronic unemployment. A wave of monetary inflation swept central and eastern Europe between 1920 and 1923. Germany's currency fell one trillion times its value in 1913, wiping out people's saving and obliging them to buy loaves of bread with wheelbarrows of cash. This crisis discredited the government of the Weimar Republic and sparked demands for more forceful leadership. Rightist groups also benefited from popular discontent over the war settlements. Italians chafed at the meager territorial rewards they received for joining the winning side, whereas Germans charged that timid politicians had rushed their country into surrender.

Fascism in Italy. Forces of the right achieved an important victory in 1922, when Benito Mussolini, a journalist and leader of the new Fascist Party, became prime minister in Italy, a constitutional monarchy. Parliamentary wrangling among a host of parties, together with rising unemployment and inflation, led first to urban violence between partisans of the left and right, then to fascist ascendancy in the legislature. Mussolini, known later as Il Duce (The Leader), became prime minister by democratic procedures, but he imposed public order from the top. Millions of Italians applauded.

Benito Mussolini marching with a group of Blackshirts in Rome, 1922. A charismatic leader, Mussolini appealed to public sentiment and emotion. Once elected as prime minister, he gutted political opposition, used secret police against his enemies, and outlawed labor strikes, securing his status as dictator by 1926. What elements of this photograph depict Mussolini as a man of the people? What elements suggest his authoritarian view of how Italy should be governed?

Like most right-wing parties, Mussolini's Fascists promoted nationalism, antiliberalism, anticommunism, military strength, and government by decisive action. He also promoted state ªcorporatism,º that is, the organizing of society into industrial and occupational interest groups that together would presumably form an organic, harmonious social whole. In fact, corporatism served mainly to undermine the influence of labor unions and protect industrial capitalists who backed Mussolini's dictatorship.

fascism A political ideology that advocates authoritarian leadership, intense national loyalty, cultural renewal, and rejection of both liberal democracy and socialism.

The term *fascism* derives from the Latin word *fasces*, an ancient Roman emblem symbolizing imperial authority. The key distinction between fascism and other forms of rightist politics was its drive to mobilize mass support. Radiating macho charisma, Mussolini deftly used newspapers, radio, and public rallies to appeal to popular longings for national unity, international respect, and a larger colonial empire. The Fascist regime kept King Victor Emmanuel III on his throne as ceremonial head of state, and the Roman Catholic Pope retained sovereignty over the 110 acres of Vatican City in the heart of Rome. But Mussolini repressed all political opposition and deployed gangs of supporters called Blackshirts to intimidate uncooperative citizens. He instructed

totalitarianism A political ideology and governing policies that mandate strong central control and regulation of both public and private thought and behavior.

Italian women to abandon their quest for equal rights and get busy producing fascist babies. Indeed, he intended the state to be **totalitarian,** organized to

penetrate and manage all levels of society down to the nuclear family.

Nationalism and authoritarian power in Turkey. In the five years following World War I, Turkey emerged from the ruins of the Ottoman empire as a new sovereign republic. It had a parliament and popular elections, but as in Italy those liberal institutions masked the entrenchment of a highly centralized authoritarian government.

Mustafa Kemal Atatürk, a Turkish hero of World War I, emerged as the chief architect of the new republic. By the terms of the postwar settlement, the former empire was compressed into a small, semisovereign country in Anatolia, the heartland of ethnic Turkey. The rest of the realm, including the Arabic-speaking Middle East, was transferred by one political arrangement or another to Britain, France, Italy, or Greece. In those humiliating circumstances, Atatürk (meaning ª Father of the Turks,º as he later became known) joined with other military officers and several resistance groups to raise rebellion against the Ottoman sultan and to defy the war settlement. In the spring of 1920, these insurgents formed a republican government, choosing Atatürk as president. Their forces routed Greek troops from western Anatolia and seized Istanbul (Constantinople), the capital city. At that point, Britain and France thought it pragmatic to renegotiate the postwar treaty. By 1923 the major European powers recognized Turkey's full sovereignty as a republic.

Atatürk abandoned the old Ottoman ideal of a multiethnic state in favor of an exclusive Turkish nationalism. He also labored throughout his fifteen-year rule to transform Turkey into a modern secular (nonreligious) nation-state

Atatürk inspecting troops in Constantinople, 1926. The Turkish president, fedora in hand, is flanked by the prime minister and the minister of war.

Turkish Views on Dress and National Identity

Across Asia and Africa, nationalist reformers sought to explain why Western countries appeared to surge ahead in military and industrial power while their own countries lagged behind. The answer, some argued, lay in European cultural practices and behavior. If people in other countries adopted European habits, the argument went, they would help their nations advance faster.

From this perspective, clothing took on particular importance. Turkish nationalists urged citizens to abandon "native dress" and copy Western styles to help instill in people a modernizing spirit. Similarly, in China, republican leaders denounced the queue, or "pigtail" that men traditionally wore as a symbol of the decadent, antimodern Qing dynasty. A modern China must be a "queue-less" China, they proclaimed, and this hairstyle eventually disappeared.

Atatürk admonished men to throw off the fez, the conical-shaped headgear that Turks had worn before World War I (even though this headgear had come into fashion in the nineteenth century as a modern replacement for the traditional turban). Many Turks took off their fezzes voluntarily, but Atatürk was not content with gradual change. In 1925 he imposed a Hat Law ordering men to put on Western fedoras or other headgear. He viewed the fez as a visual emblem of Muslim identity not compatible with modern secular society. Those who ignored the Hat Law could be imprisoned. Atatürk campaigned energetically for the new policy. The first selection below is taken from a speech Atatürk gave in 1925, a few months after the Hat Law was passed. The second selection is from an article written in 1929 by Turkish novelist, feminist, and nationalist Halidé Edib. Writing while in exile from Turkey, she explained why she considered the law misguided.

DOCUMENT 1 Atatürk, August 1925

Gentlemen, the Turkish people who founded the Turkish republic are civilized; they are civilized in history and in reality. But I tell you . . . that the people of the Turkish Republic, who claim to be civilized, must show and prove that they are civilized, by their ideas and their mentality, by their family life and their way of living. In a word, the truly civilized people of Turkey . . . must prove in fact that they are civilized and advanced persons also in their outward aspect. I must make these last words clear to you, so that the whole country and the world may easily understand what I mean. I shall put my explanations to you in the form of a question.

Is our dress national? (Cries of no!)
Is it civilized and international? (Cries of no, no!)
I agree with you. This grotesque mixture of styles is neither national nor international. . . .

My friends, there is no need to seek and revive the costume of Turan [Central Asia]. A civilized, international dress is worthy and appropriate for our nation, and we will wear it. Boots or shoes on our feet, trousers on our legs, shirt and tie, jacket and waistcoat—and, of course, to complete these, a cover with a brim on our heads. I want to make this clear. This head-covering is called a "hat."

DOCUMENT 2 Halidé Edib, 1929

The first and most spectacular of these [reforms] was the so-called "hat law," passed in 1925. It was also the most futile and superficial in comparison with the others which followed. But it was the *only one* which accomplished a change overnight even in outside appearances. In a week it made the Turks don European hats (the only part of the city-dweller's outfit which was still un-Westernized) and made them look like Westerners, although the manner in which it was accomplished was utterly un-Western. The Westernization of Turkey is not and should not be a question of mere external imitation and gesture. It is a much deeper and more significant process. To tell the Turk to put on a certain headdress and "get civilized" or be hanged, or imprisoned, is absurd, to say the least. . . . Among all the recent measures, this was the most seriously opposed in the country itself. Any opposition to the hat law was labeled as reactionary. The interesting fact connected with the substitution of the hat for the Turkish fez

is that of all the changes of the last four years it attracted the greatest attention in the Western world. The many fundamental changes taking place in Turkey have been either unnoticed or criticized, or treated as unimportant items of foreign news in Western papers. But the moment the Turks put hats on their heads, the general cry in the West was, "at last the Turks are civilized; they wear hats." Hence those who enacted the hat law might say: "We have killed a few, and imprisoned a large number, but it was good psychology: has anything in the past brought Turkey so into the limelight? Has anything brought the Turk nearer to the European in the European mind?" . . .

In Turkey, the first substantial result of the law was that it enriched European hat factories at the expense of the already impoverished Turks.

Sources: Atatürk quoted in Bernard Lewis, *The Emergence of Modern Turkey,* 2nd ed. (New York: Oxford University Press, 1968), 268±269; Halidé Edib, "Dictatorship and Reforms in Turkey," *Yale Review,* 19 (Sept. 1929): 30±32.

Thinking Critically

What kind of clothing did Atatürk regard as "civilized"? Why do you think he believed Turks should adopt this style of dress? How did Edib's views on the Hat Law differ from those of Atatürk? What do you think she meant by noting that the law was implemented in an "utterly un-Western" way? Why did she think some Turks opposed the law? Think of some countries besides Turkey and China where particular dress has served as a symbol of national identity or patriotic commitment.

modeled on those of western Europe. Turkish men (and, after 1934, women) elected a legislative assembly, which periodically chose the national president. In 1926 he replaced Islamic law (shari'a), with a civil code based on the Swiss and other European systems. On another cultural front, he ordered scholars to create a Latin alphabet for writing Turkish to replace the traditional Arabic-derived script. He made primary education compulsory, and thereafter the populaton's literacy rate soared. Convinced that symbols of change must accompany substance, he instructed Turkish men to wear European-style clothing and encouraged women to discard their traditional Muslim veils.

Like Mussolini, Atatürk used modern media to rouse nationalist feeling, and he built an authoritarian apparatus capable of suppressing any serious challenge to his grand projects. Contrary to liberal democratic principles, he banned all political parties except for the Republican People's Party, which he headed. Minority populations, especially Armenians and Kurds, lost all rights to distinctive cultural recognition. The government centralized economic policy, collaborating with private business to develop industry and agriculture, though the results remained modest. By transforming Turkey into an internationally respected nation-state, Atatürk, as authoritarian as he was, inspired young nationalists in Asia and Africa to oppose European colonial rule.

Japan's shift to the right. After 1918, Japan gradually transformed itself from a liberal constitutional monarchy with very limited popular participation into an authoritarian regime commanded by a nationalist elite of right-wing civilians and military officers. Like the United States, Japan emerged from World War I economically stronger than it had been in 1914. It tripled its export trade during and after the war, which helped finance more industrialization at home and capital investments abroad. Japan's population grew from fifty-one to seventy million between 1914 and 1940, and Tokyo rivaled London and New York as a premier world city where young urbanites crowded into movie theaters and jazz clubs. At the Washington Conference of 1921±1922, Japan agreed with the other major powers to limit naval tonnage and to renounce aggressive action against China. The Pacific rim appeared to be entering a new era of international cooperation.

Despite spectacular industrial statistics, however, Japan did not enjoy social calm in the 1920s. Business conditions fluctuated, the agricultural economy remained depressed, and urban unemployment stayed high. Amid dizzying economic change (and a devastating earthquake in Tokyo in 1923), political parties multiplied along a scale from communist revolutionaries on the left to fascist-sympathizing ultranationalists on the right. Strikes, rallies, and student demonstrations punctuated city life. Parties of both left and right attacked the national parliament (Diet) as corrupt, apathetic, and beholden to affluent property owners and professional politicians. The Diet enacted some liberal reforms, such as universal male suffrage, but its harshest critics regarded all parliamentary institutions as bankrupt. In 1928 the government carried out mass arrests of communists, unionists, and other activists, an action that took the wind out of left-wing groups but energized the political right.

In the nationalist view, Japan also faced a crisis of economic survival among major powers. Throughout the 1920s the country became increasingly dependent on food, mineral, and timber imports because domestic production could not keep up with population growth and urban demand. Japan had nearly 130,000 automobiles by 1937, but domestic wells could not come close to filling gas tanks. Japan exploited its East Asian colonial possessions, Korea, Taiwan, and part of Manchuria (northeastern China), for rice and other commodities. Amid the early symptoms of the global depression in 1930, conspiracies, political assassinations, and an attempted army takeover left the legislature immobilized and popular sympathy shifting right.

Left and Right in Latin America

Like Japan and industrialized Europe, Latin America experienced renewed economic growth after World War I. But the trend was erratic, social tensions mounted, and political groups of all persuasions struggled for power in many of the seventeen republics stretching from Mexico to Argentina. At the start of the century, a wealthy top stratum of families owning large businesses, farms, and ranches dominated political and economic affairs nearly everywhere. However, an urban bourgeoisie of bureaucrats, lawyers, managers, teachers, merchants, and intellectuals gained steadily in numbers and, during economic upswings, personal income. This rising middle class resented the lock on power that the old land-owning elite continued to possess in most countries. Latin America's population growth rate was probably the highest in the world in the interwar decades. Hopes of employment attracted Indians and mestizos from countryside to city. Many of them were illiterate and poorly skilled for anything but farming, and they crowded into apartment buildings and new shantytowns. By 1930 Buenos Aires, Argentina's capital, ranked among the top ten largest cities in the world, with 2.2 million people.

In the 1920s almost all Latin American states had import-export economies, as they had had in the nineteenth century. They supplied foodstuffs, fiber, and minerals to the industrial centers of Europe and North America, earning currency that paid for imported manufactures. World prices for commodities such as copper, petroleum, sugar, coffee, and bananas fluctuated throughout the decade, but the system worked well enough from the perspective of foreign companies and the local elites, politicians, and trading firms allied with them. Capitalists in the United States, a country awash in surplus capital after World War I, gradually supplanted British banks and firms (except in Argentina) as the principal suppliers of loans and direct investments.

Urbanization in Buenos Aires. This scene on the Calle Congalio, a retail shopping street, shows some of the consequences of urban growth in Latin America. How might this photo be interpreted as presenting either a positive or a negative view of twentieth-century urban life?

underemployed. Urban feminist organizations pressed for women's voting rights, which no Latin American country offered before 1929.

In these troubled conditions, new leaders rose to power (and often fell again) in several states in the interwar period. Political parties exploited every nationalist phrase and symbol they could think of to mobilize mass support. As in Europe, voting publics warmed to the idea of stronger presidencies, having lost faith in corrupt, squabbling parliaments. In some states, notably Argentina, Uruguay, Chile, and Costa Rica, the urban middle class replaced the old land-owning families as the government's most important constituency. In Mexico, the only Latin American country to experience sweeping social revolution in the early twentieth century (see Chapter 24), political stability returned gradually after 1917. Under the constitution of that year, the presidency commanded much more power than the legislature, and after 1929 the National Revolutionary Party extinguished all significant opposition. In spite of one-party rule, the revolution left the great land-owning families politically weakened, the Roman Catholic Church expelled from politics, and both urban workers and country peasants with stronger voices in political affairs

Colonial Rule and Its Opponents in Africa and Asia

FOCUS What political, economic, and social conditions in colonial empires contributed to the rise of nationalist resistance movements?

In 1920 close to six hundred million people lived under the rule of one or another of nine colonial states. The vast majority of dependent peoples inhabited Africa or Asia, though there were also relatively small colonial territories in the Pacific basin, the Caribbean, and South America.

Under the terms of the settlements ending World War I, the victorious Allies deprived Germany of all its foreign possessions. Those lands, however, did not gain freedom. Germany's four colonies in Africa went to Britain, France, or the Union of South Africa as League of Nations Mandates. The League authorized, or mandated, those powers to administer the former German territories until some unspecified time when they might be ready to govern themselves. To the dismay of Middle Eastern nationalists, the peace settlements also converted the former Ottoman empire's predominantly Arabic-speaking provinces into mandates run by France or Britain.

Britain gave up only one important imperial possession following the war, the southern counties of Ireland. After eight hundred years of English rule, the Irish Free State was born in 1923. Independence, however, came after more than two years of bitter fighting between British security forces and the nationalist Irish Republican Army, which wanted

Burgeoning cities progressively altered social and economic landscapes. Elite power groups could no longer easily ignore either the growing middle class or the crowds of new urbanites fresh from rural villages. Urban leaders could see that an export economy, one in which American and European trading companies exercised great political influence, would produce much less growth and fewer new jobs than an economy based on home industries. As Victor Raúl Haya de la Torre, the leader of the populist Aprista Party in Peru argued, "It is this middle group that is being pushed to ruination. . . . The great foreign firms extract our wealth and then sell it outside our country. Consequently, there is no opportunity for the middle class."[8] In cities like Buenos Aires, Santiago, Lima, and São Paulo, middle-class activists pressured wealth-dominated legislatures to broaden the democratic base. Labor unions attracted the unskilled and sovereignty for all of Ireland. More than three-quarters of the island was overwhelmingly Roman Catholic and pro-nationalist, but several northern counties, the region called Ulster, had Protestant majorities and were determined to remain within the United Kingdom. By the terms of the peace settlement, Ireland was partitioned.

Economy and Society in the Colonial Empires

In the interwar years the world's colonized peoples were overwhelmingly rural, earning their livings as farmers, herders, artisans, laborers, and traders. Nevertheless, these lands became increasingly entangled with the international economy. In Africa and Asia, colonial dependency mainly strengthened the kind of system that existed in Latin America: export of raw commodities and import of most finished goods.

All the colonial powers proclaimed the general principle that their rule should benefit both the subject population and the citizens of the **metropole**. Dependent peoples should labor for their own well-being but also advance the economic interests of the metropole's business firms, banks, and consumers. Lord Frederick Lugard, a British general who served as governor of the West African colony of Nigeria, contended that a ᵃdual mandateº should motivate colonial economic activity. He described this philosophy in the culturally arrogant terms typical of the European imperial class: ᵃ Let it be admitted at the outset that European brains, capital, and energy have not been, and never will be expended in developing the resources of Africa from motives of pure philanthropy; that Europe is in Africa for the mutual benefit of her own industrial classes, and of the native races in their progress to a higher plane.º 9

metropole The colonizer's home country and seat of supreme imperial authority.

In the decade after World War I, efforts to implement dual mandates produced substantial economic growth in some parts of colonial Africa and Asia, especially when food, fiber, and the products of minesĐ tin from Malaysia, oil from Iraq, copper from the Belgian CongoĐ commanded high international prices. But most colonial regimes discouraged local manufacturing because the products would likely compete with goods that capitalist firms wished to import. The colonizers built roads and railways, but with the partial exception of India, these transport lines served, not to internally integrate dependent economies, but to move commodities from interior regions to seaports for export, and foreign goods in the opposite direction (see Map 25.2).

Despite little industrial development in most colonies, import±export business kindled rapid economic and social change. People earned more income from wages, used money more widely, and migrated farther in search of jobs. Where foreign firms invested in plantations, mines, or railroads, they usually employed large numbers of laborers. In the early colonial decades, subsistence farmers often resisted wage labor. Consequently, imperial officers and private entrepreneurs sometimes coerced people into labor gangs or forced villages to meet quotas for saleable crops. They also pushed rural people into wage work by requiring them to pay taxes in money, not farm produce.

In several colonies, farmers who managed to stay on the land did well selling ᵃcash cropsº during the war and the early 1920s, when commodity prices were favorable. Coffee growers in Indonesia, rice farmers in Burma and Vietnam, cotton producers in Uganda, and peanut cultivators in Senegal saw their living standards rise in some years. In the British Gold Coast colony (later Ghana) in West Africa, farmers began planting cocoa trees in the 1890s. By 1917 they were exporting 118,000 tons of beans every year. For Ghanaians in the cocoa-producing regions, higher incomes meant better housing, more schools, and declining infant mortality.

During the interwar period, more people moved within and between colonies. Wage seekers tended to migrate from regions of limited economic opportunity to areas where colonial capitalists needed more workers than the local population could supply. Rubber plantations and coal mines in the southern part of French-ruled Vietnam attracted laborers from the poor but densely populated north. In Indonesia the Dutch government encouraged people, including large numbers of young women, to move from crowded Java to the less populated island of Sumatra, where they worked on tobacco plantations. Copper mines in the southern Belgian Congo and northern Rhodesia (Zambia) pulled in labor from all over central and southern Africa. A worker who traveled five hundred miles from the central Congo to the Ruashi Mine near the flourishing colonial city of Elizabethville (Lubumbashi), recorded his impressions of the harsh life in a migrant camp in the 1920s: ᵃ Yes, we lost many of our people at Ruashi, some died from work accidents, others, the majority, from diarrhea. The man who had diarrhea one day died in two or three days. All of us wanted only one thing: to terminate our contract and return to our country.º 10

In colonized lands, more men than women earned wages, though the picture was complex. When families grew cash crops, husbands typically controlled the earnings but still counted on wives to contribute labor in addition to caring for home, children, and household plots. In regions where polygyny was common, men sometimes acquired additional wives, if they could afford it, specifically to increase their cash crop output. During Ghana's cocoa boom, for example, male farmers did this so brazenly that young women launched a successful protest movement, refusing to work for their husbands, starting cocoa farms of their own, or declining to marry at all.

As in Latin America, rural men and women flocked to African and Asian towns to look for jobs as construction workers, artisans, domestic servants, clerks, or police. Rural women hoping to help the family or advance themselves found city employment as servants, food sellers, hoteliers, or sex workers. Burgeoning cities became arenas of social experimentation as newcomers sought security and new

MAP 25.2 European and African rail networks after World War I.

What geographical, political, or economic factors help explain the locations of railway construction in Africa in the 1920s and 1930s? How would you explain the differences between European and African rail networks in terms of their extent and density?

identity. Urban associations ranged from ethnic societies, sports clubs, dance groups, and military bands to labor unions and new religious denominations. In the first half of the twentieth century, both Roman Catholic and Protestant churches made large gains in tropical Africa and among Vietnamese- and Chinese-speaking populations in Southeast Asia. Islam also continued to grow in Subsaharan

Africa, often because of the proselytizing energy of Sufi associations, which served both the social welfare and spiritual needs of converts. Dozens of towns in Africa and Asia more than doubled in population in the first half of the twentieth century. Casablanca on the Atlantic coast of French-ruled Morocco, for example, grew from 20,000 people in 1897 to 257,000 by 1936. Some towns flourished next to mining or commercial farming zones, others as ports or colonial administrative centers. In some places towns that had not existed before the nineteenth century appeared suddenly. These included Nairobi, the capital of colonial Kenya, and Kuala Lumpur, which sprang up in Malaysia near tin mines.

Ways of Ruling

Colonial powers whose home governments were democratic had to justify their autocratic rule of other peoples on racial and cultural grounds. The ᵃmodern and civilized° metropole, they argued, must shepherd ᵃbackward and primitive° colonial subjects to a better future. Dependent peoples might advance toward self-government but only at a measured pace, usually estimated in decades if not centuries.

Theories of rule. All the colonial powers aimed to ensure law and order in their dependencies, but beyond that the ideas and practices of imperial rule varied widely. France, Portugal, Belgium, and Japan favored the theory of direct rule, which specified that a single chain of bureaucratic command should extend from the metropole down to the local district in the colony. Direct rule should involve removal of established monarchs or chiefs because they could not be trusted with modern administration and would obstruct the colonial work of introducing civilization to backward subjects. French colonial ideology centered on the metropole's ᵃcivilizing mission° to teach dependent peoples the French language, through which they might advance step by step toward rational learning, material progress, and eventual assimilation with the French nation.

Britain, the Netherlands, and the United States (in the Philippines) leaned toward theories of **indirect rule,** allowing existing African or Asian political authorities to govern on local or regional levels as long as they pledged loyalty to the imperial state. In contrast to their French counterparts, British rulers saw no obligation to assimilate subject peoples to British culture. Africans and Asians, they declared, suffered from cultural and indeed racial disabilities that prevented them from such conversion.

indirect rule Theory and practice of colonial government favoring the appointment of local leaders as political intermediaries between the colonizer and the indigenous population.

Colonial realities. Despite these divergent ideas about colonial governance, relations between imperial masters and their subjects were much more complicated on the ground. Day-to-day administration depended mainly on local conditions, not on policies hatched in London or Paris. The French government, despite its ideal of culturally bonding colonial populations to the metropole, offered French-language education to very few. Every colonial territory produced a small class of évolués, or ᵃevolved persons,° who spoke and wrote in French and in a few places acquired the rights of citizens. But otherwise, colonial governors ruled by an authoritarian law code that excluded most men and women from many rights that French citizens took for granted.

For its part, Britain applied indirect rule partially and erratically. In India, the regime extended self-government to a group of traditional Indian princes and, after World War I, permitted limited decision-making power to provincial legislatures. But the Indian Civil Service, whose high officials were British, directly ruled about two-thirds of India's population. Indirect rule worked quite efficiently in a region like northern Nigeria, where the Sokoto caliphate, an important Muslim empire before British conquest in the early 1900s (see Chapter 22), had a well-organized civil service perfectly capable of managing local affairs. Nigerian princes retained much of their authoritarian power over millions of people, and the British administration saved money. By contrast, in places such as Tanganyika (Tanzania) in East Africa, colonial officials dealt with thousands of self-governing villages, kinship groups, and small chieftaincies rather than with functioning states. There, indirect rule operated mainly at the local level. In fact, all colonial governments employed thousands of local men and women as village heads, soldiers, clerks, secretaries, and maintenance workers. None of the empires could have functioned without them.

Foreign Immigrants in Colonized Lands

Some colonial dependencies took in migrants from other parts of the world in sufficient numbers to significantly alter the territory's political and social character. Every colonial regime needed skilled or educated people from the metropole or other countries to serve as administrators, engineers, business agents, and military officers. Most of those expatriates, however, stayed only long enough to do business or complete a tour of duty before returning home. As of 1920, for example, British-born men and women resident in India numbered less than 0.3 percent of the total population.

Settlers from overseas. In a few parts of Africa, however, European settlers had a large impact on colonial society and government. As in the neo-European societies that developed in earlier modern centuries in North America, the southern cone of South America, Siberia, and Australia, settlers migrated to African territories, not to work or serve temporarily, but to found permanent communities where they expected to live a fundamentally European way of life and enjoy a higher standard of living than they had had at home. They went almost exclusively to colonies, or regions within colonies, where the climate was reasonably temperate and the tropical disease environment not excessively threatening. They also acquired land in those places, routinely displacing African farmers by legal or extralegal means and with colonial government support.

In the early twentieth century, British citizens migrated to Southern Rhodesia (Zimbabwe) and the temperate highlands of Kenya. At the other end of Africa, France's conquest of Algeria, which started in 1830, opened that

Muslim princes from northern Nigeria. In that region the British asserted colonial rule indirectly through local leaders like these men: the Emir of Gwanda, the Sultan of Sokoto, and the Emir of Kano. This photograph was taken in 1934, when the three men visited London. How might such a journey have strengthened their authority in Nigeria?

Mediterranean country to land-hungry French, Spanish, Portuguese, Greek, and Maltese settlers (see Chapter 22). France dismissed any idea of Algerian self-determination by annexing the territory to the French state, as if it were a province like Normandy or Brittany. Most of the country's Arabic- and Berber-speaking Muslim majority was reduced to the status of a landless, dependent wage-earning class as large European agribusinesses appropriated peasant farm land. This majority population had scant access to education or skilled jobs. European migration to South Africa was distinctive because Europeans had been settling there since the mid-seventeenth century (see Chapter 19) and because that country was a self-governing state rather than a British colony after 1910. Predominantly English-speaking settlers moved there in growing numbers in the late nineteenth century, following the discovery of diamonds and gold. By 1920 the European population numbered nearly 15 percent. The Union of South Africa had a parliamentary form of government that progressively restricted participation to the white minority, which spoke either English or Afrikaans (the language of descendants of Dutch settlers). In 1913 the all-white parliament passed the Native Land Act, which prohibited Africans from owning more than 7 percent of the country's land (later changed to 14 percent). This repressive legislation benefited white farmers and effectively pushed more Africans off the land and into white-owned gold mines and other growing industries.

In every African colony that had significant numbers of European settlers, they remained a small minority of the total population (about 11 percent in Algeria but less than 1 percent in Kenya). Nevertheless, settlers expected the European colonial government to protect them and to grant them economic opportunities and social privileges that the great majority did not enjoy, as well as access to cheap local labor for their farms and households. Settlers also exercised political influence in the colony out of all proportion to their numbers, and, having adopted the colony as their homeland, most of them became fierce opponents of any reform that might lead toward majority rule.

Overseas settlement in the interwar period was not limited to Europeans. In the 1920s millions of Chinese and South Asian men and women moved to French, Dutch, and British colonies.[11] More than 150,000 South Asians went to South Africa between 1860 and 1911, mostly to work on sugar plantations. In the late nineteenth century, Indian soldiers played a major part in Britain's seizure of East African territories, and tens of thousands of civilians arrived to build a rail line from Mombasa on the coast of Kenya to Uganda in the deep interior. South Asians came to form a socially subordinate middle group in East Africa between the African majority and the small British administrative and settler class.

Jewish settlers in Palestine. Jewish migration from Europe to Palestine, a British-ruled mandate territory in the interwar period, seriously altered the political dynamics of the predominantly Arabic-speaking Middle East. From about 1880 to World War I, millions of Jews who suffered anti-Semitic persecutions in Russia and eastern Europe migrated to the United States and other distant lands. Long-established Jewish minorities already inhabited Middle Eastern cities under Ottoman rule, but small numbers of new migrants founded farm communities in Palestine, a region within the Ottoman province of Syria before the war.

Those settlements were creations of the Zionist movement, which Theodore Herzl and other European Jews initiated in the 1880s to advance Jewish political nationalism and the idea of a modern Jewish state in Palestine, whose inhabitants were largely Arabic-speaking Muslims or Christians. During World War I the Zionist movement in London nurtured contacts with sympathetic members of the British government. In late 1917 Arthur Balfour, the British foreign secretary, announced that the government looked with favor on ªthe establishment in Palestine of a National Home for the Jewish people, and will use their best endeavors to facilitate the achievement of this object, it being clearly understood that nothing shall be done which may prejudice the civil and religious rights of existing non-Jewish communities in Palestine.º 12 When the League of Nations assigned Palestine to Britain as a postwar mandate, it also endorsed the Balfour Declaration. Zionists, arguing that Jews had a historic right to live in Palestine, worked to legitimize a national homeland there by promoting more settlement. Indeed, between 1922 and 1936, the Jewish population rose from about 93,000 to more than 382,000.

During the interwar years Arab farmers and immigrant Jews came into increasing conflict over control of Palestine's land and water. Jewish settlers, often aided by Zionist capital investment, purchased land from Arab owners, especially from wealthy notables willing to sell at advantageous prices. The British administration also urged Arab cultivators off the land by imposing steep taxes to be paid in cash. Those practices resulted in a growing class of landless Arab peasants. They partly blamed Arab landlords and the British regime for their troubles, but they also directed their anger at the growing Jewish minority.

Inept British policy made matters worse. The administration tried to walk a narrow line between Jewish and Arab interests, but the British high commissioners who governed Palestine did almost nothing to develop machinery for eventual self-governmentÐ no constitution, legislature, or elections above the local level. This meant that Jewish and Arab groups formed completely separate civic and labor organizations, which seldom communicated with each other. In 1929 and again in 1936, tensions between Arabs and Jews exploded in violence, and a large-scale Arab peasant revolt preoccupied British forces from 1937 to 1939. Both Zionists and Arab nationalists wanted the British to leave Palestine, but to completely contradictory ends: Zionists wished to clear the way for a sovereign Jewish state, the Arabs to achieve independence under majority rule. World War II provided only a momentary lull in this conflict.

Colonial Rule Contested

The imperial states liked to represent the interwar decades as a kind of colonial ªgolden ageº when peace, order, and progress reigned in their dependencies. But it would be hard to find a single moment between the late nineteenth century and the end of World War II when there were not, in one colony or another, people who resisted, disputed, or rebelled against their subjugated condition.

Persistent rebellion. After the Great War's victorious powers made clear they had no intention of extending self-determination to their African or Asian subjects, they faced both sudden rebellions and the formation of new nationalist political organizations committed to colonial reforms and ultimately to independence. In 1920, for example, rural farmers in Iraq rose up against the newly proclaimed British mandate there. In quashing the revolt, British forces killed about ten thousand Iraqis. In Syria and Lebanon, diverse religious communities joined together in 1925 to revolt against the French mandate government. The insurgency continued for two years. In the mountains of northern Morocco, Muhammad ibn Abd al-Karim (Abdelkrim), a modernizing Muslim reformer, led a rebellion against the Spanish colonial protectorate. The rising persisted from 1921 to 1926, costing the Spanish army tens of thousands of casualties at the hands of greatly outnumbered Berber fighters. The insurrection ended only when Spain got help from French troops.

City-based nationalist movements. Leaders of postwar nationalist movements, which ranged from cultural clubs to political parties, came chiefly from urban middle-class groups that had at least modest education and financial means. Colonial regimes offered more than primary education to relatively few, and they expected their well-schooled dependents to loyally serve the colonial order. In

Muhammad ibn Abd al-Karim. The Berber leader left his career in the Spanish colonial government in Morocco to organize local resistance. He established the Republic of the Rif, serving as its president from 1921 to 1926, when Spanish and French forces crushed it. Why do you think Abd al-Karim is dressed differently from the people gathered around him?

fact, educated men and women experienced more acutely than any other colonized group the contradictions of imperial rule. They typically spoke the colonizer's language, possessed special skills, and held jobs carrying serious responsibilities. Nevertheless, their rulers routinely excluded them from the upper ranks of administration and business, denied them legal equality, segregated them socially, and sometimes mocked them for aspiring to a level of ᵃcivilizationᵒ that their inferior ethnoracial identity presumably made impossible.

In Egypt, for example, a group of nationalists led by Sa'd Zaghlul, an intellectual and lawyer from Cairo, asked the British imperial administration for permission to represent Egypt at the Paris Peace Conference. When the rulers responded by deporting Zaghlul and other nationalists, Egyptians of all classes poured into the streets to demand full independence. British forces took several months to crush the rising at the cost of about eight hundred Egyptian lives. The Egyptian Revolution of 1919, Zaghlul wrote, ᵃturned the tables against the colonizing power and alerted the entire world to the fact that there is an oppressed nation calling out for justice.ᵒ[13] In 1922 Britain agreed to restore Egypt's sovereignty, but the plan was so hedged with restrictions that opposition grew more insistent.

Many interwar nationalists envisioned freedom in the shape of liberal democracy, deftly using its ideals against European masters, who claimed to have invented it. But others admired the Soviet model of worker revolution and rapid material progress. The early career of Ho Chi Minh (1890±1969) illustrates the communist appeal. The son of a poor Vietnamese scholar and a kitchen assistant working in France, Ho (who used a different name at the time) tried to present a petition to U.S. president Woodrow Wilson in Paris to plead for self-rule for Vietnam, then a harshly ruled French colony. Ho got nowhere, and the following year he forsook Wilsonian liberalism for Marxism. In 1930 he helped found the Indochinese Communist Party to work against the French regime.

India and Gandhi.

In South Asia, small groups of urban intellectuals had been petitioning their British masters for liberal reforms since the mid-nineteenth century. Those leaders took advantage of India's growing sense of national identity, which formed in connection with rapid urbanization and the colony's relatively sophisticated communication network. The Indian National Congress (INC), founded in 1885 by lawyers and other English-educated men, pressed continually for more political participation and better jobs. During World War I, when Britain needed to ensure India's

loyalty, the government announced its intention to guide the territory toward ᵃrealization of responsible government . . . as an integral part of the British empire.ᵒ[14] In 1919 the Raj, as the British colonial regime was called, approved limited changes, including transfer of certain decision-making powers to Indian provincial legislatures. But almost simultaneously it undercut those initiatives by harshly repressing nationalist activity. In April 1919, in the northern city of Amritsar, a British general ordered troops to fire on peaceful demonstrators. The notorious Amritsar Massacre, which left about 370 men and women dead, radicalized many nationalists.

That same year Mohandas K. Gandhi (1869±1948), a member of an affluent Hindu family from the western region of Gujarat, rose to prominence in the INC. He had earned a law degree in London and subsequently spent twenty years in South Africa, where he advocated for the Indian community. While he was there, he formulated a strategy of resistance to British rule founded on nonviolence, self-sacrifice, and the principle of *satyagraha*, the moral precept that conflicts

Gandhi leading the Salt *Satyagraha*, 1930. Gandhi walked for twenty-four days from his home to the seaside, joined along the 240-mile route by thousands of Indians. The marchers protested the British colonial government's monopoly on salt production. By collecting salt without paying tax, Gandhi intentionally broke what he regarded as an unjust law. This movement provoked other acts of nonviolent civil disobedience, resulting in more than 80,000 arrests.

should be resolved through shared understanding of universal truths. In a pamphlet written in 1908, he explained what he meant by ªpassive resistance,º though he later preferred the term *non-cooperation*: ª[It] is a method of securing rights by personal suffering; it is the reverse of resistance by arms. . . . For instance, the Government of the day has passed a law which is applicable to me. I do not like it. If, by using violence, I force the government to repeal the law. I am employing what may be termed body-force. If I do not obey the law and accept the penalty for its breach, I use soul-force. It involves sacrifice of self.º [15]

Between 1920 and the outbreak of World War II, Gandhi became the Indian nationalist movement's most influential leader. Removing the European-style suit and tie he had worn as a lawyer, he donned a loincloth of coarse white cotton, urging Indians to spin and weave their own cloth, a symbolic affirmation of *swadeshi,* or Indian economic self-sufficiency. To be sure, Gandhi had numerous Indian opponents and enemies, for example, nationalists who preferred armed resistance and the traditional princes whose local authority would disappear if South Asia achieved independence as a unified national state. For extended periods, especially 1920±1922 and 1930±1934, Gandhi and his supporters led boycotts, fasts, marches, and other acts of civil disobedience in protest against British rule, calmly submitting to police violence and jail sentences. In other years, the nationalist movement waned as the British made additional moderate concessions and some nationalists turned back to collaboration with the regime.

Gandhi strove to bring Hindus and Muslims, India's two giant religious groups, together in common alliance against Britain. But he also consistently argued that India should remain a society of distinct religious communities under one national umbrella. After 1922, Hindu and Muslim nationalists, the first concentrated in the INC, the second in the Muslim League, competed for political influence in particular provinces rather than working consistently together for independence. In 1935 the INC demonstrated its dominance by winning nearly half the seats in provincial legislatures. However, in the midst of global depression and looming threats to peace in Europe, Britain remained unwilling to schedule a definitive transfer of power.

The Great Depression and Its Consequences

FOCUS Why did the Great Depression occur, and what were its major social and political consequences?

The ups and downs that characterized the world economy in the 1920s did not deeply distress most economists and business leaders. In the modern world, they had learned, economic ups and downs were in the nature of things. In October 1929, however, the New York Stock Exchange crashed, and by 1933, production, consumption, trade, and employment worldwide plunged to such depths that some feared the worst. Was the modern economy disintegrating and humankind returning to the preindustrial age? The answer turned out to be no. But the Great Depression, which dragged on nearly to the end of the decade, had an enormous impact on social and political life from the industrial heartlands to the most rural colonial dependencies.

The Steep Descent

Since the 1930s economic historians have been arguing over the balance of factors that led to the Great Depression. Most scholars agree that the slump had multiple causes. They also agree that global interconnectivity had by that time become so fluid and complex that a serious recession in any industrialized region was bound to affect the rest of the world in one way or another.

An unbalanced boom. The resurgence of manufacturing and trade that took place in the mid-1920s radiated mainly from the United States. Emerging from World War I without material damage at home and with its European allies owing it more than $7 billion, the United States had abundant investment capital and a population of eager middle-class consumers. This was America's Roaring Twenties. The U.S. Congress, not persuaded that involvement in the world war had been necessary, remained in a mood of **isolationism.** Private bankers, on the other hand, pumped billions in loans into Europe and Japan, recharging

> **isolationism** The national policy or political doctrine of avoiding complex political or economic relations with foreign countries.

industry and commerce in those places. U.S. banks, under the 1924 program called the Dawes Plan, loaned the Weimar Republic hundreds of millions of dollars both to help stabilize the German economy after three years of raging inflation and to allow the regime to meet scheduled war reparation demands from France and Britain. Those two states, in turn, used reparation payments partly to reduce their war debts to the United States. This financial turnstile could work, however, only if American banks continued to grease it.

Speculation and debt in lethal combination. In 1928 the American money that financed postwar recovery in western Europe, as well as business projects all over the world, started drying up. This happened chiefly because continuing prosperity in the United States (except for farmers, who faced declining food and fiber prices) fueled a hot stock market. Millions of middle-class Americans withdrew their savings or borrowed money to join the action, and big investors started calling in loans from Europe and elsewhere in order to shift their money to Wall Street. Market speculation rose to a frenzy. When the U.S. government tried to calm it by raising interest rates, foreign capitalists and governments lost access to cheap American loans and had to pay more to service existing ones. At the same time,

Congress, still sour on economic internationalism, raised tariffs on imported manufactures, a policy that impeded industrialized Europe from earning dollars to pay down debt.

In the fall of 1929, Wall Street stocks became so overvalued that investors began selling them off. On October 24, the day called Black Thursday, the market bubble exploded. During the following two years, stock prices, banks, and industry sank together. Investors of all economic classes could no longer pay on bank loans they had taken to buy into the market. Worrying that banks might go under, depositors withdrew savings *en masse*, which produced the very results feared. In that era, no mechanisms existed for quickly moving dollars from one bank to another, there was no federal deposit insurance, and Washington politicians had no inclination to rescue private lending institutions. Thousands of banks closed their doors, deposits vanished, foreclosures multiplied, and millions of Americans suddenly had no money to spend. Because investment capital evaporated, industrial production in the United States dropped by about a third between 1929 and 1931 and employers laid off workers in record numbers. The number of automobiles produced in the United States decreased by half. One of the few industries that continued to prosper was movies. Tickets were cheap, and the unemployed had something to do in the long afternoons.

On the eve of the market crash, the United States produced more than 40 percent of world economic output. When its economy began to tumble, the crisis quickly reverberated around the world. In 1931 the banking crisis spread across Europe. That year Germany's entire financial system virtually fell apart. As factories shut down on both sides of the Atlantic, unemployment soared. By 1932, 44 percent of German workers were jobless. Similar crises struck countries like Argentina, Brazil, and Turkey, whose industrial sectors had been growing in the 1920s. In Japan the freeze on American investments and a drastic drop in the price of exported silk sent the economy into shock. In the United States and Canada a severe drought in western areas in 1932±1934 aggravated the depression. This disaster turned nearly ten million acres of fragile wheat land into a howling ªdust bowl,º forcing tens of thousands of farmers off the land and into chronic unemployment.

Keynesian economics. The magnitude of the depression, which reduced the value of world commerce from $36 billion to $12 billion in less than four years, sent most governments scrambling to salvage their own national economies as best they could. AutarkyÐ national economic self-sufficiencyÐ became the dominant credo. The major industrial states followed conventional procedures to try to halt the slide: let wages fall, raise tariffs on foreign imports, balance the budget, and wait for the crisis to pass. One after another, states defected from the international gold standard. When a country did that, the value of its national currency (no longer pegged to gold) typically declined, but this devaluation also made exports cheaper and stimulated

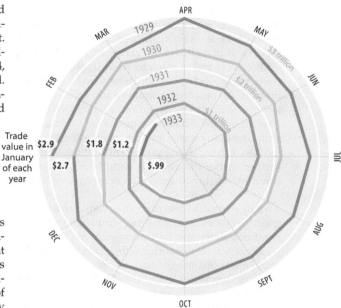

Trade value in January of each year

Value of Trade Imports (Trillions of Dollars)

Declining world trade, 1929–1933. What factors contributed to the decline in world trade shown on this chart? Source: Charles P. Kindleberger, *World in Depression, 1929–1939* (Berkeley: University of California Press, 1986), 170.

price increases. Britain, the architect of the gold standard, left it in 1931; the United States followed two years later.

The depression, however, did not reach bottom nearly as soon as the capitalist world expected, and the standard remedies did not work. The British economist John Maynard Keynes, whose philosophy achieved renown as **Keynesianism,** proposed a different and unorthodox approach. He observed that entrepreneurs and investors remained immobile out of fear that if they pumped new money into the deflated economy, others would fail to join in. Since this was a self-reinforcing trap, Keynes argued, governments had to get business moving again because they were the only institutions with the cash resources to do it, even though this meant heavy borrowing for public investment.

> **Keynesianism** Economic theories of John Maynard Keynes that promote government monetary and financial policies aimed at increasing employment and stimulating economic growth.

Leaders in the liberal democracies generally questioned Keynes's approach because it meant concentrating more power in the government and upsetting the natural functioning of the capitalist market. Nevertheless, a shift began to take place. In 1933 Sweden set the pace by introducing public works projects and unemployment assistance programs financed by government borrowing. In France the socialist government known as the Popular Front (1936±1938) enacted a barrage of new laws, including ambitious public works and the forty-hour work week. In the United States, President Franklin D. Roosevelt (in office, 1933±1945) introduced the New Deal in 1935, which gave employment to almost nine million men and women to build dams, roads, bridges, airports, parks, and public edifices and to fund arts and cultural projects. All of these programs pumped dollars into the sputtering economy. The New Deal also created a national minimum wage, federal deposit insurance for individual savings, and, later than most European states, a social security system. In short, the big slump pushed most industrialized countries further in the direction of social democracyÐ government committed to broad social and economic welfare for citizens.

The depression beyond the major industrialized regions. The effects of the big slump on the predominantly rural populations of Latin America, Asia, and Africa varied widely. Farm families that subsisted on the food they grew often managed to get through the depression years without suffering lower living standards than they already had. Nevertheless, states and colonies that produced just one or two commodities for export, such as tea, cotton, or palm oil, faced severe price drops and unemployment. In West Africa the price of cash crops overall plunged by nearly 70 percent. In Brazil the government burned coffee beans or used them to fuel rail locomotives to reduce the unsold glut. In Southeast Asia, plantations, mines, and city commerce stagnated, prompting millions of Chinese and Indian immigrants to return to their homelands. Colonial administrations had smaller budgets during the depression, so they cut back on already modest education and development spending.

Most countries whose economies relied heavily on commodity exports suffered badly when prices plummeted. In the Latin American countries of Argentina, Brazil, Chile, El Salvador, Guatemala, Honduras, and Peru, groups of military officers who thought their elected governments were incompetent to handle the crisis seized power, all within one year of the 1929 market crash. Those states and most others in the region endeavored to rouse nationalist sentiment in favor of recovery policies that included new home industries, state control of foreign trade, and long-range economic planning. In Mexico President Lázaro Cárdenas put the government at the forefront of economic development and in 1934 introduced serious reforms to give peasants more land. Four years later he nationalized Mexico's oil industry, an action that infuriated U.S. oil companies but received popular acclaim at home. In India the British regime had such great need of tax revenues during the hard times that it encouraged Indian industrialists to expand their operations. By the late 1930s India was producing enough steel to fill 70 percent of its needs.

The depression skips Russia. As we saw, Joseph Stalin put the Soviet Union on the path to extreme autarky in the mid-1920s. He shunned international economic agreements and poured massive state resources into technological modernization and heavy industry. This process started before the depression and continued straight through it. While the

Crowds celebrate the Mexican expropriation of oil, March 18, 1938. President Cárdenas used property rights established in the 1917 constitution to claim petroleum reserves beneath Mexican soil on behalf of the nation. Why might this action have prompted people to take to the streets?

United States and western Europe remained bogged in unemployment, Russia kept people working, increasing its industrial output by 500 percent between 1928 and 1937. But Stalin's rigorous Five Year Plans had harsh consequences. Rural populations suffered severe food shortages, and industrial workers had little access to consumer goods beyond the necessities. Millions of Soviet citizens performed slave labor in Siberia. Between 1928 and 1934 the Soviet prison population rose from 30,000 to 500,000.

Depression and the Continuing Trend toward Authoritarian Leaders

The United States, Britain, France, and several other states showed that liberal democratic governments could muddle through the depression intact. Nevertheless, the global trend toward authoritarianism continued without interruption in the 1930s as aspiring political leaders promised tough action and autarkic policies to save their nations. Nine more European states veered sharply to the authoritarian right, abandoning legislatures and party politics for top-down governments that were anticommunist, antiliberal, and fervently nationalist. Right-wing political groups in both Europe and Latin America emulated the style and tactics of the Italian Fascist Party. In their view, ªdemocracyº was not a matter of multiparty elections but perpetual public theaterÐ parades, flags, fiery speeches, militarized youth groups, fancy uniformsÐ to acclaim authoritarian leaders as guardians of their nations' cultural and political purity.

The political right takes charge in Japan. The onrush of depression in 1930 boosted public support in Japan for nationalist parties and military men clamoring for more imperial conquests to secure vital resources. The following year, army elements fabricated an excuse to invade and seize the whole of Manchuria. Jiang Jieshi, president of China, protested the invasion to the League of Nations, but it had no mechanism for military intervention. Also in 1931 a coalition of officers, industrialists, and high bureaucrats attained control of the Japanese legislature, adopting an ultranationalist ideology. Japan pulled itself gradually out of the depression after 1932 partly by massive state expenditure on the army and navy. In 1937 the country launched a full-scale invasion of China (see Chapter 26).

The rise of the Nazi Party in Germany. The Great Depression struck Germany harder than any other European country. Unemployment there soared from about three million in 1930 to six million in 1932. Working Germans, already devastated by astronomical inflation from 1920 to 1923, watched in dismay as their incomes and savings

Adolf Hitler at the time of the Munich Beer Hall Putsch. This 1924 photograph shows Hitler (on the left) with collaborators Emil Maurice, Hermann Kriebel, Rudolf Hess, and Friedrich Weber. Compare Hitler's appearance in traditional Tyrolean clothing to Atatürk's decision around the same time to enforce the adoption of Western business attire in Turkey. In what ways did the two men's political use of symbols of national identity differ?

disappeared once again. By this time, popular support for the postwar Weimar Republic had badly corroded. In the national legislature (Reichstag), effective decision making depended on alliances among numerous parties that invariably proved unstable.

Throughout the 1920s the Reichstag coalitions gradually shifted to the right, though not nearly fast enough in the view of groups like the National Socialist German Workers' Party, later known simply as the Nazi Party. After World War I this upstart group attracted disgruntled war veterans, among them Adolph Hitler (1889±1945), a one-time artist and street vendor from a working-class family in Austria. Demonstrating a flair for impassioned speech-making, Hitler rose to party leadership. After a bungled uprising against the Weimar government in Munich in 1923 known as the Beer Hall Putsch, Hitler spent several months in jail. The Nazi Party was banned, but it continued to campaign illegally on a platform of zealous nationalism, revenge for the Treaty of Versailles, territorial expansion, and hatred of liberals, communists, and Jews. Hitler much admired Mussolini's style of paramilitary theatrics, founding, for example, a league of fervently loyal ªstorm troopersº to bully or terrorize opponents.

When the depression hit Germany, politics became more deeply polarized than ever. In 1930 the Nazi Party took the second largest number of seats in Reichstag elections. Two years later, Nazis and communists (the far right and the far left) gained between them a majority of support among German voters. Like ultranationalist parties in other countries, the Nazis appealed especially to middle-class clerks, civil servants, storekeepers, military veterans, unskilled laborers, and farmers. These were Germans who suffered badly in the depression but also felt alienated from the industrial and financial elite on one side and powerful socialist and communist labor unions on the other.

Like Mussolini, Hitler achieved power by constitutional means. Following the election of 1932 he persuaded Paul von Hindenburg, the aging and largely powerless president of the German republic, to appoint him chancellor, that is, prime minister. Germany's traditionally conservative business elite accepted this decision, assuming that they would easily control the Austrian demagogue and his party once he took office. In short order, however, the Reichstag awarded Hitler emergency powers, which he deployed to suspend the Weimar constitution and all parliamentary institutions, effectively appointing himself dictator. Between 1933 and 1936 he gained total command of the German state and, always claiming to represent the will of the nation, moved to destroy all political opposition. In Chapter 26 we return to Nazi-ruled Germany and its part in the outbreak of World War II.

• • •

Conclusion

In the two decades after World War I, a shrewd observer of the global scene might have thought that humankind was moving simultaneously in two directions. On the one hand, interrelationships among peoples inhabiting different parts of the world continued to move along the path of greater complexity. Communication and transport technologies became ever more powerful. Professional news agencies such as Reuters, Havas, and the Associated Press made news a commodity, devoting themselves solely to gathering and disseminating information—the current cotton price in Uganda, the Tokyo earthquake, the latest Hollywood scandal. Diplomats and politicians continued to gather in capital cities to grapple with international disputes. Educated men and women traveled to international congresses to work for social and civic betterment and scientific advances. The League of Nations did commendable work around the world in cultural, health, and social welfare fields. The Olympic Games convened every four years throughout the interwar period, with four of the meets in European cities and one in Los Angeles. Uruguay hosted the first World Cup Soccer tournament in 1930.

On the other hand, the pace of global economic integration fluctuated erratically and then ground to a halt. In the depression years, industrial employment declined more than in any earlier recorded period. Middle-class incomes plunged, and the global gap between rich and poor got wider. Collectively, the world's sovereign states responded to the depression, not by doubling efforts toward economic cooperation, but by seeking more perfect autarky—freedom from economic dependence on fellow states. In the process of finding solutions to dire economic problems, dozens of governments rose and fell, often through violence.

By pulling economic and financial levers, whether big military spending (Japan and Germany) or huge new government investment programs (western Europe and the United States), states slowly pulled themselves out of the pit. These efforts did not, however, lead in the short term to a new era of growth but to another global war, this one longer and more destructive than the first.

• • •

Key Terms

autarky 738	indirect rule 746	Nazi Party 753
Black Thursday 751	isolationism 750	New Deal 752
demographic transition 731	Keynesianism 751	New Economic Policy (NEP) 736
fascism 740	League of Nations Mandates 743	totalitarianism 740
Great Depression 750	metropole 744	
Guomindang 738	modernism 731	

Change over Time

1900	Sigmund Freud's *The Interpretation of Dreams* is published.
1905	Albert Einstein announces theory of relativity.
1910	South Africa becomes a self-governing state under Afrikaner domination.
1919	German colonies and Ottoman provinces are turned over to Britain, France, or South Africa according to the League of Nations Mandate system. Egyptians demand independence from Britain in the Egyptian Revolution of 1919. Mohandas Gandhi begins activist career in India.
1920	Iraqis revolt against British rule. Turks fight for an independent Turkish Republic; Atatürk becomes president.
1921–1926	Abd al-Karim leads a rebellion against Spanish rule in Morocco.
1922	Benito Mussolini takes power in Italy. The USSR is formed.
1923	The Irish Free State is established; Northern Ireland (Ulster) removes itself from the new state.
1924	The Dawes Plan for German reparation payments goes into effect.
1927	Werner Heisenberg theorizes the "uncertainty principle."
1928	Stalin's first Five Year Plan goes into effect in the Soviet Union.
1929–1938	Economies around the world tumble in the Great Depression.
1931	Japan invades Manchuria.
1933	Hitler becomes chancellor of Germany.
1935	U.S. president Franklin Roosevelt announces New Deal.
1938	Mexico nationalizes its oil industry.

Please see end of book reference section for additional reading suggestions related to this chapter.

26 World War II and Its Aftermath

1933–1950

A shot from Leni Riefenstahl's 1934 film *Triumph of the Will* documenting a Nazi Party rally in Nuremberg.

In the first half of the twentieth century, the movie became a tool of war. Dozens of countries established national film industries, and governments took an early interest in cinema for its propaganda value. Political leaders recognized the power of moving pictures not only to report and preserve visual representations of the world but also to alter and manipulate them. During the 1930s and World War II, both democratic and authoritarian states sponsored entertainment films intended to inspire national unity, boost military morale, and report current events in ways that accentuated the good news and downplayed the bad. In Germany under Nazi Party rule, filmmakers made numerous documentaries depicting Adolf Hitler as a nationally revered superhero. In 1934 the gifted director Leni Riefenstahl made *Triumph of the Will,* a record of Hitler's appearance at a gigantic Nazi political rally in the city of Nuremberg. In this ingenious feat of propaganda, Hitler's airplane descends to Nuremberg through billowing clouds, as if from heaven, and, stepping from the plane, the Führer is engulfed in a sea of drums, trumpets, and rapturous faces. In the United States the federal government commissioned a series of seven wartime movies titled *Why We Fight.* Brilliantly editing stock newsreel footage and charging the soundtrack with patriotic rhetoric and stirring music, the films roused both troops and civilians to the necessity of total victory over the German and Japanese aggressors.

Mass persuasion through film and other modern media is just one gauge of the growing power that states acquired in the twentieth century to rally citizens behind government action. In the 1930s Japan, Germany, and, on a more modest scale, Italy marshaled their populations and national resources to build territorial empires. Britain, the United States, and other democratic countries also knew how to mobilize citizens for war and sacrifice. But the Great Depression left them wary of risking a second global conflict in order to stop this new imperialist surge.

As the world struggled out of the depression, its most powerful states did little to rebuild an international system of open trade and shared security. Rather, they flocked into competing and increasingly antagonistic regional blocs (see Map 26.1). One of these crystallized around Germany, a second around Japan, and a third around the Union of Soviet Socialist Republics. Britain and France looked to their respective overseas colonial empires for economic support. The United States dominated the business and trade of the Western Hemisphere. In 1939, tensions and antagonisms among these power groups exploded into war, first in central and western Europe and then in the North Atlantic, North Africa, Russia, the western Pacific, and Southeast Asia. The

• • •

regional blocs rearranged themselves into two giant military alliances that pitted the world's mightiest industrial states against each other. Something similar had happened in World War I, but now the opposing countries possessed far greater destructive power than they had had in 1914.

The first part of this chapter investigates the run-up to World War II in the context of Japanese, German, and Italian empire building, adventures that emerged out of the dire conditions of the Great Depression. Germany under Nazi rule, moreover, deviated from nineteenth-century imperialism because it aspired to carve its empire, not out of pieces of Africa or Asia, but from the very heart of Europe. Until 1939 the major democracies trusted that some combination of negotiations and enlightened reason would persuade Nazis, Italian fascists, and Japanese militarists to moderate their belligerent behavior. These hopes proved futile. The second part of the chapter surveys the world war from September 1939, when Germany invaded Poland, to August 1945, when American planes dropped atomic bombs on Hiroshima and Nagasaki, driving Japan to unconditional surrender. We also explore key social, technological, and environmental developments that attended the war.

A Panoramic View

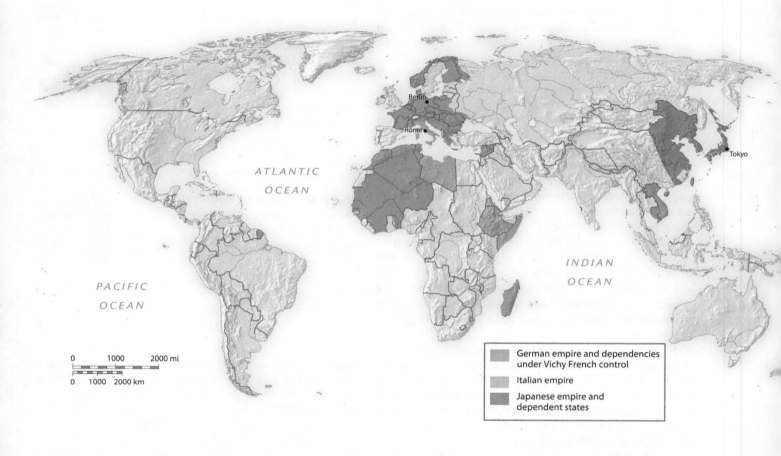

MAP 26.1 German, Japanese, and Italian empires and dependent states, early 1941.
What resources and strategic advantages did the Axis powers gain through territorial expansion? What logistical challenges did these wartime empires face?

The chapter's final section addresses events that took place in the immediate aftermath of the war, five years in which the world haltingly recovered from the conflagration. Even as the war wound down, relations between the United States and the Soviet Union degenerated into mutual recrimination and distrust. Nor could the European powers with colonial empires expect to return to business as usual. In Africa and Asia the end of the war triggered demands for new governments that would serve the popular will and end foreign exploitation.

Empire Building and Global Crisis

FOCUS How did authoritarian, ultranationalist states succeed in amassing power in the 1930s?

Some historians have lumped World Wars I and II together and called them the twentieth century's ªThirty Years' War,º playing on the conflict of that name that took place in Europe in the 1600s. From this perspective, the so-called interwar years were nothing but a partial lull in a long global struggle that reached its zenith of death and destruction between 1939 and 1945.

This interpretation has something to commend it, but the perpetrators of war in 1914 and 1939 had very different intentions. The World War I adversaries had aimed to alter the balance of power in Europe but not to drastically rewrite its map. In the decade leading to World War II, by contrast, Germany and Japan instigated violent imperial exploits far exceeding in scope and ambition the imaginings of any of the combatants in World War I. Like so many other countries in the interwar decades, Germany, Japan, and Italy exchanged liberal elective governments for authoritarian ones. They moved to the far right of the political spectrum, displaying intense nationalism, militarism, and contempt in equal measure for both communism and multiparty democracy. All three countries justified conquest as essential to the survival of the nation and aimed to achieve economic self-sufficiency partly by exploiting the labor and resources of subjugated peoples. In the late 1930s they entered into a series of accords with one another, culminating in 1940 with the tripartite alliance known thereafter as the Axis.

Empire of the Sun

In the two decades after World War I, the brilliant red disk at the center of the Japanese flag flew over a country growing impressively in population and industrial might. This power, however, depended on a continuous search for overseas resources, notably oil, which the islands did not have. For committed nationalists, Japan had either to extend its sphere of economic domination beyond Taiwan, Korea, southern Manchuria, and some Pacific islandsÐ territories it had seized between 1895 and 1910Ð or resign itself to diminishing influence among the world's industrial states.

Demands for military action, particularly against China, became more strident during the Great Depression, which hit Japan hard from 1930 to 1932 (see Chapter 25). Amid social stress, public assassinations, and attempted coups, political factions led principally by ultranationalist army officers strengthened their grip on the national legislature (Diet). In September 1931, army units already in control of part of southern Manchuria launched a full-scale invasion of that region, sweeping aside nationalist Chinese forces. Japan erected a puppet Manchurian state called Manchukuo and began to extract the region's abundant coal, iron, gold, and other chemical resources. Back in Europe, the League of Nations noisily protested the invasion but did nothing.

After 1932 Japan pulled out of the depression by spending massive public sums on industry and armaments, while leaders proclaiming an ultranationalist creedÐ unquestioning loyalty to emperor and state, renunciation of Western liberalism, and assertion of Japanese racial superiorityÐ took full control of the government. This regime improved social services, but it smothered socialist, communist, and feminist groups and suppressed nearly all democratic institutions. Expressing warm admiration for European fascism, the new leaders idealized women as patriotic mothers and homemakers who had no need for voting rights. They also envisioned Japan dominating a huge economic zone embracing all of East and Southeast Asia. According to a booklet produced by the ministry of education, that whole region was destined to be Japan's ªpaddy field.º[1]

Easy victory in Manchuria encouraged Japan to seize more territory. In 1937, land and air forces moved out from Manchuria to invade northern China on a broad front.

The Battle of Shanghai. Japanese soldiers fought their way through the city in 1937. The invasion compounded the disruption China was already suffering owing to civil war between nationalist and communist forces. What factors motivated the Japanese army to seize more Chinese territory after it captured Manchuria?

President Jiang Jieshi and the nationalist Chinese army fought tenaciously but were doubtless weakened by having spent the previous six years battling communists and other internal enemies. The invasion's ferocity drew global outrage, especially the assault on Nanjing, the nationalist capital, where Japanese troops slaughtered tens of thousands of people and indiscriminately raped women. By 1939 a million Japanese soldiers controlled most of the cities of northern and central China. However, they still did not rule about 60 percent of the country's rural population. Both nationalist and communist forces, though at odds with each other, continued to resist.

The Nazi State

While Japan pursued its dream of empire in Asia, Adolf Hitler and the Nazi Party moved to make Germany the preeminent power in Europe. Hitler became chancellor of Germany in January 1933 in conditions of alarming economic crisis, a situation that allowed him to dismiss the parliament and assume emergency powers (see Chapter 25). During his twelve years of rule, he never called the legislature back. In August 1934 he assumed the title of Führer, or Supreme Leader, effectively abolishing the German republic that had existed since 1919. Germany became informally known as the Third Reich, or the Third Empire, succeeding earlier manifestations of German imperial grandeur. Like other authoritarian rulers of the era but with special talent for commanding hero worship, Hitler represented himself as the embodiment of the nation's spirit and destiny.

An admirer of Italian fascism, Hitler took less than three years to set up a totalitarian regime more intrusive and despotic than Benito Mussolini's. For all his hatred of communism, he in fact imitated Joseph Stalin in the Soviet Union by building an apparatus of state bureaucrats, informers, secret police (the Gestapo), and elite military units (the *Schutzstaffel,* or SS). During its first six months alone, the Nazi regime imprisoned thirty thousand political opponents and other perceived troublemakers. Hitler also ordered Gestapo and SS agents to jail or execute army officers, politicians, old rivals, and even Nazi Party members he wanted out of the way.

Nazi racial dreams. Hitler set forth his peculiar world view in *Mein Kampf* (My Struggle), a rambling, hate-filled, partly autobiographical work that he compiled while in prison in 1924. For Marxists, history turned on social class struggle. For Hitler the key to past and future was the clash of races. This conflict would end when the ªAryans,º a mythical racial group of superior intelligence and hardihood, achieved dominance over all lesser forms of humanity. As Aryans, Hitler declared, the German people, or *volk,* must defend themselves at all cost against contamination by racially defective peoples. For him, racial mixing would inevitably lead to ªphysical and intellectual regression.º² He

excluded the majority of Europeans from Aryan membership, especially Jews, Roma (Gypsies), Poles, Czechs, Russians, and all other Slavs. He most emphatically excluded Africans and Asians. At one point, he expressed admiration for Britain's subjugation of millions of dark-skinned peoples but ridiculed the idea of their ever gaining self-rule. The way to deal with Indian nationalists, he is reported to have said, should be clear enough: ªShoot Gandhi, and if that does not suffice to reduce them to submission, shoot a dozen leading members of [the Indian National] Congress; and if that does not suffice, shoot 200 and so on until order is established.º³

Anti-Semitic prejudice was commonplace in interwar Europe, but to Hitler the Jews represented the single greatest threat to the German nation. Jews, he declared, had no homeland or nation of their own but worked their way into the societies of others and fed off them. Their intellectual and psychological defects were legionÐ greed, cunning, dishonesty. According to this Nazi delusion, wherever one looked for socialists, liberals, grasping capitalists, or communists, there one would find Jews.

As early as 1933 the Nazi Party took steps to cleanse the nation of the unwanted and unfit, subjecting them to imprisonment, banishment, sterilization, medical neglect, euthanasia, or execution. Alcoholics, feminists, gay people, the mentally infirm, or anyone who failed to show avid enthusiasm for the Nazi regime became targets of persecution. The project to isolate Jews got under way systematically in 1935 with proclamation of the Nuremberg Laws. These acts dispossessed Jews of German citizenship, prohibited them from marrying non-Jews, and harassed them in numerous other humiliating ways. Such zealous interference in the lives of certain groups meant that the Nazi state had in fact to watch and regulate *everyone.* Gradually, all public institutions from schools and churches to newspapers and social clubs came under strict Nazi control. ªThe right of personal freedom,º Hitler wrote, ªrecedes before the duty to preserve the race.º⁴ Like Italian fascists, Nazi leaders defined the emancipation of women as freedom to serve the state and to bear as many young Aryans as possible.

Despite its extreme authoritarianism, the Nazi government commanded growing popular support, especially among urban middle classes. By massive public spending, it pulled Germany out of the depression faster than any liberal democratic state managed to do. By 1938 Germany's jobless rate fell to less than 1 percent. The state also offered citizens generous social benefits, including housing, childcare, and medical services. Hitler revitalized heavy industry, publicly financing metallurgical, chemical, and weapons factories, even though arms manufacture violated the World War I settlement. He generally followed fascist Italy's example of collaborating with conservative business leaders and big corporations. One of his pet public projects was the autobahn, the world's first superhighway network. He also worked with Ferdinand Porsche, the German automotive

An ideal Aryan family. This Nazi-era image idealizes family life and a connection to nature through agricultural toil. This poster shares with other Nazi propaganda a celebration of motherhood and hard work. Notice the mother's tan line where her dress is open to nurse the baby. How might the Nazi government have intended Germans to respond to this poster?

that would ensure supplies of farm goods and minerals on terms favorable to Germans.

Nazi empire building. From the start of his political career, Hitler preached that Germany's salvation depended on territorial conquest. ᵃOnly an adequately large space on this earth,° he argued, ᵃassures a nation of freedom of existence.°⁵ The idea that the German nation must either enlarge its ᵃliving space° (*lebensraum* in German) or end up as a slave to other, racially polluted groups became a fundamental tenet of Nazi ideology. The regime's immediate project was to gather all German-speaking peoples, including the millions who over the centuries had migrated to various parts of central and eastern Europe, into a unitary German state. But more than that, Hitler set his sights on all of eastern Europe and Russia as ᵃthe necessary soil for our German people°Ð a great frontier of conquest and settlement extending all the way to the Ural Mountains.⁶ Once under the authority of the Third Reich, the existing, mainly Slavic populations would be transformed into a gigantic pool of forced labor. The weak and undesirable, including all Jews, would have to be either driven deep into Inner Eurasia or liquidated. Along the way to victory in the east, the Reich would naturally terminate the Russian communist state, ensuring that never again would Germany be surrounded by hostile powers, as it had been in World War I.

Until the late 1930s neither the Soviet Union nor the Western democracies took Hitler's imperial dream nearly seriously enough. The Western powers failed to intervene decisively partly because Hitler built his empire by incremental steps. They protested each act of aggression, but then reluctantly accepted it, hoping that Germany would ask for nothing more. In 1936 Hitler sent troops into the Rhineland, the industrially rich western area of Germany that had been demilitarized since 1919. In March 1938 he intimidated Austria, a predominantly German-speaking state, into accepting annexation to the ᵃGreater German Reich.° About the same time, he demanded that Czechoslovakia cede substantial parts of its territory to Germany, charging that German minorities there were being oppressed. In September 1938 he met with European leaders in Munich, where France and Britain agreed to the takeover, neither of them wanting to start a war over a small Slavic state. Neville Chamberlain, the British prime minister, declared that the Munich conference had achieved ᵃpeace in our time.° Six months later, however, Nazis collaborated with local fascist

designer, to build a small, fuel-efficient automobile priced, like the Ford Model T, for working citizens. Porsche produced a prototype of the Volkswagen, or ᵃpeople's car° in 1935, though few Germans acquired these Beetles until after the war.

Like both Mussolini and Stalin, Hitler believed that national strength and independence must be achieved through autarkyÐ economic self-relianceÐ not membership in an international system of trade and cooperation. He pulled Germany out of the League of Nations and stopped making World War I reparations to France and Britain. Envisioning Germany at the center of a great economic power bloc, he directed his agents to persuade or bully weaker states of central and eastern Europe to sign commercial agreements

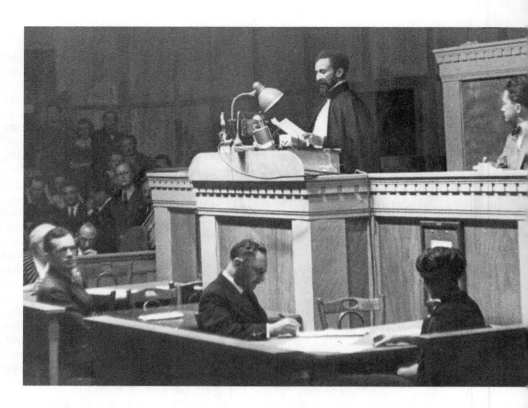

Emperor Haile Selassie addressing the League of Nations, 1936. The Ethiopian emperor's appeals to the international community to help resist the Italian invasion went unanswered. Why do you think none of the major powers were willing to come to Ethiopia's aid?

leaders to seize control of the rest of Czechoslovakia, as well as part of Lithuania in northeastern Europe.

Italy's Foreign Aggressions

Benito Mussolini, who took power in Italy in 1922, proclaimed that national solidarity required foreign conquest, imagining himself the heir of ancient Roman emperors. Italy had played a modest part in Europe's late-nineteenth-century imperialist surge, seizing Libya across the Mediterranean, as well as Eritrea and Somaliland in northeastern Africa. An Italian army had invaded Ethiopia in 1896 but suffered ignominious defeat (see Chapter 23). Mussolini spent the early years of his rule strengthening the Italian economy and army. Then in 1935 he dispatched 100,000 troops to invade Ethiopia again, equipping them with motorized transport, tanks, aircraft, and, contrary to international law, poison gas. The Ethiopian army fought resolutely but lost to carpet bombing, unbridled attacks on civilians, and mass executions. Haile Selassie (r. 1930±1974), Ethiopia's emperor, appealed to the League of Nations for help: ªOn many occasions I have asked for financial assistance for the purchase of arms. That assistance has been constantly refused me. What, then, in practice, is the meaning of . . . collective security?º⁷ The League denounced the invasion but proved no more willing to help Ethiopia than it had Manchuria in 1931. In 1939 and under cover of Hitler's assault on Czechoslovakia, Mussolini also invaded Albania, a small Balkan monarchy that he knew he could beat. Neither Britain nor France tried to stop him.

Fascist Dictatorship in Spain

Between 1936 and 1939 Spain fell into a ferocious civil war that produced between 400,000 and 1 million casualties. Spain in the 1930s was a microcosm of European ideological struggles between the political right and left. In 1931 a republican government assumed power but made little progress in solving Spain's acute problems of rural poverty and industrial exploitation of low-paid urban workers. In 1936 a shaky coalition of liberals, socialists, communists, and regional separatists, constituting a Popular Front of the political left, won parliamentary elections. Within months, however, General Francisco Franco (in office, 1938-1973) and other right-wing military officers attempted a *coup d'état* that triggered the civil struggle. The Spanish Civil War also had a colonial dimension because Franco initially based his movement in the part of northern Morocco that Spain had ruled since 1912.

The three-year war pitted the communist-dominated coalition of the left against an ultranationalist alliance of military men, land-owners, fascist paramilitary groups, and the deeply conservative hierarchy of the Spanish Catholic Church. Even though Franco was less a doctrinaire fascist than a pragmatic nationalist, the wider world perceived the war as a titanic struggle between political right and left. Stalin sent Soviet aid to the republican side. Forty thousand leftist foreign volunteers, including the Abraham Lincoln Brigade from the United States, joined the cause, many of them dying in combat. On the nationalist side, Franco got help from German air squadrons, which bombed republican-held areas. Wary that a republican victory might lead to a communist takeover, Britain and France refused to help neutralize the German intervention. But Franco's victory in 1939, together with Czechoslovakia's calamity, persuaded Britain and France to oppose further Nazi expansion.

The Greatest War

FOCUS What factors explain why a second global war occurred in the first half of the twentieth century?

The Wehrmacht, or German army, invaded Poland in early September 1939, precipitating European war. Between then and mid-1942 the Nazi empire grew to colossal size, extending from Arctic tundra to the North African Sahara and from the Atlantic coast of France to the Black Sea. Parallel to this expansion, Japanese forces overran a large part of China, almost all of Southeast Asia, and numerous Pacific islands. Only in 1942 did a large coalition of countries led by the United States, Russia, and Britain begin to confront the Axis powers. From then until 1945, battles raged on land and sea, and casualties of both soldiers and civilians soared into the tens of millions. In this chapter we survey the war's broad outline, including changes it brought in the social, economic, and environmental spheres.

The Years of Axis Victory, 1939–1942

At certain points between 1940 and early 1942, many well-informed observers thought the war was about to end in Axis victory. Germany, its allies, and its client states achieved control of more than three-quarters of Europe. Sweden, Switzerland, Spain, Portugal, and Ireland remained neutral, but all of those states except Ireland endured persistent Nazi intimidation. After German forces overran France, they created the Vichy (vee-SHEE) puppet regime, which permitted Axis collaborators to take control of France's colonies in North and West Africa and in Southeast Asia. In western Europe, only Great Britain continued fight. To the east, Japan forged an empire even bigger than Germany's, by 1942 the largest the world had ever seen, if one counts the seas that the Japanese navy patrolled.

War in East Asia and Poland. Fighting in Europe and on China's northwestern frontier announced the start of general war. In August 1939, and much to the dismay of Britain and France, Germany signed a nonaggression pact with the Soviet Union. This accord included an

arrangement to divide Poland and other eastern European states between the two powers in the event of war. Here was Stalin, the leader of the international communist movement, making common cause with the rabidly anticommunist Hitler. How did this deal come about? Stalin knew perfectly well Hitler's designs on Russian territory, but he needed to buy time. He could call up millions of soldiers, but they were poorly equipped compared to the German Wehrmacht (armed forces) divisions facing eastern Europe. Furthermore, in the late 1930s Stalin conducted a brutal purge of both army officers and Communist Party officials in order to root out political enemies, real or imagined. The purges devastated the upper ranks of the officer corps and left the entire chain of command in shambles. By pragmatically allying with Germany, Stalin aimed to rebuild the Red Army with a new generation of loyal subordinates, regain eastern European territory lost in World War I, and encourage Germany to exhaust itself fighting a war with Britain

SOMEONE IS TAKING SOMEONE FOR A WALK

The Nazi–Soviet Pact, 1939. This cartoon published in London's *Evening Standard* shows Stalin and Hitler strolling along the border they established after dividing Poland between them. How did the cartoonist portray this alliance between the Soviet Union and Germany? What details suggest that this arrangement was not stable?

and France rather than with him. The pact also bought time for Hitler. He had long believed that German conquest to the east first required eliminating France and Britain as viable enemies. He expected to perform that task in short order and then, nonaggression pact or no pact, invade Russia.

In Japan the Nazi±Soviet pact caused serious rethinking of imperial priorities. Japan and Russia had fought a war in 1905 (see Chapter 24), and they remained rivals for influence in northeast Asia. Since early 1939 the two states had been fighting an undeclared war intermittently along the border between Manchuria and Mongolia, a Soviet client state. In late August the Russian army won a decisive victory, prompting the leaders in Tokyo to cut their losses, patch up relations with Russia, and redirect military operations from northeastern Asia to the British, French, and Dutch colonies in Southeast Asia. This is exactly what Hitler hoped Japan would do.

The Wehrmacht invaded Poland in September 1939, knowing that state had to be secured before they could launch an invasion of western Europe. Despite fierce Polish resistance, Nazi forces quickly overran the western third of the country, while Russian divisions seized the eastern provinces, all according to plan. When the fighting ended, Joseph Goebbels, Hitler's propaganda chief, made clear Nazi intentions for the Polish people. They are, he wrote, ªcompletely primitive, stupid, and amorphous. . . . The Führer has no intention of assimilating the Poles. . . . This nation's civilization is not worth consideration.º⁸ Operating with this mindset, the invaders indiscriminately killed Polish civilians, burned villages, executed intellectuals, machine-gunned the disabled, and herded several hundred thousand Jews and others to ghettos in central Poland to make space for German settlers. In the eastern region, the Soviet occupiers killed or imprisoned even more people in the months after the invasion, for example, massacring about twenty-two thousand army officers and other Poles in the Katyn Forest in March 1940.

The fall of western Europe.
When the Wehrmacht assaulted Poland, Britain and France declared war, though neither had sufficient land forces to stop Hitler from driving west. Between April and the end of June 1940, German mechanized divisions supported by the Luftwaffe (air force) invaded Denmark, Norway, the Netherlands, Luxembourg, Belgium, and France one after the other. By mid-June, the Nazi swastika flew over Paris. Retreating on two fronts, British and French troops converged on Dunkirk on the northern coast of France, where a hastily arranged swarm of seacraft gathered to ferry 338,000 soldiers across the English Channel to safety. Cloudy skies limited German air attacks. ª The bad weather has grounded the Luftwaffe,º the army chief of staff complained, ªand we must now stand by and watch countless thousands of the enemy get away to England right under our noses.º⁹ Once in Britain, surviving French troops formed the Free French organization under the leadership of Charles de Gaulle (1990±1970).

Meanwhile, German forces fanned out across western Europe as far as the Mediterranean coast and the Spanish frontier. Hitler intended to absorb most conquered territory directly into the Third Reich. However, he allowed a **collaborationist** government led by Marshall Philippe Pétain, an elderly World War I hero, to administer the southern provinces of France from the small city of Vichy. The war in western Europe seemed to be over. Millions of Europeans, relieved that it had ended quickly, were quite prepared to wait and see what Hitler's victory might bring. Rosie Waldeck, a German-born correspondent living in Romania in the summer of 1940, captured the resigned public mood: ª The fall of France formed the climax to twenty years of failure of the promises of democracy to handle unemployment, inflation, deflations, labor unrest, party egoism, and what not. . . . Hitler, Europe felt, was a smart guyÐ disagreeable but smart. . . . Why not try his way.º¹⁰ Other millions, however, wanted no part of Hitler's way, and in every defeated country resistance movements of noncooperation, sabotage, and guerrilla warfare gradually took shape, though these activities tended to be scattered and out of communication with one another.

> **collaborationist** A government, a group, or an individual that cooperates with foreign enemies, usually an occupying power.

In Britain, Prime Minister Winston Churchill (1874±1965) refused to accept German domination of continental Europe in return for peace. Not yet prepared to invade England, Hitler ordered massive aerial bombing to bring the country to its knees. Royal Air Force (RAF) fighter planes fought back, however, and British scientists developed superior radar technology to track and intercept enemy aircraft. The airborne Battle of Britain raged during the fall and winter of 1940±1941, with the Luftwaffe dropping tens of thousands of explosive and incendiary bombs on British factories, cities, harbors, and ships. The RAF shot down attacking planes faster than German factories could replace them. Consequently, Hitler shelved his invasion plans, confident that he could deal with Britain once he defeated Russia. The bombing eased up, leaving Britain economically exhausted but with some breathing space to rebuild.

War in the Atlantic.
As soon as Britain and Germany went to war, their navies began to engage each other from the North Sea to the South Atlantic. By conquering France, Germany gained access to new ocean-facing ports. Its surface navy was much smaller than Britain's, but its submarines, or U-boats, roamed the Atlantic. Between October and December 1940 alone, German naval craft sank more than 700,000 tons of British shipping. The sea war brought Europe's crisis closer to the United States. Britain desperately needed North American food and war materiel, but the United States had neutrality laws prohibiting it from helping either side. The U.S. Congress was not eager for another great war twenty-three years after the first. The Franklin Roosevelt administration, however, became persuaded that if Britain fell, the U.S. navy would have to defend the North Atlantic against Germany while facing Japanese aggression in the Pacific at the same time. Public opinion also shifted

in Roosevelt's favor, and in March 1941, Congress enacted the Lend-Lease program, which effectively freed the president to offer Britain, and later Russia, billions of dollars in military aid. The following summer, the navy began escorting convoys as far across the Atlantic as Iceland. By October, American and German vessels were attacking each other, even though no state of war yet existed between the two countries.

The ªwar of annihilation° in Russia. The Nazi±Soviet nonaggression pact collapsed abruptly on June 22, 1941, when three German army groups invaded the Soviet Union simultaneously. Stalin received the news in shock. In the following seventeen months, the Wehrmacht penetrated hundreds of miles into Russia. Hitler was confident of victory because his army had already invaded Yugoslavia and Greece and pressured Hungary, Romania, and Bulgaria into joining the Axis. Moreover, Nazi race theory made no room for effective Russian resistance, a German military handbook declaring that Slavic soldiers, being ªslow-witted,° were ªincapable of decisive resistance against a well-commanded, well-equipped force.°[11] Hitler told his high command that the invasion of Russia would be a ªwar of annihilation.°

Between June and December 1941, German troops overran western Soviet defenses, destroyed the Soviet air force, and captured hundreds of thousands of prisoners. As the armies advanced, they also got busy clearing living space for the racially pure. The Wehrmacht burned thousands of villages, shot or hanged Communist Party leaders and numerous other civilians, and sent thousands of men and women to slave labor camps in Germany. The Nazi regime let upward of two million Russian war prisoners starve or freeze to death. The invaders rounded up and murdered Jews, often in village squares, and these atrocities grew rapidly in scope and ferocity. Some Ukrainians and other non-Russian minorities at first welcomed the Germans as liberators from Stalinist despotism. But instead of cooperating with these groups, Nazi officers followed Hitler's orders to ªspread such terror as to crush every will to resist among the population.°[12]

Within six months of the assault, however, it became clear that Germany would not replicate its triumphant march across western Europe. In July 1941 Stalin proclaimed that Russia would fight a ªGreat Patriotic War° of defense. Fired by this nationalist appeal, the Red Army recovered its footing and partisan guerrillas began to operate behind German lines. In December, Soviet forces stopped the Wehrmacht before it reached Moscow. Early in 1942 Hitler ordered a major offensive in southern Russia to seize Soviet oil wells in the Caucasus region. But this advance stretched German supply lines dangerously thin.

Japan at its imperial zenith. War engulfed Southeast Asia and the Pacific in late 1941, when Japan nearly simultaneously attacked Hong Kong, Malaya, Singapore, Indonesia, the Philippines, and the American naval base at Pearl Harbor in Hawaii. Germany's spectacular successes in western Europe gave Japan a golden opportunity to move against the French, Dutch, and British colonies in Southeast Asia, territories that offered rich resources in oil, rubber, tin,

For Motherland, honor, and freedom! Soviet posters during World War II urged citizens to support the "Great Patriotic War." What features of this poster might have inspired popular support for the war effort?

rice, and other critical commodities. Leaders in Tokyo proclaimed that these territories were now part of the Greater East Asia Co-Prosperity Sphere, an economic and political bloc whose conquered populations would presumably work with Japanese overlords in a spirit of Asian brotherhood. Japan's wartime needs for resources and labor, however, meant that harsh repression quickly eclipsed all schemes for ᵃco-prosperity.°

The Japanese strategy for unqualified victory assumed a free hand in both China and Southeast Asia. That meant preventing the United States from intervening. Tojo Hideki, the Japanese prime minister, assessed the situation in 1941: ᵃTwo years from now we will have no petroleum for military use; ships will stop moving. . . . I fear that we would become a third-class nation after two or three years if we merely sat tight.°[13] The U.S. government balked at war with Japan while its own naval buildup was in progress, but in July 1941 President Franklin D. Roosevelt imposed an **embargo** on trade in oil and other strategic commodities. Consequently, Tokyo resolved to attack Pearl Harbor from the air, knocking the American Pacific fleet out of action long enough to secure Southeast Asia, including the American-ruled Philippines.

embargo A legal restriction or prohibition imposed on trade.

In the first six months after Pearl Harbor, Japan's multiple amphibious and air assaults succeeded spectacularly. About 130,000 British, Australian, and Indian troops surrendered in Hong Kong, Malaya, and Singapore. In Indonesia, Dutch resistance collapsed quickly, and thereafter the archipelago's oil and rubber flowed exclusively to Japan's war industries. The U.S. public overwhelmingly supported Roosevelt's mobilization for war, even though damage to the Pacific Fleet prevented a quick military response. In support of his Asian ally, Hitler ordered that war be declared on the United States, which ensured that in due course the United States would enter the European conflict alongside Britain. Winston Churchill later reminisced that when the United States went to war with Germany, he ᵃwent to bed and slept the sleep of the saved and thankful.°[14]

Italy's early setbacks. Mussolini, Hitler's ally, declared war on Britain and France when he was convinced the Nazis had western Europe in hand. As the Battle of Britain raged,
he launched his own offensive campaigns, attacking Greece through Albania and western Egypt through Libya. His generals botched both campaigns, however, and had to fall back. Italy also quickly lost its Ethiopian colony. In early 1941 a coalition of Ethiopian fighters, units from British African colonies, Congolese troops, and both black and white South Africans drove the Italian army out of Ethiopia, Eritrea, and Somaliland. Emperor Haile Selassie returned to his throne after an exile of less than seven years.

The Years of Counteroffensive, 1942–1945

Both Germany and Japan understood that a prolonged war would pit them against states having greater long-term access to global resources. The Soviet Union had to be destroyed, Britain humbled, and the United States persuaded to let Germany and Japan have their regional empires without a fight. After three violent years, however, the Axis achieved none of those objectives.

Hitler announced a ᵃNew Order° for Europe, which some interpreted as a plan for shared economic development. But he had no thought, as it turned out, of a ᵃfamily of nations° under German leadership. Nazi officers proceeded ruthlessly to extract Europe's resources and labor to support the fighting elsewhere. Any expectation that Nazi rule might at least mean political calm and economic reconstruction dissipated rapidly. Japanese forces similarly squandered opportunities for good will in Southeast Asia, killing or imprisoning large numbers of civilians and cruelly exploiting labor, in other words, behaving worse than the European colonial rulers they had replaced.

Hitler's failure to knock the Soviet Union quickly out of the war also allowed Stalin time to mobilize the labor and resources of the Russian heartland. The Red Army and millions of workers moved whole industrial plants eastward by truck and rail to locations in Inner Eurasia that German bombers could not reach. Stalin successfully rallied the population to fight a national war, though he was no less authoritarian than Hitler. Stalin tapped Russia's deep interior for millions of draftees, including gulag prisoners herded to the front as cannon fodder. The German army simply could not kill Russian conscripts nearly as fast as they were marched to the battle lines.

Stalin scorned capitalist democracy as much as Churchill and Roosevelt disliked communism, but the three leaders transcended their deep suspicions to form a ᵃGrand Alliance° against the common aggressor. From 1942 the United States channeled huge shipments of supplies to the Red Army, mostly through northern Russian ports or Iran, which British and Russian forces jointly occupied in mid-1941. Fourteen states joined the Allied coalition early on, nine of them, including Belgium, Poland, and the Netherlands, represented by governments-in-exile. In short, Germany and Japan faced a growing coalition of enemies (see Map 26.2).

THE YEARS OF AXIS VICTORY	
1939	Nazi–Soviet nonaggression pact. German invasion of Poland.
1940	German conquest of continental western Europe. Aerial bombing of Britain.
1941	German invasion of the Soviet Union. Japanese expansion in Southeast Asia and the Pacific; attack on Pearl Harbor. Failed Italian campaigns.

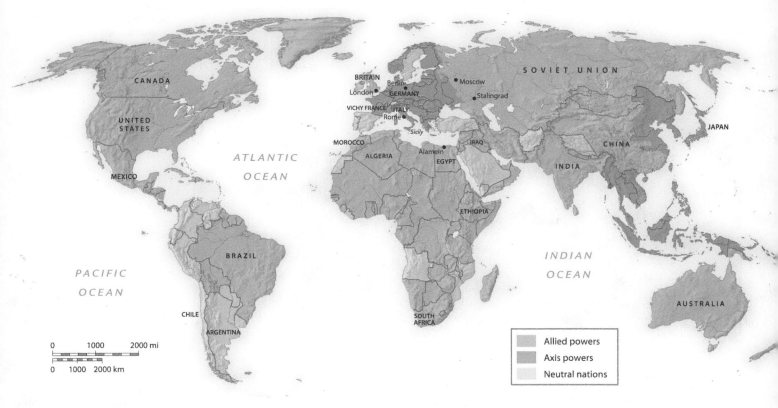

MAP 26.2 Allied and Axis states, mid-1943.

Describe the changes in territory claimed by the Axis states from early 1941 (Map 26.1) to mid-1943. Why do you think there were so few neutral states by this point in the war?

A war running on oil. The Allies moved into Iran (despite the anger of Iranian nationalists) partly to protect British-controlled oil fields there. In fact, the search for fuel energy illustrates the widening resource gap between the Allies and the Axis as the conflict dragged on. Factories, ships, tanks, and airplanes consumed colossal amounts of fossil fuel. Far more than World War I, this was a war of internal combustion engines. The United States had abundant coal and oil reserves for making numerous hydrocarbon products, including synthetic rubber. U.S. oil companies laid the Big Inch and the Little Big Inch, two pipelines that by the summer of 1943 pumped crude and refined petroleum overland from Texas to East Coast ports. Those projects reduced dependence on oil tankers, which were vulnerable to U-boat attacks. British companies rapidly expanded oil production in the Middle East. In Iraq, which devolved from a British-ruled mandate to a sovereign constitutional monarchy in 1932, pro-German nationalists seized power in April 1941. British and Indian troops, however, immediately toppled this regime and kept the Iraqi fields pumping oil to the Allies.

The oil problems of the Axis powers went from bad to worse as the war stretched on. The Wehrmacht thirsted for fuel, but Germany had almost no domestic oil. The oil fields of Romania, a Nazi client state, became the army's main source of crude. In mid-1943, however, Allied planes started bombing Romanian refineries, and the German advance in Russia lost its momentum well short of the Caucasus petroleum reserves. Japan was also an oil-poor country. It captured the wells and refineries of Indonesia, but from 1944 Allied naval attacks increasingly disrupted the long tanker routes to Japanese ports.

The turning tide of battle. Between mid-1942 and June 1944, when the Allies invaded France, the balance of fire power gradually shifted. New American aircraft carriers and battle cruisers regrouped in the central Pacific. U.S. and Japanese carrier-based planes fought their first major engagement in the Coral Sea northeast of Australia in April 1942. At the Battle of Midway the following month, an American fleet stopped Japan's Pacific advance, destroying four carriers. From that point, Japanese commanders had to shift to defending the huge Pacific perimeter they had secured only months earlier. Ferocious fighting for control of one island after another continued for more than three years.

North Africa was a theater of war from 1940 until mid-1943. After the fall of France, the entire southern shore of the Mediterranean west of Egypt became Axis territory. Italy ruled Libya, and pro-Vichy officials took charge of the French colonial governments in Tunisia, Algeria, and Morocco. Early in 1941 a German army under the command of General Erwin Rommel arrived in North Africa determined to overrun both Egypt and the Middle Eastern oil fields that lay beyond. Egypt had become a constitutional monarchy in 1922 following four decades of British rule, but Britain nevertheless retained rights to garrison the Suez Canal Zone. Consequently, British, Australian, and New Zealander troops poured into the country. Seesaw battles raged in the Libyan and western Egyptian deserts for nearly two years. But after victory at Alamein in October 1942, the Allies took the offensive, and fuel-starved Axis forces retreated to Tunisia. The following month, American, British, and Free French armies landed in Morocco and Algeria, removed the Vichy governments, and pushed eastward. Fighting in North Africa ended in May 1943, when a quarter-million Axis troops surrendered in northern Tunisia. From there, Allied divisions organized an invasion of Italy.

Just as the North African war wound down, the Red Army halted the German advance into Russia. In the deep winter of 1942±1943, more than two million German and Russian combatants clashed for control of the city of Stalingrad, an industrial and communication center that controlled the flow of oil from the Caucasus to the Russian heartland. The German Sixth Army took most of the city in November 1942 but had to rely on long supply lines from

the west. The invaders suffered both body-numbing cold and vicious hand-to hand combat in the bombed-out city center. ªMy hands are done for,º a German soldier wrote. ªThe little finger of my left hand is missing andÐ what's even worseÐ the three middle fingers of my right one are frozen. . . . The best thing I can do with the little finger is to shoot with it.º 15 Russian tank and infantry forces under General Georgi Zhukov gradually massed around the city, finally surrounding the German army and, in February 1943, forcing its surrender. The Red Army prevailed at the cost of about 110,000 dead, wounded, missing, or captured and 40,000 civilian lives. Axis casualties may have exceeded 800,000.

Stalingrad turned out to be the eastern limit of the Nazi empire, which after that defeat had no hope of capturing the Caucasus oil fields. Fighting shifted into central Russia, but at Kursk in July, the Russians smashed a German offensive in the biggest tank battle in world history, throwing the invaders permanently on the defensive. That same month an Allied army crossed the hundred-mile-wide strait between Tunisia and Sicily, launching the liberation of Italy. These gains also heartened partisan resistance movements throughout Nazi-ruled Europe. In Yugoslavia, for example, the communist leader Tito organized a guerrilla army to strike back at the German occupiers. By 1944 his commanders controlled much of the country.

China's three-cornered war. The people of China fought a civil war and a national liberation struggle simultaneously. Between 1937 and 1939 the Japanese seized most of the

Red Army soldiers marching victoriously after the Battle of Stalingrad. Soviet forces stopped German eastward expansion with this victory. What elements of this photograph from February 1943 suggest a celebration? What elements document the high price the Soviets paid for victory?

cities, industries, and transport networks of eastern China. Jiang Jieshi moved the nationalist army and government deep into the interior, safe for the time being from Japanese land forces. The Allies could help the nationalists only by airborne deliveries of arms, materiel, and advisors over the Himalayan ª hump° from India. Nationalist leaders, however, also made problems for themselves. They allied with landlords to exploit peasants, bought and sold army conscripts as if they were slaves, and winked at clandestine trade with the Japanese.

Meanwhile, communist forces under the leadership of Mao Zedong fought Japan from their own strongholds. In 1927 Jiang had launched a campaign to eradicate the Chinese Communist Party and nearly succeeded (see Chapter 25). But in 1934±1935 Mao Zedong led about twenty thousand soldiers on a six-thousand-mile journey, a legendary trek known as the Long March, from southeastern China to a safe base in the northwest. Mao had taken part in founding the Chinese Communist Party in 1921, but in contrast to most of his comrades, he abandoned urban worker organization in order to mobilize peasants for revolution. Recasting Marxist-Leninist teaching, he argued that communist cadres should both lead and learn from hardworking peasants, not just the city proletariat. In 1927 he wrote: ª If we allot ten points to the accomplishments of the democratic revolution, then the achievements of the urban dwellers and the military units rate only three points,

while the remaining seven points should go to the peasants in their rural revolution. . . . There must be a revolutionary tidal wave in the countryside.° [16] Mao and his lieutenants proved much more effective than the nationalists in redistributing land, building schools, and opening leadership positions to women. They also outmatched the nationalists in mustering peasants to fight the Japanese.

Indeed, World War II became a three-way struggle in which nationalists, communists, and Japanese all fought each other. In 1941 Jiang ordered an attack on a communist army, and after that, cooperation between these two sides collapsed. Much to the annoyance of Allied advisors, Jiang kept his best-trained divisions from fighting the Japanese, expecting that the communists would in the longer run prove the greater threat. A 1944 intelligence memo reported Jiang as saying: ª You Americans are going to beat the Japanese some day. . . . On the other hand, if I let Mao Zedong push his propaganda across Free China, we run the riskÐ and so do you AmericansÐ of winning for nothing.° [17] For their part, communist partisans seized control of extensive rural areas, which the Japanese could not effectively garrison for lack of personnel. In fact, Chinese nationalists and communists together tied down about 40 percent of the entire Japanese army.

The Axis empires under siege. From the spring of 1943 to late summer 1945, the Allied powers ground down and finally terminated the Axis empires. Italy's fascist regime was the first to go. By the time the Allies invaded Sicily in mid-1943, the great majority of Italians wanted out of the war. But because Hitler sent troops into Italy, combat continued there for another two years. Allied forces fought their way to Rome, then toward the Alps. In April 1945 Italian partisans captured Mussolini and executed him.

In the sea and air war, the Allies gradually gained supremacy. In the North Atlantic, German U-boat attacks diminished early in 1943, thwarted by a number of innovations in maritime warfare. Radar detected enemy craft on the surface, sonar used sound waves to find submarines, and electrical HF/DF equipment, known colloquially as ª huff-duff,° was used to pinpoint the source of U-boat radio transmissions. Allied aircraft operating mainly from England began bombing Germany on a large scale in the spring of 1942, not only to destroy material targets but also to terrorize and demoralize the enemy population, just as the Luftwaffe had done over Britain. German airplane factories could not keep pace with losses to their own squadrons, and by April 1944 the Allies had full air superiority.

From the summer of 1943, the Red Army advanced westward toward Germany in a series of victorious surges. In the west, Allied commanders waited until they had amassed a colossal armada in southern England before launching an amphibious invasion of France, which took place on June 6, 1944. The landing and the ensuing Battle of Normandy between June and late August cost both sides approximately

THE YEARS OF COUNTEROFFENSIVE	
1942	U.S. entry into war. Battle of Midway in the Pacific.
1943	Allies win North Africa, invade Italy. Soviet victory in Battle of Stalingrad; westward advance of Red Army.
1944	Allied victory in Battle of Normandy. Liberation of Paris. Allies stop German advance in the Ardennes Forest, Belgium.
1945	Battle of Iwo Jima in the Pacific. Execution of Mussolini. Churchill, Roosevelt, and Stalin meet at Yalta in the Soviet Union. Germany surrenders. Allies liberate the Philippines from the Japanese. Atomic bombing of Hiroshima and Nagasaki. Japan surrenders.

425,000 dead, wounded, and missing. Nevertheless, the Allies liberated Paris on August 25. The drive into western Germany, however, took nearly another year. Consequently, Russian forces had time to penetrate most of Nazi-ruled central Europe well ahead of American or British divisions. The last big air assaults on Germany took place in the winter of 1945. Finding that strategic bombing of German military and industrial targets failed to do adequate damage, the U.S. and British air forces turned to carpet bombing of several major German cities. These attacks supported the Soviet advance, and by April the Red Army had Berlin surrounded. Hitler committed suicide in his Berlin bunker on April 30, and a week later the German high command surrendered, ending the Third Reich twelve years after its founding.

In Asia, Allied submarines wreaked havoc on Japanese shipping throughout 1944. By the end of the year, Japan's petroleum supplies were running out. Beginning in June, newly developed B-29 long-range bombers attacked Japan's industrial and population centers. In October, U.S. forces, aided by local guerrillas, started the grueling campaign to take back the Philippines. As the war in Europe drew to an end, Allied forces blockaded Japan's sea routes and dropped thousands of incendiary bombs on Tokyo and other cities. When the Japanese government still refused to negotiate peace terms, Harry S. Truman (in office, 1945±1953), who became president in April 1945 on the death of Roosevelt, ordered an atomic bomb attack, first on Hiroshima on August 6 and another on Nagasaki three days later. On August 15, Emperor Hirohito, contradicting the wishes of his most diehard commanders, ordered Japan's surrender, thereby preempting the planned Allied invasion of the islands.

A mother adjusts her son's bandages in Hiroshima, October 1945. Both mother and son were injured in the atomic bomb blast. They are lying on the floor of a bank building that was converted to a makeshift hospital. The extensive damage to buildings complicated efforts to tend to survivors, many of whose wounds proved fatal. Why did images such as this one especially shock viewers around the world, even though civilian casualties were common throughout the war?

The Second Total War

The twentieth century's second great conflict mobilized populations for total war on an even larger scale than the first one. Central governments organized and regulated society and economy more rigorously. Opposing states rained many more tons of bombs and shells down on one another to destroy infrastructure and demoralize civilians. And the war provoked greater extremes of repression, persecution, and brutality than any earlier struggle in history. In World War I, military deaths totaled 8 to 10 million, but in World War II the total was 22 to 25 million.

The continuing growth of state power. Many governments accrued more power between 1930 and 1945 as leaders endeavored first to pull national economies out of depression and second to fight another global war. Germany, Italy, Japan, and Russia had authoritarian governments, which regulated national economies however they liked without much question. The Nazi regime created numerous state-owned manufacturing and financial enterprises. To control inflation it routinely intervened in the market to regulate prices and wages, even by the crudest means. According to Hitler, ᵃInflation is lack of discipline. . . . I'll see to it that prices remain stable. That's what my storm troopers are for. Woe to those who raise prices. . . . You'll see.º[18]

On the Allied side the British government took charge of industrial production and agriculture, gave scientists and engineers deadlines for new military inventions, told people to plant ᵃvictory gardens,º and put the entire population on rations. In the United States, full mobilization got under way after Pearl Harbor. Roosevelt set up the War Production Board and numerous other public agencies, the federal payroll swelled, and most Americans started paying income taxes for the first time. Government and business cooperated extensively, market forces continued to operate, and companies profited.

The war affected state attitudes toward human rights differently depending on the country. Germany, Italy, and Japan sharply curtailed private freedoms several years before the war, and Stalin consistently ignored them. In Britain and the United States, most democratic institutions continued to function, though the governments restricted the press and other forms of public expression in the interest of unity and security. The Roosevelt administration blatantly discriminated against Japanese Americans shortly after Pearl Harbor by ordering them to leave their homes in the western states for detention camps in remote places, arguing that these people, about 110,000 men, women, and children, might sympathize with the enemy. The government manifestly violated civil rights laws, pandered to anti-Asian racist sentiment, and failed to restore lost property and businesses to the detainees after the war.

Women mobilized. In all warring states, armies occupied only the top level of a sprawling pyramid of civilian and auxiliary support. In every country, the mass conscription, disablement, and deaths of adult men meant that everyone else, especially women, had to accept wartime duties. Millions of British and American women took wage and volunteer jobs or enlisted in the military. More than two million women joined the British wartime labor force; another million signed on for military or civilian defense service. In the United States the Roosevelt administration urged women to go to work as a patriotic duty, though they consistently received lower wages than men for comparable jobs. By 1944 the U.S. labor force included about nineteen million women, many of them working to make tanks, ships, airplanes, and uniforms. Rosie the Riveter emblemized national fortitude and sacrifice in image and song:

> All the day long,
> Whether rain or shine,
> She's a part of the assembly line.
> She's making history,
> Working for victory,
> Rosie the Riveter.
> Keeps a sharp lookout for sabotage,
> Sitting up there on the fuselage.

The German, Italian, and Japanese regimes were slow to send more women into wage work owing to ultranationalist ideology that idealized motherhood and family duty as anchors of the nation. Nazi leaders preferred to exploit low-paid foreign conscripts, prisoners of war (POWs), or slaves to meet German industrial demands, though many of those workers were in fact women. Japanese officials urged women to stay home and reproduce at a faster rate, though females eventually had to make up for extreme industrial labor shortages. In the Soviet Union, by contrast, the state mobilized women for war work in great numbers, partly because Communist Party ideology extolled equal opportunities for members of the proletariat, whether male or female. By 1943, women comprised more than 55 percent of the Russian industrial workforce.

Social conventions kept women out of uniformed combat in most of the belligerent states except for Russia. In Japan, women organized and managed thousands of ᵃneighborhood associations,º which distributed food, sold war bonds, and collected taxes. In the United States, about 350,000 women joined the armed services, mainly in the Women's Army Corps (WAC) and the Navy's WAVES. Thousands of military nurses served in war theaters, and women also flew new combat aircraft from U.S. factories to airfields in Britain. In countries under Nazi or Japanese occupation, women played vital roles in local resistance movements as fighters, nurses, couriers, and spies. In the Soviet Union, several hundred thousand women served at the war front as infantry, fighter pilots, snipers, and tank drivers.

If the war emancipated women in some respects, it caused terrible suffering for millions more. Prostitution, sometimes voluntary but often coerced, flourished around military bases of all countries. The Japanese conscripted about 200,000 Korean, Chinese, and Filipino girls and

Individuals MATTER

Olga Lisikova: Soviet Combat Pilot

Combat pilot Olga Lisikova

In October 1941 the Soviet Union became the first country in the world to allow women pilots to fly in combat. By the end of the war approximately 12 percent of Soviet pilots were women. The air force formed three all-female regiments, which flew a combined thirty thousand war missions. Women were also attached to mixed-sex regiments and flew alongside men.

Olga Lisikova distinguished herself as the only woman pilot in an otherwise all-male division. Trained in the late 1930s, she flew for Aeroflot, the civil aviation agency. During the 1939–1940 war between the Soviet Union and Finland, she transported injured soldiers to medical facilities, continuing to fly into her eighth month of pregnancy. When her daughter was less than a year old, Germany invaded the Soviet Union. Lisikova and her husband, also a pilot, left their child with a relative and reported for military service. She performed medical evacuations and transported cargo, in addition to ferrying officials around the country.

On one occasion in August 1941, Lisikova was flying two severely wounded soldiers to a hospital, when a German fighter plane spotted her:

> When I saw that a German fighter was on my tail, I still thought that he would see the red crosses and leave me alone. . . . But the fighter closed up on me. I had several seconds before my life would end. . . . In such extreme circumstances, a person's brain works in an unusual manner: I saw an overhang, and I literally thrust my airplane under this overhang. The burst that was launched by the fighter passed over my aircraft and cut into the other bank of the [Msta] river. . . . In these places it flowed between steep banks. I pressed the stick and flew lower and lower, flying directly over the water, darting back and forth with the river. . . . Then I came upon an airfield—Verebye, and set my aircraft down without an approach. When my aircraft stopped, I looked around. People were running up to me from all sides, shouting something and waving. I did not understand. I climbed down from the cabin, looked around, and saw that the Messerschmitt [German fighter] was burning. It had dived on my airplane and began to pull out, but the aircraft had bottomed out.[19]

Following this episode, the Soviet government awarded Lisikova the Order of the Red Banner for heroism in combat.

Surrounded by male pilots, Lisikova tried to ensure that her sex would never be held against her. Reflecting on her war service many decades later, she remembered that her division commander had warned that "where the failure of a male pilot could pass unnoticed, mine would always be under surveillance." Consequently, she resolved that "I would do everything better than the men."[20] She flew 280 combat missions during the war, eventually earning a spot in the Intelligence Directorate of the General Staff of the Red Army. In that assignment, she flew paratroopers behind enemy lines and also carried out supply drops. Like most other female pilots in the Soviet military, however, her service ended not long after the war's conclusion. She flew her last mission in 1946.

Thinking Critically

What factors do you think motivated the Soviet Union to recruit women for air combat missions in World War II, when most of the countries at war barred women from this role?

---

women to prostitute themselves as ᵃcomfort women° to male soldiers. The Germans put about ten thousand French women in concentration camps on charges of resistance activity. Only about 5 percent of them returned home. The Nazis also targeted Jewish, Slavic, and other ᵃundesirable° women of reproductive age for imprisonment or execution on the grounds that if they married or had sex with Germans, they would produce racially contaminated children.

Genocidal war. If the majority of civilians killed in the war died randomly, from bombs, shells, diseases, or lack of food, many millions were deliberately murdered. Ethnic cleansing, our contemporary term for the mass killing or expulsion of one group by another, has accompanied wars and social conflicts for many centuries. In World War II, however, premeditated brutality reached epic proportion. Systematic killing on a large scale included the Japanese army's butchery of civilians in Nanjing, China, in 1938; Stalin's deadly deportation of non-Russian ethnic groups before and during the war; and the Croatian fascist party's murder of more than 330,000 Orthodox Christian Serbs.

The Nazis, however, elevated methodical murder of particular classes of people to the level of a ghastly industrial enterprise. Implementing Hitler's grand plan to dispose of all who threatened Aryan racial destiny, the Third Reich systematically killed approximately six million Jews and about an equal number of Poles, Russians, Ukrainians, Roma, gays, and the physically or mentally disabled. During the first six weeks of the invasion of Poland, SS and other Nazi units shot or hanged more than sixteen thousand people, about five thousand of them Jews.

genocide The premeditated, purposeful killing of large numbers of members of a particular national, racial, ethnic, or religious group.

By 1942 the Nazi state marked Jews and Roma for **genocide,** while murdering Slavs, POWs, and other prisoners more haphazardly or keeping them barely alive for forced labor. To carry out their Final Solution of the ªJewish problem,° Nazi officials built new concentration camps and refitted existing ones, including Auschwitz, Treblinka, Belzec, Sobibor, and Bergen-Belsen. At some of these camps, prison guards killed men, women, and children in large gas chambers, then either buried the corpses or cremated them in ovens. Nazi officials puzzled over ways to make this complicated task run more efficiently. At the Treblinka extermination center in Poland, for example, camp technicians introduced ªtime and motion° innovations to move large numbers of the condemned from train arrival platform to gas chamber in less than forty-five minutes.[21] The language of extermination became bureaucratic and abstract. Victims were ªitems for transportation° to be ªprocessed,° ªresettled,° or given ªspecial treatment.° As the Wehrmacht began to retreat, Nazi officers worked even more zealously to round up Jews and other disposable persons from conquered territories. The Nazis killed something like 65 percent of Europe's Jews before Germany surrendered, the genocidal machinery grinding to a halt only when Allied troops approached the death camps and the staffs fled.

The spectrum of human response to the Holocaust ranged from enthusiastic participation to heroic resistance. Many captives walked into the gas chambers as they were told. But others incited riots, prison outbreaks, and insurrections, for example, the furious but hopeless uprising of the Warsaw ghetto population in April 1943. In Germany, millions of citizens blandly accepted the government's violent anti-Semitism, but others hid Jews throughout the war. Fascist governments in Romania and Hungary organized their own mass killings of Jews, but in Bulgaria more than 80 percent of the Jewish community survived because King Boris III, though allied with Germany, stopped cooperating with Nazi deportation. The documentary evidence shows that the British and American governments responded unhurriedly to a growing stream of intelligence information about Nazi death camps. Only when the Allies came face to face with emaciated inmates and piles of corpses did they proclaim the extent of the horror.

The dimensions of death. World War II lasted about a year and a half longer than World War I, and it killed twice as many people partly because of the power of its weaponryÐ automatic rifles, long-range bombers, explosive rockets, and atomic bombs. Together, combat, disease, hunger, and organized murder claimed about 2.6 percent of the 1940 global population of around 2.27 billion. In the Soviet Union, 25 million people died, about two-thirds of them civilians. In early 1945 the U.S. and British air forces, having found that strategic bombing of German military and industrial targets did insufficient damage, launched carpet bombing raids on several German cities. The firebombing of Dresden flattened the city center and killed between 120,000 and 150,000 people, mostly civilians. The nuclear attacks on Hiroshima and Nagasaki killed about 220,000. War conditions combined with poor harvests could also set

Survivors of the Buchenwald concentration camp. Emaciated slaves greeted U.S. troops who entered this camp in central Germany in April 1945. Many other prisoners died of malnutrition or starvation during the war. Notice how little bunk space each prisoner had. Some are using metal food bowls as pillows. How do you think images like this one affected the postwar settlement?

off famine. In India, for example, two million people died in Bengal in 1943 because the Japanese invasion of neighboring Burma cut off rice imports. Nevertheless, British authorities refused to divert food intended for big cities or armies. As in the case of World War I, however, massive war deaths did not produce a net global population decline because average life expectancies continued to rise (excepting frightful mortality in particular war-torn places) along with birth rates. Between 1940 and 1950, world population grew by around 11 percent.

The War beyond the Theaters of War

Before the war ended, fifty-one countries or governments-in-exile joined the Allies, though significant fighting took place in only eighteen countries. In other words, the conflict pulled in many states, not because they were attacked or contributed troops, but because the war seriously affected their political and economic interests. Profoundly disrupting the world economy and interstate relations, the war left no society completely untouched.

Latin America and the war. Except for naval battles in the western Atlantic, fighting remained as far from Latin America as it did from the United States. Nevertheless, every Latin American state joined the Allies before the struggle ended. Brazil sent an infantry force to Italy, and Mexico contributed a Pacific fighter squadron. Some countries, Argentina and Chile, for example, entered the war near its end to ensure good relations with the victorious United States and to qualify for charter membership in the United Nations.

In general, World War II served Latin American economies well. The Great Depression pushed many states to intervene more forcefully in economic affairs, and this trend continued during the war. Prices for exports rose, the United States having a huge wartime need for Latin American food and minerals. Brazilian rubber, Cuban sugar, and Venezuelan and Mexican oil were all immensely important to the Allied war effort. Latin American industries also profited by expanding manufacturing to help meet the rising middle-class demand for radios, refrigerators, and other trappings of modern urban life. This wartime growth, however, benefited mainly the middle and wealthy classes.

Colonized peoples and the war. The populations of African and Asian dependencies were invariably drawn into the conflict by their colonial masters. British colonies made vital contributions of resources, labor, and fighting skill to the struggle against the Axis. After the Germans marched into Paris, much of the French overseas empire, including North and West Africa, fell under the control of the Vichy collaborationist regime for at least part of the war. In France's central African colonies, by contrast, administrators led by Félix Éboué, the governor of Chad and a man of African descent from French Guiana in South America, declared their loyalty to the Free French. Consequently, from late 1940, Charles de Gaulle had not only an office in London but also a territorial base in Brazzaville in the French Congo. Belgium fell to the Nazis, but its gigantic Congo colony remained out of Axis reach. Congolese farmers and miners supplied the Allies with strategic materials, including uranium that American scientists used to build the atomic bomb.

Soldiers from Allied colonies fought in all the major theaters of war. Thousands of Indians put on uniforms to defend South Asia against a potential Japanese invasion through Burma. Thousands more fought under British command in the Middle East and Southeast Asia, and for the first time Indian officers were permitted to rise to high ranks. After the Allies invaded North Africa, fighters from French-ruled Morocco, Algeria, and Tunisia took part in the campaign to liberate Italy and Germany. At times, forces under Free French command were more than 50 percent African.

Even before Southeast Asians realized the fraudulence of Japan's ª co-prosperity sphere,° they began to organize resistance. In Malaya, communists and other insurgents, principally from the large Chinese minority, organized rural bases for launching guerrilla attacks against the occupiers. Filipinos set up similar operations in mountain forests. In Vietnam the nationalist leader Ho Chi Minh led the communist Viet Minh's resistance against both the Japanese and the French colonial government, which was under Vichy control. As Japanese power waned, Ho's forces seized much of northern and central Vietnam.

The War and the Global Environment

A hypothetical chart of global environmental change in the twentieth century would undoubtedly show sharp spikes during the two great wars. In those years, humans exploited, manipulated, and damaged the biosphere at an especially frenzied pace in order to achieve urgent military and economic objectives. Both the warring states and the countries they traded with accelerated economic production, thereby consuming global resources and generating waste at unprecedented levels.

Combat, including aerial bombardment, caused enormous environmental harm, if only in the short term. In places of intense fighting, such as the western Soviet Union or certain Pacific islands, flora, fauna, and soils were devastated, though they tended to recover gradually after the armies went away. Explosive and incendiary bombs nearly leveled cities like Dresden, Hamburg, Berlin, Warsaw, and Tokyo, but rebuilding commenced soon after the war. In China, nationalist forces tried to slow the Japanese advance by dynamiting levees on the Yellow River, an act of sabotage that drowned hundreds of thousands of Chinese and inundated millions of acres of farm land. Nevertheless, the dikes were rebuilt shortly after 1945.

Not all military destruction, however, was so easily set right. DDT, a chemical insecticide developed in the late 1930s, saved soldiers from typhus, malaria, and other diseases in

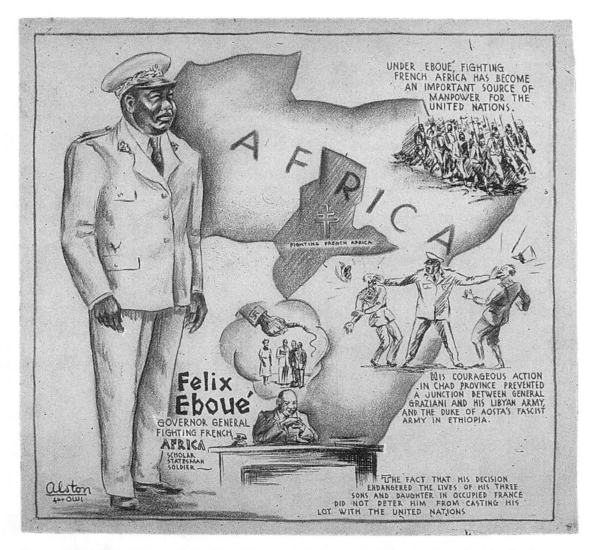

Governor Félix Eboué and the war effort in Africa. This poster by Harlem-based artist Charles Alston chronicles Eboué's contributions to the Allies in French Equatorial Africa during and after World War II. What aspects of Eboué's career did Alston choose to emphasize? What might account for those choices?

both Europe and the South Pacific. This compound, however, also permeated soils and poisoned marine and bird life, a fact not well understood until the 1960s. Toxic nuclear radiation continued to kill Japanese long after the war ended, about fifty thousand of them by 1975.

The war forced the belligerent states to initiate agricultural and industrial crash programs to feed and supply their military services. Many countries extended production of commercial food and fiber crops to steep hillsides, which in regions such as tropical Southeast Asia worsened soil erosion. More intensive farming, plus voracious consumption of timber for wartime construction, also accelerated the rate of global deforestation. In Britain the war used up about half

the country's remaining forests.[22] The Germans clear-cut huge areas of Poland and Norway to get lumber. In Japan, where woodland conservation had long been government policy, the war compelled destruction of forest stands that in some cases had been nurtured for centuries. When the conflict ended, pressure on forests worldwide only increased because so much rebuilding had to be done.

Ironically, warfare eased environmental degradation in some circumstances. All the combatant states introduced measures to conserve fuel, electricity, and food. Atlantic fish stocks recovered significantly during the war because commercial fishing boats had to stay in port. After the Allies bombed places like the Ruhr Valley and the Berlin region,

Propaganda for Wartime Conservation

During World War II, governments on both sides of the conflict rallied their citizens by commissioning propaganda posters. These posters, which typically went on display in public spaces such as courthouses and post offices, broadcast a variety of messages. The German and Japanese governments put up posters to spread their ideology of racial superiority, depicting minority ethnic or religious groups as subhuman or sinister. American and British posters portrayed Japan and Germany as dire threats to democracy and freedom. Posters exhorted citizens to mobilize for victory by joining the army or taking on extra employment.

Posters, as well as movies, radio messages, and newspaper announcements, urged citizens to support wartime production and supply by conserving resources. By deferring purchases of cars or clothing and by consuming less meat or gasoline, citizens would speed factory production of tanks, jeeps, airplanes, ammunition, and uniforms. Wartime posters reminded citizens to grow "victory gardens" to free up food supplies for soldiers. The two posters shown here promote communal sharing and conserving of resources as acts of patriotic cooperation and vigilance. After the war ended, however, such broadsides soon disappeared, superseded, especially in the United States, by private advertisements urging consumers to buy more consumer products.

British wartime poster

U.S. wartime poster

Thinking Critically

What message do you think each poster intends to deliver? How do the posters use the figure of Hitler to make their point? What does "humble pie" mean in the text of the British poster? Why do you think that conservation posters like these disappeared right after the war? Would you characterize these posters as elements of a wartime environmental movement? Why or why not? Do the messages of these posters have relevance today? If so, how?

smoke-belching factories fell silent and skies cleared. After the war, however, the factories fired up again, and a new surge of global economic growth only sped human intervention in the workings of the biosphere.

In the Wake of War, 1945–1950

FOCUS What were major consequences of World War II, and how did global political and economic conditions change in the five years after the war?

Big wars cause all sorts of trouble even after they have ended. Populations are left displaced and wandering, economies and communication systems are shattered, food and fuel are in short supply, and social disorder threatens. States that were strong are suddenly weak; others bristle with new power. Because of want, insecurity, and cravings for revenge, killing continues. All of these things happened in the half-decade following World War II. Restabilizing and rebuilding the world presented an immense task. Indeed, many leaders feared that the world might quickly plunge back into deep economic depression. Nevertheless, governments, businesses, and charitable organizations immediately took up the tasks of reconstruction and revival.

The European colonial empires that had existed before the war could not, however, be put back the way they were. The global conflict created new conditions that made imperial systems dating back to the nineteenth century or earlier much more difficult to sustain. Consequently, between 1945 and 1950 the British, French, and Dutch empires shrank significantly, and ten new sovereign states appeared in Asia. Korea regained its independence from Japan, though it shortly split into two separate states. In China, communist forces drove the nationalist government to Taiwan and proclaimed a new Chinese people's republic.

Restoring Stability, Enforcing Justice

Victory celebrations took place against a backdrop of continuing misery and violence. Across Europe, partisans and angry citizens executed hundreds of Nazi collaborators, and they stripped women accused of sleeping with Axis soldiers and then shaved their heads. Reports of Poles killing Jews even after the Nazis had left helped persuade 200,000 Holocaust survivors to leave eastern Europe forever. In the heavy

combat zones, postwar food shortages left millions malnourished or dead. About two million Russians and Ukrainians died in 1946 because of bad harvests. In Poland, Czechoslovakia, and other eastern European countries, liberated subjects of the Third Reich expelled several million German residents, both long-established minorities and those who had settled during wartime to escape the Soviet army.

The Geneva Conventions, which were rules of war that sovereign states had been drawing up since the nineteenth century, provided the legal basis for prosecuting individuals for war crimes. The Allies convened an international military tribunal in the German city of Nuremberg in 1945 and a similar tribunal in Tokyo the following year. These

French women accused of collaborating with Nazi occupying forces. After the D-Day invasion and the liberation of French cities, Resistance partisans shaved the heads of women who socialized with German soldiers, had sexual relationships with them, or were suspected of passing information to the enemy. This photograph, taken in August 1944 in Chartres, shows women walking past jeering onlookers. The baby's father was a German. Why might citizens have shaved women's heads as a form of community punishment?

courts pronounced a few dozen Nazi or Japanese leaders guilty of crimes against humanity and hanged or imprisoned the convicted. But many more Axis officers and officials escaped or were never charged. To prevent highly skilled German scientists and engineers from falling into Soviet hands, the U.S. government office known as the Joint Intelligence Objectives Agency initiated a postwar program called Operation Paperclip to bring as many of them as possible to America to work. These individuals included many former members of the Nazi Party, including war criminals. The agency, however, deliberately doctored, disguised, or hid the biographies of many of these individuals and gave them American security clearances.

The war ended with American, British, and Soviet troops in control of different parts of Germany. Those states agreed to occupy three separate military zones, plus a fourth one for France. Berlin, the bombed-out German capital, lay inside the designated Soviet zone but was to be governed jointly by the four powers. The occupiers outlawed the Nazi Party, disbanded the German army, and arrested and interrogated thousands of Nazi officials, though some escaped by joining the stream of civilian refugees. After Japan surrendered, 300,000 mostly American troops fanned out across the Pacific islands to enforce the authority of the new occupation government under its supreme commander General Douglas MacArthur.

The Two New Empires

The pattern of global power changed drastically in the five years after the war. The German, Japanese, and Italian empires vanished, and the United States and the Soviet Union emerged as the big imperial winners. American global influence in some ways echoed the ªinformal empires° of Britain and France in the nineteenth century. The United States did not directly take charge of large foreign territories, except for its temporary occupations in Germany, Japan, and other former Axis states. Rather, it entered into accords and treaties to aid and defend friendly countries, and it rose to dominate the postwar international trade and financial system. It also projected armed mightÐ a navy and air force that ranged around the world, a large concentration of troops in western Europe, and numerous foreign military bases. By the mid-1950s the United States had 450 bases in more than thirty-five countries. Within less than a decade of the war, the Central Intelligence Agency engineered or helped engineer the overthrow of elected governments in Iran (1953) and Guatemala (1954) as perceived threats to American political and corporate interests.

Despite Russia's immense wartime losses, Stalin drove the Soviet industrial economy to rapid postwar recovery. Like the United States,

Russia asserted influence abroad informally, though with particularly heavy-handed tactics in eastern Europe. Moscow made sure that friendly and cooperative Communist Party officials ruled the eastern third of Germany and, by 1948, Poland, Czechoslovakia, Hungary, Romania, Bulgaria, and Albania. (Stalin had absorbed the Baltic states of Estonia, Latvia, and Lithuania into the Soviet Union in 1940.) Finland, Yugoslavia, and Austria remained politically neutral, whereas Greece and Turkey eventually became allies of the United States. In Asia the Soviets established close, if sometimes rocky relations with the communist regimes that took control in China, North Korea, and Vietnam in the decade following the war. In the rest of the world the two new superpowers began to compete intensely for political and economic sway.

American power in action. The United States emerged from the war with much greater industrial capacity than any other country. It had abundant cheap energy, mammoth stores of foreign currency, and a banking system to which other countries owed billions. Even though at that point the country depended little on the rest of the world, the American public favored continued international engagement in much greater numbers than after World War I. Many Americans feared a replay of the catastrophic economic crisis that had fed Nazi success. If the wealthiest state in the world did little to assist the damaged economies of Europe and East Asia, social discontent might breed new versions of Hitler. The United States, internationalists argued, had much to gain by helping war-torn countries, both allies and foes, get back on the road to recovery. This would presumably strengthen

Delegates at the Bretton Woods conference, 1944. Representatives from all forty-four Allied nations signed international monetary and trade agreements intended to revive the global economy.

democratic and capitalist institutions. Most Americans also favored new international bodies that would terminate the era of protectionism and lackluster trade that had generally prevailed since 1914. The Atlantic Charter, which Roosevelt and Churchill had signed in August 1941, envisioned a postwar world in which all states would have ªaccess, on equal terms, to the trade and to the raw materials of the world.º [23]

In July 1944, less than a month after the Allied invasion of France, representatives from more than forty countries met in Bretton Woods, New Hampshire. There, they established the International Monetary Fund (IMF) and the International Bank for Reconstruction and Development (World Bank). They also formulated new rules and procedures designed to liberalize trade, prime the pump of capital investment in war-damaged countries, and stabilize the global currency exchange system.

The United States loomed over the Bretton Woods conference and the numerous international meetings that followed. In 1947 President Truman announced the Marshall Plan, named after George C. Marshall, the secretary of state, to flood Europe with reconstruction aid, eventually about $14 billion in direct grants. Truman contended that revival of international commerce and cooperation depended on Europe's robust recovery, including Germany's. Lavish aid would also presumably check the influence of Soviet-backed communist parties. For similar reasons, the United States awarded Japan an aid package of $500 million to rekindle its civilian economy.

The United Nations.

The American vision of a world of sovereign states trading freely and committed to one another's security in the framework of a capitalist world economy included support of the United Nations organization. Founded just before the end of the war, this new club of states aimed to promote international cooperation in numerous spheres, including economic development and human rights. Unlike the League of Nations, its troubled predecessor, the UN Charter assigned peacekeeping responsibilities to a fifteen-member Security Council with power to deploy troops, if necessary, to resolve international conflicts before they got out of hand. The five permanent members of the councilÐ the United States, the Soviet Union, Britain, France, and China (represented by the nationalist government)Ð retained the power to veto resolutions. In 1945 the world had high hopes that these five victorious allies would work together constructively to prevent new conflicts. Instead, the Soviet Union and the other four permanent members became immediately engaged in disputes and rivalries, even though numerous economic and cultural projects got under way.

Allies to adversaries: The early Cold War.

After the war, one event after another aggravated relations between the United States and the Soviet Union. On both sides, every tactical military move, every initiative to make new allies, and every hard-line political announcement tended to compound the antagonism until it hardened into a permanent state of affairs, a **Cold War** that stopped short of any disastrous military clash.

Even before the war ended, American and Soviet leaders viewed world prospects through different

Cold War The state of antagonism, distrust, and rivalry that existed between the United States and the Soviet Union and their respective allies from the end of World War II to the late 1980s.

geopolitical prisms. The United States and Britain agreed that Russia deserved special influence in postwar Eastern Europe considering that victory over Germany in 1945 depended on the Soviet advance to Berlin. They also knew that during the three years of fighting leading to the Allied landing at Normandy in June 1944, the Red Army had been responsible for more than 90 percent of Germany's military casualties. Shortly after the war, however, the Soviets took actions the Western powers regarded as uncooperative and intimidating. It made claims to special influence over Turkey. It took its time pulling troops out of Iran. It kept three million soldiers under arms compared to half that number in the U.S. services. Stalin positioned most of these troops between Russia and Western Europe. To him, this deployment had a compelling logic, considering that his country had been invaded from that direction just a few years earlier. When the Western European democracies looked east, however, they saw Soviet tank and infantry divisions facing them.

Moscow also saw U.S. political and economic influence growing in nearly every country in the world that Soviet troops did not actually occupy. They watched as pro-American politicians in France and Italy tried to subvert strong communist parties by denying them participation in governing cabinets. And they regarded the Bretton Woods plan for a new era of international capitalism as a threat to the Soviet socialist experiment. Stalin continued to strive for economic self-sufficiency apart from the global capitalist system. At the same time, the United States did nothing to negotiate compromises that might have led to greater Russian participation.

The two powers may indeed have come closer to violent confrontation in the immediate postwar years than at any later time. In 1946 Stalin proclaimed that armed conflict between communism and capitalism was inevitable. The following year President Truman announced that ªit must be the policy of the United States to support free peoples who are resisting attempted subjugation by armed minorities or by outside pressures.º [24] From this statement came the Truman Doctrine, a policy inspired by Secretary of State George Kennan to ªcontainº the Soviet Union within the zone of power it held at the end of the war. In the first test of this policy, Truman persuaded Congress to vote $400 million in economic and military assistance to Turkey, where Stalin wanted territorial concessions and military bases. In Greece, communist rebels who had led resistance against the German occupation continued their armed struggle against a postwar right-wing government. This regime, however, was pro-Western, and the United States gave it millions in aid to successfully suppress the communist insurgency. Stalin protested vigorously but did not intervene. Meanwhile, the Soviet Union achieved important victories. Communist parties under Russian protection seized power in Poland, Hungary, and Czechoslovakia between 1945 and 1948, despite Stalin's promises to allow multiparty elections in all three countries.

Ground zero of the early Cold War was Germany. The Soviet Union could not agree with the United States, Britain, and France on a postwar plan to create a united Germany that would remain militarily harmless. By 1948 the three Western powers started to set up a new German administration and to rebuild industry in the two-thirds of the country they occupied, as well as in their sectors of Berlin, which was surrounded by the Soviet zone. Stalin feared a strong new German state in alliance with the United States, and in April 1948 he tried to obstruct this development by blockading land access to Berlin. American, British, and French cargo pilots checked this move by dropping food and other supplies to the two million Berliners who did not live in the Soviet sector. This airlift continued for nearly a year, with planes arriving over the city at an average of three-minute intervals. Stalin condemned this operation, but both sides played out the crisis with restraint, and in May 1949 the Soviets withdrew the blockade.

Within a few months of the standoff, however, Germany was formally divided into two hostile states, the Federal Republic in the west and the Democratic Republic in the east (see Map 26.3). The Berlin blockade also impelled the United States to join with nine Western European countries and Canada to form the North Atlantic Treaty Organization (NATO), a military and political alliance to ensure the security of Western Europe. (In 1955, the Soviet Union

MAP 26.3 Central Europe, 1948.

The immediate post-World War II settlement divided Germany into four occupied zones, each administered by one of the victorious powers. Since Berlin lay entirely within the Soviet zone, why do you think the Soviets agreed to an American, French, and British military presence there?

and its Eastern European allies created the Warsaw Pact as a counteralliance.) Relations between the two sides entered an ice age of mutual suspicion and recrimination that never more than partially thawed during the following forty years.

World War II and the Challenge to Colonial Empires

National independence movements in most Asian and African colonies gained momentum in the postwar years for a number of reasons. First, colonial soldiers who had fought for the Allied cause in Europe or Asia often returned home to unemployment and almost always to continuing social discrimination. These veterans blamed colonial administrations for these conditions, and with good reason. Second, the European imperial powers wanted to keep their colonies, but they faced a dilemma. They had to address such huge rebuilding demands at home that they could afford neither to placate nationalist organizations with generous development aid nor mobilize enough armed force to try to eradicate them. Third, both the United States and the Soviet Union generally encouraged nationalist independence movements. Most Americans cared more about advancing U.S. commercial interests abroad than in shoring up old colonial systems that restricted trade with outsiders. The Russian leadership, declaring that Marxist-Leninist principles would not tolerate capitalist exploitation of conquered peoples, sided with nationalistsÐ as long as they did not raise their heads in Russia's own empire.

Finally, the war effectively destroyed the intellectual and moral rationales for European colonial rule, based as they were on an ideology of innate biological and cultural differences between ªcivilized° and ªuncivilized° peoples. Nazi genocidal horror exposed the folly of such theories of political domination. At the end of the war, these notions were a standing embarrassment to imperial states that called themselves democracies. Jawaharlal Nehru (1889±1964), the Indian nationalist leader, wrote in 1943: ªBiologists tell us that racialism is a myth and there is no such thing as a master race. But we in India have known racialism in all its forms ever since the commencement of British rule. The whole ideology of this rule was that of the . . . Master race, and the structure of government was based upon it.°[25]

New states and a new war in the Middle East. With German and Italian forces out of the Middle East and North Africa, Britain and France sought to reassert their influence in the region's affairs. The independent states of Iraq and Egypt held to a pro-British line after the war. So did Transjordan (later Jordan) after 1946, when Britain gave up its League of Nations Mandate to rule this desert monarchy. France aimed to preserve its economic and cultural clout in Syria and Lebanon while also agreeing to relinquish its mandates there.

Political circumstances in Palestine, the coastal land facing the eastern Mediterranean, were different from those in the rest of the Arabic-speaking world. Also a British-ruled mandate, Palestine had a mostly Arabic-speaking population, the majority Muslim and an important minority Christian. However, with the support of the international Zionist movement to create a national Jewish state, Jews began to migrate there in the late nineteenth century (see Chapter 25). About 300,000 arrived in the 1930s as Nazi persecutions worsened in Europe. By 1940 about 30 percent of Palestine's population of 1.53 million was Jewish.

Since World War I the British government had supported the idea of a Jewish ªhomeland° in Palestine but did almost nothing to help build national institutions through which all elements of the population might work together. Rather, Arab and Jewish political groups increasingly isolated themselves from each another, while acts of intercommunal violence proliferated. Wishing to muster Arab support for the Allies, Britain announced in 1939 that it had no policy to transform Palestine into a Jewish state. Rather, it scheduled the territory for independence in ten years, presumably with a politically dominant Arab majority.

The war suspended this plan for six years, but even before the Axis surrendered, the struggle for Palestine resumed. Under the leadership of David Ben-Gurion, Jews mobilized to drive out the British and proclaim a Jewish state. The Haganah, or Jewish defense force, launched an insurgency that included sabotage, assaults on British personnel, and, in collaboration with the Irgun and Stern Gang guerrilla organizations, staged terrorist attacks, including partial destruction of the King David Hotel in Jerusalem. World War II left Britain financially bankrupt and therefore incapable of forceful action in Palestine. Consequently, it invited the United Nations to find a solution. In November 1947 the UN General Assembly voted by a substantial majority, including the votes of both the United States and the Soviet Union, to **partition** Palestine into separate Jewish and Arab states and to internationalize the city of Jerusalem. The ªno° votes included all the members of the Arab League, a newly formed coalition of countries that vehemently opposed a Jewish polity in a region whose majority population was Arab.

partition The division of a political entity into two or more separate, autonomous territories.

When the British government announced imminent withdrawal, civil war broke out. Haganah forces moved to seize the territory that the UN partition resolution assigned to the proposed Jewish state, including plans to clear villages or urban neighborhoods that resisted. Arab residents, who still occupied much of that territory, fought back. Bombings, ambushes, and street battles multiplied. In April 1948, for example, Jewish partisans massacred 250 Arab villagers, including women and children. Arabs retaliated by killing seventy Jewish medical personnel. In the wake of this violence, hundreds of thousands of Arabs, both villagers and the urban educated classes, fled into neighboring countries. British security forces departed formally in May 1948 without transferring political authority to anyone. The

MAP 26.4 The Middle East and Egypt, 1950.

How might a look at this 1950 map have aroused fear or antagonism on the part of both Israelis and Arabs in the neighboring countries regarding the future of the region?

civil struggle ballooned immediately into regional war. Ben-Gurion declared the independence of Israel, but the armies of Egypt, Syria, Iraq, and Jordan advanced into Palestine to abort it. Over the seven months of the first Arab±Israeli War, Haganah fighters pushed back the invaders, who coordinated their operations poorly, and took control of parts of Palestine that had not in fact been allotted to Israel under the UN partition plan. The single Arab strategic success was the Jordanian army's seizure of the eastern part of Jerusalem.

Finally, in January 1949 the American UN representative, Ralph Bunche, got the warring parties to negotiate an armistice. In the months that followed, individual Arab states worked out their own cease-fire agreements with Israel, even though none of them recognized the new state. In effect, the war produced partition, but not between a Jewish state and an Arab Palestinian one. Rather, Israel took one part of the territory, Jordan occupied Jerusalem and land west of the Jordan River (known from then on as the West Bank), and Egypt held the Gaza Strip along the Mediterranean coast.

The fighting produced a massive exchange of populations. More than 700,000 Arabs fled Palestine, nearly 500,000 of them moving into refugee camps in Jordan and the Gaza Strip. Israel's Arab population fell to about 20 percent, where it remains today. The Israelis had no master plan to expel Arabs from conquered territory. Nevertheless, the Haganah instigated forced evacuations, used tactics to scare away Arabs, and attacked Arab villages that appeared hostile. The neighboring Arab states proved unwilling, mainly for domestic political reasons, to take in large numbers of Palestinians, and the Israeli government refused to allow Arabs to return home without a comprehensive peace settlement. Meanwhile, many more Jews arrived in Israel, raising the population to about one million by 1950.

Thus, the European colonial era ended in the Middle East with the region in a state of profound tension. Israel, enjoying strong American backing, insisted that the Arab states accept the new international map. Their rulers, however, knew that their own popular legitimacy depended on adamant refusal to do this. Thus, the Middle East suffered its own Cold War until 1956, when hostilities broke out again (see Chapter 26).

India: Independence and division. South Asia's wartime hardships, the great strains on colonial resources, and the bankruptcy of race-based imperial ideology worked

Palestinian refugees leave their homes. This news photograph from November 4, 1948, shows Palestinians walking to Lebanon. Israeli Jews date the founding of their independent state to 1948, while Palestinians and Israel's Arab citizens mourn the year of their defeat, which they call "al-naqba," the catastrophe. Does this photo have political relevance today? If so, in what way?

together to speed the withdrawal of Britain from India within two years of the war's end. This event marked a monumental transfer of political power from colonizer to colonized: India was nearly eighteen times larger than Britain and had more than eight times more people. Its independence also inspired comparable movements across Asia and Africa. Almost immediately, however, colonial India split into two states, India and Pakistan. This event signaled the sort of ethnic and religious strife that would trouble numerous new nations in the second half of the century.

In the interwar decades, the Indian National Congress, the colony's leading nationalist movement under the guidance of Mohandas K. Gandhi had lobbied its British overlords incessantly to share power and indeed gained expanded authority over provincial legislatures. Jawaharlal Nehru, an English-educated lawyer and committed socialist, emerged as an astute Congress leader. The outbreak of the war radicalized nationalist demands, especially after August 1942, when nationalist strikes and insurgent attacks broke out, and the British responded with armed repression and imprisonment of Congress leaders. Late in the war, however, Britain realized that it lacked the financial resources to continue to rule nearly 450 million people against their will. Consequently, the British viceroy, or governor, reopened negotiations with Congress leaders.

During the war, however, India's passage to independence became extremely complicated. In the late 1930s the Muslim League, a party dedicated to the political interests of India's large Muslim minority (about a quarter of the population), charged that Hindu political and economic interests would be favored over those of Muslims in a British-style parliamentary system. In the late 1930s Muhammad Ali Jinnah (1876±1948), the rising star of the Muslim League, advanced the idea, until then foreign to the vast majority of Indians of any religion, that the country consisted of *two* ªnations.º Hinduism and Islam, Jinnah proclaimed, constituted ªtwo different civilizations which are based mainly on conflicting ideas and concepts. . . . To yoke together two such nations under a single state, one as a numerical minority and the other as a majority, must lead to growing discontent and final destruction.º [26] If India were to remain whole, the Muslim nation must govern provinces with Muslims majorities, especially the Punjab in the northwest and Bengal in the northeast. Muslim nationalists named these territories ªPakistan,º meaning ªland of the pureº in the Urdu language. By no means did all Muslim leaders share Jinnah's two-nations vision, but more of them joined him as fears of Hindu domination grew.

Three-cornered negotiations among the Congress, the Muslim League, and the British authority resumed right after the war. But the parties could not reach agreement, and tensions mounted. In August 1946, violence broke out in Calcutta, triggering a year of sporadic Hindu±Muslim clashes across northern India. As the strife worsened, Muslims in predominantly Hindu areas fled by the millions to the northwest or to Bengal. Millions of Hindus escaped in the opposite direction.

Gandhi, Nehru, Jinnah, and Lord Mountbatten, the last English viceroy, all pleaded for restraint, but to little avail. Despairing of any other solution, Nehru and Jinnah declared the independence of India and Pakistan as separate states in August 1947. When the partition became reality, the two-way ethnic cleansing became even more violent, with mobs halting refugee trains and massacring passengers who did not share their religion. In late 1947 alone, about five million Hindus, as well as adherents of the Sikh religion, fled from the northwest into independent India; an even greater number of Muslims headed into Pakistan. The culminating irony of this calamity was the assassination of Gandhi, the apostle of nonviolence, at the hands of a Hindu extremist in January 1948. At the dawn of independence, then, both India and Pakistan faced immense problems of building stable political institutions.

Decolonization in Southeast Asia.

Within a decade of Indian and Pakistani independence, most of the colonized territories of Southeast Asia became sovereign as well. When World War II broke out, strong nationalist movements already existed in Burma, Vietnam, Indonesia, and the Philippines. Weaker ones struggled to gain traction in overwhelmingly rural Cambodia and Laos, as well as in Malaya, where ethnic tensions between native Malays and large Chinese and Indian minorities hindered nationalist unity. As in India, Southeast Asian nationalist leaders were mostly professionals, intellectuals, students, and members of affluent families. These elites typically spoke the colonizer's language and favored strategies that combined Western political ideas with local cultural and religious traditions. Most leaders drew inspiration from Gandhi. Nationalist visions of independence, however, varied widely. Many advocated European-style parliamentary governments, others wanted nations founded on Buddhist or Muslim values, and still others urged Marxist-Leninist revolution.

In some places independence came rapidly. Once the British resolved to pull out of India, they also agreed to transfer power to nationalist governments in Burma and Ceylon (later Sri Lanka) in 1948. The United States restored sovereignty to the Philippines less than a year after Japan's surrender. However, U.S. authorities largely dismissed the rural Filipino guerrillas who had helped fight the Japanese and instead turned power over to the established professional and land-owning class. This elite cooperated readily with American business interests and accepted ninety-nine-year leases for twenty-three U.S. military bases. "Our safest course," gushed Manuel Roxas, the Philippines' first president, "is in the glittering wake of America."[27]

By contrast, in the Dutch colony of Indonesia a colonial war had to be fought. The Japanese had occupied Indonesia

President Sukarno addressing a crowd, 1946. Sukarno led Indonesia's fight for independence. The Netherlands did not relinquish control until 1949, but in 2005 the Dutch government recognized Indonesia's original 1945 declaration of independence. The placard in the crowd proclaims support for the nationalist PBI, the Labor Party of Indonesia.

Postwar Hanoi under Viet Minh rule. Viet Minh soldiers stand guard as a military parade rumbles through the streets of Hanoi in northern Vietnam. Ho Chi Minh's nationalist regime controlled the city throughout the anti-colonial struggle against France, which endured from 1946 to 1954.

during the war, and the Germans had seized the Netherlands. Once the Axis powers surrendered, the Dutch wanted their colony back. Harsh Japanese rule, however, had roused both nationalist feeling and a new sense of common Indonesian identity among ethnically diverse people strung out across 13,670 islands. Ahmed Sukarno, a university graduate from a poor Muslim family, rose to the forefront of the freedom movement, preaching a loose national ideology founded on democracy, social justice, and belief in God. When nationalists declared independence, Dutch forces moved in to crush the insurgency. Both the United States and the Soviet Union pressured the Netherlands, whose postwar economy was in shambles, to follow the British example in India. Finally yielding in 1949, the Netherlands transferred sovereignty to an independent state dominated by Sukarno and Indonesia's educated and affluent class.

France also wanted its Southeast Asian possessions restored after the war. In Vietnam, however, nationalists under the leadership of Ho Chi Minh and the Communist Party already had control of much of the northern region. A founder of the Indochinese Communist Party in 1930, Ho and his comrades launched peasant resistance in northern Vietnam. After 1941 they fought both Japan and its French puppet regime. In August 1945 Ho led the communist Viet Minh (Vietnamese Independence League) into Hanoi, the French colonial capital in the north.

That success marked the start of a brutal conflict that continued for nearly a decade. The United States had aided and advised Ho in his fight against the Axis. But as the Cold War settled in, the Americans abandoned him, throwing massive aid to the French side in order to prevent a communist victory. Colonial forces, however, failed to suppress Viet Minh guerrillas, and in 1954, after a humiliating defeat at the Battle of Dien Bien Phu, France agreed to leave Vietnam. Thereafter, the country remained divided between a communist-ruled north, and an American-supported, anticommunist regime in the south, a situation that would persist for another twenty-one years.

Communist Victory in China

When Japan surrendered, China faced the resumption of a festering civil war between nationalist and communist partisans. Anxious to see Jiang Jieshi's Nationalist Party in full control, the United States helped airlift his troops into most of China's major cities. It also urged him to parley with Mao Zedong to allow the Communist Party to take part in a postwar democratic government. Jiang refused, negotiations collapsed by the end of 1946, and war broke out again in full force.

Within three years, the communists won the war after Mao's forces encircled numerous cities, bottling up nationalist troops. As communist units captured Beijing and swept into southern China, Jiang and about two million nationalist soldiers fled to Taiwan. Mao then announced the birth of the People's Republic of China, the first major communist triumph since the Russian Revolution of 1917. Meanwhile, the Soviet Union, having declared war on Japan just a week before it surrendered, sent forces into the northern half of Korea. U.S. troops occupied the southern half, and the United Nations sanctioned a provisional division of Korea at the thirty-eighth parallel of latitude.

• • •

Conclusion

From prelude to aftermath, World War II riveted humankind's attention. It cost about sixty million lives and left several of the world's important industrial centers knocked flat. It severely disrupted international trade, migration, and cultural exchange. The end of the conflict presented new and intractable problems—smoldering cities that had to be rebuilt, tens of millions of refugees to be resettled, and massive debts to be paid. Furthermore, the victorious Grand Alliance between the Western liberal democracies and the Soviet Union collapsed in bitter suspicion and rivalry.

Yet, as tumultuous as the war was, it interrupted modernity's long-term trends only briefly. On the global scale, population continued to rise at an accelerating rate. Human energy consumption continued to soar. Scientific and technological innovation surged, and many wartime novelties—radar, nuclear fission, antibiotics—found socially beneficial uses after 1945. The war set off a race between the belligerents to boost the speed and range of communication and transport. (The American test pilot Charles Yeager broke the sound barrier in a rocket-powered aircraft just two years after the war ended.) The destruction of the Axis empires had no significant impact on the continuing accumulation of power in the hands of states. The ideologies of liberal democracy and several variants of socialism, which spread around the world in the nineteenth century, found new appeal after the war. At least for a time, overtly fascist political movements were discredited. Finally, the brisk global economic growth that had characterized long stretches of the eighteenth and nineteenth centuries resumed about 1950. Before long, as we see in Chapter 27, economists were convincing themselves that the whole calamitous period from 1914 to 1945 was just a brief and unfortunate deviation from modernity's long and upward economic spiral.

• • •

Key Terms

Cold War 779
collaborationist 764
embargo 766
genocide 773
Greater East Asia Co-Prosperity Sphere 766
Hiroshima and Nagasaki 770

Holocaust 773
International Monetary Fund (IMF) 779
Marshall Plan 779
North Atlantic Treaty Organization (NATO) 780
partition 781

Third Reich 760
United Nations 774
Warsaw Pact 781
World Bank 780
World War II 760

Change over Time

1934–1935	Mao Zedong leads communist soldiers across China in the Long March.
1935	Italy invades Ethiopia.
1936–1939	Nationalists defeat a leftist coalition in the Spanish Civil War.
1937	Japan invades China.
1938	Germany annexes Austria. Munich agreement endorses German occupation of Czechoslovakia.
1939–1945	Allied and Axis powers clash in World War II.
1944	The United States hosts a global gathering known as the Bretton Woods conference, which establishes the International Monetary Fund and the World Bank.
1945	The United Nations Charter is signed. Ho Chi Minh leads the communist Viet Minh into Hanoi.
1945–1948	Communists seize power in several Eastern European countries.
1946	Jordan, Lebanon, and Syria win independence.
1947	India and Pakistan win independence.
1948–1949	Israel declares independence; the First Arab–Israeli War engulfs the Middle East. Stalin sets up Berlin blockade; Western allies airlift supplies and food.
1949	North Atlantic Treaty Organization (NATO) is founded to ensure the security of Western Europe. Indonesia wins independence. Communist forces achieve victory in China.

Please see end of chapter reference section for additional reading suggestions related to this chapter.

27 The Global Boom and Its Contradictions

1945–1975

Sputnik I, the first artificial satellite in Earth's orbit.

I n February 1945 Arthur C. Clarke, the British science writer later celebrated for such books as *2001: A Space Odyssey,* wrote to the editor of *Wireless World* magazine. He argued in his letter that World War II rocket technology had advanced to the point where "artificial satellites" could be launched into orbit around the earth. The transmitters on these devices would broadcast research data about the upper atmosphere. Almost as an afterthought, Clarke also proposed that if a satellite were placed at the correct height above the equator to make one revolution every twenty-four hours, it would remain in a stationary position relative to the ground. "Three repeater stations, 120 degrees apart in the correct orbit," he wrote, "could give television and microwave coverage to the entire planet." In other words, these satellites could hypothetically relay signals instantly from any point on earth to any other point, a feat not possible at ground level. Clarke mused that the technical hurdles to satellite broadcasting might be overcome "perhaps half a century ahead."

In fact, the Soviet Union put Sputnik, a transmitting satellite the size of a beach ball, into orbit in October 1957, just twelve years after Clarke wrote his visionary letter. The United States shot Explorer I into space the following year, and in 1962 the AT&T corporation, working with the National Aeronautics and Space Administration (NASA) launched Telstar, the first orbital satellite to relay TV signals. By 1964, governments and corporations were firing satellites into orbit at a rate of about ten a month. In 1969 three Americans landed on the moon.

The remarkable pace of satellite communication and space exploration was one expression of the extraordinary economic and technological surge that characterized the three decades after World War II. In the immediate aftermath of that devastating conflict, world leaders could not have foreseen that by 1950 both global population and economic production would veer sharply upward. The first part of this chapter explores this phenomenon, its causes, and its implications for both human social development and the planet's physical and natural health.

Scientific research animated the space age but so did the intense rivalry that developed between the United States and the Soviet Union, the subject of the second section of the chapter. The wartime Grand Alliance sealed in 1941 between the Western democracies and the Soviet Union deteriorated into acrimony even before the struggle ended (see Chapter 26). The United States and Russia never hurled

Chapter Outline

• • •

armored divisions or nuclear missiles at each other, so in that sense the conflict remained a "cold" war. But the venomous rhetoric and brinksmanship of the two political blocs, plus their strategic interventions in the affairs of numerous other states in Latin America, Africa, and Asia, kept the world in a state of chronic anxiety for nearly forty years.

The third part of the chapter investigates the relationship between expanding global growth and accelerating demands around the world for political freedom and social justice. These rising expectations among the colonized and the poor, as well as among well-fed but discontented middle classes, produced political tensions, indeed several civil wars and revolutionary movements. Between 1950 and 1975 the world as a whole advanced to unparalleled material prosperity, but the chasm between the richest and the poorest social groups and world regions continued to widen.

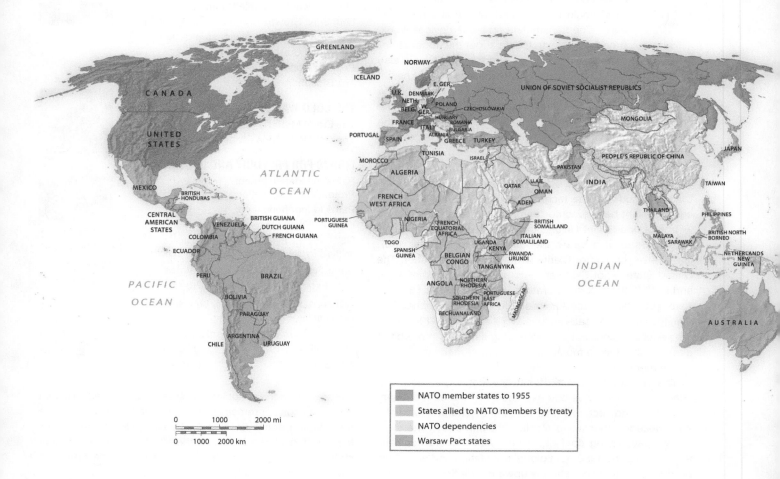

A Panoramic View

MAP 27.1 Political and military alliances, 1955.

The Cold War produced a politically bipolar global landscape. Which states remained outside the Warsaw Pact or NATO alliances? What factors might have encouraged certain states to maintain neutrality?

Population and Economy: An Era of Spectacular Growth

FOCUS Why did the world economy grow at such a rapidly accelerating rate in the three decades following World War II, and what were major social consequences of that growth?

The mid-twentieth century was a significant turning point for the global economy and the world's population. In the three decades after World War II, production of material wealth worldwide advanced at a much faster rate than it had during the previous thirty years. In some countries people consumed goods on a scale their grandparents would have thought unimaginable. Also about midcentury, the population growth rate, which had been accelerating since the eighteenth century, shot up even faster.

These two trends reinforced each other. Economic growth and new technology allowed the planet to accommodate more people, and more people meant an expanding supply of labor in places where economic success required it. In countries where population grew faster than the economy, however, living standards for peasants and workers typically declined. Stunning economic growth on the world scale proved compatible with both worsening poverty and environmental degradation in many places.

Global Population at Its Crest

In the third quarter of the twentieth century, the world's population growth rate ran higher than in any previous historical era; it also ran higher than after 1975. During those twenty-five years, some societies moved through a demographic transition (see Chapter 25). This meant that people lived longer on average (the mortality rate declined), but women had fewer children (the fertility rate also declined). The population growth rate therefore slowed. This happened in Europe and North America (north of Mexico) and a little later in Eastern Europe, Russia, Japan, and some Latin American states. In several regions, however, fertility rates remained high but mortality rates dropped faster than ever; consequently, growth rates went up. In much of Africa, Asia, and Latin America, populations grew at a rate of about 2.5 percent per year, much higher than, for example, in Western Europe. India's population grew from about 360 million in 1950 to 580 million by 1973, a number only slightly less than the world's entire population in 1600.

Several factors contributed to spiraling population after World War II. One of these was the post-World War II **baby boom**. Despite the general trend of slowing growth rates in many

baby boom A period of increased birthrates, especially in Western countries, from the end of World War II to about 1957.

Western industrialized countries, a spike occurred just after the war, as more young people, released from military service or war-related work, started families amid improving economic conditions. In the United States and Britain, for example, millions of women lost wartime jobs. Consequently, they returned in large numbers to domestic life, and new offspring soon arrived. The baby boom lasted until about 1957, when fertility rates declined again.

On the global scale, the population surge may be linked to an array of new drugs and pesticides, which pushed down mortality rates, especially in tropical and subtropical regions. Vaccination campaigns combated lethal diseases such as cholera, typhus, diphtheria, and polio, raising the survival rate of small children. Smallpox was exterminated, the last known case occurring in East Africa in 1977. DDT, the chemical pesticide first used in World War II, killed insects that transmitted typhus and malaria. Gradual postwar improvements in nutrition and water treatment, especially in large cities, also helped lower annual mortality.

The Postwar Economic Boom

Extraordinary global economic growth after World War II manifested itself in several ways: a huge expansion of capitalist industry, a resurgence of international trade and investment, continuous quickening of scientific and technical innovation, rising incomes for hundreds of millions of people, and much greater consumption of both fossil fuels and material goods. Remarkable rises in gross domestic product per capita occurred not only in the large capitalist economies but also in the communist states and at least some of the new nations that emerged from colonial dependency.

Evidence of boom times. The United States primed the growth pump worldwide. In 1945 it controlled nearly two-thirds of the globe's industrial output. However, once the Western European states and Japan dug themselves out of physical ruin, they began to register even higher growth rates than the United States. In the Soviet Union, communist economic planners showed they could also perform postwar miracles. That country's industrial output doubled between 1945 and 1950 alone and kept on growing into the 1960s. On the global scale, manufacturing grew fourfold between 1950 and 1975, and world trade doubled every ten years (see graph: Change in GDP per capita from 1914 to 1975[1]). In the major capitalist states, unemployment plunged, and workers enjoyed rising real wages. Both inflation and cyclical business downturns remained mild.

Integrating the capitalist economies. At the international Bretton Woods conference in New Hampshire in 1944 (see Chapter 26), the leading capitalist states vowed to advance global peace and prosperity by setting up postwar institutions for international cooperation, collective security, stabilization of currencies, low-tariff trade, and new investment in war-ravaged countries. When the war ended,

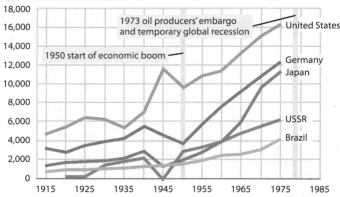

1990 International dollars

Change in GDP per capita from 1914 to 1975. Which countries experienced the greatest growth in GDP in this period? How would you characterize overall change in GDP in this period? What factors can account for the spike in U.S. GDP just after the sharp decline in Soviet GDP in 1945?

Italy, Japan, and the two-thirds of Germany that became the capitalist Federal Republic (West Germany) subscribed to the Bretton Woods plan. The countries that collaborated to promote economic integration formalized their association in 1961 as the Organization for Economic Cooperation and Development (OECD), a group that included seventeen European states, the United States, Canada, Turkey, and (within three years) Japan.

In the 1950s the United States presided firmly over this club of capitalist states and the ᵃBretton Woods system,° a set of rules that states were expected to follow in doing business with one another. Economic leaders agreed to make the U.S. dollar the world's anchor currency, pegging its value to gold at a fixed rate of $35 an ounce. Other countries then pegged their currencies to the dollar, though provision was made for states to alter the value of their currency to deal with economic or financial crises. The system worked well for nearly two decades. It discouraged disruptive currency fluctuations and stimulated international commerce and investment. Twenty-three countries established the General Agreement on Tariffs and Trade (GATT) in 1947 to sponsor successive ᵃrounds° of negotiations to lower customs duties on manufactured goods. The United States, Japan, and Western Europe all experienced huge export booms in consequence. Until the 1970s they produced together more than 80 percent of the world's manufactured exports, trading the greater part of those goods with one another.

In the postwar years, American corporations, flush with new consumer products, technologies, and disposable capital, dominated international investment. These firms put money in foreign countries by building factories and opening marketing offices. Between 1950 and 1973, U.S. corporate investment in Western Europe and Japan grew from $2 billion to $41 billion. Companies that mass-produced technologically complex products like automobiles ballooned in size. For example, Chrysler, Ford, and General Motors, the

three major American automakers, all opened plants in Western Europe. By the late 1960s they commanded more than 25 percent of that region's consumer market for cars and trucks. Eventually, European and Japanese companies penetrated foreign markets as well.

The European Economic Community. The ruin of war convinced many Western European leaders that the region must exchange autarkyÐ enclosed national self-sufficiencyÐ for economic integration, even political federation. These leaders knew that the German Federal Republic would not be held back economically for long, and they wanted it to direct its energies toward the region's economic resurgence and not into a new military buildup. The United States encouraged a pan-European partnership. John Foster Dulles, secretary of state during the Dwight D. Eisenhower presidency (1953±1960), had argued back in 1941 that when the war was over the ᵃreestablishment of some twenty-five wholly independent sovereign states in Europe would be political folly.°² European integration would presumably serve the objectives of Bretton Woods, enlarge markets for American goods, and counteract communist subversion.

Several states were ready to advance in that direction. In 1952 the German Federal Republic, France, Belgium, the Netherlands, Luxembourg, and Italy joined together to launch the European Coal and Steel Community (ECSC), an international regulatory authority that created a common market for those two resources among the member states. This was a remarkable achievement, considering that Germany and Italy had been mortal enemies of the other four members just a few years earlier. In fact, the agency worked so well that these six states negotiated a much broader common market for goods, founding the European Economic Community (EEC) in 1957 under the terms of the Treaty of Rome. By the 1960s free trade and commercial cooperation among an expanding list of members were transforming Western Europe into a global economic powerhouse.

Capitalism and the welfare state. The idea that the state has a responsibility to guarantee at least minimal economic safety nets for all citizens gained nearly universal acceptance during the twentieth century, at least as a social principle. Leaders committed to the Bretton Woods system generally understood that wage-earning citizens, including labor union members and democratic socialists, would buy into plans for greater global economic integration only if the state continued to guarantee people basic security against company failures, wage losses, layoffs, and sudden business downturns.

Consequently, the **welfare state** grew along with the global economy, though disproportionately faster in Western Europe than in the

welfare state An approach to government in which the state uses public funds to protect and promote the health and social well-being of all citizens.

United States, where public opinion remained divided about federal government activism. Owing to postwar prosperity, governments accumulated revenue to expand services such as health care, disability insurance, low-cost housing, pensions, public education, and grants to college students. In the third quarter of the century, this partnership between capitalist enterprise and social democracy worked quite well. In all the leading industrial states, poverty generally declined, worker wages rose, and leaders of the moderate left and right cooperated.

Economic Growth in Communist States

Between 1945 and 1955 the number of countries dedicated to the Marxist-Leninist brand of socialist ideology grew from oneÐ the Soviet UnionÐ to twelve, including eight in Eastern Europe, plus China, Mongolia, North Korea, and North Vietnam (see Map 27.1). The number of people living under communist governments increased by hundreds of millions. Many of these states experienced impressive economic growth in the 1950s. The Soviet economy grew faster than that of any Western capitalist country, though from a lower starting point. China enjoyed unprecedented growth from 1952 and 1957. All of these states shunned the Bretton Woods club, which, as they well knew, functioned in large measure to advance the global political and economic interests of the United States. Rather, they adopted highly centralized state planning and control generally modeled on Soviet-style socialism.

Soviet successes. Under Joseph Stalin's long rule, the Soviet economy moved to the rhythm of successive Five Year Plans, sets of government-mandated economic goals. The state, not private enterprises, owned the country's industrial plants, transport systems, and commercial institutions, as well as most of its farming. The state, not the market, determined prices and wages. After World War II, Stalin continued to mobilize the Soviet population for industrial development as if the fighting had not stopped. Living standards remained modest, and most consumer goods were available to only the *nomenklatura*Ð the upper levels of the communist civil and military bureaucracy.

The Soviet economy continued to grow under the guidance of Nikita Khrushchev (1894±1971), the brash and boisterous coal miner's son who rose to the top of the Soviet political hierarchy within two years of Stalin's death. He denounced his predecessor's harsh domestic repression and global isolation, but he had full faith in socialism to improve life for ordinary citizens. During Khrushchev's

years in command (1953±1964), he shifted some state investment from heavy industry to consumer products like shoes, clothing, and radios. He expanded low-cost housing, public services, and higher education, notably for young women. He revived Soviet farming with new machinery, fertilizers, and irrigation projects for collective farms. Gradually, rural living standards improved. Khrushchev also caught the capitalist world off guard in October 1957, when Soviet engineers launched Sputnik into earth orbit on a ballistic missile. This event sent the American public into an uproar over the country's failure to stay ahead of its communist rival in science and technology.

Khrushchev announced that within twenty years the Soviet economy would leave the capitalist states far behind. ªWhen we catch you up . . . , in passing you up, we will wave to you,º he told then±U.S. vice president Richard Nixon in 1959.[3] These confident proclamations, however, masked serious weaknesses. Many party bureaucrats despised Khrushchev's reforms and did all they could to sabotage them. State controls, though relaxed slightly, continued to stifle broad technical innovation. Despite the initial Soviet breakthrough in ballistic missile testing, Russia had only 4 operational missiles by 1962; the United States had 224.

Nikita Khrushchev and Richard Nixon discuss consumer economics. In 1959 the U.S. government opened an exhibit in Moscow featuring a typical American suburban house complete with labor-saving appliances. Touring the exhibition together, the Soviet premier and the American vice president engaged in an impromptu conversation (through interpreters) about their respective national economies. The exchange, known as the Kitchen Debate, was captured with new color videotape technology and broadcast in both countries. Why might Khrushchev and Nixon have debated household consumption as part of a larger conversation about economic ideology?

Khrushchev's political opponents forced him from office in 1964, though he had ªde-Stalinizedº the political culture enough that his successors sent him into obscure retirement, not to Siberia. Leonid Brezhnev and Alexei Kosygin then rose to leadership. They continued to make modest social reforms and greatly increased Soviet foreign trade. But they also invested heavily once again in state planning, heavy industry, and the military. During the rest of the decade, economic growth slowed steadily; by the early 1970s, the Soviet economy was close to stagnant.

China leaps forward and back. Like Stalin in Russia, Mao Zedong aimed to make the People's Republic of China a self-sufficient industrial power. The country experienced periods of impressive economic growth between 1949 and 1976, the year Mao died. During those twenty-seven years, however, the economy oscillated wildly, in large part because of deep policy disagreements within the ruling Communist Party. Mao was determined to industrialize China at breakneck speed without compromising the Marxist-Leninist vision of radical social equalityÐ no rich and poor peasants, no landlords, no capitalist bourgeoisie. Generally, when the state tried to orchestrate the economy from the

top, growth waned. When it backed off, for example, permitting rural farmers to buy and sell privately in local markets, growth accelerated but income inequalities also widened.

For a few years after its 1949 victory, the communist government left petty capitalism in the countryside mostly alone, and with generous aid from the Soviet Union the Chinese economy grew rapidly. Between 1950 and 1957, life expectancy rose by twenty-one years. The number of children in school soared, and new laws alleviated the exploitation of rural women by abolishing child marriage and permitting divorce by mutual consent.

In the mid-1950s, however, Mao and his inner circle decided that the country must ramp up farm output to sustain industrial expansion and the rapidly growing urban workforce. He therefore ordered wholesale collectivization of agriculture. Peasants were to labor for the state, not for themselves. When village-size collectives proved insufficiently productive, the regime hatched grander plans, dispatching tens of millions of rural men and women to giant irrigation projects and to huge communes where they shared dormitories, dining halls, communal nurseries, and ªhappy homesº for the elderly. To increase iron and steel production, the state also instructed peasants to build and operate miniature blast furnaces. China, Mao proclaimed, would make a ªGreat Leap Forwardº into socialist utopia.

Instead, from 1958 to 1961 the country descended into famine. Farm output on the big but inefficient communes plummeted. Backyard mills produced inferior metal and prevented peasants from tending crops. A succession of disastrous harvests left vast rural areas with no food at all. Upwards of thirty million people, unable to survive on grass, bark, and shoe leather, died of starvation and disease, probably more than perished in World War II. Soviet help also shrank because relations between the two countries soured over a range of issues, including simmering territorial disputes along their mutual border. Economic conditions became so bad that leaders who favored smaller collectives and private plots for peasants recovered political influence. For a few years, growth returnedÐ along with greater income differences.

In 1966, however, China descended again into turmoil. Mao, reacting to critics within the party and opposing any resurgence of capitalism, proclaimed the Great Proletarian Cultural Revolution. This mass popular mobilization aimed to cleanse party and society of bourgeois values, foreign influences, and ideological impurities. In effect, Mao and his hard-core supporters, including his radical wife Jiang Qing, unleashed young intellectuals, students, and workers against the very government establishment that he headed. More than two years of political tumult and economic stagnation

A worker stokes a backyard blast furnace. Chinese peasants set up over one million smelters in the "battle for steel," an attempt to make steel on an industrial scale through the collective efforts of many rural communities. Why did localized steel manufacturing not produce the results Mao expected, in spite of a long history of impressive peasant productivity?

followed. Maoist Red Guards intimidated and even murdered people even faintly suspected of bourgeois ᵃwrong thinking,° including ownership of Western pop records. Millions of educated men and women were exiled to villages where peasants instructed them in proper revolutionary attitudes. Red Guard enthusiasm began to wane in the late 1960s, and the economy revived quickly. Meanwhile, high party officials devoted themselves to vicious infighting over succession to the elderly and failing Mao. This state of affairs continued until his death in 1976.

The Worldwide Lure of Industrialization

As the postwar world economy blossomed, the idea that industrialization was the key to prosperity spread rapidly from the big capitalist and socialist economies to dozens of other states. In most of these smaller countries, leaders tried to follow a middle road between private investment and centralized planning and control. They remained leery of the Bretton Woods system, arguing that economic progress required high tariffs to protect new industries, not closer ties with foreign corporations and banks.

Economies in Latin America. During the Great Depression and World War II, when global trade shrank, several Latin American republics experimented with **import substitution industrialization, or ISI.** These programs aimed to reduce both commercial dependence on more economically developed countries and vulnerability to global economic swings. Through ISI, a country could slow the export of natural resources and reduce somewhat its reliance on foreign capital. The state, however, had to prime the development pump by investing in and managing industries and transport networks. In the 1950s ISI produced some good results. Mexico quadrupled its manufacturing output between 1945 and 1973. By the mid-1960s Brazil, which occupies nearly half the land area of South America, produced nearly all its own consumer goods. Even so, foreign investment did not wither. Between 1950 and 1965, for example, American companies invested $3.8 billion in Latin American enterprises, reaping in return profits of $7.5 billion.

> **import substitution industrialization (ISI)** Government economic policies to encourage national industries to produce finished goods that would otherwise be imported.

During and right after World War II, several Latin American states worked to strengthen democratic institutions, including voting rights for women. This trend, however, did not last. With the notable exceptions of Chile and Uruguay, authoritarian governments of one type or another, some of them military regimes, seized power, most in close alliance with the U.S. government. Typically, those governments represented pragmatic alliances among the army, business leaders, professionals, urban middle classes, and industrial workers, all groups that wanted technical modernization and industrial self-sufficiency. Between 1962 and 1966

alone, military coups took place in nine Latin American countries, including Brazil.

Even the most dictatorial governments, however, adopted nationalist and sometimes even socialist rhetoric, rallying city populations with promises of welfare services and better living standards. In Argentina, for example, President Juan Perón (in office 1946±1955, 1973±1974) kept a tight rein on power but also appealed to the urban masses and labor unions for support. Eva Duarte, the president's wife, rose from soap opera actress to brilliant advocate of the poor against the traditional land-owning class. Known affectionately as ᵃEvita,° she helped women get the vote in 1947, though also arguing that women best served the nation by staying home. Nonetheless, except in Mexico, reforms to transfer land from estate lords to peasants made little progress. In the late 1960s about 17 percent of Latin American proprietors owned about 90 percent of the land. Population also rose faster than national economies, producing inflation, rural joblessness, and swelling urban poverty in many countries.

Economic challenges in new states. In all the territories that achieved independence from colonial rule in the decade after World War II, new leaders aimed to modernize their economies by building national industries. The largest and most technically advanced of these new states was India, which in 1950 had about 372 million people, more than twice as many as in all of Latin America. In pointed contrast to most states in Asia, India achieved growth while simultaneously building a vivacious, if disorderly, democracy. Jawaharlal Nehru, who led India and the Congress Party from 1947 to 1964, was a socialist and radical modernizer devoted to rapid industrialization. He emulated the Soviet Union in launching ambitious five-year development plans, but he also collaborated with Indian capitalists, of which there were many. Huge state investment produced impressive results. In the 1950s, iron, steel, textile, and automobile industries all advanced. In the 1960s, however, the economy slowed. Like several Latin American states, India shifted too much public investment from agriculture to heavy industry when population was rising fast. Irrigating more land, using more chemical fertilizers, and planting hybrid seeds helped produce more food, but rural poverty remained pervasive, propelling millions to migrate to cities like Bombay (Mumbai), Calcutta (Kolkata), and New Delhi.

Growth varied widely in other Asia territories, though four of them began to show remarkable success in the early 1960s. South Korea, the Republic of China on Taiwan, the largely self-governing British colony of Hong Kong, and Singapore, which gained independence from Britain in 1965, rejected the Latin American model of manufacturing mainly to supply home consumers. Instead, they favored new enterprises to make finished products to export to the rest of the world. None of these countries had abundant natural resources, but by making high-quality goods and keeping costs down, they became the ᵃAsian tigers,° competing vigorously in global markets.

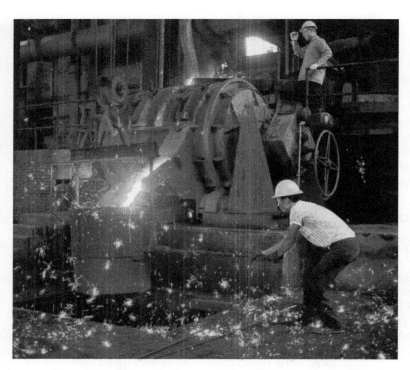

Steel workers operate a forge at the Hsin Yee Metal Industries factory in Taiwan. Like other Asian tiger economies, Taiwan increased its output of both heavy industry and consumer goods starting in the 1960s. How did this economic strategy compare to efforts to industrialize in mainland China during the same period?

Cities, Suburbs, and Shantytowns

Population and economic growth together boosted the world's city dwellers from about 25 percent in 1950 to 40 percent by 1980. At midcentury there were 67 cities with populations in excess of one million; by 1975 there were 172.[4] The distribution of big cities on the world map also changed, with Asia taking the lead from Europe and North America (see Map 27.2).

In the boom years, cities in both industrialized and developing countries became more complex and more densely populated as centers of interdependent economic activityÐ manufacturing, processing, transport, research, higher education, government administration, and a multitude of services. Cars, new roads, and public transport systems also allowed people to live farther from historic centers, transforming some cities into sprawling metropolitan regions. For example, in the Kanto area of Japan after World War II, Tokyo and several

> **megalopolis** An extensive and densely urbanized region or chain of urbanized regions.

other cities fused into one giant **megalopolis,** which today has a population in excess of thirty-six million. In North America and Europe, families with sufficient income to buy houses and cars spilled out from city centers into leafy suburbs, and businesses soon followed them. In less industrialized countries,

urban sprawl resulted much less from outward suburbanization than from inward movement of poor rural people, who erected shantytowns in widening rings around city cores. In urbanizing regions like South Asia and tropical Africa, the first generation or two of city newcomers were predominantly men; women remained in villages to carry on with farm work. Family and ethnic networks, however, continued to tie urban settlements with ancestral villages. Also, clusters of urban huts and shacks often evolved into communities made stable by more balanced sex ratios, new families, and civic and religious organizations.

Postwar Consumer Society

The continuing fossil-fuel revolution made it possible for industry to produce more consumer goods than ever before. This torrent of new products inevitably produced cultural and psychological transformations. More men and women, first in the booming industrial economies, subscribed to a ᵃculture of consumption.º This way of living, which centered on desires to acquire and display ᵃthings,º profoundly influenced economic decisions, social relations, and expectations of individual fulfillment. In fact, modern middle classes around the world came to define themselves partly by their ability to consume goods and enjoy pleasures that the lower classesÐ the great majorityÐ could not afford.

The United States exited World War II as a rich society ready to shop. Refrigerators, kitchen ranges, TVs, automobiles, and single-family homes were among the most coveted ᵃbig-ticketº items. In the 1950s consumer spending also rose exponentially in Western Europe, Canada, and Australia. In France, for example, the proportion of homes with indoor toilets rose from 25 percent in 1954 to 75 percent in 1975. In the 1960s **consumerism** hit Japan. In the Soviet Union and communist Eastern Europe young men

> **consumerism** Social and cultural values and practices centered on the accumulation and consumption of material goods.

and women persistently clamored for more goods than their governments were willing or able to supply. The regimes in Poland, Hungary, Czechoslovakia, and East Germany raised consumer production somewhat in the late 1950s, but mostly they promised full employment rather than generous wages and mountains of merchandise.

After World War II, private businesses spent much larger portions of their budgets on advertising, product testing, and customer relations strategies. The Burton's men's clothing chain in Britain exemplifies consumerist tactics. The 1953 edition of its ᵃManager's Guideº declared that salesmanship was the ᵃart of making people want what you have to sell. . . . Create desire to possess strong enough to overcome a natural antipathy to parting with money, and you will make sale after sale.º[5] Consumer capitalists also invented new credit mechanisms, notably home mortgage loans, installment buying, and store credit cards, so that customers with average

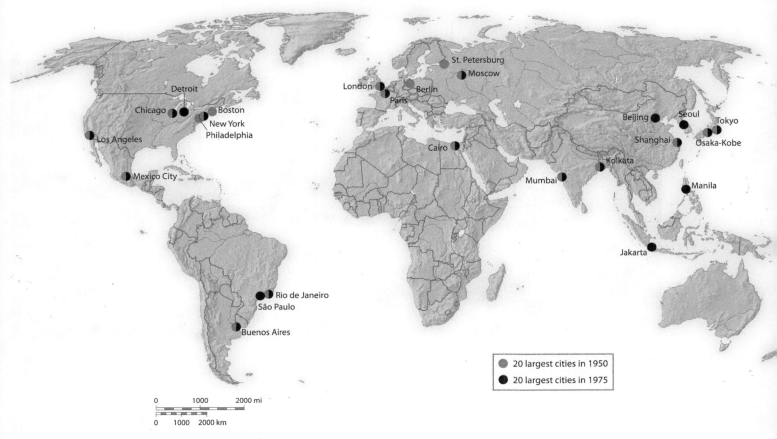

MAP 27.2 The world's twenty largest cities in 1950 and 1975.
Which of the largest cities in 1950 were no longer among the top twenty in 1975? What factors account for the shifting locations of the largest cities between 1950 and 1975?

incomes might enjoy instant gratification. Moreover, corporations devoted more research and development to inventing products designed specifically to make last year's goods seem outdated and unfashionable, a strategy known as planned obsolescence. Auto makers, for example, introduced new vehicle designs every year, hoping the Smiths would trade in their old model in order to climb a rung above the Joneses on the ladder of social prestige.

Consumption and social change. Consumerism had profound social effects in the richest societies. People could travel more freely, get better health care, and cut drudgery with work-saving technology. Economists worried at first that if the consumer economy fulfilled most desires and the welfare state kept everyone above water, then people would work less, thereby reducing productivity. In fact, the opposite happened. People tended to work harder and longer as their incomes rose, persuaded that more purchasing power would make them happier.

Economic growth and consumerism significantly changed the lives of middle- and working-class women. After a slump in female employment after the war, both married and single women poured back into wage work, squeezing homemaking into fewer available hours. Manufacturers relentlessly pursed female buyers, recognizing that they often made major domestic buying decisions. Ironically, dishwashers, ovens, and steam irons helped push women into the labor market but convinced few men that they might also master those machines. On the whole, employed women continued to earn less than men and to hit ᵃglass ceilingsº when promotions came around.

Postwar consumer culture had many critics. Social observers, especially in Europe, complained that popular yearning for material goods replaced community values with self-absorbed individualism. In the 1950s, European intellectuals saw the United States as a gigantic material culture pump, flooding the world with its movies, comic books, plastic doodads, and other spirit-numbing wares. In the 1960s, however,

Consumer advertising proliferated in the 1960s. A scene at a London train station illustrates the opportunities a diverse range of advertisers had to reach future customers, both women and men. What income levels and demographic groups do you think the advertisers in this picture were hoping to reach?

fears of an American cultural invasion largely evaporated in Western Europe, as people there adopted their own distinctive consumer cultures. They drove smaller cars to navigate the narrow streets of ancient European cities. Their filmmakers competed energetically with Hollywood, the Italian director Sergio Leone, for example, making idiosyncratic American ªwesterns° on location in Spain. The cultural invasion in fact reversed direction when British music and fashion hit American shores, and European corporations sold American consumers on the glamour of European goods.

The Biosphere in Distress

Humans altered and exploited the earthly biosphere at a rapidly accelerating rate in the postwar decades. Energy from fossil fuelsÐ coal, petroleum, and natural gasÐ drove a threefold jump in global gross domestic product between 1950 and 1973. A parade of technological innovationsÐ better chemical refining processes, high-pressure pipelines, larger tanker shipsÐ allowed for the massive exploitation of fossil-fuel reserves. By 1975 humankind was consuming 2.3 billion tons of oil per yearÐ up from 10 million in 1890. The Middle East joined Russia, Romania, Mexico, Venezuela, and the United States as a major oil-producing region. Fossil-fuel combustion, along with turbo-generating dams,

fed most of the world's insatiable appetite for electricity. In the mid-1950s the Soviet Union, the United States, and Britain began to tap nuclear power for everyday use. From then until the 1980s, nuclear power plants multiplied in several other countries, notably France.

In the postwar decades, rapid economic and demographic growth had a much greater impact on the planet's physical and natural environment than anyone seems to have understood at the time. There is no doubt that degradation of the planet's soils, water systems, and atmosphere advanced steadily.

Manipulating soil, water, and seed. History's earliest farmers began to deplete the planet's thin soil layer by disturbing it with sticks and hoes. By the twentieth century, mechanized farming, lumbering, mining, and building caused billions of tons of soil to wash or blow away every year. Serious erosion could be checked to some extent by reforestation or other expensive measures that peasants could seldom afford. In mountainous Rwanda in East Africa, for example, population density increased from 80 to 180 people per square kilometer between 1948 and 1978. Farmers there waged a constant struggle to slow hillside soil loss. In postwar Brazil, commercial growers clear-cut millions of acres of forest to expand coffee production, causing massive soil runoff.

Expanding metallurgical and chemical production after the war generated mountains and rivers of toxic waste from mines, factories, smelters, and refineries. By 1950 most cities in developed countries had safe drinking water, but in much of the world urbanization far outpaced construction of enclosed sewers and water treatment plants. Consequently, water-borne diseases like cholera and typhoid continued to kill millions, especially small children. Even in places with good water treatment, businesses, governments, and private citizens tended to regard lakes and rivers as convenient cesspits. In the 1950s, for example, heavy industry made a fast recovery in northern Europe's Rhineland, but this also transformed the lower Rhine River into a chemical and metallurgical gutter largely devoid of aquatic life. Serious cleanup efforts began only in the late 1970s.

Soil and water degradation was also an unintended consequence of immense dam and irrigation projects. Between 1950 and 1980, irrigated land worldwide increased by close to 200 million acres.[6] Irrigation could vastly increase crop yields and therefore raise peasant incomes and promote exports. But it also presented long-term problems. Chemical fertilizers seeped from irrigated land back into canals and rivers, stimulating the buildup of algae and other nutrient-devouring plants, which clogged channels and starved aquatic life.

One example is particularly poignant. In Egypt, Gamal Abdel Nasser, the military ruler from 1952 to 1970, ordered construction of a high dam at Aswan on the middle Nile River, an enormous project that started in 1960 and took a decade to complete. The dam stopped the Nile's annual summer flood, which had sustained Egypt's agrarian civilization for five thousand years. Instead, downstream flow was regulated to allow crop irrigation all year round. Presumably, Egypt would then be able to feed its rapidly growing population and to export large surpluses of cotton and other commodities. Signs of trouble, however, soon appeared. The millions of tons of silt that for millennia had flowed across the lower valley and the Nile delta every summer accumulated instead in Lake Nasser, the huge reservoir behind the dam. Consequently, farming downstream depended on massive annual infusions of chemical fertilizer, much of which had to be purchased abroad. Riotous blooms of algae and water hyacinths clogged irrigation canals and even water delivery to Cairo. In the absence of annual silt flow, Mediterranean sea water pushed deeper inland, threatening the farm-rich Nile delta. Nasser had hoped for agricultural self-sufficiency, but today Egypt imports as much as 60 percent of its annual food supply.

Global population could not have increased at the rate it did after the war without an accompanying rise in food production. In the postwar decades, scientists and engineers applied modern technology to ramp up farm yields, in some places by a factor of ten. Bioengineers developed new strains of wheat, rice, and maize (corn) bred specifically

Building the Aswan High Dam. A worker pauses to change his shoes at the site of this ambitious project, which involved both massive manual labor and heavy machinery. Partly funded by the USSR, the dam was to be a big step toward Egypt's food and energy self-sufficiency. What role might nationalist appeals have played in arousing popular support for the project?

to produce luxuriant crop yields, but only in the presence of chemical fertilizers, pesticides, and immense volumes of irrigation water. This **Green Revolution,** which got under way slowly in the 1930s, spread from the United States to Mexico, where wheat harvests tripled between 1944 and 1960. In the following two decades, many populous countries, including Turkey, India, Pakistan, Indonesia, China, South Korea, and the Philippines produced enough wheat or rice to keep up with the pace of population growth.

Yet unintended consequences multiplied. In much of Asia, Africa, and Latin America, technology that raised farm productivity tended to benefit large-scale landlords and companies disproportionately relative to individual farm families. Gasoline-powered machinery, fertilizers, and irrigation water represented enormous inputs of energy and capital that only big land-owners could usually afford. Hybridized seeds produced high-yield food plants, but the seeds of those plants were sterile. Consequently, farmers had to buy new seeds every year from firms that owned patents to them. This state of affairs hugely benefited biotechnology corporations but not small farmers in developing countries. Nor could family farmers compete easily with big growers capable of producing crops in volume and therefore keeping

market prices down. In the 1970s millions of farmers, especially in Asia, left the land to find subsistence wage work.

Air pollution. Early in the twentieth century, a London physician coined the term *smog* to describe the ªsmoky fogº that hung over large cities. The word came to mean the atmospheric haze that forms when sunlight chemically reacts with the nitrogen oxides and hydrocarbons emitted by internal combustion engines. Smog causes eye and respiratory maladies, and it harms many types of flora. During the postwar boom, factories, mines, farms, and motor vehicles spewed record tonnages of chemical contaminants into the atmosphere. Only in the 1960s, however, did scientists begin systematically to measure air contamination in big cities and industrial regions. By then, the richer countries were taking steps to bring urban air pollution under at least partial control. London roused itself to action after December 1952, when a combination of weather conditions shrouded the city in a weeklong toxic fog. The Great Smog caused nearly four thousand deaths from respiratory diseases. In the 1950s and 1960s, contamination affecting whole regions reached appalling levels in places like the São Paulo area in Brazil and the Ruhr valley in northwestern Europe.

Even the most technologically innovative countries were slow to address pollution from motor vehicles, whose numbers in the world grew from 50 million in 1930 to 500 million by 1985. Some metropolitan areas, for example, Mexico City, Los Angeles, Athens, and Tehran, began to suffer acutely

Daytime traffic during the Great Smog. A bus navigates the streets of London in December 1952, as commuters brave foul conditions caused by hydrocarbon emissions. Why did air quality deteriorate so much before residents of industrialized countries began to take measures to counteract pollution?

because cars became so numerous, the sun shines many days a year, and surrounding mountains prevent smog dispersion. Also, beginning in the 1920s, oil corporations improved gasoline efficiency by adding lead, which caused toxic elevations in human blood streams. Concerted efforts to reduce tailpipe contamination got under way in the late 1960s, but urban pollution worldwide was still getting worse as of 1975.

In 1962 Rachel Carson, an American zoologist, published *Silent Spring,* an indictment of the chemical industry for selling DDT and other pesticides that killed animal life. Despite intense corporate opposition, her work roused scientific and public consciousness about the environment. Not until the following decade, however, did governments and public interest groups begin to make commitments to retard and if possible reverse numerous forms of environmental degradation (see Chapter 28).

The Cold War Wears On

FOCUS How did the Cold War affect political and economic relations among the world's peoples in the three decades following World War II?

The Cold War, whose early years we described in the context of World War II's aftermath (see Chapter 26), may be conceived as a struggle between two contrasting political and economic visions. The United States aspired to lead the world to economic prosperity through democracy and capitalism. The Soviet Union, China, and other communist states were equally determined to shun capitalist internationalism. The communist regimes, rather, aimed to demonstrate that Marxist-Leninist teachings, together with central planning, economic self-sufficiency, and subordination of private interests to the state, would produce material well-being and social equality for all. On the ground, Europe remained divided at what Winston Churchill called the iron curtain: The armies of the United States and its Western European NATO stood nose to nose with divisions of the Warsaw Pact, the military alliance that the Soviet Union formed with its Eastern European junior partners in 1955 (see Map 27.1).

The Era of Mutually Assured Destruction

The existence of nuclear weapons shaped all international relations after 1945. The world's most powerful states had gone to war in both 1914 and 1939 on the assumption that whatever the cost, winners would eventually emerge from the wreckage and start to rebuild. A war fought with atomic bombs, however, threatened to snuff out the human species altogether. Who would rebuild after that? The United States, which showed what even small fission bombs could do to two Japanese cities, held a monopoly on atomic technology for four years. But Stalin ordered a nuclear crash program

that yielded a successful atomic test on the Inner Eurasian steppes in 1949.

The Korean War as test case. The war that erupted in Korea in 1950 might have provoked a nuclear confrontation, but it did not. Like Germany, Korea found itself divided at the end of the world war, a Soviet-allied communist government installed in the north, and a U.S.-backed republic in the south, the two states separated by an arbitrary border at the thirty-eighth parallel of latitude. But as soon as both major powers withdrew their troops from the Korean peninsula in 1948±1949, north and south threatened to attack each other.

The Soviet Union, having signed a mutual defense pact with Mao Zedong and perhaps hoping to discourage postwar Japan from drawing too close to the United States, gave Kim Il-Sung, the leader of North Korea, a green light to invade the south and reunify the peninsula under communist rule. He thought the United States would not interfere. Instead, the U.S. government convinced the United Nations Security Council (on a day when the Soviet delegation was absent) to authorize military intervention. The ensuing war lasted just over three years. At the start, North Korean forces nearly overran the peninsula, but a counterassault under General Douglas MacArthur drove close to North Korea's border with China at the Yalu River. Believing such provocation could compromise his own hold on power, Mao ordered 300,000 Chinese troops to cross the Yalu in October 1950. That onslaught pushed American and allied divisions back, but then the war degenerated into grinding stalemate. Neither Stalin nor U.S. president Harry Truman wanted to

Troops of the People's Liberation Army, North Korea, October 1950. Chinese forces sent to support the communist North Korean government were unequally equipped to battle United Nations forces led by the United States. Notice the ragtag uniforms and the soldiers in the front row wearing only sandals. Nevertheless, these troops managed to halt UN advances and bring the war to a stalemate. Why might Mao have risked sending poorly equipped soldiers to war?

drop atomic bombs to decide the future of Korea, and in July 1953 the adversaries signed an armistice, leaving the peninsula still divided. Something like 2.8 million Koreans died in the war. The conflict aggravated mistrust between the United States and Russia and sent American relations with China into deep freeze for more than two decades.

Cold War fears and hopes. The Korean War also intensified the nuclear arms race. In 1952 the United States tested the first hydrogen bomb, which worked on the principle of nuclear fusion. The detonation in the South Pacific produced a 10.4 million ton explosion, five hundred times larger than the blast over Nagasaki. The Soviets evened that playing field the following year. Between 1952 and 1974, Britain, France, China, Israel, and India all joined the nuclear club, though their arsenals remained relatively small. By the mid-1960s both Russia and the United States had submarine fleets armed with enough nuclear missiles to kill hundreds of millions of people in a single afternoon.

Leaders in both Washington and Moscow could imagine the likely consequence of an all-out missile exchange, and it scared them from the start. When Mao Zedong remarked in 1957 that China could lose three hundred million people in a nuclear strike and still recover nicely, Soviet and Americans leaders were equally appalled. In 1959 President Dwight Eisenhower mused darkly that if missiles started flying ªyou might as well go out and shoot everyone you see and

> **mutually assured destruction (MAD)** The doctrine aimed at preventing nuclear war between the United States and the Soviet Union by shared knowledge that, if either side attacked, both would suffer mass destruction.

then shoot yourself.º⁷ In the early 1960s the United States openly proclaimed a policy of **mutually assured destruction,** or **MAD,** the dubious theory that if no one expected to come out of a nuclear war alive, then no one would start one.

The Cold War in the 1950s and 1960s had a strange inconsistency. On the one hand, the adversaries continued to expand their military arsenals and spy networks. Each side warned the other that it would answer an attack with a rain of nuclear fire. In the 1950s, however, American intelligence revealed that the United States had far greater nuclear and long-range missile capability than Russia did. The Soviets knew this, too, which drove them to turn up the volume of threats. The U.S. propaganda machines responded in kind. On the other hand, both powers proclaimed their commitment to peaceful coexistence. They held periodic summit meetings and organized cultural exchanges. Trade between the Soviet bloc and the Western industrial states grew rapidly in the 1960s. In 1963 the United States and the Soviet Union signed the Limited Test Ban Treaty, which prohibited nuclear testing in the atmosphere. Additional agreements followed, culminating in the 1972 Anti-Ballistic Missile Treaty, which banned nuclear states from developing defenses against incoming rockets.

The European stalemate. After Stalin lifted the land blockade of West Berlin (see Chapter 26), the Cold War adversaries moved toward a cautious understanding that neither would attack or otherwise destabilize the other's half of Europe, barring the most extreme provocation. For example, in 1956, Hungarian citizens, angered over repression and poor progress in living standards, revolted against their communist government, demanding withdrawal from the Soviet bloc. Within a few days, however, the Red Army moved in to suppress the insurgency, at a cost of some twenty thousand Hungarian lives. The United States and its allies denounced the aggression but did nothing more, confirming, to the dismay of street fighters in Budapest, their policy of nonintervention in the affairs of Soviet satellites.

Then, in 1961, the Soviet Union collaborated with the communist-ruled German Democratic Republic (GDR) to build a wall, first of barbed wire, then of concrete, to seal East Berlin and the rest of the GDR from West Berlin. Unable to stop citizens, especially skilled and educated ones, from fleeing to booming West Berlin, the GDR put up the barrier as a measure of desperation. The Western allies protested but also knew that the wall just might reduce tensions in central Europe. John F. Kennedy, recently inaugurated as U.S. president (in office 1961±1963), conceded that ªit's not a very nice solution, but a wall is a hell of a lot better than a war.º⁸

The Cold War Goes Global

An irony of the Cold War is that even though American and Soviet missiles remained on their launch pads, something like fifty-five wars of varying scope, both civil and international, either started or were already in progress between 1950 and 1975. Both superpowers intervened in several of these conflicts, hoping to cultivate new allies and advance their own strategic and ideological interests. The Cold War therefore played out across Asia, Africa, and Latin America, often with unforeseen consequences.

In Iran, for example, the government of Prime Minister Muhammad Mosaddiq tried in the early 1950s to build a constitutional democracy that limited the powers of the hitherto authoritarian monarchy of Muhammad Reza Shah (reigned, 1941±1979). To reduce foreign control over the economy, Mosaddiq nationalized the Anglo-Iranian Oil Company. Fearing both disruption of oil deliveries to Europe and Mosaddiq's tolerance for communist political activity, the U.S. Central Intelligence Agency (CIA) conspired with British operatives and conservative Iranian military officers in 1953 to overthrow the regime. Reza Shah returned to full power, and the United States gained a close ally. But the people of Iran got twenty-seven more years of royal despotism. Similarly, in 1954 the United States collaborated with right-wing army officers in Guatemala to oust President Jacobo Arbenz (in office 1951±1954). He had not only enacted land reforms that offended the United Fruit Company, an American corporation, but also cultivated friendly ties with communist governments. Following the coup, Guatemala descended into decades of military dictatorship and civil war.

On the Soviet side, Khrushchev and his successors also saw opportunities to project Soviet imperial power in informal ways. He energized Russian foreign policy, offering economic and military aid to friendly or neutral countries and exploiting unstable situations. The Cold War reached a critical turning point in 1962, when the Soviets installed intermediate range missiles in Cuba. Three years earlier, Fidel Castro (in office 1959±2008) and a guerrilla army dedicated to radical, Marxist-inspired social reform had emerged from mountain hideouts to overthrow the oppressive government of Fulgencio Batista, a close ally of American business. When Castro confiscated $1 billion worth of American property, the United States broke diplomatic relations. Having nowhere else to turn, Castro asked the Soviet Union to buy Cuban sugar, its main export, and to provide technical and military aid. In response, President Kennedy authorized the CIA and Cuban exiles to invade the island at the Bay of Pigs, a wretchedly planned operation that ended in disaster. Nevertheless, Kennedy continued to try to destabilize Castro's regime, including a trade embargo.

The Cuban revolution surprised Soviet leaders because a Marxist-Leninist regime had come to power in the Western Hemisphere without them having done anything to make it happen. Khrushchev apparently thought that by placing missiles in Cuba he would simultaneously protect his new client and encourage communist revolutionaries elsewhere in Latin America. ªIt was clear to me,º he later wrote, ªthat we might very well lose Cuba if we didn't take some decisive steps in her defense.º 9 When Kennedy learned that Soviet rockets were to be installed ninety miles from Florida, he saw no choice but confrontation. In October 1962 he announced to jittery television audiences around the world that a Soviet missile launch on any target in the Western Hemisphere would provoke immediate retaliation. But rather than ordering air strikes on the rocket sites, he dispatched a naval flotilla to block Soviet supply ships from reaching Cuba. Knowing well that the United States far outgunned him in numbers of intercontinental missiles, Khrushchev backed down. The crisis did not end, however, in American triumph. Khrushchev negotiated removal of the missiles already in Cuba for withdrawal of U.S. nuclear weapons from Turkey and Kennedy's promise not to invade the island again.

The Cuban missile crisis had important political consequences. Both superpowers grasped more urgently the need to keep lines of communication open between them to prevent mutual misunderstandings, however loud the public rhetoric. Though the Soviets agreed to tread lightly in Latin America, the two powers ratcheted up their rivalry in the young states of Asia and Africa. Meanwhile, Castro's light shone brighter than ever among leftist and communist leaders around the world because he had stood up to his mighty capitalist neighbor.

Fights for Freedom and Justice

FOCUS In what ways did global economic and political change in the three decades after World War II affect the development of movements for colonial independence and social reform?

The fact that some societies in the postwar world enjoyed rising living standards and reasonably responsible governments roused yearnings for similar life benefits nearly everywhere else. In colonial dependencies and in states with relatively small economies, disappointed economic hopes among middle and poorer classes aggravated social tensions and helped stir popular revolutions, civil struggles, and violent protests. After a cluster of newly independent states joined the United Nations between 1946 and 1950, there was a five-year lull. The second wave of colonial flag-lowering started in 1955, continuing steadily, especially in Africa, during the following two decades. In 1950 the United Nations had 50 members; by 1975 it had 144 (see Map 27.3). In addition to movements against colonial rule,

Khrushchev pulls his rockets out of Cuba. This cartoon, originally published in the *Hartford Times*, parodies the Soviet Union's decision to withdraw its ballistic missiles from Castro's Cuba. Edmund Valtman, the artist, won the Pulitzer Prize for editorial cartoons in 1962. How does this image portray the relationship between Cuba and the USSR?

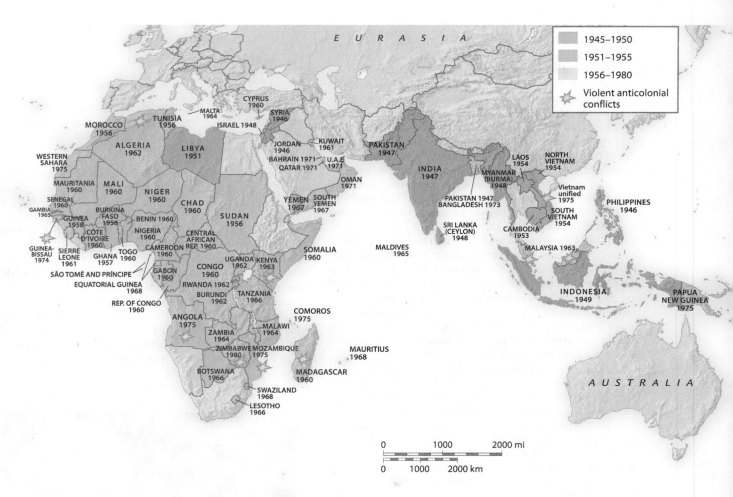

MAP 27.3 New sovereign states in Afroeurasia, 1945–1980.
Why did many Asian dependencies achieve independence between 1945 and 1956 and so many African ones only after 1956? What political or cultural similarities and differences do you notice among the dependencies that had violent struggles before achieving independence?

millions of people in sovereign states, including the richest countries in the world, took to the streets to register dissent over inequality and oppression. Popular protest around the world reached a crescendo in 1968.

Paths to Independence: Protest and Negotiation

Between 1956 and 1980 forty new states emerged in Africa. In most cases the decolonization process took place without battlefield violence. Nationalist parties waged their struggles with petitions, marches, strikes, boycotts, and short urban uprisings, tactics that produced death and injury, but not on a grand scale. In no African colony did nationalist leaders wish to break up the territory or wreck its governing apparatus. Rather, nationalists aimed initially to assume full control of the same administrative organs and the same territorial boundaries that European invaders had created earlier.

None of the imperial powers in AfricaÐ Britain, France, Belgium, Portugal, and SpainÐ expected to leave as soon as they did. After World War II, Britain and France proclaimed new economic and political development programs, expecting that small minorities of men and women with Western educations would willingly collaborate to improve, at a gradual pace, the living standards of poor majorities. Most nationalists, on the contrary, regarded every useful economic project and every small political reform as an argument for full independence sooner rather than later. Moreover, between 1950 and 1975, one imperial power after another (the last being Portugal) conceded that they could no longer afford their empires, neither the expense of relentless suppression of nationalist opposition nor the costs of serious economic development.

To politicians in London and Paris, the alternative of letting leaders of new nations largely finance their own development, while at the same time cultivating friendly business relations with them, looked increasingly attractive.

Britain, moreover, was willing to defer to the United States in formulating strategies to keep communists or other anti-capitalist radicals from getting control of nationalist movements or seizing power in new states.

New states in British Africa.

Great Britain had fifteen dependencies in Africa, the largest of them Nigeria, which had a population in 1960 of nearly forty million, eight times more people than in Scotland. Since the interwar decades, British administrators had been working with small educated elites to expand, without any sense of hurry, indigenous participation in political institutions like advisory councils, local governments, or civil services. But after 1945, independence movements gained momentum. In the British Gold Coast, renamed Ghana after independence, Kwame Nkrumah (1909±1972) emerged in the late 1940s as tropical Africa's first larger-than-life nationalist hero and mass organizer. Educated in the United States and inspired by Gandhi's nonviolent resistance strategies in India, he formed the Convention People's Party (CPP), which coordinated rallies, marches, strikes, and boycotts to push relentlessly against the British regime.

In 1951 Britain agreed to a general election, hoping that the radical CPP would lose it. That did not happen, and colonial officials had no choice but to appoint Nkrumah, who was in jail at the time, ªleader of government business.º In 1954, African American writer Richard Wright visited Ghana. Attending a CPP rally, he bore witness to Nkrumah's remarkable ability to rouse urban crowds and personify the nationalist cause.

The speaker [one of Nkrumah's supporters] threw a challenging question in English requiring a yes or no answer, for he wanted the audience to participate in the meeting . . .

ª Nkrumah has led you this far and he will lead you on! . . . You must believe that he'll never let you down! He went to prison for you; he suffered for you; he'll lay down his life for you! . . .

ª Will *he* fight for you?

ª Yes!

ª Will *you* fight for him?

ª Yes!

ª And what are we fighting for?

ª FREEÐ DOOOOM! FREEÐ DOOOOM!º [10]

Three years later, Ghana achieved independence under Nkrumah's presidency. Between then and 1965, Britain dispossessed itself of ten other dependencies in Africa, including enormous Nigeria, without prolonged violence.

New states in French Africa.

Shortly after World War II the newly constituted French Fourth Republic declared that it had no intention of shedding its Asian and African empire. By the end of 1954, however, the Viet Minh nationalist army had forced France to leave Vietnam (see Chapter 26), and Muslim nationalists had started an insurrection in Algeria. Those developments inspired educated elites, trade unions, and urban youth in France's immense tropical African territories to press for self-rule. The people of those colonies also watched nationalists in Morocco and Tunisia win independence from France in 1956 with warm support from the United States.

As in the British case, France's postwar government announced plans to develop its tropical African dependencies and to expand the number of *évolués*Ð Africans considered culturally ªevolvedº because they had French-style educationsÐ to be permitted to stand for election to the French National Assembly. As in the British colonies, however, nationalists, with some encouragement from French

Voters cast their ballots in Senegal, 1956. Africans in French colonies voted for representatives to the French National Assembly, but this limited civic participation did not quell nationalist resistance to colonial rule. Some Africans tore up their ballots to protest the lack of African control of local government, arguing that representation in Paris was no substitute for independence. How did the timing of voting rights for women in French-ruled Africa compare with that of women's enfranchisement in France (see the section called "Feminist movements").

Frantz Fanon on the Shortcomings of the National Bourgeoisie

One of the most influential texts to emerge from colonial independence movements is Frantz Fanon's The Wretched of the Earth. *Fanon (1925–1961) came from a middle-class family on the French Caribbean island of Martinique. During World War II he went to North Africa to join the Free French resistance against the Germans. He was wounded in battle and awarded the Croix de Guerre. After the war he studied medicine and psychiatry in France. There, he became starkly aware of the limits of social assimilation. Though he had grown up in a thoroughly French environment and fought for the country, whites never viewed him as an equal. His interest in the psychological effects of colonialism resulted in his first book,* Black Skin, White Masks *(1952).*

In 1953 Fanon accepted a position at an Algerian psychiatric hospital and gave support to FLN revolutionaries. He became acutely aware, through experiences of his patients, of the violent foundations of French colonial rule. In 1956 the French government expelled him from Algeria. He then moved to Tunisia where he continued his work on behalf of Algerian independence.

Suffering from terminal leukemia, Fanon wrote The Wretched of the Earth *in 1961. The book attracted notoriety for its apparent approval of violence as a means to end colonial rule. Fanon recognized, however, that both perpetrators and victims of violence can never escape its psychological effects. In subsequent essays he explained that revolutionary violence must be short lived, or it will destroy all whom it touches.*

In the excerpt below, he discusses how the nation (here referring to a body of people with shared political goals) must negotiate the transition from colonialism to independence. Within a general Marxist framework of class struggle, Fanon argues that the indigenous colonial bourgeoisie are ill equipped to lead the nation because they have identified with the values of their capitalist colonial oppressors and lost touch with the masses.

The national middle class which takes over power at the end of the colonial regime is an under-developed middle class. It has practically no economic power, and in any case it is in no way commensurate with the bourgeoisie of the mother country which it hopes to replace. . . .

Seen through its eyes, its mission has nothing to do with transforming the nation; it consists, prosaically, of being the transmission line between the nation and a capitalism, rampant though camouflaged, which today puts on the masque of neocolonialism. The national bourgeoisie will be quite content with the role of the Western bourgeoisie's business agent, and it will play its part without any complexes in a most dignified manner. But this same lucrative role, this cheap-jack's function, this meanness of outlook and this absence of all ambition symbolize the incapability of the national middle class to fulfill its historic role of bourgeoisie. Here, the dynamic, pioneer aspect, the characteristics of the inventor and of the discoverer of new worlds which are found in all national bourgeoisies are lamentably absent. In the colonial countries, the spirit of indulgence is dominant at the core of the bourgeoisie; and this is because the national bourgeoisie identifies itself with the Western bourgeoisie, from whom it has learnt its lessons. It follows the Western bourgeoisie along its path of negation and decadence without ever having emulated it in its first stages of exploration and invention, stages which are an acquisition of that Western bourgeoisie whatever the circumstances. . . . The national bourgeoisie will be greatly helped on its way towards decadence by the Western bourgeoisies, who come to

it as tourists avid for the exotic, for big-game hunting and for casinos. . . . Because it is bereft of ideas, because it lives to itself and cuts itself off from the people, undermined by its hereditary incapacity to think in terms of all the problems of the nation as seen from the point of view of the whole of that nation, the national middle class will have nothing better to do than to take on the role of manager for Western enterprise, and it will in practice set up its country as the brothel of Europe. . . .

If you really wish your country to avoid regression, or at best halts and uncertainties, a rapid step must be taken from national consciousness to political and social consciousness. . . . The battle-line against hunger, against ignorance, against poverty and against unawareness ought to be ever present in the muscles and the intelligences of men and women. . . . There must be an economic program; there must also be a doctrine concerning the division of wealth and social relations. . . . It is only when men and women are included on a vast scale in enlightened and fruitful work that form and body are given to that consciousness. . . . The living expression of the nation is the moving consciousness of the whole of the people; it is the coherent, enlightened action of men and women. . . . No leader, however valuable he may be, can substitute himself for the popular will; and the national government, before concerning itself about international prestige, ought first to give back their dignity to all citizens.

Source: Frantz Fanon, *The Wretched of the Earth,* trans. Constance Farrington (New York: Grove Press, 1965), 149, 152±154, 203±205.

Thinking Critically

Why, in Fanon's view, does the national middle class feel a stronger relationship to the colonizer than it does to others in its own country? What do you think Fanon means by saying that the middle class will turn its country into the "brothel of Europe"? What do you think he means by the term "neocolonialism"? What problems must a new nation first address to ensure its viability? From this selection, what can you infer about Fanon's views of those taking power in newly independent countries? In what ways, if any, does the selection reveal the influence of Marxism on Fanon's thought?

communists and socialists, agitated for one reform and compromise after another. Urban laborers, dissatisfied with pay, working conditions, and social discrimination, continued to organize strikes, and a stream of young men and women in big cities like Dakar and Abidjan joined nationalist political groups. In 1956 the government in Paris responded by dividing French West Africa and French Equatorial Africa, its two big colonial federations, into smaller political units, hoping to fragment and weaken nationalist elites. This scheme had little effect, and in any case revolutionary violence in Algeria spread to France, bringing the Fourth Republic to its knees in 1958. Charles De Gaulle, leader of the Free French in World War II, came out of retirement to proclaim the Fifth Republic and preside over a new constitution. He made one last effort to keep the African colonies within the French fold but by then had run out of persuasive arguments. In 1960 fourteen new republics in West and Equatorial Africa, plus the island of Madagascar, achieved full sovereignty.

Paths to Independence: Insurgency and Revolution

Among the dozens of territories that sought and won independence in the third quarter of the century, only a few witnessed prolonged fighting between colonizer and colonized. One example is the British East African colony of Kenya, where a small but politically powerful European settler population adamantly opposed African independence. There, violence broke out in 1952. African guerrillas, mainly Kikuyu-speaking peasants and urban poor frustrated over landlessness, unemployment, and low-wage labor on European-owned coffee and tea estates, set up rebel bases in central Kenya's forests. Colonial forces, which gave the uprising the derogatory name Mau Mau, launched counterinsurgency operations and imprisoned tens of thousands of men and women. The fighting ended in 1955, after 95 Europeans and at least 11,500 Africans lost their lives. Shortly afterward, however, London decided to negotiate decolonization before another violent outbreak occurred. Kenya became independent in 1963 under the presidency of Jomo Kenyatta.

The Algerian Revolution. Algeria was different from all other French overseas colonies because its inhabitants included about one million people of European origin. They constituted a minority of about 15 percent of the population, which was predominantly Arabic- or Berber-speaking Muslims. Most European settlers fiercely opposed Algerian self-rule under any authority except its own, and the Fourth Republic regarded the territory, not as a dependent colony, but as a permanent part of France. The economic and social gulf between the privileged, mostly city-dwelling European minority and the Muslim population of peasants, urban workers, and small entrepreneurs was immense. Under great settler pressure, successive French governments refused to make any significant moves toward majority rule.

The consequence was eight years of bitter war. In November 1954, just a few months after France withdrew from Vietnam in defeat, Algerian insurgents instigated a countrywide rebellion. The National Liberation Front (FLN), which orchestrated the rising, demanded a sovereign, democratic, and socialist Algeria guided by Islamic ideals. The French authorities responded with brutal repression, which only spread the revolutionary fire. By mid-1957 the colonial army appeared to be winning the war, but the FLN continued to operate from havens in neighboring Morocco and Tunisia. Facing both colossal costs and nothing but intransigence on the part of settler leaders, De Gaulle opened negotiations with the FLN in 1960. Independence came two years later. About 85 percent of the European population refused Algerian citizenship and fled the country in near panic during the final months of the war. The new nationalist regime took over a country in a state of physical and economic collapse.

Southern Africa. Armed struggles broke out in three southern African colonies in the 1960s. The British dependency of Southern Rhodesia (Zimbabwe after independence) had a European settler population of only about 5 percent, but this minority dominated politics and the export economy. Watching Britain give up one African possession after another and counting on support from white-ruled South Africa, Southern Rhodesia's white leaders made a Unilateral Declaration of Independence in 1965 to perpetuate their authority. Britain protested but did not send troops. Zimbabwe's African nationalist parties stepped up guerrilla operations. Meanwhile, armed resistance also intensified in the two big Portuguese colonies of Angola and Mozambique. In those cases the metropolitan government, itself an authoritarian dictatorship under António Salazar, refused all negotiation with nationalist leaders. In 1974, Portuguese officers, weary of protracted African wars of no discernible benefit to tiny Portugal, overthrew Salazar, paving the way for democracy at home and independence for the colonies in 1975. In consequence, Zimbabwe's guerrilla fighters were able to take advantage of sanctuaries in Angola and Mozambique, which led to negotiated independence under majority rule in 1980.

Struggles for Stability in Young States

In the 1950s and 1960s new states celebrated independence flush with hope for rapid economic development. Few of these states had much industry. Rather, they exported food and mineral commodities, as they had during the colonial era. During the postwar global boom, however, world prices for many commodities rose higher, which translated into at least modest growth for many new countries. In Ghana, the Ivory Coast, and Kenya, among other states, society made impressive gains in health care, life expectancy, and education.

Yet rising gross domestic product seldom produced long-term political calm. Few of the states that started out as presidential republics or constitutional monarchies followed India's path to democracy. In the 1950s and 1960s military officers seized power in many states. Eighteen coups took place in Africa alone. In several countries, elected presidents transformed themselves into dictators, banning all political parties except their own. In a few states, debilitating civil wars broke out.

Upon gaining independence, nationalist leaders took over the civil services, police, and communication networks that the colonial regimes had left behind. Most new governments also put themselves in control of economic resources with the goal of creating a more equitable society. In most of these countries, however, development plans lost steam. Highly skilled workers, up-to-date technology, and investment capital were usually in short supply. Railway, telephone, and electrical networks did not improve nearly fast enough after decades of colonial neglect. Government-paid jobs mushroomed, but industrialization projects did not. By the mid-1960s the global boom had passed its peak. Revenue from export commodities, typically a young state's biggest income source, began to drop. Where top leaders had failed to secure their own power, disgruntled political groups, often military men (the army being the only organization with plenty of guns) threw the old nationalist leaders out.

In Ghana, for example, Kwame Nkrumah, the founding president, lost power to a military faction in 1966 after the price of cocoa, the country's leading export, began to plummet. That same year, Nigeria, suffering from severe tensions among regional political groups, experienced the first of a long series of military takeovers. Competition for control of newly discovered oil made matters worse and led directly to a three-year civil war (1967±1970) in which the southeastern region tried unsuccessfully to form a separate state named Biafra.

The Congo fell into civil turmoil just two weeks after it celebrated independence from Belgium in June 1960. In contrast to Britain and France, Belgium not only banned all nationalist political activity in its enormous colony until the mid-1950s, but also permitted only a handful of Africans to get responsible government jobs or even high school educations. When popular riots broke out in the capital city of Leopoldville (Kinshasa), the Belgian regime organized slapdash elections to a new Congolese legislature, then abruptly abandoned the colony.

Independent Congo unraveled almost immediately. More riots broke out, army units mutinied, and in the copper-rich southern province of Katanga rebels in alliance with European mining interests declared a separate state. Just before independence, Patrice Lumumba (1925±1961), a former postal clerk, founded a national political party dedicated to transcending the country's complex ethnic and linguistic divisions. But as the Congo's first prime minister, he faced an agonizing task of restoring order. There is no evidence that Lumumba was a communist, but his radical denunciation of Belgium and a plea to the Soviet Union to send aid moved the United States to support a UN peacekeeping force.

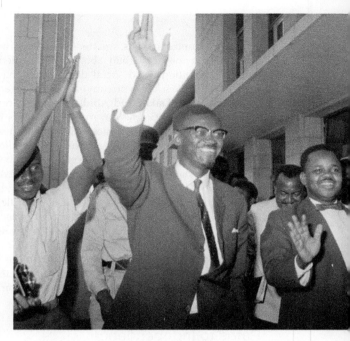

Patrice Lumumba, Congo's first prime minister, leaving the National Senate, 1960. The first democratically elected leader of Congo faced huge challenges during his twelve-week term in office. In this photo Lumumba celebrates the 41–2 vote of confidence, called in response to his handling of the Katanga succession. In 2002, Belgium issued an apology to Congo for Lumumba's murder in 1961.

Lumumba agreed to this plan, but in 1961, Joseph Mobutu, a rising Congolese military star, conspired with Belgian operatives and the U.S. CIA to have the prime minister murdered. UN troops extinguished the Katanga rebellion in 1963, and two years later, after about a million Congolese had died in violent upheaval, Mobutu seized full power. There he remained for more than thirty years, keeping the country unified, cooperating with capitalist mining enterprise, and adamantly opposing the slightest democratic reform.

The turbulent Middle East. The era of formal European colonial rule ended in most of the Arabic-speaking Middle East shortly after World War II. Even so, continuing hostility between the Jewish state of Israel and its neighbors, concentrations of hundreds of thousands of Palestinian refugees in camps in Egypt and Jordan, and the rising international stakes for access to Middle Eastern oil made for volatile postcolonial conditions. Popular opinion in the Arab states overwhelmingly regarded Israel as a foreign intruder and proxy for continuing Western imperial domination. Israel gained international credibility by winning the 1948 war with its Arab neighbors and believed it deserved regional acceptance. But tensions remained high, including chronic fighting along the border between Israel and Egypt. Arab leaders dealing with pressing economic problems at home had no wish to undermine their own authority by moving to normalize relations with Israel.

Arab national governments, some ideologically socialist, others pro-Western and conservative, quarreled intensely with each other, but they also joined together to fight three more wars with Israel, in 1956, 1967, and 1973. In Egypt, President Gamal Abdel Nasser put himself forward as champion of regional unification, promising to absorb Israel into a large pan-Arab state. In 1956 he negotiated with the British to end their occupation of the Suez Canal Zone, but shortly thereafter he suddenly nationalized the canal's operation. Two-thirds of Western Europe's oil supplies passed through the waterway, and in October, Britain, France, and Israel devised a secret plan to take back the canal and overthrow Nasser. When the military operation got under way, the United States, seeing the situation from a wider regional perspective, refused to back its allies. ªHow could we possibly support Britain and France,º President Eisenhower protested, ªif in doing so we lose the whole Arab world?º[11] The Soviet Union, which had good relations with Nasser, threatened nuclear retaliation if the attack did not stop. Neither Britain nor France could afford to defy U.S. opinion. Within a few weeks they and the Israelis pulled out of Egyptian territory, ending the Suez Crisis. The war made Nasser a regional hero. On its side, Israel demonstrated once again its military strength but also reinforced

the Arab conviction that Israel had no genuine desire for peace with its neighbors.

Shaky calm prevailed for eleven years, but in the spring of 1967 tensions reached a boiling point once again. Nasser continued to seek Arab unity by vowing to extinguish Israel, while the Soviet Union sent both Egypt and Syria cargos of weapons. The United States proclaimed its commitment to Israel's defense while tending carefully to its oil interests elsewhere in the region. Following a succession of miscues between Israel and its neighbors over who intended to do what, Israeli jets simultaneously attacked Egypt, Syria, and Jordan on June 5, destroying the air forces of all three countries. Israeli forces then invaded the Sinai Peninsula, Gaza, the Golan Heights in Syria, and the West Bank (Jordanian territory west of the Jordan River). Israel's victory in this Six Day War (or June War) discredited all the Arab regimes, especially Nasser, whose army lost twelve thousand soldiers, the Sinai oil fields, and revenue from the Suez Canal, which remained closed to shipping until 1975. Israel occupied 28,000 square miles of new territory, which included 300,000 Arabs, many of them impoverished refugees from the 1948 conflict (see Map 27.4). The war compounded regional hostilities and strengthened the hand of Palestinians determined to wage guerrilla warfare against Israel. The

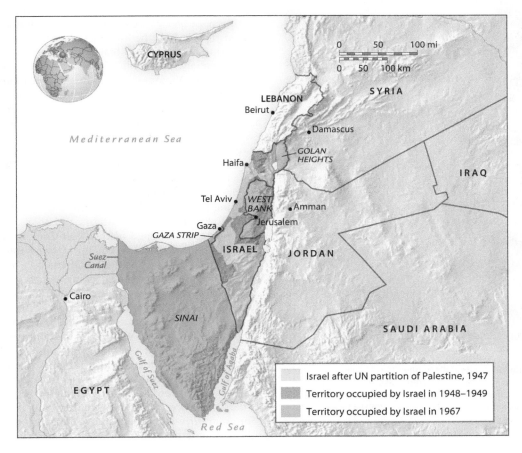

MAP 27.4 Israel and its occupied territories.

What aspects of physical geography might have affected the course and outcome of the 1967 Arab–Israeli War?

Legend:
Israel after UN partition of Palestine, 1947
Territory occupied by Israel in 1948–1949
Territory occupied by Israel in 1967

fourth war of the era broke out in 1973, an event associated with the economic crises to be described in Chapter 28.

Vietnam between civil war and Cold War.

Vietnam achieved independence in 1954, several years sooner than most of France's colonies, because communist Viet Minh forces under the leadership of Ho Chi Minh humbled the French army in battle. Vietnam, however, did not achieve unification. Ho's Indochinese Communist Party controlled the north but not the south, where anticommunist sentiment remained strong, especially among the land-owning elite and the politically influential Roman Catholic minority population. Terms of Vietnam's independence (the Geneva Accords) projected reunification in 1956, following an election. But no vote took place because the United States, replacing France as patron of pro-Western political groups throughout Southeast Asia, engineered the installation of Ngo Dinh Diem, a staunch anticommunist, as president of South Vietnam.

In the north, Ho's regime, with aid from both the Soviet Union and China, adopted socialist prescriptions of one-party control, state-led industrialization, and land reforms to give private estate lands to peasants. In the south, by contrast, the Diem government allied itself with the land-owning class and made policies that favored Catholics over the Buddhist majority. Despite injections of American money, Diem steadily lost popular support, while pro-communist elements in the countryside organized the National Liberation Front (NLF), or Viet Cong, to incite revolution. Vowing to reunite Vietnam, Ho supported the NLF, provoking all-out war between north and south by the early 1960s. Both the United States and the Soviet Union came to see this struggle as a microcosm of their own global contest. The U.S. government declared that it would not stomach any more communist regimes in Asia, while the Soviets intensified their strategy to support not only communist but radical leftist governments wherever they could.

In 1963 the United States allowed South Vietnamese officers to overthrow and kill Diem, although political leadership continued to deteriorate. The Saigon government moved rapidly into the informal American imperial orbit, depending on the United States for as much as 80 percent of its economy. When NLF forces seized control of about half of South Vietnam, U.S. military forces took on more of the fighting. U.S. president Lyndon Johnson (in office 1963±1969) saw the war as a test of U.S. credibility. ªIf we are driven from the field in Viet-Nam, then no nation can ever again have the same confidence in American promise, or in American protection.º¹² From 1965 to 1973 Presidents Johnson and Richard Nixon (in office 1969±1974) tried successively to achieve victory by military escalation, including deployment of more than 500,000 troops and strategic bombing of both North and South Vietnam, plus NLF and North Vietnamese sanctuaries in Cambodia.

These tactics stopped neither Viet Cong operations nor the movements of North Vietnamese troops into the south. In 1968 the NLF launched the Tet Offensive, a militarily unsuccessful but nonetheless shocking series of urban guerrilla assaults that reached the gates of the U.S. embassy in Saigon. After that, American public opinion shifted steadily against the war as a waste of life and resources. Nixon attempted to get out of Vietnam with honor by dropping more bombs while at the same time withdrawing troops and opening negotiations with the North Vietnamese. The adversaries finally concluded a ceasefire agreement in 1973. But two years later, the South Vietnamese army collapsed, as northern forces overran the country, finally reuniting it. More than fifty-eight thousand Americans and about four million Vietnamese died in the war.

A refugee runs with her possessions during the Tet Offensive. Vietcong and North Vietnamese fighters launched urban assaults in January 1968, destabilizing Saigon and several other cities. Although the U.S. and South Vietnamese armies regained control of Saigon by March, the battle signaled a turning point in American opinion of the war. How might photos like this one have affected American attitudes?

High Expectations and Social Protest

Peoples who were subjects of neither foreign colonial masters nor rapacious dictators but nonetheless suffered discrimination, powerlessness, or poverty found new voice in the 1960s. Young people, many of them college students, added to the wave of social discontent with protests against the war in Vietnam, stifling conformism in education, and the failure of parents and other authority figures to understand the anxieties and aspirations of a generation that grew up enveloped in material plenty. If a single thread ran through the social protest movements of this period, it was the conviction that societies that congratulated themselves for being prosperous and democratic failed too often to guarantee the social equality and individual freedom that a world without fascist empires was supposed to offer. The movements that sprang up in the 1960s generally adopted the symbols and rhetoric of the political left, though the ideological spectrum ran from moderate democratic socialism to the radical revolutionism inspired by Mao Zedong.

Discrimination and racism in the post-Nazi decades. To the global majority, systems of social inequality founded on a hierarchy of superior and inferior races looked especially antiquated and hateful in the post-Nazi era. In a few places, however, such systems held on after the war. In the United States, Martin Luther King, Jr., and others led the nonviolent, Gandhi-inspired civil rights movement to end legalized racism in the southern states. The movement set in motion a series of legislative and court actions culminating in the Civil Rights Act of 1964, which guaranteed all adult Americans the right to vote. These new laws were partial victories, and in the later 1960s, social dissenters focused on economic discrimination against blacks and other minorities, especially in the inner cities of the North and West.

The most notorious case of institutionalized racism was South Africa, where the dominant population of European descent represented, not the majority as in the American South, but a minority of about 20 percent of a total 1950 population of 12.4 million. Africans, the group subject to the most drastic repression and discrimination, numbered about 68 percent. Minorities of ªColoreds° (people of mixed race) and Asians had only slightly better legal status. Like the European minority in Algeria, South African whites, who spoke Afrikaans or English, regarded themselves as home-grown citizens of their country, not as foreign colonial rulers. The great majority of them believed white domination to be rooted in the natural order of things.

Nevertheless, South Africa was changing fast after World War II. The mineral and farm export economy boomed, and Africans poured into the cities and mining areas, seeking wage work and relief from life on parched and unfertile rural land. As their numbers grew, these urban dwellers became increasingly impatient with pervasive racism. In 1948, however, the ultraconservative National Party won a majority in the parliamentary government, an election in which blacks could not vote. The new government responded to

rapid social transformations by fortifying the existing system with new laws known collectively as **apartheid,** or ªseparation.° These measures aimed to deny Africans any rights to live permanently in cities. Rather, the state required them to have legal residence in designated rural ªhomelands,° or Bantustans, where they constituted giant pools of labor to be moved temporarily in and out of cities or mines as needed. Apartheid laws also included strict social segregation, bans on interracial marriage, and requirements that African men and women carry ªpass books° authorizing them to travel from one place to another. In the 1950s the government spent twelve times more per capita on the education of white children than on Africans, a large percentage of whom did not attend school at all.

> **apartheid** The political and legal system in force in South Africa from 1948 to 1994 designed to ensure the domination of the white minority over the majority population.

In a resource-rich country whose continuing industrialization required increasing economic flexibility and integration, apartheid was utterly irrational. It was founded ultimately on well-justified white fears that Africans despised the racist order. From the late 1940s onward, in fact, South Africa descended into festering civil conflict punctuated by strikes, boycotts, and marches. State authorities responded harshly, for example, shooting sixty-nine Africans at an anti±pass law rally at Sharpeville in 1960. After that incident, the African National Congress (ANC) and the more radical Pan-African Congress, the two major African nationalist parties, organized armed units that carried out acts of sabotage. The white government banned the ANC and in 1964 sent Nelson Mandela (1918-) and other nationalist leaders to serve life sentences on desolate Robben Island in the South Atlantic. At his trial on charges of sabotage, Mandela explained why he had taken recourse to violence: ªWe were placed in a position in which we had either to accept a permanent state of inferiority, or to defy the government. We chose to defy the law. . . . When . . . the government resorted to a show of force to crush opposition to its policies, only then did we decide to answer violence with violence.° [13]

The imprisonment of ANC leaders seriously hurt the resistance movement, but in the meantime more Africans managed to gain literacy and even attend universities, though within the framework of segregated ªBantu education.° This group became increasingly politicized and internationally connected. In 1976, radicalized students spearheaded a new and ultimately successful mass movement for freedom (see Chapter 28).

In other parts of the world, efforts to fight oppression had mixed results. In Northern Ireland, which remained part of the United Kingdom after the Republic of Ireland achieved independence in 1922, Roman Catholics organized mass demonstrations in 1968 to protest economic inequality and the political domination of the Protestant majority. This initially peaceful action degenerated into fighting between

Protesters flee from police gunfire in Sharpeville, South Africa. Police used live ammunition to disperse participants in a peaceful demonstration organized by the Pan-Africanist Congress to protest race-based pass laws. Many of the sixty-nine dead were shot in the back. How might this event have radicalized both black South Africans and international opposition to the white minority government?

Catholic and Protestant paramilitary bands, which provoked British military intervention. Peace was not achieved until 1998. In Latin America, left-leaning Roman Catholic clergy came to the defense of poor Indian and *mestizo* majorities, proclaiming a new ªliberation theology° dedicated to alleviating poverty, hunger, disease, and class discrimination. Most activists in this movement assisted poor neighborhoods and villages, but religious and political conservatives branded them as disguised Marxists. The movement faded in the 1970s when Pope John Paul II, a fierce anticommunist, turned against it.

Radicalism in the 1960s. Between 1964 and 1970, young activists representing the most advantaged populations in the world took to the streets, mobilizing an assortment of radical movements for equality and justice. Underlying this radical turn was the coming of age of the baby-boom generation, the relatively large demographic group born in Europe and North America in the decade after World War II. Responding to the postwar economic upswing, baby boomers flooded into colleges and universities. The rising incomes of working parents, the declining demand for youthful farm labor, and the opening of many new public universities propelled this development. The United States led the way in mass higher education, but Western European student enrollments also rose, depending on the country, anywhere from 300 to 900 percent between 1960 and 1980.

Middle-class students of the postwar decades tended to have high expectations of both satisfying careers and the world's material and moral progress. By the 1960s, however, disappointment and skepticism began to set in. Political and cultural leaders appeared to endorse spirit-sapping consumerism rather than creativity, ªestablishment politics° rather than participatory democracy, capitalist profits rather than social justice, and threats of nuclear annihilation rather than global peace. Universities as semi-enclosed intellectual and social communities proved to be warm incubators for radicalism, the more so when educational authorities tried to contain free expression. Student activists trended to the political left ideologically, specifically to the New Left, a movement for social justice that was as wary of doctrinaire, state-controlled communism as it was of capitalist materialism.

Radical organizations and spontaneous protests sprouted across the industrialized world and among urban middle-class youth nearly everywhere. Television broadcasts of demonstrations, marches, and confrontations between protesters and police reinforced the impression of a worldwide community of young people who shared a common fight for justice, a global cohort that, according to a slogan of the times, ªdid not trust anyone over thirty.° In the United States, the civil rights movement fueled broader-based radicalism that targeted the Vietnam War, the draft, and corporations that built weapons. Students in Europe, Japan, Mexico, and many other places took up similar causes but also protested the failure of governments to expand university access nearly fast enough to meet demand.

Student and, in some countries, worker protests reached a crescendo in the spring and summer of 1968. In the United States, public opinion turned against the Vietnam quagmire,

A May Day rally in Paris, 1968.
Thousands of workers and students marched across the city. Their banners demand peace in Vietnam, higher wages, and an end to the state of emergency the French government imposed in an attempt to quell protests.

Protesters arrested in Mexico City. Demonstrations turned violent on October 3, 1968, as university students clashed with police. The event, known as the "Massacre of Tlatelolco" after the urban plaza where it occurred, killed as many as three hundred people, though Mexican media reported only 27 dead at the time. How would you characterize the range of government responses to popular protests in the 1960s in different countries?

Alexander Dubček: Leader of the Prague Spring

Alexander Dubček addresses factory workers in Prague, August 1968.

Shortly after Alexander Dubček (DOOB-chehk, 1921–1992) assumed the office of secretary of the Czechoslovakian Communist Party in January 1968, he promised reforms to establish "socialism with a human face." In the following months, he announced new social and economic freedoms. But on August 21 he watched in alarm as Soviet army forces invaded his country, abruptly ending what became known as the Prague Spring.

Dubček was born in Czechoslovakia's eastern Slovak ethnic region in 1921, but he spent his early years with his family in the Soviet Union. There he enjoyed a quiet childhood and, despite Joseph Stalin's repressive rule, acquired a strong faith in Soviet communist leadership. He returned to Czechoslovakia in the late 1930s and during World War II took part in anti-German resistance. After the war he became a leader in the Slovak wing of the Czechoslovakian Communist Party and in the 1950s was selected to study at a political institute in Moscow. His time there coincided with Nikita Khrushchev's de-Stalinization campaign, a strategy that in Dubček's view showed the party could relax controls on economic and political life without jeopardizing its authority. He returned to Czechoslovakia in the late 1950s determined to work for similar reforms at home.

A retiring individual without notable speaking skill, Dubček nonetheless rose in 1963 to leadership of the Slovak Communist Party. During the next several years, Slovakians enjoyed more freedom of expression than their ethnic Czech counterparts, who lived under the hardline leadership of Antonín Novotný. Resisting all economic or social reforms and charged with corruption, Novotný yielded his party leadership to Dubček in January 1968. The new secretary moved quickly to loosen authoritarian controls on Czech citizens, authorizing new workers' councils and relaxing laws governing public speech and foreign travel. He pursued a program to implement "democratic socialism" within ten years, but he also insisted on firm party control and solid allegiance to the Soviet Union. Consequently, Dubček had to perform an intricate balancing act between popular pressure for liberalizing reforms and Russian wariness that Czechoslovakia could gradually slip out of the Soviet bloc. Dubček also faced rising criticism from other Eastern European communist leaders, who feared their own citizens' attraction to Czech-style reforms.

Dubček held talks with the Soviets in the summer of 1968 but refused to call off a planned conference to reform the party structure or agree to garrison Soviet troops on Czechoslovakian territory. This was too much for Leonid Brezhnev, general secretary of the Soviet Communist Party. On the night of August 20, Russian tanks, supported by small units from other Soviet bloc states, rolled across the Czech frontier and occupied Prague without encountering armed resistance. In the following months, Dubček tried to salvage some reforms, and Czechs launched a campaign of passive resistance. But in April 1969, he was stripped of party membership and the following year was sent to an obscure job in the forestry service, where he remained for nineteen years.

By suppressing the Prague Spring, the Soviet Union baldly reasserted its hegemony over Eastern Europe. But it severely damaged Soviet claims to leadership of the global communist movement. Romanian, Yugoslavian, and Chinese communist leaders all deplored the invasion. So did the communist parties of Western Europe and the leaders of student protest movements worldwide. As for Dubček, he returned to public life during Czechoslovakia's 1989 Velvet Revolution, when communist rule ended. He was elected chairman of the Czecho-Slovak parliament, a position he held until his death in 1992.

Thinking Critically

How do you think Dubček reconciled his commitment to the exclusive authority of the Communist Party in Czechoslovakia with his conviction that the country needed political and economic reforms?

and countrywide campus demonstrations helped persuade President Johnson to renounce a bid for reelection that year. In Paris students barricaded streets and took over parts of the city, while workers staged wildcat strikes. In the aftermath of these disturbances, President Charles De Gaulle retired to his country home, where he died a few months later. In Czechoslovakia, student demonstrations played a part in the ªPrague Spring,º a brief period of political liberalization that ended when Soviet and Eastern European armies sent in tanks to restore full subservience to Moscow. Student activism, along with the accompanying counterculture of rock music, flamboyant dress, long hair, drug taking, communal living, and declarations of sexual freedom, continued at a high pitch until 1970, when it lost steam quite rapidly, owing less to repression than to general exhaustion and bitter splits and conflict among various protesting groups.

Feminist movements. In the aftermath of World War II, people yearned for social stability. For the great majority of male leaders, return to normalcy meant restoring conventional family life: Women should step down from the wage jobs they had during the war and partner with breadwinning husbands to bring up young citizens and make wise consumer choices. As Cold War tensions worsened, Western leaders also contended that families in the care of modest and morally upright women offered the country's best defense against communist agents of class warfare. In the socialist countries, postwar normalcy generally meant that women should continue to work at factory and farm jobs as they had before the war, while performing the same domestic duties they always had. In most newly emerging states, male elites insisted that women who had served nationalist movements as political organizers or guerrilla fighters help build the nation on a bedrock of strong families. In Algeria, for example, the image of women as revolutionary fighters, bomb makers, and spies gave way after independence to the ideal of the Muslim woman at home teaching children proper nationalist and Islamic values.

In the industrialized countries, however, the ideal of stay-at-home wife and mother flew in the face of facts. Throughout the 1950s and 1960s the number of females, including married women, in the paid workforce grew steadily. So also did the number of women seeking higher education. Women sought greater sexual freedom as courts and legislatures became more tolerant of birth control and family planning, notably in Europe and Japan, where wartime fears of population decline receded. Women also gained full voting rights shortly after the war in France, several Latin American countries, and most new postcolonial states.

Social and economic progress, however, did not keep pace with legal changes. In the environment of universities and competitive workplaces, women increasingly challenged the hypothesis, relentlessly urged by consumer business, that women who were not content with family care, home beautification, and personal appearance somehow suffered from psychic or emotional deficiencies. In the United States and Europe, feminist writers, including Betty Friedan, Simone de Beauvoir, and Gloria Steinem, persuaded more women that they had permission to seek opportunity and satisfaction beyond house and neighborhood. ªWe can no longer ignore,º Friedan wrote in *The Feminine Mystique* in 1963, ªthat voice within women that says: `I want something more than my husband and my children and my home.'º [14]

In the 1960s, women began to organize on a number of fronts to advocate fairness at work, reproductive choice, and attention to prostitution as a social affliction. These associations, for example, the National Organization for Women (NOW) founded in the United States in 1966, proliferated first in Western countries. They appeared shortly thereafter in Asian and African cities. This feminist wave was just gathering force in 1975, when the United Nations proclaimed ªInternational Women's Yearº and sponsored the first major international conference on women's rights in Mexico City.

• • • •

Conclusion

The third quarter of the twentieth century is still so recent that any estimation of its most important developments for the world's history must remain tentative. Consider just three factors—population, economy, and environment. The global population growth rate reached its all-time peak during those twenty-five years. It might conceivably soar again in the future, but many demographers believe that it is likely to fall in the coming century owing to the continuing decline of both mortality and birthrates.

The global economic growth rate also reached its highest historic level during that quarter-century, a feat that increased living standards in much of the world but did not prevent a widening breach between the richest and poorest populations. Since the early 1970s, global economic growth has been more volatile (see Chapter 28).

Regarding the environment, humans consumed nonrenewable energy and manipulated the biosphere on an unprecedented scale between 1950 and 1975. Human action greatly sped up ecological degradation in several different physical and natural systems. After 1975, however, humans for the first time became acutely aware of the potential damage they were causing. Consequently, some political, business, and civic leaders took action to slow environmental deterioration, though at a far more leisurely pace than seems justified from our present vantage point.

• • •

Key Terms

apartheid 811
Asian tigers 795
baby boom 791
Bretton Woods system 792
consumerism 796
Cuban missile crisis 803
feminist movement 815
Great Leap Forward 794

Great Proletarian Cultural Revolution 794
Green Revolution 800
import substitution industrialization (ISI) 795
iron curtain 801
Korean War 801
megalopolis 796

mutually assured destruction (MAD) 802
Prague Spring 815
Six Day War 809
Suez Crisis 809
Vietnam War 812
welfare state 792

Please see end of book reference section for additional reading suggestions related to this chapter.

Change over Time

1948	The South African government institutes apartheid.
1950–1953	The Korean War pits the Soviet-backed north against U.S.-backed south.
1952	The United States tests the first hydrogen bomb. London's Great Smog raises awareness of air pollution.
1952–1955	Kenyan guerrillas fight British colonial forces in the Mau Mau rebellion.
1953	With help from U.S. and British operatives, military officers in Iran overthrow the Mosaddiq government and reinstate the king, Reza Shah.
1954	France withdraws in defeat from Vietnam.
1954–1962	Algerian insurgents battle French authorities in the Algerian Revolution.
1955	Soviet-allied states form the Warsaw Pact.
1955–1975	Vietnam becomes the theater of a civil war and Cold War conflict.
1957	Ghana achieves independence from Britain under Kwame Nkrumah. The Soviet Union launches Sputnik, the first artificial satellite to orbit the globe. The European Economic Community is founded.
1958–1961	Mao Zedong initiates the "Great Leap Forward" to speed China's industrialization.
1960	Fourteen former French colonies in Africa win independence.
1961	A number of capitalist states form the Organization for Economic Cooperation and Development (OECD). The German Democratic Republic attempts to stop emigration with the Berlin Wall.
1962	Rachel Carson's *Silent Spring* raises awareness of the environmental toll of pesticides. The United States and Soviet Union face off in the Cuban missile crisis.
1963	The United States and the Soviet Union sign the Limited Test Ban Treaty.
1965	Britain, France, and Israel's plan to take back the Suez Canal from Egypt leads to the Suez Crisis.
1967	Israel defeats its Arab neighbors in the Six Day War.
1967–1970	Competition for control of oil leads to civil war in Nigeria.
1968	Worldwide student demonstrations coalesce around social justice issues. Soviet and Eastern European armies put an end to the Prague Spring in Czechoslovakia.
1970	The Aswan High Dam in Egypt begins operation.
1975	Portuguese African colonies gain independence. The United Nations proclaims International Women's Year.

28 Countercurrents of Change

1970 to the Present

A representation of global Internet traffic, in which each line is a data path.

Tim Berners-Lee thought about calling the software he created for sharing scientific documents between different computers the "Mine of Information" or the "Information Mesh." He finally decided on the "World Wide Web." Electronic communication had preoccupied him since childhood. Growing up in England, he built make-believe computers out of cardboard boxes, and while he was studying physics at Oxford University, he constructed a real computer using an old TV set and a soldering iron. In 1989 he went to work as a consultant at CERN, the renowned nuclear physics research center in Geneva, Switzerland.

There, he discovered that collaborating scientists had no efficient way to locate and study particular documents or data sets on one another's computers. "I found it frustrating," he later wrote, "that in those days, there was different information on different computers, but you had to log on to different computers to get at it. . . . Often it was just easier to go and ask people when they were having coffee."[1] The Internet was already available to researchers as a system for connecting computers, but scientists lacked convenient ways to share information while they sat at their individual machines.

In 1990 Berners-Lee set out to develop a relatively uncomplicated coding system for hypertext, that is, text on a computer that has embedded in it links to other text residing on the same or other computers.

His design had three fundamental elements. One was code for creating hypertext that could be used on different types of computers. He named that system HyperText Markup Language, or HTML. The second was a standard code for identifying and viewing a body of content, or "page" displayed on a computer screen. He called a page's "address" its Uniform Resource Locator (URL). Third, he worked out code for moving around the Internet from one URL to another. This was the HyperText Transfer Protocol (HTTP).

When Berners-Lee's colleagues saw that this World Wide Web (www) worked well, some of them argued that people should pay CERN a fee to use it. Berners-Lee adamantly opposed this option, insisting that the system be free because science would likely benefit in direct proportion to the number of professional users. The web was to have no central database or manager but rather to exist as an imaginary place in cyberspace where anyone who accepted the coding rules could read other people's web sites or put their own site "online."

Berners-Lee created the first World Wide Web site (http://info.cern.ch) in 1991, and thereafter web pages multiplied rapidly. The application passed quickly beyond the confines of science to the wider public. In 1992 he uploaded the first photo, a color image of Les Horribles Cernettes, a women's rock band that CERN employees started. The topic of that site suggested the web's immense possibilities beyond the networks of scientific exchange. And so it has come to pass. By mid-2012 the world had more than 4.2 billion Internet users and about 190 million active web sites.

Electronic innovations and their applications to science, energy production, manufacturing, human health, social organizations, and many other things continue to multiply at hyperspeed. In this book we have taken the view that human history is a story of growing complexity, both in the nature of interconnections among individuals and groups and in relations between people and their natural and physical environments. The pace at which humans have created and become enmeshed in new forms of complexity began accelerating faster with the fossil-fuel revolution of the eighteenth century. The rapidity of global change in the past few decades sometimes astounds and bewilders us. The term *globalization* has entered the language to encapsulate the idea that, first, human society is continuously restructuring itself in all sorts of ways and, second, human interconnections are becoming continuously more elaborate and intense.

Among animal species, humans possess a uniquely powerful aptitude for creating complexity because of what world historian David Christian has called "collective learning," the capacity to accumulate, share, organize, preserve, and transmit larger and larger amounts of information—so far without any limit in sight. In the past forty years the process of collective learning has sped up primarily owing to

Chapter Outline

• • •

the invention of complex electronic systems. These systems underlie or influence almost all other forms of change in the past few decades. The first part of this chapter therefore explores the revolution in electronic technology and its transforming effect on the ways people broadcast, analyze, and store information on a planet whose population has nearly doubled in the past forty years.

More than any other material factor, electronic innovation has powered the accelerating trends in the world toward integration and connectedness, and these trends have benefited humankind in countless ways. At the same time, however, innovation has not prevented, indeed it has contributed to, severe inequities in the way people live, as well as social anxieties, international rivalries, political violence, criminal behavior, and environmental degradation. To flourish as a species, humankind has created—appears to need

A Panoramic View

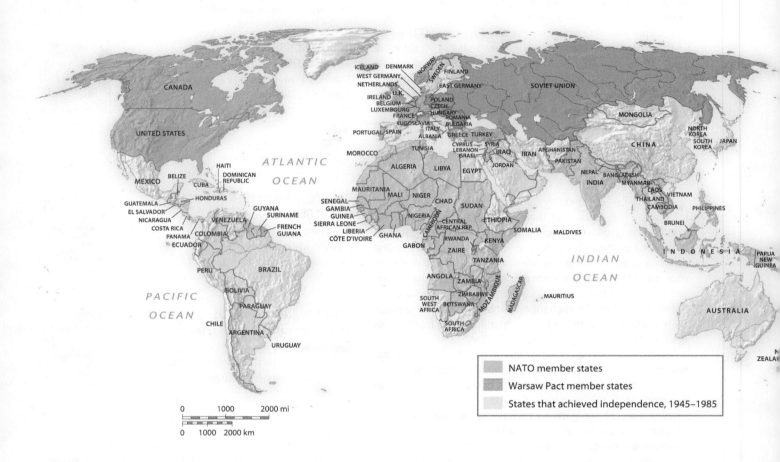

MAP 28.1 The geopolitical world, 1985.
The Cold War was often characterized as an east–west conflict. How does a global perspective encourage you to also think about north–south differences?

to create—increasingly complex systems, networks, and institutions. But as these structures become denser and more tangled, the more prone they become to instability, malfunction, or breakdown. (Indeed, scientists argue that the coherence and stability of all physical and natural systems, not just human ones, require constant inputs of energy to keep them from falling apart.) In the remaining parts of this chapter we explore human experience in the past forty years in the economic, political, and environmental realms, examining both trends of global integration and the countercurrents that have produced fragmentation, conflict, and dysfunction.

An Electrified World

FOCUS How has electronic technology transformed human communication systems and scientific and medical knowledge in the past four decades?

Electricity became a servant of human communication in the nineteenth century, when inventors discovered how to convert electrical impulses transmitted through copper wires into coded language that individuals at each end of the wire could understand. The first useful application was the telegraph. Since its advent in the 1830s, humans have put electrical charges to work energizing thousands of kinds of machines, especially those that transmit and store information.

The Era of the Integrated Circuit

In the 1950s engineers began replacing the vacuum tubes that had previously controlled electrical current in computers and other electronic appliances with much smaller solid state transistors that had semiconducting propertiesÐ the potential to conduct electricity under certain conditions. A transistor is fundamentally an electronic device that controls the flow of an electrical current and is used principally as an amplifier or a switch. Transistor technology formed a happy marriage with the binary number system, which involves only *ones* (switch on) and *zeros* (switch off) sequenced precisely to carry programmed instructions. In the 1960s scientists discovered ways to link transistors together in integrated circuits, channeling electrical energy to perform complex operations. Invention of the microchip, a wafer of silicon inscribed with numerous transistors and other electronic components, set off a contest among engineers to reduce the size of integrated circuits. The more components a chip could carry, the more data it could process. The Intel company produced a chip in 1971 that held 2,300 transistors. Today, engineers using a sophisticated technology called photolithography can place more than two billion transistors on a single chip. Integrated circuitry has become essential to nearly every type of technological advance of the past half-century that uses electricity.

The shrinking computer. During World War II, British and American scientists devised an electronic calculator to break German war codes. In the following two decades, computer research expanded in scope to take on problems of electronically processing, storing, and transmitting large quantities of data for many purposes. At first, mostly scientists, governments, and big companies used computers. The United States and the Soviet Union deployed them to fight the Cold War. The U.S. government, for example, contracted with International Business Machines (IBM) to develop early warning defenses against a Soviet air attack. Early computers were huge. The SAGE system for detecting Soviet bombers

involved forty-eight computers in different locations, each one taking up about an acre of space. In the 1970s microchip circuitry solved the problem of making much smaller and more powerful computers that could perform many new tasks. The Apollo space program, including six manned moon landings between 1969 and 1972, depended on small computers. All these missions together, however, used about as much computational power as it takes today to carry out a single Internet search on a search engine like Google.

In the later 1970s young electronics experts around San Jose, CaliforniaÐ the Silicon ValleyÐ launched the personal computer industry. Knowing that millions of Americans already had televisions and typewriters, these inventors built user-friendly machines that incorporated screens and keyboards instead of complex programming cards and tapes. In 1976 Steven Jobs and Stephen Wozniak introduced the Apple II, a personal machine housed in a plastic case. In 1980 IBM entered the personal computer market, adopting the MS-DOS operating system (the software to perform the computer's fundamental tasks) created by Bill Gates and Paul Allen, founders of the Microsoft Corporation. In 1985 MS-DOS gave way to Windows. Laptops became available in the mid-1980s, and personal computer sales soared. About one billion of them came into use worldwide between 1980 and 2008.[2]

In the early 1970s the U.S. Department of Defense initiated a project to link computers at different locations to facilitate collaborative research. The result was the **Internet,** a ªnetwork of networksº that allowed scientists and military personnel to communicate with one another's

> **Internet** A global computer network connecting smaller networks, all of which use the same set of communication formats and rules.

machines. As this technology advanced, public pressure grew to make it available to all. Among the scientists who helped build the system, Radia Perlman began work in the 1980s to improve the way messages were routed from one computer to another, winning her the title ªMother of the Internet.º As we saw in the chapter introduction, Tim Berners-Lee invented the World Wide Web, which greatly simplified data sharing. In 1993, engineers at the University of Illinois introduced Mosaic, a program that nonspecialists could easily use to ªbrowseº for information on the Internet. Mosaic provided the primary model for later generations of browsers, including Netscape Navigator, Internet Explorer, Firefox, and Google Chrome. By 1996 forty million people were using the Internet to access the web and connect their own sites to it.

Streams of data. In the 1970s technical barriers to moving information nearly instantaneously from one part of the world to another fell in rapid order. Satellite technology, first demonstrated in 1957 when the Soviet Union launched Sputnik (see Chapter 27), advanced quickly. Between that year and 1989, the Soviet Union, the United States, and a few other countries launched 3,196 satellites. Engineers invented increasingly ingenious ways for satellite transmitters connected to earthbound computers to process telephone calls and television signals and to monitor weather, map the earth's surface, and detect the locations of weapons and troop movements. In 1993 twenty-four satellites linked together activated the first Global Positioning System (GPS). Within several years, personal navigation devices became available to millions of consumers at relatively low cost.

In the 1980s engineers began laying networks of fiber optic cable. Constructed of thin strands of refined glass bundled together, these lines could transmit pulses of light that were converted into electrical signals carrying messages and images at near light speed. As of 2013 a single cable could transmit thirty million phone calls across the Atlantic Ocean in one second. In the 1970s scientists first devised machines that connected telephones through localized radio ªcellsº rather than wires. The city of Tokyo built the first cellular phone network in 1979. Since then, many rural and relatively poor regions in the world have skipped directly from no telephone service at all to cellular technology. Powerful

handheld computers dubbed ªsmartphonesº appeared on the market early in the new century. Their Internet connections and applications (apps) can perform thousands of functions. Some owners even use them to make telephone calls! As communication technology has become more sophisticated, its cost has also fallen rapidly. Consequently, the webs of world communication have become much more efficient and incalculably dense. In 1945 a three-minute phone call from Britain to the United States cost about $75. Today, a software application like Skype allows voice and video communication between computer users anywhere in the world at no direct charge.

The Electronics of Transport

Although humans can transmit information at lightning speed, they cannot move themselves from place to place much faster than they could in 1960. (Rocket travel in space is much speedier, but so far fewer than six hundred men and women have experienced it.) Electronic systems, however, have greatly advanced both the reliability and efficiency of

Satellites orbiting the earth perform many tasks. Among numerous other functions, satellite communication helps auto commuters avoid traffic congestion and shows scientists trends in urban air pollution. How have you recently benefited from satellite technology to communicate with someone or retrieve information?

A digital representation of the human genome. A museum displays a complete map of our genetic code. A team of scientists from six countries collaborated on the project. They announced this significant breakthrough fifty years after Watson and Crick first documented the double helix structure of DNA molecules.

transportation. In the late 1960s engineers invented metal containers of standard size to move cargo between ships, rail cars, and truck trailers without unpacking and repacking. Container shipping has reduced costs significantly, but the system works only because computers keep accurate track of the locations of millions of boxes. When the 1967 Arab±Israeli War closed the Suez Canal for eight years, supertankers were built to ship crude oil from the Middle East. These enormous vessels, which typically carry two million barrels of oil, depend on such sophisticated electronic navigation, meteorological, and monitoring systems that they sail with crews of as few as twenty people.

Computers have become fundamental to the design and operation of trains, automobiles, and airplanes. Auto companies began installing onboard computers in cars in the early 1980s, mainly because high oil prices and rising pollution demanded greater attention to fuel efficiency. By the 1990s computers controlled ignition, timing, fuel injection, and exhaust emissions. Auto mechanics also learned to analyze computer data to improve performance and diagnose malfunctions. The fuel-efficient hybrid vehicles that appeared on the roads after 2000 depended on computers to smoothly transfer the propulsion source back and forth between the electric motor and the gasoline engine. More recently, automotive engineers have experimented with vehicles that virtually drive themselves, transforming cars into wheeled robots. The airplane industry tells a similar story. In 2011 the Boeing company began delivering the 787 Dreamliner, an intricately computerized plane designed for high fuel efficiency. Partly owing to aeronautic advances, as well as electronic reservation and boarding systems, the number of daily air travelers worldwide quadrupled between 1975 and 2009 to about 7.7 million.

Computers and the Body

Electronic technology has largely driven advances in science and engineering in recent decades, remarkably so in medical research and practice. Magnetic resonance imaging and other visualizing devices can peer into the deep recesses of the human body, discovering cancers in their early stages. Scientists can better understand the structure of molecules linked to diseases by modeling them on computers in three dimensions. In the 1980s researchers began to theorize the potential of nanotechnology, including ways to manipulate individual atoms or molecules to build miniscule ªchipsº of extraordinary precision. This field will have practical medical applications in the near future. Computers have already revolutionized health care systems in industrialized countries. People can get instant access to their medical records, hospital personnel can more accurately diagnose and monitor patients, and health professionals having different kinds of expertise can share information no matter where they are in the world.

Ever since the scientists James Watson and Francis Crick produced a model of the structure of deoxyribonucleic acid (DNA) at Cambridge University in 1953, advances in the study of the genes resident in human cells have come one after another. In the 1970s molecular biologists in the United States invented techniques for splicing strands of DNA, typically from different organisms, then recombining them to produce DNA that can alleviate genetically related diseases. In 1990 the U.S. government formally launched the Human Genome Project, an international endeavor to sequence the human body's approximately 100,000 genes, as well as the three billion or so base pairs, that is, strands of DNA that are bonded together in the shape of a double helix. The Human Genome Project was completed in 2003, a task that would have been impossible without immense computational power. Since then, the genome ᵃmap° has provided researchers with remarkable tools for understanding genetic factors in disease. The new field of pharmacogenomics, for example, aims to demonstrate how an individual's precise genetic constitution may affect the body's reaction to particular drugs, leading the way to drug designs customized for particular individuals.

Unintended Consequences of Electronic Innovation

The electronic revolution has generated not only amazement but also a host of worries. Like all systems in the universe, electronic ones tend to become more fragile and unpredictable as they advance in complexity. By the 1990s it became apparent that electronic networks held the world together in vital ways but that society also had to expend great mental and physical energy to keep networks functioning and to meet global demand for even more complex systems. Fears that computer glitches could set off false attack alarms haunted the Cold War. Near the end of the twentieth century, software engineers theorized that global communication systems might collapse because computer clocks had not been designed to switch from ᵃ19° to ᵃ20° years. In the few years leading up to New Year 2000, businesses and governments spent billions of dollars correcting code to solve the ᵃY2K° problem. A media barrage predicting that a general computer collapse might take place anyway caused a serious global cyber panic. The crisis was short-lived, however, because no major electronic meltdown took place.

The Internet developed in the 1990s into an enormous public space with no rules to determine who may enter it and for what purpose. Personal computers connected to the Internet became windows on the world but also receptacles for floods of unwanted messages from advertisers, interest groups, and pornographers, as well as targets for electronic vandals, fraudsters, identity thieves, and clandestine corporate intelligence gatherers. The term ᵃcomputer virus° to describe programs that self-replicate, often for malevolent purposes, came into use after 1984. Electronic communications have vastly enlarged humankind's capacity for collective deception and propaganda. National armies have become thoroughly dependent on computer systems. Indeed, military personnel have distanced themselves more successfully than ever from war's death and destruction with the help of surveillance satellites, smart bombs, and attack drones piloted from thousands of miles away. Cyber warfare has become a reality. For example, Stuxnet, a set

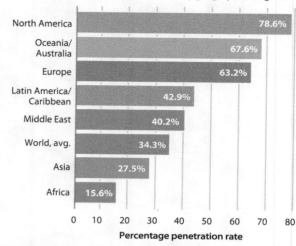

World internet penetration rates by geographical regions

Region	Percentage penetration rate
North America	78.6%
Oceania/Australia	67.6%
Europe	63.2%
Latin America/Caribbean	42.9%
Middle East	40.2%
World, avg.	34.3%
Asia	27.5%
Africa	15.6%

Percentage penetration rate

World Internet penetration rates, 2012. This bar graph shows the estimated number of Internet users as a percentage of the total population. What economic and social factors might account for the regional differences in Internet penetration indicated on this graph?

of variant computer codes designed to infect and disable Iran's uranium enrichment centrifuges, was deployed by the United States and Israel as early as 2007. Corporations, governments, and home computer users alike continue to spend billions of dollars every year defending electronic systems against data theft, malicious control, and sabotage.

Global access to electronic networks has, like standards of living, also suffered from severe regional imbalance. Some governments, including China, North Korea, and Iran, have deliberately blocked citizen access to particular Internet sites to try to limit political dissent and control public opinion. A larger problem is that many people around the world, especially poor people, still have little access to electronic resources other than radio and television. The number of Internet users in the world grew from a little more than 360 million in 2000 to 2.4 billion by 2012. That still left about 66 percent of humankind without it. In 2012 nearly 80 percent of North Americans had access but less than 16 percent of Africans did. The potential economic, cultural, and health benefits of personal computers and Internet access to poor farmers, for example, far outweigh the risks and aggravations of going online.

Countercurrents in the Global Economy

FOCUS Why have some regions of the world developed economically and raised standards of living more successfully than others in recent decades?

In the modern era, humans have commanded far more energy, material wealth, and knowledge than in any earlier time. Today, our species has access to about one hundred times more useful energy than it did before the fossil-fuel energy surge. The global trend of the past century has been a spectacular rise in gross domestic product (GDP) from about $2.7 trillion in 1913, the eve of World War I, to $75 trillion by 2013. To be sure, growth has followed a bumpy course. GDP plunged during the Great Depression of the 1930s, then rose again. During the long economic boom after World War II, GDP growth followed a nearly steady upward trajectory (see Chapter 27). Since the 1970s, however, the track has become more jagged. Business cyclesÐ short-term phases of growth and stagnationÐ have followed one another at intervals of usually less than a decade. A severe drop occurred between late 2007 and 2009, and global recovery proceeded slowly thereafter. Serious economic fluctuations in recent years have invariably had global impact, in large part because electronic systems have linked national economies tightly together, a phenomenon that has vastly sped up financial transactions but also enhanced the risks of instability and loss of managerial control. Nonetheless, many economists argue that the global economy will continue its long-term upward trend because human society has the technical capacity and creative ingenuity to generate increasing amounts of energy and wealth for at least another century.

The fundamental countercurrent to this narrative of growth has been the widening gap between rich and poor. Despite numerous technological miracles and many worthy plans to advance economic justice, the *distribution* of global wealth has become increasingly lopsided. In the past forty years, the world's population *as a whole* has by the measures of income and life expectancy become better off. But economic growth has benefited some people and some countries far more than others. Hundreds of millions of people continue to suffer unemployment, malnutrition, illiteracy, social oppression, and early death.

The 1970s: An Economic Turning Point

The financial system that the United States and its wartime allies set up at the Bretton Woods conference in New Hampshire in the waning months of World War II began to run into trouble by 1970 (see Chapter 27). The mechanisms that pegged the currencies of capitalist countries to the U.S. dollar at a fixed rate of $35 to an ounce of gold stabilized international monetary transactions. But as war-damaged economies recovered, currency exchange rates needed more flexibility. Recuperating states like Britain, France, the German Federal Republic, and Japan could better serve their own national economic goals by uncoupling their currencies from the dollar. For example, a country could decrease the value of its currency relative to the dollar and thereby make its exports cheaper on the world market. In the late 1960s, the real value of the dollar declined relative to other currencies despite the fixed gold price. Foreign banks and investors began selling dollars and buying gold, draining American gold reserves. In response, the United States took steps in 1971 to leave the gold standard; more countries soon followed. This development gave states greater economic

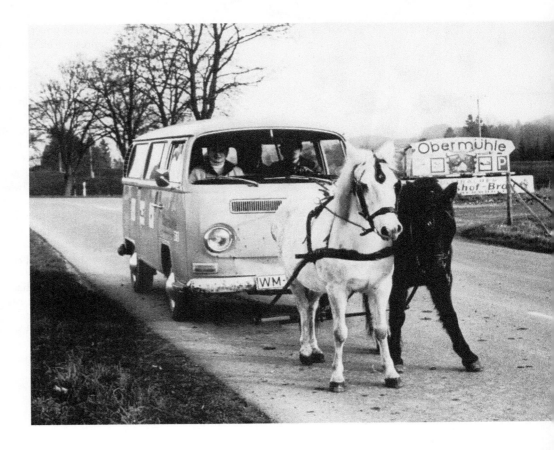

Consumers adapt to the 1973 oil shock. This horse-drawn Volkswagen was a creative German response to a nationwide vehicle ban on Sundays. Rationing at gas pumps encouraged more people in the United States and Western Europe to walk, ride bicycles, and take public transportation. To what extent did the crisis change consumers' fuel consumption behavior in the long term?

freedom. But it also ushered in an era when global finance became more complicated, exchange rates more unstable, and monetary coordination among countries more difficult.

The end of Bretton Woods freed states to print more money and pump it into their economies, but these poli-

> **inflation** An upward trend in the prices of goods and services.

cies aggravated **inflation,** and consumer purchasing power subsequently fell. A military crisis in late 1973 worsened the inflationary spiral and sparked a serious global recession. In October, Egypt and Syria launched an attack on Israel. They aimed to recover national territory that had been under Israeli occupation since 1967 and persuade the United States to force a settlement of the long-running Arab±Israeli conflict. The war lasted less than three weeks, though at a cost of nearly fourteen thousand lives on both sides. In support of Egypt and Syria, the Arab members of the Organization of Petroleum Exporting Countries (OPEC), an association to coordinate petroleum policies, declared an oil embargo against states that supported Israel, vowing to enforce it until Israeli forces withdrew from all occupied territories. As the embargo took hold, international demand for petroleum rose far beyond available supplies, prices for all sorts of goods rocketed up, world trade slumped, and the global

economy stagnated. In 1978±1979 a second ªoil shockº struck when a popular revolution in Iran replaced the autocratic king Muhammad Reza Shah with a government dominated by Shi'a Muslim clerics. The accompanying social upheaval disrupted Iranian oil production, and world oil prices soared again, triggering another worldwide economic slide.

After the first oil crisis, most major capitalist economiesÐ the United States, Japan, and the Western European statesÐ contracted the economic disease called ªstagflation,º an alarming combination of inflation, sluggish business activity, and falling employment. Near the end of the decade, however, the United States introduced monetary policies that pushed short-term interest rates from near zero to 10 percent and higher. This ªtight moneyº strategy obliged companies to cut borrowing and hold down both prices and wages. Inflation eased, and several European states followed the American lead. The new policies set off another recession, but the major capitalist states recovered gradually without inciting another inflationary surge. Nevertheless, inflation continued to plague particular countries and regions, for example, Latin America throughout the 1980s.

Conflicting Capitalist Doctrines

The economic troubles resulting from oil shocks and rampant inflation ignited furious debates among economists and politicians over the benefits of the modern welfare state. After World War II, Western political leaders broadly agreed that capitalism could thrive even though governments spent heavily on social programs such as pension security and health care to protect citizens from jarring economic ups and downs. John Maynard Keynes, the most influential economist of the mid-twentieth century, argued that in times of recession governments should spend more to counteract the depressive effects of low private investment and high unemployment. Beginning in the late 1970s, however, economically conservative leaders, notably Prime Minister Margaret Thatcher in Britain (in office 1979±1990) and President Ronald Reagan in the United States (in office 1981±1989), contended that the welfare state had become bloated and that too much public spending dampened business confidence in long-term economic growth. The private sector, so the argument ran, would by itself generate healthy revenue and raise employment. These **neo-liberals,** as they came to be called, claimed the heritage of nineteenth-century economic liberalism, which urged limited government and the sanctity of private

> **neoliberalism** An economic and political ideology advocating reduced government intervention in economic matters, privatization of state-owned enterprises, free trade, open markets, and deregulation of business.

property (see Chapter 21). They championed policies to reduce taxes, trim regulations, lower tariffs, privatize certain services, and encourage individual self-sufficiency.

Since the 1980s capitalist economies around the world have tended to swing from Keynesian to neoliberal policies erratically and inconsistently. For example, neoliberal

Ronald Reagan and Margaret Thatcher speak to reporters, 1982.
The U.S. president and the British prime minister forged a formidable political alliance. Their terms in office overlapped for eight years. The two largely agreed on neoliberal domestic agendas and assertive foreign policies.

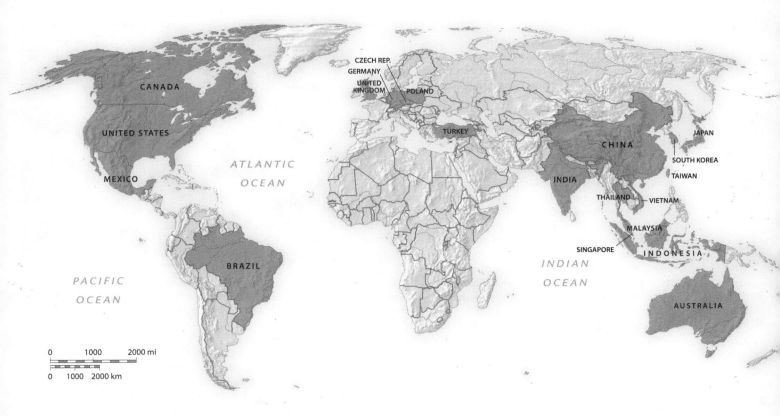

MAP 28.2 The twenty most competitive manufacturing countries, 2013.
Which countries would not have been on this map in 1975? What factors help explain the global shift in manufacturing?

leaders advised big public spending cuts, but most industrialized states nonetheless accrued unprecedented deficits in the 1980s. Under Reagan the U.S. deficit rose from $60 to $220 billion between 1980 and 1986, owing mostly to military spending. The Great Recession of 2007±2009 and the slow recovery that followed in most capitalist states called forth contradictory solutions. Neoliberals demanded draconian cuts in both government budgets and taxes to restore business confidence and spur investment. Keynesian economists advocated large infusions of borrowed public money into economies to stimulate employment, consumer demand, and therefore growth, leaving the issue of deficit reduction until good times returned.

Shifting Centers of Economic Power

After the Bretton Woods system was dismantled, international capital flow sped up as countries exported more goods. Neoliberal strategies gained more public support in many industrialized countries, and governments took steps to free up market activity by trimming regulations on banks, airlines, and multinational corporations. More developing states abandoned quests for economic self-sufficiency and waded into the global market, cutting import

tariffs, privatizing industries, and generally deregulating economic activity. Since the 1990s nearly every state in the world (the few exceptions include North Korea and Cuba) has sought integration into the capitalist world system. International financial markets, which deal in currency exchange, investment, and borrowing, grew spectacularly from about $160 billion in 1973 to $140 *trillion* by 2012.

In fact, loan transactions have climbed to unprecedented levels of volume and complexity. In the past few decades, corporations have borrowed immense sums to expand operations or acquire other companies, and governments have paid for armies and public services by borrowing many billions more than they collect in revenue. For example, the United States borrowed heavily after 2001 in connection with the Afghanistan and Iraq wars, rising social service costs, and the recession of 2007±2009. From 2007 to 2012, U.S. debt rose on average $3.93 billion a day.

This advance toward global financial complexity inevitably altered the lineup of major economic players. In the 1950s and 1960s the states of North America and Europe, plus Japan, produced about 90 percent of the world's manufactured goods and sold them mainly to each other (see Map 28.2). Most of Asia, Africa, and Latin America remained solidly agrarian, marketing food, fiber, minerals, and the labor of their own citizens as foreign workers. Since the 1970s, however, new manufacturing centers have emerged and international exchange has become much more elaborate.[3] Corporations have more routinely opened and closed manufacturing plants depending on the comparative costs of materials and wages in particular countries. Manufacture of product components has become globalized, so that, for example, the laptop a student buys in an American electronics store may be the product of research undertaken in Japan, investment secured in Germany, rare metals mined in Congo, and skilled assembly performed in Taiwan.

A Korean worker tests electronic components. This 1987 photograph shows a Samsung computer and television factory in Seoul. What social or cultural factors in Korea might have encouraged or permitted women to take factory jobs?

Asian tigers and tiger cubs. Beginning in the late 1960s, Taiwan, South Korea, Hong Kong, and Singapore, all of them places short on exportable raw commodities, followed Japan's lead in building export-oriented manufacturing industries (see Chapter 27). These four ªAsian tigersº invested generously in new electronic technology and education, and they benefited from women's economic productivity. By the 1980s women constituted more than 30 percent of the labor forces in these countries, though generally earning lower wages than men for comparable work. South Korea achieved the most impressive economic miracle, transforming itself from an impoverished, mostly rural state in 1960 to a builder of automobiles and the wealthy host of the 1988 Olympic Games. The tigers also sponsored new industries in other states where they could employ workers at lower wages than they could at home. In the 1990s those investments helped several ªtiger cubs,º notably Indonesia, Malaysia, the Philippines, and Thailand, jumpstart export industries. Vietnam made its first market reforms in 1986, barely a decade after the end of the Vietnam War and the country's unification under Communist Party rule. Owing primarily to looser trade controls, the value of Vietnam's exports rose from $14.3 billion in 2000 to $114.6 billion 2012.[4]

China in the global market. Economic transformations began to take place in China in 1978, when Deng Xiaoping (1904±1997), the leader of the Chinese Communist Party, vowed to revive and modernize the economy, after nearly three decades of central planning and wildly oscillating economic performance under Mao Zedong. He and his political allies initiated market reforms that allowed Chinese farmers, local businesses, and, after about a decade, large industries to buy and sell goods privately. In 1980 China opened fourteen coastal cities to foreign capital investment, which poured in. This influx triggered successive surges of economic growth and exploding urbanization. Both the government and private entrepreneurs began investing surplus earnings abroad, notably in Subsaharan Africa and Latin America. Before the mid-eighteenth century, China had the largest manufacturing output in the world. By 2010 it claimed that status again by slightly surpassing the United States. The Chinese Communist Party, however, eagerly joined the capitalist world economy while refusing to enact significant democratic and civil rights reforms. Mass demonstrations against party intransigence in April 1989 ended in the People's Liberation Army massacring about 1,300 citizens in Beijing's Tiananmen Square. The country has since remained an authoritarian state, though the ruling party's Marxist-Leninist ideology has lost all meaning.

India and its Silicon Valley. Ironically, India, a democratic state with a large private sector, tried to keep its economy sheltered from the gales of international commerce and finance longer than its giant communist neighbor did. For forty years after independence from Britain (1947), the social democratic approach of the Indian National CongressÐ self-sufficiency, strong central government controls, food subsidiesÐ guided the economy. However, faced with soaring national debt and anemic exports, the government gradually adopted more market-oriented policies starting in 1991. By the end of that decade, foreign investors were arriving in force, including people of South Asian origin who had earlier emigrated to the United States and founded successful companies there, including Sun Microsystems and Hotmail. Business innovators found a special market niche producing and exporting information technology. At first, they profited from **outsourcing** operations such as data processing or call-in support services. In the new century, however, Indian firms have expanded research and development into a variety of electronic fields. The city of Bangalore has been labeled India's Silicon Valley. Among the top manufacturing countries in the world in 2009, India

outsourcing The business practice of reducing costs by transferring work to outside contractors, including foreign companies.

An Artist's Comment on Capitalism in China

Under Mao Zedong, chairman of the Communist Party of China from 1949 to 1976, party leaders tightly controlled artistic expression. During the height of the Great Proletarian Cultural Revolution in 1966–1968, when Mao roused Chinese youth to cleanse the country of all signs of "capitalist revisionism," visual artists mass produced graphically striking posters that celebrated socialist solidarity and sacrifice. The image on the left is one example. Young revolutionaries, however, forbade all art that hinted of "bourgeois values."

After Mao's death in 1976, the new party leaders who gradually opened China to the world economy allowed artists and writers wider creative scope. In the 1980s Chinese visual artists began to attract international attention as they explored numerous new themes and media and founded new creative movements. One of these was Political Pop, a movement that drew on the aesthetic style of American Pop Art of the 1960s and 1970s to comment on the stark political and social contrasts between Mao's China and the era of capitalist enterprise and consumption that has followed. Wang Guangyi, a native of northeastern China who witnessed the most radical phase of the Cultural Revolution as a boy, emerged in the 1990s as a leading Political Pop artist. In a series of paintings he called the Great Criticism, he combined Cultural Revolution poster imagery with references to the Western consumer products that newly affluent Chinese were eager to buy.

In the Great Criticism *image on the right, Wang depicts two figures similar to those on the Cultural Revolution poster—forward-looking, radiant, and happy workers. In both images the red-covered book* Quotations from Chairman Mao Zedong *appears. Wang appropriates the dominant red color in the Cultural Revolution work, but he paints in a style reminiscent of the work of Artists like Andy Warhol. The numbers scattered across the painting represent serial numbers that workers stamp on manufactured products. Wang's image evokes both the old China and the new, but as in other paintings in this series, he leaves the viewer with questions about his intentions.*

Thinking Critically

In terms of subject matter and artistic style, what similarities and differences do you find in the two images? Why do you think Wang chose to reference Coca-Cola in this image? Do you think he is criticizing China's embrace of capitalism? Or might he be ridiculing the Cultural Revolution and its propaganda? Do you think Wang's image throws light on the China of the late 1990s? In what way?

A political poster from the Cultural Revolution. It says, "Strive to collect scrap metal and other waste materials!"

Wang Guangyi's *Great Criticism: Coca-Cola*, 1993.

New Year's celebrations on the remains of the Berlin Wall, 1990. Crowds began to breach the wall and demolish it with sledge hammers in November 1989. In the distance revelers stand atop the Brandenburg Gate, a nineteenth-century peace monument located in East Germany. Why do you think pieces of the wall remain potent symbols of protest even today?

came in twelfth, just four ranks below Britain, its former colonial master.[5]

The end of central planning in Russia and Eastern Europe.

Like China before 1978, the Soviet Union and its Eastern European allies pursued a socialist model of economic development and self-sufficiency. Government employeesÐ planners, managers, and techniciansÐ determined prices, wages, and the distribution of economic resources. Directed by this bureaucracy, the Soviet economy slowed in the 1970s and became increasingly dependent on trade with Western countries for food and finished goods. The Soviet GDP in 1980 was more than 80 percent smaller than that of the United States, though oil exports permitted Moscow to fund a gigantic army. In 1981 President Reagan ramped up U.S. military spending, eventually including a Strategic Defense Initiative, popularly called ªstar wars,º to build a complex missile defense system. The Soviet Union could not keep pace and indeed headed toward economic exhaustion. In 1985 Mikhail Gorbachev (in office 1985±1991), named general secretary of the Soviet Communist Party, launched a campaign of bold political reforms (*glasnost)* and economic liberalization (*perestroika).*

In the socialist states of Eastern Europe, popular demands for economic and political reform rapidly intensified after Gorbachev announced that the Soviet Union would no longer send in tanks to suppress public protests, as it had done in Czechoslovakia in 1968. In the German Democratic Republic (East Germany), government confusion and paralysis over citizen demands for uninhibited international travel led border guards to open gates in the wall that divided the eastern and western sectors of Berlin. In November 1989, jubilant crowds started pulling down the wall. In the following months, Germany was reunified and elections across Eastern Europe ended the communist party monopolies that had prevailed since the end of World War II.

The fifteen federated republics that made up the Soviet Union answered to Moscow, but in several of them, the nationalist sentiments of peoples speaking languages and cherishing ethnic traditions other than Russian lay just beneath the surface. Watching the dissolution of the communist regimes in Eastern Europe, those nationalists questioned the advantages of remaining part of the economically anemic Soviet Union. Early in 1991, Lithuania, a Soviet republic that had once been a sovereign Baltic state, declared its independence. In the ensuing months all fifteen republics formally separated from one another without great violence. Gorbachev had planned to introduce limited Western-style reforms, not to dismantle the Soviet Union. Nevertheless, it ceased to exist on December 25, 1991.

MAP 28.3 Geopolitical change in Eastern Europe and Inner Eurasia, 1985 and 2013.
What historical developments account for major changes on the political map of this region between 1985 and 2013?

Those tumultuous events led to a decade of disarray in both the former Soviet Union and Eastern Europe, as new political regimes attempted to reinvent their societies and economies. In the new Russia (the Russian Federation), upstart capitalist entrepreneurs, many of them former Soviet bureaucrats and industrial managers, bought up state-owned property at fire-sale prices and, often in league with Western business interests, got immensely rich. By contrast, the standard of living plunged for the great majority. In the new century, however, most Eastern European states built stable, mostly democratic governments, and several of them achieved impressive growth as Western investors flocked into Hungary, Poland, and Czechoslovakia to exploit new markets and cheap labor. Russia associated itself with capitalist Europe more tentatively, and since 2000 has not proceeded far in broadening its export economy beyond oil, natural gas, and other primary commodities. Under Vladimir Putin's presidency and prime ministership

(2000±present), it has continued to struggle for balance between forces favoring multiparty democracy and the country's long tradition of authoritarian rule.

The European Union as an economic power. Economic integration in the world's oldest center of fossil-fuel industrialization has proceeded gradually but persistently since six Western European states formed the European Economic Community in 1957 (see Chapter 27). The organization's membership grew to twelve between 1973 and 1986. The scale of economic cooperation rose after 1992 when, by the terms of the Maastricht Treaty, the federation changed its name to the European Union (EU) and formulated complex rules and institutions for moving goods, capital, and workers freely among member states. The treaty also strengthened the authority of the European Parliament headquartered in Brussels. In 1998 eleven member states agreed to adopt the euro as a common currency issued by the European Central

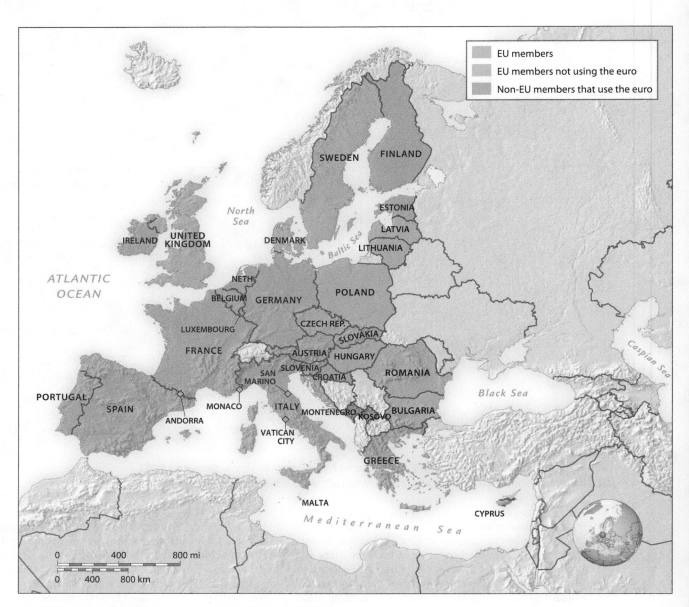

MAP 28.4 The European Union and the Eurozone, 2013.

This map of treaty agreements represents the greatest extent of interstate cooperation achieved in this region. How would you account for differences in the policies of particular states regarding EU membership and euro use?

Bank. Formation of the Eurozone, which currently has seventeen members, demolished more impediments to the rapid flow of goods and money from one state to another. Between 2004 and 2007 most Eastern European states joined the European Union, taking membership to twenty-eight by 2013 (see Map 28.4).

Nevertheless, the union is still a work in progress. The question of national sovereignty remains at the heart of debates over its future. Some leaders have long argued for full economic and even political integration leading to a United States of Europe, though an initiative to create an EU constitution failed in 2004. Every member country has *euro-skeptics*, political parties and individuals that fear the loss of national independence and identity. Some parties argue for less EU interference in members' internal affairs (regulation of food safety or genetic engineering, for example), others for total withdrawal from the organization. British governments have remained consistently ambivalent about their country's economic marriage to continental Europe. Britain is a member of the EU, but it has not joined the Eurozone and has a vocal euroskeptic minority.

The seventeen members that adopted the euro did not at the same time thoroughly integrate their financial and banking systems. Because euro members have no national currency, they cannot alter monetary policy or print money to address problems of high debt or weak economic performance. Yet the economically healthiest members have no formal obligation to redistribute part of their national wealth to troubled members. The viability of the Eurozone came under threat starting with the 2007±2009 recession, which worsened economic imbalances between the richest members (especially Germany and France) and several struggling ones (Greece, Ireland, Italy, Spain, Cyprus). As one informed observer remarked, ª The basic problem is that the EU is not a true union but more a collection of states that have not in any real sense ceded decision-making power to a central authority. The result is chaos fed by conflicting national objectives. . . . Instead of preserving sovereignty and nurturing democracy, it has created a situation where paymaster nations like Germany seek to impose the policy preferences of German voters on other states without regard to economic circumstances.º⁶ Despite these serious problems, the European Union remains a colossus on the world stage. It represents the largest economy in the world, and it unites nearly 504 million people in a unified market and a single domain of social and cultural exchange.

The Persistence of Poverty

The global economy has grown in most years since the end of World War II but so has the gap between the richest and poorest segments of the world's population. This is the fundamental economic contradiction of the recent past. In 2011, 42 percent of total global income went to the richest 10 percent of the world's population, and 1 percent went to the poorest 10 percent.[7] Within many individual countries, income gaps have also continued to widen. A country may achieve impressive economic growth over several years and still show widening income inequality if the growth benefits predominantly upper-income citizens. This condition has existed not only in very poor countries like Mozambique and Cambodia but also in the United States, Russia, and China. In 2011 the income gap between rich and poor was wider in the United States than in any European country.[8] If the middle sector in relatively wealthy countries cannot afford equal access to education, health care, or career mobility, productivity is certain to erode and social welfare costs will go up. The capitalist world economy cannot

Demonstrations against Greek austerity measures. Protesters in Athens' Syntagma Square threw stones at police in October 2011 as lawmakers imposed job, pay, and pension cuts on civil service workers, as well as imposing higher taxes, in an effort to keep the Greek government solvent. What factors may have led initially peaceful protests to turn violent?

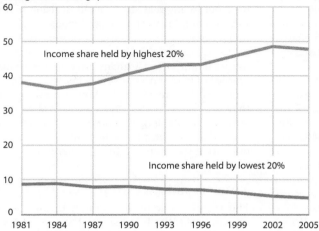

Income share held by highest 20%

Income share held by lowest 20%

The changing income gap in China, 1981–2005. How did the proportion of income taken home by the highest 20 percent of Chinese wage earners change in this period? How did this figure change for those in the bottom 20 percent of wage earners? How would you account for the widening income gap after 1984?

sustain growth if billions of people are too poor to consume more than a small part of what it produces.

Because of recent economic successes in some countries, notably China, the percentage of the world's population living on less than $1.25 a day has declined somewhat since 1990. But at present nearly 1.3 billion people live on that amount or less, and most of them, especially in Africa, suffer from ªmultidimensional poverty.º This means that they have little access to many things that affect the quality of livingÐ healthful nutrition, clean water, sanitation, medical services, cooking fuel, education, or expectation of reasonably long life. Women living in such poverty also typically lack access to contraception, prenatal consultations, or professional help during birth.

Foreign invasions, civil wars, famines, floods, earthquakes, refugee displacement, and global or regional recessions all impoverish people, at least temporarily. The world economy, however, remains potentially productive enough to feed everyone. Multidimensional poverty, rather, is mainly a consequence of institutional and political factors that perpetuate grossly unequal *distribution* of global wealth.

Prospects for demographic transition. If the population of a country grows at a faster rate than its economy, living standards are likely to fall or remain stagnant. Since the early twentieth century, a growing number of states have moved through a significant demographic transition, in which people live longer but women have fewer children. That causes the population growth rate to level off (see Chapter 27). Unfortunately, quite a few states, especially in Africa and the Middle East, have remained in the early stages of that transition. Consequently, population has continued to grow at higher rates than economic expansion.

Reversing this condition requires strategies both to reduce fertility rates and to achieve real economic development, which means growth that benefits the great majority.

Perils of the market economy. In the 1970s, states that faced soaring fuel costs sought large international loans to finance development. Oil riches impelled Middle East statesÐ Saudi Arabia premier among themÐ to put billions of ªpetrodollarsº in the hands of big banks to loan out to developing countries, which spent part of that money to buy even more oil. The International Monetary Fund (IMF) and the World Bank, two institutions created as part of the Bretton Woods system, became important lenders. The IMF loans money to countries in particularly difficult straits, while insisting on economic and financial reforms. The World Bank provides funds to jumpstart development projects and attract private investors.

By the early 1980s many developing states began to experience severe debt crises. International lenders, fearful of never being repaid, turned off the money spigot. In Latin America, for example, prices for many exports began to fall in the 1980s. This reduced funds available for interest payments on loans. When lenders backed off, growth decelerated, food prices soared, and poverty worsened in much of the region. Mexico discovered rich oil deposits in 1978, prompting President José López Portillo to boast, ªThere are two kinds of countries in the world todayÐ those that don't have oil and those that do. We have it.º[9] Foreign investors eagerly rushed in with huge loans to feed the fossil-fuel bonanza. But after 1980, oil prices declined rapidly, plunging Mexico into deeper debt, recession, and worsening impoverishment. In the 1990s the countries of Africa as a whole used 40 percent of their earnings from exports simply to service loans.[10] Even though quite a few states reduced their debt burdens in that decade or later, massive borrowing has remained a key part of the global economy.

In the face of rising public debt, many states began in the 1980s to move from centrally planned systems to market economies and exchanged state welfare doctrines for neoliberal ones that encouraged corporate investment from abroad, reduced public spending, economic privatization, and export growth. The results have been mixed. Even in countries that have achieved impressive growth rates, poverty has worsened in connection with cutbacks in public employment and services and the diversion of national income to political elites and international corporations. Foreign investors have tended to favor projects in developing countries that bring short-term profits rather than to commit to long-term development of infrastructureÐ roads, rail lines, Internet connections, education, brand new industriesÐ on which solid economic development must rest. In addition, rich states have given poorer ones much less aid as a percentage of their GDP than they promised back in the early 1970s. In 2008 the United States offered more economic aid than any other country in absolute dollars but gave only 0.19 percent of its GDP, about five times less than Sweden contributed.

Barriers to trade. Big industrialized states have had a habit of lecturing developing countries on the benefits of open markets. At the same time, they have imposed high tariffs on imports or awarded cash subsidies to their own farmers or manufacturers to help them keep costs and prices down. These policies have prevented producers in developing countries, especially farmers, from selling commodities to rich countries at competitive prices. For example, African farmers are expert producers of rice, wheat, cocoa, and textiles, but trade walls and subsidies have kept these goods out of potentially huge overseas markets.

Wealth and political power. In too many states, political leaders have regarded public wealth not as development capital but as the means to sustain a hierarchy of power in which a small group at the top redistributes public funds or private income to loyal followers, often members of their own extended families or ethnic communities. Conversely, citizens having economic grievances have sometimes abandoned civic activism for strategies to connect themselves to powerful patrons who might send bits and pieces of wealth their way. Such systems are inevitably corrupt, and foreign governments and firms have too willingly rewarded elites in return for access to the official cooperation they need to run profitable enterprises. Countries with great economic potential have suffered from the ªcurse of oil,º a vice that leads powerful people to use profits from fossil fuel or other extractive industries to lubricate the wheels of patron-client relationships rather than economic transformation. This has happened in Nigeria, for example, where vast offshore oil revenues have so far done little to benefit the population as a whole.

Women in the economy. Nearly half of the adult women in the world do not participate in the paid labor market. On the global scale, women earn about 75 percent of what men receive for comparable work. Low literacy levels and lack of job or entrepreneurial opportunities for women are less a consequence of formal religious teachings than of traditional practices that rigidly perpetuate male social and cultural domination. Many developing countries have only recently begun to mobilize the productive capacities of

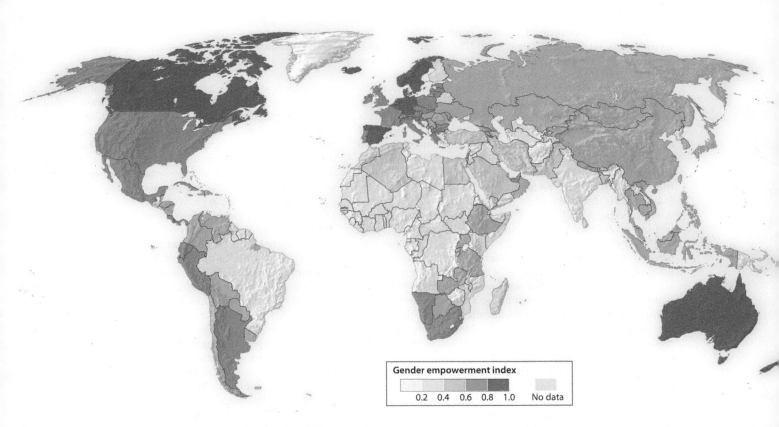

Gender empowerment index

0.2 0.4 0.6 0.8 1.0   No data

MAP 28.5 UN gender empowerment index, 2012.

Based on data from the UN Development Program, this index focuses on economic empowerment measured in terms of women's shares of legislative seats, shares of senior management positions, and income levels compared to men. The higher the score, the greater the level of women's empowerment. What economic and political characteristics might countries with high levels of empowerment have in common? What different characteristics might countries with lower levels of empowerment share?

women more effectively (see Map 28.5). More leaders may be recognizing that, as Hillary Clinton said in 2011, ªThere is a stimulative and ripple effect that kicks in when women have greater access to jobs and the economic lives of our countries. . . . By harnessing the economic potential of all women, we boost opportunity for all people.º[11]

Migration and the Global Economy

Migration of large numbers of people from one part of the world to another has been a prominent feature of the modern centuries. The numbers have grown spectacularlyÐ from about 2 million migrants in 1850 to 214 million in 2012. This trend faltered significantly only during the Great Depression and the two world wars. In the past forty years, mass migration has continued to accelerate despite the actions of most major receiving countries to restrict and manage immigration. These border controls aim generally to protect national sovereignty and the economic security of citizens. More specifically, they aim to select immigrants for their potential social and economic worth, prevent tourists from taking up permanent residence, and block migrants who have no economic resources or who pose criminal or political threats. The United States, for example, imposed much more stringent border and visa controls following the terrorist attacks of September 11, 2001. The immigration policies of some governments also cater to popular prejudices against immigrants as cultural aliens and troublemakers.

Border monitoring, however, has not been nearly as efficient as governments would like nor has it seriously impeded population mobility worldwide. Since 1970, mass migration has been an inevitable accompaniment to rapid economic and political change. Several developments have helped to accelerate population movement: the steady expansion of new industries and the rise of new manufacturing centers; the acceptance of capitalist market economics in almost all states; the need for immigrants or temporary workers to perform low-skill jobs; the fall of Eastern European and other authoritarian regimes that had previously restricted emigration; the steady flow of poor farmers and laborers into cities; political upheavals that have generated refugees; the improving efficiency of both travel and mechanisms for migrants to transmit money; and the development of electronic media that allow far-flung families and friends to stay in close communication. Interestingly, the *rate* of global migration in recent decades has not much exceeded the rate in the 1920s. The planet, however, supports five billion more people today than it did then.[12]

As in earlier decades of the twentieth century, the great majority of recent migrants have moved from less developed to more developed countries and to states rich in oil. And since 1970 many more countries have been sending citizens abroad, including China (since the 1980s), Southeast and South Asia, Eastern Europe (since the 1990s), Latin America, and both North and Subsaharan Africa. In many source countries, rising population, rapid urbanization, underemployment, and lack of opportunity even for

Syrian children in a refugee camp near the Turkish border. Syrians displaced by the civil war that began in 2011 wait in camps like this one to cross into Turkey or other neighboring countries. Hundreds of thousands of people in improvised settlements like this one have struggled for adequate sanitation, clean water, and medical care. What other recent conflicts in the world have bred large refugee camps?

well-educated people have driven emigration. In fact, the populations of relatively rich receiving states would decline if immigrants did not arrive. The fertility rate in the European Union as a whole has for several decades been too low to keep the population growing by natural increase (the difference between the number of births and number of deaths per year). Population growth, rather, depends on immigration. In 2005 the EU population rose by 1.9 million, but the inflow of people born outside it accounted for about 84 percent of that number.[13] In the oil kingdoms of the Middle East, large percentages of the workforces are foreign born, mainly temporary migrants. In Kuwait about 47 percent of the current population of 2.7 million is non-Kuwaiti, and foreigners hold 60 percent of the jobs.[14] In 2013 Qatar, a country smaller than New Jersey, had 250,000 citizens and 1.2 million foreign workers, mostly from South and Southeast Asia.[15]

Female migrants, especially single women and girls, have been subjected to labor exploitation and abuse in many countries. In an age when slavery and slave trading have been legally abolished throughout the world, human trafficking in women and girls has flourished. Illicit traffickers operating either within countries or across international borders deceive women into leaving home on the promise of a good job, persuade impoverished families to sell daughters, or simply kidnap vulnerable victims. According to a 2009 UN report, sexual exploitation, predominantly of women and girls, accounts for 79 percent of trafficking. Forced labor accounts for most of the remaining 21 percent.

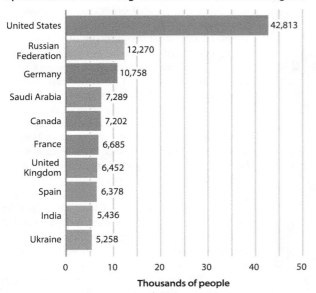

Top ten countries with the largest number of international immigrants

Country	Thousands of people
United States	42,813
Russian Federation	12,270
Germany	10,758
Saudi Arabia	7,289
Canada	7,202
France	6,685
United Kingdom	6,452
Spain	6,378
India	5,436
Ukraine	5,258

Countries with the largest number of international migrants, 2010. These ten countries received 52 percent of the world's migrants. What geographical, political, and economic factors might account for migration to these particular states?

In recent years, migrant women in several countries have become more politically active, publicly protesting discrimination or exploitation. These include Filipino women employed in domestic service jobs in the Middle East.[16]

Countercurrents in the Search for Global Order

FOCUS In what ways have systems for keeping order in the world changed since the 1970s?

In the past four decades, world population has grown by about 3.1 billion, humans have consumed finite energy resources on a colossal scale, and change has accelerated in virtually every sphere of life. These circumstances have put great pressure on societies to create more effective systems of global order. In one direction, human economic and technical structures have become larger and more complex. And keeping those structures going has required more complex and global-scale systems of cooperation and management. In the opposite direction, and in response to the very conditions we call **globalization,** humans continue, as they always have, to gather together in relatively small groups to

globalization The process by which peoples around the world have become increasingly interconnected through rapid communication and transport, resulting in both general acceleration of change and endeavors to strengthen the bonds of local community and identity.

seek security, well-being, and social identity. The communities that people form range from nuclear families, neighborhood societies, and local religious groups to nation-states and large international organizations. Cooperating communities also compete with one another, again as they always have, for material resources, sometimes in violent and irrational ways. Our species has good reason to want to perpetuate the immensely complex global systems it has created, especially institutions and networks that make life better. Yet these systems have not so far engendered world peace, environmental health, or anything close to global economic equality or justice. Consequently, there continues to be great tension between globalizing, integrating forces on the one hand and human urges to huddle together in communities to resist these forces, protect finite resources, and preserve shared rights and identity, on the other hand.

In the modern era, sovereign states have served as the primary institutions for maintaining social and political order. In the nineteenth century, nationalism proved to be a powerful new ideology for building states that not only exercised power but also sheltered a community bound together by shared language, culture, history, and destiny. Also in that century, states took the first shaky steps to create or encourage organizations dedicated to resolving conflicts, improving international communication, and promoting the world's economic, social, and cultural welfare. In the twentieth century, and especially since World War II, these organizations have multiplied and flourished in response to the colossal challenges of managing complex systems and addressing countless global problems.

The World State System since 1970

In the thirty years after World War II, the major colonial powers dismantled their empires. Consequently, the number of sovereign states in the world rose dramatically (see Chapter 27). Since 1975, dozens more colonial territories, mostly small ones, have achieved independence. In 1991, as we have seen, the Soviet Union broke into fifteen states. As of 2013 the United Nations had 193 sovereign members. These states range vastly in population, form of government, ethnic diversity, domestic resources, military power, and territorial size. (Russia is 813,000 times bigger than the sovereign state of Nauru in the Pacific Ocean.) Nevertheless, all of them claim the privilege of diplomatic equality with one another in accord with principles of sovereignty first worked out in Europe back in the seventeenth century. They also claim the right to govern and defend themselves without external interference.

Some political analysts argue that organizing the world in nearly two hundred separate states inhibits beneficial global integration and makes an already complicated world more unstable and dangerous. Other observers, however, claim that because states form, or aspire to form, national communities founded on cooperation and shared identity, they are still the most stable platforms on which to build democracy, advance human welfare, and protect individual rights.

Nelson Mandela addresses supporters in a Soweto soccer stadium. This rally occurred shortly after his release from prison in 1990. He was incarcerated for twenty-seven years for opposing the minority apartheid government. In 1994 he led the once-banned African National Congress to electoral victory in South Africa's first nonracial election. How might different segments of South African society have reacted to seeing Mandela, once branded as a terrorist, speak in public?

In fact, several organizations have in recent years published annual reports evaluating every state in the world in terms of its success at democratic governance and commitment to citizens' rights.[17] These surveys have found that over the past forty years the number of states that may be characterized as partially if not fully democratic has grown significantly, while the number of authoritarian states has declined. This trend has been moderate, not spectacular. Some states have not improved their flawed records very much. Others have in recent years allowed democratic

institutions to deteriorate, for example, Russia, Hungary, and Mali. But in still others, governments that not many years ago tyrannized their citizens have since mended their ways. In Eastern Europe most of the states that had one-party communist regimes before 1990 have made transitions to authentic parliamentary systems and free elections. The great majority of South American countries have transformed themselves from military or civilian dictatorships into societies where people vote in contested elections and enjoy more secure civil rights than they previously did. South Africa achieved majority rule in 1994 under the presidency of Nelson Mandela after a long winter, stretching back to the seventeenth century, when a white minority dominated society in every respect.

The end of bipolar politics. The possibility of nuclear annihilation loomed over the Cold War era, but some historians have suggested that international relations were more stable than after the freeze ended. The two superpowers and their allies, so the argument runs, had straightforward geopolitical aims: The future of the world rested on the triumph of either of two ideological visions. One was liberal democracy and free-market capitalism; the other was socialist society under the direct management of the state. The international politics of both alliances turned primarily on the objective of winning and holding the friendship of so-called third-world or nonaligned states.

The Cold War's bipolar politics were dangerous nonetheless. In the mid-1960s the United States and the Soviet Union entered into a period of improved relations known as *détente* (relaxation). Through the Helsinki Accords of 1975 they resolved outstanding issues over post±World War II frontiers in Europe, and they made progress limiting long-range missiles and nuclear warheads. The United States also normalized relations with the People's Republic of China following President Richard Nixon's decision, despite his avowed anticommunism, to visit Beijing in 1972. After 1975, however, Soviet±American relations worsened again over rivalry for influence in developing countries, nuclear disarmament failures, and tit-for-tat missile emplacements in Europe. The political temperature dropped further in June 1979, when Soviet forces invaded Afghanistan, an intrusion aimed at saving a friendly socialist regime there. In 1981 Ronald Reagan became U.S. president, vowing to increase military spending. Superpower relations reached bottom between 1982 and 1984, years in which strategic arms talks broke down and the Soviet Air Force shot down a Korean commercial airliner, claiming it was an American spy plane.

The Soviet economy generated little growth in those years, and Mikhail Gorbachev came to power in 1985 intent on reviving *détente* and implementing economic and political reforms. In the following two years, he pulled Soviet forces out of Afghanistan, where guerrilla fighters aided by the United States had kept up a war of resistance for eight years. In the rush of events leading to the dissolution of the Soviet Union, he was sidelined by Boris Yeltsin, who favored the breakup and who emerged as president of the newly declared Russian Federation. The Cold War ended abruptly by default as the Communist Party regime in Moscow crumbled (see Map 28.3).

The American giant. Some observers expected that bipolar politics (free world vs. communist world) would give way to a multipolar system in which several large statesÐ the United States, Russia, China, Japan, and the EU countriesÐ would share global leadership, and military power would be more diffused. In fact, the United States remained top dog not only in military might but also in its armed presence on land and sea around the world. Russia struggled economically to the end of the twentieth century and cut back its armed forces. The European Union moved toward commercial and monetary integration in the 1990s but proved reluctant to deploy military forces to deal with a crisis in its own backyard, the collapse of the multiethnic republic of Yugoslavia. That event in 1991±1992 led to three years of vicious interethnic warfare mainly among Serbs, Croats, and Bosnian Muslims. When Bosnian Serbs threatened wholesale ethnic cleansing of the Muslim population and UN peacekeepers proved ineffective, the United States intervened, coaxing its European NATO allies to launch air strikes to stop the carnage. In 1995 U.S. president Bill Clinton (in office 1993±2001) presided over an accord among the several states that by then had partitioned Yugoslavia. As for China, its new market economy grew spectacularly after 1978, but its military power remained technologically far behind that of the United States.

In the first decade of the new century, the United States faced no serious challenges to its global military supremacy. The attacks on New York and Washington, D.C., on September 11, 2001, raised popular fears that the country was nonetheless vulnerable to terrorist assaults. The administration of president George W. Bush (in office 2001±2009) consequently announced a ªwar on terror,º particularly on al-Qaida, an international, though uncentralized revolutionary organization. Osama bin Laden, a wealthy Saudi who established a base in Afghanistan, emerged as al-Qaida's leader. American and other NATO contingents invaded Afghanistan in the fall of 2001, joining with Afghan rebels there to overthrow the Taliban regime, which sheltered al-Qaida. The mission succeeded quickly, but more NATO troops arrived to help secure a new, presumably pro-Western government. Progress on that front moved slowly, and thirteen years after the 2001 military campaign, there were still more than 87,000 NATO-led troops in Afghanistan, 60,000 of them Americans.

In 2003 the United States invaded Iraq, gathering a coalition of allies but also acting without securing the approval of the UN Security Council. The U.S. government's announced objective was to preempt the regime of President Saddam Hussein from collaborating with al-Qaida and from using chemical or other weapons of mass destruction. In fact, Hussein had not previously had friendly relations with al-Qaida, and weapons of mass destruction were never found. The invaders overthrew the Hussein regime in a matter of weeks, but the war quickly mutated into a combination civil conflict and anticoalition resistance movement that dragged on for eight years. When American troops finally departed in late 2011, Iraq's attempt to build multiparty democracy was in a fragile state and its economy operating far below its potential.

American actions in both Afghanistan and Iraq aggravated relations with the Russian Federation. Under the leadership of Vladimir Putin, Russia initiated a more assertive foreign policy, especially in opposition to the expansion of NATO to include most of the former Soviet Union's Eastern European allies. Putin fiercely objected to NATO membership for Ukraine and Georgia, both former Soviet republics, and to American plans to place ballistic missile defense hardware in the Czech Republic and Poland. U.S. president Barack Obama (in office 2009±) suspended both of those initiatives, but in 2008 Russia fought a brief war with Georgia to protect two pro-Russian breakaway provinces of that country. The status of these provinces has remained unresolved and a continuing source of Russian±American strain.

A World of Organizations

Political scientists have characterized the sovereign state system as fundamentally a condition of *anarchy*Ð a word of Greek origin meaning ªabsence of rulersºÐ in the sense that no overarching central authority, no world government, imposes laws on states that they must obey. Global complexity, however, has impelled states to cooperate with one another more effectively and on larger scales. They must do this partly to manage rapid change and partly to prevent the institutions and organizations that world order requires from falling apart. Since World War II, international organizations have multiplied by the hundreds. Through these institutions, sovereign governments work together under agreed sets of rules and procedures to achieve goals of mutual interest, whether collective security, tariff reduction, or improved communications nets. Global complexity, however, has also demanded more **transnational organizations** that promote order, stability, and well-being in the world. Their work often involves exerting pressure on sovereign states to change their policies or account for their actions.

> **transnational organization**
> An association of individual citizens or private groups that collaborates across national frontiers to carry out particular activities or programs.

In the nineteenth century, states in Europe began to collaborate more systematically to manage their complex interrelations, founding, for example, the international Red Cross (1863); the Universal Postal Union (1878); and the Hague Conference (1899), which formulated procedures for resolving international conflicts. Such organizations proliferated in the twentieth century, as the two world wars demonstrating plainly the urgency of building institutions that bound states together in dense networks of cooperation and mutual dependence.

Red Cross workers unload a boat in Katanga province, Congo. Food and medical supplies supported families returning to the region in 2006 after being displaced by civil war. Why have transnational organizations such as the Red Cross taken on increasingly visible roles in the world in the past half-century?

The United Nations. Since 1945 the United Nations has served as the world's preeminent institution for guiding and harmonizing international relations. Member states, which today include every sovereign polity in the world except Taiwan and Vatican City, must agree to abide by the articles of the UN Charter. That treaty set forth the fundamental purposes of the United Nations to uphold international peace and security, address international problems of all kinds, encourage amicable relations among states, and foster respect for human rights. The charter refers to both the relations among states and the rights and welfare of ªpeoples.º Advocates of a strong United Nations have contended therefore that the organization has authority to intervene in the internal affairs of member states if they grossly oppress or abuse their citizens. In that sense the institution has challenged one of the principles of national sovereignty, freedom from external interference.

From its inception the UN Security Council, currently comprised of five permanent and ten rotating members, has had the authority to undertake military missions. In contrast to the League of Nations, its pre±World War II predecessor, the United Nations gives special powers to the Security Council's permanent members (today the United States, Britain, France, Russia, and China) and a majority of the full council membership to ªtake such action by air, sea, or land forces as may be necessary to maintain or restore international peace and security.º[18] In the Cold War years, however, incessant rivalry among the United States,

the Soviet Union, and their respective allies drastically limited UN military action. The five permanent members had power to veto resolutions that came before them, and one or another member did so on substantive issues 193 times between 1945 and 1990. The council authorized armed intervention in Korea in 1950 only because the Soviet Union temporarily boycotted the proceedings. UN forces, made up of volunteers from member states, also undertook a number of peacekeeping operations, for example, creating a line of separation between Egyptian and Israeli troops following the Suez Crisis of 1956 (see Chapter 27).

After the cold war ended and the world's two biggest military powers stopped butting heads over nearly every proposed UN military operation, many more peacekeeping missions were launched. These operations included the dispatch of UN forces to try to end or contain calamitous civil wars. The Security Council also authorized the large coalition that drove Iraq out of Kuwait in 1991. This campaign boosted the United Nations' prestige and suggested an expanding role in preventing or repelling state aggression. Soldiers wearing the organization's signature blue helmets have had several peacekeeping, indeed peacemaking, successes, notably overseeing the resolution of long-running civil wars in Cambodia (1970±1991) and El Salvador (1979±1992). Attempted interventions in wars in Rwanda, Bosnia, Somalia, and Angola, however, had little success. In 1999 NATO deployed airpower to prevent Serbia from attacking its own Albanian-speaking citizens in the Kosovo region because

ERADICATE
EXTREME POVERTY
AND HUNGER

ACHIEVE UNIVERSAL
PRIMARY EDUCATION

PROMOTE GENDER
EQUALITY AND
EMPOWER WOMEN

REDUCE
CHILD MORTALITY

IMPROVE MATERNAL
HEALTH

COMBAT HIV/AIDS,
MALARIA AND OTHER
DISEASES

ENSURE
ENVIRONMENTAL
SUSTAINABILITY

A GLOBAL
PARTNERSHIP FOR
DEVELOPMENT

The UN Millennium Development Goals. How do you think UN development goals might have been different in 1950? What features do you think these goals have in common?

Russian opposition prevented the Security Council from approving intervention. UN prestige as a peacekeeper dropped again in 2003 after the United States invaded Iraq without Security Council authorization.

The UN Charter (Article 1.3) enjoins members ᵃto achieve international cooperation in solving international problems of an economic, social, cultural or humanitarian character.º The number of UN agencies and projects dedicated to human rights and welfare has increased steadily since 1945, though member states have on the whole substantially reduced their contributions to these institutions. Nevertheless, UN organizations have carried on their benevolent work without receiving the media notoriety that armed missions have attracted. The organization has been a party to the striking progress made in nuclear and strategic arms control since 1990. It has sponsored numerous conferences of member states to address issues of human rights, population growth, the status and opportunities of women, and environmental degradation. In 2000 the United Nations outlined eight Millennium Development Goals that include cutting extreme poverty rates in half and providing primary education to the children of all member states. Progress has been made toward many of these goals, but it has slowed in the past few years owing to the complexity of the challenges and the inadequacy of funds from donor states.

International organizations on the regional scale. States in particular regions of the world have also grouped themselves into organizations to address a range of issues. During the Cold War, regional initiatives tended to be linked to one superpower bloc or the other. Since 1990, more regional organizations have formed, sometimes to strengthen collective security but also to take on social and economic problems having a particular regional character, for example, cooperation among African states to reduce high levels of HIV infection. Nearly every state in the world has become party to one or more regional organizations to reduce tariffs. These include the South American Common Market (Mecosur, 1991) and the North American Free Trade Agreement (NAFTA, 1992). No regional organization, however, has advanced as far as the European Union toward political and economic integration.

Transnational organizations. After World War II, more world leaders accepted the fact that national governments, even acting in close partnership with one another, could not address many complex global problems as effectively as more flexible, task-oriented, private organizations could. Transnational associations aim to serve human welfare apart from the interests of states or governing elites. The scholar Akira Iriye has written of the gradual emergence in the past century or so of an ᵃinternational civil societyº in which individuals and private groups band together to better the human condition in a variety of ways. He refers to networks ᵃthat are based upon a global consciousness, the idea that there is a wider world over and above separate states and national societies, and that individuals and groups, no matter where they are, share certain interests and concerns in that wider world.º [19]

Many transnational associations may be categorized as international nongovernmental organizations (INGOs). These institutions have multiplied into the thousands to serve human welfare in areas such as conflict resolution, disarmament, humanitarian assistance, economic development,

TABLE 28.1. Examples of International Nongovernmental Organizations

Organization	Location	Mission
Acumen Fund	United States	Economic development
APOPO	Tanzania	Humanitarian services, landmine clearance
Ashoka	United States	Economic development, social entrepreneurship
Barefoot College	India	Education, skills training
BRAC	Bangladesh	Economic development
CARE International	Switzerland	Economic development, humanitarian services
Ceres	United States	Environmental sustainability
Clinton Health Access Initiative	United States	Public health
Cure Violence	United States	Antiviolence intervention
Danish Refugee Council	Denmark	Humanitarian services
Doctors without Borders	Switzerland	Public health services
Handicap International	France	Humanitarian services
Heifer International	United States	Economic development
International Rescue Committee	United States	Humanitarian services, refugee services
Landesa	United States	Land tenure rights
Mercy Corps	United States	Humanitarian services
One Acre Fund	Kenya	Economic development
Partners in Health	United States	Public health services
Root Capital	United States	Economic development
Wikimedia Foundation	United States	Education, knowledge dissemination

Source: *The Global Journal,* ª The Top 100 NGOs 2013,º h ttp://theglobaljournal.net /top100NGOs/.

cultural exchange, environmental protection, and human rights (see Table 28.1). Many influential INGOS, such as international labor unions and faith-based groups, have memberships numbering in the millions, that is, more than the populations of many sovereign states. Electronic media also permit INGOs to disseminate information rapidly, archive millions of documents, and lobby governments and corporations to take action or modify policies. Dozens of INGOs have formal affiliation with the United Nations. For example, the delegations to the Kyoto conference on climate change in 1997 included 161 states and 236 transnational entities. In short, there are many public ªactorsº on the world stage today besides states.

Transnational groups have made especially important contributions to human rights. Since the United Nations adopted the Universal Declaration of Human Rights (1948) in response to the revelation of atrocities committed during World War II, sovereign states have come to accept that universal rights are a proper subject of international concern. In the past several decades, states have entered into numerous treaties and protocols that commit signers to ensuring the rights of citizens to equality before the law, protection against government abuse, freedom of speech and assembly, rights to political participation, freedom from racial and sexual discrimination, access to health care and education, and several other rights and liberties. States, however, have also been the principal abusers of human rights, especially authoritarian or weak regimes but sometimes democratic states as well.

The international mechanisms for enforcing human rights *inside* states are meager. Governments have tended to pick and choose the human rights violations they wish to protest, depending on their own political self-interests. This was especially true during the Cold War, when the United States and Russia looked the other way when their ideological and strategic allies committed serious abuses. INGOs unaligned with the political interests of particular states have worked effectively using persuasion and publicity to pressure governments to improve their human rights records. For example, Amnesty International, which grew rapidly in the 1970s and today has more than two million members, identifies and draws public attention to individuals imprisoned for political reasons. Other major INGOs include Human Rights Watch, the International Federation for Human Rights, and MADRE, a network of women's rights organizations.

Disorder and Breakdown in an Era of Global Integration

The demise of the Cold War brought a rush of hope for a new era of international peace and cooperation. Indeed, in the past quarter-century the world's strongest military powers have remained at peace with one another. And far fewer people have died in wars than in the mere six years of World War II. According to one study, the number of war deaths (both military and civilian) in the first ten years of the twenty-first century averaged about 55,000 people a year, compared to 180,000 a year between 1950 and 1989.[20] In those decades the Korean and Vietnam conflicts raged, and Iraq and Iran fought a border war, partly for control of oil fields, that dragged on for eight and a half years (1980±1988) and cost about 650,000 lives. Since then, no wars have reached that scale of violence, though 160,000 people died in Iraq during the American occupation of 2003±2011, nearly 80 percent of them Iraqi civilians.[21]

Wars after the Cold War. Nevertheless, more than one hundred relatively small wars have erupted since 1990, a few of them between states but mostly internal struggles for control of resources and power. Paradoxically, processes of global integration have themselves bred conflicts that have resulted in political and social disintegration. World demand for oil, rare minerals, illicit drugs, and many other commodities; the thriving international arms trade;

explosive growth rates of the urban poor; and the disproportionate flow of wealth to a minority of the world's population have made wars an inevitable corollary of globalization. If wars since 1990 have been less deadly than in previous years, they have nonetheless killed hundreds of thousands of men, women, and children and generated millions of refugees. Their horrors have included genocidal campaigns and civilian massacres, conscription of child soldiers, torture and execution of prisoners, and the rape, murder, and displacement of millions of women.

Most wars since 1990 have happened in relatively small or poor states where political disorderÐ marked by rebellions, interethnic clashes, rivalries between local warlords, and in some cases the intervention of foreign powers or hired mercenariesÐ has involved appalling violence (see Map 28.6). Several factors, always varying from one case to another, have operated to undermine central state authority. These have included chronic rural poverty, high unemployment rates of urban youth, rivalry for resources that command high world market demand (diamonds, rare earths, timber, cocaine), pervasive political corruption, and

oppressive governments that have sometimes endured only with the support of foreign patrons. Also, long-simmering social tensions rose to the surface in a number of states after the Cold War ended. That happened in part because oppressive or weak governments could no longer count on economic and military support from a Cold War patron to guarantee their power. Moreover, rulers who tried to build national unity on a platform of either anticommunism or anticapitalism discovered that these ideologies lost much of their popular appeal. In some countries, discontented political groups have had greater success than their own national governments in drawing on local ethnic or religious sentiments to foment rebellion.

Political identity and violence: Two cases. In the former Yugoslavia, regional ethnic and religious identities proved stronger than national allegiance when the country descended into crisis. A large majority of Yugoslavia's population shared a common secular culture and the Serbo-Croatian language. But the country was part Serbian Orthodox Christian, part Roman Catholic, and part

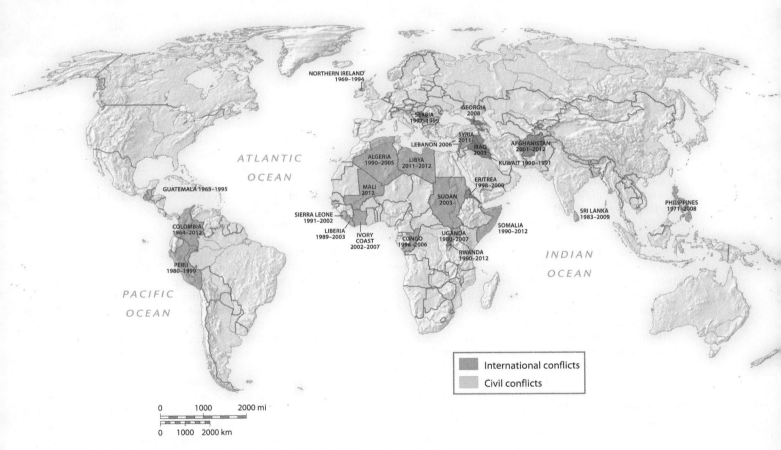

MAP 28.6 Twenty-five international and civil conflicts since 1990.
Which regions have largely escaped armed conflict since 1990? What factors might account for the proliferation of war in some regions and relative peace in others?

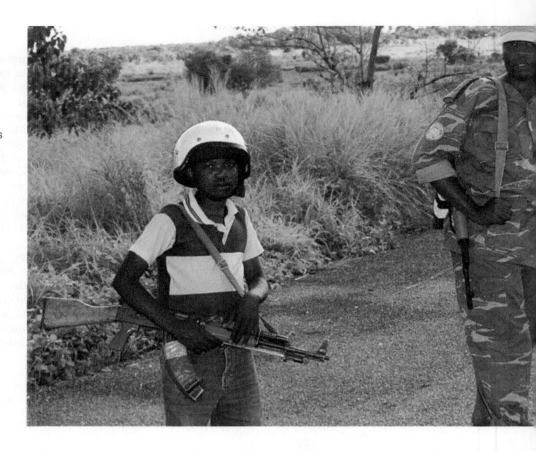

A UN peacekeeper watches a child soldier of the United Revolutionary Front in Sierra Leone. As local conflicts proliferated after the Cold War, rival factions fighting to control their country's resources or government increasingly used young boys and girls as armed combatants, cooks, porters, messengers, and sex slaves. What aspects of this boy's appearance do you find remarkable?

Muslim. In 1991±1992, shortly after the breakup of the Soviet Union, Yugoslavia fragmented, mainly over differences between leaders of the large Serbian minority, who insisted on dominating the state, and the other ethno-religious groups. After the breakup, regional cultural identities became much more politically useful than Yugoslav nationalism as leaders sought to build and defend several new republics from the wreckage of the old one. In the region of Bosnia, rivalry for land and power led to three years of war in which Bosnian Serb and Muslim communities revived ancient justifications for despising each other's cultural and historical identities and for clinging more fervently to their respective religious traditions than many of them had done when they were citizens of multiethnic Yugoslavia.

In the small East African state of Rwanda, the Belgian colonial administrators who ruled there until 1962 favored the aspirations of the Tutsi minority population, which traditionally herded cattle, over the majority of Hutu farmers. Even though both groups spoke the same language and shared much of their culture, tensions between them festered following national independence. Competition for land in conditions of rapidly rising population aggravated social friction, and the assassination of the Hutu president Juvénal Habyarimana in the spring of 1994 triggered Hutu armed attacks on Tutsis. Those assaults exploded quickly into a genocidal rampage that in the short span of three months took between 800,000 and 1 million lives. The victims also included many Hutu who opposed the genocide or who had marriage or other connections to their Tutsi neighbors. Neither the United Nations, the Organization of African Unity, nor any major world power took decisive action to stop the killing, which ended only when a Tutsi force seized the capital. After 1994 Tutsi and Hutu leaders achieved an uneasy reconciliation at home, though the Rwandan army and a variety of armed militias became involved in chronic and ongoing fighting in the neighboring Congo Democratic Republic.

Terrorism. The world had no trouble branding the September 11 attacks on the World Trade Center in New York and the Pentagon in Washington, D.C., as terrorism. The perpetrators carried out these airborne assaults to broadcast *political* grievances, not just to commit crimes. They aimed their strikes on civilians and on prominent symbols of powerÐ bastions of global capitalism and American military might. They intended to instill fear and confusion, demoralize their adversary, or provoke a disproportionate militaristic response, probably all of those things. They professed an extreme ideology of change through violence, in their case a vision of Islam having little relationship to what millions of Muslims believe and practice. Finally, the aggressors demonstrated that the weak could inflict pain on the strong without their necessarily having any more ambitious strategic goal than that.

Terrorism is by no means a new tool of war. It was an element in both world wars and in anticolonial resistance movements. From the 1960s to the 1980s, extremists of various ideological persuasions hijacked airplanes, set off bombs, took hostages, and carried out assassinations and suicide missions. In the past two decades, however, terrorist violence has taken some new directions. First, more terrorist operations have transnational dimensions. Even if perpetrators planned attacks on single targets, they frequently have built networks that recruit, plan, raise money, and procure weapons in several countries simultaneously. Al-Qaida emerged as a guerrilla organization fighting Afghanistan's Soviet occupiers, but after 1989 it morphed into an international network of cells to combat Western military and cultural intrusions in the Muslim world.

Terrorist attack on New York's World Trade Center towers. The south tower erupts in flames after a hijacked commercial passenger plane crashed into it on September 11, 2001. Another commandeered plane had already struck the smoking north tower. A total of 2,937 people died in the attacks on the world trade towers and the Pentagon. Another forty passengers and crew members were killed in the crash of a fourth hijacked plane near Shanksville, Pennsylvania.

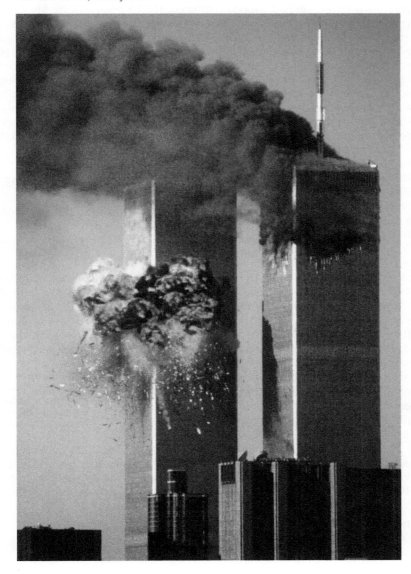

Second, terrorist groups have benefited immensely from the electronic revolution, using mobile phones, computers, and web sites to communicate plans, coordinate activities, and disseminate their messages. Third, at least a few sovereign states have given sanctuary and material support to terrorist groups at one time or another, notably Iran, Libya, and Syria. Fourth, throughout most of the twentieth century, anti-imperialist or Marxist-Leninist opposition to bourgeois capitalist oppression motivated many terrorist acts. Since 1990, however, terrorism has become a specialized weapon of underemployed, politically alienated young males in Asia and Africa, notably radicals who profess an ᵃIslamistᵒ religion characterized by rigid, puritanical ideology and a rhetoric of apocalypse and martyrdom. Fifth, terrorism has by definition represented a tactic of war wielded by a few against many. Consequently, terrorist conspiracies have frequently come to nothing, operations have failed regularly, and successful attacks have more often than not achieved little of benefit to the perpetrators. Nevertheless, the world has come to fear that terrorists may acquire portable weapons of mass destruction capable of killing tens or hundreds of thousands of people. The Japanese Aleph cult demonstrated the possibilities when in March 1995 its operatives released toxic sarin gas on five trains in the Tokyo subway system, killing thirteen and injuring hundreds more. Thus, global anxiety remains high that, despite vigorous police and military campaigns to root out extremists before they strike, civilian populations remain acutely vulnerable to terrorist violence on unprecedented scales.

Finally, terrorism, like other forms of warfare in the contemporary world, is a complex phenomenon requiring explanation. As reprehensible as it is, politically motivated violence springs from real social grievances and injusticesÐ economic frustration or destitution, government oppression, lack of opportunity for political participation, spiritual or moral disquiet over an increasingly decadent and materialist world, and sheer anxiety over the complexity and speed of change. Political analysts continue to debate the relative importance of the cultural, economic, and social conditions that turn men and women to careers of political violence. In the case of the September 11 attacks, Osama bin Laden and other al-Qaida leaders offered precise rational explanations for plotting mayhem: American failure to address the aspirations of Palestinians in their conflict with Israel, Western economic sanctions against Iraq and their grim consequences for the Iraqi people, Western support for corrupt Middle Eastern regimes, and the posting of American troops in Saudi Arabia, an affront to Muslims who worship in the holy cities of Mecca and Medina.

Palestinians and Israelis

Terrorist acts have figured prominently in the long-running and agonizing conflict between the state of Israel and the Arabic-speaking peoples of Palestine. Israel has fought four wars with neighboring Arab states (1948, 1956, 1967, 1973), and to date it has established full diplomatic relations with only two of them, Egypt (1979) and Jordan (1994). In the aftermath of its victory in the 1967 war, Israeli forces occupied Egyptian, Jordanian, and Syrian territories. Israel returned the Sinai to Egypt (1980±1982) but continued to occupy the West Bank (lands west of the Jordan River that had been part of Jordan) and the Gaza Strip (formerly within Egypt). These lands already had large populations of Palestinian Arabs, most Muslim but also a significant Christian minority. Since the war of 1973, the region has seen two Israeli invasions of Lebanon to root out Palestinian and other Arab fighters (1982±1984 and 2006), two major Palestinian uprisings (1987±1991, 2000±2002), Iraqi missile attacks on Israel during the Gulf War (1991), a violent split between the two major Palestinian political parties (2006±2007), extensive fighting in Gaza (2008), and throughout those years a nearly steady drum beat of Arab terrorist attacks and violent Israeli military reprisals

The fundamental issues perpetuating this conflict have not changed greatly in the past sixty-some years. Jewish immigrant settlers founded Israel in a land where Arab farmers and townspeople had made their homes for many centuries. Following the 1967 war, Israel imposed its rule on millions more Palestinians in the West Bank and Gaza. Today, there are about 4.4 million Palestinians in the occupied territories (another 1.4 in Israel). But no sovereign Palestinian state exists. There is only the Palestinian Authority, created in 1994 under terms of the Oslo Accords between Israel and the Palestinian Liberation Organization (PLO), to administer Gaza and parts of the West Bank. In addition, successive Israeli governments have also allowed Jewish Israelis to settle in the West Bank in increasing numbers, even though that territory lies outside the state of Israel. (The government dismantled Jewish settlements in Gaza in 2005.) Thus, 4.4 million Palestinians continue to live in a state of political limbo. Several million more Palestinians have status as refugees in Jordan, Lebanon, and Syria but do not hold citizenship in those countries.

The past forty years have also seen intermittent peace talks between the Israeli government and Palestinian representatives, usually under the sponsorship of the United States. None of these parlays has solved several seemingly intractable problems: Who should govern and under what conditions the city of Jerusalem, a place holy to Muslims, Jews, and Christians alike? How should the borders between Israel and a new Palestinian state be drawn? Under whose authority should Jewish settlers in the West Bank

live? Should Palestinians ever be permitted to return to homes they left behind in Israel more than sixty-five years ago? Who will support a Palestinian state's much-needed economic development?

To complicate matters further, elections in 2006 for a legislature under the Palestinian Authority put members of Hamas, a radical party, in control of Gaza, which Israeli troops have not occupied since 2005. Hamas does not formally recognize Israel's right to exist and has broken ties with the more moderate PLO in the West Bank. In the past few years, the contending parties have made no significant progress toward a ªtwo state solution.º And looming over the fluctuating political scene are three trends that will have to be addressed. One is unsettled conditions in the region following the so-called Arab Spring of 2011, which triggered the overthrow of existing authoritarian regimes in Tunisia, Egypt, Yemen, and Libya and the outbreak of civil war in Syria. No observer, however well informed, can confidently predict the long-term political complexion of new governments in those countries or how their relations with Israel and the Palestinian people will play out. A second issue is the near certainty that in Israel and the Palestinian territories combined, the Arabic-speaking Muslim population will soon outnumber Israeli Jews, leading to a condition in which a Jewish minority politically dominates and denies full citizenship rights to a Palestinian majorityÐa serious predicament for Israelis committed to democratic government. A third problem is worsening environmental stresses in the whole region, especially declining supplies of water, which Israeli industry and agriculture use in great quantities. A dropping water table threatens future economic growth in both Israel and a prospective Palestinian state.

Into the Anthropocene

FOCUS In what circumstances did the global environmental movement emerge, and how much success has it had slowing or reversing environmental degradation?

In recent years a number of environmental scientists have endorsed a startling idea: Sometime in the nineteenth century, the world entered a new age in which human beings, rather than slow-moving geological and climatic forces, became the primary agents of change in the earth's biosphere. In 2000 Paul Crutzen, a chemist and Nobel Prize winner, popularized the term AnthropoceneÐa word from the Greek *anthropo* referring to ªhumanº and *cene*, meaning ªnewºÐto describe this era. In his view

Anthropocene The era beginning in the nineteenth century in which human beings have become the primary agents of change in the earth's biosphere.

the Anthropocene is superseding the Holocene, the post±Ice Age epoch in which we have been living for the past twelve thousand years. Crutzen and two colleagues have written, ªHuman activities have become so pervasive and profound that they rival the great forces of Nature. . . . The Earth is rapidly moving into a less biologically diverse, less forested, much warmer, and probably wetter and stormier state.º²²

Environmentalists have predicted that human society has reached such a level of complexity that it will soon lose the capacity to manage and control the vast material waste that complexity inevitably generatesÐ carbon dioxide emissions, pesticide residue, stored radioactive plutonium, plastic bottles, and obsolete electronic devices. Humans will then have either to discover much better technological solutions to the problem of unhealthful, nature-destroying waste or else dismantle at least some complex systemsÐ an unlikely prospect on a planet of seven billion people and counting. As we pointed out at the beginning of the chapter, if humans lose the ability to hold complex structures together through constant effort, those structures will inevitably break down of their own accord. One writer has observed that in the past two centuries humans have by their actions already undermined the complexity of animal life on the planet. They have done this by forcing thousands of species into extinction while vastly increasing the populations of a few speciesÐ cattle, sheep, pigs, chickensÐ that they want for their use.²³ Could our species eventually manipulate and alter natural and physical processes so much that its own existence as a complex organism becomes untenable?

Environment and Environmentalism

Humans have been modifying the planetary environment since our species emerged 200,000 years ago. As society became more complex, this intervention intensified. In Chapter 27 we described the connection between unprecedented economic growth in the thirty years after World War II and accelerating environmental change, much of it harmful. As a consequence of human economic activity, forest lands shrank, soil washed away, rivers and lakes turned poisonous, pollutants thickened the air, fresh water tables dropped, and more animal and plant species disappeared. Some types of environmental degradation had immediate and harsh effects on human well-being. But others altered landscapes and natural systems in ways that most of the world largely ignored. In the past four decades environmental change has become far more evident, in part because a drastic shift in public attitudes began to take place in the 1970s.

In the post±World War II years, political and economic leaders nearly everywhere, whether they were communists, capitalists, or nationalists in new developing countries, believed that sustained and accelerating economic growth would ultimately make life better for all. Consequently, those leaders ignored, either willfully or not, mounting scientific evidence of the serious and long-term environmental damage that unfettered economic growth might inflict. Or, if they recognized that human industry, agriculture, and

A solar array in Spain harvests the sun's energy. At this solar plant, mirrors follow the sun's track, reflecting light onto the central tower, which generates steam to power an electrical turbine. Spain was home to 40 percent of the world's solar installations in 2008.

urban crowding could injure the earth, they assumed either that nature would heal its own wounds or ingenious technologists would find ways to limit the destruction without getting in the way of growth.

The environmental movement. Public awareness of agricultural and industrial contamination grew moderately in the 1960s following publication of Rachel Carson's best-selling book *Silent Spring*, which exposed the lethal effects of widespread pesticide use (see Chapter 27). The year 1970 marked a watershed in environmental awareness in the United States. That year Democratic and Republican party leaders joined together to organize the first Earth Day, an event that mobilized about twenty thousand Americans to demand solutions to worsening environmental ills.

The Earth Day movement inspired many more public interest initiatives and helped awaken world consciousness to the problems and complexities of the emerging Anthropocene. The oil crisis of 1973 generated global anxiety over chronic fossil-fuel shortages and the lack of alternative or cleaner sources of energy. Under public pressure, governments in the Western democracies began to organize agencies and enact legislation to address environmental degradation. The United States offered a model for other countries by establishing the Environmental Protection Agency in 1970 and subsequently passing laws to clean up air and water. By the 1980s the governments of many other states, including young developing countries, began to organize environmental ministries and take action on some level to restrain forest cutting, protect wildlife, and reduce pollution. Also in that decade, politically minded environmentalists organized Green Parties in several Western countries.

Once the new earth consciousness became rooted, major disasters could no longer occur without massive public reaction. In December 1984, for example, the accidental release of methyl isocyanate gas and other toxic chemicals from a pesticide factory in Bhopal, India, killed about fifteen thousand people. The Bhopal disaster and its aftermath cast a long shadow over the Union Carbide Corporation, whose subsidiary owned the factory. Two years later, a disastrous explosion at the Chernobyl nuclear plant in the Soviet Ukraine contaminated to one degree or another most of Europe and caused the illness or deaths of thousands of people exposed to radioactive fallout. This calamity also exposed the communist state's bureaucratic incompetence and probably hastened the Soviet Union's collapse in 1990. An environmental movement bloomed in the new Russia, and it helped expose the appalling environmental damage wrought by Joseph Stalin and his Soviet successors. That movement has continued to grow despite scant encouragement from the central government, which has continued to pin the country's future on massive production of fossil fuels and minerals.

As early as the 1960s, governments negotiated bilateral and multilateral agreements on pollution reduction and other environmental issues. The United Nations held its first major conference on the human environment in Stockholm in 1972, producing a declaration of twenty-six principles on economic development and defense of the biosphere. Other international meetings followed, for example, the Copenhagen climate summit in 2009. In the past forty years, hundreds of INGOs have been founded to advance environmentalist agendas. These organizations, including Friends of the Earth, Greenpeace, and the Sierra Club, have persistently taken both governments and corporations to task for environmental mismanagement, including rampant deforestation and waste dumping. They have also monitored deficiencies in safety technologies and regulations that have caused such disasters as the Deepwater Horizon oil rig blowout in 2010, which killed eleven people and disgorged two hundred million gallons of crude oil into the Gulf of Mexico.

China's spectacular economic growth curve since the 1980s has coincided with the rise of global environmentalism. The timing here has been bad. Chinese leaders are perfectly aware of multiple environmental degradation crises, but they do not want to slow China's climb to the top rank of economic powers. Rapid reform of industrial practices will

Humans and wildlife suffer the consequences of environmental disasters. A local government official rescues a contaminated bird along the Louisiana coast after an explosion on BP's Deepwater Horizon drilling rig caused a massive oil spill. How might this 2010 event have set back or benefited the environmentalist movement?

be difficult. Lung-destroying air pollution hit record levels in northern China in 2013, and growing quantities of dust, mercury, and carbon monoxide have been wafting eastward over the Pacific to fall back to earth in North America.

Environmentalist success. Nevertheless, environmental activism has made impressive achievements. In many countries, especially the wealthiest, cleanup projects have partially cleared skies over big cities and brought dead waterways back to life. Some wild animal species have returned from the brink of extinction. Europe has recovered forest land to the extent it had a century and a half ago when the industrial revolution was going full speed.[24] Some industrialized countries have significantly reduced sulfur dioxide and lead emissions into the atmosphere. Many large corporations have begun, after years of resistance, to introduce more environmentally responsible policies and procedures; almost all of them have launched campaigns to refashion their public images as friends of the earth. In the 1980s and 1990s a remarkable international effort persuaded many states to reduce production of chlorofluorocarbons (CFCs), an organic compound used as a refrigerant, spray propellant, and solvent. When released into the atmosphere, CFCs disrupt and pierce holes in the ozone layer, the thin chemical blanket in the stratosphere that absorbs most of the sun's ultraviolet radiation. If that radiation reaches the planet's surface in significant amounts, it damages oceanic plankton essential to the health of the biosphere. It also afflicts humans with eye diseases and skin cancers. Fortunately, international cooperation has reduced CFC contamination so much that the ozone layer appears to be on the mend, though its full restoration will take decades.

The quest for energy sources to supplement fossil fuels has also advanced. Nuclear power has remained highly controversial in the aftermath of Chernobyl and, more recently, the 2011 earthquake and tsunami that severely damaged the nuclear plant in Fukushima, Japan. Nevertheless, about 11 percent of total energy production came from nuclear power in 2009, and today nearly 450 plants are in operation, the greatest number in the United States, France, and Japan. In the 1970s the potential of geothermal, solar, and wind power was known but hardly developed. In recent years science and engineering have raised the efficiency and lowered the cost of these energy producers, resulting, for example, in a fivefold increase in available solar power. Electric automobiles, which proved too costly and cumbersome to compete with internal combustion engine vehicles throughout the twentieth century, are now appearing on the road.

The Perils of Climate Change

The Holocene is an interglacial geological era, a period when the earth's surface temperature warms slightly in the interval between one ice age and another. But compared to the small temperature fluctuations that have accompanied most of the Holocene, the increase of about one degree Fahrenheit in the course of the twentieth century is ominous.

Wangari Maathai: Environmental Activist and Nobel Laureate

Kenya is one of those African countries whose population has grown stupendously since the early twentieth century. In the 1920s Kenya had about 2.7 million people. By 2013 numbers had risen to more than 44 million. This growth has put great pressure on land and water resources. The country has suffered extensive deforestation as Kenyans have cut down trees for fuel and lumber.

By the 1970s the negative effects of this deforestation were becoming apparent. Wangari Maathai (1940–2011), a professor of veterinary anatomy at the University of Nairobi and an advocate for women's rights at the institution, became concerned about the environmental destruction she was witnessing in her country. She began to combine her feminist activism with environmental advocacy, using her position in the National Council of Women of Kenya to launch a community-based tree planting program. Maathai encouraged women to plant and nurture tree seedlings in exchange for a small stipend, seeing this project as a way to steward the environment and create jobs for women at the same time. "It's the little things citizens do," she observed. "That's what will make the difference. My little thing is planting trees."[25] In 1977 she established the Green Belt Movement (GBM), a non-governmental organization dedicated to planting trees on a much larger scale. Though the GBM received some financial and logistical support from Kenya's Ministry of Forestry, it got crucial assistance from international organizations like the UN Environment Program. Backed by international groups, the GBM did not have to depend on the Kenyan government's good graces for its survival.

The government indeed proved to be an unreliable partner. In the late 1980s Maathai began to speak out against the increasingly repressive single-party regime of President Daniel arap Moi. She first confronted Moi in 1989 when she campaigned to block the construction of a sixty-story business tower on the grounds of Uhuru Park in central Nairobi. Moi and his government repudiated her efforts and subjected her and the GBM to harassment. Nevertheless, Maathai and her supporters successfully lobbied international investors to withdraw their funding from the project, and Moi had to cancel it.

Throughout the 1990s Maathai and the GBM worked to enact democratic change in Kenya by registering voters and calling for constitutional reform. Maathai also protested multiple government attempts to transfer public land to commercial developers, often drawing international attention to these schemes and shaming the government into abandoning them. She was arrested numerous times and publicly criticized by Moi for not playing her part in society as an obliging and submissive woman.

Moi retired from office in 2002. He also saw his party lose the presidential election to a candidate from the National Rainbow Coalition, an alliance of parties that counted Maathai among its members. In the same election she stood as a candidate for parliament, winning 98 percent of the vote in her constituency. The following year, she took office as assistant minister for environment, natural resources and wildlife. In 2004 Maathai became the first African woman to win the Nobel Peace Prize, awarded to her for her impact on sustainable development, peace, and democracy. When she died of cancer in September 2011, she left behind a multidimensional legacy of service to democracy, feminism, human rights, and environmental conservation. "You cannot protect the environment," Maathai wrote, "unless you empower people, you inform them, and you help them understand that these resources are their own, that they must protect them."[26]

Wangari Maathai addresses the UN summit on climate change, 2009.

Thinking Critically

Wangari Maathai's activism addressed environmental degradation, women's empowerment, and democratic governance. Why do you think this combination of issues gave Maathai great public influence?

The world's scientific community is nearly unanimous in ascribing this remarkable surge to human action. If our species can significantly and for a long time alter planetary temperature, then we have clearly left the Holocene behind and entered the Anthropocene.

The heat the earth receives from the sun is radiated back toward space, but greenhouse gases, mainly water vapor but also carbon dioxide, methane, ozone, and nitrous oxide, trap most of the heat there. It then radiates back to the earth to warm its surface to a temperature that sustains life (59°F, on average). This greenhouse effect is therefore essential to life. Human intervention, however, has resulted in greater quantities of greenhouse gases rising into the lower atmosphere. The carbon dioxide concentration there has increased by

TABLE 28.2. Future Impacts of Global Warming in Three Regions

Africa	Australia and New Zealand	North America
Increased water stress for 75–250 million people by 2020	Intensified water security problems in southern and eastern Australia and parts of New Zealand, by 2030	Western mountains: decreased snowpack, more winter flooding, and reduced summer flows
Loss of arable land, reduced growing seasons, and reduced yields in some areas	Further loss of biodiversity in ecologically rich sites, by 2020	Increasing impacts on forests due to pests, diseases, and fire, with an extended period of high fire risk and large increases in area burned
Threats to low-lying coastal areas posed by sea-level rise	Increased risk from sea-level rise, more severe and more frequent storms, and coastal flooding in the Cairns region and southeast Queensland (Australia), Northland to Bay of Plenty (New Zealand), and other coastal communities, by 2050	In early decades of the century, during moderate climate change, 5 to 20 percent increase in total agricultural yields, with important regional variations; major challenges for crops with limited access to water or those near the warm end of their suitable range
Further degradation of mangroves and coral reefs	Some initial benefits in western and southern New Zealand, such as longer growing seasons, less frost, and increased rainfall	Increased intensity, duration, and number of heat waves in cities historically prone to them
Decreased fish stocks in large lakes	Decreased yields from agriculture and forestry by 2030, due to increased drought and fire, in much of southern and eastern Australia and parts of eastern New Zealand	Coastal areas: increased stress on people and property, due to climate change impacts interacting with development and pollution

Source: Adapted from University Corporation for Atmospheric Research, "Future Global Warming Impacts, by Region," h ttp://www.ucar.edu/news/features/climatechange/regionalimpacts-text.jsp; interactive map based on M. L. Parry, O. F. Canziani, J. P. Palutikof, P. J. van der Linden, and C. E. Hanson, eds. *Contribution of Working Group II to the Fourth Assessment Report of the Intergovernmental Panel on Climate Change, 2007* (New York: Cambridge University Press, 2007). © University Corporation for Atmospheric Research.

about one-third in the past two centuries. The chief cause of buildup has been fossil-fuel burning in factories and vehicle engines. Between 1990 and 2012 world petroleum production rose from nearly 66,500 to more than 89,000 barrels per day. The number of cars on the world's roads jumped from about 170 million to more than 1 billion between 1970 and 2012. Other important sources of gases that float into the atmosphere are wood burning, rice cultivation, chemical fertilizers, and livestock manure. Global deforestation also reduces the amount of carbon dioxide that living plant matter absorbs.

The effects of rising global temperature are not simply hotter weather but climatic instabilityÐ more rain in some places, worse drought in others, more frequent cyclone activity, loss of polar ice caps and glaciers, and a rise in sea levels. The Intergovernmental Panel on Climate Change has predicted a global temperature increase of anywhere from 2.5 to 10 degrees Fahrenheit in the next century. As the temperature climbs, the consequences will become more extreme, including rising seas that inundate low-lying islands and densely populated continental coasts (see Table 28.2).

Most of the world's political leaders remain fundamentally committed to the philosophy of continuous growth that has dominated economic thought since the industrial revolution. For example, in 2001 the administration of U.S. president George W. Bush, a champion of neoliberal economics, repudiated the 1997 Kyoto protocol to reduce greenhouse gas emissions on the grounds that it would interfere with American business growth. Even leaders who advocate strong environmental protection laws find it much easier to convince citizens to support short-term remedies rather than address long-term restructuring. Proper stewardship of the earth is also complicated by global commercial integration, which has intensified humankind's demand for more material goods, which must be grown or manufactured. We can hope that human ingenuity, coupled with serious if not drastic readjustments in the way we live, may prove sufficient to slow the pace of change, thereby avoiding massive social disruption and a forced return to simpler times.

• • •

Conclusion

This book has to have an ending, but the stories we have told in this final chapter have no conclusions. We cannot see the full shape of the world-scale developments that have taken place in the past four decades because they are still in progress. We have identified what we think are important developments in the technological, economic, political, and environmental spheres. But we cannot know whether people living a hundred, fifty, or even just ten years in the future will think those developments are as important as we do now.

Scholars who study "big history," a relatively new field of inquiry that situates the human story in the much longer narrative of cosmic history from the Big Bang to the present, have demonstrated that we can predict the future of human society in the very long term with greater confidence than we can forecast, say, the next five years. Drawing on the evidence of astrophysics, for example, these "big historians" assure us that within probably less than two billion years, the sun will begin to expand, bombarding the earth with so much radiation that all living organisms will be extinguished. Our own species will almost certainly have already disappeared by then, probably within no more than a few million years from now. If the longevity of most other species is a valid measure, our extinction is likely to happen even if we tread far more lightly on the earth than we do now. In short, on very large scales of time, our fate is quite easy to foresee.

Let us drop down to the tiny scale of just the coming one hundred years and focus on human beings and their complex activities, relationships, and networks. We can predict from the experience of the previous century that the pace of change will continue to accelerate at a fast clip and that our numerous, intermeshed systems will become even more complex. We cannot, however, forecast with much precision the directions change will take. Will the acceleration of global population growth continue to slow down as much as demographers think? Will the income gap between the ultra-rich and the very poor get wider, or will it close at least a little? Will sovereign states matter even more in the twenty-second century than they do now? Or will regional and global associations that group people together for many different purposes replace states? Will the ideology of nationalism die away, or will it fuel even more conflicts between communities? Will the number of war deaths go up or down? How much will the earth's surface temperature rise, and in what ways will society have to restructure itself as that happens? No one can answer these questions with much assurance.

One change is almost certain to occur in the next century, or two at most: Our species will use up most of what remains of the fossil-fuel-energy jackpot it has enjoyed since the nineteenth century. If we as a species continue to consume nonrenewable energy at anything close to the current rate, the underground supplies of it, as well as the uranium that powers nuclear plants, will decline precipitously. Back in Chapter 21 we introduced the idea of the biological old regime, the long span of human history before the nineteenth century, when most of the energy humans used came from the shining sun, the renewable energy source that animates living things. When the fossil-fuel bonanza ends—the only major nonrenewable energy source capable of sustaining a human population in the billions—our species will be obliged to rely once again on the sun's renewable energy. A return to the biological old regime does not necessarily mean we will have to dismantle the complex systems we have been erecting at a frantic pace over the past two centuries. But we will have to achieve two objectives: First, we must develop technology to harvest energy from solar radiation on a far larger scale and at more manageable costs than we have done so far. Second, we must drastically reduce the rate at which we pollute and scar the earth, plunder its resources, and destroy its life-forms. Doing that will not require us to lower the global population by billions or abandon all complexity. We will not all have to be foragers, hunters, or subsistence farmers. But we will almost certainly have to retreat in some measure from the computer-driven, car-loving, and product-consuming way of life that so far remains a global aspiration.

• • •

Key Terms

al-Qaida 839
Anthropocene 846
détente 838
European Union (EU) 832
Eurozone 833
glasnost 830
globalization 837
Green Belt Movement (GBM) 849

greenhouse effect 849
inflation 825
international nongovernmental organization (INGO) 841
Internet 821
neoliberalism 826
Organization of Petroleum Exporting Countries (OPEC) 825

outsourcing 828
perestroika 830
stagflation 825
terrorism 844
transnational organization 839
UN Security Council 839

Change over Time

Year	Event
1972	The United Nations holds its first major conference on the environment in Stockholm.
1973	The OPEC oil embargo precipitates first global "oil shock."
1978	China initiates changes to modernize its economy.
1979	Tokyo activates the first cellular phone network.
1989	Crowds dismantle the Berlin Wall.
1991	The Soviet Union is officially dissolved. India begins to adopt more market-oriented policies. Tim Berners-Lee creates the first World Wide Web site.
1992–1995	Civil war rages in Bosnia after the breakup of Yugoslavia.
1993	The first Global Positioning System (GPS) is activated.
1994	Apartheid ends in South Africa. Hutu groups in Rwanda target Tutsis and sympathizers for genocidal mass slaughter.
1998	Eleven members of the European Union adopt the euro as a common currency.
2001	Al-Qaida terrorists hijack planes and strike the U.S. Pentagon and World Trade Center towers.
2003	The Human Genome Project identifies and maps genes and DNA sequences.
2003–2011	United States and coalition forces occupy Iraq.
2007–2009	Many countries experience an economic recession.
2011	An earthquake and tsunami severely damage the nuclear plant in Fukushima, Japan. Authoritarian regimes in Tunisia, Egypt, Yemen, and Libya are overthrown in the Arab Spring.

Please see end of book reference section for additional reading suggestions related to this chapter.

Student Quick Tips

Use this Student Quick Tips guide for a quick and easy start with McGraw-Hill Connect. You'll get valuable tips on registering, doing assignments, and accessing resources, as well as information about the support center hours.

How to Access Connect using the Code Inside of your McGraw-Hill Create™ PRINT textbook.

NOTE: *If you are using an eBook, please see the next set of instructions below.*

Getting Started

TIP: You will need a 20 digit unique code which comes with the purchase of your McGraw-Hill Create™ print textbook. This code is **located on the inside back cover** of your printed textbook.

Registration and Sign In

1. Find the ISBN of your Create textbook. This can be found on Connect instructions page which is the last printed page of your book (begins with 978…)
2. Visit www.mcgrawhillcreate.com/shop
3. Search for the 13 digit ISBN found in step 1 (978XXXXXXXXXX).
4. The book should match your course (i.e. school, instructor, course name/number) and should say "Free With Access Code." Enter your unique 20 digit code found on the inside back cover of your textbook.
5. Register as a new user or sign-in if you already have a McGraw-Hill account

TIP: Remember this username and password as you will need it when you get to Connect

6. Open a new browser and go to the unique URL provided by your instructor
   (example: http://www.mcgrawhillconnect.com/class/instructorname_section_name)

> Sample of Connect Web Address
> http://www.mcgrawhillconnect.com/class/instructorname_section_name

7. Click the Register Now button and sign in using the same email address and password you created on the McGraw-Hill Bookstore (Step 5).

How to Access Connect Using the Code Inside of your McGraw-Hill Create™ eBOOK.

If you are viewing this page in your purchased Create ebook, then you only have a few more steps to complete your registration.

1. Open a new browser and go to the unique URL provided by your instructor
   (example: http://www.mcgrawhillconnect.com/class/instructorname_section_name)

> Sample of Connect Web Address
> http://www.mcgrawhillconnect.com/class/instructorname_section_name

2. Click the Register Now button and sign in using the same email address and password you created on the McGraw-Hill Bookstore when you purchased/accessed your eBook.

Trouble Logging In?

- Ensure you are using the same email address you used during registration

- If you have forgotten your password, click on the "Forgot Password?" link at your Instructor's Connect Course Web Address

- When logged into Connect, you can update your account information (e.g. email address, password, and security question/answer) by clicking on the "*My Account*" link located at the top-right corner

Home (Assignments)

TIP: If you are unable to begin an assignment, verify the following:

- The assignment is available (start and due dates)

- That you have not exceeded the maximum number of attempts

- That you have not achieved a score of 100%

- If your assignment contains questions that require manual grading, you will not be able to begin your next attempt until your instructor has graded those questions

TIP: Based on the assignment policy settings established by your Instructor, you may encounter the following limitations when working on your assignment(s):

- Ability to Print Assignment

- Timed assignments – once you begin a "*timed assignment*," the timer will not stop by design

TIP: "*Save & Exit*" vs. "*Submit*" button

- If you are unable to complete your assignment in one sitting, utilize the "*Save & Exit*" button to save your work and complete it at a later time

- Once you have completed your assignment, utilize the "*Submit*" button in order for your assignment to be graded

Library

TIP: The *Library* section of your Connect account provides shortcuts to various resources.

- If you purchased ConnectPlus, you will see an *eBook* link, which can also be accessed from the section information widget of the *Home* tab

- *Recorded Lectures* can be accessed if your instructor is using *Tegrity Campus* to capture lectures. You may also access recorded lectures when taking an assignment by clicking on the projector icon in the navigation bar

- Many McGraw-Hill textbooks offer additional resources such as narrated slides and additional problems, which are accessible through the *Student Resources* link

Reports

TIP: Once you submit your assignment, you can view your available results in the *Reports* tab.

- If you see a dash (-) as your score, your instructor has either delayed or restricted your ability to see the assignment feedback

- Your instructor has the ability to limit the amount of information (e.g. questions, answers, scores) you can view for each submitted assignment

Need More Help?

CONTACT US ONLINE

Visit us at:

www.mcgrawhillconnect.com/support

Browse our support materials including tutorial videos and our searchable Connect knowledge base. If you cannot find an answer to your question, click on "Contact Us" button to send us an email.

GIVE US A CALL

Call us at:

1-800-331-5094

Our live support is available:
Mon-Thurs: 8 am – 11pm CT
Friday: 8 am – 6 pm CT
Sunday: 6 pm –11 pm CT

Glossary

A

absolutism A political doctrine asserting that in a monarchy the ruler holds sole and unquestionable power by divine authority.

Afroeurasia The land masses of Africa and Eurasia, together with adjacent islands, as a single spatial entity.

agrarian society A society in which agriculture, including both crop production and animal breeding, is the foundation of both subsistence and surplus wealth.

agricultural revolution The transition from collecting food in the wild to domesticating and producing particular plants and animals for human consumption.

Anthropocene The era beginning in the nineteenth century in which human beings have become the primary agents of change in the earth's biosphere.

apartheid The political and legal system in force in South Africa from 1948 to 1994; designed to ensure the domination of the white minority over the majority population.

asceticism The principle and practice of renouncing material comforts and pleasures in pursuit of an elevated moral or spiritual state.

australopithecines Several species of the earliest bipedal hominins, now extinct, whose remains have been found in eastern Africa.

autarky A country that aims to achieve economic independence and self-sufficiency, especially freedom from dependence on external trade or assistance; also autarkic.

authoritarian monarchy A state, headed by a king, a queen, or an emperor, whose ruling class demands strict authority over the rest of the population.

B

baby boom A period of increased birth rates, especially in Western countries, from the end of World War II to about 1957.

biological old regime Human history before the nineteenth century, when economic production depended almost entirely on capturing flows of energy from the sun.

biomass Plant matter, including wood, brush, straw, and animal waste, used especially as a source of fuel.

biosphere The zone of the earth that can support life.

bipedal Walking upright on two legs, one skill among others that distinguishes hominins from apes.

bishopric In the Catholic Church organization, a district (diocese) under the authority of a bishop.

Black Death An infectious disease, probably plague, that caused significant population decline in parts of Afroeurasia in the mid-fourteenth century.

bourgeoisie The social category of town-dwelling artisans, merchants, and bankers who occupied a position between rural peasants and the aristocratic class; in modern usage, the ª middle classº; in Marxist thought, the property-owning class that oppresses the working class.

bronze age The era centered on the third and second millennia B.C.E. when bronze making was the most advanced metallurgical technology in the world.

bureaucracy A hierarchy of officials within a government that carries out the laws, decrees, and functions of the state.

business cycle A sequence of economic activity typically characterized by recession, fiscal recovery, growth, and fiscal decline.

C

caliph In Sunni Islam, the deputy or successor of the Prophet Muhammad as leader of the Muslim community.

canon law A code of laws and regulations governing a Christian church or denomination, especially in matters of faith, worship, moral behavior, and church administration.

capitulations International agreements in which one state awarded special privileges within its borders to subjects or citizens of another state.

caravel A type of light, highly maneuverable sailing vessel used by Iberian sailors in the Atlantic in the fifteenth and sixteenth centuries.

carrack An oceangoing ship, larger than a caravel, used extensively by Iberian mariners in the Atlantic and Indian Oceans in the fifteenth and sixteenth centuries.

caste A social class more or less rigidly separated from other classes by distinctions of heredity, occupation, wealth, or degree of ritual purity.

cathedral A church that serves as the seat, or headquarters, of a Christian bishop; typically, a large church that attracts worshipers and pilgrims from a wide surrounding region.

caudillos Autocratic political bosses or dictators, especially in the post-independence period in Latin America.

cavalry The part of a military force trained to fight mounted on horses or camels.

charter A document in which a state or other political authority granted specific rights or privileges to an individual, town, guild, or other organization to carry out particular functions.

chartered company A type of corporation in which the state granted specific rights and obligations to private investors to engage in exploration, commerce, or colonization.

chattel slavery A type of slavery in which the bonded individual has the social and sometimes legal status of a unit of property and therefore no formal rights or privileges in law.

city-state A politically sovereign urban center with adjacent agricultural land.

clan A type of social organization in which a group of people claim shared identity as descendants of a single, usually distant ancestor. Clan organization is common among pastoral nomadic societies.

clergy In Christianity, people ordained for religious vocations, as distinguished from ordinary worshipers.

codex A set of pages of parchment or other material stacked together and bound along one edge or, alternatively, a continuous strip of material folded accordion-style to form pages; a codex is to be distinguished from a scroll.

Cold War The state of antagonism, distrust, and rivalry that existed between the United States and the Soviet Union and their respective allies from the end of World War II to the late 1980s.

collaborationist A government, a group, or an individual who cooperates with foreign enemies, usually an occupying power.

collective learning The process whereby humans accumulate and share complex knowledge and transmit it from one generation to the next.

Columbian Exchange The transfer of living organisms, including plants, animals, microorganisms, and humans, between Afroeurasia and the Americas starting in 1492.

commercial diaspora Merchants who share cultural identity but who live among alien communities to operate networks of trade.

communism A dimension of socialist thought that advocates revolution to eradicate capitalism and establish the universal triumph of the proletariat.

complex society A type of society, also called a ªcivilization,º possessing most of the following features: dense population, an agricultural economy, cities, a complex social hierarchy, complex occupational specialization, a centralized state, monumental building, a writing system, and a dominant belief system.

constitutional monarchy A type of government in which a monarch, usually a member of a family that enjoys hereditary succession, serves as head of state. Under the terms of a constitution or body of laws, however, the monarch surrenders part or all of his or her

governing power to a legislature and a judiciary.

consumerism Social and cultural values and practices centered on the continuous accumulation and consumption of material goods.

corvée labor Unpaid labor required by a ruler, an estate lord, or another authority, usually for road work or other construction.

cosmopolitan Characteristic of a place where people of diverse origins come together or of an individual who travels widely.

coup d'état The sudden overthrow of an existing government by a small group. A ªstroke of stateº in French.

creole A person of African or European descent born in the Americas.

D

debt peon A laborer, usually on a farm or plantation, who works under obligation to repay a loan.

deindustrialization An economic process in which a state or region loses at least part of the capability it previously had to manufacture goods, especially owing to foreign competition or intervention.

demographic transition The stabilization of population level in a society resulting from the decline of both fertility rates and death rates.

deurbanization A social process in which cities in a particular region decline or disappear.

dynasty A sequence of rulers from a single family.

E

ecosystem A biological system in which living organismsÐ plants, animals, microorganisms, humansÐ interact with one another and with nonliving elements such as air, sunlight, soil, and water.

El Niño Southern Oscillation (ENSO) A warming of ocean surface temperatures that occurs about every five years in the equatorial Pacific Ocean. An El Niño episode produces unusual, sometimes extreme weather in various parts of the world. A Pacific cooling cycle is called La Niña.

embargo A legal restriction or prohibition imposed on trade.

empire A type of state in which a single political authority, often identified with a particular kinship, linguistic, or ethnic group, rules over peoples of different ethnic or linguistic identities.

encomienda A grant from the Spanish crown to its conquistadors or other Spanish settlers in the Americas, giving them the rights to the labor services and tribute payments of the indigenous people in a particular area.

energy revolution The massive increase of useful heat energy made available to humans by extracting and burning fossil fuels.

entrepôt A port or other urban center where merchants of different origins exchange goods and ship them onward.

equal-field system The Chinese system for state distribution of land; the state assigned fixed acreages of crop land to families on the basis of labor, both adult males and animals, available to work it.

eunuch A castrated male who typically served as a functionary in a royal court, especially as an attendant in the female quarters (harem).

evangelism The practice of propagating the Christian gospel by preaching, personal witnessing, and missionary work.

F

fascism A political ideology that advocates authoritarian leadership, intense national loyalty, cultural renewal, and rejection of both liberal democracy and socialism.

feudalism A hierarchical system of social and political organization in which an individual gives grants of land to other individuals in return for allegiance and service.

fief An estate of land an individual holds on condition of allegiance and service to the grantor.

filial piety The quality in children of showing respect and care for their parents and all ancestors.

fisc The treasury of a sovereign state; a state department concerned with financial matters; also fiscal.

flagellants In Christian Europe in the thirteenth and fourteenth centuries, individuals who whipped, or flagellated, themselves as an act of public penance for sin.

Fordism A system of technology and organization, named after Henry Ford, that aims both to produce goods at minimal cost through standardization and mass production and to pay wage workers rates that allow them to consume the products they make.

fossil fuels Hydrocarbon deposits, especially coal, crude oil, and natural gas, derived from the remains of once-living plant and animal organisms; these deposits are burned to produce heat energy.

free trade An economic doctrine contending that trade among states should be unrestricted, principally by lowering or eliminating tariffs or duties on imported goods; factors of supply and demand should mainly determine price.

freeholders Farmers who own the land they cultivate.

G

galleon A large, multidecked sailing vessel used for both war and commerce from the sixteenth to the eighteenth century.

genocide The premeditated, purposeful killing of large numbers of members of a particular national, racial, ethnic, or religious group.

geoglyph An image, a character, or a set of lines imprinted on a landscape, usually on a large scale, by moving rocks or soil or by cutting into the ground surface.

globalization The process by which peoples around the world have become increasingly interconnected through rapid communication and transport, resulting in both general acceleration of change and endeavors to strengthen the bonds of local community and identity.

glyph A graphic figure or character that conveys information, often a symbol carved or incised in relief.

Great Arid Zone The belt of arid and semiarid land that extends across Afroeurasia from the Sahara Desert in the west to the Gobi Desert in the east. It has been home both to pastoral nomadic communities and to farming societies where sufficient water is available.

Green Revolution Acceleration of world agricultural production, especially from the 1960s, resulting from use of high-yielding varieties of food crops, synthetic fertilizers, pesticides, and expanded irrigation systems.

H

Hellenistic Relating to the interaction between Greek language and culture and the languages and cultural forms of peoples of Southwest Asia, the Nile valley, the western Mediterranean, and the Black Sea region.

heresy In Christianity, beliefs or practices that contradict the church's official doctrine.

hominin The primate subfamily that includes all species of the genus *Homo*. Scientists commonly use ªhominidº to refer to the family that includes both the *Homo* and the large ape species.

humanism European movement of the fourteenth to sixteenth centuries dedicated to rediscovering, investigating, and reinterpreting ancient Greek and Roman civilization.

I

ice age Any geological epoch, most recently the **Pleistocene** era (1.6 million to 12,000 years ago), when glaciers covered a large part of the world's surface.

imam In Islam in general, the individual who leads congregational worship and carries out other duties such as officiating at marriages.

import substitution industrialization (ISI) Government economic policies to encourage national industries to produce finished goods that would otherwise be imported.

indirect rule Theory and practice of colonial government favoring the appointment of local leaders as political intermediaries between the colonizer and the indigenous population.

industrial revolution The technological and economic processes whereby industrialization based on fossil-fuel energy, steam engines, and complex machines led to worldwide economic, social, and environmental transformations.

inflation A rise in the level of prices of goods and services over time. Rising inflation means that the purchasing power of a given unit of currency declines.

informal empire A situation in which a powerful state protects its interests in a foreign society by exerting political and economic influence but without assuming the costs of territorial control.

Inner Eurasia The interior land mass of Eurasia, whose dominant features are flat or rolling regions of grassy steppe or forest, interrupted by deserts and highland areas.

insurgency An organized, usually internal rebellion against a government or its policies, sometimes employing guerrilla or terror tactics.

interglacial A period of global warming and retreating glaciers between ice ages. Our current geological epoch, the **Holocene,** is an interglacial.

Internet A global computer network connecting smaller networks, all of which use the same set of communication formats and rules.

Isolationism The national policy or political doctrine of avoiding complex political or economic relations with foreign countries.

J

janissaries An elite infantry corps in the Ottoman Turkish state whose members were conscripted as boys from Christian families in southeastern Europe.

junta A committee or council that seizes control of a local or national government, especially following civil upheaval or revolution.

K

Keynesianism Economic theories of John Maynard Keynes that promote government monetary and financial policies aimed at increasing employment and stimulating economic growth.

khanate A state ruled by a khan; a Turkic or Mongol monarchy.

kinship The quality or state of being related by shared genealogical descent or by marriage. Kinship may also be claimed among a group of people for social or cultural reasons even though no biological relationship exists.

L

language death A process in which the number of native or fluent speakers of a particular language declines over time until no community of speakers remains.

latitude The imaginary east±west lines that circle the earth and that indicate distance in degrees north and south of the equator, which has the value of 0 degrees.

liberalism A set of economic and political doctrines advocating individual freedom, unrestricted market competition, free trade, constitutional government, and confidence in human progress; sometimes called ᵃclassical liberalism.º

lingua franca A spoken or written language that facilitates commercial or diplomatic communication across cultural frontiers.

Little Ice Age A trend of climatic cooling that affected weather conditions chiefly in the Northern Hemisphere approximately from the late thirteenth to the mid-nineteenth century.

liturgy The established forms of public worship, especially the order of services, including rituals, prayers, readings, and hymns.

longitude The imaginary north±south lines that extend between the North Pole and the South Pole and that run perpendicular to lines of latitude. By international agreement the line with a value of 0 degrees, called the Prime Meridian, passes through Greenwich, England.

M

madrasa A center of higher learning dedicated mainly to the study of Islamic religious and legal subjects.

mamluk In Muslim states, a slave or freedman having primarily military or administrative duties.

manor In medieval Europe, a landed estate; also the main house or castle on the estate.

matrilineal succession The practice of tracing descent or the transmission of property or authority primarily through female relatives.

megalith A large stone sometimes roughly carved and used to build a structure often having religious significance.

megalopolis An extensive and densely urbanized region or chain of urbanized regions.

mercantilism An economic doctrine based on the idea that the world's exploitable wealth could not expand and that a state should therefore erect barriers to keep rival states out of its circuits of trade with its colonies.

meritocracy A government or other institution in which individuals are awarded office and responsibility based on their meritÐ intelligence, talents, or educationÐ rather than merely on their social status or circumstances of birth.

Mesoamerica The region comprising southern Mexico plus the seven small Central American states.

metropole The colonizer's home country and seat of supreme imperial authority.

microlith A small blade of flaked stone used as a tool.

military slavery The personal bondage of an individual to a ruler or other authority with an obligation to provide military service.

milpa In Mesoamerica a farm plot created by cutting or burning forest and planted with maize, squash, beans, and other crops.

modernism The movement in the arts and humanities that embraces innovation and experimentation and rejects adherence to traditional forms and values.

monotheism The doctrine or belief that there is one supreme and universal deity.

monsoon winds The seasonally reversing winds that governed long-distance sailing in the Indian Ocean and China seas.

movable type printing A technology in which characters, especially alphabetic letters and punctuation, are individually carved or cast on pieces of wood, ceramic, or metal and then assembled into a text, inked, and printed on paper or other material.

mutually assured destruction (MAD) The doctrine aimed at preventing nuclear war between the United States and the Soviet Union by shared knowledge that, if either side attacked, both would suffer mass destruction.

mysticism The individual pursuit of knowledge or consciousness of spiritual truth or divine reality, through meditation, prayer, study, or ecstatic experience; also, mystical religion, teaching, or practice.

N

nation-state A sovereign territorial state whose inhabitants share, or are ideally expected to share, common language, cultural traditions, history, and aspirations for the future.

nationalism An ideology centered on the natural rights of a people or ᵃnationº to constitute a sovereign state.

natural philosophy A method of scientific and moral inquiry founded on the idea that fundamental laws governing nature, including human behavior, may be discovered through the exercise of logic, reason, or careful observation.

natural rights Universal and inherent rights of human beings bestowed by nature or divine power.

neo-Europe A region outside of Europe, predominantly in temperate latitudes, where people of European descent came to make up a large majority of the population.

neoliberalism An economic and political ideology advocating reduced government intervention in economic matters, privatization of state-owned enterprises, free trade, open markets, and deregulation of business.

neolithic era The ᵃnew stone ageº extending from about 10,000 to 4000 B.C.E. and characterized by refined stone toolmaking and the development of agriculture.

new imperialism The campaigns of colonial empire building that several European powers plus Japan and the United States undertook in the late nineteenth and early twentieth centuries against other societies, especially in Africa and Southeast Asia.

O

Oceania (also, the Island Pacific) The enormous region centered on the tropical Pacific Ocean and its islands. This definition of the region excludes Australia, though not New Zealand.

old regime The political and social system in France and other European monarchies between the sixteenth and eighteenth centuries; characterized by a rigid class hierarchy and rulers' claims to absolute authority.

oligarchy A political system in which a relatively small number of individuals or families control the government.

outsourcing The business practice of reducing costs by transferring work to outside contractors, including foreign companies.

P

paleoanthropologist A scientist concerned with the study of human evolution and the physical and behavioral characteristics of early humans and their biological ancestors.

paleolithic Meaning "old stone age," this period dates from approximately 2.5 million years ago, when hominin species first devised stone tools, to about 12,000 years ago, when humans started experimenting with agriculture.

pandemic An infectious disease that moves quickly from one region to another, affecting large numbers of people.

partition The division of a political entity into two or more separate, autonomous territories.

pastoral nomadism A type of economic and social organization in which livestock raising is the principal means of subsistence. Pastoral nomadic communities typically migrate seasonally in search of pasture and water.

pastoralism A type of economic and social organization involving the breeding and raising of domesticated hoofed animals, or livestock.

patriarch In the early Christian centuries, the title of the bishops of Rome, Constantinople, Jerusalem, Antioch, and Alexandria; in later centuries, the title of the highest official of the Greek Orthodox Church, as well as other Asian or African Christian churches.

patriarchy A society in which males dominate social, political, and cultural life.

patriotism An emotional or sentimental attachment to a place, an ethnic people, or a way of life; in modern times, the attachment is often to one's national homeland.

patron–client system A vertical social and political system in which individuals possessing relative degrees of power, wealth, or social status offer protection or economic benefits to other individuals in return for personal loyalty and services.

peasants The social and economic class of farmers or herders who hold relatively small amounts of productive land as owners, rent-paying tenants, or serfs bound to a particular estate.

phalanx A military formation in which soldiers march and fight in closely packed, disciplined ranks.

pogrom A violent attack on a minority community characterized by massacre and destruction of property; most commonly refers to assaults on Jews.

polis (plural, poleis) The ancient Greek term for a sovereign state centered on a single city; a city-state.

polytheism A belief system that incorporates multiple deities or spirits.

pope The title used from about the ninth century to designate the head of the Christian church in western and central Europe.

popular sovereignty The doctrine that the sovereignty or independence of the state is vested in the people, and that the government is responsible to the will of the citizenry.

price revolution A period of sustained inflation in Europe in the sixteenth and seventeenth centuries.

primogeniture The legal or customary right of the firstborn child, usually the firstborn male, to inherit a family's entire estate, sometimes including a noble title or office, to the exclusion of younger children.

principality A sovereign state or dependent territory, usually relatively small, ruled by a person with a noble title of high rank, for example, prince, princess, duke, or duchess.

proletariat The working class; in Marxist theory, the class that must overthrow the capitalist bourgeoisie to achieve control of the means of production.

proselytize To convert or attempt to convert an individual or group to one's religion.

protectorate A type of colonial relationship in which a foreign power takes control of the top levels of government in the colonized territory but permits it to retain formal, if largely fictional sovereignty.

pueblo A Spanish word meaning "village" or "small town." Spanish colonizers used this term to describe multistory stone or brick compounds that the Ancestral Puebloans (Anasazi) built in the American Southwest.

putting-out system A production method in which employers distributed raw materials to individuals or families, who then made finished goods, typically woolen or cotton yarn or cloth, and returned these goods to the employer for payment.

R

real wages Wages estimated in the amount of goods those wages will buy rather than in the face value of money paid.

regent An individual who administers the affairs of a state when the ruler is absent, is disabled, or has not reached adulthood.

reparations The act of making amends or giving satisfaction for an injustice or injury; payment of compensation by a defeated state for presumed damages inflicted on another state as a result of war between them.

republic A type of government in which supreme power rests with a body of citizens possessing rights to vote to approve laws and to select public officials and representatives.

Romanization The spread within the Roman empire, especially among elite classes, of a style of social and cultural life founded on practice in Roman Italy.

S

satrapy An administrative unit of the Persian empire under the authority of a satrap, or provincial governor.

scholastic theology In medieval Europe, systematic investigation of the relations between the authority of spiritual revelation and the claims of human reason; a method of disputation drawing on philosophy, particularly the works of the ancient Greek thinker Aristotle; also, scholasticism.

secular ruler In the Christian tradition, a monarch or other ruler who is not an ordained priest and does not formally represent the authority of the church; a temporal, as opposed to spiritual, leader.

self-determination The idea put forth during and after World War I that a society sharing common language, history, and cultural traditions should have the right to decide its own political future and govern its own affairs.

serfdom A system of labor in which farmers were legally bound to work for and pay fees to a particular landlord in return for protection.

service nobility A privileged governing class whose members depended entirely on the state rather than on inherited property and titles for their status and income.

shaman A man or woman who the community believes has access to supernatural forces or beings and who can appeal to the spirit world to discern the future, bring good fortune, or perform physical healing.

shari'a The body of Islamic laws and moral precepts principally the Quran and the sayings and actions of the Prophet Muhammad.

shifting agriculture A method of crop production in which a farmer clears and cultivates a plot of land until the soil loses its nutrient value, and then moves on to clear and plant a new field, allowing the first one to lie fallow and recover.

Sinification The spread within East Asia, especially among elite classes, of a style of social and cultural life founded on practice in China.

slavery The social institution in which an individual is held by law, custom, or simply coercion in servitude to another individual, a group, or the state.

social bondage A condition in which an individual or a group holds rights to a person's labor or services, whether for a limited period or for a lifetime. Social bondage may take a variety of forms, including slavery, serfdom, or indentured servitude.

socialism A variety of ideologies that advocate social equality and justice and the community's collective control and management of economic institutions; in Marxist thought, socialism follows capitalism in society's transition to communism.

southern seas The China seas and the Indian Ocean, including the Arabian Sea and the Bay of Bengal.

soviet Revolutionary workers' councils that served during the Russian Revolution as local units of government and civil order. The term was applied later to legislative bodies within the communist regime.

split inheritance The practice of dividing the estate of a person among different heirs.

syncretism In religion, the blending of beliefs or practices from two or more different belief systems; also the incorporation of beliefs or practices of one belief system by another.

T

tax farming A system in which a government awards the right of tax collection to a private individual or group in return for a fee or a percentage of the taxes gathered.

tectonic plates Irregular blocks of solid rock that make up the earth's lithosphere and that constantly shift and change shape.

terra preta A type of nutritionally rich soil that farmers of Amazonia produced by mixing charcoal, organic matter, and pottery shards. Literally, ª black earthº i n Portuguese.

three estates The principal social classes or orders constituting societies in premodern Europe: the Roman Catholic clergy, the titled nobility, and everyone else.

tribute Wealth in money or material goods paid by one group to another, often a conquered group to its conquerors, as an obligation of submission or allegiance.

total war Warfare, especially characteristic of World Wars I and II, in which the opposing states mobilize their civilian populations and all available resources to achieve victory; also a wartime policy intended to damage or destroy both the enemy's military forces and its economic infrastructure and social fabric.

totalitarianism A political ideology and governing policies that mandate strong central control and regulation of both public and private thought and behavior.

transnational organization An association of individual citizens or private groups that collaborates across national frontiers to carry out particular activities or programs.

treaty ports Sea or river ports in China where, as a consequence of diplomatic and military pressure, foreigners gained special privileges to engage in trade and enjoy exemptions from Chinese laws and courts.

tribe The largest social group in a region whose members claim shared descent.

U

ulama Muslim religious scholars, judges, teachers, and mosque officials.

universal empire A multiethnic state whose ruler claims a right to authority over all of humankind.

universalist religion A religion whose doctrines and practices aim to appeal to all people irrespective of their language, ethnicity, social class, or political affiliation.

V

vassal An individual who is subordinate to or dependent on another individual; in feudalism, an individual who holds land given by a lord in return for loyal service.

vernacular language The native language commonly spoken by ordinary people in a region.

viceroy An official appointed by a monarch to govern a colonial dependency as the sovereign's representative. *Vice* is a Latin prefix meaning ª in place ofº a nd *roy* means king. The territory administered by a viceroy is called a viceroyalty.

W

welfare state An approach to government in which the state uses public funds to protect and promote the health and social well-being of all citizens.

Recommended Reading

General Works on World History

Jerry H. Bentley. *Old World Encounters: Cross-Cultural Contacts and Exchanges in Pre-Modern Times.* New York: Oxford University Press, 1993.

Jerry H. Bentley, ed. *The Oxford Handbook of World History.* New York: Oxford University Press, 2011.

Jerry H. Bentley, Renate Bridenthal, and Anand A. Yang, eds. *Interactions: Transregional Perspectives on World History.* Honolulu: University of Hawai'i Press, 2005.

J. M. Blaut. *The Colonizer's Model of the World: Geographical Diffusionism and Eurocentric History.* New York: Guilford Press, 1993.

Cynthia Stokes Brown. *Big History: From the Big Bang to the Present.* New York: New Press, 2007.

Edmund Burke III, David Christian, and Ross E. Dunn. *World History: The Big Eras, A Compact History of Humankind for Teachers and Students.* Los Angeles: National Center for History in the Schools, 2012.

Tertius Chandler. *Four Thousand Years of Urban Growth: An Historical Census.* Lewiston/Queenston, ON: St. David's University Press, 1987.

David Christian. *Maps of Time: An Introduction to Big History.* Berkeley: University of California Press, 2004.

David Christian. *This Fleeting World: A Short History of Humanity.* Great Barrington, VT: Berkshire Publishing, 2007.

Pamela Kyle Crossley. *What Is Global History?* Malden, MA: Polity, 2008.

Ross E. Dunn, ed. *The New World History: A Teacher's Companion.* Boston: Bedford St. Martin's, 2000.

Marnie Hughes-Warrington, ed. *World Histories.* New York: Palgrave Macmillan, 2005.

Neil MacGregor. *A History of the World in 100 Objects.* New York: Viking, 2011.

Angus Maddison. *The World Economy: A Millennial Perspective.* Paris: Organization for Economic Co-operation and Development, 2001.

Patrick Manning. *Navigating World History: Historians Create a Global Past.* New York: Palgrave Macmillan, 2003.

John R. McNeill and William H. McNeill. *The Human Web: A Bird's-Eye View of World History.* New York: Norton, 2003.

William H. McNeill. *The Rise of the West: A History of the Human Community; with a Retrospective Essay.* Chicago: University of Chicago Press, 1992.

Douglas Northrup, ed. *A Companion to World History.* Hoboken, NJ: Wiley-Blackwell, 2012.

Chapter 15. Calamities and Recoveries across Afroeurasia

John Aberth. *The First Horseman: Disease in Human History.* Upper Saddle River, NJ: Pearson Prentice Hall, 2007.

Timothy Brook. *The Troubled Empire: China in the Yuan and Ming Dynasties.* Cambridge, MA: Belknap Press of Harvard University Press, 2010.

Peter Burke, *The Renaissance,* 2nd ed. New York: St. Martin's Press, 1997.

Norman F. Cantor. *In the Wake of the Plague: The Black Death and the World It Made.* New York: Free Press, 2001.

Kenneth Chase. *Firearms: A Global History to 1700.* New York: Cambridge, 2003.

Samuel K. Cohn, Jr. *The Black Death Transformed: Disease and Culture in Early Renaissance Europe.* London: Arnold, 2002.

John W. Dardess. *Ming China, 1368±1644: A Concise History of a Resilient Empire.* Lanham, MD: Rowman & Littlefield, 2012.

Brian Fagan. *The Little Ice Age: How Climate Made History, 1300±1850.* New York: Basic Books, 2000.

George Holmes. *Europe: Hierarchy and Revolt, 1320±1450,* 2nd ed. Medford, MA: Blackwell, 2000.

Lisa Jardine. *Worldly Goods: A New History of the Renaissance.* New York: Norton, 1996.

William Chester Jordan. *The Great Famine: Northern Europe in the Early Fourteenth Century.* Princeton, NJ: Princeton University Press, 1996.

H. H. Lamb. *Climate, History and the Modern World,* 2nd ed. New York: Routledge, 1995.

Heath W. Lowry. *The Nature of the Early Ottoman State.* Albany: State University of New York Press, 2003.

Beatrice Forbes Manz. *The Rise and Rule of Tamerlane.* Cambridge: Cambridge University Press, 1989.

D. R. SarDesai. *India: The Definitive History.* Boulder, CO: Westview Press, 2008.

Chapter 16. Oceans Crossed, Worlds Connected

Leonard Y. Andaya. *Leaves of the Same Tree: Trade and Ethnicity in the Straits of Melaka.* Honolulu: University of Hawai'i Press, 2008.

Giancarlo Casale. *The Ottoman Age of Exploration.* New York: Oxford University Press, 2010.

Noble David Cook. *Born to Die: Disease and New World Conquest, 1492±1650.* New York: Cambridge University Press, 1998.

Alfred W. Crosby. *The Columbian Exchange: Biological and Cultural Consequences of 1492.* Westport, CT: Greenwood Press, 1972.

Jared Diamond. *Guns, Germs, and Steel: The Fates of Human Societies.* New York: Norton, 2005.

Felipe Fernández-Armesto. *Before Columbus: Exploration and Colonization from the Mediterranean to the Atlantic, 1229±1492.* Philadelphia: University of Pennsylvania Press, 1987.

Charles C. Mann. *1493: Uncovering the New World Columbus Created.* New York: Alfred A. Knopf, 2011.

Michael Pearson. *The Indian Ocean.* New York: Routledge, 2003.

William D. Phillips, Jr., and Carla Rahn Phillips. *The Worlds of Christopher Columbus.* New York: Cambridge University Press, 1992.

Kenneth Pomeranz and Steven Topik, eds. *The World That Trade Created: Society, Culture, and the World Economy, 1400 to the Present,* 3rd ed. Armonk, NY: M. E. Sharpe, 2013.

Matthew Restall. *Seven Myths of the Spanish Conquest.* New York: Oxford University Press, 2003.

Matthew Restall and Felipe Fernández-Armesto. *The Conquistadors: A Very Short Introduction.* New York: Oxford University Press, 2012.

A. J. R. Russell-Wood. *The Portuguese Empire, 1415±1808: A World on the Move*. Baltimore: Johns Hopkins University Press, 1998.

Sanjay Subrahmanyam. *The Portuguese Empire in Asia*. New York: Longman, 1993.

John. K. Thornton. *Africa and Africans in the Making of the Atlantic World, 1400±1800*, 2nd ed. New York: Cambridge University Press, 1998.

James D. Tracy, ed. *The Rise of Merchant Empires: Long-Distance Trade in the Early Modern World, 1350±1750*. Cambridge: Cambridge University Press, 1990.

Chapter 17. Afroeurasia and Its Powerful States

Jeremy Black. *War in the Early Modern World*. Boulder, CO: Westview Press, 1999.

Fernand Braudel. *Civilization and Capitalism, 15th±18th Century*. New York: Harper & Row, 1981±84.

Kenneth Chase. *Firearms: A Global History to 1700*. Cambridge: Cambridge University Press, 2003.

Stephen Frederic Dale. *The Muslim Empires of the Ottomans, Safavids, and Mughals*. New York: Cambridge University Press, 2010.

Natalie Zemon Davis. *Trickster Travels: A Sixteenth-Century Muslim between Worlds*. New York: Hill and Wang, 2006.

David Eltis. *The Military Revolution in Sixteenth-Century Europe*. New York: I. B. Tauris, 1995.

Jack A. Goldstone. *Revolution and Rebellion in the Early Modern World*. Berkeley: University of California Press, 1991.

Victor Lieberman. *Strange Parallels: Southeast Asia in Global Context, c 800±1830*. New York: Cambridge University Press, 2003.

William H. McNeill. *The Pursuit of Power: Technology, Armed Force, and Society since A.D. 1000*. Chicago: University of Chicago Press, 1982.

Harbans Mukhia. *The Mughals of India*. Malden, MA: Blackwell, 2004.

Geoffrey Parker. *Europe in Crisis, 1598±1648*, 2nd ed. Malden, MA: Blackwell, 2001.

Richard L. Smith. *Almad al-Mansur: Islamic Visionary*. New York: Pearson, 2006.

James D. Tracy. *Europe's Reformation, 1450±1650*. Lanham, MD: Rowman & Littlefield, 1999.

Merry E. Wiesner-Hanks. *Early Modern Europe, 1450±1789*. New York: Cambridge, 2006.

Merry E. Wiesner-Hanks. *Religious Transformations in the Early Modern World: A Brief History with Documents*. Boston: Bedford St. Martin's, 2009.

Chapter 18. The Expanding Global Economy: Expectations and Inequalities

Timothy Brook. *Vermeer's Hat: The Seventeenth Century and the Dawn of the Global World*. New York: Bloomsbury Press, 2008.

Alfred W. Crosby. *Ecological Imperialism: The Biological Expansion of Europe, 900±1900*, 2nd ed. New York: Cambridge University Press, 2004.

Philip D. Curtin. *The Rise and Fall of the Plantation Complex: Essays in Atlantic History*, 2nd ed. Cambridge: Cambridge University Press, 1998.

Jan De Vries. *Economy of Europe in an Age of Crisis, 1600±1750*. New York: Cambridge University Press, 1976.

Dennis O. Flynn and Arturo Giráldez, eds. *Metals and Monies in an Emerging Global Economy*. Aldershot: Variorum, 1997.

Andre Gunder Frank. *ReOrient: Global Economy in the Asian Age*. Berkeley: University of California Press, 1998.

Trevor R. Getz and Liz Clarke. *Abina and the Important Men: A Graphic History*. New York: Oxford University Press, 2011.

Jack P. Greene and Philip D. Morgan, eds. *Atlantic History: A Critical Reappraisal*. New York: Oxford University Press, 2009.

Karen Ordahl Kupperman. *The Atlantic in World History*. New York: Oxford University Press, 2012.

Patrick Manning. *The African Diaspora: A History through Culture*. New York: Columbia University Press, 2009.

Patrick Manning. *Slavery and African Life: Occidental, Oriental, and African Slave Trades*. New York: Cambridge University Press, 1990.

Kenneth Pomeranz. *The Great Divergence: China, Europe, and the Making of the Modern World Economy*. Princeton, NJ: Princeton University Press, 2000.

Marcus Rediker. *The Slave Ship: A Human History*. New York: Viking, 2007.

John F. Richards. *The Unending Frontier: An Environmental History of the Early Modern World*. Berkeley: University of California Press, 2003.

Stuart B. Schwartz, ed. *In Tropical Babylons: Sugar and the Making of the Atlantic World, 1450±1680*. Chapel Hill: University of North Carolina Press, 2004.

James Sweet. *Domingos Álvarez, African Healing, and the Intellectual History of the Atlantic World*. Chapel Hill: University of North Carolina Press, 2011.

John K. Thornton. *A Cultural History of the Atlantic World, 1250±1820*. Cambridge: Cambridge University Press, 2012.

Chapter 19. The Changing Balance of Wealth and Power

William Beik. *Louis XIV and Absolutism: A Brief History with Documents*. Boston: Bedford St. Martin's, 2000.

Jane Burbank and Frederick Cooper. *Empires in World History: Power and the Politics of Difference*. Princeton, NJ: Princeton University Press, 2010.

Luke Clossey. *Salvation and Globalization in the Early Jesuit Missions*. New York: Cambridge University Press, 2008.

Pamela Kyle Crossley. *The Manchus*. Malden, MA: Blackwell, 2002.

Richard Maxwell Eaton. *The Rise of Islam and the Bengal Frontier, 1204±1760*. Berkeley: University of California Press, 1993.

J. H. Elliott. *Empires of the Atlantic World: Britain and Spain in America, 1492±1830*. New Haven, CT: Yale University Press, 2006.

Richard Elphick. *Kraal and Castle: Khoikhoi and the founding of White South Africa*. New Haven, CT: Yale University Press, 1977.

John Henry. *The Scientific Revolution and the Origins of Modern Science*, 3rd ed. New York: Palgrave Macmillan, 2008.

David Igler. *The Great Ocean: Pacific Worlds from Captain Cook to the Gold Rush*. Oxford: Oxford University Press, 2013.

Margaret C. C. Jacob. *The Scientific Revolution: A Brief History with Documents*. Boston: Bedford St. Martin's Press, 2009.

Daniel R. Mandell. *King Philip's War: Colonial Expansion, Native Resistance, and the End of Indian Sovereignty*. Baltimore: Johns Hopkins University Press, 2010.

Peter C. Perdue. *China Marches West: The Qing Conquest of Central Eurasia*. Cambridge, MA: Belknap Press of Harvard University Press, 2005.

George Saliba. *Islamic Science and the Making of the European Renaissance*. Cambridge, MA: MIT Press, 2011.

Yuri Slezkine. *Arctic Mirrors: Russia and the Small Peoples of the North.* Ithaca, NY: Cornell University Press, 1994.

Alan Taylor. *American Colonies.* New York: Viking, 2001.

John K. Thornton. *The Kongolese Saint Anthony: Dona Beatriz Kimpa Vita and the Antonian Movement, 1684±1706.* New York: Cambridge University Press, 1998.

Kerry Ward. *Networks of Empire: Forced Migration in the Dutch East India Company.* Cambridge: Cambridge University Press, 2009.

Chapter 20. Waves of Revolution

Benedict Anderson. *Imagined Communities: Reflections on the Origin and Spread of Nationalism.* New York: Verso, 1991.

Nigel Aston. *The French Revolution, 1789±1804: Authority, Liberty and the Search for Stability.* New York: Palgrave Macmillan, 2004.

Daniel A. Baugh. *The Global Seven Years War, 1754±1763: Britain and France in a Great Power Contest.* New York: Longman, 2011.

C. A. Bayly. *The Birth of the Modern World, 1780±1914.* Malden, MA: Blackwell, 2004.

Thomas Bender. *A Nation among Nations: America's Place in World History.* New York: Hill and Wang, 2006.

Jack R. Censer and Lynn Hunt. *Liberty, Equality, Fraternity: The French Revolution.* University Park: Pennsylvania State University Press, 2001.

John Charles Chasteen. *Americanos: Latin America's Struggle for Independence.* New York: Oxford University Press, 2008.

Laurent Dubois. *Avengers of the New World: The Story of the Haitian Revolution.* Cambridge, MA: Belknap Press of Harvard University Press, 2004.

Susan Dunn. *Sister Revolutions: French Lightning, American Light.* New York: Faber and Faber, 1999.

Geoffrey Ellis. *The Napoleonic Empire.* New York: Palgrave Macmillan, 2003.

David Patrick Geggus. *Haitian Revolutionary Studies.* Bloomington: Indiana University Press, 2002.

Eric J. Hobsbawm. *The Age of Revolution, 1789±1848.* New York: Vintage, 1996.

Gary B. Nash. *The Unknown American Revolution: The Unruly Birth of Democracy and the Struggle to Create America.* New York: Viking, 2005.

Simon Schama. *Citizens: A Chronicle of the French Revolution.* New York: Alfred A. Knopf, 1989.

James D. Tracy, ed. *The Rise of Merchant Empires: Long-Distance Trade in the Early Modern World, 1, 350±1750.* Cambridge: Cambridge University Press, 1990.

Chapter 21. Energy and Industrialization

John Bezis-Selfa. *Forging America: Ironworkers, Adventurers, and the Industrial Revolution.* Ithaca, NY: Cornell University Press, 2003.

Alfred W. Crosby. *Children of the Sun: A History of Humanity's Unappeasable Appetite for Energy.* New York: Norton, 2006.

Harry Gregor Gelber. *Opium, Soldiers and Evangelicals: Britain's 1840±42 War with China, and Its Aftermath.* New York: Palgrave Macmillan, 2004.

Jack Goldstone. *Why Europe? The Rise of the West in World History, 1500±1850.* New York: McGraw-Hill, 2009.

Eric J. Hobsbawm. *Industry and Empire: The Birth of the Industrial Revolution,* new ed. New York: New Press, 1999.

J. E. Inikori. *Africans and the Industrial Revolution in England: A Study in International Trade and Economic Development.* New York: Cambridge University Press, 2002.

Margaret C. Jacob. *Scientific Culture and the Making of the Industrial West.* Oxford: Oxford University Press, 1997.

Penelope Lane, Neil Raven, and K. D. M. Snell, eds. *Women, Work and Wages in England, 1600±1850.* Rochester, NY: Boydell Press, 2004.

Robert B. Marks. *The Origins of the Modern World: A Global and Ecological Narrative from the Fifteenth to the Twenty-first Century,* 2nd ed. Lanham, MD: Rowman & Littlefield, 2007.

Sidney W. Mintz. *Sweetness and Power: The Place of Sugar in Modern History.* New York: Penguin, 1985.

Joel Mokyr. *The Gifts of Athena: Historical Origins of the Knowledge Economy.* Princeton, NJ: Princeton, University Press, 2002.

Ian Morris. *Why the West RulesÐ for Now: The Patterns of History, and What They Reveal about the Future.* New York: Farrar, Straus & Giroux, 2010.

Giorgio Riello. *Cotton: The Fabric That Made the Modern World.* New York: Cambridge University Press, 2013.

Vaclav Smil. *Energy in World History.* Boulder, CO: Westview Press, 1994.

Dava Sobel. *Longitude: The True Story of a Lone Genius Who Solved the Greatest Scientific Problem of His Time.* New York: Penguin Books, 1995.

Peter N. Stearns. *The Industrial Revolution in World History,* 2nd ed. Boulder, CO: Westview Press, 1998.

Chapter 22. Coping with Change in the New Industrial Era

Joyce Appleby. *The Relentless Revolution: A History of Capitalism.* New York: Norton, 2010.

Jeffrey Auerbach and Peter H. Hoffenberg, eds. *Britain, the Empire and the World at the Great Exhibition of 1851.* Burlington, VT: Ashgate, 2008.

Sven Beckert. *The Empire of Cotton.* New York: Macmillan, 2007.

John Charles Chasteen. *Born in Blood and Fire: A Concise History of Latin America.* New York: Norton, 2001.

Emma Christopher, Cassandra Pybus, and Marcus Rediker, eds. *Many Middle Passages: Forced Migration and the Making of the Modern World.* Berkeley: University of California Press, 2007.

Carter V. Findley. *Turkey, Islam, Nationalism, and Modernity: A History, 1789±2007.* New Haven, CT: Yale University Press, 2010.

Steven R. Fischer. *A History of the Pacific Islands.* New York: Palgrave, 2002.

Mervyn Hiskett. *The Sword of Truth: The Life and Times of the Shehu Usuman dan Fodio.* New York: Oxford University Press, 1973.

Adam Hochschild. *Bury the Chains: Prophets and Rebels in the Fight to Free an Empire's Slaves.* Boston: Houghton Mifflin, 2005.

Dirk Hoerder. *Cultures in Contact: World Migrations in the Second Millennium.* Durham, NC: Duke University Press, 2002.

Howard N. Lupovitch. *Jews and Judaism in World History.* New York: Routledge, 2010.

James M. McPherson. *Battle Cry of Freedom: The Civil War Era.* New York: Oxford University Press, 1988.

Jonathan D. Spence. *God's Chinese Son: The Taiping Heavenly Kingdom of Hong Xiuquan.* New York: Norton, 1996.

Jonathan Sperber. *The European Revolutions, 1848±1851,* 2nd ed. New York: Cambridge University Press, 2005.

Peter N. Stearns and Herrick Chapman. *European Society in Upheaval: Social History since 1750,* 3rd ed. New York: Prentice Hall, 1992.

Barbara Taylor. *Eve and the New Jerusalem: Socialism and Feminism in the Nineteenth Century.* New York: Pantheon Books, 1983.

Steven Topik, Carlos Marichal, and Zephry Frank, eds. *From Silver to Cocaine: Latin American Commodity Chains and the Building of the World Economy, 1500±2000.* Durham, NC: Duke University Press, 2006.

Chapter 23. Capital, Technology, and the Changing Balance of Global Power

A. Adu Boahen. *African Perspectives on Colonialism.* Baltimore: Johns Hopkins University Press, 1989.

Edmund Burke III. *Prelude to Protectorate in Morocco: Precolonial Protest and Resistance, 1860±1912.* Chicago: University of Chicago Press, 1976.

Philip D. Curtin. *Death by Migration: Europe's Encounters with the Tropical World in the Nineteenth Century.* New York: Cambridge University Press, 1989.

Philip D. Curtin. *The World and the West: The European Challenge and the Overseas Response in the Age of Empire.* New York: Cambridge University Press, 2000.

Dennis O. Flynn, Lionel Frost, and A. J. H. Latham. *Pacific Centuries: Pacific and Pacific Rim History since the Sixteenth Century.* New York: Routledge, 1999.

Daniel R. Headrick. *The Tools of Empire: Technology and European Imperialism in the Nineteenth Century.* New York: Oxford University Press, 1981.

Eric Hobsbawm. *The Age of Empire, 1875±1914.* New York: Vintage Books, 1989.

Adam Hochschild. *King Leopold's Ghost: A Story of Greed, Terror and Heroism in Colonial Africa.* Boston: Houghton Mifflin, 1999.

Peter J. Hugill. *Global Communications since 1844: Geopolitics and Technology.* Baltimore: Johns Hopkins University Press, 1999.

Marius B. Jansen. *The Making of Modern Japan.* Cambridge, MA: Belknap Press of Harvard University Press, 2002.

Harold G. Marcus. *The Life and Times of Menelik II: Ethiopia, 1844±1913.* Lawrence, NJ: Red Sea Press, 1995.

David A. Northrup. *Indentured Labor in the Age of Imperialism, 1838±1914.* New York: Cambridge University Press, 1995.

Timothy Parsons. *The British Imperial Century, 1815±1914: A World History Perspective.* Lanham, MD: Rowman & Littlefield, 1999.

Emily S. Rosenberg, ed. *A World Connecting, 1870±1945.* Cambridge, MA: Harvard University Press, 2012.

Nicholas Tarling. *Imperialism in Southeast Asia: ªA Fleeting, Passing Phase.º* New York: Routledge, 2001.

Theodore R. Weeks. *Across the Revolutionary Divide: Russia and the USSR, 1861±1945.* Malden, MA: Wiley-Blackwell, 2011.

H. L. Wesseling. *The European Colonial Empires, 1815±1919.* New York, Pearson/Longman, 2004.

Chapter 24. Innovation, Revolution, and Global Crisis

John M. Barry. *The Great Influenza: The Epic Story of the Deadliest Plague in History.* New York: Viking, 2004.

Ian F. W. Beckett. *The Great War, 1914±1918,* 2nd ed. New York: Pearson Longman, 2007.

Myron Echenberg. *Plague Ports: The Global Urban Impact of Bubonic Plague, 1894±1901.* New York: New York University Press, 2007.

Daniel R. Headrick. *The Tentacles of Progress: Technology Transfer in the Age of Imperialism, 1860±1940.* Oxford: Oxford University Press, 1988.

Peter J. Hugill. *Global Communications since 1844: Geopolitics and Technology.* Baltimore: Johns Hopkins University Press, 1999.

Nikki R. Keddie. *Modern Iran: Roots and Results of Revolution.* New Haven, CT: Yale University Press, 2006.

John Keegan. *The First World War.* New York: Alfred A. Knopf, 1999.

Alan Knight. *The Mexican Revolution.* Cambridge: Cambridge University Press, 1986.

John H. Morrow. *The Great War: An Imperial History.* New York: Routledge, 2004.

Michael S. Nieberg. *Fighting the Great War: A Global History.* Cambridge, MA: Harvard University Press, 2006.

Richard Pipes. *A Concise History of the Russian Revolution.* New York: Alfred A. Knopf, 1995.

Hew Strachan. *The First World War in Africa.* New York: Oxford University Press, 2004.

Robert Strayer. *The Communist Experiment: Revolution, Socialism, and Global Conflict in the Twentieth Century.* New York: McGraw-Hill, 2007.

Peter Zarrow. *China in War and Revolution, 1895±1949.* New York: Routledge, 2005.

Chapter 25. Turbulent Decades

A. Adu Boahen. *African Perspectives on Colonialism.* Baltimore: Johns Hopkins University Press, 1987.

Richard Evans. *The Coming of the Third Reich.* New York: Penguin Books, 2005.

Jeffry A. Frieden. *Global Capitalism: Its Rise and Fall in the Twentieth Century.* New York: Norton, 2006.

Daniel R. Headrick. *The Invisible Weapon: Telecommunications and International Politics, 1851±1945.* New York: Oxford University Press, 1991.

Richard L. Johnson, ed. *Gandhi's Experiments with Truth: Essential Writings by and about Mahatma Gandhi.* Lanham, MD: Lexington Books, 2006.

Ian Kershaw. *Hitler.* New York: Longman, 2001.

Pericles Lewis. *The Cambridge Introduction to Modernism.* New York: Cambridge University Press, 2007.

David Lindley. *Uncertainty: Einstein, Heisenberg, Bohr, and the Struggle for the Soul of Science.* New York: Doubleday, 2007.

Erez Manela. *The Wilsonian Moment: Self-Determination and the International Origins of Anticolonial Nationalism.* Oxford: Oxford University Press, 2007.

Mark Mazower. *Dark Continent: Europe's Twentieth Century.* New York: Viking, 2000.

Michael S. Nieberg. *Fighting the Great War: A Global History.* Cambridge, MA: Harvard University Press, 2005.

Robert Paxton. *The Anatomy of Fascism.* New York: Alfred A. Knopf, 2004.

C. R. Pennell. *A Country with a Government and a Flag: The Rif War in Morocco, 1921±1926.* Boulder, CO: Middle East and North African Studies Press, 1986.

Dietmar Rothermund. *The Global Impact of the Great Depression, 1929±1939.* New York: Routledge, 1996.

Thomas E. Skidmore, Peter H. Smith, and James N. Green. *Modern Latin America,* 7th ed. New York: Oxford University Press, 2010.

Chapter 26. World War II and Its Aftermath

Franz Ansprenger. *The Dissolution of the Colonial Empires.* London: Routledge, 1989.

Christopher Bayly and Tim Harper. *Forgotten Armies: The Fall of British Asia, 1941±1945.* Cambridge: Cambridge University Press, 2005.

Martha Byrd. *A World in Flames: A Concise History of World War II.* Tuscaloosa: University of Alabama Press, 2007.

Richard Evans. *The Third Reich at War.* New York: Penguin Press, 2009.

Richard Evans. *The Third Reich in Power, 1933±1939.* New York: Penguin Press, 2005.

John Lewis Gaddis. *The Cold War: A New History.* New York: Penguin Books, 2007.

John Keegan. *The Second World War.* New York: Penguin, 2005.

Peter Longerich. *Holocaust: The Nazi Persecution and Murder of the Jews.* New York: Oxford University Press, 2010.

Mark Mazower. *Hitler's Empire: How the Nazis Ruled Europe.* New York: Penguin Press, 2008.

William Murray and Allan R. Millett. *A War to Be Won: Fighting the Second World War.* Cambridge, MA: Harvard University Press, 2000.

Andrew Roberts. *The Storm of War: A New History of the Second World War.* New York: Harper, 2011.

Martin Shipway. *Decolonization and Its Impact: A Comparative Approach to the End of Colonial Empires.* Malden, MA: Blackwell, 2008.

Charles D. Smith. *Palestine and the Arab-Israeli Conflict: A History with Documents,* 7th ed. Boston: Bedford St. Martin's, 2010.

Anders Stephanson, *Manifest Destiny: American Expansion and the Empire of Right.* New York: Hill and Wang, 1996.

Jill Stephenson. *Women in Nazi Germany.* New York: Longman, 2001.

Chapter 27. The Global Boom and Its Contradictions

Michael Adas, ed. *Essays on Twentieth-Century History.* Philadelphia: Temple University Press, 2010.

David Birmingham. *The Decolonization of Africa.* Athens: Ohio University Press, 1995.

Matthew Connelly. *A Diplomatic Revolution: Algeria's Fight for Independence and the Origins of the Post-Cold War World.* New York: Oxford University Press, 2002.

Gerard J. De Groot. *The Sixties Unplugged: A Kaleidoscopic History of a Disorderly Decade.* Cambridge, MA: Harvard University Press, 2008.

Eric Hobsbawm. *The Age of Extremes: A History of the World, 1914±1991.* New York: Pantheon Books, 1995.

Tony Judt. *Postwar: A History of Europe since 1945.* New York: Penguin Books, 2005.

Walter LaFeber. *America, Russia, and the Cold War, 1945±2006,* 10th ed. Boston: McGraw-Hill, 2008.

Mark Atwood Lawrence. *The Vietnam War: A Concise International History.* New York: Oxford University Press, 2008.

John R. McNeill. *Something New under the Sun: An Environmental History of the Twentieth Century.* New York: Norton, 2000.

David Reynolds. *One World Divisible. A Global History since 1945.* New York: Norton, 2000.

Edward Roux. *Time Longer Than Rope: A History of the Black Man's Struggle for Freedom in South Africa.* Madison: University of Wisconsin Press, 1964.

Bonnie G. Smith, ed. *Global Feminisms since 1945.* New York: Routledge, 2000.

John Springhall. *Decolonization since 1945: The Collapse of European Overseas Empires.* New York: Palgrave, 2001.

Anders Stephanson. *Manifest Destiny: American Expansionism and the Empire of the Right.* New York: Hill and Wang, 1995.

Odd Arne Westad. *The Global Cold War: Third World Intervention and the Making of Our Times.* Cambridge: Cambridge University Press, 2005.

Chapter 28. Countercurrents of Change

Daron Acemoglu and James A. Robinson. *Why Nations Fail: The Origins of Power, Prosperity, Poverty.* New York: Crown Business, 2012.

F. Gerard Adams. *Globalization, Today and Tomorrow.* New York: Routledge, 2011.

Andrew J. Bacevich, *The American Empire: The Realities and Consequences of U.S. Diplomacy.* New York: Holt, 2008.

John Baylis, Steve Smith, and Patricia Owens. *The Globalization of World Politics: An Introduction to International Relations,* 5th ed. New York: Oxford University Press, 2011.

Edmund Burke III and Kenneth Pomeranz. *The Environment and World History.* Berkeley: University of California Press, 2009.

Peter Calvocoressi. *World Politics since 1945,* 9th ed. New York: Pearson Longman, 2009.

Stephen Castles and Mark J. Miller. *The Age of Migration: International Population Movements in the Modern World,* 4th ed. New York: Guilford Press, 1993.

Paul E. Ceruzzi. *Computing: A Concise History.* Cambridge, MA: MIT Press, 2012.

Akira Iriye. *Global Community: The Role of International Organizations in the Making of the Contemporary World.* Berkeley: University of California Press, 2002.

Victor K. McElheny. *Drawing the Map of Life: Inside the Human Genome Project.* New York: Basic Books, 2010.

Steven Pinker. *The Better Angels of Our Nature: Why Violence Has Declined.* New York: Penguin, 2012.

Joachim Radkau. *Nature and Power: A Global History of the Environment,* trans. Thomas Dunlap. Cambridge: Cambridge University Press, 2008.

William L. Cleveland and Martin Bunton. *A History of the Modern Middle East.* 5th ed. Boulder, CO: Westview Press, 2013.

Fred Spier. *Big History and the Future of Humanity.* Malden, MA: Wiley-Blackwell, 2011.

Peter N. Stearns. *Globalization in World History.* New York: Routledge, 2010.

References

chapter 15

1. Henry S. Lucas, "The Great European Famine of 1315, 1316, and 1317," *Speculum* 5 (1930): 365±366.

2. Ibn Khaldun, *The Muqaddimah: An Introduction to History*, trans. Franz Rosenthal, 3 vols. (Princeton, NJ: Princeton University Press, 1958), 1:64.

3. Giovanna Morelli et al., "*Yersinia Pestis* Genome Sequencing Identifies Patterns of Global Phylogenetic Diversity," *Nature Genetics* 42 (Dec. 2010): 1140±1145.

4. Ewen Callaway, "Plague Genome: The Black Death Decoded," *Nature* 478 (2011). Retrieved from http://www.nature.com/news/2011/111025/full/478444a.html.

5. Michael Dols, *The Black Death in the Middle East* (Princeton, NJ: Princeton University Press, 1977), 69.

6. Giovanni Boccaccio, *Decameron*, trans. John Payne, revised and annotated by Charles S. Singleton (Berkeley: University of California Press, 1982), 1:14±15.

7. Ibn Abi Hajalah, quoted in Dols, *Black Death in the Middle East*, 238.

8. Dols, *Black Death in the Middle East*, 265.

9. *The Chronicles of Jean Froissart*, trans. Lord Berners, selected, edited, and introduced by Gillian and William Anderson (Carbondale: Southern Illinois University Press, 1963), 138.

10. F. W. Mote, *Imperial China, 900±1800* (Cambridge, MA: Harvard University Press, 1999), 744±745.

11. Sally K. Church, "Zheng He: An Investigation into the Plausibility of 450-Ft Treasure Ships," *Monumenta Serica* 53 (2005): 1±43.

12. H. A. R. Gibb, trans. and ed., *The Travels of Ibn Battuta, A.D. 1325±1354*, Vol. 4, translation completed with annotations by C. F. Beckingham (London: Hakluyt Society, 1994), 814.

13. Kritovoulos, *History of Mehmed the Conqueror*, trans. Charles T. Riggs (Princeton, NJ: Princeton University Press, 1954), 25.

14. Kritovoulos, *History of Mehmed the Conqueror*, 66±67.

chapter 16

1. Al-Umari, quoted in D. T. Niane, ed., *General History of Africa*, Vol. 4: *Africa from the Twelfth to the Sixteenth Century* (Paris: UNESCO, 1984), 664±665.

2. Tertius Chandler, *Four Thousand Years of Urban Growth: An Historical Census* (Lewiston, NY: St. David's University Press, 1987), 477.

3. Antonio Galvão, *A Treatise on the Moluccas*, quoted in Anthony Reid, *Southeast Asia in the Age of Commerce, 1450±1680* (New Haven, CT: Yale University Press, 1988), 146

4. Tomé Pires, *The Suma Oriental*, trans. Armando Cortesão, 2 vols. (London: Hakluyt Society, 1944), 2:286.

5. Tomé Pires, *Suma Oriental*, 1:41±42.

6. Duarte Barbosa, *Livro* (London: Hakluyt Society, 1918±1921), 76±77.

7. Duarte Pacheco Pereira, *Esmeraldo de Situ Orbis*, trans. and ed. George H. T. Kimble (London: Hakluyt Society, 1937), 144.

8. Pedro Cieza de Leon, *The Second Part of the Chronicle of Peru*, trans. and ed. Clements R. Markham (London: Hakluyt Society, 1883), 57.

9. Quoted in Basil Davidson, *The African Past: Chronicles from Antiquity to Modern Times* (New York: Grosset & Dunlap, 1964), 192.

10. Michele de Cuneo, quoted in Noble David Cook, *Born to Die: Disease and New World Conquest, 1492±1630* (New York: Cambridge University Press, 1998), 28.

11. Luis de Figueroa and Alonso de Santo Domingo, quoted in Cook, *Born to Die*, 61.

12. Cook, *Born to Die*, 61.

13. *The Broken Spears: The Aztec Account of the Conquest of Mexico*, edited and with an introduction and new postscript by Miguel León-Portilla, expanded and updated edition (Boston: Beacon Press, 1992), 30.

14. Quoted in Robert McCaa, "Spanish and Nahuatl Views on Smallpox and Demographic Catastrophe in Mexico," *Journal of Interdisciplinary History* 25 (1995): 428±430.

15. Bernal Díaz del Castillo, *The True History of the Conquest of New Spain*, trans. Alfred Percival Maudslay (London: Hakluyt Society, 1908), 244.

16. *Reports on the Discovery of Peru*, trans. and ed. Clements R. Markham (New York: Burt Franklin, 1872), 56.

17. Quoted in Sanjay Subrahmanyam, "The Connected Histories of the Iberian Overseas Empires, 1500±1640," *American Historical Review* 112, no. 5 (Dec. 2007): 1368.

18. Quoted in Glenn J. Ames, *Vasco da Gama: Renaissance Crusader* (New York: Pearson Longman, 2005), 74.

19. Hans Mayr, *The Voyage and Acts of Dom Francisco*, quoted in G. S. P. Freeman-Grenville, *The East African Coast: Selected Documents* (London: Rex Collings, 1974), 111±112.

20. Dom João de Castro, quoted in Subrahmanyam, "Connected Histories," 1 373.

chapter 17

1. Al-Ifrani, *Histoire de la dynastie saadienne au Maroc, 1511±1670*, trans. and ed. O. Houdas (Paris, 1886), 160±162, quoted in E. W. Bovill, *The Golden Trade of the Moors* (London: Oxford University Press, 1968), 165±166.

2. Antonio Monserrate, *The Commentary of Father Monserrate, S. J., on His Journey to the Court of Akbar*, trans. from Latin by J. S. Hoyland and annotated by S. N. Banerjee (London: Oxford University Press, 1922), 198.

3. Toyotomi Hideyoshi, *101 Letters of Hideyoshi: The Private Correspondence of Toyotomi Hideyoshi*, ed. and trans. Adriana Boscaro (Tokyo: Sophia University, 1975), 31.

4. Quoted in Edward William Bovill, *The Golden Trade of the Moors: West African Kingdoms in the Fourteenth century*, with a new introduction by Robert O. Collins (Princeton, NJ: Markus Wiener, 1995), 147±148.

5. William Eckhardt, "War-Related Deaths since 3,000 BC," *Bulletin of Peace Proposals* 22 (Dec. 1991): 437±443.

6. Weston F. Cook, *The Hundred Years War for Morocco: Gunpowder and the Military Revolution in the Early Modern Muslim World* (Boulder, CO: Westview Press, 1994).

7. Quoted in Barton C. Hacker, "Women and Military Institutions in Early Modern Europe: A Reconnaissance," *Signs* 6, no. 4 (1981): 648.

8. Quoted in Nicola Di Cosmo, "Did Guns Matter? Firearms and the Qing Formation," in *The Qing Formation in World-Historical Time*, ed.

Lynn A. Struve (Cambridge, MA: Harvard University Press, 2004), 142.

9. Richard Hellie, ªRussia, 1200±1850,º in *The Rise of the Fiscal State in Europe, c. 1200±1850*, ed. Richard Bonney (Oxford: Oxford University Press, 1999), 493.

10. Charles Tilly, *European Revolutions, 1492±1992* (Oxford: Blackwell, 1993), 156.

11. Russ Rymer, ªVanishing Voices,º *National Geographic* (July 2012), http://ngm.nationalgeographic.com/2012/07/vanishing-languages/rymer-text.

12. Quoted in Paul A. Russell, *Lay Theology in the Reformation: Popular Pamphleteers in Southwest Germany 1521±1525* (Cambridge: Cambridge University Press, 1986), 203.

13. Quoted in Nicholas Ostler, *Empires of the Word: A Language History of the World* (New York: HarperCollins, 2005), 404±405.

14. Quoted in ibid., 465.

15. Matteo Ricci, *China in the Sixteenth Century: The Journals of Matthew Ricci: 1583±1610*, trans. Louis J. Gallagher (New York: Random House, 1953), 21.

chapter 18

1. Gemelli Careri, quoted in Henry Kamen, *Empire: How Spain Became a World Power, 1492±1763* (New York: HarperCollins, 2003), 205.

2. William S. Atwell, ªInternational Bullion Flows and the Chinese Economy, circa 1530±1650,º in *Metals and Monies in an Emerging Global Economy*, ed. Dennis O. Flynn and Arturo Giráldez (Aldershot: Variorum, 1997), 147.

3. Andre Gunder Frank, *ReOrient: Global Economy in the Asian Age* (Berkeley: University of California Press, 1998), 131.

4. Vazquez de Espinosa, ªCompendium and Description of the West Indies,º quoted in Alfred W. Crosby, Jr., *The Columbian Exchange: Biological and Cultural Consequences of 1492* (Westport, CT: Praeger, 2003), 84.

5. Garcilaso de la Vega, quoted in Charles C. Mann, *1491: New Revelations of the Americas before Columbus* (New York: Alfred A. Knopf, 2005), 314.

6. Dennis O. Flynn and Arturo Giráldez, ªBorn with a `Silver Spoon': The Origin of World Trade in 1571,º *Journal of World History* 6, no. 2 (Fall 1995): 201±221.

7. Antonio Vázquez de Espinosa, *Compendium and Description of the West Indies*, trans. Charles Upson Clark (Washington, D.C.: Smithsonian Institution, 1942), 542±543.

8. Dennis O. Flynn and Arturo Giráldez, eds., *Metals and Monies in an Emerging Global Economy* (Aldershot: Variorum, 1997), xxiii.

9. Angus Maddison, *The World Economy: A Millennial Perspective* (Paris: Organization for Economic Co-operation and Development, 2001), 241, 243.

10. Ibid., 54.

11. Quoted in Carlo M. Cipolla, *Before the Industrial Revolution: European Society and Economy, 1000±1700*, 3rd ed. (New York: Norton, 1993), 239.

12. Quoted in Richard Von Glahn, *Fountain of Fortune: Money and Monetary Policy in China, 1000±1700* (Berkeley: University of California Press, 1996), 128±129.

13. Von Glahn, *Fountain of Fortune*, 126.

14. Quoted in Geoffrey Parker, ªEurope and the Wider World, 1500±1700: The Military Balance,º in James D. Tracy, ed., *The Political Economy of Merchant Empires* (Cambridge: Cambridge University Press, 1991), 179±180.

15. David Eltis, ªFree and Coerced Transatlantic Migrations: Some Comparisons,º *American Historical Review* 88, no. 2 (April 1983), 255.

16. Philip D. Curtin, *The Rise and Fall of the Plantation Complex* (Cambridge: Cambridge University Press, 1990), 39±40.

17. Paul E. Lovejoy, *Transformations in Slavery: A History of Slavery in Africa*, 2nd ed. (New York: Cambridge University Press, 2000), 47.

18. Ibid., 63.

19. Venture Smith, *A Narrative of the Life and Adventures of Venture, a Native of Africa* (New London, CT: C. Holt, 1798), 10±11.

20. G. I. Jones, ed., ªOlaudah Equiano of the Niger Ibo,º in Philip D. Curtin, ed. *Africa Remembered: Narratives of West Africans from the Era of the Slave Trade* (Madison: University of Wisconsin Press, 1968), 95.

21. Geoffrey Parker, ªCrisis and Catastrophy: The Global Crisis of the Seventeenth Century Reconsidered,º *American Historical Review* 113, no. 4 (Oct. 2008): 1053±1079.

chapter 19

1. William H. Dall, ªA Critical Review of Bering's First Expedition, 1725±30, Together with a Translation of His Original Report upon It,º *National Geographic Magazine* 2, no. 2 (1890): 141.

2. Rein Taagepera, ªSize and Duration of Empires: Systematics of Size,º *Social Science Research* 7 (1978): 108±127.

3. Emperor Yongzheng, quoted in Mark C. Elliott, *The Manchu Way: The Eight Banners and Ethnic Identity in Late Imperial China* (Stanford, CA: Stanford University Press, 2001), 241.

4. Emperor Qianlong, letter to King George III of Great Britain, 1793, in E. Backhouse and J. O. P. Bland, *Annals and Memoirs of the Court of Peking* (Boston: Houghton Mifflin, 1914), 328.

5. Richard Steckel and Michael Haines, eds., *The Population History of North America* (New York: Cambridge University Press, 1997).

6. Alexander von Humboldt, *Political Essays on the Kingdom of New Spain*, 4 vols. (London: Longman, Hurst, Rees, Orme, and Brown, 1811), 3:463±464.

7. Jean Domat, ªOn Social Order and Absolute Monarchy,º *Modern History Sourcebook*, http://www.fordham.edu/Halsall/mod/modsbook.asp.

8. James I, Speech in the Star-Chamber, 1616, quoted in G. W. Prothero, ed., *Select Statutes and other Constitutional Documents Illustrative of the Reigns of Elizabeth and James I* (Oxford: Clarendon Press, 1898), 400.

9. Quoted in Alan Taylor, *American Colonies: The Settling of North America* (New York: Penguin, 2002), 98.

10. *The Harvard Charter of 1650*, Harvard University Archives, http://hollis.harvard.edu/?itemid=|misc/via|olvwork368905.

11. Robert Gray, *A Good Speed to Virginia* (London, 1609), quoted in Kate Aughterson, ed., *The English Renaissance: An Anthology of Sources and Documents* (New York: Routledge, 1998), 529.

12. N. S. Orlova, cited in Yuri Slezkine, *Arctic Mirrors: Russia and the Small Peoples of the North* (Ithaca, NY: Cornell University Press, 1994), 14.

13. James C. Armstrong and Nigel Anthony Worden, ªThe Slaves,º in *The Shaping of South African Society, 1652±1840*, 2nd ed., ed. Richard Elphick and Hermann Giliomee (London: Maskew Miller Longman, 1989), 129.

14. Leonard Guelke, ªFreehold Farmers and Frontier Settlers, 1657±1780,º in Elphick and Giliomee, *Shaping of South Africa*, 66.

15. Laetitia Matilda Hawkins, ªLetters on the Female Mind, Its Powers and Pursuits. Addressed to Miss H. M. Williams, with Particular Reference to Her Letters from France, 1793.º Reprinted in Vivien

Jones, *Women in the Eighteenth Century: Constructions of Femininity* (New York: Routledge, 1990), 118.

16. Samuel Johnson, *A Dictionary of the English Language,* 1st ed. (London: Times, 1983).

17. Michael Pearson, *The Indian Ocean* (New York: Routledge, 2003), 173.

18. John McManners, *The Oxford Illustrated History of Christianity* (Oxford: Oxford University, 2001), 310.

19. John K. Thornton, *The Kongolese Saint Anthony: Dona Beatriz Kimpa Vita and the Antonian Movement, 1684±1706* (New York: Cambridge University Press, 1998), 211±213.

part 6

1. George Modelski, *World Cities, ±3000 to 2000* (Washington, D.C.: Faros2000, 2003), 63, 69±72.

2. David Christian, *Maps of Time: An Introduction to Big History* (Berkeley: University of California Press, 2004), 146±148.

chapter 20

1. Ronald Findlay and Kevin H. O'Rourke, *Power and Plenty: Trade, War, and the World Economy in the Second Millennium* (Princeton, NJ: Princeton University Press, 2007), 292.

2. Paul Kennedy, *The Rise and Fall of the Great Powers* (New York: Vintage Press, 1989), 149.

3. Prasannan Parthasarathi, *Why Europe Grew Rich and Asia Did Not: Global Economic Divergence, 1600±1850* (New York: Cambridge University Press, 2011), 37±46.

4. Quoted in Jack R. Censer and Lynn Hunt, *Liberty, Equality, Fraternity: The French Revolution* (University Park: Pennsylvania State University Press, 2001), 88.

5. Quoted in Alan I. Forrest, *Soldiers of the French Revolution (Bicentennial Reflections on the French Revolution)* (Durham, NC: Duke University Press, 1990), 157.

chapter 21

1. Frances Ann Kemble, *Records of a Girlhood* (New York: Henry Holt, 1879), 283.

2. Rolf Peter Sieferle, *The Subterranean Forest: Energy Systems and the Industrial Revolution* (Cambridge, UK: White Horse Press, 2001).

3. Henry Booth, *An Account of the Liverpool and Manchester Railway* (Philadelphia: Carey & Lea, 1831), 197, 198.

4. Angus Maddison, *The World Economy: A Millennial Perspective* (Paris: Organization for Economic Co-operation and Development, 2001), 241, 264.

5. Patrick Colquhoun, *A Treatise on the Wealth, Power, and Resources of the British Empire,* 2nd ed. (New York: Johnson Reprint Corp., 1965 [1815]), 68±69.

6. Quoted in Prasannan Parthasarathi, ª Rethinking Wages and Competitiveness in the Eighteenth Century: Britain and South India,º *Past and Present* 158 (Feb. 1998): 79.

7. Margaret Bryan, *Lectures on Natural Philosophy* (Cambridge: Cambridge University Press, 2011), 16.

8. Thomas Tryon quoted in Sydney W. Mintz, *Sweetness and Power: The Place of Sugar in Modern History* (New York: Penguin Books, 1985), 47±48.

9. Kenneth Pomeranz, *The Great Divergence: China, Europe, and the Making of the Modern World Economy* (Princeton, NJ: Princeton University Press, 2000), 274±276.

10. Quoted in Margaret C. Jacob, *Scientific Culture and the Making of the Industrial West* (New York: Oxford University Press, 1997), 110.

11. E. A. Wrigley and R. S. Schofield, *The Population of England, 1541±1871: A Reconstruction* (Cambridge, MA: Harvard University Press, 1981), 208±209.

12. Elizabeth Bentley, ª Evidence Given before the Sadler Committee,º *Parliamentary Papers,* 1831±1832, Vol. XV, 44, 95±97, 115, 195, 197, 339, 341±342.

13. Maxine Berg, ª What Difference Did Women's Work Make to the Industrial Revolution,º in *Women's Work: The English Experience, 1650±1914,* ed. Pamela Sharpe (London: Arnold, 1998), 161.

14. J. F. C. Harrison, *Society and Politics in England, 1780±1960* (New York: Harper & Row, 1965), 71±72.

15. Quoted in Sieferle, *Subterranean Forest,* 170.

16. Michael Chevalier, *United States: Being a Series of Letters on North America* (Boston: Weeks, Jordan and Co., 1839), 169.

17. Maddison, *World Economy,* 263.

18. Karl Marx and Frederick Engels, *The Communist Manifesto* (New York: Verso, 2012), 39.

19. Kennedy, *The Rise and Fall of the Great Powers,* 140.

20. Ssu-yü Teng and John K. Fairbank, *China's Response to the West: A Documentary Survey, 1839±1923* (Cambridge, MA: Harvard University Press, 1982), 19.

21. John Stuart Mill, *On Liberty* (New York: Penguin Books, 1986), 13.

22. David Christian, *Maps of Time: An Introduction to Big History* (Berkeley: University of California Press, 2004), 141; I. G. Simmons, *Changing the Face of the Earth: Culture, Environment, History,* 2nd ed. (Cambridge, MA: Blackwell, 1996), 27.

23. J. R. McNeill, *Something New under the Sun: An Environmental History of the Twentieth-Century World* (New York: Norton, 2000), 315.

24. Vaclav Smil, *Energy in World History* (Boulder, CO: Westview Press, 1994), 226.

chapter 22

1. Quoted in Robert Hughes, *The Fatal Shore: The Epic of Australia's Founding* (New York: Alfred A. Knopf, 1987), 278.

2. Quoted in Walton Look Lai, ª Asian Contract and Free Migrations to the Americas,º i n David Eltis, ed., *Coerced and Free Labor Migrations: Global Perspectives* (Stanford, CA: Stanford University Press, 2002), 246.

3. Benedict Anderson presented the idea of the nation as ª imagined communityº in *Imagined Communities: Reflections on the Origin and Spread of Nationalism* (New York: Verso, 1983).

4. Karl Marx, *Manifesto of the Communist Party,* authorized English translation edited and annotated by Frederick Engels (London: W. Reeves, 1888).

5. Poncianto Arriaga, quoted in E. Bradford Burns, ed., *Latin America: Conflict and Creation, A Historical Reader* (Englewood Cliffs, NJ: Prentice Hall, 1993), 96.

6. Raja Rammohun Roy, ª A Letter on English Education,º i n *English Works,* Part IV (Calcutta: Sadharan Brahmo Samaj, 1945), 33±36.

7. Michael Geyer and Charles Bright, ª Global Violence and Nationalizing Wars in Eurasia and America: The Geopolitics of War in the Mid-Nineteenth Century,º *Comparative Studies in Society and History* 38 (Oct. 1996): 619±657.

8. Abraham Lincoln, *Speeches and Writings,* ed. Don E. Fehrenbacher, 2 vols. (New York: Viking, 1989), 2:403.

chapter 23

1. Angus Maddison, *The World Economy: A Millennial Perspective* (Paris: Organization for Economic Co-operation and Development, 2001), 264.

2. T. H. Von Laue, "A Secret Memorandum of Sergei Witte on the Industrialization of Imperial Russia," *Journal of Modern History* 26 (March 1954): 66.

3. Maddison, *The World Economy*, 185.

4. Daniel R. Headrick, *Tentacles of Progress: Technology Transfers in the Age of Imperialism, 1850±1940* (New York: Oxford University Press, 1988), 55; W. Dean Kinzley, "Merging Lines: Organizing Japan's National Railroad, 1906±1914," *Journal of Transport History* 27, no. 2 (Sept. 2006): 48±49; Andrew M. Regalsky, "Foreign Capital, Local Interests and Railway Development in Argentina: French Investments in Railways, 1900±1914," *Journal of Latin American Studies*, 21, no. 3 (Oct. 1989): 427; A. G. Ford, "Capital Exports for Argentina," *Economic Journal* 68, 271 (Sept. 1958): 592.

5. C. T. McClenachan, *Detailed Report of the Proceedings Had in Commemoration of the Successful Laying of the Atlantic Telegraph Cable* (New York: Edmund Jones and Company, 1863), 48.

6. Elisabeth Aryton, *The Cookery of England* (Harmondsworth, UK: Penguin, 1974), 429±430, quoted in Sidney W. Mintz, *Sweetness and Power: The Place of Sugar in Modern History* (New York: Viking, 1985), 120.

7. Quoted in Sven Beckert, "Emancipation and Empire: Reconstructing the Worldwide Web of Cotton Production in the Age of the American Civil War," *American Historical Review* 109 (Dec. 2004): 1405±1438.

8. C. A. Bayly, *The Birth of the Modern World, 1780±1914* (Malden, MA: Blackwell, 2004), 189; Eric Hobsbawm, *The Age of Empire, 1875±1914* (New York: Vintage Books, 1989), 29.

9. Quoted in Mike Davis, *Late Victorian Holocausts: El Niño Famines and the Making of the Third World* (London: Verso, 2001), 107.

10. Niall Ferguson, *Empire: The Rise and Demise of the British World Order and the Lessons of Global Power* (New York: Basic Books, 2002), 201±202.

11. Quoted in Robert G. Athearn, *William Tecumseh Sherman and the Settlement of the West* (Norman: University of Oklahoma Press, 1956), 223.

12. Quoted in Ferguson, *Empire*, 188.

13. Oration of the Ndebele leader Somabulana, quoted in T. O. Ranger, *Revolt in Southern Rhodesia, 1896±97* (Evanston, IL: Northwestern University Press, 1967), 122.

14. Quoted in David K. Wyatt, *Thailand: A Short History*, 2nd ed. (New Haven, CT: Yale University Press, 2003), 197.

part 7

1. J. R. McNeill, *Something New under the Sun: An Environmental History of the Twentieth Century* (New York: Norton, 2000), 15.

2. *World Urbanization Prospects: The 2011 Revision* (New York: United Nations, 2012).

chapter 24

1. John Maynard Keynes, *The Economic Consequences of the Peace* (London: Macmillan, 1919), 101.

2. George Modelski, *World Cities: -3000 to 2000* (Washington, D.C.: Faros2000, 2003), 63.

3. R. Hume, "From Ahmednagar," *New York Times*, November 22, 1896, quoted in Mike Davis, *Late Victorian Holocausts: El Niño Famines and the Making of the Third World* (New York: Verso, 2001), 144.

4. Hermann Buhr Gillomee, *The Afrikaners: Biography of a People* (Charlottesville: University of Virginia Press, 2003), 152.

5. Lionel Kochan, *Russia in Revolution, 1890±1918* (New York: New American Library, 1967), 99.

6. Qiu Jin, "Preoccupation (Written while in Japan)," *Women Writers of Traditional China: An Anthology of Poetry and Criticism*, ed. Kang-I Sun Chang and Haun Saussy (Stanford, CA: Stanford University Press, 1999), 642±643.

7. Ian F. W. Beckett, *The Great War, 1914±1918*, 2nd ed. (London: Pearson Longman, 2007), 438.

8. Siegfried Sassoon, *Counter-Attack and Other Poems* (London: William Heinemann, 1918), 18.

9. Beckett, *The Great War*, 237.

10. Lev Trotsky, *My Life* (Harmondsworth, UK: Penguin, 1975), 351.

11. William Eckhardt, "Water-Related Deaths since 3000 bc," *Bulletin of Peace Proposals*, 22, no. 4 (1991): 437±443.

12. Erez Manela, *The Wilsonian Moment: Self-Determination and the International Origins of Anticolonial Nationalism* (Oxford: Oxford University Press, 2007).

chapter 25

1. Gross domestic product estimates are based on Angus Maddison, Historical Statistics, http://www.ggdc.net/maddison.

2. Angus Maddison, *The World Economy: A Millennial Perspective* (Paris: Organization for Economic Co-operation and Development, 2001), 243.

3. Michael Williams, *Deforesting the Earth: From Prehistory to Global Crisis* (Chicago: University of Chicago Press, 2003), 396.

4. Quoted in Pericles Lewis, *The Cambridge Introduction to Modernism* (Cambridge: Cambridge University Press, 2007), 1.

5. Quoted in Linda Nochin, *Impressionism and Post-Impressionism, 1874±1904* (Englewood Cliffs, NJ: Prentice-Hall, 1966), 8±9.

6. M. M. Khatayevich, quoted in Robert Conquest, *Harvest of Sorrow: Soviet Collectivization and the Terror-Famine* (New York: Oxford University Press, 1986), 261.

7. "A Declaration of Beliefs by the New Youth," in Dun J. Li, ed., *The Road to Communism: China since 1912* (New York: Van Nostrand Reinhold, 1969), 40.

8. Victor Raúl Haya de la Torre, quoted in Thomas E. Skidmore and Peter H. Smith, *Modern Latin America*, 6th ed. (New York: Oxford University Press, 2005), 219.

9. Frederick J. D. Lugard, *The Dual Mandate in British Tropical Africa*, quoted in Philip D. Curtin, ed., *Imperialism* (New York: Harper & Row, 1971), 317.

10. Yogolelo Tambwe ya Kasimba, "*Mission de recrutement des travailleurs de lU.M.H.K. au Kivu-Maniema (1926±1928)*," M.A. thesis, National University of Zaire, quoted in Bruce Fetter, ed., *Colonial Rule in Africa: Readings from Primary Sources* (Madison: University of Wisconsin Press, 1979), 117.

11. Adam McKeown, "Global Migration, 1846±1940," *Journal of World History* 15, no. 2 (June 2004): 167.

12. "Balfour Declaration," quoted in Charles D. Smith, *Palestine and the Arab-Israeli Conflict: A History with Documents*, 8th ed. (Boston: Bedford St. Martin's Press, 2013), 93±94.

13. Quoted in Erez Manela, *The Wilsonian Moment: Self-Determination and the International Origins of Anticolonial Nationalism* (Oxford: Oxford University Press, 2007), 142.

14. Edwin Montagu, Secretary of State for India, quoted in D. George Boyce, *Decolonization and the British Empire* (New York: St. Martin's Press, 1999), 89.

15. M. K. Gandhi, *Indian Home Rule*, 5th ed. (Madras: Ganesh, 1922), 87.

chapter 26

1. ªThe Way of Subjects,º reprinted in Otto D. Tolischus, *Tokyo Record* (New York: Reynal & Hitchcock, 1943), 409, 427.

2. Adolf Hitler, *Mein Kampf,* trans. Ralph Manheim (Boston: Houghton Mifflin 1943), 286.

3. Quoted in Niall Ferguson, *Empire: The Rise and Demise of the British World Order and the Lessons for Global Power* (New York: Basic Books, 2004), 279±280.

4. Hitler, *Mein Kampf,* 255.

5. Ibid., 643.

6. Ibid., 666.

7. Quoted in Haile Selassi, ªAddress to the League of Nations,º in Molefi Kete Asante and Abu S. Abarry, *African Intellectual Heritage: A Book of Sources* (Philadelphia: Temple University Press, 1996), 668.

8. Fred Taylor, trans. and ed., *The Goebbels Diaries, 1939±1941* (New York: G. P. Putnam, 1983), 16, 20.

9. Quoted in William L. Shirer, *The Rise and Fall of the Third Reich* (New York: Simon & Schuster, 1960), 736.

10. R. G. Waldeck, *Athene Palace* (New York: Robert M. McBride, 1942), 124.

11. Quoted in Mark Mazower, *Hitler's Empire: How the Nazis Ruled Europe* (New York: Penguin Press, 2008), 140±141.

12. Quoted in ibid., 144.

13. Quoted in Alvin D. Coox, ªThe Pacific War,º in Peter Duus, *The Cambridge History of Japan,* Vol. 6: *The Twentieth Century* (Cambridge: Cambridge University Press, 1988), 336.

14. Winston Churchill, *The Second World War,* Vol. 3 (Boston: Houghton Mifflin, 1948±1953), 539.

15. ªThe Battle of Stalingrad,º The History Learning Site, http://www.historylearningsite.co.uk/battle_of_stalingrad.htm.

16. Conrad Brandt, Benjamin Schwartz, and John K. Fairbank, eds., *A Documentary History of Chinese Communism* (Cambridge, MA: Harvard University Press, 1952), 83, 84.

17. Quoted in Gabriel Kolko, *The Politics of War: The World and United States Foreign Policy, 1943±1945* (New York: Random House, 1968), 205.

18. Quoted in Gerald D. Feldman, *The Great Disorder: Politics, Economics, and Society in the German Inflation, 1914±1924* (New York: Oxford University Press, 1993), 855.

19. Interview with Olga Mikhaylovna Lisikova, conducted by Oleg Korytov and Konstantin Chirkin, English translation by James F. Gebhardt, St. Petersburg, Dec. 11, 2007, http://lend-lease.airforce.ru/english/index.htm.

20. Quoted in Anne Noggle, *A Dance with Death: Soviet Airwomen in World War II* (College Station: Texas A&M University Press, 1994), 241.

21. Jean-Francois Steiner, *Treblinka* (New York: Simon & Schuster, 1979).

22. J. R. McNeill, *Something New under the Sun: An Environmental History of the Twentieth-Century World* (New York: Norton, 2000), 346.

23. ªThe Atlantic Charter,º August 14, 1941, North Atlantic Treaty Organization (NATO), http://www.nato.int/cps/en/natolive/official_texts_16912.htm.

24. Edmund Jan Ozmanczyk, *Encyclopedia of the United Nations and International* Agreements, 3rd ed., Vol. 4 (New York: Routledge, 2004), 2379.

25. Jawaharlal Nehru, ªReveries in Jail,º in *Nehru: The First Sixty Years,* ed. Dorothy Norman, Vol. 2 (New York: John Day, 1965), 142.

26. Quoted in Stephen Ha, ed., *Sources of Indian Tradition,* 2nd ed., Vol. 2, *Modern India and Pakistan* (New York: Columbia University Press, 1988), 230.

27. Quoted in Alfred W. McCoy, ªIndependence without Decolonization,º in Robin Jeffrey, ed., *AsiaÐ The Winning of Independence* (New York: St. Martin's Press, 1981), 26.

chapter 27

1. J. Bolt and J. L. van Zanden. ªThe First Update of the Maddison Project; Re-Estimating Growth Before 1820.º Maddison Project Working Paper 4, 2013.

2. Ronald Pruessen, *John Foster Dulles: The Road to Power* (New York: Free Press, 1982), 309.

3. Richard M. Nixon, *The Challenges We Face: Edited and Compiled from the Speeches and Papers of Richard M. Nixon* (New York: McGraw-Hill, 1960), 220.

4. Tertius Chandler, *Four Thousand Years of Urban Growth: An Historical Census* (Lewiston, NY: St. David's University Press, 1987), 507, 511, 512.

5. Quoted in Frank Mort and Peter Thompson, ªRetailing, Commercial Culture and Masculinity in 1950s Britain; The Case of Montague Burton, the `Tailor of Taste,'º *History Workshop Journal* 38 (1994): 113.

6. Clive Ponting, *A New Green History of the World: The Environment and the Collapse of Great Civilizations* (New York: Penguin, 2007), 258.

7. Andrew P. N. Erdmann, ª'War No Longer Has Any Logic Whatever': Dwight D. Eisenhower and the Thermonuclear War,º in John Lewis Gaddis et al., eds., *Cold War Statesmen Confront the Bomb: Nuclear Diplomacy since 1945* (Oxford: Oxford University Press, 1999), 113.

8. Michael R. Beschloss, *The Crisis Years: Kennedy and Khrushchev, 1960±1963* (New York: Edward Burlingame, 1991), 278.

9. Nikita S. Khrushchev, *Khrushchev Remembers,* ed. and trans. Strobe Talbot (Boston: Little, Brown, 1970), 493.

10. Richard Wright, *Black Power: A Record of Reactions in a Land of Pathos* (New York: Harper & Brothers, 1954), 75±76.

11. Douglas Little, *American Orientalism: The United States and the Middle East since 1945,* 3rd ed. (Chapel Hill: University of North Carolina Press, 2008), 179.

12. John T. Woolley and Gerhard Peters, The American Presidency Project [online], Santa Barbara, CA, http://www.presidency.ucsb.edu/ws/?pid=27116.

13. Nelson Mandela, *In His Own Words* (New York: Little, Brown, 2003), 28.

14. Betty Friedan, *The Feminine Mystique* (New York: Norton, 1963), 32.

chapter 28

1. Tim Berners-Lee website, http://www.w3.org/People/Berners-Lee/.

2. Worldometers, Real Time World Statistics, http://www.worldometers.info/computers.

3. *2013 Global Manufacturing Competitiveness Index,* Deloitte LLP and U.S. Council on Competitiveness.

4. Index Mundi, Historical Data Graphs per Year, http://www.indexmundi.com; U.S. Central Intelligence Agency, World Factbook, Vietnam, https://www.cia.gov/library/publications/the-world-factbook.

5. Greyhill Advisors, ªManufacturing Output by Country,º http://greyhill.com/manufacturing-by-country/.

6. David C. Unger, ª Who Can Bring the E.U. to Its Senses?º *New York Times,* March 30, 2013.

7. The Conference Board of Canada, ª World Income Inequality,º September 2011, http://www.conferenceboard.ca/hcp/hot-topics /worldinequality.aspx.

8. Organization for Economic Cooperation and Development, StatExtracts, Income Distribution-Inequality, http://stats.oecd .org/Index.aspx?DataSetCode=INEQUALITY.

9. Quoted in Thomas E. Skidmore, Peter H. Smith, and James N. Green, *Modern Latin America,* 7th ed. (New York: Oxford University Press, 2010), 69.

10. United Nations, Office of the Special Adviser on Africa, ª External Debt in Africa,º P olicy Brief No. 3 (October 2010).

11. Quoted in ª Where Women Are Winning,º *Newsweek Magazine,* Sept. 18, 2011.

12. Jose C. Moya and Adam McKeown, ª World Migration in the Long Twentieth Century,º i n *Essays on Twentieth-Century History,* ed. Michael Adas for the American Historical Association (Philadelphia: Temple University Press, 2010), 34.

13. Stephen Castles and Mark J. Miller, *The Age of Migration: International Population Movements in the Modern World,* 4th ed. (New York: Guilford Press, 1993), 119±120.

14. U.S. Central Intelligence Agency, World Factbook, Qatar, https:// www.cia.gov/library/publications/the-world-factbook.

15. Richard Morin, ª Indentured Servitude in the Persian Gulf,º *New York Times,* April 14, 2013.

16. United Nations Office on Drugs and Crime, *Global Report on Trafficking in Persons,* Feb. 2009, http://www.unodc.org/documents /Global_Report_on_TIP.pdf.

17. *The Economist,* Economist Intelligence Unit, ª Democracy Index 2012,º http://www.eiu.com; Freedom House, ª Freedom in the World 2013,º www.freedomhouse.org; World Democracy Audit, worldaudit.org.

18. United Nations Charter, Article 42.

19. Akira Iriya, *Global Community: The Role of International Organizations in the Making of the Contemporary World* (Berkeley: University of California Press, 2002), 8.

20. Joshua S. Goldstein, ªT hink Again: War,º *Foreign Policy,* Sept.±Oct. 2011, http://www.foreignpolicy.com/articles/2011/08/15/think _again_war?page=0,0.

21. ª Iraqi Deaths from Violence, 2003±2011,º I raq Body Count, http:// www.iraqbodycount.org/.

22. Will Steffen, Paul J. Crutzen, and John R. McNeill, ªT he Anthropocene: Are Humans Now Overwhelming the Great Forces of Nature?º *Ambio* 36, no. 8 (Dec. 2007): 614±621.

23. Fred Spier, *Big History and the Future of Humanity* (Malden, MA: Wiley-Blackwell, 2011), 187±88.

24. John Richards, ª Land Transformation,º i n *The Earth as Transformed by Human Action,* ed. B. L. Turner et al. (Cambridge: Cambridge University Press, 1990), 164.

25. Wangari Maathai, quoted in Nobel Women's Initiative, ª Meet the Laureates,º http://nobelwomensinitiative.org/meet-the-laureates /wangari-maathai/.

26. Wangari Maathai, quoted in *Los Angeles Times,* September 27, 2011.

Credits

LINE ART/TEXT

Chapter 15

p. 431: M. J. Müller, ªIbnulkhatib's Bericht über die Pest,º Sitzungsberichte der Königl. Bayerischen Akademie der Wissenschaften, 2 (1863): pp. 2±12. Translated from the Arabic with assistance from Dr. Walid Saleh. In John Aberth, *The First Horseman: Disease in Human History,* 1st Edition, pp. 44±46, © 2007. Reprinted by permission of Pearson Education, Inc., Upper Saddle River, New Jersey.

Chapter 18

p. 537: Richard Ligon, *The True and Exact History of the Island of Barbadoes, 1657,* ed. J. Edward Hutson (St. Michael, Barbados: Barbados National Trust, 2000), pp. 64, 66±67, 75, 76. Reprinted by permission of the Barbados National Trust.

Chapter 20

p. 598: C. L. R. James, *The Black Jacobins: Toussaint L'Ouverture and the San Domingo Revolution,* 2nd ed. Rev. (New York: Vintage Books, 1963), pp. 195±197. Reprinted by permission of Curtis Brown Group Ltd. (London).

Chapter 22

p. 651: Susan Gilson Miller, trans. and ed., *Disorienting Encounters: Travels of a Moroccan Scholar in France in 1845±46: The Voyage of Muhammad As-Saffar,* pp. 108, 110, 153, 190, 193±194. Copyright © 1992 by The Regents of the University of California. Reprinted by permission of the University of California Press.

Chapter 24

p. 710: Qiu Jin, ªPreoccupation (Written while in Japan)º from *Women Writers of Traditional China,* edited by Kang-i Sun Chang and Haun Saussy. Copyright © 2000 by the Board of Trustees of the Leland Stanford Jr. University. With the permission of Stanford University Press, www.sup.org; p. 714: Extracted from ATTACK by Siegfried Sassoon by kind permission of the Estate of George Sassoon.

Chapter 25

p. 751: Charles P. Kindleberger, *World in Depression, 1929±1939,* p. 170 (Figure 10). © 1973, 1986 Deutscher Taschenbuch Verlag. © 1986 Charles P. Kindleberger. Reprinted by permission of the University of California Press.

Chapter 26

p. 771: *Rosie the Riveter:* Words and Music by Redd Evans and John Jacob Loeb. Copyright © 1942 (Renewed 1970, 1998) by Fred Ahlert Music Corporation and John Jacob Loeb Music Company/Administered by BMG Rights Management (US) LLC and Music Sales Corporation (ASCAP). International Copyright Secured. All Rights Reserved. Used by Permission. Reprinted by permission of Hal Leonard Corporation and Music Sales Corporation.

Chapter 27

p. 806: Excerpts from *The Wretched of the Earth* by Frantz Fanon, translated from the French by Constance Farrington, copyright © 1963 by Présence Africaine. Used by permission of Grove/Atlantic, Inc. Any third party use of this material, outside of this publication, is prohibited.

Chapter 28

Table 28.2: © University Corporation for Atmospheric Research.

PHOTOS

Front Matter

Page vii(top): Photo by Jordan Catapano; p. vii(bottom): © Graham Proctor; p. ix: © The Metropolitan Museum of Art. Image source: Art Resource, NY; p. x: © Dea/G Dagli Orti/Age Fotostock; p. xii: © Leo Hol; p. xiii: © akg-images; p. xiv: © The Trustees of the British Museum/Art Resource, NY; p. xv: © SSPL/Science Museum/Art Resource, NY; p. xvii: © eye35.pix/Alamy.

Chapter 15

Opener: © Erich Lessing/Art Resource, NY; p. 425(1): ©Werner Forman/HIP/The Image Works; p. 425(2): © British Library Board/Robana/Art Resource, NY; p. 425(3): © ullstein bild/The Image Works; p. 429(top): John Montenieri/CDC; p. 429(bottom): © Getty Images/Digital Vision RF; p. 430: © Werner Forman/HIP/The Image Works; p. 432: © British Library Board/Robana/Art Resource, NY; p. 435: © Michael Klinec/Alamy; p. 436: © British Library Board/Robana/Art Resource, NY; p. 437: © The Art Archive at Art Resource, NY; p. 438: © Interfoto/Alamy; p. 440: © Robert Harding Picture Library/SuperStock; p. 441: © Imaginechina/Corbis; p. 442: © Dinodia Stock Connection Worldwide/Newscom; p. 443: © Roland and Sabrina Michaud/akg/The Image Works; p. 444: © ullstein bild/The Image Works; p. 445: © Fogg Art Museum, Harvard University Art Museums, USA/Gift of Sir Joseph Duveen/The Bridgeman Art Library; p. 447: © Italian School, (15th century)/Museo de Firenze Com'era, Florence, Italy/The Bridgeman Art Library; p. 449: © National Gallery, London, UK/The Bridgeman Art Library.

Chapter 16

Part Opener: © The Trustees of the British Museum/Art Resource, NY; p. 454: With permission of the Royal Ontario Museum © ROM; p. 455(1): © The Power of Forever Photography/Getty Images; p. 455(2): © Sofia Pereira/LusoimagesÐ Palaces/Alamy; p. 455(3): © Mireille Vautier/Alamy; p. 455(4): © Werner Forman/UIG/Age Fotostock; p. 458: © J E Bulloz/DEA/Age Fotostock; p. 460: © Album/Kurwenal/Prisma/Newscom; p. 461: © The Trustees of the British Museum/Art Resource, NY; p. 462: © The Granger Collection, New York; p. 463: © The Power of Forever Photography/Getty Images; p. 465: © Sofia Pereira/LusoimagesÐ Palaces/Alamy; p. 467: © Everett Collection/Newscom; p. 468(top): © Bridgeman-Giraudon/Art Resource, NY; p. 468(bottom): © North Wind Picture Archives/Alamy; p. 473: © The Granger Collection, New York; p. 474: © Mireille Vautier/Alamy; p. 475: © The Granger Collection, New York; p. 476: © De Agostini/A. Dagli Orti/Getty Images; p. 480: © Werner Forman/UIG/Age Fotostock; p. 481: © Werner Forman/Art Resource, NY.

Chapter 17

Opener: © De Agostini Picture Library/Getty Images; p. 485(1): © TopFoto/The Image Works; p. 485(2): © Historical Archive, Turin, Italy/Index/The Bridgeman Art Library; p. 485(3): © bpk, Berlin/Kupferstichkabinett, Staatliche Museen/Jorg P. Anders/Art Resource, NY; p. 488: © Giulio Veggi/Science Source; p. 490: © The British Library Board/The Image Works; p. 491: dbimages/Alamy; p. 492: © The Granger Collection, New York; p. 493: © Digital Vision/Punchstock RF; p. 494: © Interfoto/Alamy; p. 495: © TopFoto/The Image Works; p. 498: © De Agostini Picture Library/akg-images; p. 499: © Archivart/Alamy; p. 500: © Ian Nellist/Alamy RF; p. 501: © Historical Archive, Turin, Italy/Index/The Bridgeman Art Library; p. 503: © Private Collection/The Stapleton Collection/The Bridgeman Art Library; p. 508: © bpk, Berlin/Kupferstichkabinett, Staatliche Museen/Jorg P. Anders/Art Resource, NY; p. 509: © Album/Prisma/Newscom; p. 510: © The Jewish Museum, New York/Art Resource, NY.

Chapter 18

Opener: © National Geographic/Getty Images; p. 515(1): © Fotosearch/Getty Images; p. 515(2): © Peter Newark Pictures/The Bridgeman Art Library; p. 515(3): © The Granger Collection, New York; p. 518: © National Maritime Museum, London/The Image Works; p. 519: © Fotosearch/Getty Images; p. 521: © Photo12/UIG/Getty Images; p. 523: © akg-images; p. 524: David Beck, Louis De Geer Photo © Nationalmuseum, Stockholm; p. 525: © The Metropolitan Museum of Art. Image source: Art Resource, NY. Detail; p. 527: © BeBa/Iberfoto/The Image Works; p. 528: © Werner Forman/Art Resource, NY; p. 529: © Peter Newark Pictures/The Bridgeman Art Library; p. 534: © The Granger Collection, New York; p. 536: © Corbis; p. 538: © Art Resource, NY; p. 539: © The Trustees of the British Museum/Art Resource, NY.

Chapter 19

Opener: © North Wind Picture Archives/Alamy; p. 543(1): © Universal History Archive/Getty Images; p. 543(2): © North Wind Picture Archives/Alamy; p. 543(3): © Academy of Natural Sciences of Philadelphia/Corbis; p. 546: © The Metropolitan Museum of Art. Image source: Art Resource, NY; p. 547: © Universal History Archive/Getty Images; p. 548: © Hermitage, St. Petersburg, Russia/The Bridgeman Art Library; p. 549: © The New York Public Library/Art Resource, NY; p. 550: © Breamore House, Hampshire, UK/The Bridgeman Art Library; p. 552: © National Gallery, London/Art Resource, NY; p. 553: © RMN-Grand Palais/Art Resource, NY; p. 554: © Museumslandschaft Hessen Kassel/The Bridgeman Art Library; p. 555: © Mansell/Time Life Pictures/Getty Images; p. 559: © North Wind Picture Archives/Alamy; p. 560: © akg-images/Laurent Lecat/Newscom; p. 561: © The Gallery Collection/Corbis; p. 564: © North Wind Picture Archives/Alamy; p. 565: © Academy of Natural Sciences of Philadelphia/Corbis; p. 569: © akg-images/Gilles Mermet/Newscom; p. 570: © Archivio Storico di Propaganda Fide; p. 571: © Dutch School/Getty Images.

Chapter 20

Part Opener: © SSPL/Science Museum/Art Resource, NY; p. 576: © The Trustees of the British Museum/Art Resource, NY; p. 577(1): © V&A Images, London/Art Resource, NY; p. 577(2): © akg-images/Newscom; p. 577(3): © The Granger Collection, New York; p. 580: © V&A Images, London/Art Resource, NY; p. 582: © De Agostini/Getty Images; p. 585: © Fine Art Images/Age Fotostock; p. 586: © Fotosearch/Getty Images; p. 588: © RMN-Grand Palais/Art Resource, NY; p. 590: © Photo12/UIG/Getty Images; p. 591: © akg-images/Newscom; p. 592: © John Parrot/Stocktrek Images/Getty Images RF; p. 595: © akg-images/Newscom; p. 597: © Bettmann/Corbis; p. 599: © Stock Montage/Getty Images; p. 600: © The Granger Collection, New York; p. 601: © Gianni Dagli Orti/The Art Archive at Art Resource, NY; p. 603: © Jose Caruci/AP Photo.

Chapter 21

Opener: © Gianni Dagli Orti/The Art Archive at Art Resource, NY; p. 607(1): © Universal History Archive/Getty Images; p. 607(2): © Giraudon/The Bridgeman Art Library; p. 611: Library of Congress, Prints and Photographs Division [LC-USZC4-11219]; p. 612: © Universal History Archive/Getty Images; p. 613: © akg-images/Newscom; p. 616: © Erich Lessing/Art Resource, NY; p. 618: © National Maritime Museum, London/The Image Works; p. 620: © Image Asset Management Ltd./Alamy; p. 621: © Pictorial Press Ltd/Alamy; p. 623: © Archives Charmet/The Bridgeman Art Library; p. 625: © Fotosearch/Getty Images; p. 626: © Giraudon/The Bridgeman Art Library; p. 629: © Hulton Archive/Getty Images; p. 631: Library of Congress, Prints and Photographs Division [LC-USZ62-101759].

Chapter 22

Opener: © SSPL/Getty Images; p. 635(1): Library of Congress, Prints and Photographs Division [LC-USZ62-105116]; p. 635(2): © Hulton Archive/Getty Images; p. 635(3): © Roger-Viollet/The Image Works; p. 635(4): © The Granger Collection, New York; p. 638: © Culver Pictures/The Art Archive at Art Resource, NY; p. 639: Library of Congress, Prints and Photographs Division [LC-USZ62-105116]; p. 641: © Stapleton Collection/Corbis; p. 642: © North Wind Picture Archives/AP Photo; p. 644: © The Granger Collection, New York; p. 645: © Francois Rude/The Bridgeman Art Library/Getty Images; p. 646: © Hulton Archive/Getty Images; p. 647: © Bettmann/Corbis; p. 649: © Interfoto/Alamy; p. 650: Library of Congress, Prints and Photographs Division [LC-USZ62-77267]; p. 653: Yale Collection of Western Americana, Beinecke Rare Book and Manuscript Library; p. 654: © Roger-Viollet/The Image Works; p. 655: © BL/Robana/Age Fotostock; p. 656: © ullstein bild/The Granger Collection, New York; p. 659: © The Granger Collection, New York; p. 661: © Mary Evans Picture Library/The Image Works.

Chapter 23

Opener: © akg-images/Newscom; p. 665(1): © ullstein bild/The Granger Collection, New York; p. 665(2): © Amoret Tanner/Alamy; p. 665(3): © Silvio Fiore/TopFoto/The Image Works; p. 667: © ullstein bild/The Granger Collection, New York; p. 669: © The Granger Collection, New York; p. 671: © ullstein bild/The Granger Collection, New York; p. 672: © Mary Evans/Grenville Collins/The Image Works; p. 674: © DeAgostini/Getty Images; p. 675: © Amoret Tanner/Alamy; p. 677: © Bettmann/Corbis; p. 678: © HIP/The Image Works; p. 679: Image from Honda, Kinkichiro, Kiyochika Kobayashi, Ai Maeda, and Isao Shimizu. 1985. *Jiyu minkenki no manga*. Tokyo: Chikuma Shobo: p. 35. Photo: Library of Congress [JC599.J3 J58 1985 Japan]; p. 680: © adoc-photos/Corbis; p. 683: © Cultural Heritage Images/Universal Images Group/Newscom; p. 685: © Corbis; p. 686: © Lordprice Collection/Alamy; p. 688: © Albert Harlingue/Roger Viollet/Getty Images; p. 690: © Hulton Archive/Getty Images; p. 691: © Silvio Fiore/TopFoto/The Image Works.

Chapter 24

Part Opener: © eye35.pix/Alamy; p. 696: © Corbis; p. 697(1): © Corbis/Age Fotostock RF; p. 697(2): © Bettmann/Corbis; p. 697(3): Library of Congress, Prints and Photographs Division [LC-USZC4-11161]; p. 700: © Corbis/Age Fotostock RF; p. 701: © Image Asset Management Ltd./Alamy; p. 702: © The Gallery Collection/

Corbis © 2013 Estate of Pablo Picasso/ Artists Rights Society (ARS), New York; p. 704: © Ariadne Van Zandbergen/ Alamy; p. 705: © Gardiner F. Williams/ National Geographic Creative/Corbis; p. 706: © Ingram Publishing RF; p. 707: © akg-images/RIA Nowosti/Newscom; p. 709: © The Granger Collection, New York; p. 710: © Xia Gongran Xinhua News Agency/Newscom; p. 712: © Bettmann/ Corbis; p. 713: © Bettmann/Corbis; p. 716: © Roger Viollet/Getty Images; p. 717: © Robert Hunt Library/Mary Evans/The Image Works; p. 718: Library of Congress Prints, and Photographs Division [LC-USZC4-11161]; p. 720: © Mary Evans/ Meledin Collection/The Image Works; p. 721: © akg-images/Alamy; p. 723: © The National Archives UK.

Chapter 25

Opener: © The Art Archive/Kharbine-Tapabor/Coll. Perrin; p. 729(1): John Gordon Rideout (American, 1898±1951). Radio, 1930±1933. Plaskon (plastic), metal, glass, 11¾ × 8⅞ × 7½ in. (29.8 × 22.5 × 19.1 cm). Brooklyn Museum, Purchased with funds given by The Walter Foundation, 85.9; p. 729(2): © Corbis; p. 729(3): © akg-images/The Image Works; p. 732: John Gordon Rideout (American, 1898±1951). Radio, 1930±1933. Plaskon (plastic), metal, glass, 11¾ × 8⅞ × 7½ in. (29.8 × 22.5 × 19.1 cm). Brooklyn Museum, Purchased with funds given by The Walter Foundation, 85.9; p. 733: © UPPA/Photoshot © 2013 Artists Rights Society (ARS), New York/ProLitteris, Zurich; p. 734: © Keystone-France/Gamma-Keystone via Getty Images; p. 736: © Bettmann/Corbis; p. 737: © Corbis; p. 738: © Bettmann/ Corbis; p. 739: © Underwood & Underwood/Corbis; pp. 740, 743: © Bettmann/ Corbis; p. 747: © Robert Sennecke/ullstein bild/The Image Works; p. 748: © Bett-mann/Corbis; p. 749: © akg-images/The Image Works; p. 752: © Keystone-France/ Gamma-Keystone via Getty Images; p. 753: © Popperfoto/Getty Images.

Chapter 26

Opener: © ullstein bild/akg-images; p. 757(1): © DIZ Muenchen GmbH, Sueddeutsche Zeitung Photo/Alamy; p. 757(2): © Laski Diffusion/Getty Images; p. 757(3): © Bettmann/Corbis; p. 759: © ullstein bild/ The Granger Collection, New York; p. 761: © bpk, Berlin/Art Resource, NY; p. 762: © DIZ Muenchen GmbH, Sueddeutsche Zeitung Photo/Alamy; p. 763: © Top-Foto/The Image Works; p. 765: © Laski Diffusion/Getty Images; p. 768: © SZ Photo/Scherl/The Image Works; p. 769: © Sovfoto/UIG via Getty Images; p. 770: © Hulton-Deutsch Collection/Corbis; p. 772: © Oleg Korytov Collection via Ilya Grinberg; p. 773: National Archives and Records Administration [NWDNS-208-AA-206K(31)]; p. 775: National Archives and Records Administration [NWDNS-208-COM-189]; p. 776(left): © Eileen Tweedy/The Art Archive at Art Resource, NY; p. 776(right): © Peter Newark Military Pictures/The Bridgeman Art Library; pp. 777, 778: © Bettmann/Corbis; p. 783: © AP Photo; p. 784: © John Florea/Time & Life Pictures/Getty Images; p. 785: © Bettmann/Corbis.

Chapter 27

Opener: © Detlev van Ravenswaay/Science Source; p. 789(1): © National Railway Museum/SSPL/The Image Works; p. 789(2): Library of Congress, Prints & Photographs Division, drawing by Edmund S. Valtman [LC-DIG-ppmsc-07978]; p. 789(3): © Keystone-France/Gamma-Keystone via Getty Images; pp. 793, 794: © Everett Collection/Age Fotostock; p. 796: © Paul Almasy/Corbis; p. 798: © National Railway Museum/SSPL/The Image Works; p. 799: © National Geographic/ Getty Images; p. 800: © TopFoto/The Image Works; p. 801: © Bettmann/Corbis; p. 803: Library of Congress, Prints & Photographs Division, drawing by Edmund S. Valtman [LC-DIG-ppmsc-07978]; p. 805: © Keystone-France/Gamma-Keystone via Getty Images; p. 808: © Bettmann/Corbis; p. 810: © Nik Wheeler/Corbis; p. 812: © Africa Media Online/The Image Works; p. 813(top, bottom): © AP Photo; p. 814: © CTK/Alamy.

Chapter 28

Opener: © CAIDA/Science Source; p. 819(1): © JG Photography/Alamy RF; p. 819(2): © Patrick Robert/Sygma/Corbis; p. 819(3): Courtesy United Nations Development Programme (UNDP); p. 819(4): Photograph by Markel Redondo for Greenpeace; p. 822: © JG Photography/Alamy RF; p. 823: © Mario Tama/Getty Images; p. 825: © Keystone Pictures USA/ZUMAPRESS/ Newscom; p. 826: © AP Photo; p. 828: © Patrick Robert/Sygma/Corbis; p. 829(left): © David Pollack/Corbis; p. 829(right): © Paul Strawson/Alamy; p. 830: © Wolfgang Kumm/dpa/Corbis; p. 833: © Thanassis Stavrakis/AP Photo; p. 835: Map by Zara Matheson, Martin Prosperity Institute, "The Geography of Women's Economic Opportunity," *The Atlantic Cities*; p. 836: © AA/ABACA/Newscom; p. 838: © AP Photo; p. 840: © Lionel Healing/AFP/ Getty Images; p. 841: Courtesy United Nations Development Programme (UNDP); p. 844: © Seyllou Diallo/AFP/Getty Images; p. 845: © Sean Adair/Reuters/Corbis; p. 847: Photograph by Markel Redondo for Greenpeace; p. 848: © Gerald Herbert/AP Photo; p. 849: © Richard Drew/AP Photo.

Index

Booth, William, 654
Boris III (king of Bulgaria), 773
Bosch, Carl, 700
Bosnia, 844
bourgeoisie, 445, 647. *See also* middle class
Boxer Rebellion (China), 709, 711
Brahe, Tycho, 564
Brazil
  deforestation, 798
  immigration, 732
  independence, 599, 602
  industrialization, 795
  macombos, 536
  Portuguese colonization of, *477*, 478, 532, 534
  revolution (1848), 648
  slavery, 478, 534, 637, 638, 642
  sugar production, 533, 534
  urbanization, 699, *700*
  War of the Triple Alliance, 658
  women's rights movement, 648
Bretton Woods institutions, 778±779, *778*, 791±792, 825±826, 834
Brezhnev, Leonid, 794, 814
Britain
  1550±1700 c.e., 522, 530, 534
  abolition of slavery, 637, 638
  agriculture (1750±1850 c.e.), 615±616
  Anglo-Chinese Wars, 631, 659, 667, 670
  baby boom, 791
  Black Death, 429
  Boer War, 705
  Crimean War, 657
  Enlightenment, 567, 568
  and European unification, 833
  fifteenth-century recovery, 446
  and French Revolution, 590
  and gold standard, 699
  Great Exhibition of the Industry of All Nations, *634*, 635, 636
  and Holocaust, 773
  Hundred Years' War, 434±435, 437±438
  industrialization, 611±618, 628, 667
  and Iran, 708
  middle class, 679±680
  military technology and strategy, 504
  and Muhammad Ali's Egypt, 626
  opium trade, 629, 631, 667, 675
  rural rebellions (1300±1500 c.e.), 434
  and Russian empire, 682
  scientific revolution, 617±618
  Seven Years' War, 577, *578*, 583±584, 585±586
  sixteenth century, 497, *499*, 500
  Suez crisis, 809
  trade (nineteenth century), 628
  trading companies, 517±518
  vernacular language, 510±511
  women's rights movement, 648
  World War I, 713, 714, 715±716
  World War II, 764, 766, 771, 774, 775
  and World War II buildup, 761, 763
  See also British government; British imperialism/colonialism
British Anti-Slavery Society, 637
British East India Company, 579, 583, 628, 631, 655, 660, 673. *See also* British India
British government
  1650±1750 c.e., 554±556, 559

and American Revolution, 586
and Enlightenment, 567, 568
fifteenth century, 447
Glorious Revolution, 556, 559, 567, 568, 586, 616
and industrial revolution, 616±617, *616*
reform movements (1830±1870 c.e.), 648
sixteenth century, 500
British imperialism/colonialism, 681
  Africa, 629, 683, 686, 688±689, 704, 705, 746, 747, 804±805, 807
  China, 629, 631, 659, 667, 670, 708, 709, 711
  Ireland, 555±556, 743±744
  Middle East, 722, 743, 748, 781
  Oceania, 684
  Southeast Asia, 684, 691, 784
  and southern seas trade, 504, 583, 629
  See also British India; British North America
British India
  1720±1830 c.e., 583
  1860±1914 c.e., 667, 672±673
  agriculture, 675
  communication/transportation systems, 673, 701±702
  deindustrialization, 628, 672±673, 675
  famine (1860±1914 c.e.), 677, *677*, 701±702, 704
  and global migrations, 641
  government, 746
  Great Depression, 752
  Great Indian Rebellion (1857), 660, 673
  Hitler on, 760
  independence, 782±784
  resistance, 655, 749±750, *749*
  South Asian immigrants, 747
  textile industry, 611, 628, 672±673
  and World War I, 716, 749
  and World War II, 774, 783
British North America, 557±559, *559*
  American Revolution, 568, 584, 585±587, *586*, 588, 589, 645
  Enlightenment, 568, 586
  and industrial revolution, 616
British Raj, 660. *See also* British India
Bruegel, Pieter the Elder, 525
Brunelleschi, Filippo, 448
Bryan, Margaret, 613, 618
Buddhism, 496, 505, 585
Buenos Aires, 699, 742, *743*
Bukhara, 530
Bulgaria, 444, 773
Bunche, Ralph, 782
bureaucracy, China, 545
Burj Khalifa (Dubai), *694*
Burma (Myanmar), 496±497, 511, 684, 691, 774, 784
Busbecq, Ogier Ghiselin de, 489
Bush, George W., 839, 850
business
  Fordisim, 702
  globalization (1860±1914 c.e.), 680
  and science, 681
  See also economic policies; trade
business cycles, 676, 699, 825
Byzantine empire, 444±445, *444*, 449, 459

C

Cabral, Pedro Álvares, 478

Cairo, 429
Calcutta (Kolkata), 530, 583
Calvin, John, 506, 507, 555
Cambodia, 497, 684, 691, 840
Canada, 557, 584, 674, 715
Canary Islands, 460, *460*, 469
cannons. *See* artillery; firearm technology
Canton (Guangzhou), 546±547, 704
Cape of Good Hope, 466, 469, 478±479, 529, 530, 561
Cape Town, 530
Cape Verde Islands, 461
capitalism
  1720±1830 c.e., 579
  corporations, 680
  and liberalism, 631±632
  neoliberalism, 826±827, 834
  See also global economy; trade
capitulations, 490
Capuchin order, 570
caravels, 464±465, *465*, 517
Cárdenas, Lázaro, 752
Caribbean Islands
  colonization of, 471±472
  contract labor, 641±642, *642*
  French colonies, 584, 588
  slavery, 533, 534, *534*, 537
Carolingian empire. *See* Frankish empire
carracks, 465, 517
Carson, Rachel, 801, 847
Cartwright, Edmund, 612
Casablanca, 745
Cassatt, Mary, 735
castas, 550, *550*
Castro, Fidel, 803, *803*
Catherine de Medici (queen of France), *498*
Catherine II the Great (Russian tsar), 548, 567, 584±585
Catherine of Siena, 445, *445*
Catherwood, Frederick, 549
Catholic Church
  1300±1500 c.e., 435±436
  1830±1870 c.e., 654
  China, 505, 571
  Counter Reformation, 508±509
  and Enlightenment, 565
  evangelism, 654
  and French Revolution, 589, 590
  Ireland, 744
  Japan, 528±529
  Latin America, 652, 712, 743
  Napoleonic era, 593
  North America, 558
  papacy, 435±436, 445, 505, 506, 740
  Philippines, 569
  and Protestant Reformation, 506, 507
  and Renaissance, 448
  and scientific revolution, 564
  sixteenth century, 498, 499, 506, 507
  and Spanish Civil War, 762
  and Spanish colonies in the Americas, 478, 549, 569±571, *569*
  and Vietnam War, 810
  and wars of religion (sixteenth century), 498, 499
Catholic Reformation (Counter Reformation), 508±509

The way we once learned history . . .

. . . IS NOW HISTORY

Just as a panoramic image provides a broad view, *Panorama* provides a ground-breaking, broad view of the world's history by reaching across regional boundaries and highlighting large-scale, global patterns. *Panorama's* easily understood chronology, coupled with its innovative, proven digital tools, ensures that learners are always moving forward as they study change and continuity across time, assess knowledge gaps, and mold critical thinking skills. The result is improved course performance through greater understanding of our world's past, its large-scale global trends, and its impact on and relevance to 21st-century students.

ARCTIC OCEAN

30°E 60°E 90°E 120°E 150°E 180°

Arctic Circle

SWEDEN
FINLAND

R U S S I A

60°N

ESTONIA
LATVIA
LITHUANIA
BELARUS
POLAND
CZECH.
SLOV.   UKRAINE
AUS. HUNG.   MOLDOVA
SLO.   ROMANIA
CRO. BOS.   SERB.
MONT. KOS. BULGARIA
ITALY ALB. MACE.
GREECE   TURKEY

KAZAKHSTAN

MONGOLIA

N. KOREA
S. KOREA   JAPAN

PACIFIC
OCEAN

MALTA

GEORGIA
ARMENIA AZERBAIJAN
CYPRUS   SYRIA
LEBANON
ISRAEL   IRAQ   IRAN
JORDAN

UZBEKISTAN
KYRGYZSTAN
TURKMENISTAN
TAJIKISTAN

AFGHANISTAN

C H I N A

LIBYA
EGYPT

SAUDI
ARABIA
UNITED ARAB
EMIRATES   OMAN

KUWAIT
BAHRAIN
QATAR

PAKISTAN

NEPAL
BHUTAN

BANGLADESH

INDIA

MYANMAR
(BURMA)
LAOS

Taiwan

Tropic of Cancer

Mariana Is.
(U.S.)

Wake I.
(U.S.)

30°N

CHAD
SUDAN

ERITREA YEMEN
DJIBOUTI

CENTRAL
AFRICAN REP.
SOUTH
SUDAN   ETHIOPIA

THAILAND
CAMBODIA   VIETNAM

SRI
LANKA

PHILIPPINES

Guam
(U.S.)

MARSHALL
IS.

CAMEROON
CONGO
DEM. REP.
OF THE
CONGO

UGANDA
RWANDA
BURUNDI
KENYA

SOMALIA

MALDIVES

BRUNEI

PALAU

FEDERATED STATES
OF MICRONESIA

TANZANIA

SEYCHELLES

SINGAPORE

MALAYSIA

I N D O N E S I A

Equator

NAURU

0°

ANGOLA
ZAMBIA

MALAWI
COMOROS

PAPUA
NEW GUINEA

SOLOMON
IS.

KIRIBATI

TUVALU

NAMIBIA
ZIMBABWE
MOZAMBIQUE
MADAGASCAR
MAURITIUS
Réunion
(Fr.)

INDIAN
OCEAN

TIMOR-LESTE

VANUATU

New Caledonia
(Fr.)

SAMOA

FIJI

TONGA

BOTSWANA

Tropic of Capricorn

AUSTRALIA

SOUTH
AFRICA

SWAZILAND
LESOTHO

30°S

ABBREVIATIONS	
ALB.	ALBANIA
AUS.	AUSTRIA
BELG.	BELGIUM
BOS.	BOSNIA AND HERZEGOVINA
CRO.	CROATIA
CZECH.	CZECH REPUBLIC
DEN.	DENMARK
HUNG.	HUNGARY
KOS.	KOSOVO
LIECH.	LIECHTENSTEIN
LUX.	LUXEMBOURG
MACE.	MACEDONIA
MONT.	MONTENEGRO
NETH.	NETHERLANDS
SERB.	SERBIA
SLOV.	SLOVAKIA
SLO.	SLOVENIA
SWITZ.	SWITZERLAND

Tasmania
(Aust.)

NEW
ZEALAND

60°S

Antarctic Circle

30°E 60°E 90°E 120°E 150°E 180°

Online Supplements

Connect 1-Term Online Access for Panorama

McGraw-Hill Connect is a digital teaching and learning environment that improves performance over a variety of critical outcomes. With Connect, instructors can deliver assignments, quizzes and tests easily online. Students can practice important skills at their own pace and on their own schedule.

HOW TO REGISTER

Using a <u>Print Book</u>?
To register and activate your Connect account, simply follow these easy steps:
1. **Go to the Connect course web address provided by your instructor or visit the Connect link set up on your instructor's course within your campus learning management system.**
2. **Click on the link to register.**
3. **When prompted, enter the Connect code found on the inside back cover of your book and click Submit. Complete the brief registration form that follows to begin using Connect.**

Using an <u>eBook</u>?
To register and activate your Connect account, simply follow these easy steps:
1. **Upon purchase of your eBook, you will be granted automatic access to Connect.**
2. **Go to the Connect course web address provided by your instructor or visit the Connect link set up on your instructor's course within your campus learning management system.**
3. **Sign in using the same email address and password you used to register on the eBookstore. Complete your registration and begin using Connect.**

Note: Access Code is for one use only. If you did not purchase this book new, the access code included in this book is no longer valid.

Need help? Visit mhhe.com/support